AREA HANDBOOK

for

THAILAND

Co-Authors

Harvey H. Smith

Donald W. Bernier

Frederica M. Bunge

Frances Chadwick Rintz

Rinn-Sup Shinn

Suzanne Teleki

Research and writing were completed on
May 31, 1967

Published

September 1968

(This pamphlet supersedes DA Pam 550–53, June 1963.)

12,645

For sale by the Superintendent of Documents, U.S. Government
Printing Office, Washington D.C. 20402—Price $4   +0'.

FOREWORD

This volume is one of a series of handbooks prepared by Foreign Area Studies (FAS) of The American University, designed to be useful to military and other personnel who need a convenient compilation of basic facts about the social, economic, political and military institutions and practices of various countries. The emphasis is on objective description of the nation's present society and the kinds of possible or probable changes that might be expected in the future. The handbook seeks to present as full and as balanced an integrated exposition as limitations on space and research time permit. It was compiled from information available in openly published material. Extensive bibliographies are provided to permit recourse to other published sources for more detailed information. There has been no attempt to express any specific point of view or to make policy recommendations. The contents of the handbook represent the work of the authors and FAS and do not represent the official view of the United States Government.

An effort has been made to make the handbook as comprehensive as possible. It can be expected, however, that the material, interpretations and conclusions are subject to modification in the light of new information and developments. Such corrections, additions and suggestions for factual, interpretive or other change as readers may have will be welcomed for use in future revisions. Comments may be addressed to—

The Director
Foreign Area Studies
The American University
5010 Wisconsin Avenue, N.W.
Washington, D.C. 20016

PREFACE

This is the second revision of the 1957 *Area Handbook for Thailand,* which was prepared under the Chairmanship of Wendell Blanchard by the Washington Branch of Human Relations Area Files (HRAF), the predecessor of the present Foreign Area Studies of The American University. An earlier monograph prepared for HRAF in 1956 was directed by Professor Lauriston Sharp and was edited by Dr. Frank J. Moore and Dr. Walter F. Vella; it was of great value in preparing the 1957 edition of the handbook. This earlier study drew extensively on the field notes and the firsthand knowledge of the members of the Southeast Asia Program of Cornell University. In 1963 the first revision of the handbook, which was under the Chairmanship of Dr. George L. Harris, brought to the study the benefit of research and writing developed during the intervening 6-year period.

The present revision deals with the political, social, economic and military developments since 1963, which have contributed to Thailand's continuing national stability and progress and to the strengthening of Thailand's position as a bulwark against Communist expansion in Southeast Asia.

Special credit is given to Professor Frederick Mote of the Department of Oriental Studies of Princeton University for his observations, advice and perceptive comments based on experience as a ministerial adviser and as an observer in the field. Especially helpful was his firsthand information on the Chinese and other ethnic minority problems. Particular appreciation is also extended to the staff of the Military Assistance Institute of the American Institutes for Research for their extensive cooperation in providing the use of facilities and important source materials and for their valuable advice and assistance on many parts of this study. Mr. George E. Aurell, who drew on his extensive field experience, contributed useful information and provided timely advice and suggestions.

Grateful acknowledgment is also due many persons within and outside the United States Government who are too numerous to mention individually but who gave of their time and special knowledge to provide data and objective criticism of preliminary chapter drafts.

A glossary is included as an appendix for the reader's convenience. Wherever possible the place names used are those established by the United States Board on Geographic Names for Thailand as of April 1966.

COUNTRY SUMMARY

1. COUNTRY: Kingdom of Thailand, originally known as Sayam. Name changed in the 1850's to Siam and so known until 1939 when title of Thailand (land of the free) was adopted. Name reverted to Siam from 1945 to 1949, when it was changed back to Thailand. A kingdom throughout its history; has never experienced colonial rule.

2. GOVERNMENT: Under the governing Interim Constitution of 1959, is still a constitutional monarchy, with King exercising nominal power. Actual responsibility for public affairs is centralized in Council of Ministers headed in 1967 by Prime Minister Thanom Kittikachorn; permanent constitution planned.

3. POPULATION: About 34.2 million; annual growth rate, approximately 3.4 percent; density averaging about 132 per square mile; some 40 percent of total live in 30 percent of land area. *Composition.* More than 98 percent born in Thailand; 97 percent speak Thai; more than 93 percent are Buddhists. Most important minority, ethnic Chinese. Other minorities include Malays, Khmers (Cambodians), non-Thai hill peoples, and some Vietnamese living in Northeast Region. *Immigration.* Controlled after World War II by quota system, 200 a year for any nationality. In 1964, approximately 2,100 permanent immigrants and 346,000 temporary residents arrived. *Migration.* Extensive between ethnically related people across the Mekong River, which for over 600 miles forms boundary between northeastern Thailand and Laos.

4. SIZE: Area, 200,000 square miles; greatest north-south distance, 1,000 miles; east-west, 500 miles.

5. TOPOGRAPHY: Four natural regions: Northern Region, about 42,000 square miles, mountainous area in the north with peaks rising to 8,500 feet; Northeast Region, about 66,000 square miles, comprised mainly of Khorat Plateau; Central Region, about 62,000 miles, the fertile and populous basin of the Chao Phraya River; Southern Region (peninsular Thailand), about 30,000 square miles, extending some 500 miles south to Malaysia.

6. LANGUAGES: Official national language is Siamese Thai, a variant of closely related and mutually understandable Thai and

Lao; spoken by more than 90 percent of population. Principal other languages: Chinese, spoken by 2.6 million; Malay, by one million speakers. English predominates among the Western languages.

7. RELIGION: Official religion is Theravada Buddhism, in contrast to Mahayana Buddhism of China and Japan. Other religions represented include: Brahmanism, Islam, and Christianity as well as Confucian teachings; animism among the hill peoples.

8. EDUCATION: Literacy rate rising, varies between 50 and 70 percent. In 1966, vocational training was provided for 45,000 students in 210 schools. Total university enrollment in 1964: 45,980 with almost 5,000 graduating.

9. HEALTH: Conditions improving, but much remains to be achieved. Between 1957 and 1964, death rate dropped from 9 to 7.9 per 1,000 population; infant mortality rate, from 62 to 37.8 per 1,000 births. Malaria, the leading cause of death until early 1960's, decreased considerably. Principal diseases: diarrhea and dysentery; typhoid and paratyphoid, influenza and other respiratory ailments, and parasitic worm infestations.

10. CLIMATE: Tropical, monsoonal with rainy season from May to end of September; dry season for rest of year.

11. JUSTICE: Independent judiciary headed by President of the Supreme Court. Three-level court system: Courts of First Instance; Court of Appeal; and Supreme Court. Jury system not used.

12. ADMINISTRATIVE DIVISIONS: *Civil.* Provinces (71), districts (520), subdistricts (21), communes (4,926), villages (41,630), and municipalities (120); all largely centrally directed from Bangkok. *Military.* Army maintains a system of regional area commands for administrative and tactical purposes.

13. ECONOMY: Prosperous agrarian type; grew at rate of 7 percent a year during 1960–65. Rice continues to be the most important economic product.

14. INDUSTRY: Minor but of increasing economic importance; contribution of manufacturing to gross domestic product rose from 11 to 13.5 percent, 1950–65. Confined largely to processing agricultural products (mainly rice milling) and fabricating a few consumer products.

15. LABOR: Force estimated in 1966 to be 15 million, aged 15 years and over. About 80 percent engaged in farming, fishing, forestry and related occupations; commerce, 7 percent; services, 5.5 percent; and manufacturing, 4.7 percent.

16. EXPORTS: Steadily increasing but pattern changing. From 1950 through 1960, four principal exports—rice, rubber, tin and teak—accounted for 89 percent of all export earnings. Significant increases: corn, jute and kenaf, tapioca and other agricultural products.

17. IMPORTS: Largely manufactured goods, machinery and transport equipment, chemicals and pharmaceuticals, petroleum products, food and beverages. Foremost category, manufactured consumer goods.

18. FINANCE: *Currency*. Remarkably stable. Unit is the baht; divided into 100 satang. Solidly backed by gold, foreign exchange and securities. In 1966, baht was revised upward from 20.80 to 20.71 for 1 United States dollar. *Banks*. Stringently controlled by legislation and Ministry of Finance regulations, which give the Central Bank—Bank of Thailand—extensive powers over commercial banks.

19. COMMUNICATIONS: *Telephone and Telegraph*. Telehones numbered 55,220 in 1963, almost 85 percent in Bangkok and vicinity; telegraph lines, 8,550 miles. *Radio*. Government controlled. Stations, approximately 160; receiving sets, 3.5 million, mostly in Bangkok and other urban centers. *Television*. Virtually a government monopoly. Receiving sets about 300,000. Operating stations, five in 1966.

20. RAILROADS: Government-owned and operated meter-gauge system totaling 2,500 miles, single track except for 56-mile stretch running north from Bangkok.

21. ROADS: Approximately 7,800 miles, highway and provincial. Many unpaved except in Central Region. Maintenance generally poor; large sections impassable during rainy season.

22. PORTS AND PORT FACILITIES: Only port accommodating oceangoing vessels is Bangkok, 17 miles from sea on Chao Phraya River. No deepwater seaports. Other ports include: Sattahip, 75 miles southeast of Bangkok; Songkhla, on eastern shore of Peninsula, about 150 miles north of Malaysia; Pattani, about 50 miles south of Songkhla; Phuket, on island off Peninsular west coast.

24. AIRFIELDS: Don Muang, about 16 miles north of Bangkok, adequate for large modern aircraft. About 80 smaller fields suitable only for light planes; generally poorly surfaced, lacking in adequate fueling and communications facilities, and inoperative for extended periods during rainy season.

25. PRINCIPAL AIRLINES: Government-owned Thai Airways Company, Ltd. (TAC) the only domestic airline. In addition,

Thai Airways International Ltd., a joint venture with Scandinavian Airlines System (SAS).

26. INTERNATIONAL AGREEMENTS AND TREATIES: *Civil.* Two agreements with the United States: for exchange of students under the Fulbright Act, and an Economic and Technical Cooperation Agreement, signed in September 1950. *Military.* Limited to those agreements inherent in the Southeast Asia Treaty Organization.

27. AID PROGRAMS: *Civil.* Numerous and varied, consisting generally of loans, grants and technical assistance for specific purposes or projects. Biggest single donor is the United States, mostly through the United States Agency for International Development (AID). Other assistance, technical and financial, from West Germany, Denmark and Japan. International organizations giving assistance total at least 13 including Colombo Plan and Southeast Asia Treaty Organization. *Military.* Mainly from United States AID and from United States Military Assistance Program.

28. INTERNATIONAL OBLIGATIONS AND MEMBERSHIPS: Admitted to the United Nations in December 1946; supports its principles and participates in 10 of its subsidiary organizations.

29. THE ARMED FORCES: Total strength approximately 130,000: Air Force (21,000), Navy (21,000), Army (88,000), including its Marine Corps component. National Police, under the Ministry of the Interior, are to support the armed forces in national emergencies. Conscription: 2-year period. Budget: about 15 percent of total budget.

THAILAND

TABLE OF CONTENTS

LIST OF ILLUSTRATIONS

LIST OF TABLES

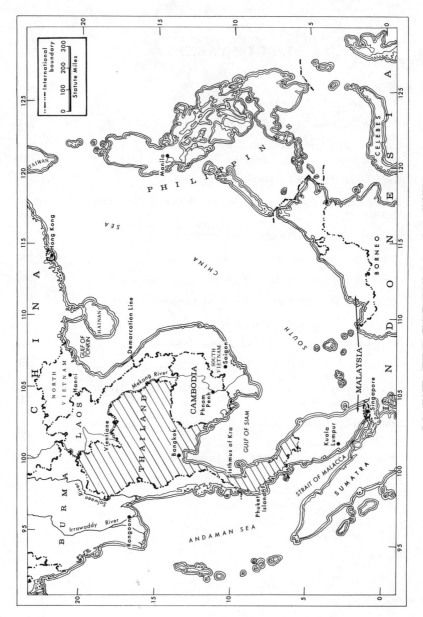

Figure 1.—Position of Thailand in Southeast Asia.

SECTION I. SOCIAL

CHAPTER 1

GENERAL CHARACTER OF THE SOCIETY

Although the Thai peoples had been drifting south into northern Thailand for at least two centuries, the modern state grew out of an independent kingdom called Sukhothai. It was formed in the middle of the thirteenth century by those Thai who chose to move southward out of their long-established Kingdom of Nanchao, in present-day Yunnan, China, rather than accept the rule of the conquering Mongols under Kublai Khan. This kingdom extended from northern tributaries of the Chao Phraya River, across the broad fertile Chao Phraya Plain, into the narrow Malay Peninsula, to the Isthmus of Kra.

During the next 500 years, under several successive dynasties, Thai power alternately receded and advanced in struggles against the Khmer (Cambodians) and the Burmese. Meanwhile, contacts with European powers began early in the sixteenth century and gradually increased. Diplomatic envoys were exchanged, treaties were concluded and numerous foreigners were employed to help reform governmental administration and to assist in the development of natural resources. The state in its present form came into being shortly after the mid-eighteenth century when General Chakri, who was a prominent leader in the struggle to liberate the country from Burmese domination, ascended to the throne in 1782. As Rama I, he founded the dynasty which has reigned since that time.

In its early history the country was known to foreigners as Sayam. This designation was eventually changed to Siam, which was officially adopted in the 1850's by the government. The Thai people, however, felt that the name did not properly apply to them or to their country. In 1939 it was officially changed to Thailand (land of the free), but in 1945, as a concession to foreign influence, it was again changed to Siam. Popular senti-

1

ment soon prevailed, and in 1949 the name Thailand was again adopted.

The country, situated entirely within the northern tropical zone in the center of the Indochinese Peninsula, has four distinct geographic regions, each of which has strongly influenced the shaping of Thai society and its relationships with neighbors and the rest of the world. The Central Region, which is the great fertile plain of the Chao Phraya River, comprises about 30 percent of the country's total area and contains about 40 percent of its population. This region has been stripped of natural cover and converted into a vast rice paddy that provides the country's stable food and principal source of foreign exchange. It has a large proportion of the country's nascent industry and contributes more than 50 percent to the gross domestic product.

Bangkok, in the Central Region, in addition to being the nation's capital, is the commercial, political and industrial center. It is the chief port of entry for goods from the outside world. Highways, railroads and airplanes carry products to Bangkok from the interior; some are used locally, and others are routed to foreign markets. It is the nation's cultural center and the site of its principal institutions of higher learning.

The Northern Region, in which Chiengmai, the second largest city in Thailand, is located, is a mountainous region that is not easily accessible from the Chao Phraya Plain to the south. The relatively sparse population includes numerous but small communities of non-Thai hill peoples, most of whom live in the highlands. Boundaries with Burma and Laos are indistinctly marked, and the movements of local groups across the borders are the subject of occasional discussions with these two countries. The bulk of the population, however, is composed of Thai, who live in the narrow alluvial valleys separated by high ridges and covered with forests that yield valuable products, such as teak and various resins, both of which are commercial assets to the country. These northern Thai speak with a distinct dialect but display only minor cultural differences from the Central Thai.

The Northeast Region, whose principal town is Khorat, is a seasonably arid plateau. Lack of water and poor soil make much of it unsuited to wet-rice farming. Its living standards and per capita productivity are lower than in other regions. Poverty, relative isolation from the rest of the country and cultural affinities with neighboring Laos account for some of the differences between the people of this area and the Central Thai. The ease of communication with Laos attracts the Thai of the Northeast Region toward their ethnic kin across the river. In contrast, the Phetchabun Mountains rimming the plateau on the west have been an impediment to communication with the Chao Phraya Valley. Nevertheless, the great majority of the people living in the Region reportedly consider themselves Thai, not Lao. Toward the south the ill-defined and sometimes disputed boundary with Cambodia extends along the Phanom Dongrak Range. Charges and countercharges of border violations and minor incursions have been detrimental to relations between Thailand and Cambodia. The government's Five-Year Plan for National Economic and Social Development (1967–71) gives high priority to projects and programs designed to improve conditions in the Northeast Region and to draw the people living there into the orbit of Thai national life.

The fourth natural region is the Southern Region, or Peninsula, which is a narrow mountainous strip running down the west side of the Gulf of Siam to Malaysia. It is a land of rubber plantations and tin mines, whose products are sent into world markets. The Peninsula was gained by conquest, and much of it is being integrated rather slowly into Thai culture. A heavy concentration of Chinese work in the tin mines. About 1 million, or 70 percent, of the population of the four southernmost provinces are ethnic Malays, who are Moslems and who are related to the inhabitants of Malaysia's northern provinces. In the past ethnic Malays have harbored Irredentist sentiments that have led to rebellions in the 1920's and earlier. The anti-Malaysian Communist terrorists on the Thai border have tried to appeal to these Malay sentiments but without much success. The border situation has caused concern in Thailand and Malaysia, and both governments have cooperated in efforts to maintain public order in the area.

Although differences of speech and custom exist among the Thai in the various regions, the Central Thai speak the dialect that has become the official national language. Customs and speech differentiate the non-Thai, and there are some minor physical differences. Overshadowing these variations, however, are the common features of language, way of life and outlook that have long identified the predominant Thai as one nation.

Efforts to modernize the concepts and procedures of government began in the mid-nineteenth century. These were accompanied by many social and economic measures, such as the abolition of slavery, the establishment of modern defense forces, the construction of railways and roads and the improvement of irrigation methods; thus, the country entered a phase of progressive development based on Western patterns. The Chakri kings, like their predecessors, continued to rule as absolute monarchs until 1932, when a coup d'etat made the king a constitutional monarch and introduced certain parliamentary features into the system of government. Although every administration since that time has reaffirmed the intention to establish democratic processes, successive governments have not been strong, and military leaders have been in control much of the time.

The Thai people, historically accustomed to authoritarian rule, retain their traditional reverence for their king and are proud that their rulers were able to maintain their country's independence despite pressures from colonial powers. Thailand's historical record of some seven centuries of unbroken independence as a people has been of great significance in conditioning the nation's adjustment to the modern world. In contrast to many former colonial countries, the Thai have felt free to accept, reject or modify the ideas, practices and institutions of the West and have not suffered from feelings of inferiority which have handicapped some former colonial peoples. The processes of change have been presided over by Thai and have never been forced on a reluctant people by alien administrators. The successive dynasties were, therefore, able to maintain Thai traditions while accepting Western ideas which appealed to them. For a century the elite of Thailand have been obtaining their advanced education in the West. Modern concepts of progressive government are generally promoted in Thailand by the elite, whereas the mass of people are generally less progressive and more traditional, though not xenophobic.

The essence of the many alterations made in the political order since 1932 was that the locus of power was shifted from the king and the aristocracy, which surrounded him, to a succession of groups of military officers and associated civil officials whose commanding position was the result of their influence among the armed forces, the police and the bureaucracy. Despite the adoption of Western constitutional structures and parliamentary practices, the operation of government and politics was not abruptly changed, and Thailand's officialdom, both civil and military, is generally professionally educated according to Western models or in the West and is experienced in career service in which promotion depends mainly on performance.

After 1932 the people were enfranchised, but this power was largely unasserted by the electorate, qualified by the Constitution and frequently either diverted or nullified by military coups. National elections were instituted as the formal method of political change, but the coup d'etat remained a more significant means of replacing one regime with another. Since 1932 there have been about 25 coups or attempted coups, which have set the pattern for changes in government. Political parties were allowed to exist only periodically, and they were more a means of promoting the personal ambitions of their leadership than of expressing and advancing the interests of their adherents. Although a national legislature was established, its composition was usually controlled, at least partly, by the ruling group, and even its limited powers were never fully developed or employed. The country's constitutions—there have been seven—have been of little importance, except as an indication of the government's announced policies and as a means of legitimatizing its authority.

The governmental system as functioning in mid-1967 was established in 1968 after a coup d'etat led by Marshal Sarit Thanarat, who controlled the armed forces. Some of his first acts were the suspension of the Constitution, proclamation of martial law, dissolution of the legislature and prohibition of political parties. Since 1958 the legislature has been reconstituted on terms that allow the government to appoint its entire membership, and an interim constitution legitimizing the new regime has been put into effect. Virtually no change in government resulted when Sarit died in December 1963 and was succeeded by his deputy, General Thanom Kittikachorn. In mid-1967 the ban on political parties had not been lifted.

Controlling all important sources of power and facing no serious domestic opposition, Prime Minister Thanom's government, which is regarded as an extension of the government of former Prime Minister Sarit, has been one of the most stable and long lived since the elimination of the absolute monarchy in 1932. Though technically under martial law, all governmental functions are still carried on through normal civil channels. The Thai judiciary prides itself on its adherence to its code of law. The Thai press is, with rare exceptions, independently owned, and it is constantly at variance with the government on popular issues in spite of the government's power—rarely exercised—to close newspapers which it considers pro-Communist or irresponsible.

The continuance of political power in the hands of Thailand's present elite not only has been sanctioned by the nation's history but facilitated by the present complexion of the society. The people are generally indifferent to national politics and public affairs, and they have great tolerance for a broad and vigorous exercise of government power. The basically agrarian society in this relatively homogeneous nation has not favored the establishment of significantly different values, the development of highly structured interest or pressure groups, or the growth of varied political organizations and attitudes, which might promote the formation of organized popular opposition to governmental authorities. The strong position of the ethnic Chinese in commerce and finance gives them potential economic influence, which they have exercised through the common device of aligning themselves with prominent Thai political and military leaders. One beneficial side effect of this practice has been a merging of the ethnic Chinese commercial elite with the ruling Thai elite. Intermarriage is common in the younger generation, and they have common education and aspirations. The elite has shown an impressive ability to overcome or assimilate actual or potential opponents, and political competition has been confined to maneuverings by groups or individuals within the ruling circles.

The characteristics of an integrated and unified national society are present to a greater extent in Thailand than in other countries of Southeast Asia. The great majority of the people, almost 90 percent, share a common or related ethnic origin. Their ancestors, the Thai, after migrating from the north, completely absorbed the earlier inhabitants they encountered in the area of present-day Thailand. They now regard themselves as belonging to a single nation, which has its religious, political, social and economic center in Bangkok. Some variations do exist, however, between the rural and urban peoples and between the inhabitants of the densely populated Central Region and those of the Northern and Northeast Regions. Several non-Thai minority groups are found in various sections of the country.

Members of the largest minority group, the Chinese, have settled mainly in urban areas and have closely blended with the predominant Thai. In the nineteenth century Chinese immigration began to be encouraged to meet the growing need for non-agricultural labor that was created by the country's rapidly expanding foreign commerce. The Thai lack of interest in anything besides traditional pursuits allowed the Chinese to acquire prominent positions in trade, banking and industrial enterprises. Since the 1930's Chinese immigration has been severely curtailed; legal restrictions have been imposed on the economic activities of aliens; and Chinese schools have been required to conform to the Thai curriculum. By 1967, 90 percent or more of the ethnic Chinese in Thailand were born there and were Thai citizens. The government's long-range policy was aimed at assimilation. There were signs, especially on the upper levels of the Chinese community, that the policy was having a remarkable degree of success. The native ethnic Chinese in Thailand speak Thai, often use Thai names, especially if they are prospering, give their children Thai and Western educations and aspire to prominent social and official positions as Thai. An extremely high percentage of Thailand's urban population is of mixed Sino-Thai blood.

The remaining groups consist primarily of the Malay living in the south, the Vietnamese in the Northeast and the hill peoples living mostly in the north. Except for the Chinese, most of whom are engaged in commerce and have a strong influence in economic affairs, the non-Thai groups have exerted only a minor influence on the country's economic and political system. The various hill peoples, who live virtually independent existences in isolated or separated groups, constitute semiautonomous societies.

A contributing factor in the distinctly cohesive quality of national society is the Thai language, which is commonly used by most persons and spoken as a second language by many others. More important, however, is the influence of Buddhism, which has prevailed in Thailand for more than 700 years. Theravada Buddhism is the state religion prescribed by the constitution, which stipulates that the king must profess the Buddhist faith and must uphold religion. Although complete religious freedom is guaranteed, Thailand is a secular society, and there is a definite separation of state and church.

Under the absolute monarchies, the secular society was hierarchically ordered into hereditary nobles, appointed government officials and a largely rural population of freemen and slaves. The Buddhist monastic order, or Sangha, which most men entered for at least a short period of study and contemplation at some time in their lives, was regarded as standing apart from and above the mundane world, but it too was organized into an elaborate hierarchy. The concern with rank and status penetrated every sector of the society. Besides the aristocracy, which was united by pride of kinship with the royal family, the preoccupation with rank did not group people into categories or classes but tended to place each individual on a scale of status that literally put everyone with whom he came in contact socially above or below him. The criteria for these differences were not simply economic but included age, sex, education, reputation for wisdom and religious merit, and a host of personal qualities. This concept is strongly supported by Theravada Buddhism, which holds that salvation is attained through the accumulation of individual merit. Two other characteristics of the traditional pattern were an elaborate etiquette for the expression of respect, deference or condescension and a tendency for the relationship between persons of different status to take a paternalistic form.

Throughout modern history, the Thai have been exposed to and have borrowed from the many civilizations with which they have come in contact. Characteristically, they have preserved their identity, which is an indication of pride in their common heritage of ethnic origin, language and religion. The Mongoloid physical type shows they are racially related to the Chinese, but the nature of the relationship has not been established clearly. Their speech also shows Chinese influence. These Chinese connections, which were important among the early Thai, were later overshadowed by direct and indirect borrowings from Indian civilization and from the Indian-influenced cultures of Cambodia and Burma. During this process, which affected almost every sphere of thought and activity, the Thai acquired their Theravada Buddhist religion, their traditional concept of an absolute and divine monarchy, their elaborate hierarchy of social status, their writing and the subject matter of their classical literature and the form and content of much of their art and architecture. The borrowed items, however, underwent a transformation in which they became unmistakably Thai. Buddhism in Thailand, for example, is almost inextricably bound with retained folk beliefs and observances. The absolutist principle in government was usually tempered by mildness in practice. Some of the formalities of Indian social customs were received along with other Indian influences, but the caste system itself was ignored.

The modern period has brought many changes, such as the abolition of slavery, the end of royal absolutism, the introduction of commercialization of agriculture, the beginnings of industry and the dissemination of new knowledge, ideas and values through the public school system. The elite is no longer a closed circle composed of the royal family and the traditional bureaucracy, but it includes all those who have been able to rise to the top in government, business, religious and other professional life. The base of the social structure is formed by the village farmers and a large group of artisans and unskilled laborers. Of great potential importance is a small but growing group of middle- and lower-level civil servants, merchants, white-collar and skilled industrial workers. The trends in this process of change are expected to continue.

The pattern of the traditional order, as it is distinguished from its particulars, remains in many respects intact. A period of service in the Sangha (see Glossary) still confers a prestige that can be gained in no other way. A constitutional executive exercises powers hardly less qualified than were those of his counterpart under the absolute monarchy, and civil or military office continues to overshadow all other careers. To the bulk of the population, however, farming remains not merely an inherited way of life but a desirable, although demanding, occupation providing an independence and a dignity that are not

8

associated with commercial or service pursuits. Throughout the society individuals continue to measure themselves and each other against a complex scale of status and to follow a paternalistic model in seeking patronage from above and in offering it to those below.

The economy of the country in mid-1967 was characterized by accelerating growth, particularly after 1961 when the Six-Year Economic Development Plan (1961–66) went into effect. It was a prosperous agrarian economy based mainly on rice. The agricultural output accounted for approximately one-third of the gross domestic product, and the annual growth rate rose from 5 percent during the previous decade to 7 percent for the 1960–65 period. The goal announced for the Plan, which was to raise the standard of living by building a firm foundation for a broadly developing economy, apparently had been achieved. In its application special efforts were directed toward various fields, such as the diversification of agriculture to lessen the dependence on rice as a major export item and a source of foreign exhange; the expansion of industry by constructing added facilities for smelting tin, refining oil and manufacturing needed light industrial products; the development of basic public utilities, including those for hydroelectric power; and the expansion and improvement in communications, transportation, mining, construction, irrigation and flood control. Surveys were initiated to discover and exploit new or additional natural resources in oil, iron, antimony, tungsten and other minerals.

These projects were undertaken mostly with the aid of foreign grants and loans. The inflow of private capital from foreign and domestic sources is increasingly attracted by government encouragement, a stable currency, political stability over the past decade, a sensible financial policy and sound economic planning. Vigorous efforts by governmental authorities were required in the attainment of these goals. There have been no significant pressures by the people for economic development. Most of them are reasonably well fed, comfortably clothed and adequately housed for the tropical climate in which they live. Almost 90 percent of the population lives in small self-sustaining villages or hamlets, and they seem to realize that the country has enough resources to maintain their standard of living.

Government efforts to ensure continued economic growth, which is sufficient to keep pace with a population increasing at the annual rate of about 3.4 percent, were reflected in the Plan for National Economic and Social Development (1967–71). This new Plan, which was promulgated in the autumn of 1966, envisages a continued annual growth rate of 8.5 percent in the gross national product and an increase in expenditures for development programs that will be 50 percent more than that of the Six-Year Plan. Particular efforts will be devoted to the improvement and the expansion of communications, transportation, irrigation projects and agricultural productivity. The Plan also includes provisions for reforms in the school system, for increasing the period of compulsory attendance, for expanding courses and for vocational and technical training facilities needed to produce the literate manpower, who are qualified in vocations, science and technology, required by a rapidly growing economy.

Thailand's foreign relations, which are based primarily on national defense requirements, have been characterized by a friendly attitude toward almost all non-Communist countries except Cambodia. Diplomatic relations in mid-1967 were maintained with only two Communist states, the Soviet Union and Yugoslavia.

The foreign policy of Thailand has been pro-Western, particularly since 1950 when a battalion was sent to help United Nations forces in Korea and a Military Assistance Agreement was signed with the United States. After the French defeat by Communist forces in 1954 in Indochina, Thailand, as a charter member of the Southeast Asia Treaty Organization (SEATO), became allied with the United States, Great Britain, Australia, New Zealand, the Philippines, France and Pakistan. It is firmly anti-Communist in its external policy, and it has consistently supported Western positions in international and regional organizations. Thailand strongly supports resistance to Communist aggression in Southeast Asia, and in January 1967 the prime minister announced that some 2,400 men would be sent to aid the South Vietnamese later in the year.

A critical test of Thailand's alliance policy under SEATO was presented by the instability of the neutralist coalition government in neighboring Laos, where the military operations of the Communist-led Pathet Lao forces in May 1962 and April 1963 moved toward the Thai frontier and threatened its security in the Northern and Northeast Regions. In 1962 the swift deployment in Thailand of military forces from the United States, Great Britain, Australia and New Zealand allayed Thailand's fears, but the country's leadership expressed dissatisfaction with SEATO's response. In March 1962 Secretary of State Rusk and Foreign Minister Thanat Khoman issued a joint statement in which the United States declared its treaty obligation to Thailand under SEATO to be individual as well as collective.

Because of the mounting Communist threats, the government has recognized the need for modernizing its defense establishment and has signed various assistance agreements with the United States. Under these agreements, relatively large-scale military assistance has included advice, training and materiel. Military support under SEATO arrangements has also included small troop contingents from Great Britain, Australia and New Zealand.

The economic aspects of the country's foreign relations are emphasized by its interest and activity in various international bodies. The Economic Commission for Asia and the Far East (ECAFE) headquartered in Bangkok coordinates the work on the Mekong River Development Plan and the Asian Highway, a section of which passes through Thailand. The Association of Southeast Asia (ASA) was formed by Thailand, Malaysia and the Philippines in 1961 to encourage trade arrangements and technological cooperation. The Asia and Pacific Area Council (ASPAC) includes nine Asian countries: Australia, Japan, the Philippines, South Korea, South Vietnam, Malaysia, New Zealand, the Republic of China and Thailand. Its goal, defined at its first meeting in August 1966 in Bangkok, has been increased economic and technical cooperation among its members. Beside trade agreements with West Germany and Japan, assistance is received either directly or indirectly through arrangements with the International Monetary Fund (IMF), the International Finance Corporation (IFC) and several specialized agencies of the United Nations.

CHAPTER 2

PHYSICAL ENVIRONMENT

Thailand, situated in the heart of Southeast Asia, has an area of about 200,000 square miles. It has common frontiers with Laos on the north and east, with Burma on the north and west and with Cambodia on the south and east (see fig. 1). To the south of mainland Thailand and to the east of peninsular Thailand lies the Gulf of Siam. Peninsular Thailand is bounded on the south by Malaysia, on the west below latitude 10° by the Strait of Malacca and above latitude 10° by Burma, which also touches the remainder of the country's western perimeter.

The country's greatest distance from north to south is about 1,000 miles and from east to west is 500 miles. It has about 950 miles of coastline on the Gulf of Siam, where the country's main harbors are located and into which the Chao Phraya River drains. On the western side of the peninsula the coastline of about 350 miles along the Strait of Malacca is rugged and without adequate harbor facilities. Along both coasts lie numerous jungle-covered islands. The largest and most important, Phuket, at the northern end of the Strait of Malacca, is the center of the country's tin industry.

There are three natural inland boundaries: the Mekong River, which flows between Thailand and Laos for about 50 miles on the north and for more than 450 miles on the east; the watershed of the Bilauktaung Range, which lies between Thailand and southern Burma; and the Salween River, which flows between northwestern Thailand and Burma for a short distance. The boundaries of modern Thailand have varied considerably since 1900 as the result of modifications set forth in treaties and agreements made with the British and French (see ch. 3, Historical Setting).

In 1967, Thailand was free from boundary disputes with all neighboring states except Cambodia. This dispute was a challenge to Cambodia's claimed sovereignty over a ruined temple in the eastern sector of the Phanom Dongrak Range, which separates the two countries south of the Khorat Plateau. Boundaries are generally respected by the population except certain mountain groups along the Burma border in the north and the Lao people along the Mekong in the northeast. These groups pay little heed to frontier-crossing formalities and frequently create problems for the Border Patrol Police units in these areas (see ch. 27, Public Order and Safety).

The country is administratively divided into 71 provinces (*changwat*), including one island province, Phuket. These are subdivided into districts (*amphur*), communes (*tambons*) and villages (*muban*). In the mid-1920's a government act created 70 provinces. The present number has existed since early in the 1950's. Historically, the provinces have served as an extension of central government agencies in the outlying areas. The boundaries have remained virtually unchanged. The factors determining their locations appeared to include administrative convenience, population density and economic considerations. The name of a province corresponds to the name of its capital, except in the case of Phra Nakhon, whose capital is Bangkok. The provincial seat of government is generally the traditional community center in its area, and there appears to be no significant pressure, political or otherwise, for changes in site or modifications of jurisdiction (see fig. 2).

The country is tropical but presents a regionally varied landscape in which the dominant features are forested mountains, relatively dry plateaus and fertile river plains. A broken mountain upland in the north rises above the low platform of the Khorat Plateau in the northeast. West of the plateau is the Central Plain, stretching from the mountains in the north some 300 miles to the Gulf of Siam and from the scarp of the Khorat Plateau on the east 150 miles to the foothills of the Bilauktaung Range west of Bangkok and the southern slopes of the Tanen Taunggyi mountians south of Chiengmai.

On the Central Plain, which is the basin of the Chao Phraya River and its tributaries, most of the country's staple food crop and principal export, rice, is produced in the fertile soil deposited by these rivers. This area has long been the center of the country's national life, and the capital, Bangkok (Krung Thep in the vernacular, Khra Nakhorn in the official form) is situated above the mouth of the Chao Phraya River about 15 miles north of the Gulf of Siam. Peninsular Thailand is an extension of the mountain range to the west of the Central Plain.

The climate is monsoonal and has a pronounced rainy season from about May to the end of September. A dry season exists the rest of the year, although there is considerable local variation in the amount and seasonal pattern of rainfall. It is coolest in December and January and hottest in April. Only on the peninsula is the rainfall adequate for rice cultivation throughout the year, but the soils there are generally unsuitable for rice. During the dry season in other parts of the country the farmer depends on irrigation.

The village is the most prevalent form of settlement. The largest and fastest-growing cities are Bangkok and adjacent Thon Buri. Chiengmai in the Northern Region and Nakhon Ratchasima in the Northeast Region—both in the center of the developing transportation network—have undergone much growth since 1963. Because waterways were at one time the principal means of transportation, village settlements are usually strung along one or both sides of a river, canal or roadway. Provincial towns grew out of the larger settlements on a web of waterways, where some of the houses were built on pontoons.

The prominent role of waterways as arteries of mainland travel accounts for the relatively late start in the use of modern means of transportation. Railroads—first opened in 1891—have been important in the economic, administrative and cultural consolidation of the country. In 1967 they were extensively used for reliable, all-weather transportation, and the railway network is being further expanded.

Beginning in 1950 the government launched extensive highway construction programs, but by 1967 only a limited number of roads outside the Bangkok-Thon Buri metropolitan area and those connecting the large provincial cities were suitable for year-round use by buses, trucks and automobiles. In the rural areas rivers and canals were still prominently used for conveying produce to the markets. In the sparsely populated mountain areas the traditional means of waterborne transport was supplemented by animal-drawn carts, pack trains and human carriers.

Most ocean traffic is handled by Bangkok and Shongkhla, although both are shallow-water ports, and their facilities are inadequate to handle the growing number of ships on call. Sattahip, located on the Gulf of Siam about 75 miles southeast of Bangkok, is being developed as a major port to relieve congestion and difficult berthing at the silted, riverine port of Bangkok (see ch. 28, The Armed Forces).

Bangkok, served by the Don Muang airport, 16 miles north of the city, has become an important stopover for tourists traveling on international flights. The government-owned Thai Airways Company, Ltd. (TAC), serves 21 provincial centers and maintains an international service to the major urban centers of Southeast Asia.

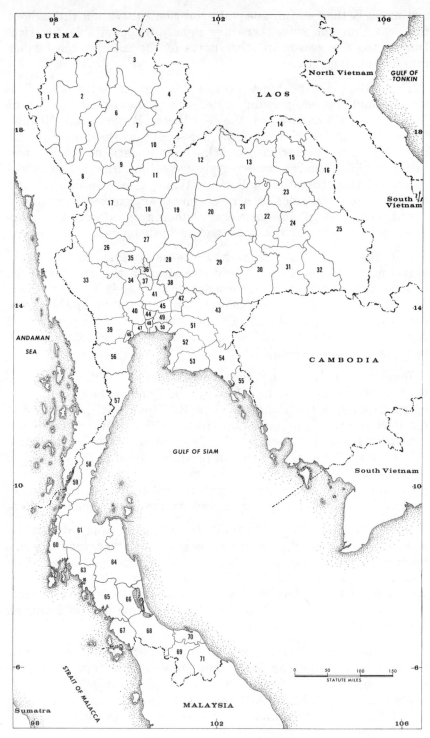

Figure 2.—Provinces of Thailand.

MAJOR GEOGRAPHIC REGIONS

Four natural regions are delineated by the pattern of rivers and mountains: the Northern Region, the Northeast Region (principally the Khorat Plateau), the Central Region (Chao Phraya basin) and the Southern Region (Peninsula). These regions have no significance in civil or military administrations, but their descriptive names are frequently used in presenting various types of information and in defining locations (see fig. 3).

With the exception of the Southern and Northeast Regions the political geography of the nation is oriented toward one major river system, the Chao Phraya (commonly referred to as "Menam," the Thai word for river). Historically the Thai gradually mover down the tributaries of the Chao Phraya and onto the plain of the river itself, which became the center of Thai civilization and political power.

The Northern Region

The mountainous Northern Region, which has an area of about 42,000 square miles, is drained by numerous streams. Those of the extreme north join the Mekong; those of the extreme west join the Salween River. The majority, however, flow southward and eventually join the Chao Phraya. The terrain is marked by a series of parallel north-south mountain ridges and deep, narrow, alluvial valleys. Except where they are scarred by the clearings of the mountaineers or interrupted by masses of bare rock, the ridges are covered with thick forests that yield valuable timber.

The average height of the peaks in the Northern Region is 5,200 feet; southwest of Chiengmai the country's highest mountain, Doi Intharnon, rises to an elevation of about 8,500 feet above sea level. The westernmost ridges continue southward to form the backbone of the Malay Peninsula. In the east the northern sector of the Thai-Laotian border follows the crest of the Luang Phra Bang Mountains.

The Northeast Region (Khorat Plateau)

The 66,000 square miles of the Northeast Region are almost one-third of the country's total area. Its long dry season and relatively scarce rainfall make it the least favored region in the country. Natural vegetation is limited to scrub forests, weeds and grasses. The poor communications and impoverished mixed

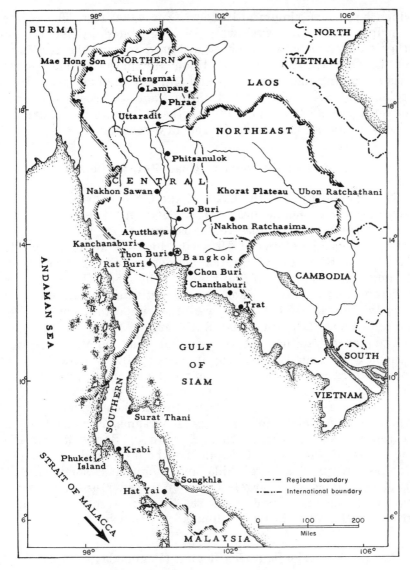

Figure 3.—Natural Regions and Place Names of Thailand.

farming and stockraising there pose a serious challenge to the national authorities in their economic planning (see ch. 20, Agriculture; ch. 21 Industry; ch. 9, Living Conditions).

The plateau is essentially a large basin slightly tilted to the north and east toward the Mekong River. It is rimmed on the south by the Phanom Dongrak Range, a mountain chain rising to between 1,000 and 2,500 feet above sea level on the Cambodian boundary, and on the west by the Phetchabun Mountains,

19

which have a maximum altitude of over 4,000 feet. The region's principal river, the Mun, which is augmented by the Chi and other smaller tributaries, flows eastward to join the Mekong at the Laotian frontier east of Ubon Ratchathani. The marshy flats extending along the Mun and Chi are the only areas in the region that are well watered throughout the year. Elsewhere, the level ground is swampy during the rains and forms dried up wastes of grass and reeds in the dry season.

The Central Region (Chao Phraya Basin)

The Central Region, the basin of the Chao Praya River, is the political and economic heart of the nation. It has an area of about 62,000 square miles and stretches from the foothills of the northern mountains at Uttaradit to the Gulf of Siam. It is flanked on the west along the boundary with Burma by the Bilauktaung Range and on the east by the Khorat Plateau. Bangkok and adjacent Thon Buri constitute the largest urban area in the region, but there are other important centers, such as Ayutthaya, Lop Buri and Rat Buri.

The general flatness of the alluvial basin is interrupted occasionally by small but abruptly rising hills. Jutting into the southeastern part of the region is an extension of the Cardamom Mountains of southwestern Cambodia. The low gradient of the river valley makes it a catch basin for the heavy monsoon rains which slowly drain into the sluggish streams. Belts and patches of jungle occur to the north and south of Bangkok and along the coast of the Gulf of Siam. To the east and southeast of Bangkok a small area of hills and mountains, some rising to 3,000 feet, is covered largely by a dry forest. Most of the valley, however, consists of wide expanses that are treeless or sparsely grown with tall palms and clumps of bamboo.

The Southern Region (Peninsula)

Peninsular Thailand, an area of about 30,000 miles, was acquired in the expansion of the Thai Kingdom down the Malay Peninsula between the fifteenth and nineteenth centuries. The population is predominantly Moslem Malay with small numbers of Thai and Chinese. The economy is based on tin mining, rubber and other tropical crops. The only good soils and harbor facilities are on the Gulf of Siam (see ch. 5, Ethnic Groups; ch. 21, Industry).

The region, noted for its natural scenery, is mountainous with narrow valleys cut by turbulent streams plunging to the coast.

The strip between lower Burma and the Gulf of Siam is in some places less than 12 miles wide, and the land rises steeply from the coast to the mountains of the Burma frontier. Farther south the peninsula is divided by a central range.

RIVERS

From the mountain complex of Tibet ridges and spurs extend through southwestern China and Burma into Thailand where they define the drainage pattern (see fig. 4).

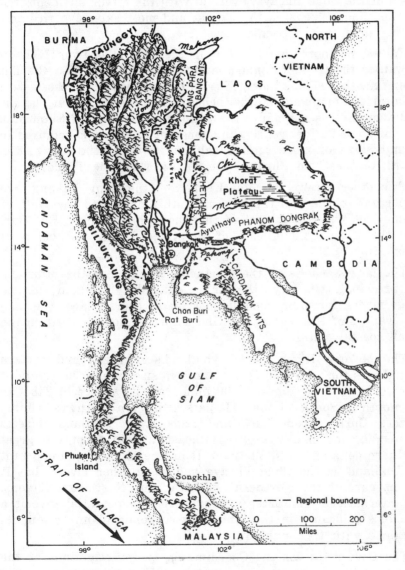

Figure 4.—Landforms and Drainage in Thailand.

In the upper valleys of the Northern Region three major rivers originate, all flowing south: the Ping and its tributary, the Wang; the Yom and the Nan, which combine above Nakhon Sawan to form the Chao Phraya. Farther east a fourth stream, the Pa Sak, also flowing south, joins an eastern branch of the Chao Phraya at Ayutthaya. A distributary of the Chao Phraya, the Nakhon Chai Si, roughly parallels the main stream south of Nakhon Sawan to the Gulf of Siam, which it enters about 25 miles west of the mouth of the Chao Phraya. The amply watered basin of the Chao Phraya, overlaid with the fertile silt deposited by the annual floods, is the richest and most extensive rice-producing area in the country.

Falling no more than 75 feet in the 150 miles from Nakhon Sawan to the Gulf of Siam, the river flows slowly, and the flat plain on either side is indented with backwaters and crossed with tributaries, manmade feeder channels and irrigation canals. Sedimentation is extending the plain into the Gulf of Siam at a rate of 15 or 20 feet yearly, and constant dredging is required to permit ships of more than 2,000 tons to cross the bar at the mouth of the Chao Phraya (see ch. 23, Domestic Trade).

Two other rivers, the Mai Klong and the Bang Pakong, are important in the Central Region. Both empty into the Gulf of Siam—the Mae Klong west of the Chao Phraya below Rat Buri and the Bang Pakong east of the Chao Praya and north of Chon Buri.

The largest rivers in the Northeast Region are the Mun and its principal tributary, the Chi. Peninsular Thailand has no large rivers, but numerous small streams course down the narrow valleys of the region, creating a serious flood hazard on the small coastal plains.

The Mekong River marks Thailand's northern and eastern boundaries for some 500 miles. Tenth in size among the rivers of the world, it flows almost 3,000 mile from its source in Tibet to its mouth in South Vietnam. It passes through southwest China, divides Burma from Laos and Laos from Thailand, bisects Cambodia, and finally veers southeastward to form the great southern delta of South Vietnam. It has never been as important to Thailand as the Chao Phraya and some other rivers, but it drains part of the Northern and all of the Northeast Regions. Its international character and hydroelectric potential give it a special significance in the kingdom's economic planning and its relations with its neighbors.

The Committee for the Coordination of Investigations of the Lower Mekong Basin was created in 1957 by invitation of the

Economic Commission for Asia and the Far East (ECAFE). Surveys have led to plans for dams, irrigation canals and dikes, powerplants and improved navigation. The plans were to be implemented with the cooperation of the five riparian countries (Thailand, Burma, Laos, Cambodia and South Vietnam) and financial assistance from the United Nations and 11 countries, including the United States. In 1958 the United States financed a research program to obtain technological data for the establishment of a hydrologic network in the Lower Mekong Basin and to begin the training of personnel in the operation of the network. The project was started in mid-1963.

Plans were also made for an irrigation project and multipurpose dam (the Pa Mong dam) on the Mekong in the Northeast Region some 25 miles upstream from Vientiane, the capital of Laos. The new dam, which has a capacity of over 1 million kilowatts of power, will control floods as well as increase water levels during the dry season. It will also aid navigation and irrigate about 2.5 million acres of land. A study regarding the feasibility of this project was in progress in 1965 (see ch. 21, Industry).

The Nam Pung Dam, which was completed northeast of Udon Thani in November 1965, also provides irrigation, electrical power and flood control. A hydroelectric power and irrigation plant on the Phong River, a tributary of the upper Chi River in the Northeast Region, opened in March 1966. Situated approximately 50 miles southwest of Udon Thani, the plant generates 25,000 kilowatts of electricity and irrigates about 90,000 acres of land.

The Yanhee multipurpose project, which is located 260 miles northwest of Bangkok just above the confluence of the Ping and Wang Rivers, centers on the construction of a multipurpose dam that will create a reservoir holding more than 14 million cubic yards of water. The dam will also control flooding and aid navigation in the Chao Phraya Basin, make possible a second crop in a large area during the dry season and supply water for the irrigation of more than 500,000 acres of new riceland (see ch. 21, Industry).

CLIMATE

The climate of the country is one of regularity in which the transitional periods between the two distinct seasons offer only a slight variation. The high- and low-pressure masses which alternate in continental Asia in the vicinity of Lake Baykal (conventional Baikal—located in the Soviet Far East) are the governing climatic factors. From late March or early April to September the low-pressure area over Lake Baykal and a similar high-pressure area over the Indian Ocean cause warm, moist winds to be drawn from the southwest across the Bay of Bengal and into Thailand, bringing the moisture that precipitates over the landmass. In the remaining months of the year (September to March) a high-pressure system over Lake Baykal sends dry continental winds from the northeast toward the lows of the Indian Ocean, and the "dry monsoon" is dominant. During this time the Thai peasant farmer in the Central Plain depends upon the river for his water.

The "wet monsoon" of March through September is the more distinct season because the winds are constant and the precipitation is regular. The direction and speed of the winds are not as constant during the dry monsoon.

Climatic variations are most important in terms of rainfall, especially in the districts that are not affected by the annual flooding of the Chao Phraya. Only in the Peninsula is there adequate rainfall for rice cultivation, but rice soils are rarely found there (see fig. 5).

In the Central Region (the Chao Phraya Basin) at least 90 percent of the rainfall occurs during the wet monsoon from May to October. This percentage is reasonably constant for the entire country. Chiengmai receives 85 percent of its precipitation from May to September; in October the Northern Region is beyond the reach of coastal variables that might bring showers, but it is susceptible to cyclonic and landform variations particularly in March, April and December.

Although the dominant rainfall distribution pattern is based upon the monsoon winds and the location of the mountains, cyclonic variations occur. Thailand is influenced by side eddies from the southern Asiatic winter cyclonic storm belt which extends from northeastern India to southwestern Communist China. The summer cyclonic storm belt has no effect except in the far northwest.

The mountain slopes are crucial to the regulation of the Chao Phraya watershed because they are still thickly forested, and normally insignificant amounts of rainfall are effective. On the western slopes of the basin showers occur about 3 weeks before the summer monsoon, thus raising the level of the streams high enough for the peasant to find water to soften his land in preparation for plowing. Showers occurring during local cyclonic variations have the same effect.

24

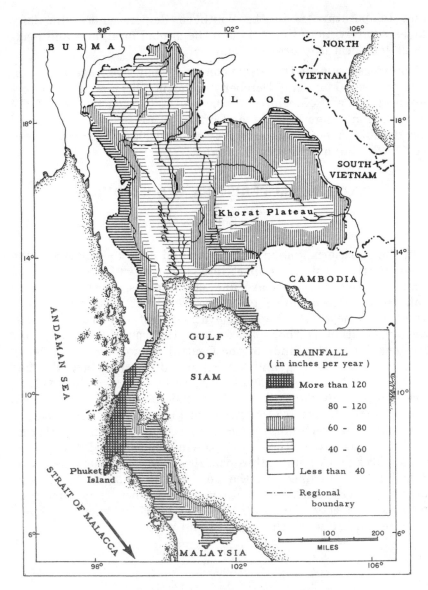

Figure 5.—Rainfall in Thailand.

From March to September, the period of the wet monsoon, the mean maximum temperature in the Central Region is near 98° F., but there are records of readings above 100°; the minimum temperature is about 80°. In the dry season the maximum temperature goes above 90° although the mean is considerably lower; the minimum temperature is near 57°. In the north and northwest the variation is much greater. Chiengmai has a mean annual temperature of 77.8° and a mean range of 14°. The most constant temperature is in the Southern Region where the daily range is rarely more than 14° and the annual minimum and maximum temperatures are 68° and 95°.

Thunderstorms in the afternoon and early evenings are common between May and October in the northern areas and between March and November in the south. Toward the end of the dry season and again at the end of the rainy season typhoons of considerable violence sweep across the Indochina peninsula from the South China Sea into Thailand.

LAND CHARACTERISTICS AND RESOURCES

Soils

In the Northern Region dark clays and alluvial deposits found along the river valleys support intensive rice cultivation. On the Khorat Plateau the soils are fine sandy loams. Most are low in plant nutrients, and some are saline. Deeper and richer soils are found on some of the higher elevations, but the prevailing natural vegetation is the sparse grass that provides forage for livestock. In the lowlands of the Central Region the basic heavy dark clays are varied, and superimposed on them are the fine sandy and silty soils deposited by the Chao Phraya floodwaters. Rice can be grown on all the flood plains, and the lighter soils along the riverbanks are favorable for growing fruit trees, sugarcane, jute and vegetables. The deep red soils of the southeast coastal plains are suitable for growing rubber and fruit trees and sugarcane. Coconut palms can also be raised where this type of soil is well drained. In the northern part of the Peninsula some soils are saline, but farther south rubber trees thrive on the sand and clay loam soils. The fertile river valleys support the rice culture (see ch. 20, Agriculture).

Minerals

The country's wide variety of minerals is being exploited unevenly. Tin in peninsular Thailand and on Phuket Island is the most important mineral. It amounts to about 16 percent of the non-Communist world's tin reserves. Tin deposits of lesser importance occur also in the northwestern part of the country in a narrow strip along the Burmese border (see fig. 6).

Antimony is found in the Northern Region, southeast of Chiengmai in Lampang and Phrae Provinces, and in Surat Thani in the Southern Region. The size of the reserves has not been established, but it is not thought to be large. There is some tungsten in the Bilauktaung Range and on the islands of Phangan and Samui, which are 80 miles north of Nakhon Si Thammarat along the eastern shoreline of the Gulf of Siam. The most important deposits discovered are in the estreme northwest (Mai Hong Son Province) and in Kanchanaburi Province, west of Bangkok.

Copper reserves are located mainly in the Northern Region, west and southwest of Lampang. Gold has been reported in 26 provinces. The best-known deposits are at Kabin Buri in the hills about 70 miles east of Bangkok, To Mo on the Malaysian border and the area east of Nakhon Sawan in the Central Region. Ilmenite, the source of titanium, is found in beach deposits in many places along the east and west coasts of peninsula Thailand. Lead and zinc occur and are mined near Lampang southeast of Chiengmai, in the Bilauktaung Range mountains of Kanchanaburi Province and in association with tin and tungsten on the Malaysian border. Tungsten with tin also occurs in the Bilauktaung Range and farther north along the Burma border southwest of Chiengmai.

Manganese is found in several small deposits west of Chanthaburi, on the Peninsula just north of the Malaysian border and north of Kanchanaburi along the upper reaches of the Mae Klong River. Gem stones that include sapphire, ruby, topaz and zircon are mined from several deposits in the mountains southeast of Bangkok along the Cambodian boundary and north of Kanchanaburi in western Thailand.

Molybdenum is found southeast of Chanthaburi near the Cambodian border. Monazite and Ilmenite occur on the west coast of the Peninsula north of Phuket Island and on the Gulf of Siam coast, north and south of Phet Buri and south of Songkhla.

Coal deposits, some with a high sulfur content, are known to be in 17 localities in 8 provinces. The most important are on the Peninsula near Surat Thani and on the western coastline north and south of Krabi. Important deposits are also found in the Northern Region southwest of Chiengmai and east of Lampang. The coal found in the Lampang area is lignite or brown coal; total reserves of this deposit are estimated at 15 million metric tons.

Oil shale is present in substantial quantity, probably exceeding 2 million tons, in the basin around Mae Sot, in the northwest highlands near the Burma border. Oil content ranges roughly between 7 and 70 gallons per metric ton of shale. Petroleum with a naphthalene base has been found at tar seeps and in shallow wells

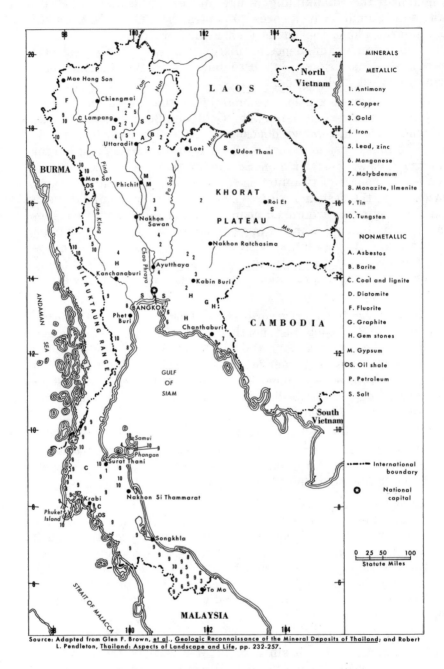

Source: Adapted from Glen F. Brown, et al., Geologic Reconnaissance of the Mineral Deposits of Thailand; and Robert L. Pendleton, Thailand: Aspects of Landscape and Life, pp. 232-257.

Figure 6.—Mineral Resources in Thailand.

in the northernmost tip of the northwest highlands. Reserves are estimated to be about 22 million barrels.

Asphaltic sand is quarried from the tar seeps for highway surfacing. A reserve of asphalt-impregnated sand and gravel near the seeps is estimated to be 5 million cubic yards (see ch. 21, Industry). Iron ore (hematite-magnetic) is mined only at Thap Kwai hill in the Central Region, 55 miles southeast of Nakhon Sawan, although the largest reserves (approximately 30 million tons) occur 35 miles northeast of Kanchanaburi. Other fields exist at Loei west of Udon Thani in the Northeast Region, on Samui Island in Surat Thani Province and just north of Bangkok.

Asbestos and barite are known to be present north and northeast of Uttaradit. Barite is also found near the Burma border north of Mae Sot. Deposits of diatomite are found southeast of Lampang; fluorite is present southwest of Chiengmai. The area south of Kabin Buri near the Cambodia border shows some graphite deposits. Known gypsum reserves of more than 10 million tons are located in Phichit Province, about 220 miles north of Bangkok; other deposits are reported in several localities, including some of the Southern Region.

Although the evaporation of sea water from the saltponds built at the head of the Gulf of Siam provides the major source of salt, a number of salt springs are scattered throughout the Northern Region and the Khorat Plateau in the northeast. The most important springs are those east of Lampang in northern Thailand and on the Khorat Plateau, a few miles northwest of Udon Thani and southeast of Roi Et.

Vegetation

Forests cover almost 60 percent of the total area of the country. In general, tropical evergreen forests are found at elevations above 3,200 feet, and deciduous forests are located in uncultivated areas at lower levels; in the Northern and Northeast Regions some coniferous growth occurs down to an altitude of 2,400 feet. Thorn and bamboo thickets grow in all regions except in the north (see fig. 7).

In the Northern Region are the evergreen forests which provide valuable teak and redwood timber. In the Northeast Region evergreen forests cover the low mountains fringing the southern and western perimeters of the Khorat Plateau. The remainder of the plateau is covered mainly with thorny shrubs, stunted trees and bamboo, and sparse grass. Most of the natural vegetation has disappeared from the lowlands of the Central Region except along

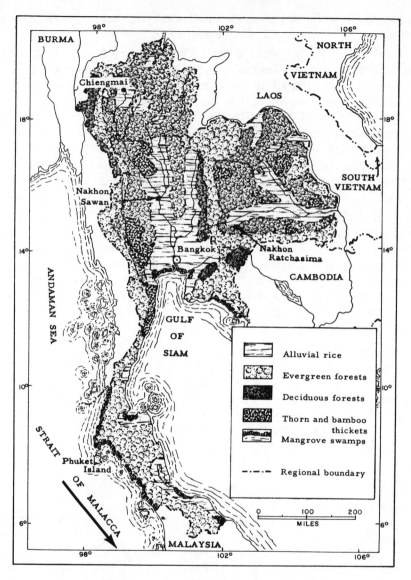

Figure 7.—Vegetation of Thailand.

the Gulf of Siam coast, which is lined with mangrove swamps, trees of various types or bamboo thickets. Most of the Peninsula is covered with tropical evergreens. The country has a wide variety of tropical, wild fruit trees and flowering plants.

Animal Life

Thailand is endowed with a rich and varied fauna. Wild elephants roam the limestone hills of the Northern Region and the woodlands of the Southern Region. They can be tamed for work in the timber areas, and they are protected by law. The gaur or kating, a large wild ox, grazes in the uplands of the north and northwest. Both the single- and double-horned rhinoceros existed in the Southern Region until the early years of this century when they appear to have become extinct. The tapir is occasionally seen in the forests along the Malaysian border, and the wild hog and several types of deer are common in the wooded areas.

Other forest dwellers are the big cats—tigers, leopards and panthers—and many small predators. The large Himalayan black bear and the smaller Malay bear are found in the mountain ranges. Gibbons and several species of monkeys are widely distributed. Of the 50 kinds of snakes, about a dozen are poisonous, including cobras, coral snakes, kraits and vipers. Sea snakes and lizards abound; crocodiles and several species of turtles are also present.

The waters of the area, fresh and salt, are rich in fish. Offshore fishing is a developing industry, and farmers raise and catch fish in artificial ponds and the flooded ricefields. The catch from the rivers is sizable (see ch. 20, Agriculture).

SETTLEMENT PATTERNS

Rural

Between 85 and 90 percent of the people reside in small, long-established, self-sustaining hamlets and villages. They fall roughly into three types: strip villages, cluster villages and dispersed villages.

The strip village is the most common. Typically, such a settlement stretches along one or both sides of a river, canal or roadway. House orientation within this strip shows no particular pattern. The larger strip villages may be several miles in length, with the ricefields lying behind the single line of dwelling compounds. In densely settled areas villages may form a continuous line, for a considerable distance, with no apparent demarcation among them. In such cases administrative units may not coincide with social community units. Within the strip villages the local orientation of the villagers may be based on the position of the local *wat* (see Glossary).

Cluster villages, prevalent in the valleys of the Northern Region, are usually set back several hundred yards from the main thoroughfare—a river, navigable canal, railroad line, branch road or main highway. Villages of this type are ordinarily situated in and around a grove of fruit trees and coconut palms.

The third type, the dispersed village, accounts for less than one-tenth of the villages in the country and is found only in the delta region around Bangkok. There isolated farms or groups of several households, each widely separated from its neighbors on its own small piece of high ground, have appeared in conjunction with the development of intensive commercialized rice cultivation on relatively large landholdings. Between 10 and 50 of these widely separated farmsteads are grouped together for administrative purposes as a village, each with an elected headman.

Urban

Bangkok, the country's only city with a population of more than 100,000, is one of the great metropolitan centers of Southeast Asia. In 1960 its population was estimated to be about 1.6 million, of which 1.3 million lived in Bangkok proper and the remainder in Thon Buri, the principal suburb. In 1965 it was reported that Bangkok had a population of about 2 million.

The city is situated on the east bank of the Chao Phraya River, about 15 miles from the Gulf of Siam. The river divides the Bangkok-Thon Buri metropolitan area, which covers a total of about 173 square miles. Bangkok, on the east side of the Chao Phraya River, occupies three-fourths of the municipal land.

Low, level ground interspersed with waterways characterizes the topography of the area. The interior of Bangkok is laced with *klongs* (canals) that carry much of its traffic and give it a distinctively aquatic character. *Klongs* were formerly utilized extensively for waterborne travel, but since the late 1950's they have been used mainly for carrying produce to markets.

Historically, the hub of the city was the Grand Palace. This oldest section of Bangkok, located in a deep bend of the river, was constructed by King Rama I (1782–1809) with the labor of thousands of Cambodian prisoners of war.

Thon Buri, the largest suburb, is on the west bank of the Chao Phraya opposite the central part of Bangkok proper, to which it is joined by several bridges. This suburb is most densely populated along the river and the principal canal. Small commercial establishments have begun to appear as the population increases.

Each of the city's districts and quarters, with its own temples and markets, functions almost as a self-contained small town. The Chinese Sampeng district is the only minority quarter. Almost everywhere thatched houses and rice paddies are in close proximity to shops, Western-style houses and modern government buildings. There is relatively little formal separation of industrial, commercial and residential areas; the only exceptions are the newer residential districts of Ban Kaphi to the north and Bang Su to the east.

Bangkok is an important international port and the center of the internal transport system. All of the country's principal highways and rail, water and air routes converge upon it. Its large and well-equipped airport at Don Muang is one of the principal international air route junctions in the Far East.

Extensive building and reconstruction of roads have been carried out, and many narrow, *klong*-lined sections of road have been superseded by broad highways. The main road to and through the important suburb of Ban Kaphi is now a commuters' highway. Another modern road links the city with the Don Muang airport, 16 miles to the northeast. The ban on *samlors* (pedicabs) within the city limits and their replacement by small three-wheeled taxis have eliminated one important cause of traffic congestion (see ch. 23, Domestic Trade).

Bangkok has also become a major shopping and amusement center. Whereas it once offered little more than temples and picturesque floating markets, by the mid-1960's the city had modern hotels, new restaurants and other tourist accommodations. The contribution of tourism to the country's foreign exchange is considerable (see ch. 24, Foreign Economic Relations).

Chiengmai, with a population of 72,600 in 1963, is regarded as the second largest city in Thailand. It is about 500 miles north of Bangkok and lies along the Ping River in a valley about 15 miles wide. About 1,000 feet above sea level, it is situated 4 miles from the base of Doi Suthep—a peak rising over 5,000 feet. Perched 3,500 feet up the mountainside is the famous Temple of Wat Doi Su Thep, established in 1383 and visited by Buddhist pilgrims from all over the world.

Chiengmai was founded in 1296 by King Meng Rai (Prince of Chieng Saen) and was a city-state for centuries. As recently as 100 years ago it was virtually independent. Crumbling brick walls hem in its older portion on the west bank of the river; on the east bank is the modern section. Nearby are teak forests, where elephants are used to roll logs to the river where they are floated as rafts to Bangkok.

Nakhon Ratchasima (sometimes called Khorat), the largest town in the Northeast Region and the fourth largest in the country, is about 145 miles northeast of Bangkok. The town is situated in a saucer-shaped area at the edge of the Khorat Plateau, which is characterized by rolling, low-altitude hills interspersed with small bodies of water. During the rainy season (from July through October) large parts of the area are flooded because the low relief causes slow ground-water drainage.

With a population of approximately 43,000, the city has outgrown its walls, and its old main gate now stands in the center of the town. It is the distribution center for the Northeast Region, and its railway workshops service the rail lines running east to Ubon Ratchathani and north to Nong Khai, which is across the Mekong River from the Laotian capital of Veintiane.

Hat Yai, with a population of almost 36,000, is situated 475 miles southwest of Bangkok, about 20 miles inland from the port city of Songkhla in peninsular Thailand. The commercial center of the south, it is the headquarters of wealthy rubber and tin traders and of numerous overseas commercial firms. The general aspect of the town is more Malay than Thai.

TRANSPORTATION

Railroads

In 1966 railroad service was provided by a meter-gauge (3 feet 3⅜ inches) railway system totaling 2,275 miles in length. All lines were single track except a 56-mile double-track stretch running north from Bangkok (see fig. 8).

The first railroad line, opened in 1891, provided passenger service between Bangkok and Samut Prakan, located on the Gulf of Siam coast about 20 miles south of the capital. When this venture proved successful, the government launched its first major railway-building program connecting the city of Ayutthaya, in the Chao Phraya lowlands about 40 miles north of Bangkok, with Nakhon Ratchasima in the Northeast Region. This line was opened in 1901, and by 1926 it was carried to Ubon Ratchathani near the Laotian border. A branch line, running north from Nakhon Ratchasima across the Khorat Plateau to Udon Thani, was later added. The completion of this line northward to Nong Khai on the Mekong River was delayed, however, until 1955.

Another line toward the east, running directly east from Bangkok to the Cambodian border, was completed in 1926. The main line from Bangkok to the Northern Region was completed in 1921. It passes through a mile-long tunnel 25 miles southeast of its terminus at Chiengmai.

Railway transport from Bangkok to peninsular Thailand also started in the early 1900's. The Bangkok-Phet Buri line was opened in 1903. The southward extension of this line was completed in 1922 when connections were established with the Malay-

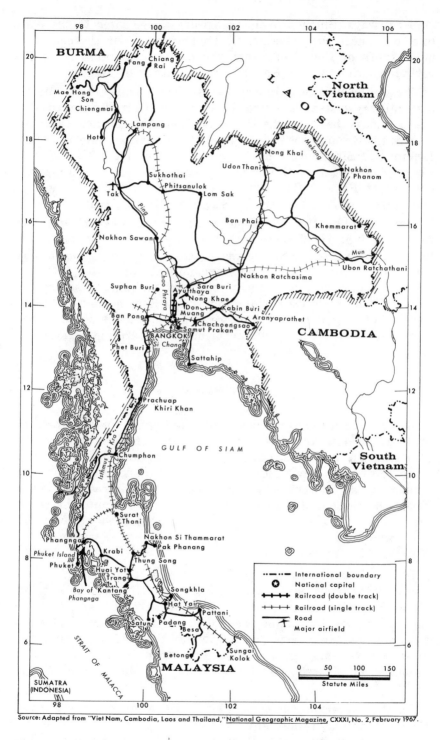

Source: Adapted from "Viet Nam, Cambodia, Laos and Thailand," National Geographic Magazine, CXXXI, No. 2, February 1967.

Figure 8.—Transportation Routes, Ports and Major Airfields in Thailand.

35

sian railways. Short branch lines were added later to the main line to connect with Nakhon Si Thammarat, near the coast 340 miles south of Phet Buri, with the port of Songkhla 100 miles farther south and with Kantang on the Strait of Malacca.

The southern railway line connects with a branch of the Malaysian railway system at Sungai Kolok on the Gulf of Siam coast at the boundary between the two countries. This branch continues southward through the central part of the Malay Peninsula to the Republic of Singapore. The Songkhla branch of the Thai railway line extends in a southwestern direction to join the Malaysian railway at Padang Besa. This section of the Malaysian system continues southward along the Strait of Malacca coast.

Plans to extend the railway network were considerably retarded by World War II. Money allotted in the national budget for the building of railroads and loans extended by the International Bank for Reconstruction and Development were used to repair existing facilities and to renew obsolete equipment (see ch. 25, Public Finance). Specific plans were made during the early 1960's for the building of an additional railroad line on the western coast of the Peninsula, but in 1967 information regarding the status of this project was unavailable.

Waterways

The inland waterways, which are navigable for shallow-draft craft, total approximately 3,700 miles and are now secondary in importance to railways. Concentrated mostly on the plains of the Chao Phraya lowlands, north of Bangkok, they constitute an interconnected network of rivers, canals and branch streams. Nearly 80 percent of the rice crop is moved to the mills via waterways; however, the great fluctuation of water levels caused by the rainy and dry seasons handicaps much of the river traffic (see ch. 23, Domestic Trade).

In the Central Region the Chao Phraya River, its tributaries and distributaries, and a network of connecting canals are used by boats of all sizes throughout the year. Much of the local trading activity on the plains just north and northeast of Bangkok takes place on shop-boats, which display their wares as they float down rivers and canals. Ayutthaya, about 50 miles north of Bangkok, is a well-known center of "floating markets" (see fig. 4).

Farther north, in the Chao Phraya Basin, much rice is moved by water although there are fewer canals and rivers are less suitable for water transport. During the fall harvesttime the boats are towed upstream by tugs, and the loaded ones float downstream to Bangkok when high water conditions prevail.

On the Khorat Plateau the Chi River and its tributaries may be used for boat transport only during the flood season in September and October.

In the Northern Region river travel is very limited. Short boat trips are possible during the rainy season, although streams and creeks tend to flow in torrents.

River transport is exceedingly difficult on the Mekong, which forms much of the country's eastern boundary. Passengers and goods are transported by river streamers from the Laotian border town of Vientiane to Khemmarat, 300 miles downstream. Below Khemmarat there are numerous dangerous rapids navigable only by small boats from May to August.

Roads

Modern highway and road construction began in the late 1930's. Priority has generally been given to the construction of roads which serve as feeders to the railway lines. In late 1966 there were approximately 7,800 miles of highways and provincial roads. Some of these roads were built under the Seven-Year Provincial Highway Development Program (1964–70) (see ch. 23, Domestic Trade).

Road maintenance is generally poor, and during the rainy season large sections are impassable because of flooding. According to government statistics in 1963, the majority were unpaved in all but the Central Region. The surfaces often break up under heavy loads because of construction defects and poor drainage. Only about 35 percent of the existing roads in 1965 were suitable for all-weather travel.

In the Northern Region the most important highway is the road leading from Bangkok northward 300 miles through Nakhon Sawan, then northwest about 100 miles into the mountains to Ban Tak and north through Lampang to Chiang Rai. From Chiang Rai the road continues north into Burma. About 50 miles north of Ban Tak a road branches off northwestward to Chiengmai and then north to Fang, near the Burmese border. The mountainous area west of Chiengmai, including the upper Ping River valley, is severly handicapped by the lack of roads; however, a map published in 1965 by the Thai National Statistical Office shows a road about 50 miles north of Chiengmai branching westward to Mae Hong Son near the Burmese border. Another branch road runs from Chiengmai some 50 miles in a southwesterly direction to Hot, only about 25 miles west of the main north-south highway.

An important highway in the Northern Region leads from Ban Tak about 50 miles east to Sukhothai and then to Phitsanulok. From the latter a good, hard-surface road runs about 80 miles to Lom Sak, located at the foot of the Phetchabun Mountains. Called the East-West Highway, the road was completed in 1965 with United States aid.

In the Khorat Plateau a major road, almost 250 miles long, runs northward from Nakhon Ratchasima to Nong Khai on the Mekong River. Several other roads run eastward from rail junctions on this road, notably from Ban Phai about 90 miles north of Nakhon Ratchasima and from Udon Thani about 30 miles south of Nong Khai.

From Bangkok the Khorat Plateau may be reached by a highway, about 152 miles long, that runs from the capital in a north-eastern direction to Sara Buri and then to Nakhon Ratchasima. The Sara Buri-Nakhon Ratchasima stretch, about 92 miles long, is a good, all-weather road completed with United States aid in 1965. Another road linking the capital to the eastern provinces runs through Nong Khai, 48 miles northeast of Bangkok, to Aranyaprathet on the Cambodian border. The road is usable throughout the year and connects with two major highways in Cambodia.

To provide a direct approach, which bypasses Bangkok, from the Gulf of Siam to the Khorat Plateau, a new road was opened in 1966. It runs from Chachoengsao, about 25 miles north of the Gulf of Siam, for 50 miles in a northeastern direction through Kabin Buri to Nakhon Ratchasima. Built with substantial United States aid, the road cuts through approximately 145 miles of jungle forests and ricefields.

The major road to the Peninsula runs west about 48 miles from Bangkok, to Ban Pong, then south about 250 miles through Phet Buri and Prachuap Khiri Khan to Chumphon, where it traverses the Isthmus of Kra and continues along the western coast south-ward through Phangnga to Krabi. At Krabi it swerves from the coastline in a southeastern direction to the railroad junction of Huai Yot (Khao Khao) and then to Kantang on the Strait of Malacca coast.

From Kantang the Peninsula may be traversed by a highway, roughly 100 miles long, running northeast to Trang, Thung Song, Nakhon Si Thammarat and then Pak Phanang on the coast of the Gulf of Siam. South of Trang a relatively extensive road network serves the mines and rubber plantations in the southernmost part of the Peninsula and on Phuket Island. A good road crosses the Peninsula from the port of Songkhla on the Gulf of Siam via the railroad junction of Hat Yai to Satun, 10 miles from the western coastline. About 20 miles south of Hat Yai two roads extend farther south and connect with the highways of Malaysia. One of the roads runs in a relatively straight southern course and crosses the Malaysian border 40 miles south of Hat Yai. The other branches off to the east 20 miles south of that city and leads to Pattani on the eastern coast of the Gulf of Siam. From Pattani a road runs south about 100 miles through an important tin and rubber region, and it connects with Malaysian highways after crossing the border near Betong.

Ports

There are no natural deepwater ports on the country's 1,550 miles of shoreline. Bangkok is the only major port, but its docking facilities, which were mostly built between 1939 and 1954, are inadequate. Because it is a riverine port, situated 17 miles from the sea at the mouth of the Chao Phraya, most large oceangoing vessels have difficulty passing through the entrance channel. Dredging operations to enlarge the channel have proved expensive and only partially effective. The growing volume of ocean traffic has created much congestion in the harbor although wharf facilities have been enlarged since 1965. Some of the large vessels berth in the upper reaches of the Gulf of Siam at Si Chang Island, but lighters must be used to move their cargoes to the mainland.

In order to relieve the overburdened capacity of Bangkok construction of a major port in Sattahip, 75 miles southeast of Bangkok, began in 1966. In 1967 dredging operations were in progress to deepen the harbor. When it is completed, Sattahip will offer berthing facilities to four to seven ships simultaneously and will have repair shops for major commercial and military vessels (see ch. 28, The Armed Forces).

Songkhla, on the eastern shore of the Peninsula about 150 miles north of the Malaysia border, ranks second in importance after Bangkok. Oceangoing vessels, however, may call only during the rainy season from April to September because of the shallow water in the port. Following a survey made in 1963 by a United States firm recommendations were made to construct a deepwater port in Songkhla, but in 1967 information on the status of this project was unavailable.

Pattani, 50 miles south of Songkhla, is the other major port on the eastern shore of the Peninsula, and it serves an important rubber and coconut exporting area. Because of limited facilities and shallow water conditions Pattani offers only limited service, and large vessels must anchor about 5 miles offshore. Improvement of the port facilities has been planned to facilitate the landing of deep-draft vessels.

Phuket, on Phuket Island, faces east on the Bay of Phangnga. The port is shallow, providing service for small vessles only. A major tin port, Phuket also serves the town of Phangnga and its environs on the mainland north of Phuket. Funds were authorized in 1956 to dredge a deep channel and basin to accommodate large lighters and medium-sized, coastal vessels.

Airports

The government-owned Thai Airways Company Ltd., (TAC) provides domestic service to 21 points within the country. There are TAC international flights to India, Burma, Hong Kong, Taiwan, Japan, Cambodia, South Vietnam, Laos and Malaysia.

The only airport adequately maintained to provide continuous service for four-engine aircraft is at Don Muang, about 16 miles north of Bangkok. Government plans in 1967 called for the expansion of its facilities and for the building of an additional airport to serve the growing air traffic in the Bangkok area.

The country has approximately 30 additional airfields, but they are suitable for light planes only. These fields are generally poorly surfaced and lack adequate fueling and communications facilities. Moreover, they are inoperative for extended periods during and immediately following the rainy season. Projects to improve the airfields at Ubon, Ratchathani, Nakhon Ratchasima, Udon Thani, Tak and Chiengmai were underway in 1965.

CHAPTER 3

HISTORICAL SETTING

The Thai word for history means "biograhy of the kings," and this is the character of most Thai historical writing. There is much about war and conquest, palace intrigue and kingly exploits but almost nothing about the social and intellectual history of the people. The Thai historical record, for the most part, has been based on orally repeated legends rather than on factual investigation.

In recent years there has been official encouragement of historical scholarship, which has been inspired by a growing national consciousness. A few Western and Thai writers have begun to take greater interest in the history of the country, and a number of partial studies have appeared. The version of Thai history taught to schoolchildren, however, continues to be based largely on the legends of past Thai glory and greatness. It is much more specific in its dates and descriptions than non-Thai scholars have considered verifiable.

Knowledge of the earliest Thai history is derived almost exclusively from the little that appears in ancient Chinese annals. The people seem to have lived in tribal groupings in areas corresponding roughly to the present-day province of Yunnan in southwest China. No written history of the Kingdom of Sukhothai, which arose in the area of present-day northern Thailand after numbers of Thai had emigrated from China, has ever been discovered; historians must depend entirely on the chronicles of neighboring countries, a few ancient and obscure manuscripts, and three stone inscriptions.

Accurate and fairly complete records date only from the Bangkok Era (1767–1932); when the Burmese took Ayutthaya for the second time in 1767 they destroyed many of the official records and annals. Subsequent efforts to reconstruct the history of Ayutthaya have resulted in a work called the *Phongsawadan*. This work was developed in several versions, which were variously dated and differed widely in content, and the compilers failed to preserve the documents from which they had drawn their information. Speaking of these annals, King Mongkut (1851–68) said that they were "full of fable and not of satisfaction for belief." Nonetheless, these sources proved useful in shedding light on the history of the Ayutthaya period.

From the time of Nanchao, the earlist known Thai state, to the present, certain historical consistencies exist. The economy of the Thai has always been based on rice cultivation, and the religion has been a mixture of Buddhism and animism. Government has been a function of the elite, and rulers have not in any real sense been accountable to the people. Except for compulsory labor on public projects and military service the people have been little oppressed or disturbed by their rulers. There are no recorded instances of peasar.. revolts or class warfare. Except for rare and brief intervals the state has not been subject to foreign rule.

While the Thai have vigorously guarded their political independence, they have liberally borrowed cultural elements from other peoples. Warfare and trade have brought them into contact with many rich and highly developed civilizations—Chinese, Indian, Kh..ier (Cambodian), Burmese and European. The Thai have shown a striking ability to recover from adversity and to accept from others whatever suited their needs.

Even the briefest period in Thai history cannot avoid frequent references to war and combat. The Thai first appeared in history as warriors and migrants. Wars have been the concern of kings and nobles, and the ordinary people who have been frequently called to combat have not been fond of fighting and have not cherished the military virtues.

Thailand has a long record of conflict with neighboring powers. Boundaries were frequently changed by force of arms. In the north and northeast Chiengmai and Lan Xang (in present-day Laos) were often at war with Ayutthaya. In the east, Cambodia periodically rebelled against Thai suzerainty, and the Vietnamese, especially during the late eighteenth and early nineteenth centuries, were a frequent threat. Burma, long the chief adversary, mounted attacks that threatened the very existence of the Thai state. In 1568 and again in 1767, Burma destroyed Ayutthaya and subjected Thailand to its control.

Wars were fought not only for territory but over questions of dignity and power. A struggle might be precipitated by the desire for white elephants, which were thought to bring their possessors prestige and good fortune. Rulers coveted them because the presence of many white elephants during a king's reign was regarded as a most auspicious sign of divine favor.

To the turmoil of these external struggles was added the confusion of internal strife when a provincial lord revolted against the central authorities or when members of the royal family disputed succession to the throne.

The almost incessant warfare inevitably had important social effects. People fled before advancing armies or were forcibly transplanted by the victors; this accelerated the cultural diffusion and increased the ethnic complexity of all the states of Southeast Asia. The demands of war created systems of slavery and increased the burden of compulsory military and labor service. Warfare also worked in the usual way to limit population growth. Thousands of troops were lost in combat, and thousands of civilians died in the devastation caused by the invading armies. Disease ravaged besieged towns and wasted whole provinces. Some authorities estimate that only in recent years has Thailand exceeded the population it had in the sixteenth century before the conflicts with Burma began.

Thailand's history falls into five main periods: the Nanchao Era (c. A.D. 650–1253), the Sukhothai Era (c. 1238–1350), the Ayutthaya Era (1350–1767), the Bangkok Era (1767–1932) and the Constitutional Era (1932–   ). All except the first and last periods derived their names from the capital cities of the time (see fig. 9).

THE NANCHAO ERA (c. A.D. 650–1253)

Chinese annalists of the sixth century B.C. made frequent references to the "barbarians" south of the Yangtze River. Many different tribes were probably included in this designation, and some of them in southwest China appear to have been Thai peoples. Little is known about their earliest history, but according to a few sources they seemed to have physically resembled the Chinese people in some respects and to have spoken a tonal language related to Chinese (see ch. 5, Ethnic Groups).

Legend has it that by the mid-seventh century A.D. the Thai had established the powerful military Kingdom of Nanchao, which was centered in the region of Lake Tali in the Chinese province of Yunnan. Many Western scholars do not recognize this kingdom as being as large or long-lasting as the Thai legend indicates. An eminent German Sinologist states that the Thai of Yunnan were bands led by chieftains rather than an organized state. The Chinese annals, however, do refer to Nanchao although little is known about the extent of its boundaries or its period of duration.

Nanchao is said to have successfully resisted Chinese efforts

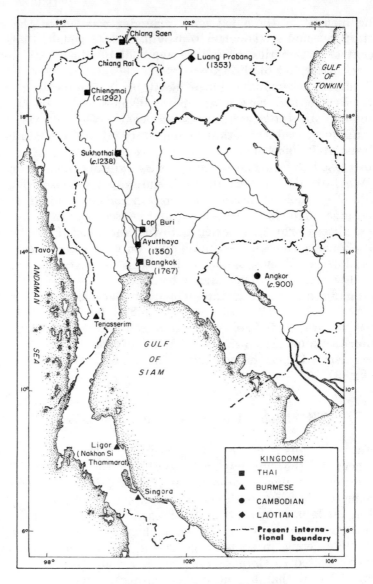

Figure 9.—Kingdoms Affecting Thai History.

at reconquest in 751 and 754. After asserting its independence from the Chinese, Nanchao slowly extended its territory to the south and east; in 862–63 it invaded Tonkin (present-day North Vietnam). By the end of the ninth century Nanchao appears to have accepted Chinese overlordship on the basis of a tributary relationship, and in 1253 the Thai were driven out of Nanchao by the Mongol-Chinese armies under Kublai Khan.

Thai culture in the Nanchao period was heavily influenced by the Chinese with whom the Thai had frequent contact through tributary missions, trade and war. Thai rulers sought marriage with aristocratic Chinese families and sent their sons to Chinese centers to study. In 829 the Thai armies captured a large number of Chinese artisans and brought them to Nanchao. Chinese chronicles of the T'ang dynasty (A.D. 618–907) and Marco Polo, during and after his stay in China (1275–1292) recorded the similarity in customs, dress and administration between the Chinese and Thai peoples.

According to Thai accounts, Nanchao achieved a fairly sophisticated political organization and an official class which included ministers of state, censors, recorders, judges, court chamberlains and military officers. Most of the people were rice farmers. Land was distributed according to the rank and size of families, and taxes were paid chiefly in rice. Gold was mined, and handicrafts included the weaving of cotton and silk. All adult males were required to perform military service. Prisoners of war were enslaved, but during this period slavery and forced labor were only slightly developed among the Thai themselves (see ch. 22, Labor). Religion was believed to be a mixture of animism and Buddhism (see ch. 12, Religion).

THE SUKHOTHAI ERA (c. 1238–1350)

Movement Southward

Long before the fall of Nanchao, Thai peoples had begun drifting southward along the rivers of central Indochina, and tiny, independent Thai principalities began to emerge in northern Indochina. Early in the twelfth century small Thai states dotted the upper Chao Phraya valley (see ch. 2, Physical Environment). During the thirteenth century, the stream of movement became a flood that was released by the defeat of Nanchao and by the weakening of the Khmer (Cambodian) power in the south.

In the Chao Phraya valley there were, in addition to the small Thai states, two Mon-Khmer kingdoms: Dvaravati, a Khmer vassal in the south, and Haripunjaya, an independent kingdom in the north. In 1238 these Mon-Khmer states were defeated by two powerful chieftains of the small Thai states that had developed in the upper Chao Phraya Basin at Chiang Rai and Chiengmai. One of the chieftains established at Sukhothai what was to become a mighty and vigorous, although short-lived, Thai kingdom. The other chieftain established at Chiengmai a city-state kingdom.

By 1300 the Thai had settled all the valleys of the principal river systems, the Irrawaddy, Salween, Chao Phraya and Mekong, and dominated most of the peninsula to the south. One branch of the Thai family, the Shan, controlled much of the area of present-day Burma; another branch, the Lao, consolidated their petty states into the Empire of Lan Xang, in 1353, and dominated an area considerably larger than present-day Laos.

The capture of Sukhothai from the Khmer was a major event in Thai history. The first Thai king of Sukhothai, whose original name was Phra Ruang, is regarded as the national hero who delivered his people from the Khmer. He took the Khmer throne-name of Pho (father) Khun (lord) Sri Indraditya. The events of his life and reign are shrouded in myth and legend. He is popularly believed to have been of lowly birth and to have possessed superhuman and magical powers. In Thailand today to say that a man has a mouth like Phra Ruang means that he can make things happen at will. In his honor four later kings of Sukhothai took the name of "Phra Ruang," but it is the first Phra Ruang who is enthroned in Thai legend.

Cultural Borrowings

The Sukhothai Era is regarded by the Thai as marking their origin as a distinct people. It was a period of great cultural development when they absorbed elements of the various civilizations with which they came in contact. Relations were maintained with China, and Chinese artisans were brought to establish the famous pottery works of Sawankhalok, 25 miles north of Sukhothai. From Cambodia came new cultural elements, concepts and patterns. Sukhothai traded with northern India, and Thai art, sculpture and literature reflected strong Indian influences. Artistic activity was also influenced by the Mon and the Burmese to the west (see ch. 11, Artistic and Intellectual Expression).

The height of this era was reached under Rama Khamhaeng (Rama the Great) the third king of Sukhothai. His reign of 42 years (1275–1317) saw a great extension of Thai power, covering an area that corresponded to much of present-day Thailand. He maintained friendly relations with the neighboring Thai kingdom of Chiengmai and introduced a new system of Thai writing.

The original Thai writing apparently had been based on Chinese characters and lost in the long trek south from Nanchao. Other forms of writing had appeared, but under King Rama Khamhaeng the Khmer script, which originated in southern India, was adapted to the Thai language. It became the basis of modern Thai writing. From the Khmer, Sukhothai also took Brahmanic concepts and rules of law as well as the principles and practices of government. For military organization the kingdom turned to the Mongolian dynasty of Yüan (1271–1368) in China. In addition, King Rama Khamhaeng made Theravada Buddhism the state religion to which the Thai have adhered ever since. This religion had entered Thailand from India in successive states via Java, Burma and Ceylon (see ch. 12, Religion).

THE AYUTTHAYA ERA (1350–1767)

After the death of King Rama Khamhaeng, Sukhothei began to decline and was finally conquered by a new power, Muang U Thong (the City of King U Thong), northwest of modern Bangkok. Muang U Thong was evacuated in an epidemic, and a new capital, destined to last much longer than its predecessor, was built at Ayutthaya in 1350. Under the Prince of U Thong, who was proclaimed King Rama Thibodi I, Ayutthaya grew in wealth and strength. It seized the Khmer possession of Lop Buri to the north and Chanthaburi to the southeast, and it eventually asserted its authority over other Cambodian vassal states. Tributary relations were established with China, and the term "Siam" came into use, although the Thai preferred to call their country by the name of the capital, Krung Sri Ayutehaya. The word "Siam" did not receive official approval until the reign of King Mongkut in the nineteenth century.

At the height of its power, Ayutthaya controlled most of the territory of Sukhothai, the area south and west to Rat Buri and Phet Buri, and up the Gulf of Siam as far as modern Bangkok. Down the Malay Peninsula its domain included Tenasserim, Nakhon Si Thammarat (Ligor) and Songkhla (Singora). In 1432 the Thai captured the Cambodian capital of Angkor, ending the Angkor peroid of Cambodian history (802–1432). To escape the threat of growing Thai power Malacca became a tributary to China when Ayutthaya did. Meanwhile, the last kings of Sukhothai presided over the little that was left, consoling themselves with the memory of former glory and a personal reputation for piety.

King Rama Thibodi I, revered as a great lawgiver, promulgated the first recorded Thai laws. Most of his legislation was later submerged in additions from the Hindu Code of Manu that was introduced under Burmese domination, but some of the provisions give insights into the society of the time. The Law of Evidence (1350) excluded numerous categories of persons from giving evidence. The Law of Offenses Against the Government

(1351) set severe penalties for violations; an official who stole government funds was liable to one of eight punishments, ranging from death to degradation and 25 strokes of the rattan, to fines and suspension from office. The Law of Abduction (1356) contained a reference to the frequent attempts of slaves to excape to Sukhothai, where slavery was rare, indicating that this institution was well-developed in King Rama Thibodi's domain. The Law of Husband and Wife (1359) recognized polygamy and provided for easy divorce.

Foreign Cultural Influences

The rise of Ayutthaya intensified the exposure of the Thai to the civilizations of Cambodia and India. Since Ayutthaya had once been part of the Khmer empire, Cambodian influences with Indian coloration were strong. In the last decade of the fourteenth century the King of Cambodia invaded the Chon Buri and the Chanthaburi districts southeast of Bangkok and removed about 7,000 of the inhabitants to Cambodia. In retaliation King Ramesuen sacked Angkor in 1431, and no less than 90,000 Cambodians were taken as prisoners to Ayutthaya.

Ayutthaya benefited richly from the knowledge and skills of its captives, many of whom were artisans, scholars and former high officials. One of the most important Cambodian-Indian ideas adopted was divine kingship, which was added to the traditional, paternalistic conception of kingly rule under the Sukhothai kings. It is recorded that King Rama Khamhaeng had hung on the palace gates at Sukhothai a great bell that could be rung by any subject who was wronged; when the bell rang, the King came forth to inquire into the matter and to deliver personal justice to the injured. Although in the ancient concept the king was absolute and derived none of his power from the people, he was expected to lead in war, dispense justice and protect the kingdom's economic and social well-being. These ideas of kingship did not entirely die with Sukhothai. To them was added the doctrine of the king as a divine or nearly divine personage with the attributes of a Brahmanic deity. He was protected by the sanctions of Brahmanistic doctrine, magical regalia and sacred ritual and was surrounded by sycophantic officials. The monarch, sacred and remote, was no longer accessible to the people; the few who were permitted to speak to him could do so only in a special language of deference. Art portrayed him only under supernatural aspects.

Social Institutions

Until the fifteenth century the authority of even the strongest Thai rulers did not extend much beyond a circle of territory around the capital. In the countryside, powerful local chiefs often paid only nominal homage to the central authority. Effective centralized control came with King Trailok (1448–88) who adapted the Cambodian model and instituted a series of government reforms that endured until the nineteenth century.

King Trailok organized the central administration on a departmental basis. Civil departments, which were separated from the military, included: the Ministry of the Interior, the Ministry of Local Government, the Ministry of Finance, the Ministry of Agriculture and the Ministry of the Royal Household. The military administration was also divided into departments under officers of ministerial rank.

In theory there were seven ranks of officials, although the lower ranks were often not appointed, but only the first and second ranks were of major importance. The first rank was "lord of the front palace"; since the holder of this position was often designated the heir apparent to the throne he came to be called, especially by foreigners, the "second king," or "vice-king." Many authorities feel that the term "second king" was too strong because, although he had unlimited access to the treasury, he could not encroach upon the power of the monarch. This practice of designating an heir apparent during the king's lifetime proved to be a stabilizing factor because it saved Thailand from the bloody struggles for succession that led to the downfall of many kingdoms elsewhere. Under the new administrative system the second important official rank was called "lord of the rear palace," and its holder was known as "duplicate second king."

King Trailok's other contribution was the perfecting in 1450 of the Palace Law that codified the operation of the Royal Household and set the customs of the Court in a pattern which lasted until the decline of the absolute monarchy in the twentieth century. The law defined various noble ranks and the rights and duties pertaining to each. The law described Court ceremonies, and rules of etiquette were set forth in detail.

Severe penalties were exacted for violations of the law. A man guilty of illicit relations with a lady of the palace was to be tortured 3 days and then killed; the lady was also to be put to death. The death penalty was prescribed for shaking the king's boat, for letting stray dogs into the palace and for whispering during a royal audience. Princes of high rank could be restrained, but only with golden fetters; silver shackles were used for lesser aristocrats. When a prince was to be executed he had to be placed in a large sack of fine material and beaten to death with a sandalwood club.

King Trailok also regulated the old *sakdi na* grading system that determined the amount of land a man might own, according to his official rank or class status. He revised the system by prescribing rules that redefined the various grades and by specifying the amount of land allotted to each instead of a salary. The amounts of land ranged from the equivalent of 4,000 acres for the *chao phraya*, the highest level of officialdom, to 10 acres for the lowest class of free peasants (see ch. 7, Social Structure). In theory, all land still belonged to the king; in practice, landholders were soon exercising rights of ownership.

As it evolved the *sakdi na* system, which survived until recent times, supplied a viable framework for the society. Before officials were granted salaries in the nineteenth century it set the amount of their income; in court cases it provided a graduated scale from which fines were determined; and, since the population remained small in relation to the amount of arable land, it could assure the members of the lowest grades enough land for subsistence. The system was prevented from hardening into rigid class stratification by the inheritance law that allowed all members of the family to inherit a portion of the family wealth and by a law that dissolved titles of nobility in the royal line after the fifth generation.

King Trailok did not, however, create a modern and responsible government. The government remained distant from the people and had little concept of political and social responsibility. Its demands for labor, military service and taxes were considerable, and the peasant might give as much as a third of his time to public projects under the compulsory labor system. Often the people owed service not only to the central government but also to local lords, who were left largely undisturbed in the use of their powers as long as they remained loyal to the royal authority and fulfilled their quota of taxes and service. The structure was semifeudal in the ties of mutual obligation that bound those below to those above.

Debt slavery became widespread and was recognized in law by the early seventeenth century when about 25 percent of the population was enslaved for debt. In addition, there were large numbers of enslaved war prisoners who, unlike the debt slaves, had no hope of freedom. In theory and often in practice the debt slave could buy his freedom by paying the debt or by finding another master to take his debt if the first proved to be oppressive. Apparently the system carried no social stigma, and many voluntarily entered slavery to escape the burden of compulsory labor or to simply relieve themselves of responsibility for their own maintenance. Aristocrats and monks were not included in the system of labor service obligation and slavery; monks were also spared from military service.

Early Western Contacts

During the reign of King Rama Thibodi II (1491–1529) Ayutthaya received its first European envoys. Affonso de Albuquerque, Viceroy of Portuguese India, took Malacca in 1511 and sent Duarte Fernandez, the first European to visit the country, to Ayutthaya as envoy. In 1516 a treaty granting the Portuguese permission to reside and trade in the kingdom was concluded between Ayutthaya and Albuquerque. Somewhat later they were given religious freedom and allowed to erect a crucifix in a public place. Portuguese mercenaries served effectively in Ayutthaya's armies and taught them the skills of cannon making and fortification. The first foreign missionaries to arrive in the country were two Dominicans from Malacca in 1555. In 1606 a Portuguese missionary entered the kingdom. During the first quarter of the seventeenth century, however, Portuguese influence declined as Dutch and English influence grew.

Foreign contacts increased at the beginning of the seventeenth century. Portuguese, Japanese, Dutch, French, English and Spanish mercenaries and traders entered the realm in large numbers. In 1609 a Siamese mission was sent to the Netherlands; in 1686, during King Narai's reign (1657–88), a similar mission was sent to Versailles. The first French missionaries arrived in 1662. King Narai gave them permission and materials to build a church and school. He disappointed them, however, in their hope of converting him by stating that although Catholicism was a fine religion so was Buddhism.

Although foreigners were cordially received, King Narai skillfully played one power against another—the French against the British and the Dutch against the French. Internal instability also helped to shield Ayutthaya from European economic pressure; the country was so torn by civil and foreign wars that external trade was repeatedly halted. The early demands of the foreign traders for extraterritorial rights were accepted without resistance, and the first treaty made the resident members of the Dutch East India Company subject only to the Dutch courts.

Toward the end of King Narai's reign the attitude regarding foreigners became less tolerant. In their competition for special advantage, the trading companies had not hesitated to intervene in domestic politics, and fear of European military power, the French in particular, was growing. In his conduct of foreign relations King Narai was greatly influenced by a Greek adventurer, Constantine Phaulkon, who was one of his more powerful advisers. Through Phaulkon, French traders and Jesuit priests were able to enlarge their sphere of influence, but they aroused the suspicions and resentment of the Thai aristocracy and the Buddhist clergy.

The situation became a crisis in 1688 when King Narai fell ill. Phaulkon, who was isolated, was arrested by his enemies at the Court and was put to death. His allies were crushed, and ruthless persecution of foreigners followed. Only a few Dutch and Portuguese remained after this incident. For nearly a century and a half thereafter the Thai cut themselves off from the West.

The Fall of Ayutthaya

In the middle of the sixteenth century the series of wars with Burma that were to end two centuries later with the destruction of Ayutthaya began. In 1569 the capital, which was threatened for the second time, fell to the Burmese after a yearlong siege. Its fortifications were razed and its inhabitants were removed. Elsewhere in the war-ravaged country, especially in the north, whole communities were enslaved or transplanted, and the people, who were forced to pay heavy tribute to their conquerors, were reduced to the worst conditions in their history. During its 20 years of vassalage the country received from Burma the Hindu Code of Manu, the Burmese calendar and many other items of culture.

Liberation came with Naresuan the Great, a Thai prince who had been taken to Burma as a hostage in 1564 and was released on the occasion of his sister's marriage to the Burmese monarch. Naresuan, then known as Pra Naret (the "Black Prince"), effectively crushed Burmese power in Siam in 1584; thereafter he was preoccupied with a Cambodian incursion until 1590 when his father died and he succeeded to the throne. In 1590 he met and defeated at the frontier an invading Burmese army of 200,000. Two years later the Burmese returned to the attack with an army of 250,000. Not only were the Burmese armies routed, but Prince Naresuan challenged the Crown Prince of Burma and killed him in hand to hand combat on elephants.

King Naresuan next turned to Cambodia, which had renounced its vassalage to Ayutthaya in 1569. In 1593 a Siamese army invaded Cambodia, reestablished Siamese suzerainty and brought back to Siam numerous prisoners and many of the Thai who had been carried off previously by the Cambodians.

Also in 1593 the Siamese seized Burmese Tenasserim and Tavoy, two important centers of foreign trade from which the Siamese kings subsequently received much revenue. The Kingdom of Chiengmai accepted Siamese suzerainty in 1599 after several years of renewed warfare with the divided and weakened Burmese. King Naresuan invaded Burma with the intention of reducing it to vassalage, but he was forced to content himself with control of the area south of Martaban. In May 1605 he fell ill and died while leading an army in central Burma against the King of Ava, who was the strongest of several Burmese monarchs ruling in different parts of the country. He has been remembered as the most celebrated of the warrior-heroes and as the liberator of his people from the Burmese.

The struggle between the Thai and the Burmese did not end but surged back and forth during most of the seventeenth century. Neither side could win a decisive advantage, and both suffered from incessant depredations. In Ayutthaya the population declined, economic production fell and foreign trade nearly halted. The Burmese in a gradual revival of power captured Chiengmai and incorporated it as a province. Cambodia threw off the Siamese vassal yoke. Internally the Thai kingdom was further weakened by the struggle engendered by Phaulkon's activities. A period of relative prosperity and serenity under King Boromakot (1730–58) was only the prelude to a disaster, which was once again at the hands of the Burmese.

The young and ambitious King of Burma, Alongphaya, having reunited most of Burma, launched an unsuccessful assault on Ayutthaya in 1760. He returned to the attack in 1765. After a year and a half of siege the Burmese, aided by corruption and disunity within the city, triumphed. Ayutthaya was burned; its records were destroyed; its works of art were spoiled or removed; and its aristocracy was decimated. Siamese captives, estimated at 30,000 to 200,000 were taken to Burma.

THE BANGKOK ERA (1767–1932)

The Thai found a new leader in Phraya Taksin, a man of Thai-Chinese extraction, who with 500 followers had escaped the ruins of Ayutthaya. He fled to the eastern shore of the Gulf of Siam for a counteroffensive. Later in 1767 he built a new capital in Thon Buri, across the river from modern Bangkok, and proclaimed himself king the following year at the age of 34.

King Taksin brought under his control the five independent states into which the country had been fragmented after the destruction of Ayutthaya. He also successfully warded off Burmese and Cambodian counterthrusts. By 1782 his domains embraced all of the former Kingdom of Ayutthaya except Tenasserim and Tavoy; he held Battambang and Siem Reap in northwestern Cambodia and dominated almost all the Lao states including Luang Prabang. It was this king who encouraged the Chinese immigration that paved the way for the important Chinese role in subsequent Thai economic life.

At the age of 48, King Taksin developed paranoid delusions of personal divinity. His actions become so erratic and extreme that his ministers had him executed in the interests of the state. His accomplishments, however, won him a secure place among Thailand's national heroes.

The Chakkri Dynasty

King Taksin was succeeded by General Chakkri, who had taken a leading part in the struggle against Burma. As Rama I (1782–1809) he founded the present-day ruling monarchy. Rama IX, His Majesty Bhumibol Adulyadej, King of Thailand since 1946, descends in unbroken line from the founc r. The Chakkri Dynasty produced a number of outstanding rulers, most notably King Mongkut, Rama IV (1851–68), and King Chulalongkorn, Rama V (1868–1910). It also witnessed the transformation of the royal institution from absolutism to the limited constitutional monarchy of the present day.

Historic trouble with Burma persisted during the reign of Rama I. The Burmese invaded the country three times between 1785 and 1788. In 1797 the Thai drove the Burmese from Chiang Saen on the Burma border north of Chiengmai. Conflict with the Burmese continued during the reign of Rama II (1809–24), which was also a period of renewed foreign contacts.

In 1818 Carlos Manual Silvera, a Portuguese envoy, concluded a trade agreement with Bangkok. The Thai seizure of Kedah, in present-day northern Malaya, in 1821 was to become a cause of discord with England until it was ceded, along with Kelantan and Trengganu in northern Malaya, to the English in 1909. Dr. John Crawfurd of the British East India Company visited Bang kok in 1822 and was followed soon afterward by John Hunter, the first English resident merchant. In 1824 the first Anglo-Burmese war broke out. It ended 2 years later with the cession by the Burmese of Arakan, along the northeast coast of the Bay of

Bengal, and Tenasserim to Great Britain; thus, a stronger power gained provinces over which Thailand and Burma had disputed for centuries.

The reign of King Rama III (1824–51) was relatively quiet, except for the suppression of a revolt in Kedah. Trade, carried on mainly by Chinese merchants, increased with the West. Bangkok concluded a commercial treaty with Captain Henry Burney of the East India Company in 1826 and made its first treaty with the United States in 1833.

Modernization

King Mongkut and King Chulalongkorn are the dominant figures in recent Thai history. Both recognized that the country could hope to retain its independence in the face of the expanding European colonial system only by mastering and adapting the knowledge, techniques and institutional forms of the West. Their success is obvious because only Thailand in Southeast Asia remained independent of European rule.

King Mongkut, who is the subject of two novels, *An English Governess at the Court of Siam* and *Anna and the King of Siam*, and who is more popularly known in the West through the motion picture, "The King and I," attempted with modest success, to have the princes and officials of the realm learn foreign history and languages. He brought numerous foreigners into the country to advise the government and to assist in the development of natural resources. Chinese were permitted to enter freely and to engage in commercial enterprises.

At least part of this remarkable monarch's willingness to accept Western innovations is attributable to his education. For 27 years, before ascending to the throne, he lived as a Buddhist monk studying Western sciences, history and languages. Deeply interested in new knowledge and conscious of European power, he felt it wiser to accept those Western institutions that suited Siam's needs.

In 1855, King Mongkut, overruling many of his advisers, concluded with Great Britain a treaty of friendship and commerce which is known as the Bowring Treaty. Similar treaties were made in 1856 with the United States and France. In these and other conciliatory undertakings the Western powers were given extensive trade privileges and extraterritorial rights. These measures, however, failed to stop France's expansion into Cambodia, over which Siam had claimed suzerainty. In 1867, Bangkok was forced to cede Cambodia to France; the two provinces of Battambang and Siem Reap were not acquired by the French until 1907.

King Chulalongkorn was still a minor at the time of his father's death in 1868. A regency carried on the work of government until young Chulalongkorn, who was traveling, reached his majority in 1873. At his coronation he read a decree which set the tone of his reign. It abolished the ancient practice of prostration before the King. The King considered the act unsuitable in a modern state because it humiliated the subject and induced arrogance in the ruler. The young monarch next proclaimed that children born to slaves were free and that no one could sell himself into slavery for debt. By 1905, toward the end of his reign, the King had completely abolished slavery as an unpleasant remnant of the past and as unbecoming in any advanced civilization.

Other royally sponsored modernization measures included the establishment of more effective central authority throughout the domain by replacing the feudal lords in distant regions with appointed governors, by reorganizing the central government into 12 ministries along European lines and by building postal and telegraph systems, railroads and an arsenal. In addition, the principle of religious toleration was decreed; a land survey program was developed; the taxation system was improved with the assistance of foreign advisers; and a program of legal reform was initiated. To ensure the success of these reforms King Chulalongkorn sent nationals abroad to study and brought in foreign advisers and specialists from various countries so that no single country could exert excessive influence on the Court.

Externally the reign of King Chulalongkorn coincided with the troublesome phase of European expansion in Asia. In dealing with powerful France and Great Britain he chose the prudent strategy of making concessions rather than direct confrontations. In 1893, when Siam was threatened by a French naval blockade of Bangkok, it relinquished to France the traditional claim to all Laotian territory east of the Mekong and agreed to maintain no military establishments within the provinces of Battambang and Siem Reap.

These cessions brought France and Great Britain, which had firmly established itself in Burma by the end of the 1880's, into direct confrontation in upper Burma and upper Laos. The vagueness of the frontier between them constituted a potentially dangerous situation. Out of mutual jealousy and suspicion the two powers agreed in 1893 to neutralize Siam as a buffer state between their respective colonial possessions, Laos and Burma, to the east and west. This agreement did not affect the Khorat Plateau, the provinces of Battambang and Siem Reap or the Malay Peninsula. Although Siam was not consulted by the two powers, this Anglo-French agreement is generally credited with having ensured the continued independence of Siam.

Nonetheless, the agreement did not immediately check the expansionist momentum of the two powers into Siamese domains. In 1902, 1904 and 1907, Bangkok had to relinquish to France Bassac, Battambang, Siem Reap, Sisophon, Luang Prabang and other points on the west bank of the Mekong. Similarly, in 1909, Siam surrendered its traditional suzerainty over the four Malay states of Kelantan, Trengganu, Kedah and Perlis to Great Britain. In return Siam received from these powers minor territorial retrocessions and other concessions on matters of extraterritoriality.

The reign of King Vajiravudh, Rama VI (1910–25), was relatively quiet, although there were some signs of internal opposition to the monarchy. The King was more interested in cultural pursuits than in government, and he is remembered as a writer, translator and patron of the arts. During his reign, Thailand entered World War I on the side of the Allies and sent a small detachment to Europe. Toward the end of his reign a series of treaties, the last with Great Britain in 1925, provided for the ultimate fiscal autonomy of the nation.

THE CONSTITUTIONAL ERA (1932–   )

The Coup of 1932

The long era of absolute monarchy came to a sudden end during the reign of King Prajadhipok, Rama VII (1925–35). On June 24, 1932, a coup d'etat was initiated against the government of the royal family by a group of officials and army officers, most of whom had been educated in Europe in the 1920's. The coup, like most of the others that have since punctuated the course of Thailand's political life, was almost without bloodshed. A provisional constitution, which was Thailand's first, was promulgated on June 27, 1932, and it made Rama VII the first constitutional monarch of the country (see ch. 14, The Governmental System).

The coup was motivated by a combination of forces which had been afoot in the previous two decades. Antimonarchical sentiment was clandestinely expressed as early as 1912 by a small European-trained group of army and navy officers, who had resented King Vajiravudh's policy of favoring certain "palace guard" organizations (see ch. 28, The Armed Forces). The King's policy of appointing commoners to high government posts also earned him the enmity of powerful princes. Moreover, his personal extravagance and fiscal mismanagement caused many government officials and intellectuals to lose faith in the system of absolute monarchy.

One of the first acts of the new monarch, King Prajadhipok, was to dismiss the favorites of his predecessor. He established a Supreme Council, which was composed of five of the most important princes, and princely bureaucrats soon monopolized virtually all important government posts. In the sweeping fiscal retrenchments that followed, numerous officials in the lower ranks of the civilian and military services were dismissed. A special tax on government salaries weighed heavily on those who remained, and after 1930 conditions became worse as the country felt the impact of a worldwide depression.

The coup's conspirators, who were led by the French-educated Pridi Phanomyong, found the liberally inclined King Prajadhipok almost disconcertingly ready to accept a constitutionally limited monarchy. Like his father and grandfather, he had been influenced by Western ideas and was politically prepared to go further than either of them in adopting new patterns. Perhaps in a circumscribed constitutionalism he saw a welcome opportunity to diminish the considerable power of the princes by broadening the participation of commoners in the government. By 1931 he had reportedly decided to establish limited suffrage and a parliament in order to relax royal authority gradually as the people gained political experience. Apparently he had refrained from acting, however, at the urging of the princes.

Modern Thailand

Constitutionalism closed the long chapter of royal absolutism, but it left the king the fountainhead of political authority and legitimization. Although largely symbolic, the monarchy continues to retain the aura of semidivine kingship, especially among the peasants.

The various constitutional documents have articulated the ideal of popular rule, which is to be achieved either at once or in the future. Governments established by the several constitutions, however, have tended to be tutorial rather than representative, and the exercise of power has continued to be oligarchic.

The country has enjoyed relative stability and prosperity since the early 1950's. Beginning in the mid-1950's, however, it has been confronted with the problem of internal security because of the Communist movement that is apparently directed and controlled by North Vietnam. Anticommunism has become one of the principal governmental policies at home and abroad. In September 1954, Thailand joined in the establishment of a mutual defensive pact called the Southeast Asia Treaty Organization

(SEATO) (see ch. 16, Foreign Relations). Internally Thailand has initiated a series of measures designed to foil Communist insurgency efforts, particularly those among the economically depressed elements along the Laotian border in the northeast and among the Moslem groups near the Malaysian border in the south (see ch. 15, Political Dynamics).

CHAPTER 4

POPULATION

The total population at the time of the latest census, April 1960, was 26,258,000, exclusive of the semisedentary hill peoples in the Northern and Northeast Regions. The previous census, in May 1947, enumerated 17,442,000 persons. Based on an annual growth rate of approximately 3.4 percent, calculated from census records, the country's population in mid-1967 was estimated to be about 34.2 million and was expected to exceed 37.7 million by 1970.

Improvements in the standard of living and advances in medical services and public hygiene could make possible an increase even greater than estimated. This rapid growth was reflected in the youthfulness of the population, about half of which was under 18 years of age, because of a rising birth rate and a drop in the infant mortality rate.

The vast majority of the people are rice farmers of Thai ethnic origin, who follow the Buddhist faith. According to the census of 1960, more than 98 percent of the total population was born in Thailand; about 97 percent could speak Thai; and more than 93 percent was Buddhist. In all respects the most important minority community was that of the ethnic Chinese, conservatively estimated in 1967 to comprise about 8 percent of the population. Smaller minorities included the Malays living in the four southernmost provinces; the Khmer; the Kui; Miao (Meo), Akha and other so-called hill people along the borders with Burma and Laos; and the Vietnamese refugees, most of whom were in Nakhon Phanon Province just west of the Mekong River (see fig. 2).

STRUCTURE

Age distribution is similar to that of other Southeast Asian countries, with a high ratio of children to the total population. According to the 1960 census, the median age was between 17 and 18. Children under 10 years of age made up 22 percent of the total population; those under 15 accounted for 43 percent of the total. The age structures for the four major geographic regions of the country show no striking differences from this national average.

Over 50,000 more males than females were enumerated in the 1960 census. Among persons under 50 years of age, males outnumbered females in all age groups except one (25- to 29-year-old group); in the older age groups women invariably outnumbered men, reflecting greater life expectancy for women than for men. The disparities were greatest among persons between the ages of 45 and 49. In this group the ratio was 102.2 men per 100 women, and among persons 65 and over it was 79.9 men per 100 women. In geographical distribution the variation from the national pattern was most apparent in the Southern Region. In Ranong Province, for example, 113 males were counted for every 100 females; in Krabi Province, the ratio was 108 males to 100 females. In Trang Province, by contrast, the ratio was only 95.9 males to every 100 females. The causes for these variations were not explained by the authorities. Urban areas in all parts of the country reported a slight predominance of males.

In 1963 about 3.9 million people (more than 13 percent of the estimated population) were reported to be living in areas classified as municipal. The comparative number for 1960 was 3.3 million (about 12.5 percent). The figure, however, does not give an accurate picture of the urban-rural ratio. All municipalities have some characteristics generally recognized as urban, but many include so much of the surrounding countryside that their population is more rural than urban.

Average population density, as calculated from the 1960 census, was about 132 per square mile. Comparative figures in 1962 were 236 for North and South Vietnam and 87 for Cambodia. The lowest density was in the mountainous Northern Region, where it did not exceed 83 per square mile, and highest in the Central Region, where it was about 169. The Central Region, with approximately 30 percent of the total land area, had about 40 percent of the population (see fig. 10). This settlement reflects the high agricultural production of the area—one of the finest ricegrowing regions in the world.

The heaviest concentrations, averaging more than 200 inhabitants per square mile, are found in the Chao Phraya valley north of Bangkok and the valleys of the Mun and Chi Rivers in the Northeast Region. Since only 18 percent of the total area is cultivated, there is more significance in the average density per cultivated square mile, which is close to 550. The Chao Phraya valley has more than 700 persons per square mile of cultivated land and in certain sections of the narrow peninsular coast, over 3,000.

Some indication of the size of various national minorities is evident in the registration wth the Police Department in the Ministry of the Interior of resident aliens, aged 12 and over. The 1964 listing included: Chinese, 351,000; Indians, 5,500; Vietnamese, 3,200; other Asians, 3,400; Europeans and Americans, 8,800; and the remainder, unknown. In 1966 more than 30,000 American military were reported to be in the country. The apparent size of these minority communities differs widely, however, from figures based on ethnic origin rather than citizenship. For example, in the mid-1960's a leading authority on the Chinese in Thailand estimated the total number of ethnic Chinese to be 2.6 million persons; other estimates range from 3 million to 4 million.

Chinese are found in all regions of the country, but there is a major concentration in the Thon Buri sector of the greater Bangkok metropolitan area, where they make up about a third of the total population. Another major concentration is in the central part of the Southern Region, where many are employed in the tin mines and on the rubber plantations. The Moslem Malays, distinguished from the predominantly Buddhist Thai majority, are found chiefly in the southern provinces. The other nationalities live mainly in the capital area and in the provinces bordering Burma and Laos. Important groups include the Khmer and the Mon. The Vietnamese, for example, numbering about 45,000 in 1966, are concentrated in the Northeast Region near the Laotian frontier (see ch. 5, Ethnic Groups).

A census has never been taken of the hill peoples in the mountains of the Northern Region and the uplands northwest of Bangkok. An estimated 250,000 persons belonging to various non-Thai groups are distributed along the border with Burma and Laos. They live mainly by hunting and farming; an important crop for many is the opium poppy. There are six major ethnic groups, of which the Karen, probably numbering about 75,000, is the largest. Other major groups include the Miao, Akha, Kha Htin, Lisu and Yao (see ch. 5, Ethnic Groups).

DYNAMICS

Estimates based on incomplete data suggest that the birth rate in 1964 was 37.7 per thousand; the death rate, 7.7 per thousand. The infant mortality rate was 37.9 per thousand live births. The birth and death rates were lower than those reported for neighboring Laos and Burma. This favorable trend

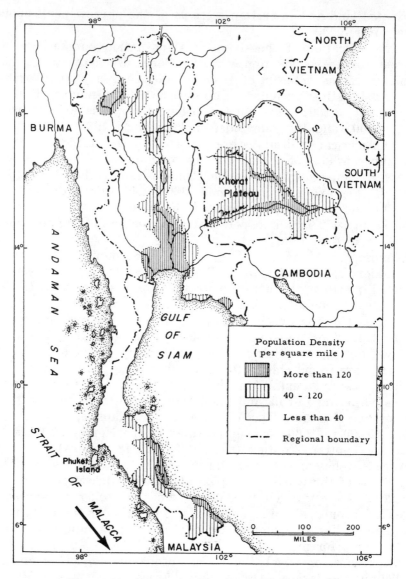

Figure 10.—Population Density of Thailand, 1960.

reflected improved conditions of public health since 1957, such as the utilization of modern pharmaceuticals and insecticides and the greater availability of medical care to the rural population. Mortality rates have declined steadily from an estimated 31 per thousand in 1930–34, to 28 per thousand in 1935–39, to 22 per thousand in 1950–54 and to 13 to 14 per thousand in 1960.

Mobility

The government in the mid-1960's was giving some impetus to internal migration. It had become involved on a small scale in resettlement activities in which it supported the movement of families from one part of the country to another, either for improvement of their economic opportunities or for internal security reasons. Five thousand persons, for instance, were scheduled to be moved from remote villages in Nakhon Phanom Province in the Northeast Region to localities closer to major towns, to safeguard them from Communist terrorists. Meanwhile, other families were shifted from their native villages in the overcrowded provinces in the Central Region to villages in the Southern Region, where they were given a small plot of land plus a loan of 6,000 baht (see Glossary) to get started in farming.

Immigration

Historically, war, trade and the drift of peoples in search of land have brought Laotians, Cambodians, Burmese, Malays, Indians and Chinese into Thailand, and Europeans began to arrive in the sixteenth century. Only the Asians, however, contributed any significant elements to the country's population, and of these the Chinese from China's southern provinces have been numerically by far the most important. As early as the seventeenth century the Chinese were migrating to Thailand at the rate of 4,000 to 5,000 annually. By 1900 the rate had increased to 19,000.

Until the end of World War I the vast majority of the Chinese immigrants were single males who came to engage in the commercial activities in which the Thai showed little interest. These early migrants either returned to China with their savings or married Thai women and founded families, many of which in a generation or two became ethnically Thai. After about 1920, however, an important change took place. In 1920–22 females made up 15 percent of the total arrivals, and by 1936–37 some 27 percent of the arrivals were women. Of all Chinese immigrants since World War II, 70 percent have been women and children.

There has been movement back and forth across the boundaries with the neighboring states of Laos and Cambodia by Thai, Laotian and Cambodian nationals. Droughts in the Northeast Region force numbers of men into the towns, especially Bangkok, in search of temporary employment. For some the move becomes permanent, but many eventually return to their villages. In contrast the Chinese, willing to go to any part of the country in pursuit of work or business opportunity, have been relatively mobile.

In 1960, 87.3 percent of the population were found to have been born in the province in which they were enumerated. Slightly over 10 percent was born in another province; 1.5 percent was born in China; and the remainder was born in other foreign countries or unknown places. Phra Nakhon Province (where Bangkok is situated), with 63.4 percent, and nearby Thon Buri Province, with 58.4 percent, had the lowest percentages of locally born residents.

Before World War II the Chinese were free to enter Thailand with little more than the requirement that they pay a small entrance fee. After the war a quota system was established. In 1947 the Chinese quota was fixed at 10,000 a year; each of the other nationalities was given a quota of 200, a figure that also applied to the Chinese after 1948. These controls appear to have been fairly effective. Several thousand refugees from Communist China have been permitted to enter the country for an indefinite period as "temporary residents." Of the estimated 2.5 million persons of Chinese extraction in the country in the mid-1960's the great majority were born in the country and were Thai citizens.

In 1964, the most recent year for which data were available, 2,100 permanent immigrants and 346,000 temporary residents arrived in the country. Among the latter group the greatest numbers came from Malaysia, Australia, the United States, Great Britain and Japan.

The 40,000 to 45,000 Vietnamese in the Northeast Region are the vestiges of an influx of refugees who fled from North Vietnam during and immediately after the Indochina War (1946–54). Estimates of the original size of this refugee community range from 60,000 to more than 80,000. The Thai Government at first welcomed the refugees, helping them get established in their new surroundings; but, as North Vietnamese Communist attempts to influence the group became increasingly apparent, the Thai made efforts to repatriate them. Through negotiations between the Red Cross societies of the two countries aided by the International Committee of the Red Cross, a repatriation program was put in effect, and the numerical strength of the group was reduced, as some 40,000 returned to their homeland—in most cases to North Vietnam. Repatriates to North Vietnam reportedly were selected by Hanoi from among those who had learned useful industrial skills in Thailand, showed promise as trainees for work as Communist propagandists or been considered to be in need of political reeducation. The repatriation program was suspended in the mid-1960's, however, because the government of North Vietnam refused to accept more returnees and the refugees themselves evidenced no interest in repatriation. North Vietnam claimed that the bombing raids over its territory made repatriation activities unsafe. Nevertheless, most Vietnamese in Thailand retained family ties with persons in North Vietnam, and the common assumption among Thai was that they sympathized with the regime of Ho Chi Minh (see ch. 5, Ethnic Groups).

A similar problem was facing the Thai Government in the mid-1960's with respect to its Laotian neighbors. In terms of ethnic origin the Thai people of the Northeast Region are closely related to, if not identical with, the Thai in Laos (see ch. 5, Ethnic Groups). They speak the same language and share with each other many cultural traits which set them apart from Thai in other parts of the country. Relations between the people of the Northeast Region and their Laotian neighbors are maintained by trade and migration. The Mekong River, which for over 600 miles forms the eastern border of Thailand, facilitates rather than impedes communications between settlers on both banks. Because of the constant movement of large numbers of people across it, the few thousand border police can give only limited attention to the supervision of river traffic, and the task of checking infiltration of Communist terrorists has been difficult.

According to leading Thai officials, the major portion of Communists moving into Thailand in the mid-1960's was coming via Laos across the Mekong. Government officials stated also that Cambodia had begun to allow Communist agents to pass through its territory into Thailand. To offset Communist influence in the outlying areas, particularly the critical Northeast Region, the government has been taking the initiative in many ways including, for example, the reassignment of some of its most able civilian and military administrators to the area.

CHAPTER 5

ETHNIC GROUPS

Although local and regional differences existed, language, culture and physical type made the majority of Thailand's population unmistakably one people. Of the country's estimated 34.2 million inhabitants in mid-1967, 30 million, or approximately 87 percent, were ethnic Thai. A minority of about 13 percent of the total population consisted of Malay, Khmer (Cambodian), Vietnamese and other South and Southeast Asian communities, small enclaves of Westerners and more than 2.6 million persons of Chinese extraction. There were an estimated one-quarter million non-Thai hill peoples inhabiting the border areas along Burma and Laos, who have been largely untouched until recently by modern Thai civilization.

The Thai generally show Indonesian-South Chinese physical features, although their features show a great admixture with other types in the Southern Region. They are divided into a number of regional subgroups of varying size that correspond to former political divisions and subdivisions. These are the Central Thai, or Siamese, the Lao of the Northeast Region, the Yuan of the Northern Region and the Pak Thai in the extreme Southern Region. Because they were the founders of modern Thailand the Central Thai became culturally and politically dominant over the other groups. Basic Thai culture patterns are common, however, to all the regional and subregional groups; they overshadow the minor cultural differences among those groups.

Many ethnic minority groups derive from populations which lived within the boundaries of modern Thailand before the Thai invasions of the thirteenth and fourteenth centuries or which were taken prisoner in war. Others, particularly the Chinese, entered the country more recently for predominantly personal and economic reasons. Most of the latter groups originally did not intend to remain, although many became permanent residents. To the extent that they and their descendants retain their own cultural and national identity, they are regarded by the Thai as aliens and temporary residents.

The government has long regarded all persons born in Thailand, including those of alien parentage, as Thai citizens, unless the births were registered with the embassy of the parent's country of origin. Although the census enumerates current resident aliens by nationality, it gives no indication of the number of descendants of earlier immigrants who have preserved their ethnic and cultural distinctiveness from the Thai. The 1960 census, for example, indicated that approximately 469,500 persons of alien citizen ship resided in the country; 409,500 held Chinese citizenship; about 7,000 were citizens of India, Pakistan or Ceylon; some 45,000 persons were citizens of Vietnam, Laos, Cambodia, Burma, Malaya or Singapore. About 5,000 came from Europe and America, and nearly 3,000 came from other countries.

The Chinese are the most important ethnic minority—socially, economically and politically. Since 1910, when Chinese women began immigrating into Thailand in substantial numbers, the Chinese have been developing a culturally distinct community within the Thai majority. They are set apart by their growing economic power and their political orientation. This circumstance has been a source of great concern to the Thai elite, and since 1932 control of the Chinese economic and political threat has been an implicit policy of every government.

In 1967 the great majority of the Chinese in Thailand had been born there, and the government's long-range policy was aimed at assimilation. Second- and third-generation Chinese themselves were seeking and achieving acculturation in Thai society. In fact, ethnic Chinese had reached a greater degree of assimilation with the dominant Thai society than had the Chinese in other Southeast Asian countries.

Another important minority is the ethnic Malays, who comprise some 1 million persons concentrated in the five southernmost provinces of Satun, Songkhla, Yala, Pattani and Narathiwat. Official efforts to absorb the Malay population into the Thai culture have met with little success.

In the mountainous areas bordering on Burma and Laos, there are varied groups of hill peoples differentiated from each other and from the Thai in their customs and language. All these groups have close ethnic ties in the countries across the border. Although numerically insignificant, the hill peoples are of political importance as unassimilated groups who are susceptible to exploitation by subversive or insurrectionary forces. The major tribes include the Karen (Karieng), Miao (Meo), Akha (Ekaw), Lisu (Lisaw), Lahu (Mussuh) and the Yao.

70

THAI

Major Groups

Historically, the Thai peoples first appeared in the inland valleys of South China, and they are referred to in Chinese annals by such names as Chuang, Lao-Chua, Tai Yai and others. By A.D. 650 the Thai established two kingdoms, Nanchao and Mong Mao, within the present-day Chinese province of Yunnan. In succeeding years numbers of persons migrated from these two kingdoms into the area of modern Thailand, where they eventually settled and intermarried with the Mon and other peoples already living there (see ch. 3, Historical Setting).

At the end of the fourteenth century there were three flourishing Thai kingdoms in the area which includes modern Thailand and Laos: the Kingdom of Ayutthaya, the (Northern Lao) Kingdom of Chiengmai and the Kingdom of Lan Xang, which included most of the middle Mekong Valley, Laos and the Khorat Plateau. Ayutthaya, Chiengmai and part of Lan Xang were united in the nineteenth century to form modern Thailand. In spite of extensive population shifts over the centuries, current regional differences among the Thai reflect this ancient division into three kingdoms.

Regional differences among the Thai are gradually becoming less significant with the development of modern means of communication, the improvement of the national school system and the growing influence of the central government throughout the country. Because of the urging of the government, the people of the Northern and Northeast Regions are beginning to acquire a national rather than a solely local orientation; however, they may still occasionally refer to themselves by a local name (see ch. 29, Subversion).

The Thai, Malays, Khmer, Burmese, South Chinese, Filipinos and Indonesians all belong to the Southern Mongoloid racial stock. It is extremely difficult to distinguish one from another by observation of physical characteristics without the aid of additional cultural clues. Indians and Westerners are the only peoples in the country clearly distinguishable from the Thai in physical type. The Thai make distinctions among themselves and between themselves and other groups, but such distinctions are based more on observable cultural and social criteria than on physical traits. If a person says he dislikes people of other ethnic groups, therefore, the reason is not that they are racially different from himself but that they behave in ways which are not in accord with the Thai concept of proper behavior.

Central Thai

The Central Thai, or Siamese, are those people of the Chao Phraya Valley, around and to the north of Bangkok, who speak the Central Thai dialect that is the official national language. The geographical proximity of most of this group to Bangkok and the relative ease of communication resulting from the network of waterways in this flood plain have exposed these Central Thai more than their countrymen to modern urban influences.

As founders of the nation the Central Thai dominate the social and political life of the country. Although members of other regional groups freely enter these hierarchies, they must meet the standards set by this dominant group. These include such things as degree of education, adoption of Central Thai attitudes, values and behavior patterns and allegiance to the nation-state. The cultural patterns of the Central Thai, especially those found in Bangkok, have become the standard of modern, urbane behavior, but the patterns of other groups, particularly those of the villages, are considered rustic and old fashioned.

Khorat Thai is the Siamese term for the Thai speakers who occupy most of Nakhon Ratchasima province. They dress and live like the Central Thai, with whom some authorities classify them, but they speak with some distinctive mannerisms. They are reportedly descendants of the Thai troops who seized this area in the fourteenth century and their Khmer women.

Lao

Thai-speaking persons living on the Khorat Plateau are generally referred to as Lao. The term is sometimes used to include the Thai-speaking population in the Northern Region around Chiengmai and Chiang Rai, although locally these persons are known as Yuan. In the mid-1950's the Lao in northeastern Thailand were said to number approximately 3.5 million. The Lao are distinguished from the Central Thai by certain stylistic differences in religious architecture and writing and by a cultural tradition that is common to various middle Mekong principalities, which existed untouched until the nineteenth century.

The area inhabited by the Lao includes much of the Khorat Plateau in northeastern Thailand and modern Laos. There has long been a constant flow of population back and forth across the Mekong River, which marks the frontier between Thailand and Laos. Many of the Lao in Thailand were forcibly brought into the country as prisoners of war a century or more ago. In the mid-1960's border traffic was heavy and was marked by the infiltration of armed subversives from North Vietnam through Laos into Thailand (see ch. 27, Public Order and Safety).

Yuan

The term Yuan, or Thai Yuan, is generally used to refer to the indigenous Thai speakers in the Northern Region, especially in the Chiengmai locality. Justification for this grouping lies in the historical distinctiveness of the area reflected in its centuries of freedom from Central Thai control and in the differences in local speech between this area and the Lao area to the east. The Yuan area comprises the modern provinces of Chiang Mai, Lamphun, Lampang, Phrae and Nan and contains a population of 2.1 million persons.

The cultural traits setting the Yuan apart from the Central Thai are those which also distinguish the Lao and other Central Mekong River groups, such as certain distinctions in temple architecture and religious script and polite speech. Most scholars distinguish them from the Lao on the basis of dialectical differences (see ch. 6, Languages and Communication).

Pak Thai

The Pak Thai, which is a group of more than 1.5 million Thai speakers in the Southern Region, is differentiated from other Thai groups by a few relatively insignificant traits. Although they are predominantly Thai, they represent some intermixture of peoples, including Malay, Mon-Khmer and Negroid pygmy strains. The Pak Thai includes some persons who appear slightly darker than other Thai. They are concentrated in the provinces of Chumphon and Nakhon Si Thammarat. A patois called Dambro is used by the Pak Thai.

Minor Groups

Phuthai are found in extreme northeastern Thailand, near the Laos border, and probably number over 100,000. They came into Thailand in the early nineteenth century from Laos and settled in compact communities, primarily in the provinces of Nakhon Phanom, Sakon Nakhon, Kalasin, Udon Thani and Sisaket. In dress, agricultural techniques and domestic architecture they are much like the neighboring Lao. Their Buddhist faith is intermixed with superstitious practices.

The Shan of Thailand are ethnically part of the more numerous and important group living in the Shan States in Burma. At one time the Shan, or Thai Yai or Thai Long (Great Thai) as they call themselves, controlled all of Burma and large parts of northern Thailand, but since the fifteenth century they have formed a minority group in both countries. In Thailand the Shan, whom the Central Thai call Ngio (Ngiaw), reside principally northwest of Chiengmai in Mae Hong Son and Tak provinces. Their customs are generally similar to those of the Thai, but the men's costumes are distinctive. They engage actively in trading in many parts of the country.

Other lesser known Thai peoples in the country include the Lu, who have emigrated from the Yunnan province of Communist China into nearby areas of Burma, Thailand and Laos. They are found principally in Chiang Rai and Nan provinces of the Northern Region. The Lu share many cultural traits with the Lao and the Yuan. Other Thai groups in the Northern and Northeast Regions show differences of speech and custom but share with each other, with the Lao and with the Central Thai many features of cultural life.

NON-THAI

The Chinese

The Chinese are the largest ethnic minority in the country and are the greatest minority problem for the government. A leading authority on Chinese society in Thailand estimated the number of ethnic Chinese—persons who consider themselves Chinese in most social situations—in 1955 at about 2.3 million persons. In mid-1965 he estimated that the number reached 2.6 million, or 8.5 percent of the estimated total population for that year. Estimates by other scholars of the Chinese minority in Thailand range as high as 4 million persons.

The vast majority of this group are Thai citizens because citizenship is given automatically to all persons born in the country, unless a claim of foreign citizenship is established by consular registration, and because naturalization proceedings are encouraged for all permanent immigrants. Less than a half million ethnic Chinese were registered in the 1960 census as citizens of either Communist or Nationalist China. Most Chinese speak one or another of several Chinese dialects used in Thailand and conform to Chinese cultural and behavioral patterns. There are a number of Thai who have Chinese ancestors on at least one side of the family, but these persons have adopted Thai culture. They are no longer distinguishable from other Thai in their way of life, speech or behavior.

The largest concentration of Chinese is in the Bangkok-Thon Buri metropolitan area. Perhaps one-third of the total population of this region is Chinese. Other Chinese are found in substantial numbers in the Southern Region, especially in the Isthmus of Kra area, which is the center of the tin and rubber industries. Betong, which is a town of 30,000 persons in Yala province near the Malaysian frontier, has the greatest proportion of Chinese of any urban area in Thailand; more than half of its 30,000 people are Chinese.

The remainder of the Chinese are scattered throughout the market towns and villages of the country. Their distribution reflects their economic influence. Ethnic Chinese are dominant in finance, commerce and industry. They operate at least 80 percent of the rice mills and run a considerable portion of the export-import, wholesale and larger retail establishments. They also supply the bulk of the industrial labor force.

Initially, Chinese immigrants were welcomed because they provided the industrial labor and skills and the commercial enterprise that were needed to advance the country along the modernizing course set by King Mongkut (1851–68) and King Chulalongkorn (1868–1910) and that were uncongenial to the agrarian Thai. Beginning in the seventeenth century with approximately 4,000 to 5,000 immigrants annually and increasing after 1860 to roughly 19,000 in 1900, Chinese immigration consisted almost entirely of unmarried males, who came with the expectation of accumulating savings and eventually returning to China. Many, however, married Thai women and founded families which in several generations became assimilated with the Thai.

In 1920 enough Chinese women had come to Thailand to constitute a significant proportion of the immigrants. This increase permitted the establishment of homes in which a purely Chinese atmosphere could be maintained and the Chinese family and lineage system could be recreated and continued. The founding of Chinese schools in the previous decade also helped to separate the Chinese and Thai societies by enabling the Chinese children to obtain a Chinese rather than a Thai education. By 1921 Chinese newspapers had been established, and the formation of a Chinese Chamber of Commerce permitted cooperation among the various components of the Chinese community and between the community as a whole and the Thai Government. Outlook, values and prestige could then be defined in terms without reference to the surrounding Thai society. Occupational differences reinforced the growing separation of the two groups, and the rapid growth of the Chinese population, because of natural increase and continued immigration, made the separation of the Chinese community more conspicuous.

There had been sporadic outbreaks of trouble between the Thai authorities and the Chinese during the nineteenth century. A Chinese general strike, which was organized in 1910 by the Chinese secret societies to protest a change in the tax on the

Chinese, caused the Thai Government to realize the strength of the Chinese economic position. Prompt action was taken against the secret societies, which had lost one of their reasons for existence after the overthrow of the Manchu dynasty in China, and they either changed into benevolent societies or disappeared. There were at that time no major restrictive measures imposed on the general Chinese population.

The interest of the Chinese community in the events in mainland China and the agitation of both Chinese Communist and Nationalist (Kuomintang) agents during the late 1940's aroused the concern of the Thai Government about the loyalty of the large Chinese population. In addition, the Thai awareness of their commercial dependence on the Chinese led to measures restricting immigration and limiting the growth of Chinese economic power.

Government restrictions applied in the 1920's and 1930's sometimes had the effect of strengthening Chinese self-identification. Government restrictions on immigration began with the first Immigration Act of 1927, which limited the number of Chinese women eligible to enter Thailand. The government hoped to reverse the trend toward all-Chinese homes. Other measures taken at this time included stricter enforcement of education laws, requiring all schools (mission schools as well as Chinese) to provide a Thai educational program, broadening of treason and riot laws and promulgation of a more stringent press law. The first immigration control law, however, was not sufficiently effective, and in 1947 it was revised to sharply reduce immigrant quotas.

After World War I, Thailand's trade with Japan grew steadily, and it was to her advantage to maintain good relations with Japan. The Chinese, however, had become antagonistic toward Japan because of the increase in Sino-Japanese incidents, particularly after the Japanese invasion of Manchuria in 1931. Because Thailand wished to maintain good relations with Japan and the Chinese minority wished to help the homeland, clashes of interest between the government and the minority, which reached a peak after the outbreak of war between China and Japan in 1937, were almost inevitable.

During the 1930's government policy continued to encourage assimilation and the gradual loosening of Chinese control of the Thai economy. This was the conscious motive of the education laws, the immigration laws and the other steps that were designed to weaken Chinese ties with China. Chinese born in Thailand were automatically Thai citizens; foreign-born Chinese of good character, who had been in Thailand for 5 years and were self-supporting, were eligible for naturalization. No restrictions were placed on the freedom of the Chinese to travel within Thailand or to own or rent land. In theory, Chinese were equal to Thai before the law, although they were at a political disadvantage. The government's handling of strikes and its imposition of literacy and wealth requirements for immigration were partly aimed at replacing Chinese labor with Thai. Because raising revenue was also a part of the government's Chinese policy, this sometimes produced inconsistencies with the general emphasis on encouraging assimilation.

The pro-Japanese sympathies of the first administration of Phibun Songkhram, which dated from December 1938, resulted in the ethnic policy of the government changing from an emphasis on assimilation to containment and restriction. A series of decrees and laws intended to curb Chinese dominance of important trades and businesses was enacted between December 1938 and May 1939. In addition, the Chinese school curriculum was forced further into the Thai mold, and many schools ceased operation. The efforts to curb Chinese economic dominance included an active propaganda campaign which called on patriotic Thai to buy only things grown or manufactured by Thais and to help each other to get started in trade or industry. All Nationalist organizations and activities designed to help China in its struggle with Japan were suppressed by the Thai police in the first 6 months of 1939. All but 1 of 10 Chinese newspapers were closed. In January 1940 civil servants were officially advised not to marry aliens.

Legal immigration was discouraged by the regulations, but illegal immigration became a serious problem. Junks loaded with Chinese began landing their passengers on quiet beaches along the 1,200-mile coastline of the Gulf of Siam. Some were prosecuted and deported, but the government was not able to stop the illegal immigration. World War II finally stopped immigration, although some Malay Chinese may have preferred to take their chances in Thailand rather than in Singapore or Malaya.

In 1946 the Chinese problem was considered by the postwar government. Earlier restrictions were in force, but inflation had reduced the effectiveness of fees and fines. In 1947 violence erupted between Communist and Nationalist sympathizers within the Chinese community. The government used this clash as justification for deporting 400 Chinese and for drastically reducing the immigration quota to 200 per year. During the mid-1950's an additional problem developed in the Northern Region where an influx of several thousand Haw, or Yunnanese Chinese, infiltrated portions of Thailand's border zone and subsequently established permanent villages in that area.

Since World War II ethnic policy generally has been oriented toward promoting assimilation. Restrictions on the Chinese have been relaxed. The alien tax, which was raised from 20 to 400 baht (see Glossary) in the immediate postwar period, has been reduced to 200 baht. Because the Chinese community is split within itself over the political situation in Communist China, it has been exerting itself to build amicable relationships with the Thai.

In the mid-1960's Chinese assimilation was again increasing. The social limits for most of the middle-class Bangkok Chinese are their own community organizations, but the upper-class Bangkok Chinese have extensive business and social contacts with the Thai because of the necessity for rapprochement between managerial and governmental elements of the society. Chinese business leaders now have social connections with Thai officials; their children attend Thai or mission schools; and their families are marrying into the Thai elite. Many Sino-Thai clubs have been established. Assimilation is proceeding at a faster rate on the higher levels of Chinese society than it is on lower economic levels, where the advantages of assimilation are less obvious. Significantly, more Chinese have been assimilated into Thai society than into any other society in Southeast Asia.

Indians, Pakistani and Ceylonese

Economically, the most important non-Thai resident minority beside the Chinese is composed of immigrants from Ceylon, the western coastal areas of India and, to a lesser extent, northern and eastern India. The 1960 census lists 6,700 residents from India, Pakistan and Ceylon; this does not include persons born in Thailand of Indian, Pakistani or Ceylonese parentage. There were an estimated 5,000 ethnic Indians in the country in the mid-1960's. About 60 percent of this Indian community lived in the Bangkok (Mookherji) area.

The Indians engage in commercial and service activities in Bangkok and the larger towns. Many are retail merchants who specialize in textiles, jewelry, precious metalwork or fancy groceries. Another group, most of whom presumably belong to the Chettyar caste of Madras, consists of moneylenders and moneychangers. A large number of Indians are employed as chauffeurs and taxi drivers, and the traditional occupations of the Sikhs are those of night watchmen and bank guards. A low-caste group living on the outskirts of Bangkok supplies the milk for the large quantity of ice cream consumed in the city.

In all of these economic activities, except dairying, the Indians are in competition with the Chinese and often with the Thai. Although they do not seem to be the object of positive dislike, they are not particularly popular with their Thai neighbors. Because they are conspicuously different from the Thai in physical type, they are considered a transient group. This attitude is expressed in the common and mildly derogatory reference to the Indians as "guests." They perform no economic function that urban Thai feel they could not perform equally well; hence, their competition may at times be somewhat resented.

Vietnamese

The majority of the Vietnamese in Thailand are survivors of the refugees who fled their country during the Indochina War. They number probably 40,000 to 45,000 and are concentrated in the northeast border provinces. Scattered groups of Vietnamese are found in a few other areas, such as the descendants of Vietnamese Catholics who fled religious persecution in Annam in the middle of the nineteenth century and who form a relatively unassimilated farming community of a few thousand persons in Prachin Buri Province, near the Cambodian border.

Initially, the refugees were welcomed by the Thai authorities. The government facilitated their settlement in the underpopulated Northeast Region, gave them land and established them in villages of their own. Social welfare and administrative agencies were established by the Vietnamese themselves, under Thai supervision. In 1950, however, the political climate shifted, and the government became more friendly toward the French and more suspicious of the North Vietnamese Communists. The Thai Government worked assiduously to halt the influx of refugees and to collect and send back those Vietnamese who had already entered Thailand. A repatriation program was begun in 1959 that eventually reduced the Vietnamese in Thailand to half their original number. North Vietnam refused to accept more repatriates, alleging that bombing attacks made it impossible to ensure the safety of the returnees. South Vietnam has also been unwilling to accept any of the refugees, who themselves have evidenced no interest in leaving their new life in Thailand (see ch. 4, Population; ch. 16, Foreign Relations).

Many of these Vietnamese have been very successful in adjusting to their new circumstances and are prospering. Because of a greater ambition and frugality than the Thai and a business acuity reportedly at least as great as the Chinese, they have established flourishing retail businesses or services, become dealers in local produce, rented land and planted truck gardens.

Nonetheless, they still remain isolated from their Thai neighbors. They are usually required to live in restricted sectors of certain villages, and their activities are closely scrutinized. Few have become citizens because few have shown much interest in citizenship and because the Thais have not made it easy for them to change their status. Most Vietnamese have learned to speak Thai as a matter of economic necessity. Their children, however, do not usually attend Thai schools, and there is not any significant social contact with the Thais.

Mon, Khmer, Kui and Others

Another grouping of minority peoples is those speaking Mon-Khmer languages. Among these communities are the Mon, whose origins are Burmese; the Khmer (Cambodians) and the Kui, with whom they have intermarried; the Lawa, who are found in the northern hills; and such small groups as the Kaleung, Kha Brao, So and Sek, who are immigrants who crossed the Mekong from the mountains of Laos.

Although the early inhabitants of the Chao Phraya Valley and much of the Northern Region were Mon, they were completely assimilated by the incoming Thai. The present ethnic minority is descended either from prisoners of war or from the relatively recent migrations of Mon refugees from Burmese oppression in the fifteenth, sixteenth and seventeenth centuries. Today, all allegedly understand Thai, and some apparently know only Thai. Most of them live near Bangkok and elsewhere in the Central Plain, but some are scattered along the valley of the Khwae Noi (a tributary of the Mae Klong) up to the Burmese border. Estimates of their number range from 60,000 to 100,000.

The Khmer, or Cambodian, minority resides principally in the provinces east and southeast of Bangkok and in the southern Khorat Plateau along the border with Cambodia—territory that was once Cambodian and later became Thai. A few communities west of Bangkok are composed of the descendants of Khmer prisoners of war. The Khmer differ only slightly from the Thai in both their manner of life and their Buddhist religion. Their language, however, belongs to a different stock than Thai. Estimates of the size of the Khmer minority in 1960 vary from 160,000 to 400,000.

The Kui, or Soai, are found in the hills along both sides of the Thailand-Cambodia border. Most of them are in the provinces of Roi Et, Surin, Ubon Ratchathani and Sisaket. The estimated size of the group is over 100,000. They are small-scale farmers like their Lao and Khmer neighbors from whom they have adopted the practice of permanent wet-rice cultivation.

Malays

The ethnic Malays, totaling approximately 1 million persons, are concentrated in the Southern Region, especially in the southernmost provinces of Satun, Songkhla, Yala, Pattani and Narathiwat. They constitute the majority of Thailand's Moslem population. The remainder of the Moslems consist of ethnic Thai and a small group of Pakistani immigrants.

The ethnic Malays differ from the Thai ethnic majority in religion, in language and in customs. They represent the farthest extension of the latter-day movement of Malay people up the Peninsula. They are Thai citizens because their settlements were incorporated into the expanding Thai kingdom. They speak Malay almost exclusively; their dialect differs from that spoken in adjacent Malaysia only in its use of more Thai words. They are mainly small-scale coconut planters, rubber planters and tappers, farmers and fishermen.

The Malays in Thailand represent a fairly homogeneous minority that has been highly resistant to assimilation into the national culture. Except at the official level, they have little contact with their Thai neighbors. Brigandage and ethnic isolationism, which are complicated by Communist terrorism along the Thai-Malaysian border, add to the gap between the ethnic Malay and the Thai majority that already exists because of language and religion (see ch. 27, Public Order and Safety).

The Thai Government has followed a policy of complete religious tolerance toward its Moslem minority. It did attempt, however, to assimilate the group through education, the requirement that Buddhist ethics be taught in the schools and the use of Thai as the language of instruction. These requirements were strongly resisted by the Malays, and, subsequently, a compromise was reached that allowed instruction in Malay and in the Islamic religion in Malay schools.

Before World War II the Malays evidenced little desire to assert their status as a homogeneous minority with special interests, and they appeared to neither want nor expect differential treatment by the government authorities. Postwar economic hardship—much of it blamed on the alleged malfeasance of Thai officials—and the spread of nationalist sentiment for Islamic Malaya and Indonesia changed the outlook of the Thai-Malay, and they began to make various demands.

In mid-1967 the Thai-Malaysian border districts were relatively quiet, in spite of occasional acts of terrorism by armed Communist guerrillas hiding in the area. Living conditions in the area were gradually improving as the government attempted to eliminate the terrorists and carried on a program of regional development, which was designed to eradicate the basic causes of unrest. Modern medical care, land resettlement, better roads and expanded educational facilities were being increased in the area.

In addition to the predominantly Malay population in the Southern Region, there are a few scattered jungle peoples, including the Semang (Ngok or Ngo). The Semang, who are Negroid pygmies, are found primarily in the foothills of the main range of the Malay Peninsula. They live principally by slash-and-burn agriculture, which is supplemented by fishing, hunting and gathering. Politically, they are organized into autonomous local groups or bands, which move within a well-defined area and which make use of caves and other natural shelters for short stays. For more permanent housing they build a shelter constructed of three poles to which underbrush and vines are attached.

Hill Peoples

The so-called hill peoples, who live mainly in the deep jungle of the foothills and high in the mountains of the border areas along Burma, Laos and Malaysia, number collectively about 250,000 persons. They may be found at elevations from 2,600 to 6,500 feet, but they prefer the 3,200 to 5,000 foot altitudes. The major groups are the Karen, the Akha, the Lisu and the Lahu, whose ethnic ties are with groups in Burma, and the Miao (Meo) and Yao, whose ethnic origins are in China. Each of these groups, in addition to the lesser ones, forms a distinct community with a life and culture of its own. Despite these divergencies, relations among the various groups are generally friendly.

The basis of the economy of the hill peoples is slash-and-burn agriculture. This involves making a clearing in the woods or jungle by fire, planting and raising crops on the land until the land is exhausted and then moving on. The average stability of residence varies considerably among the various minorities. The Lahu tend to move the most frequently; they usually change the location of their villages every 5 to 8 years. The Meo ordinarily remain in the same locality for 10 or 15 years. Exhaustion of the land is not the sole reason for moving a village. Friction between families, the appearance of too many outsiders or a sudden panic caused by superstitious fears may necessitate a move.

Rice, poppy and maize are the major field crops. The poppy is the main cash crop. Cultivation and trading in opium remains a fundamental aspect in the local economy. Hill families average an annual income of about $150 from the sale of opium. The Thai Government is currently making vigorous efforts to suppress trade in the drug, which is an illegal practice. Most of the opium traffic is handled by Haw and Thai merchants, upon whom the hill peoples are financially dependent. Because they are afraid to appear in the lowlands to sell their produce clandestinely, they rely on these traders from outside to sell their poppy crop. With the cash raised by this means they buy from the traders various consumer goods that they now consider necessities, including matches, batteries, clothing, betel nuts and canned goods (see ch. 23, Domestic Trade).

Many of the hill peoples are quite prosperous, and most families in the mountains bordering Burma live at least as well as the Thai peasants in the lowlands. Their substantial houses are built of planks and are not usually on piles. They keep pigs, poultry, dogs, oxen and ponies.

The hill peoples who have been in Thailand the longest, notably the Lawa, are becoming assimilated to Thai culture. In many instances, Lawa men have gone to the lowlands to work. The majority, however, including nearly all the groups who have entered the country mainly within the last century—the Meo, Yao, Lahu and Akha—remain culturally and socially distinct from the Thai and from each other. Nonetheless, these hill villages are no longer self-contained units that are cut off from the outside world because political events and the need to engage in commercial exchange have forced them to engage in broader relations with outside groups. Economic reasons, for example, have prevented many Karen from moving to valley areas, where they are no more isolated than other town dwellers.

Karen

The Karen (Karieng) are a Sino-Tibetan-speaking people who live along Thailand's western border between approximately 12° to 20° north. The greatest concentrations of Karen are in Chiang Mai and Mae Hong Son provinces. They are the largest of the minorities in the hills and number about 75,000 persons. The total number of Karens in Thailand and Burma together is believed to be well over 1 million. Those living in Burma have acquired a formidable reputation for their resistance to the authority of the Burmese Government. Information on the attitude of the Karen toward the Thai Government is lacking.

The Karen are a well-built, sturdy race, who average 5 feet 2 inches in height, with strong features. Recent studies divide them into four groups: Skaw Karen, the P'wo Karen, the B'ghive Karen and the Taungthu. The latter two are only sparsely represented in Thailand.

Rice forms the basis of Karen agriculture. It is supplemented by vegetables, fruits and tobacco, which are grown in small gardens, as well as by hunting, fishing and the gathering of wild plant foods. Pigs and chickens are raised by women. Some Karen owning paddy land also own buffalo, and some others speculate in cattle. Rice is grown for domestic use, but certain products are sold for cash.

The Karen live in small villages, which are usually located rather high up the mountainsides. These villages average 25 households and ideally consist of a few groups of sisters, their married daughters and unmarried children, in addition to the husbands of the married women. The usual household consists only of the simple, or nuclear family of husband, wife and children, which among the hill Karen, occupies an apartment in the longhouse. The longhouse is usually located in the village of the wife's parents. The Karen apparently trace descent and transmit property through both males and females.

The village is the most important unit, both politically and socially. It is presided over by a headman, who is selected by the villagers. He arbitrates village disputes, conducts religious ceremonies and presides over village affairs with the assistance of a council of elders.

Karen religion is animism, with a thin overlay of Thai Buddhism. In villages having contacts with the Thai the influence of Buddhism is causing changes in traditional moral behavior and religious practices. This results in some conflicts between the older, more conservative people and the younger, more Thai-influenced people. Some Karen have also been converted by Christian missionaries.

Miao (Meo)

The Miao, who number about 50,000, are concentrated in the provinces of Chiang Mai, Chiang Rai and Nan. They share ethnic and cultural ties with other Miao groups in Laos, Vietnam and southern China. Politically, they present a problem of greater concern to the Thai Government than do other hill peoples because they occupy the most remote and mountainous sector of the border region and because they have nearly 4 million ethnic kin in mainland China. No formal social or political structures, however, link the Miao in Thailand to those in Burma, China or Laos.

In contrast to the Karen the Miao kinship system is patrilineal. The household typically includes not only a man and wife and their minor children but also the married sons to age 30 and their wives and children. Authority is vested in the oldest living male, who is usually the father or the oldest brother. Beyond the extended family, the lineage unit joins all persons tracing descent from a common ancestor through the male lines.

84

The village, which is the basic political unit, is presided over by a chief, most of whom have been legally installed by the Thai Government. Traditionally, the Miao were ruled by "great chieftains," who held sway over a substantial territory that sometimes included as many as 20 villages. These territories were organized primarily as defense units, and the inhabitants of one would declare war on those of another. Such politico-military organization no longer exists.

Although the Miao are slash-and-burn cultivators, their villages are relatively permanent and are moved only every 15 years or more. Opium is still an important cash crop. Handicrafts are well developed, and a lively barter trade is carried on between the villages. Many Miao regularly visit nearby valley towns, where they buy and sell various items among the Thai.

Some Miao have become Christians, but the religion of most is an unsystematic body of belief and propitiatory practice connected with a host of spirits, including both good and bad and the spirits of the dead.

Yao

The Yao, of whom there were estimated to be 10,000 in 1966, are linguistically related to the Miao. They speak a Sino-Tibetan tongue. The Yao generally establish their villages along watercourses and prefer heights of 3,000 to 3,500 feet. The typical household consists of an extended family, including up to 20 or more individuals, which is located in the village of the husband's parents. A village chief, who is selected by a council of elders, presides over local affairs.

Their main sources of cash income as slash-and-burn farmers are opium and livestock, although near Chiang Rai there are many Yao who have learned specialized craft skills from the Thai villagers.

Akha

Numbering roughly 28,000 in 1965 the Akha, who are a Sino-Tibetan-speaking group, have immigrated from Burma. A few have come from Laos, where they are found in greater numbers. They are said to be one of the most isolated and primitive of all the hill peoples and build their villages on ridgetops at elevations of over 4,000 feet. In their animist religious beliefs the Akha attach considerable importance to the souls of the dead; hence, a house is generally abandoned at the death or serious illness of a member. The Akha are alleged to reckon descent through the male line, and family property, after the death of the father, passes to the oldest son. The position of village chieftain is hereditary through the male line.

Lahu

The Lahu (Musso, Mussuh, or Musser) came into the country from Burma and Laos in the early twentieth century, and are estimated to number at least 17,000 persons. Their traditions place them close to the Karen, with whom they claim to have once been "brothers of the same clans." They believe in a supreme being, who created all good things, and in a host of good and evil spirits. Their religious leaders have great authority—in some villages they apparently possess more than the headman. Occasionally, the posts may be held simultaneously by the same man. Villages built on flat ridgetops above 4,000 feet often break up when a leader can no longer retain the loyalty of his followers. Leaders may be either self-selected with the tacit consent of the community or formally chosen by a council of elders. The Lahu raise both opium and food crops, and they are also skilled hunters.

Lisu

The Lisu, who total 19,000 or more, live at elevations above 5,000 feet, which is higher than either the Lahu or Akha. They are reputed to be gifted linguists. Lisu men are usually fluent in Lahu, Yunnanese, Shan, Yuan and Akha in addition to their own tongue. Their animist religion emphasizes the propitiation of the souls of the dead. Opium is the most important cash crop. The office of village headman was formerly hereditary, but the village elders have apparently acquired the right to choose and depose headmen. Important decisions, however, must have the approval of the elders. In contrast to the situation among the Lahu, strong clan loyalties are said to prevent the fissioning of the villages over disputes. Nevertheless, the Lisu villages are inclined to feud with each other and with neighboring Lahu communities.

Lawa

The estimated 9,000 Lawa in the country speak a Mon-Khmer language. They are linguistically related to the Wa tribes of northern Burma and southern Yunnan. The Lawa are found chiefly in Mae Hong Son and Chiang Mai provinces in the Northern Region. They are primarily wet-rice cultivators. The principal official is the village headman, who is usually appointed by the Thai Government but is selected by a village council in some of the remote areas. Although they are allegedly Buddhist, the Lawa are greatly influenced by animist beliefs.

Westerners

Westerners form a minute portion of the total population, but they are of considerable importance because of their diplomatic, commercial, technical and educational activities. Most Westerners live and work in Bangkok for several years and return to their own countries. Some 35,000 Americans were on active military duty in Thailand in mid-1967.

Because Thailand has chosen to modernize on the Western rather than on the Communist pattern, Westerners are closely observed, and their habits, dress and ideas are often imitated or adapted by the Thai. Although association with Westerners gives prestige and Westerners are generally admired, the educated, upper-class Thai have reservations and misgivings about many aspects of Western society and culture. Many feel it is too materialistic and destructive of traditional Thai values and artistic expression. The Thai once feared the Chinese might swamp them numerically, and some now fear the West may overwhelm them culturally. This possibility, however, does not seem to worry the rural part of the population, which concerns itself almost exclusively with local issues and problems.

The West, particularly the United States, is regarded in one sense as a big brother who gives benefits and assistance to a smaller brother in return for fellowship and services. The arrangement is one of mutual advantage, and most Thai see the alliance in that light. They do not expect pure altruism, and they are not fearful that the West is practicing a new colonialism.

The Eurasian population is small. Some Western men who have lived in Thailand for a long period have married Thai women, and a few Thai who have studied abroad have brought back Western spouses. Thai parents tend to disapprove of a daughter marrying a Westerner because they fear that she might be abandoned when he goes home and that it would be difficult for her to remarry. There is no such fear regarding sons. The Eurasian children of such marriages have no difficulty in being accepted as fully Thai if they so identify themselves. In fact, Eurasians are often admired for their physical appearance because Western standards of physical attractiveness have been combined with the older ideal of beauty, which is described in the *Ramayana* and other literary works of Indian origin.

ETHNIC POLICY

Until the mid-twentieth century, the government's policy toward the hill peoples was to leave them alone, to give them freedom to occupy land as they chose and move from one place to another and to live undisturbed according to the dictates of their traditional social organization and customs. After World War II, however, these minority groups received special attention. This attention was motivated by humanitarian considerations and by official concern over the destruction of forests and watersheds, which was caused by the shifting cultivation system and the continued and illegal cultivation of opium by these groups, and by their strategic location in the northern border areas adjacent to Laos and Burma.

The government is attempting to expose the minority groups to a broader view of Thai society and its cultural and material attainments. The Border Patrol Police for some time have conducted development work in remote parts of the Northern Region, along with other government departments and agencies. Since 1960 the Department of Public Welfare, operating through a fully organized Hill Tribes Division, has been operating land settlement projects and development and welfare centers in the Northern Region. Special programs for the hill peoples are also being broadcast over local radio facilities by the government (see ch. 9, Living Conditions; ch. 27, Public Order and Safety).

CHAPTER 6

LANGUAGE AND COMMUNICATION

More than 90 percent of the population speaks either Thai or Lao. Both languages have many dialects, some of which are similar, while others vary enough so that persons from different sectors of the country find it difficult at first to understand one another. In spite of distinctive variations between Thai and Lao, they are closely related and mutual understanding between native speakers of the two tongues is possible. Siamese Thai, the variant spoken by the inhabitants of Bangkok and the Central Region, is the official national language. The government is pressing for its adoption throughout the country.

Thai or Lao speakers include not only the approximately 30 million ethnic Thai, but large numbers of ethnic Chinese, most of the Vietnamese and a few representatives of other ethnolinguistic minorities. Only where an ethnic minority is overwhelmingly predominant in a given area, as the Malays are in the four southernmost provinces, is it unessential for the ordinary non-Thai to speak the national language. Even then some members of the group must be able to speak Thai to provide middlemen between the minority community and national government representatives.

The Chinese-speaking community comprises some 2.6 million persons, concentrated in the Central Region and in the Peninsula. Malay, with an estimated one million speakers, is the next most important single language. Other minority languages are encountered among the hill peoples along the borders with Burma and Laos; the scattered Mon communities of the Central Region; the Khmer communities of the Northeast; and the several small linguistic groups in the Peninsula. Many of these languages are themselves divided into dialects spoken by groups of various sizes.

English predominates among the Western languages spoken by transient alien residents and it has long been taught as the required foreign language in the governmental school system. The languages of neighboring Southeast Asian countries and of the Indian subcontinent are spoken by immigrant communities, many of whose members are in trade and service occupations. The 40,000 to 45,000 Vietnamese concentrated in the Northeast continue to use their native language.

The government is actively promoting the spread of Thai in all sections of the country through the compulsory education law which makes Siamese Thai the language of instruction in all schools, public or private. This language is also employed by government officials in dealing with each other and, when possible, with ordinary citizens. Earlier efforts to end instruction in the language of the ethnic minorities met with considerable resistance from the Malays and Chinese. A compromise permits instruction in their languages for a certain number of hours a week in the schools of these two minority groups. Thus, while the various minorities may continue to use their own languages among themselves, the government is ensuring that present and future generations of schoolchildren will be at least nominally bilingual.

THAI

Linguists disagree as to where Thai should be assigned among language families. Some assign it to a Chinese-Thai branch of the larger Sino-Tibetan language family. A recent study, however, places it in a family of Tai-Kadai languages.

Languages and dialects of the Tai-Kadai family and their interrelationships have not been fully explored, but certain broad lines of development are clear. In Thailand, the major variants of Thai encountered are those heard in the Central, Northern and the Southern Regions, while Lao predominates in the Northeast.

Siamese Thai, spoken in Bangkok and in the Central Region and used in official communications throughout the country, is the standard spoken and literary language. It is spoken with distinct mannerisms among the Thai Khorat, around Nakhon Ratchasima. Indigenous Thai speakers of the Northern Region, particularly in the Chiengmai area, are known locally as Thai Yuan (Yun or Yun Thai) and by the Central Thai as Lanatai. Scholars generally associate Yuan with a dialect cluster made up of such groups as the Lu and Khua and sometimes extended to include Lao. These groups are distributed within the Mekong River valley, from southern Yunnan Province in southwestern China, through northern Burma and northwestern Laos into northeastern Thailand. The Pak Thai, Thai speakers in the extreme southern provinces, use a patois termed *dambro*.

Siamese Thai is the language of government, education, the press, the motion pictures and the radio. The influence of

Siamese Thai, as it is spoken in Bangkok, has increased significantly in all of the dialect areas outside the Central Region. Although in these areas its common use is still largely restricted to official and semi-official situations or to conversations with foreigners and persons from other dialect areas, words from Siamese Thai are frequently borrowed to express concepts for which the local dialect has no satisfactory words. The dialects are mutually intelligible for the most part, and young people in all parts of the country have received instruction in Siamese Thai and can understand and speak it with varying degrees of fluency. In other dialect areas real fluency is more common among urban dwellers than it is among the rural villagers, who have both less exposure to Siamese Thai and less need to know it well. Although regional and local dialects are by no means vanishing more and more persons are becoming acquainted with Siamese Thai.

Thai, in its various forms, has more speakers than any other language of mainland Southeast Asia and is spoken over an extensive geographical area including Assam in India, Burma, Laos, North Vietnam and parts of South China. This linguistic affinity with peoples outside the borders of the country has been an element in irredentist movements, such as, the sponsored by the first administration (1934–38) of Phibun Songkhram. Since the early 1950's another such movement has been sponsored by Communist China.

The Thai language is tonal, uninflected and predominantly monosyllabic. Each syllable has an inherent tone which, no less than the consonants and vowels, determines the meaning of the syllable or word. In Siamese Thai there are five tones. Many Thai-dialects are distinguished primarily by the number and distribution of tones they possess and secondarily by vocabulary differences. Thus, the word "rice" (khaw) is pronounced with a rising tone in Siamese Thai and with a high tone in northern Thai. Even within a single dialect many words are distinguished only by their tone, thus *ma* may mean horse, dog or come, depending on the tone used.

Since Thai words are uninflected, that is, do not indicate grammatical function by changes in the word itself as in many European languages, grammatical functions are shown by the word order of the sentence, much as in English, and by words whose meanings are primarily or solely grammatical. Most of the multisyllabic words in the vocabulary are either compounds of simpler one-syllable words or have been borrowed from Khmer, Sanskrit or Pali, along with the elements of culture they identify. The government has also coined words from these languages to translate concepts and innovations borrowed from other cultures for which the Thai language had no terms, rather than to make new compounds of the simpler monosyllabic words.

Status Usages

In all dialects a complex vocabulary is used to express the fine gradations of deference, intimacy, condescension of humility appropriate to conversations between persons of differing status. Personal pronouns indicate the relative status of the speaker, the person spoken to or the person spoken about. Status particles of varying degrees of formality, corresponding somewhat to "yes sir" or "no ma'am," are added at the end of sentences to indicate varying degrees of courtesy and respect. There are synonyms for many common nouns and verbs; the particular synonym used depends on the relative ranks of the persons involved in the conversation. Thus, *kin* (to eat) is used by common people among themselves or by an upper-class person speaking to or referring to his servant; *rapprathan* (also meaning "to eat") is more formal and polite and is generally used by, and in reference to, people of higher social rank. In writing, even for a popular audience, and in public speaking, formal language is invariably used, so that a foreigner with a good knowledge of colloquial Thai may have difficulty in understanding publications or radio broadcasts. When there are two or more synonyms, the one of Khmer or Sanskrit origin usually has more prestige than the word of Thai origin.

A still more formal vocabulary is used in addressing members of the Buddhist priesthood (Sangha). For royalty, a different language is used. This "royal language" is used when speaking to or about the king and the highest nobility. In ordinary conversations commoners would use terms of respect in referring to royalty rather than speak entirely in the royal language, which they would probably know only imperfectly. This royal language is based on Sanskrit with strong Khmer and Pali influences. It was never formally taught but was acquired through study of the literary classics dealing with royalty and through use in court circles. Today most people learn some of the forms and vocabulary from reading the classics or stories from them at school and from newspaper articles about royalty. It is spoken only on very formal occasions and within the king's household. The imperfect knowledge of the royal language leads to circumlocutions and sometimes to improvisations when the use of ordinary polite Thai might be considered inappropriate or disrespectful.

Respect and affection may be expressed in colloquial Thai by the use of kinship terms in speaking to non-relatives. For example, someone may address an elderly man as "uncle" or "grandfather" or friends may call each other *phi* and *nong,* the terms for older and younger sibling. These terms illustrate another feature of Thai social relations— the emphasis on age rather than on sex.

Foreign Influences

The earliest historic mention of the Thai language occurs in the Chinese annals of more than 2,000 years ago which preserve a few words, mainly names and titles of kings, that are still recognizably Thai. During the second millennium B.C., 8 words of the language of the Pang people were recorded, of which 5 are recognizably Thai. In A.D. 1172, a Chinese scholar (of Kuanghsi) gave a list of 9 words, of which 3 are recognizable as Shan and 3 as Annamite. Another scholar lists 19 words, of which 12 are found to be Thai and the remainder Annamite. Little else is known of the language until the Thai kingdom of Sukhothai arose in the area of present-day Thailand about the middle of the thirteenth century. Although the Thai had apparently been filtering into the area for some centuries, it was only about this time that they became powerful enough to establish a state of their own. Before this, they were settlers in already establish Mon and Khmer kingdoms, and were heavily influenced by these peoples in language as well as culture.

The Indian character of Mon-Khmer culture accounts for the fact that many of the words taken over by the Thai were of Sanskrit origin and were borrowed along with Mahayana Buddhism. Pali words were introduced with the conversion of the Thai, during the Sukhothai Era, to Theravada Buddhism. Later direct contact with Ceylon and India by religious missions further facilitated the introduction of Pali and Sanskrit words.

More recently, when contact with the West and other Asian countries increased, the introduction of new concepts and objects led to the incorporation of Chinese, Malay and European words into Thai. This tendency was particularly strong during the latter half of the nineteenth century when Western educational, scientific and administrative methods were being accepted enthusiastically in Thailand.

During the reign of King Vajiravudh (Rama VI—1910–25), an upsurge of nationalism led to attempts to replace Western terms with Thai equivalents formed either from native Thai elements or from Sanskrit or Pali roots. Again during the intensely nationalistic period of Phibun Songkhram's first administration, Western terms were in disfavor, and Thai, Pali or

Sanskrit translations were found for many European scientific and technical expressions. Today, although only a few except the most ardent nationalists are concerned with language purity, in official writing Thai is used for European words that are commonly accepted in colloquial speech; for example, officially, *thannakan* is used instead of *baeng* (bank) and *rongraem* instead of *hoten* (hotel). Committees are maintained in certain government ministries to find words for new concepts, usually taking them from Pali or Sanskrit.

Foreign words taken into Thai conform to the Thai language structure. The inflectional endings of words adopted from Pali or Sanskrit have often been dropped, or if retained, do not serve in Thai the grammatical function they had in their original language. Many foreign polysyllabic words are abbreviated in pronunciation in order to make them conform more closely to the monosyllabic pattern of Thai. Pronunciation of foreign words, moreover, is adapted to Thai sound patterns which vary in a number of ways from the sound patterns of Indo-European languages. Thus, hotel becomes *hoten;* tennis, *tennit;* whiskey, *witsake;* and beer, *bia.*

Writing Systems

Although the origin of the Thai script is not clear, its characteristics definitely align it with early Mon or Khmer scripts of South Indian origin, which were used extensively throughout the mainland of Southeast Asia. The first known instances of the use of such a script for Thai are in inscriptions dating from the reign of King Rama Khamhaeng (A.D. 1275–1317), to whom the adaptation of the Mon-Khmer script to the Thai language is attributed. This alphabet was further modified in the reign of King Lu Thai, the son of King Rama Khamhaeng and it is this modification which is used today.

The modern alphabet consists of 44 consonant symbols and 28 vowels and diphthong forms. The vowel and diphthong symbols are written as in other Indian-derived scripts, that is, above, below, before or after the consonants which, in pronunciation, they follow. Vowel symbols indicate both short and long vowels as well as diphthongs. The number of consonant symbols in the Thai alphabet is greater than the number of consonant sounds, some being paired duplicates for a set of consonant sounds. While these duplicate symbols have the same consonant sounds, each symbol has its own effect on the tone of the syllable in which it occurs, thus creating another element of difficulty for the foreigner in learning to read and write the language.

Tones are also indicated by special tone markers, or diacritics, in some but not all cases. There are four of these tone markers, and the absence of a diacritic or one of the paired duplicate consonants also indicates a tone. In addition, there is a special diacritical mark to indicate that a written syllable should not be pronounced. This is used frequently in writing words of Sanskrit or Pali origin, which are shortened in spoken Thai.

In writing, Thai words are not separated by spaces which serve instead to indicate the ends of phrases and sentences. The use of question marks, exclamation points and quotation marks has been borrowed from Western languages, probably from English, and their use is now common although not absolutely essential for understanding.

Most of the early writing was religious and was used principally in monasteries. Except for some inscriptions on stone, writing was usually incised on palm leaves with a sharp instrument; ink was applied to the leaf and then rubbed off, leaving the scratches filled; the leaves were then strung together to make a kind of book. These early writing materials, as well as the first printing press, set up early in the nineteenth century, and the Thai typewriter developed by American missionaries in 1981, have been important in determining the evolution of Thai letters to their present form.

Transliteration

Aside from the transcription of the actual sounds of spoken Thai, the method used by linguists and modern textbooks on spoken Thai, there are two main systems for writing Thai in Roman letters. In one, each Thai letter is replaced with a Roman alphabet equivalent. Unlike Thai notation, this method does not indicate which syllables are not pronounced. Moreover, since Thai has some sounds not indicated by special symbols in Western languages, their representation in this method is often somewhat ambiguous. The other method ignores both Thai spelling and pronunciation, and transliterates the borrowed Sanskrit and Pali words in their original form, as found in those languages. In transliterating words of purely Thai origin, this method is not different from the other.

Names and Naming Patterns

Family names have come into use in Thailand only within the past half century. In 1916 King Vajiravudh decreed that every family must have a name. He bestowed surnames on the minor royalty and officials, but villagers were obligated to choose a surname from a list prepared by the King. Villagers state that some people did not know what name to choose and were given humorous names, such as "Dances Behind the Hill," but such stories are probably apocryphal. In some cases surnames indicate the district of origin of the family or past connections with royalty (see ch. 7, Social Structure). It is not uncommon to find several families in a small village bearing the same surname, although they may disclaim blood relationship. In other villages, however, the lack of family records and the disinterest in tracing ancestry (unless the family is descended from nobility) have resulted in the possession of a common surname being considered sufficient evidence for putative if untraceable kinship.

Within the family infants are sometimes not given proper names until they are several months old; in the meantime they are referred to as "little one," the sex being indicated by the use of modifiers. In the Central Region they may be given animal nicknames, for example, "little pig" or "little mouse" or they may be called "Red," a word implying rawness. Originally this was an attempt to confuse malicious spirits which were believed to cause the deaths of very young children (see ch. 12, Religion). Proper names are selected by the village abbot after careful considerations of the astrological portents, although some younger parents may choose the name themselves. In either case care is taken to ensure that the name be auspicious. Proper names sometimes reflect the parents' hopes for the child's future, although they are usually just "lucky" names. Unlike Latin languages, boys' names are not distinguished from those of girls by grammatical endings (which are lacking in Thai) but can be distinguished only, if at all, by common usage. In the schools the use of terms corresponding roughly to "Miss" and "Mister" must be used in the records in order to distinguish the sex of some students, who have names that may be given to either sex. Children are often named on an alliterative basis; that is, the names of all the brothers and sisters may begin with the same syllable, often the same one with which a parent's name begins.

More elaborate names derived from Pali or Sanskrit are popular in urban upper-class circles, whereas shorter and simpler purely Thai names are common in rural circles and among poorer urban people. Names that are acceptable in some dialects are often vulgar or unflattering in the Siamese Thai dialect, and the bearer of such a name will feel obliged to change it should he come into frequent contact with speakers of Siamese Thai.

Individuals address older relatives by their kin term and younger relatives by name. When speaking of a sibling to an outsider, the villager and often urban people frequently use the kinship term rather than the given name. Quite frequently, boys will refer to their girl friend as a "younger sister." Presumably, the girl reciprocates by referring to him as her "older brother." This is perhaps in imitation of the custom by which married couples from 20 to 30 years of age refer to each other as younger sister and older brother. This pattern is no longer followed consistently by married couples, who may use each other's given name. Ideally, husband and wife should refer to each other by different terms according to the age group to which they belong. In some parts of Thailand the husband and wife, after their children have received names, may refer to each other as the mother or father of "so and so." As they reach middle age they may begin to address each other simply as "you," and when they reach the age of retirement from the responsibilities of life, they often begin to call each other by their given names.

In Siamese Thai a person in a superior position many address males in inferior positions by the term *nai* (Mister), which is also used by newspapers and government communications in referring to citizens without special titles; for example, military rank, official titles, or acquired or inherited titles. Although *nai* is the official written form of "Mister," it should not be used in polite discourse between equals or by subordinates addressing their superiors. Polite modern usage requires the use of the word *khun* for all except priests and royalty, who are given special titles. Similarly, the terms *nangsao* for unmarried girls and *nang* for married women are found in written sources, but these terms, and also the word *nai*, should not be used as terms of address in conversation unless one wishes to emphasize the social distance between oneself and the persons addressed, and such assumption of superiority may be resented as unjustified. Male students, for example, in speaking to teachers may refer to each other as *nai*, or may be so referred to as by the teachers. Female students, however, would probably be called by their first names without the use of a qualifying title.

Titles of respect based on religious service and on age are used with an individual's given name or with the kinship term that identifies him. If a man has served as a novice or priest, his name throughout the rest of his life will include a term of respect denoting this service. Use of this special form will be followed by his immediate family as well as by fellow villagers, or others who know of his service. As a villager reaches old age, younger villagers will address him by the kinship terms for grandfather or grandfather as a mark of respect, even though the speaker is not related to the old person. Often an additional term meaning "very old" is added to the kinship term to indicate even greater respect for the old person.

Under the monarchy, when a person entered government service and held an official position, he was given a title (which could not be inherited) and a new name to match the title. In ascending order of importance, these titles were *khun* (which is not the present polite word meaning "Mister" or "you"), *luang, phra, phraya* and *chao phraya*. With the receipt of a title and a new name, the name received in childhood was abandoned, and the man was, henceforth, known by his title name. These titles were discontinued with the advent of the constitutional monarchy, but those who had received titles and title names under the old regime continued to use them. Families related to title holders, past or present, continue to take pride in and draw prestige from them and may attempt to keep track of relatives in the male line of descent, in imitation of noble families related to a king.

Conventions and Proverbs

The people have always been fond of using poetry to express their thoughts and emotions in speech and writing. The simplest of all poetical forms is the *like'* poem, which even the illiterate know how to compose, but poetry is not limited to this formal expression. Even in everyday conversation poetic language is frequently used (see ch. 11, Artistic and Intellectual Expression). Thai lends itself well to alliteration, and words are frequently chosen to obtain a pleasing and rhythmic sound pattern; syllables may be repeated, changing the vowel on repetition, partly for emphasis and partly to make the words more pleasant to the ear. People who speak well in rhyme and rhythm are much admired and are called "masters of poetry." Similes are frequently used in both the spoken and written language, and parables are popular, especially in training children.

The Thai have a great appreciation for the humor in subtleties of language. Play on words and puns are achieved by exchanging vowels or consonants between two words or shifting tones. Double meaning and vulgarity are often expressed in this way, particularly by the clowns of the *like'* drama, and are regarded as extremely funny. Skill at puns and other word games is rated highly; clumsiness brings ridicule. Mispronunciations by announcers and public speakers bring considerable laughter, even when the result is meaningless.

Proverbs are common and their generally cautionary character suggests that the Thai are less carefree and ingenuous than might appear from superficial observation of their outward behavior. Some proverbs are: "Face like a doe—heart like a tiger"; "Pretty outside but not inside"; "The ancients said, if someone tells you of a fortune in a faraway land you should not go according to his word"; and "He who spits toward the sky gets it back in his own face."

LAO

Lao dialects are more similar to each other than to Siamese Thai which, unlike them has borrowed heavily from Khmer, Pali and Sanskrit. However, the Lao dialects and Siamese Thai remain mutually intelligible, for although the Khmer, Pali and Sanskrit borrowings in the latter have greater prestige than the original Thai terms they replaced, the older words for the most part are still known and are only dialectally different from current Lao usages.

The scripts of the Lao of the Northeast and of the North are somewhat different from that used by the Siamese Thai, but all seem to derive from the same Indian sources. The script of the Northern Thai dialect, showing some Burmese influence, has 45 consonants plus a letter sometimes classed as a nasal vowel and vowel and diphthong symbols. Only half of the consonant letters are needed to represent all the consonant sounds; the others, as in the Northeast, being paired duplicates which indicate different tones. The Northeastern script appears to be identical with or very similar to that used in Laos. At least Northeasterners who know this script have no difficulty in reading Laotian.

Neither of the local scripts is taught in the schools. They are still taught in local *wats* (walled compound containing a Buddhist temple and associated buildings) which have collections of the Buddhist scriptures, the Jataka stories (legends of previous incarnations of Buddha which teach a moral lesson as well as provide entertainment) and other works in these scripts. As a result, only men with extensive temple service are able to read these scripts with any fluency. Laymen who have learned one of them in the course of temple service enjoy special prestige as learned men.

CHINESE

In terms of native speakers the various dialects of Chinese rank second in importance among the languages of Thailand. Chinese, according to recent estimates, is habitually spoken by 2.6 million people in Thailand.

Several dialects of southern China reflecting the places of origin of the immigrants are spoken. Like Thai, they are monosyllabic and tonal, but they and Thai are mutually unintelligible. The Chinese system of ideographs is also completely different from the alphabetic writing system of the Thai. Although Teochiu, Hakka, Hainanese, Hokkien and Cantonese, the main dialects found in Thailand, all use the same system of writing, they are as different from each other as are European languages and the community tends to be compartmentalized along dialect lines.

Since the Chinese have virtually preempted the role of the trading middle class, and since business is dominated by speakers of Teochiu, this dialect has become the language of trade and the lingua franca of the Chinese minority.

Although many of the Chinese, especially those born and raised in Thailand, know Thai well and use it outside their own ethnic community, even Thai businessmen find it expedient to have at least some knowledge of Teochiu if their business dealings bring them in frequent contact with Chinese businessmen. In areas of heavy Chinese concentration, such as Bangkok, most Thai pick up a few words of Teochiu—enough to bargain with Chinese peddlers and merchants—and many of the common Teochiu expressions tend to become absorbed into the Thai language as slang.

Mandarin, officially the national language of China, is increasingly used for communication among educated Chinese of different dialect groups and, as the national language, is taught in all Chinese schools. The regional languages, however, retain their importance as the primary means of communication within the Chinese community and as a major basis for social and occupational alignments. Each major dialect group maintains a regional association for social purposes and for mutual aid. The regional associations maintain private schools; they aid members in time of crisis; they may publish newspapers and provide recreational facilities. Above all, they serve as official representatives in dealings with the authorities. For the majority of the Chinese, who have no occasion for close contact with the Thai, these linguistic associations, rather than the family, the trade union, or the nation in which they live, are the largest functional unit of the social community.

There is also in the Chinese community a distinct correlation between speech group and occupation. Thus, Teochiu dominate banking, the rice trade, insurance, rubber manufacture and many other occupations. The great majority of tobacco manufacturers and leather workshop proprietors are Hakka; sawmillers are chiefly Hainanese; Hokkien dominate the tea and rubber trades; Cantonese are prominent as restaurant owners. This traditional occupational specialization on the basis of regional and linguistic origin is apparently beginning to break down, however. The Teochiu, especially, are gradually expanding into other occupations, and the more successful find it possible to become associated with and assimilated to the Westernized Thai of the Bangkok elite.

Language is an obvious factor in the adjustment of the Chinese to life in Thailand. The non-Teochiu Chinese who have arrived in Bangkok in recent decades have had to adjust not only to Thai patterns but also to the dominant Teochiu patterns. Those who learn Thai best are well on the way to assimilation to the patterns of the larger Thai society; those who learn Mandarin and English well are likely to be heading toward the cosmopolitan culture emerging in the upper strata of Bangkok society. Those who learn Teochiu only are more or less committed to one of the Chinese classes and a life largely immersed in the Chinese quarter; those who learn no foreign language well are restricted in effective social relations to those of their own speech group.

MALAY

The Malay language is spoken by about 1,000,000 Thai nationals who are ethnic Malay; most of them live in the southernmost provinces which border on Malaysia: Narathiwat, Pattani, Yala and Satun. Malay, the native tongue of about 70 percent of the population in these provinces, belongs to the Malayo-Polynesian language family. It is a nontonal language and different in structure from Thai and Chinese. The Malay spoken in Thailand differs little from that of Malaysia. There is some admixture of Thai words, but the people on both sides of the border can readily communicate. In Thailand, Malay is written in Arabic script.

Although Thai, the official language of the country, is used by the provincial and local governments, by the courts of law in most types of disputes, and in the schools, many Malay have only a slight knowledge of it. This largely reflects the opposition among the Malay-speaking Islamic people to learning a language which they consider to be associated with Buddhism—a religion other than their own. Malay is still the predominant language of trade in the Southern Region, and Chinese and Thai businessmen in that area need a basic knowledge of it in their daily work. Area specialists estimate that of late 1965 no more than 25 percent of the Malay population spoke Thai, and in the same group, no more than 40 percent of those in the 10 to 19 year old bracket.

ENGLISH

English is the only European language widely known in Thailand. In many private schools it is taught from the elementary grades on; in public secondary schools it is usually chosen to fulfill the compulsory foreign language requirement. In practice, English is often the only foreign language taught, especially in government schools. Almost all high school graduates in Thailand have had at least 6 years of English language courses. However, since aptitude and motivation vary from student to student, this does not mean that most of them know English well.

English is used particularly in Thai elite circles; it is the language of cosmopolitan Bangkok society and of Thai international trade. Well-educated Thai, both in Bangkok and the provinces, know English and use it with foreigners. In the provinces even people without a secondary school education may know a few words of English acquired from friends and advertisements of American and British products. The lack of modern technical terminology in the Thai language and the limited number of textbooks in Thai have made the use of English almost unavoidable in the universities, especially for higher technical education. The opportunities for students to receive part of their education in the United States or Great Britain have brought about an increasing awareness among students of the desirability for fluency in English.

There is thus an increased demand for training in English at all levels of society, because of its prestige value and its importance as a channel to modern ideas and techniques. This demand is shown in the enthusiastic response to the opportunities for learning English that are available today. The classes in English offered by the American University Alumni Association Binational Language Center and by the British Information Service are crowded, and waiting lists for enrollment are long.

Although English is and long has been the most widely known foreign language, the government, for a period before and during World II, when it was pursuing a strongly nationalistic course, attempted to "purify" the language of European influences. Official publications were no longer printed in both Thai and English, and Thai numerals were used in preference to Arabic numerals. Since then English has returned to favor as the principal second language, and the government is actively promoting knowledge of it among teachers and students. Many official documents are again published in Thai and in English versions, which may be bound separately or as one volume. The Ministry of Education, through the National Teacher's Institute publishes *Public Education* (a magazine for schoolteachers), which contains brief readings, questions and exercises in English.

OTHER LANGUAGES

Pali, related to Vedic Sanskrit, is not a spoken language, but it is important in Thailand (as it is in Burma and Cambodia) as the written medium of Theravada Buddhism, which all ordained monks must study. Along with Sanskrit, Pali is the source of many linguistic borrowings and innovations, especially in Siamese Thai. Borrowed words in common speech dealing with religion generally derive from Pali, whereas those referring to the secular realm are apt to be of Sanskrit origin. The degree to which Thai dialects have borrowed from these two languages of India, and tonal shifts account for an important part of the differences among them.

The Karen, the largest group of Thailand's mountain peoples speak a Sino-Tibetan language, whose position among the language families of the world is still uncertain. Some linguists say that it is closely related to the Tibeto-Burman group of languages while others assert that it constitutes a separate major division (Karenic) within the Sino-Tibetan group. Thailand has about 75,000 Karen, among a total of approximately 1½ million in southeastern Asia as a whole. The most important of the Karen dialects in Thailand are Skaw and P'wo.

The Miao-Yao peoples, numbering collectively about 60,000 in Thailand, have close Chinese affinities. Scholars have not agreed on the linguistic position of their languages, but they are sometimes represented as a separate major division within the Sino-Tibetan group. Rather wide linguistic differences distinguish Thailand's main groups of Miao: the White Meo (Meo Khao) and the Blue Mao, who in turn subdivide themselves into Black Meo (Meo Dam), the Striped Meo (Meo Lai) and the Flowery Meo (Meo Dawk). These dialects are to some extent mutually intelligible, but Lao, the language of the Northeast is used as a lingua franca and some of the older men speak Yunnanese. The Yao, whose tongue is closely related to that of the Miao, are a far smaller group and are concentrated in Chiang Mai province.

The Lisu, Lahu and Akha mountain peoples, the bulk of whom still live in southern Yunnan province of mainland China, speak languages belonging to the Tibeto-Burman branch of the Sino-Tibetan family. The Lisu and Akha each comprise a single dialect group, but the Lahu are subdivided into two major and two minor subgroups. Lahu, a monosyllabic language with three tonal variations, has similarities with Akha and Lisu, with additional borrowings from Chinese, Burmese and Thai.

Other small linguistic groups found in Thailand include the Lawa, a Mon-Khmer speaking group long established in the area, and the Haw, recent Chinese immigrants who live in the border areas of the Northern Region. In addition, in the lowlands, small but significant groups of Mon, Khmer and Vietnamese-speaking peoples are represented (see ch. 5, Ethnic Groups).

THAI LINGUISTIC POLICY

The Thai Government has long been aware of the importance of language barriers as an obstacle to the assimilation of ethnic minority groups. Since the ultimate objective of Thai policy is to eliminate minority problems by absorbing the minority populations into the national culture, great emphasis has been placed on weakening the linguistic roots of the ethnic minorities and on promoting knowledge of Thai among all residents.

Education is viewed as an important instrument in the assimilation process. Schooling is both free and compulsory for 7 years, though in many rural areas the children in fact attend for only 4 years (see ch. 10, Education). The law requires that this education be given in the Thai language in all schools, regardless of the ethnic background of the children enrolled. In Chinese schools, this requirement is relaxed to the extent that 10 hours of a 30-hour weekly curriculum may be taught in the Chinese medium.

Among the Chinese, the education process provides scant impediment to assimilation. Not only is instruction in Chinese limited to a few hours per week, but no child may attend a Chinese school for more than 4 years beyond kindergarten. Thus, secondary education is exclusively Thai. Moreover, in the first place, more than 95 percent of ethnic Chinese children attend Thai government schools rather than those operated by their own community.

Among the Malays, completion of the basic course of religious instruction offered at the local mosque is expected of every village child, but only a minority attend the village schools. In these school for more than 4 years beyond kindergarten. Thus, sec-requiring that instruction be in Thai, while others, recognizing the difficulties this presents to the Malay-speaking children, continue to teach in Malay. The Thai government is trying to develop better language instruction programs in the Malay-speaking area. Efforts toward this goal include the introduction of experimental programs where Malay teachers are given intensive seminar courses in the national language, with prizes for the outstanding students offered as incentives. Despite this and other endeavors in the direction of meeting the special needs of the Malays, there is still strong resistance to government education.

The government maintains two types of schools for children from remote areas who cannot attend the regular government schools in the villages and towns. One type of school is established locally and staffed by the Border Patrol Police in the areas they patrol. The other type is composed of several boarding schools to which certain young people from the ethnic minorities are brought to study. In either type the objective is to introduce the Thai language and culture and other useful information to the ethnic minorities in order to increase their participation in national life and to encourage their assimilation. The government hopes to accomplish this through these students who are expected to become of increased importance in their home communities as contact of the minorities with the Thai increases with the passage of time.

The government's linguistic policy, then, is two-fold. It promotes the knowledge of English as a technical and scientific tool in the development of Thailand, and it is attempting to establish Siamese Thai as the standard national language used by all citizens. In both cases, concern for the nation, its development and unification is at the basis of the policy.

CHAPTER 7

SOCIAL STRUCTURE

Thai society is composed principally of ethnic Thai, who are a relatively homogeneous people with a sense of common identity based on a shared language and cultural tradition. Because they constitute the overwhelming majority of the population, the Thai have made their attitudes and values the dominant influence in the social organization. Together with the ethnic Chinese with whom they are closely related through intermarriage, they completely dominate national life. Other social groups, including the sizable Malay minority in the Southern Region, the hill peoples of the Northern Region and the Vietnamese refugees in the Northeast Region, constitute separate subsocieties whose identities and social patterning are distinct from that of the national society.

In spite of ethnological variations in ethnic affiliation, the principal social division is between the urban and rural segments of the population. Some 30 million villagers comprising nearly 90 percent of the population constitute the base of the social pyramid. Most of the rural inhabitants are ethnic Thai peasant cultivators, who own and operate small farms. Although they are fully aware of the existence of political and economic institutions beyond the local level, they participate only marginally in national affairs (see ch. 15, Political Dynamics).

Distinguished from them in nearly all aspects of social outlook is a small urban population that is concentrated almost exclusively in Bangkok, which is Thailand's single large city and the center of its social, commercial and political life. The upper level of this urban society is a small ruling elite, which constitutes the apex of the social pyramid and has almost exclusive access to political authority and capital resources. Between the base and the apex of the social pyramid stand the urban-based minor officials and petty functionaries, among whom bureaucratic rank comprises the principal criterion of individual status.

Besides this rural-urban dichotomy, the most significant aspect of the social order is the presence of a culturally distinct Chinese community. Large numbers of Thai nationals are wholly or partially of ethnic Chinese extraction. Fusion of ethnic Chinese and ethnic Thai through intermarriage has often made the line between the two groups indistinguishable.

The estimated size of the Chinese community varies according to what identifying criteria are used. In legal terms the Chinese community is small and numbers less than one-half million. In circumstances when it could be advantageous to claim Chinese ancestry, however, almost 4 million Thai nationals could qualify themselves as Chinese. The pressures to behave in Thai ways are great, and persons who are even partly Chinese can generally be expected to participate in society in their Thai rather than in their Chinese identities.

Since ancient times Thai forms of social organization have been relatively simple and informal. Individualism and personal liberty have been stressed. Among ethnic Thai there is little tradition of private organizations. Change of social position has been sanctioned by Theravada Buddhism, according to which social status is seen as the result of merit that was acquired in previous lives. Traditionally, the Buddhist order and the governmental bureaucracy were the chief means of social mobility.

Although there were no social classes as such, the Thai were extremely status conscious. Every social relationship was understood in terms of inferior and superior participants, and the subordinate was expected in each case to defer to and obey his superior. Until the first quarter of the twentieth century, there existed fixed hierarchies of status, which were structured in terms of delicate differences of power, prestige and obligation. The rank and status of officials, who formed the top level of this grading system, were also defined in other ways.

THE TRADITIONAL SETTING

The basic features of Thai society persisted with only slight modification from ancient times until well into the nineteenth century. In the centuries before the interaction with the West eroded the old order, Thailand was a stable, integrated society, which was composed principally of village-dwelling rice farmers. Land was readily available, and every freeman could lay claim to 25 rai (10 acres) as his own domain.

Individual families were the key social and economic units. Occasionally, the physical requirements of wet-rice farming and the need for mutual security necessitated the cooperation of a larger group. This group was composed of voluntary work units within a village and informal cooperation between villages. Later such public projects as bridge and road building were undertaken by the government, which used manpower obtained through a system of compulsory labor service (the *corveé*).

Critically important in this traditional society were two formal organizations—the Sangha (the Buddhist Order) and the absolute monarchy, including its attendant officialdom. Both of these institutions originally represented cultural borrowings from other civilizations, but in time each developed a distinctive Thai character.

Theravada Buddhism was established as the state religion during the era of the first Thai Kingdom of Sukhothai (A.D. 1238–1350). As the dominant religious faith, it has helped sustain the society since that time. From it has come the moral basis for a hierarchical social order in which individual status was regarded as the consequence of religious merit acquired in previous lives.

At the summit of the social hierarchy was the king, who was surrounded by a retinue of princes and officials. He was regarded as the "Lord of the Land" and the "Lord of Lives," and his authority was absolute. Brahmanic concepts borrowed from the Khmer and elaborate accompanying rites sustained his rule. Further reinforcement for the prestige of the throne came from the philosophical concept of the *devaraja*, or god-king, which is common to both Hindu and Buddhist traditions. According to this view, which assumes a moral and social order that ranks men by virtue and power, the king was a surrogate god and was, therefore, regarded as both more powerful and more virtuous than other men.

Society was broadly divided into three groups: the governing elite, freemen and slaves. The king, members of his family and a hierarchy of officials constituted the ruling group, which was distinguished from the remainder of the population by its power, prestige and control over productive resources. The Buddhist Order comprised a separate subsegment of the society.

Although it constituted only a tiny fragment of the population, the ruling elite dominated national life and gave society its meaning and its goals. The remainder of the population was divided between freemen and slaves; the ratio was about 3 to 1. Freemen were subject to taxation, the *corveé* or military service, but slaves were exempt from such obligations. Slavery held no stigma, and the position of many slaves was apparently no worse than that of many freemen. Persons who became slaves out of indebtedness could buy their freedom after payment of their obligations.

From the reign of King Trailok (A.D. 1448–88) until 1932, an elaborate system existed for designating rank that, in its broadest sense, included every member of society. This was known as the *sakdi na,* or dignity marks system, that assigned every one in the kingdom from the unredeemable slaves to the eldest sons of the king a given number of dignity marks. All commoners except those holding posts in the bureaucracy had dignity marks of 25. For them the *sakdi na* was a designation of social status alone, but for members of the ruling elite it also designated function and reflected their position in the administrative hierarchy. Petty functionaries had *sakdi na* ranging from 400 to 10,000, depending on their position and degree of relationship to the king.

The various levels of bureaucracy represented delicate gradations of status and prestige. Each carried explicit obligations and duties as well as privileges. The *sakdi na* system was only one of several methods of classification that were used to group and identify officials. Others included a series of honorific titles and such visible status symbols as royally conferred palanquins.

The ruling elite was further divided into two related but distinct hierarchies—civil officials and military officers. This distinction, however, was largely superficial because it seems to have had little significance in matters of function, training and general outlook.

The impact of the West, which dates from the late nineteenth century, caused sweeping changes in the old order. The aura of sanctity that for centuries had been associated with the throne was greatly diminished. After the establishment of the constitutional monarchy in 1932, active control of the government passed from the king to a military oligarchy. The old *sakdi na* system of social and functional rank was abandoned.

The personnel needs of an expanded bureaucracy stimulated the growth of public education. Because the administrative structure grew, greater numbers of petty functionaries were needed, and because opportunities for promotion developed, the possibility of moving upward in the social scale increased for a considerable number of persons. Although entrance to the top echelon of the ruling elite generally remained closed, in the remaining levels of the bureaucracy the opportunities for advancement multiplied rapidly. Initially, Buddhist temple schools were the primary source for a substantial number of candidates for these lower-level bureaucratic posts, but in the early twentieth century the foundation of a national system of popular education through the university level was laid. Educational institutions abroad provided training for many potential senior officials.

Another aspect of changing social organization in the early twentieth century was the influx of massive numbers of Chinese immigrants, especially between 1900 and 1930. The ethnic Chi-

110

nese, who first came as wage laborers to work on the railroads, construction projects and in the tin and rubber industries, were quick to see the possibilities for exploitation in the commercial sector of the economy. The result was the rapid consolidation of a predominantly Chinese entrepreneurial group that devoted itself to the development of the commercial sector of the economy. The ethnic Thai during the same period absorbed themselves increasingly in administrative and political work.

URBAN SOCIETY

Bangkok is the only city of substantial size in the country, and its population, which is about 5 percent of the national total, comprises the major urban segment of the society. All parts of the country are in varying degrees of subordination to the capital. Its residents set standards of behavior, outlook, dress and physical comfort, which are imitated in different degrees by the rural inhabitants.

Because the Chinese community is essentially urban, much of Bangkok's population is Chinese or partly Chinese. Acculteration to Thai behavior patterns is widespread among the second and third generation Chinese. Such persons typically use Thai personal and family names and are fluent in both Thai and the minority language. Chinese dominate the commercial sector of the economy; hence, most business leaders are of Chinese extraction. Ethnic Chinese are liberally represented in the medical, legal and journalistic professions and on the faculties of the major universities.

Some persons of Chinese or partial Chinese ancestry are found in the bureaucracy, although most administrative and political positions are monopolized by ethnic Thai. Both Thai and Chinese are represented, however, in other forms of urban employment, including clerical occupations, shopkeeping, skilled and unskilled work in factories, workshops and service occupations.

Groups of persons in the same occupations and with relatively equal incomes tend to form clusters at certain points on the status ladder. In the strictest sense, however, these are not social classes. The Thai tend to think of status differences existing between individuals rather than between corporate groupings with collective interests and goals. Because of the consolidation and the increasing exclusiveness of the ruling elite, the beginnings of a class structure are probably emerging in Bangkok.

The ruling group is distinguished by its monopolization of political authority and capital resources and its privileged access to such status symbols as a degree from a foreign university. It consists primarily of top-ranking government officials, many of whom have military backgrounds. The elite also includes the most powerful commercial leaders, key figures of the aristocracy and a small number of professional men. A single individual may fill several of these roles simultaneously. Consequently, the group is extremely small and probably comprises no more than 1 percent of the total population.

For several decades the leading Chinese entrepreneurs and the Thai bureaucratic elite have maintained a cooperative arrangement that has linked the political and economic bases of Thai society. In this arrangement successful Chinese merchants share part of their acquired wealth with leading Thai politicians and military men through business alliances in exchange for the protection and the assistance of these influential men in government.

Lesser officials in the higher ranks of the civil service and some prosperous businessmen, mostly Chinese, compose a substrata of this element of society. Although wholly a part of it, they maintain a close relationship with the ruling group and are able to exert some small influence on the course of national affairs. This group is minute and consists of less than 1 percent of the population.

Minor civil servants, small shopkeepers and other white collar workers take their social standards from the elite, on whose continuing favor many of their positions depend. Until the establishment of the constitutional system, government service was the only avenue to higher status. In recent years new channels have developed, but government service is still the principal one.

The occupation stratum below the white collar group is overwhelmingly Chinese in composition. It is composed mostly of craftsmen and skilled laborers—artisans, technicians, workers in service industries and the lowest-paid government workers. The Chinese and Thai in this category tend to pattern themselves after their counterparts in the group just above them. Among the Chinese great value is attached to occupational skill and the accumulation of sufficient capital to permit an upward move. The Thai, on the other hand, is more likely to place great value on obtaining some kind of white collar job.

At the bottom of the urban social scale is a large group that consists of unskilled laborers, domestic servants and vendors. It is doubtful that there is any strong sense of shared circumstance or common interest within this category. Many of the Thai are recent or temporary migrants from rural areas, and their primary identification continues to be with their home villages rather than with any social entity in the towns. The Chinese members of this lowest group generally strive to elevate themselves by accumulating sufficient capital to establish small businesses of various types.

Except in the Chinese sector, urban society is characterized by a notable lack of private social organization. Thai social structure because of its emphasis on hierarchy and vertical relationships between pairs of individuals provides little foundation for groups based on lateral or egalitarian relationships among large numbers of individuals. In addition, the government has temporarily banned several types of organizations, such as trade unions and political parties, because it regards them as counter to the public well-being and other national interests.

A number of formal associations, which are private and voluntary in the West, are government sponsored in Thailand and obligatory for all persons in a particular category. Consequently, all primary school boys are members of the Boy Scouts, and all teachers are members of the Teacher's Institute.

The Chinese have a strong tradition of private organization, which is reflected in the existence of a proliferation of dialect groups, benevolent societies and business federations. The most important of these are the dialect associations and the Chinese Chamber of Commerce, which is an organization intended to promote Chinese business interests. The dialect associations are composed of persons who speak one or another of the several Chinese dialects in use in Thailand.

Teochiu is spoken by the largest number of persons and is the principal dialect in use in the Bangkok region. The Teochiu Association, to which several smaller regional subdivisions are attached, runs a large primary school in Bangkok, maintains a graveyard for its members and publishes a monthly magazine. It is the largest and most powerful of the dialect associations. Other dialect associations have varying numbers of subdivisions of different sizes. Surname organizations exist but are less important.

All of these organizations have a variety of self-help functions, including education, political protection, insurance, charity, maintenance of cemeteries and mediation of disputes among members. Although the actual members were born mainly in China, they represent most of the Bangkok Chinese and exercise a profound influence on the entire ethnic Chinese community.

There is considerable evidence that the traditional Chinese secret societies still exist in Thailand, particularly among the laborers. Some are apparently branches of societies with international extensions in other Asian countries. These organizations, about which little is known, perform some of the functions of labor unions and have certain protective and benevolent functions. They also fulfill the psychological desires for ritual and secretiveness.

The Chinese Chamber of Commerce plays an important role as the representative of the interests of the entire Chinese community to the government. The Chamber intercedes with the authorities for individuals and groups who are in financial need or trouble, and it strives to moderate government actions that are seen as detrimental to the interests of the Chinese community. Because Thailand does not recognize Communist China, it has used the Chamber as an intermediary in arranging deportations of Chinese to the Communist-controlled mainland.

The Cosmopolitan Club and the Silom Club are two clubs important in bringing together the Chinese and the Thai elements of the new elite. The Rotary International and the Junior Chamber of Commerce also serve this purpose.

An evident trend in Chinese voluntary social organization in the mid-1960's was the disappearance of internal divisions and a consolidation of forces at the national level. The Chinese community in the past had been organized into many different dialect associations and their local subdivisions. Now, centralization within the framework of the powerful Bangkok-based Teochiu Association is taking place. Even the Hokkien-speaking population of the Southern Region, whose cultural links were with Malaysia, was being oriented toward Bangkok. In commercial life, too, activities were being increasingly structured in the direction of the Central Region and the national framework. There were even indications of the emergence of a cosmopolitan Chinese elite, who uses Mandarin as its official dialect.

RURAL SOCIETY

Rural society in the latter part of the twentieth century reflected the effect of the traditional pattern of landownership. It was composed principally of small-scale independent farmers, who live in villages no larger than 3,000 persons. These small landholders in general had little hope for quick improvement of their own financial position; economic and social advancement of individuals began with their abandonment of the rural economy and their emigration to the cities. The landholdings did, however, provide most of the rural inhabitants with a stable subsistence and relative economic security. This circumstance was reflected in the popular indifference to national politics and an inarticulate acquiescence to administration policies.

Rural society was characterized by the absence of readily discernible social classes and by a relative lack of complexity and formal institutions. Variations in wealth were everywhere apparent, and all social relationships were hierarchically patterned. In every person-to-person encounter there was assumed to be a superior and an inferior, and the delicate gradations in wealth, age or religious experience served as the basis for status differentiation. These distinctions pointed to the absence of clearly defined social classes—groups of persons who are conscious of their corporate identity and who share a set of ideals and traditions differentiating them from other classes. The individual tended to feel a strong sense of identification with only a small number of social groups—the nuclear family, the extended kin group and the nation. To a lesser extent, or at certain times in his life, he might feel a strong tie to the village school or the monastery. In addition to these, however, there were no major social institutions at the village level.

The basic unit of rural society was the household, which was composed of a man, his wife and children and frequently included other relatives. Beyond the household and the extended family, the principal social units were the local temple and the village school, both of which provided opportunities for social advancement to the young. Joining the preisthood, even for a short period, was a path to good moral standing in the community for the ordinary village boy. To the extremely poor but very ambitious it was a means of acquiring enough education to move to Bangkok and begin the climb on the bureaucratic ladder.

All members of the Buddhist clergy, both permanent and temporary, stand apart from secular Thai society and enjoy a special status position. Their saffron robes symbolize their role as exemplars and transmitters of the *dharma,* which is the truth taught by Buddha. Because they are monks they receive deference and signs of respect even from the king, who ranks above all others in the secular world. They are considered to be outside the secular affairs of the community, but they tend to be much more involved in worldly affairs than their urban counterparts.

In the villages the line between sacred and secular activities is not usually sharply drawn, and in this social setting many monks find it difficult to maintain the ideal state of scholarly seclusion and meditative spirituality. The *wat* contains the temple and the residence of the monks and is both the social center of the community and the site of most religious observances. These ceremonies, whether Buddhist religious services at the temple or family ceremonies in the household, always include food and conversation.

Many secular activities are associated with the *wat* to lend an aura of supernatural meritoriousness, which helps to ensure their success. When money is being raised to finance a local project, such as a bridge or a village road, the contributions may be put into the safekeeping of the *wat;* thus, secular contributions to the project are linked with the merit-earning contributions to the *wat* itself.

Whether they are active or passive participants in village life, monks are at the top of the village prestige scale, and their potentiality as instigators or guides of social action and change is considerable. Although their support is not always necessary, their opposition would doom any project.

Very few villagers have access to politically or economically powerful men or positions. The pattern of life and the general outlook of most villagers are much the same. Nearly all share the same occupation of farming because the village has few full-time specialists other than the monks, schoolteachers, a few tradesmen and perhaps a small-scale ricemiller. Other specialists, such as barbers, carpenters or ironmongers, netmakers and practitioners of herbal or magical folk medicine, are primarily farmers, who usually practice their special skills only on request.

In rural society people generally deal with one another in a manner appropriate to the close personal relationships that exist in a small community where most neighbors are also relatives. The villager verbally treats everyone in the village as a relative of greater or lesser closeness. He considers the age and sex of the person, his moral or religious qualities, his personality, his occupation and his special skills and then addresses the individual casually or formally as a subordinate, an equal or a superior. Some individual roles—teacher, headman or governmental official —command formal respect without regard to personal qualities, but the essence of the system is the hierarchical ordering of persons according to personal qualities rather than economic categories.

Formally, the young are considered to be subordinate to the old; women subordinate to men; and laymen subordinate to monks. There are language conventions which reflect these relationships. A *phu yai* (big person) is one in a superordinate position, and a *phu noi* (little person) is a person in a subordinate position. All relationships depend on the relative status and the personal feelings of the particular individual involved. An inferior who does not like a superior must, nevertheless, show the outward forms of respect. Like his urban counterpart, the villager is an expert in subtle innuendo incorporated in outwardly correct etiquette.

Wealth can be important as a source of influence in Thai rural society. A villager who is generous and tolerant and who excels in Buddhist virtue is more highly respected in his community than the wealthy farmer who has few or none of these qualities. The wealthy farmer, however, may have more actual power and influence because of the favors he can bestow and the obligations of his clients and debtors than someone who is more highly respected.

That "one person is as good as any other" is an unrealistic notion to the Thai. The conception of reincarnation according to one's acquired virtue excludes a belief in the equal status of all persons. Nevertheless, because anyone can acquire or lose merit and improve or diminish his position in some future life, there is no belief that one's subordinates are inherently inferior. Each person having been born to a particular status must recognize the limitations it imposes on him. Everyone from the highest to the lowest is subject to the law of rebirth until he achieves *nirvana*, and he must recognize that he has superiors as well as inferiors. Even the king is limited by conventions and customs, and in the old days he was believed to be subordinate to the Brahmanic pantheon. The human in the lowest social status is superior to the animals, which can be reborn as men. All human beings are capable of eventually reaching *nirvana*, and they, therefore, have an ultimately equal religious value.

CHAPTER 8

FAMILY

The predominant forms of family organization and behavior are those of the ethnic Thai, most of whom are rural residents and adherents of Buddhism. Details of practice vary among different components of this ethnic majority, especially between its rural and urban segments. Nevertheless, overall similarities exist in such matters as negotiation of marriage contracts and customs relating to residence, inheritance and childrearing. Other patterns of family life prevail among the ethnic Chinese, whose society reflects its Confucian heritage, and among the ethnic Malays in the Southern Region, who subscribe to the principles of Islamic law. Still other family systems are encountered among the hill peoples in the Northern Region.

In marriage ethnic Thai are more inclined to emphasize individual independence and dignity than family solidarity. The nuclear family, in which the father, mother and their unmarried children live together in permanent union, is the ideal, this status being sought and achieved by most young couples within a few years after marriage. Men and women are regarded as equals, and children, while impressed with the obligation of deference toward their elders, are not rigidly disciplined. Dissolution of families through divorce or separation is fairly common.

In the modern period there is an evident trend toward greater self-sufficiency for nuclear families, with a corresponding decline in the role of larger kin groups. When groups of the latter type actually do cooperate, as in the observance of various ceremonials involving family members, it appears to be more out of the expectation of reciprocal and mutual benefits than from a strong sense of family solidarity and cohesion. A purely functional approach is also encountered in other aspects of family life. Economic criteria, for example, are major determinants in the negotiation of marriage contracts, choice of residence and the composition of households.

THE THAI BUDDHIST FAMILY

The Thai Buddhist family is the predominant type in most sectors of the country, except the Southern Region where Malay

Moslem communities predominate, and parts of the Northern Region, where the strikingly different family systems of the hill peoples are encountered. Details of customs may differ from place to place, however, as in the matter of the much more conservative courtship rules which exist in the Central Region, compared with some villages in the Northern Region.

Structures and Function

The nuclear family is the ideal and the most often encountered form of family life. In one village in the Central Region, for example, nuclear families represent 60 percent of all households in the community. Larger groups of kinsmen cooperate for such activities as the ceremonial observance of transition points in the life cycle or for planting and harvesting rice, but the arrangement is temporary. For most purposes the nuclear family can function independently, and it constitutes the basic economic and social unit of Thai society.

Whereas the nuclear family is the ideal, many households include less closely related members. Because of economic necessity, for example, it is commonplace for a couple to take up residence after marriage with either set of parents. Other households may include aged persons, children and unmarried siblings of the head of the family brought into the group because of the dissolution of their own families through death, divorce or impoverishment. Individuals live along only in exceptional cases, such as when they have no relatives or have been abandoned by them. Polygynous marriage formerly contributed to the diversity of quite a few households, but in the modern period most marriages are monogamous.

In the Northeast and North, where the traditional pattern persists most strongly, the compact communities tend to be composed of persons related by blood and marriage, since more than half of all marriages are between persons born in the same village. Thus, neighbors are often also kinsmen. In these small and relatively stable communities, kinship ties tend to become extremely complex.

Young couples who do not establish independent households immediately after their marriage are more likely to stay with the wife's parents than with those of the husband. Usually they are given a room in the parents' house in return for which the husband helps in working their land. Most such arrangements continue for only 3 or 4 years, although the youngest daughter in the family often lives with her husband under the parental roof until their death. In recognition of the care she has given them in their old age, she generally inherits the family residence along with a share of the land equal to that of the other siblings.

Whether the couple establishes permanent residence near the husband's or the wife's family is determined primarily by economic considerations. If the wife is the sole heir to her parents' estate, or in the unusual circumstance that her parents are much wealthier than are her husband's parents, they generally settle in or near the compound of her family. Otherwise, in most cases, they will move near the husband's family.

Property considerations determine where the couple will live in the case of second marriages as well. A widower with growing children and an established farm, for example, will simply introduce his new wife into the existing household.

In rural areas, at least, fragmentation or dissolution of the family group is by no means uncommon. This phenomenon is accounted for in part by patterns of seasonal labor. In villages of the Central Region, many heads of households absent themselves for 4 to 5 months at a time while temporarily employed in Bangkok. Besides this, families with large numbers of children may send one or more children to stay with relatives, neighbors or, in the case of boys, to the monastery, where in return for their exposure to righteous ways of behaving, they act as servants to the monks. Still other families, too poor to justify their remaining together as an economic unit, simply disperse. Again, the children may be taken in by kinsmen or other villagers; the adults will return to their parents' households or become residents in a monastery.

People feel that it is more important to know lateral kin—living relatives on the mother's or father's side—than it is to be able to identify one's ancestors beyond the grandparents. Families have acquired surnames only within the last 50 years, as a result of a royal decree, and the fact that family names are seldom used among the villagers themselves (either in direct address or in referring to other villagers) suggests their lack of interest in genealogy.

The most significant deviation from the family patterns typical of the great majority of ethnic Thai occurs in some wealthy urban families. At marriage, sons usually reside in separate households built in their father's compound. The father's household also tends to include unrelated servants and retainers as well as more distant kinsmen. Within the aristocratic family, in which Brahmanic influences resulting from long contact with the Indianized Khmer predominate, the male tends to have greater authority and women to have correspondingly less freedom of action and movement than is true in other Thai families. There are also minor variations resulting from the differences in wealth. In families of the ruling elite, for example, there is no need for the woman to make an active economic contribution to the household, and she can devote herself to artistic and other similar activities.

The family of the new elite tends to be influenced either by the model of the aristocratic family or by Western concepts of family life which are felt to be more in tune with the modern world than are traditional patterns. It would appear, however, that the families of wealthier and more influential members of the new elite are more likely to be modeled upon the patterns of the traditional elite, rather than those of the West. In this circle the family extends its patronage and influence not only to kinsmen but also to unrelated persons of potential utility, who are thus analogous to the retainers of the old ruling family. There is also a correspondingly greater emphasis on the authority of the father and the importance of his side of the family.

Among the middle- and lower-income groups the urban family tends to be as much like the rural family as circumstances permit. A shortage of housing, the greater expense of building or renting a house, the higher cost of living, a higher degree of impersonal relationships and a greater number of extra-family institutions, which take over functions met in the village by the family, contrast with the conditions of village life and tend to make it difficult or impossible for poorer families to follow completely the rural patterns. Among the very poor, then, the nuclear family household probably shows little tendency to include married children, even on a temporary basis. Many of the Bangkok poor live in single-room apartments in large barnlike structures, which provide only visual privacy and minimum amenities. Under such semi-slum conditions traditional family patterns are not preserved. However, in the outskirts of Bangkok the conditions are less intensely urban, and rural patterns will correspondingly be more or less well preserved, depending largely upon the size and population density of the particular urban area.

Family connections beyond the immediate circle have less meaning than in the past; yet they still have significance in special circumstances or on particular occasions. For example, several brothers and sisters living in different communities may alternately share the care of an elderly relative who spends several months of the year in each household. Kinship, too, is the basis for organizing sizable groups of people for transplanting and harvesting rice. Besides this, kin connections are sometimes the first to be exploited in cases of financial distress. Parents or wealthier brothers and sisters are often the first persons to whom an individual turns when in need of money; if they are unable to help, aunts, uncles or cousins may be approached.

Interaction and cohesion between households are most conspicuously demonstrated through the common celebration of the New Year festival and of various ritual observances, particularly conferring of holy orders and cremations. Cremations, for example, are extremely expensive, and uncles, aunts and cousins of the deceased person, as well as his or her own spouse and all surviving children, are expected to cooperate in defraying the expense.

Relative age is a matter of critical importance in the internal regulation of family life. The guiding principle for all relationships within the family circle is that the elder member has authority over and is responsible for the younger member, even in the case of siblings only a year or two apart. Terms employed in addressing not only members of the older generation but also of the individual's own generation reflect the age of the speaker in comparison to that of the person to whom he is speaking. Basic to the family system is the concept of a mutual exchange of loving care for loving obedience between older and younger, the relationship being reinforced by the right of either person to withdraw from the arrangement if unsatisfied with it. This principle, slightly remodified, can be seen in operation throughout Thai society.

In general, family obligations are recognized and met. It is felt that a man should repay his parents for having brought him into the world and cared for him in infancy and that elder siblings are owed a debt of gratitude. Moreover, during the time a newly married young man resides with his wife's parents, he is considered to have obligations to them which take precedence over those to his own parents. Conflict between obligations to different sets of kin or between family obligations and self-interest might be expected to arise from time to time, but in fact people seem largely able to keep the sentiments apart.

The Marriage Contract

Persons who take meals around the same hearth are considered a family, and marriage within this group is forbidden. First cousins living in different households, however, may marry although many parents disapprove of such marriages. Where the match is encouraged, it is favored as a means of keeping property within the same family. In contrast with the ethnic Malays in the Southern Region, who almost invariably marry a partner from a different village from their own, the ethnic Thai have no strong precedent either way. In one village in the Central Region, the ratio of marriages between persons from the same village and persons from different villages was about equal.

Traditionally the parents choose the marriage partner for their children, not necessarily considering the preference of the young persons involved. Among ethnic Thai, beauty, family background and wealth of the prospective bride were chief among criteria considered. Horoscopes of the prospective couple were compared as well, with the hope of avoiding making a match between persons who were temperamentally incompatible. In the modern period the tendency for selection by the young people themselves is becoming widespread.

During courtship it is considered proper for a boy to talk about his love for a girl, to sing songs to her or to flirt with her. In the Northern Region, sexual liaisons may occur before marriage. Elsewhere, however, even the suggestion of physical intimacy is avoided, for such intimacy is regarded as appropriate and permissible only within the framework of marriage. Promiscuity in either sex is disapproved but is especially condemned in women. An illegitimate child, however, is not blamed for the behavior of his parents and will be reared by relatives as one of their own.

Buddhist nuptial ceremonies, elaborate in the case of well-to-do families, lead to the formal installation of the newly wedded couple in their new residence, where they begin married life. The marriage is consummated at that time rather than delayed until the groom has completed a ritual return to his own village, as among the Malays. Elopement—usually with the parents' tacit consent—has become a common means of avoiding the expense of a formal ceremony and wedding feast. Persons who marry for the second time often dispense with all ceremony and simply begin living together.

Divorce and remarriage are by no means uncommon. Marriage bonds are relatively easily dissolved, especially before a child is born, and in the villages many persons have been married several times. Most separated partners remain on friendly terms, particularly when there are children. Unless the marriage has been registered, a formal divorce is not necessary, mutual agreement by husband and wife being sufficient. Abandonment is also equivalent to divorce. Upon separating by mutual agreement or by formal divorce, each takes the property he or she brought to the marriage, whereas joint property is divided equally. Children remain with the mother, especially when they are small.

Although the overwhelming majority of Thai have always been monogamous, polygamy has been and, in the form of concubinage, still is practiced by some wealthy men as a symbol of status. Formerly, a second wife would live in the household subordinate to the first wife, but such an arrangement would be acceptable to few women today. Accordingly, the husband must bear the considerable expense of maintaining two establishments. Moreover, the second woman no longer has the legal status of a wife but is merely a concubine or mistress, and she is not likely to agree to this unless the economic return is considerable. From the man's standpoint the concubine must be exhibited if prestige is to be accorded, but such exhibition is increasingly regarded as bad taste. Furthermore, wives resent the lower living standard for themselves and their children caused by the outlay required to maintain a concubine and her children. The government discourages polygamy by refusing the second wife legal status and by requiring the husband to recognize formally his children by the concubine if they are to be included among his legitimate heirs. It also propagandizes to persuade women to reject the status of concubine.

Childhood and Youth

The newborn infant is sponged by the midwife, wrapped in swaddling clothes and placed in a shallow bamboo basket. A sacred thread may be wound around the basket to ward off evil spirits. Baby boys often are given a string of small phallic images to wear about the waist. After a month the baby is transferred to a wooden or bamboo cradle, which is hung from the ceiling. Temporary hammock cradles are sometimes improvised from a man's bathing cloth. During the first few months the baby is regarded as having only a tenuous hold on life—a reflection of the high rate of infant mortality—and is protected as much as possible from its environment.

In general the young child is treated permissively. It is nursed whenever it cries, is weaned and toilet-trained gradually, and is often fondled. The baby is introduced to solid premasticated food early to supplement its mother's milk. Complete weaning occurs late, and even after the birth of a second child the first may be nursed in order to comfort it. As soon as the baby can hold up its head alone, it is carried straddled on the hip of the mother or older sister, supported by the left hand—a carrying position which requires active muscle participation by the baby instead of merely passive relaxation. Motor skills, such as walking, climbing and eventually swimming, are largely acquired through the child's own efforts and at its own pace, although it may receive some encouragement.

A baby is officially recognized as a member of the community at the age of several months, when it receives a name and is

registered in the headman's records. The name is usually selected by the village abbot after an analysis of astrological conditions. Previously the baby may have been called by a diminu-
tive, such as "little one," "little pig" or "little mouse," and
these names may be used by close relatives until the individual
reaches maturity.

At about 2 years of age, usually after the birth of another
infant, the child is brought to realize that it is no longer the
baby of the family. By the age of 3 or 4, deliberately naughty
acts are punished, although severe corporal punishment is rare.
The child also begins to learn the proper forms of address for
older and younger brothers and sisters, older and younger
cousins and older and younger aunts and uncles and to accept
its place in the family hierarchy. The basic gesture of obeisance
is taught; later the different degrees in which it may be extended—clasped palms raised to the forehead for monks and
the Buddha; to the nose, for village elders—are inculcated. The
basic respect-prestige pattern of Thai culture, based on age differentiation, is instilled at this time.

Until the third or fourth year the Thai child stays entirely
with the family, playing nude in the family compound. After the
age of 3, the girls begin to wear skirts; the boys may run naked
in the house and yard until they are 5 or 6. At about 4 the
children begin to play with their age-mates in the village. They
soon segregate into sex groups and roam freely through the
village. Boys play at farming, fly kites, shoot arrows or play
blindman's bluff; girls nurse wooden dolls, make mudpies to sell
in make-believe markets and cook meals of weeds in toy clay
pots. In general, childhood is a carefree, happy time, and until
they are 7 or 8 years old, children have no regular chores except
caring for their baby brothers and sisters. At this age girls
must begin to help around the house, and boys are given such
tasks as watching the family buffaloes. At 7 the child enters the
government primary school and attends classes until he has completed the required primary course, or reaches 14 years of age
(see ch. 10, Education).

Partially grown children are frequently adopted, especially
by childless couples, and such children are not distinguished
from their own children in marriage arrangements and inheritance provisions. The adopted child does not inherit from
his real parents in such cases. Sometimes an older boy or girl
will be adopted to help a man and his wife manage their farm
when their own children are too young to help. In return for
this assistance the foster parents, or patrons, guarantee eventual
support in establishing the young person's own household.

126

As the children approach the end of their primary schooling, the pressure to assume an adult workload becomes progressively greater; by 15 or 16 most have taken on a full load. Along with this greater involvement in adult economic activities, adolescents begin flirtations which eventually lead to the selection of potential marriage partners. Before marriage, which usually occurs in the boy's early or middle twenties, he may wish to enter the Brotherhood of Monks (Sangha) as a novice or, if he is over 20 years of age, as a monk. If he is able to do so, the experience will bring him special respect and deference throughout his life and qualifies him to take a place of leadership in the religious affairs of the community. For a family to have a son enter the Sangha often involves considerable economic sacrifice for them, for he has only recently been able to do an adult's work; but in return this brings them much merit. The most auspicious time for a boy to enter the Sangha, moreover, is during Phansa, which covers the 3 months' rainy season when the crops are growing. Membership at this season brings more merit than an equivalent period at other times of the year, for service during Phansa counts as an entire year. Whether a man decides to remain in the Sangha for a few days, during the whole of Phansa or for a much longer time depends on his personal choice and other circumstances (see ch. 12, Religion).

At the age of 18 all men must register for military service and generally are called for service at 21. For many of those who are drafted, the period of military service is the only time they are away from their home districts and in extensive contact with urban life. At the end of the training period, recruits return to their villages and soon resume the rural routine, since probably most continue to regard themselves as farmers and expect to end their days as such.

For a village girl, entry into adolescence and adulthood comes in more gradual and less marked steps, but certain significant transitional phases can be observed: being allowed to mill rice with a girl friend at night in the compound, to go by herself to market, to have a permanent wave when she is 15 or 16 and to receive suitors unchaperoned on the veranda of her parents' house. Courtship is also carried out at dusk around the rice mill, when the girls are pounding rice for the family meals and in the work groups at planting and harvest time and at the festivals. On these occasions there may be considerable banter, but by themselves the young people tend to be extremely shy. The young men go in pairs or groups to visit girls at their homes, but once a girl has indicated her preference the friends drift away. The boy may then serenade the girl, recite love poems or talk nonsense.

A formal marriage ceremony provides the wealthier families with an opportunity for social display, but the degree of elaboration depends on the resources and status of the families involved. The ceremony itself, as distinguished from the festivities, is very simple. A sacred thread symbolically binds the couple together while water is poured over their hands. As this is merely a civil ceremony, its form is variable. The crucial fact is that it is witnessed and sanctioned by members of the community who, after the speeches of advice and the pouring of water, escort the couple to the wedding feast, where the occasion is celebrated with food and merriment.

The full responsibilities of adulthood begin with the establishment of a new household, and most young couples begin to prepare for the event after marriage while they are living with the parents of one or the other. In the case of a couple that is to reside in the wife's family house or compound until she inherits the property, the new household is not established until after the death or retirement of her father. Thereafter, the opinions of the pair are listened to as their own and not those of the parents. The wife in particular gains in stature. She always does most of the buying for the family in the local markets. Through the sale of eggs, fruits, vegetables and small livestock, she produces a sizable portion of the family cash income. She always has an important voice in the handling of the family's finances and not infrequently holds the purse strings. In the commercialized delta area, however, where large amounts of money are brought in by the sale of rice, the husband seems to keep control of the income himself. In most families income earned by the teenage children remains their own property, though they may turn it over to the mother for safekeeping.

The period of active adulthood continues through the years of rearing children. The government has officially set the age of 60 as the final year for retirement from office, and this seems to correspond with the Thai understanding of the beginning of old age.

OTHER FAMILY SYSTEMS

Various types of family organization are found among Thailand's ethnic minorities. These tend to differ from the Thai family to the degree that the minorities as a whole maintain their cultural distinctiveness and to the degree that individual families in the ethnic minority groups have assimilated Thai cultural patterns. The most important types are those of the

Chinese and Malay minority groups, although the families of the hill peoples often are strikingly different from the Thai family type. The hill peoples are generally characterized by patrilineal family organizations.

The Chinese family traditionally tends to be strongly patrilineal in character, with descent and inheritance coming through the father, who is the center of authority in the family. A number of families related in the male line are linked together in lineages, the members of which trace descent from a common male ancestor. Arranged marriages, ancestor veneration and polygamy are also features of the traditional Chinese family. This pattern has undergone changes among the ethnic Chinese of Thailand, and individual families vary widely between the traditional patterns of the Thai and of the Chinese types. Although few Chinese families in Thailand maintain the traditional ancestral shrines or tablets in their homes, all who still consider themselves Chinese adhere to the practice of honoring their ancestors at the time of the Chinese New Year. Conditions of urban life in Bangkok put limits upon the extent to which a Chinese family can follow traditional patterns, just as it limits a Thai family in following traditional Thai patterns. Speech group associations appear to have taken over many of the welfare and benevolent functions commonly assigned to lineage organizations in the traditional society of mainland China. This action probably is a result of difficulties encountered in attempts to reconstitute traditional Chinese structural arrangements in a Thai environment.

Certain other traditional features have endured. Descent and inheritance are still through males, and the husband is unquestionably the head of the family. Whenever possible, sons bring their wives into the parental home. Kinship within the family continues to regulate a person's responsibilities, rights and expectations on the basis of generation, age and sex, just as in old China. Conditions of urban life, however, prevent frequent realization of the traditional ideal of "five generations under one roof."

Larger kinship units, however, are less important than in the traditional society of South China, although they continue to define the group of people whom one may not marry. They exert little influence on the direction of community affairs, which are controlled by business groups and by regional or dialect associations. Although the overseas Chinese continues to be a member of a clan organization in China, he is isolated from it in terms of practical control and protection, and his bonds with it are thus weakened. The immigrant often finds few kinsmen beyond his immediate household group in Thailand and must rely on organizations. One such organization is the "surname group," which differs from the lineage in that the specific kin ties can seldom be traced among its members and that it lacks the ancestral tablets traditionally maintained by the lineage. Its leaders are chosen on a basis of wealth and ability rather than age and kinship relationships. It also lacks many of the welfare, educational, religious and protective functions of the South China lineage. Such groups also appear to be declining in importance and in membership, as second and later generation Chinese lose interest in them and look to the regional or dialect associations to supply welfare functions and to occupational and business associations for leadership and protection.

The Malay family resembles that of the Thai in a number of ways. Among both peoples kinship is reckoned bilaterally. Among both, the nuclear family ideally housed in its own separate dwelling is the basic social unit. Frequently among the Malays the youngest child will bring his or her spouse to live in the parental home, and the young couple will eventually inherit the parental home and farm. The primary relationships are those between members of the nuclear family. More distant kinship, however, does permit individuals to establish a relationship as individuals more easily than if they were not kinsmen.

The Malay kinship system differs somewhat from that of the Thai in the way it categorizes relatives. Unlike the Thai system, cousins are distinguished from brothers and sisters in the formal terminology. In common usage, however, they are usually addressed as siblings. All grandparents are called by a single term, and the children of a sibling are called by the same term as one's own children. There are some differences in kinship terms between Malay fishing villages and Malay farming villages, which largely result from property considerations and inheritance patterns. Until recently bride and groom always had to come from different villages, and the couple would live alternately in each village until they made a final choice. In the mid-1960's, however, young men in fishing villages tend to rely heavily on fishing for their income, so they are increasingly less well equipped to become farmers in an inland village and thus tend to insist on living in their own villages, where they can continue to be fishermen.

Among the major hill peoples it is customary for newlyweds to live with or near the family of the husband rather than that of the wife. A new household, however, is not usually established until some time after the recognition of the marriage. Among the Meo, for example, a married son usually continues to live in a section of his father's house until he has reached the age of 30. Among the Lisu the eldest son generally continues to live with his parents, but younger sons may set up independent households or, in exceptional instances, live briefly with the wife's family until the bride-price has been paid.

The composition of the average household ranges from 3 persons to 20 or more. Large households, sheltering an extended family, include a man and his wife together with their children, married and single, and their children's children. Polygamy is permitted, so that second wives and their children may also be present, although this occurs relatively seldom as only the wealthy can afford to have several wives.

The family is the basic social and economic unit. The eldest male has supreme authority in the household. Family members comprise a production unit, working together to clear fields and raise crops. Religious worship, as well as recreational and educational activity, is also a family function.

CHAPTER 9

LIVING CONDITIONS

By Southeast Asian standards the level of welfare in Thailand is, in general, high. Nearly everyone is adequately fed, clothed and housed. Unemployment is not a problem in the relatively small wage-earning segment of the population, and a tolerable level of living can be achieved by nearly everyone willing to work. Rich natural resources and the gentle climate offer relatively comfortable living conditions to the farming majority, although the land is not uniformly fertile or well watered.

The per capita gross national product, estimated to be 2,400 baht (see Glossary) in 1965, has been increasing by approximately 3 percent annually since 1957. Incomes are still low by Western standards, but most Thai are able to spend small cash surpluses on luxury goods.

The idea of accumulating wealth for its own sake has been alien to the Thai outlook in the past, although since World War II it seems to have been gaining acceptance. The desire to possess certain types of goods, both for the contribution they make to personal comfort and as status symbols, is apparent, especially in the larger towns.

Least well off are the more than 9 million inhabitants of the Northeast Region. Agricultural production is handicapped by a long, dry season and sandy soils. Per capita income is less than one-half of the national average, and villagers generally lack health and community services. Many of the roads are poor and during the rains often become impassable. Communicable diseases and malnutrition are more prevalent there than in other parts of the country. In 1962, however, the government launched a major development program in the Northeast to improve living conditions and to strengthen the political allegiance of its inhabitants. Several major roads and feeder roads have been built; crop improvement and irrigation programs have been initiated; mobile health units have been dispatched; and many schools were opened (see ch. 17, Public Information).

Traditionally, the individual relied on close relatives, friends or neighbors or turned to the local Buddhist temple in time of need. Systematic welfare activity by the government goes back only to 1940, when the Department of Public Welfare was organized in the Ministry of the Interior. In 1966 the government spent more than 14 percent of its annual budget on welfare and public health services. Its efforts in these fields are supplemented by more than 50 private charitable organizations and by various international welfare organizations, particularly local branches of the specialized agencies of the United Nations.

A marked improvement in health conditions and medical facilities has taken place since World War II. Between 1957 and 1964 the crude death rate dropped from 9 per 1,000 population to 7.9 per 1,000, and the infant mortality rate from 62 per 1,000 births to 37.8 per 1,000. The incidence of malaria, which until the early 1960's was a leading cause of death, has decreased considerably. Infectious diseases were the leading causes of death in 1967, although some of them have declined rapidly as a result of mass immunizations. Military personnel and most schoolchildren are vaccinated against smallpox, and the country has been free of the disease since 1962. Schoolchildren also receive routine immunization against tetanus and tuberculosis, but not all schools are within the reach of the immunization programs. Mass immunizations have also been undertaken against cholera.

The government's Six-Year Economic Development Plan (1961–66), which went into effect in early 1961, contained further measures to expand health facilities, including provincial hospitals; to improve sanitation; and to reduce the incidence of communicable disease. The Plan emphasized the extension of rural health programs and the continuation of efforts to control malaria, tuberculosis and leprosy.

Despite considerable advances much remains to be done in the field of public health and sanitation. Many parts of the country, especially the Northeast, suffer from chronic water shortages, and sewage systems are inadequate in most areas. Diseases caused by poor sanitation are one of the leading causes of illness and death. In addition, because more than half of the country's hospitals and most of its Western-trained physicians are found in or around Bangkok, the mass of the people lack modern medical care and continue to rely on traditional remedies and on practitioners of Chinese medicine.

The United States Operations Mission (USOM), the overseas arm of the Agency for International Development (AID), has given large-scale financial support and technical assistance to health and welfare projects. USOM assistance to Thailand in 1966 totaled $43.3 million, of which over $10.3 million were allocated to rural development, including environmental sanitation; more than $3.8 million to malaria eradication, the rural health program and medical education; and $1.5 million to potable water improvement projects.

STANDARDS OF LIVING

Growing industrialization and the Western influence in recreation and on the pace of living in general have tended to sharpen the contrast between rural and urban conditions. It has been reported that a village not far from the capital "may as well be on another planet." Bangkok, with its traffic congestion, crowded housing, the many bars and other establishments of amusement, resembles somewhat the industrial boomtowns of the Western world. A similar atmosphere has begun to prevail in some cities of the North and Northeast, especially in those near United States military bases and construction projects. Some villagers express the belief that conditions in the cities are better than in the countryside, but in general they do not seem to envy the city dwellers' way of life.

Rural Areas

The food supply in rural areas, except in parts of the Northeast, is abundant, although the diet is limited in variety. Agricultural surpluses and export demands have made the average Thai farmer a commercial producer. A bad year means a reduction in his small cash income, but usually he and his family will have food. Accordingly, he worries about the price of rice, the timing and quantity of the harvest, and the related factor—important even in the fertile Central Region—of fluctuation in the annual cycle of monsoon rains. Relatively secure in his basic way of life, however, he has shown few signs of frustration arising from unfulfilled wants.

Eating habits change according to personal requirements. For instance, the peasant usually eats two meals a day, but has frequent snacks. Meal hours are irregular; the family eats when it gets hungry, except when the work of the planting and harvesting seasons demands breakfast at dawn and supper at dusk.

Many people enjoy the mild stimulation derived from chewing betel nut and take pride in the quality of the equipment used to prepare the betel paste. Teeth stained by betel were once generally considered attractive. Recently, however, there have been indications that the use of betel is passing out of favor with the younger generation. The disapproval of Buddhist functionaries has not persuaded the people to give up the consumption of either tobacco or alcohol. Cigarette smoking has risen steadily during the 1960's. The trend is reflected in a gain of nearly 8 percent in cigarette sales between 1965 and 1966.

A gradual revolution in dress has been occurring as the people come more and more to adopt Western clothing or Asian variations of Western fashions. Traditional Thai dress is rapidly disappearing except in the interior and among the elderly peasants. In these groups both men and women wear the *phanung* (a length of material wrapped around the waist in the manner of a skirt; the men draw one end of the piece between their legs and tuck it in at the belt line, causing the *phanung* to cling to their legs and thus appear to be breeches). The *phasin*, a skirt-like garment popular among northern Thai women, was introduced into the rest of the country during the reign of King Vajiravudh (Rama VI—1910–25). It is worn with a blouse or with a scarf which is worn wrapped around the bosom and shoulders. When possible, the village men wear Western clothes for more formal occasions.

The climate is so mild that elaborate shelter is not required, and heating is necessary only at high elevations. A housing problem has developed since World War II in the more densely settled areas, as building materials have become more scarce and expensive. Teak is beyond the reach of all except the most wealthy; other hardwoods have become less available as they have acquired export value; and even bamboo and palm matting have risen in price. Furthermore, less often than in the past are rural houses built by the cooperative effort of relatives and neighbors, and more and more construction is being done by hired Chinese carpenters.

The most common type of rural house is a rectangular structure with palm matting walls, thatched roof and a bamboo or wood-slat floor. Supported on posts, it may be from 2 to 10 feet above the ground and reached by a ladder. The space beneath the more elevated houses provides shelter for livestock and a storage area. The finest rural houses are made entirely of teak and may be roofed with tile, but they are increasingly rare, even in the teak-growing Northern Region; elsewhere, a new teak house is a mark of wealth.

Whatever the material used, the basic house style is the same —a single rectangular room and, in larger dwellings, several sleeping rooms. Cooking is done in the main room or in a space partitioned off as a kitchen; more prosperous families have kitchens built away from the main dwelling. Furniture and household goods include a low table or two, a brick or earth-and-box stove, earthenware pots and water jars, porcelain or brass bowls and pots, bamboo baskets, kapok mattresses for sitting and sleeping, wooden chests, a Buddha statue and perhaps a loom. In the houses of the well to do, these items are of finer quality— brass rather than porcelain bowls, teak chests rather than those of less expensive wood, an iron stove rather than a homemade one. Prosperous families usually have some pieces of Western furniture.

Another indication of wealth is the size of the farm compound and the number and variety of outbuildings in it, such as granaries, animal sheds, a bathing shed, storage huts, houses for domestic servants, perhaps a kitchen and privy, and possibly a house for a married son or daughter living at home. Some possessions not only carry prestige but also provide sources of income. Rich families invest in additional farm animals, which are rented to neighboring farmers. Radios, engines for irrigation use, farm implements, kerosene lanterns, gasoline generators and pumps, sewing machines, motor-driven canal boats and bicycles are also within the reach of some farmers.

Consumer commodities are available in even the most remote villages. The itinerant Chinese peddler carries his merchandise, by boat, cart, pack cattle or ponies, into the markets and village fairs, selling for cash or bartering for farm produce. In the Central Region even the smallest villages have shops. From the peddlers or the shops the villager gets needles, cloth, tobacco, salt, cooking utensils, sweets and condiments, hardware and simple tools, cosmetics, jewelry and many other items. During the 1960's transistor radios have come within the financial reach of many; peasants are often seen carrying the sets with them on the way to work in the fields.

Marriages and funerals are as elaborate as a family can afford and are indications of wealth (see ch. 8, Family). Similarly, contributions to the *wat* (walled compound containing a Buddhist temple and associated buildings) enhance the donors' prestige among friends and neighbors. The richer families endow new *wats* because it is considered more advantageous from the point of view of Buddhist merit-making to endow a new *wat* than merely to support an old one. People generally spend liberally on the education of their children, which helps the child's chances for social and economic advancement and contributes to the family's prestige.

Living conditions of the Moslem Malays living on the Peninsula differ little from those of the Thai farmers. The Malays tend to be self-sufficient in foodstuffs, and their other main necessities, cloth and cigarettes, are inexpensive. Life is considered satisfactory if they own a small farm, a house on stilts near the water and some fruit or palm trees.

The hill peoples of the Northern and Northeast Regions are generally self-sufficient with regard to the production of their food supply. Rice, garden vegetables, corn, potatoes and chili are grown and livestock bred in quantities sufficient to supply family and village needs. A few villages grow a small quantity of vegetables and fruits for sale. The main cash crop, however, is opium, which is sold to traveling opium dealers or bartered for such necessities as matches, clothing, shoes, tea, sugar, kerosene and batteries (see ch. 5, Ethnic Groups).

Urban Areas

Urban eating habits differ but slightly from those in the countryside. In Bangkok and vicinity more vegetables and meat products are eaten, and canned goods are in demand. Among the old elite cooking has traditionally been an art, and women take pride in their skill in preparing sauces, savories, curries, condiments, sweets and desserts. Most upper-class urban families have adopted the Western pattern of three meals a day. Bangkok has witnessed an increase in the number of restaurants since World War II because of the growth of a salaried middle-income group. Restaurants serving Thai food are less popular than those specializing in Chinese, Western and Malay foods, in that order. Foods and soft drinks consumed in the United States have been much in demand since the 1960's, not only in Bangkok but also in provincial towns where United States personnel are stationed.

Members of the upper- and middle-income groups wear Western clothes, but traditional Thai attire is being increasingly seen on formal or special occasions, a trend inspired by the Queen. Members of the lower class ordinarily wear a combination of Thai and Western garments or—less commonly, as among members of the older generation—strictly Thai apparel, the best clothes of both sexes in the cities are Western style. Uniforms are worn by all schoolchildren and some members of the civil service, as well as by persons in the military service and the police.

Middle- and upper-class men wear their hair cut in Western fashion; lower-class men continue to crop theirs close to the head. Western hair styles are popular with younger women, and cosmetics are used even in remote villages.

Urban housing since 1962 presented problems of crowding and of a proliferation of substandard accomodations. The problems have been most outstanding in Bangkok, which experienced a considerable influx of population from the provinces in search of profitable, if temporary, occupations. The number of foreigners stationed in or visiting the capital has also been growing steadily. To alleviate the shortage, the government has started constructing various housing projects for middle-income groups. One of the projects has been undertaken jointly with United States business firms at the cost of over $5 million for the construction of 800 two-storied apartment buildings in a Bangkok suburb.

Housing standards in the capital present extremes of squalor and luxury. Thousands of families live in the restricted quarters of houseboats. The poorest people rent space in structures built from bamboo scrap lumber, packing boxes and the tin salvaged from oilcans. Many of the shacks in the lower sections of the city are swept away by the floods of the Chao Phraya or destroyed by fire, but landlords quickly replace them as a profitable investment. There are no sanitation facilities; water is obtained from public taps. The canals serve as the sewage disposal system and constitute a serious health hazard during the dry season.

The typical house of the middle-income family in Bangkok is a small two-storied structure with wooden walls and a tile roof. A large veranda or room at the entrance, generally Western in style, is used for receiving guests. It may contain a table, chairs, some framed pictures, a cane rack and a raised platform with mat and pillows for lounging. There may be one or two private rooms on the ground floor. The kitchen is invariably apart from the house but connected to it by a covered passage. The family rooms and a receiving room for guests are upstairs; these are generally furnished in Thai style with a low table, mats and chests.

The houses of the elite, scattered about the city and its suburbs, are set in walled compounds which also contain separate quarters for servants. Most compounds have their own water tanks and electric generators.

The poorer Chinese in Bangkok live in houseboats, tenements and shacks. In the Peninsula Region, Chinese workers on the pepper and rubber estates live in their own compounds. The Chinese shopkeeper usually lives above his establishment. The interiors of Chinese households generally show strong Thai and Western influences.

Living conditions in the provincial towns of the North and Northeast Regions have undergone considerable changes during the 1960's, largely as a result of the presence of United States personnel. In the northeastern town of Udon Thani near the Laotian border, hotels, restaurants, souvenir shops and nightclubs have been added to the town center formerly consisting of a few government buildings, *wats* and schools. Newly established shops carry a variety of consumers goods, usually at considerably higher prices than in Bangkok. Hotel shops feature an abundance of souvenirs, including elephants carved of teakwook, a favorite item usually purchased by tourists. Recorded, Western-type music is played in the restaurants, many of which serve foods and drinks typical of the diet in the United States. Enterprising townspeople have found occupations as entertainers, as porters in the new establishments or as street vendors.

CONSUMPTION LEVELS

Consumption levels among the Thai are relatively high by Asian standards. Many families in all income categories seem to feel little restraint about spending, and there seems to be a preference for accumulating goods rather than for saving money. The Chinese, who are mainly shopkeepers and businessmen, have acquired a formidable reputation for financial acquisitiveness and prudence. Among both the Thai and the Chinese, however, consumer spending for luxury and prestige items has been increasing in most parts of the country.

The rise of the cost-of-living index has been a relatively low 5 percent since 1961, although the prices of beef, pork and many essential nonfood items have created hardships for persons in lower- and middle-income groups, especially in the cities. A considerable portion of household expenditures in 1965 was used for food. Since 1957, however, private spending on other items has grown rapidly so that the sum spent on food as a percent of the total household budget has declined from 47.7 percent in that year to 46.3 percent in 1965. About 8 percent of private budgets were spent on clothing and footwear. The price of these commodities has been generally stable and even decreased slightly in 1965.

The proportion of private income spent on transportation and communication in 1965 almost equaled that spent on clothing, and officials have indicated that, as a result of improvements being made on roads, railroad and bus lines, families will soon spend as much or more on communication and travel as on clothing. Rising incomes and growing urbanization are reflected in the upward trend of private spending on recreation, which rose over 10 percent between 1964 and 1965. Private expenditures on health care, fuel, beverages, tobacco, furniture and household equipment showed an increase of 49 percent between 1957 and 1965.

SOCIAL WELFARE

The sick, aged and destitute are usually taken care of by members of their immediate families. Nearly everyone has some relative to whom he can turn in an emergency or who will feed and shelter him should he be unable to provide for himself. In rural areas needy persons are often assisted by wealthy residents of the village in which they live or by the village *wats*. The monks will supply shelter and food to vagrants, disabled persons, the mentally ill and the infirm if they have no families or if their families cannot help them. The *wat* or the *wat* committee sometimes lends money to help families through crises.

Christian missionaries have long been active in relief and welfare work in the country. Orphanages, hospitals and medical teams, financed by European and American missionary and lay groups, were established in Bangkok and in some provincial centers in the nineteenth century. Free medical services were offered for the first time by Christian hospitals.

Indigent or destitute members of the Chinese community rely on the assistance of the many Chinese benevolent associations. Operating throughout the country and officially recognized and encouraged by the government, these associations offer economic and social assistance, including legal advice. Some of them finance schools, hospitals, temples and cemeteries and act as intermediaries between the government and the Chinese community. Others help new Chinese immigrants from abroad to find employment and provide social security for the poor and elderly.

The Department of Public Welfare, the key governmental agency for social service, was established in 1940. Under the Ministry of the Interior, it consists of an Office of the Secretary and nine divisions—Finance, Social Studies, Housing Welfare, Social Security, Child and Youth Welfare, Welfare Assistance, Occupation Assistance, Disaster Relief, and Community Service. Supplementing the Department activities and also under its jurisdiction are the Self-Help and Settlement Bureau and the Community Development Department. Lack of funds and trained personnel greatly handicaps the field operations of the Department and its coordinated agencies.

A number of voluntary private charitable and religious groups carrying on welfare activities, including the Thai Red Cross Society (of which Queen Sirikit is president), the Young Men's Christian Association, the Young Women's Christian Association, the Family Welfare Association of Thailand, the Crippled Children's Welfare Center, and a number of organizations of the Catholic Church, including the Catholic Association of Thailand and the Catholic Family Movement. There are also private foundations for the crippled, the deaf and the mentally retarded. The Council of Social Welfare of Thailand was organized in 1960 to support and coordinate welfare programs sponsored by the government and by private groups. The Council, a member of the International Conference of Social Workers and of the International Union of Child Welfare, includes committees on youth activities, voluntary services, and family and child welfare.

Assistance from abroad has been provided by the United Nations Children's Fund (UNICEF); the World Health Organization (WHO); the United Nations Educational, Scientific and Cultural Organization (UNESCO); and by various programs of the USOM.

Housing

The influx of persons into the large cities during World War II intensified an existing housing shortage. A modest, government-financed building program in urban areas was begun in 1948, but in 1967 much of the population of Bangkok and adjacent Thon Buri, as well as in some of the provincial towns, lived in crowded and dilapidated dwellings.

The building of apartment houses and family houses has been assisted by the government through the Department of Public Welfare, the government Housing Project Fund and the government Housing Bank. These agencies have constructed public housing units for rent or for sale on a rental-purchase plan and have made loans to private persons to enable them to build or to improve their own dwellings. The National Police Department, under the Ministry of the Interior, the Royal Irrigation Department, under the Ministry of National Development, and several other government agencies have carried out small housing programs for the benefit of their own employees.

Public housing has benefited a small number of families, but the overall program has suffered from lack of planning and coordination by the various public agencies concerned. For example, the residents of newly established housing projects have sometimes been left without schools, medical clinics or other needed public services.

The Six-Year Economic Development Plan calls for the continued construction of public housing projects for low-income groups. Private investment in housing has also been encouraged, but in general little progress had been made in public housing by 1967.

Child Welfare

The Department of Public Welfare operates 6 children's institutions, including 2 for juvenile delinquents, and some 30 foster homes. In 1963 these establishments cared for approximately 1,000 children from infancy to 17 years of age. The Central Juvenile Court and the Central Observation and Protection Center, under the Ministry of Justice, are responsible for juvenile offenders before trial and after, unless they are placed in one of the three reformatories operated by the Department of Corrections, administered by the Ministry of Justice. The Court, which deals with minors under 17 years of age, operates a children's home, a training school for boys and a training school for girls. After their release many former inmates are placed with families and provided with jobs (see ch. 27, Public Order and Safety).

Other government and private agencies are also active in child welfare work. The Ministry of Education, for example, maintains special education facilities for handicapped children, and UNICEF and WHO have played an important role in establishing maternal and child health centers.

Family assistance is provided, under legislation in force in 1967, to families with many children. A family of five children in which the head of the family earned an average monthly income of approximately 800 baht received a maximum monthly allowance of about 120 baht; the sum of the benefit increases with the number of children, but at a diminishing rate.

Social Security

A project to introduce extensive social security legislation was under study in 1966. The legislation is to call for a contribution from employees of 1.5 percent of their salaries which is to be matched by 3 percent from the employer and by another 1.5 percent from the government. In the case of workers earning 15 baht or less per day employers must assume full responsibility for payments. The program is to be introduced at first in the Bangkok-Thon Buri area only.

Rural Development

Living conditions in the Northeast Region and a few provinces in the Peninsula Region are generally poorer than in other parts of the country. Roads are poor; electricity is lacking; and water is scarce. Modern medical care is for the most part unavailable, and the relative incidence of malaria, hepatitis, jaundice, respiratory ailments and leprosy is high.

Since 1962 the government, with substantial aid from USOM, has initiated various projects designed to raise the standards of living in these areas. In 1963 the Accelerated Rural Development Program was launched with emphasis on the northeastern provinces of Ubon Ratchathani, Nakorn Phanom, Sakon Nakhorn, Udon Thani, Loei and Nong Khai. The program called for road construction and the building of potable water facilities and small-scale public works, such as dams. The program also provided for expanding marketing facilities and organizing crop and livestock improvement projects. By 1965 the cash income of many farmers in the area had risen as a result of the sale of new tobacco and fruit crops. The program in 1966 received extensive support from USOM, including a $10.3 million grant in addition to machinery and training services.

Supplementing the program are the mobile development units of the National Security Command. The units move from village to village, initiating improvement projects, including digging wells and fishponds, establishing schools and building water reservoirs and latrines. The local population is then trained to continue these projects and to initiate others. The units also offer medical and veterinary aid and give courses in hygiene, in sanitation and in crop and livestock improvement techniques. Select groups of villagers receive special training in self-government and administration.

Rural development efforts were further strengthened by the dispatching, in April 1966, of young people with backgrounds similar to those working in the United States Peace Corps to assist in the implementation of community development projects in Northeast and Peninsula Regions.

Control of Social Problems

The illegal use of narcotics is a problem, particularly among the Chinese. Opium-smoking is widely practiced among the hill peoples of the Northern Region, where the opium-yielding poppy is an important cash crop. The consumption of opium in the form of heroin represents an increasingly serious problem, especially in the cities. After the passage of the Harmful Habit-Forming Drugs Act of 1961, the police began an active campaign against persons dealing in or using narcotics. In 1963, 13,934 persons were convicted for violating the law. In connection with educational campaigns initiated by the Ministries of Education and of Public Health, it was announced that the identity of addicts who voluntarily applied to hospitals and police stations for cures would be kept secret if they desired. A rehabilitation center was established at the government-operated hospital at Pathum Thani, northwest of Bangkok, where addicts receive medical care and vocational training.

The Act for the Abatement of Prostitution, passed in November 1960, made prostitution illegal, but it reportedly continues in Bangkok and in other towns. Begging, once quite common, was banned in Bangkok and in certain other cities by the Beggars Control Act of 1941. The government has established four homes for former beggars, destitutes and vagrants where they are given vocational training. The homes are in Bangkok and in the Southern, Northern and Northeast Regions.

Indigent handicapped persons are admitted to the Pra Pradang Home (near Bangkok), which has a capacity of 500 and offers health care and rehabilitative vocational training. Needy, aged persons are accommodated in government-run homes for the aged located near Bangkok and in the provinces of Chiang Mai and Nakhon Ratchasima.

Another form of assistance to the indigent is provided through the land settlement program. Destitute persons, from rural and urban areas, are resettled in communities established on newly opened farmlands. Each family receives, in addition to a plot of land, a small grant to help defer the costs of moving, house construction and purchasing tools, seeds and livestock. By 1964 there were 37 self-help land settlements in 30 provinces, with about 150,000 persons working newly allocated plots. The principal settlements were in the provinces of Chiang Mai, Chiang Rai and Loei. In 1965 additional land plots were allocated to Malay fishermen on the peninsula whose fish catch was insufficient for subsistance.

By 1967, although no official policy had been established regarding birth control, officials in the Ministry of Public Health permitted or tacitly encouraged the dissemination of birth control information and devices under the Family Health Program. In 1966, 10 hospitals in Bangkok and 6 provincial hospitals offered family planning services free of charge. It was estimated in 1967 that about 5 percent of the 4 million women of from 20 to 44 years of age practiced birth control. Some Cabinet members disapprove of limiting the size of families, on the grounds that numerous offspring guarantee national strength, especially in the presence of the prolific Chinese community in the country.

PUBLIC HEALTH

Diet

In 1967 most Thai appeared to have had enough to eat. The daily per capita intake in 1965 was 2,120 calories, which is superior to many other countries in Southeast Asia. Nutritional deficiency diseases, however, were prevalent in many areas. These diseases resulted from an inadequate intake of proteins, vitamins and calcium, because of the reliance on a practically all-rice diet.

Rice, which is commonly believed to impart stength and health, supplies almost 80 percent of the daily caloric intake. The average rice consumption in 1964 was almost 340 pounds. In rural areas the per capita rice consumption is greater than in the cities, where foods are more varied.

The method of processing is an important factor in the nutritional value of rice. Traditionally, it was home-pounded by the peasants for their own consumption by a technique which retained a good deal of the bran covering of the grain and, with it, the vitamin B_1, the lack of which results in beriberi, a vitamin deficiency disease. More recently, however, machine-milled, polished rice has become popular. In Bangkok it is sold only in this form, and in the rural areas farmers are increasingly sending their paddy (the unmilled grain) to a local mill. Small mechanical hullers which produce a polished rice have been introduced in the villages and have increased the incidence of beriberi.

Artificial methods of preserving or restoring the vitamin content of polished rice have been tried. One method involves soaking the grain in hot water, steaming it and drying it before milling. The process forces the vitamins from the bran into the grain itself. Parboiled rice has not become popular, however, presumably because people object to its odor and off-white color. A method of enriching rice was introduced in the late 1950's by the government-owned Thai Rice Company. Special grains containing concentrated thiamin, niacin and riboflavin (all member of the vitamin B complex) and other vitamins and minerals were mixed with ordinary rice. Demand for this product was limited, however, because of its relatively high cost in comparison with non-enriched brands.

Rice remains the basis of all meals at all income levels. As a result of increased prosperity during the 1960's the diet has included more fish, meat, eggs, vegetables and fruit. Regional culinary variations are slight. The more prosperous city dwellers have acquired some Western food habits. Fish is a major source of protein, although it is often unavailable in the Northern and Northeast Regions. Pork, beef and poultry are preferred by urban residents. In the poorer rural areas the meat of aged draft animals is also eaten. Sauces, curries, condiments and sweets add to the variety of the rice diet. Many types of spices are used in the preparation of meat dishes. Fish is salted, dried, pickled, fermented, boiled or eaten raw. Coconut is used extensively in the preparation of sweets. Milk and dairy products are rarely consumed.

In an effort to raise the general level of nutrition by diversifying the average diet, the Food and Agriculture Organization (FAO) and USOM have encouraged the development of high-grade herds of dairy cattle and the use of modern techniques in sterilizing, handling and distributing milk. Various Thai educational and research institutions are engaged in activities in the field of nutrition, such as the Division of Nutrition of the Ministry of Public

Health, the Ministry of Industry, the Faculty of Public Health at the University of Medical Sciences, the Army Quartermaster Subsistence Division and Kasetsat University (University of Agriculture). WHO has organized various nutrition surveys among civilians and military personnel.

Sanitation

The prevalence of waterborne and filth-borne diseases reflects the generally poor conditions of sanitation, especially in rural areas. In 1965, 80 percent of all diseases and 40 percent of all deaths were caused by poor sanitary practices and contaminated water supplies. Most people are without safe drinking water or indoor bathing facilities.

In the cities garbage and trash are disposed of indiscriminately, and the basic rules of sanitation are widely ignored in the handling and storage of food. In the villages rainwater is generally stored in large jars for cooking and drinking, but ponds, shallow wells and canals are resorted to in the dry season. Drinking water is rarely boiled. Although most people prefer not to drink the polluted canal water, villagers and the poorer townsfolk bathe and wash clothes in it. Only about 10 percent of the rural population have latrines; the canals and fields serve the purpose for the rest of the people. In the cities many of the larger buildings have septic tanks, but there is no public sewage system. In Bangkok and other large cities open sewage storm drains are used which discharge untreated sewage into rivers or canals.

Most markets are unsanitary and crowded and are without refrigeration and piped water. Food sanitation is poor in most restaurants. In Bangkok, however, the large restaurants and some of the markets are reasonably clean and sanitary.

The USOM has undertaken a number of programs to help the government improve environmental sanitation and to develop potable water supplies. By 1964 over 4,500 wells had been dug and 108,000 latrines constructed under these programs. About 600 villages are to benefit from a community water-supply project launched in 1965. During the same year, 6,700 villages were to carry out sanitation programs, and special teams of sanitarians were to be trained to initiate such programs in an additional 5,700 villages near the Laotian and Malaysian borders. Similar programs have been started in the southern provinces of Pattani, Yala, Satun and Songkhla.

The water supply for Bangkok is drawn from the Chao Phraya River and chemically treated at a municipal plant before being piped to public water taps and private dwellings throughout the city. Some contamination of the water, indicated by periodic bacterial counts, is caused by seepage into the pipes and from unchlorinated deep-well water pumped into the system at various points. The volume of water is also inadequate. During the day, when demand is heavy, pressure drops, and certain sections of the city are left temporarily without water.

A health hazard is created in Bangkok, as in most of the rest of the country, not only by the fact that many canals are used for the disposal of garbage and wastes, but also by the fact that these same canals are used for bathing, laundering and swimming. Improvement of sanitation in the city is made difficult by the existence of a high water table which prevents the absorption of excrement by the soil and greatly increases the expenditure required to build an adequate sewage system.

The rapidly increasing population has placed heavy demands on the municipal water supply in Bangkok, and water shortages were noted several times during 1966. During the same year municipal authorities drafted a plan to improve and expand existing water supply facilities. The plan called for the installation of new chlorinators and filters and for the digging of additional artesian wells so that water may be pumped 24 hours a day. The ultimate goal is to furnish 140,000 cubic meters of water daily for Bangkok, and an additional 30,000 cubic meters for Thon Buri. These amounts are believed to be sufficient to supply the population of the capital, which is expected to reach at least 4.5 million within 30 years.

Diseases

Available statistics do not accurately reflect health conditions in the country. Causes of death in the villages are usually determined and reported by headmen and lay practitioners who are not qualified to make accurate diagnoses. In most of the country only major epidemic diseases, such as cholera, plague, smallpox, cerebrospinal meningitis and yellow fever must be reported to the authorities. Typhoid, leprosy, diphtheria and poliomyelitis are required to be reported only in the Bangkok-Thon Buri area. Statistics from Bangkok, which has a disproportionately high percentage of the country's few doctors, are generally more reliable and comprehensive than elsewhere.

In the mid-1960's communicable diseases continued to be the major causes of illness and death. Chronic and degenerative ailments, however, including diabetes, hypertension and cerebrovascular diseases, have become increasingly frequent. In 1964 heart disease was the fifth leading cause of death. Bladder stones are endemic in certain areas of the Northeast, and patients with carcinoma of the liver are frequently reported.

Diarrhea and enteritis, tuberculosis, pneumonia and diseases

148

of early infancy were the chief causes of death in 1964. Intestinal diseases, malaria, diseases of pregnancy and childbirth, nutritional disorders and venereal diseases are common throughout the country.

It has been reported that at any given time, more than half of the population suffers from diarrhea and dysentery. Debilitating and, in its severe forms, often fatal to adults, this class of ailments takes its greatest toll among infants and young children. Epidemics of dysentery occur regularly on the Peninsula and in the Northeast Region. Typhoid and paratyphoid are endemic and reach epidemic proportions in parts of the country during the dry season. A major cholera epidemic occurred in 1958 and 1959, when about 20,000 cases and 2,400 deaths were reported. No cases were reported between 1959 and 1962, but the disease reoccurred in 1963 and 1964, when there were 1,500 and 1,100 reported cases, respectively. A study of enteric diseases completed in 1966 in Chiengmai traced most cases to the city's contaminated water supply.

Tuberculosis, causing a reported 9,000 deaths per year, is one of the principal infectious diseases in the country. About 10 percent of the deaths occur in Bangkok. Nearly all reported cases represent tuberculosis of the respiratory tract. Surveys of the disease in the cities of Bangkok, Khon Kaen and Chiengmai indicated that, in 1964, about 7 percent of the inhabitants were infected by tuberculosis. An antituberculosis vaccination campaign was carried out from 1953 to 1959, concentrating mainly on schoolchildren and contacts of active carriers of the disease. A more inclusive antituberculosis drive in 1966 announced the establishment of vaccination and tuberculosis control centers in Bangkok and in various provincial towns, including Chiengmai, Khon Kaen and Yala. In addition, seven mobile chest clinics of the Ministry of Public Health operated in Bangkok.

The country has only one tuberculosis hospital, a 400-bed institution at Nonthaburi, just north of Bangkok, maintained by the Ministry of Public Health with the assistance of UNICEF. WHO maintains a tuberculosis epidemiological center in a congested area of Bangkok, which conducts case-finding and treatment programs on a limited basis. Outpatient care is provided by chest clinics in Bangkok, Chiengmai and Khon Kaen.

Venereal diseases represent a health problem of long standing. They occur less frequently in the rural areas, but the rate of infection is believed to be high in Bangkok and other cities. The Bureau of Disease Prevention and Control, under the Ministry of Public Health, operates about 36 venereal disease control units, and 20 additional units have been organized by other government agencies. In 1964 the 36 control centers reported 20,000 cases. This number represents only a small part of the countrywide rate since many cases are unreported and undetected.

Pneumonia ranked high among the causes of death in 1964, with a rate of 23.8 per 100,000. Common colds, influenza and other respiratory ailments are prevalent during the peak of the rainy season from July through August.

Until the mid-1950's malaria debilitated and killed more persons than any other disease, causing some 40,000 deaths annually—among them, 14,000 children under 4 years of age. The prevalence of one variety of malaria-carrying mosquito, *Anopheles minimus,* in the pools, eddies and streams of the northern mountains has caused many Thai to refer to malaria as "northern fever." Other varieties of malaria-carrying mosquitoes, including *Plasmodium falciparum,* breed in the swamps and still waters of the Central Plains and on the peninsula. It was reported in 1964 that about one-third of infections caused by the *Plasmodium falciparum* have shown resistance to chloroquine, a widely used antimalarial drug.

The first antimalaria measures were started in 1950 with the assistance of WHO and UNICEF. These organizations provided demonstration teams and began to train technicians. The National Malaria Eradication Project was inaugurated in the same year, by the Ministry of Public Health, with extensive assistance from USOM. For the purposes of the project the country was divided into 30 zones. The zones were divided into 8 to 12 sectors, and these, in turn, into five squad areas, each with about 16,000 inhabitants. Three or four spray technicians were assigned to each squad. In the squad areas entire villages were sprayed with DDT in the weeks before and immediately after the beginning of the rainy season in May. Malaria control teams inspect houses and streams for the presence of mosquitoes, examine villagers to determine whether they have been infected and distribute drugs for treatment. If professional supervision is not available, a responsible village leader is entrusted with the administration of the drugs. A large-scale public education program has also been carried out, by means of lectures, posters, mobile exhibits and motion picture units.

By 1964 the death rate from malaria had fallen to 18.2 per 100,000 as compared to 53.3 in 1956. According to government reports almost 25 million people were reached by malaria eradication and surveillance activities in 1966. The government hopes to eliminate the disease by the early 1970's.

Health specialists estimated in 1964 that about 80 percent of the population in most areas suffer from helminthiasis (parasitic worm infestation). The most common are roundworms, hookworms and whipworms. In the Northeast Region, along the Mekong, as many as 80 percent of some village populations are reported to be infected by another parasitic organism, the liver fluke. Infestation by roundworms afflicts about 60 percent of the population of the peninsula.

Leprosy is prevalent in the Northern and Northeast Regions. In 1964, of the almost 90,000 cases reported and treated, 70,000 were in the Northeast. Health authorities estimated that there may have been as many as 100,000 undetected cases in the country. Some 5,000 cases are segregated in two government-run leprosaria and in 13 leprosy colonies. A large-scale campaign to treat the disease was begun in 1953 with the aid of WHO and UNICEF.

Rabies, contracted from rabid stray animals, poses a serious health problem. Because the Buddhist code of ethics forbids the willful killing of living creatures, the efforts of local officials to destroy dogs and other animals afflicted by the disease have rarely succeeded. Rabies vaccines are available at the Pasteur Institute in Bangkok, but most victims go untreated. About 200 to 300 deaths caused by rabies are reported yearly, but it is believed that the actual incidence is at least double this figure.

Medical Services and Facilities

The activities of the government in the field of public health date from the establishment in 1888 of the Medical Department. Initially concerned mainly with problems of sanitation and epidemic disease, the Department steadily acquired broader responsibilities. In 1918 it became the Department of Public Health, and in 1942 the Ministry of Public Health.

The Ministry administers public medical facilities; furnishes vaccines for contagious diseases; sets standards for the medical, dental and pharmaceutical professions; and supervises public sanitation. Headed in 1967 by Phra Bamras Naradura, it is organized into the Office of the Under Secretary of State; the Department of Medical Services, which administers government hospitals; and the Department of Health, concerned mainly with sanitation, communicable disease control and health education. The administration of activities at the regional level is carried out by regional medical officers and a corps of provincial and district health officers.

According to official reports in 1964, 87 government-owned general hospitals, with a total of 8,900 beds, were operated by the Department of Medical Services of the Ministry of Public Health. There were seven mental hospitals, with 5,100 beds. There is at least one hospital for each province, located usually in the provincial capital.

The Department of Health of the Ministry of Public Health operates rural health centers. Depending on the extent of their facilities, the centers are grouped in three categories. Each of the first-class centers has from 10 to 25 beds and is staffed by one doctor and three assistants (a nurse, technician and midwife). Second-class centers, of which there were 734 in 1964, are staffed by paramedical personnel only and have no beds. The third-class facilities are midwife centers and have only a midwife and some lay assistants in attendance. The number of midwife centers in 1964 was 1,135.

In addition, in 1964 about 25 hospitals were owned by government agencies other than the Ministry of Public Health, and several others were operated by private individuals or charitable organizations. More than 80 private hospitals, with a total of about 1,300 beds, were in the Bangkok-Thon Buri areas. Many private practitioners in the metropolitan area operated small clinics, each with about 20 beds. Health specialists estimated that, in 1964, on a countrywide basis, the total of hospital beds was about 20,000, or 0.8 beds per 1,000 population.

Sirraj Hospital, the country's largest, in 1966 was operated by the University of Medical Sciences, under the jurisdiction of the Office of the Prime Minister, and had a capacity of over 1,000 beds. Three hospitals, with a total capacity of about 325 beds, were operated by the Chinese community in Bangkok. In 1966 the government announced the expansion of the 200-bed Central Hospital of Bangkok to a 1,500-bed facility. A 300-bed obstetrics department is to be added to Vajira Hospital, also in Bangkok. Construction of a large, modern hospital in Chiengmai was completed in 1967, with substantial assistance from USOM.

A number of laboratories carry on diagnostic and bacteriological work. The Pasteur Institute in Bangkok prepares vaccines and snakebite-antivenins (some 2,000 persons a year require treatment for snakebite). The Department of Medical Sciences of the Ministry of Public Health operates a central diagnostic laboratory with branches in the provinces. The government laboratory and laboratories of the armed forces produce pharmaceuticals and biologicals.

The government requires the registration of physicians and other medical personnel, including practitioners of traditional medicine. A vast number of the latter—herbalists, spirit doctors, self-taught dentists and part-time healers—remain unregistered; also in this category are numerous Buddhist monks to whom villagers often turn for medical as well as for spiritual guidance.

According to official records of the Ministry of Public Health, the country had some 4,054 physicians with modern medical training in 1964, or 1 to about every 8,000 persons. More than two-thirds of them practice in Bangkok, and for economic and other reasons, few are willing to leave the area. Most are staff associates in government hospitals; only a few are in full private practice. In the same year there were only 378 registered dentists, of whom all but about 50 were in Bangkok. Crude dentistry is performed by traditional practitioners. Nurses and midwives are also in short supply. In 1964 there were only 4,924 graduate nurses, 5,821 nurse-midwives and 970 midwives.

Medical training is offered at the University of Medical Sciences in Bangkok, which includes the Chulalongkorn Medical School and Hospital; the Sirraj Medical School and Hospital in Thon Buri; Schools of Dentistry, Pharmacy, Public Health, Medical Technology, Medical Science and Tropical Medicine; and the new medical school in Chiengmai. The University of Medical Sciences graduated 321 physicians in 1964.

Medical education has received considerable assistance from UNICEF, WHO and the United States. In addition to the efforts of UNICEF and WHO in the training of personnel for the maternal and child health centers of Bangkok and Chiengmai, US-OM has established the Health Training and Demonstration Center at Thon Buri for public health workers. Under a contract financed by USOM, the University of Illinois College of Medicine has supplied a two-man team to the Chiengmai Medical School and to its teaching hospital to upgrade the curriculum and develop a research program.

The prestige enjoyed by traditional practitioners is gradually being transferred to doctors, nurses and health technicians, although the process is a slow one in the countryside, where most of the people rarely come into contact with the thin scattering of modern health workers. Wherever they are available, however, the new health services are eagerly sought out.

Popular Beliefs and Practices

Traditional Thai medicine is a mixture of Chinese and Indian theories, Buddhist and animist beliefs, and techniques developed through trial and error. Many common afflictions are recognized and easily diagnosed as being of physical origin. Others are thought to be the work of evil spirits which from whim or malice enter the body, with detrimental or fatal effects. Sorcerers are frequently thought to be responsible for the freeing of these spirits.

153

Little attention has been given to the prevention of illness, although Buddhist or animistic amulets and charms are used as protection against specific ailments; injuries and misfortune in general. Among the talismans most frequently worn are Buddha images; metal cylinders containing slips of paper with magic spells or Pali inscriptions and hung as pendants from the neck; and cotton strings tied around the wrists or ankles of a baby or made into necklaces for persons threatened by evil spirits. The use of tattooing as insurance against disease is practiced to a limited extent in some regions, particularly among the hill peoples in the North.

Some villagers, particularly those in the Central Region, believe that young children can be assured good health by cutting their hair in a particular way. When a baby is a month or so old, several clay dolls are made, one with shaved head, one with top-knot, one with two pigtails, and so on. They are placed on the ground in front of the child, who reaches for one. The child's hair is then arranged like that of the chosen doll in the belief that he will thus avoid the children's diseases that might otherwise plague him.

The house spirit is believed by many to be the most important protection against sickness or other misfortune. Building a spirit dwelling on the occasion of a housewarming and propitiating the spirit at other times are believed to ensure the inhabitants' good health.

In connection with the Buddhist belief in acquiring merits, it is felt that treating the monks well and going frequently to the *wat* will increase one's chances of avoiding sickness. Religious observances are not seen as a guarantee of good health, however, since they cannot overcome the adverse ethical consequencies of one's evil acts (see ch. 12, Religion).

Traditional methods of therapy include many home remedies and favored food and herbal mixtures which may be known generally or by a single family. These are usually prepared by the person who is ill or by a member of his family and taken without ritual thought of spiritual intervention. Medicines of the Chinese pharmacist, if there is one in the community, or from the itinerant drug peddler are also popular. They include traditional Chinese medicaments, modern patent medicines and such drugs as aspirin, quinine and sulfanilamide.

In cases of more serious illness the patient or his family may decide to try propitiation of the house spirit or may solicit the help of the local practitioner. The latter may be a certified practitioner of traditional medicine (of whom there are about 34,000), but he is more likely to be an unregistered nonprofessional, charging little or nothing for his services and working most of the time at some other occupation. He may be a man reputed to have magical curing abilities or one who has devoted himself to the study of herbal medicines. Whether the cure is primarily medical or ritual depends on the diagnosis and presumably to a large extent on the specialty of the practitioner. If the sick person seems to be having difficulties with an evil spirit, offerings may be made to cool the spirit's anger, or elaborate gifts may be promised in the event of a speedy recovery. In more stubborn cases of spirit possession, exorcism may be deemed necessary. In such cases the ritual may consist of incantations and sprinkling or bathing the patient in lustral water, perhaps accompanied by traditional offerings of incense, candles and flowers. A more rigorous treatment involves beating the patient to force out the evil spirit.

A rite performed, with variations, in many parts of Thailand, involves placing a clay doll on a tray with other objects, food and some item closely associated with the sick person (such as nail parings, hair or a piece of clothing). The spirit is coaxed, by incantations and perhaps some stroking or beating of the patient, to come out and eat from the tray. The tray is then taken quickly to a crossroads and left there. The theory is that the spirit, when he has finished eating, will enter the clay doll thinking that it is the sick man. By the time the spirit has decided which is the proper road to take back to the afflicted person, the patient will be well on the way to recovery.

Buddhist monks serve in many areas as medical therapists. They either use traditional medicines or, like the spirit doctors, rely on animistic ritual cures.

Most village women, in bearing their children, are still attended by midwives employing traditional methods. Childbirth usually takes place in the home. In the absence of a midwife the pregnant woman's mother or some other relative will aid in the delivery. Traditional postnatal care consists of the mother's staying indoors for 6 to 8 weeks, lying near an open fire.

Chinese oriental medicine is widely practiced not only among members of the Chinese community (commonly estimated to number up to 4 million persons), but also among the Thai. Chinese practitioners are popular especially in the provincial towns. Patent medicines compounded by Chinese practitioners and labeled in terms of traditional oriental medicine are widely sold in the villages.

CHAPTER 10

EDUCATION

Education is one of the principal concerns of the government, as shown by the substantial investment of public funds in education and the formulation of long-range plans for educational reform.

The educational level of the population has risen considerably since the 1940's. Official figures show that in 1947 the literacy rate was only 40 percent among women and 67 percent among men; whereas, in 1960 the comparative figures were 61.8 and 80.-6 percent, respectively. For children between 10 and 14 years of age the illiteracy had dropped from 39 percent in 1947 to 14 percent in 1960. Estimates for the total literacy rate for the whole kingdom in 1966 varied between 55 and 70. In some of the remote rural areas, however, the literacy rate might have been as low as 20 percent.

Education is provided by the state through a centrally controlled school system arranged according to preprimary, primary, secondary and higher levels. Fraternal associations of the Chinese community and Christian mission groups provide additional educational opportunities, especially on the preprimary and secondary levels where they play an important role. Common to both public and private schools are teaching methods which rely heavily on memorization and rote learning.

The Six-Year Economic Development Plan of 1961–66 contained extensive measures for educational reform. The main reforms contemplated were extension of compulsory education from 4 to 7 years and revision of the curricula so that the subjects taught would be in furtherance of individual needs and national goals. The extension of compulsory schooling was expected to be fully implemented in 1970. Traditional school instruction was geared primarily to the preparation of a small elite for entrance into civil service; the new plan called for emphasis on a combined academic and vocational program designed to be of practical use to the majority of the people. Specific educational planning was being directed to bring secondary education into alignment with the country's manpower needs. The Educational Planning

Office of the Ministry of Education in the early 1960's conducted a survey of secondary education, on the basis of which it developed a program to be implemented by 1971.

The new educational policy appeared, by the end of 1966, to be at least partially successful in achieving the government's objectives. This was evident in the increased enrollment on all school levels and in the literacy rate (an estimated 70 percent in 1966) which already compared favorably with those of other Southeast Asian countries, and which continues to rise. In 1966 the number of students enrolled in the lower and upper grades of primary schools exceeded 4.7 million, or about 15 percent of the population. As early as 1963, the government under its new policy was making special efforts to extend education to the hill peoples of the North and Northeast, where the principal aim of educational efforts was to encourage economic and social development and to counteract Communist insurgency and propaganda activities.

Noteworthy progress had been made by mid-1967, despite delays in the implementation of reform measures. Vocational schools were not providing up-to-date training, mainly because of inexperienced staffs and inadequacy of equipment. There was also a shortage of qualified teachers, and secondary school facilities were insufficient for the growing number of students who wished to continue their education beyond the primary grades. Continued progress is envisaged, however, in the Second Five-Year Plan (1967–71) approved by the Economic Development Council, December 2, 1966. This plan provided for an annual output of approximately 9,800 teachers by 1971 (compared to about 1,750 in 1964) and for the number of students in all classes to increase from 5.3 million in 1966 to 6.35 million in 1971.

The government regards the educational system as an important instrument for developing feelings of national unity. Article 34 of the draft constitution provides that a person "enjoys full liberty with respect to education, so far as it is not contrary to his duties as a national, as provided by the laws governing education and organization of educational institutions." Regulations have been designed to ensure that the entire citizenry be literate in Thai and loyal to the government. This policy has antagonized some Chinese and Thai-Malay, who view it as an infringement of their rights.

The country has joined international projects designed to improve and to expand education. It is a participant in the Karachi Plan drafted in 1960 and supported by the United Nations. The Plan represents a long-term effort to align education on all levels more closely to the country's need for manpower trained in certain skills. The government also participates in the Colombo Plan which provides scholarships and training abroad, exchanges experts in the field of education and offers assistance to member countries in obtaining educational supplies. Membership is also maintained in the Association of Southeast Asian Institutions of Higher Learning (ASAIHL), which encourages the exchange of information and teaching staffs among member countries, which include Malaysia, Singapore, Hong Kong, South Vietnam, India, Ceylon, Indonesia, and the Philippines.

The United States Operations Mission (USOM) has sent about 300 education experts to the country since 1963, initiated joint projects between Thai and United States universities and launched vocational training projects. The country has also benefited by USOM's Southeast Asia Regional English Language Teaching Project. The West German government sent machinery and tools to the Technical Institute of Bangkok, and awarded scholarships for study in Germany. Japan has provided expert personnel and equipment in vocational training and also has awarded scholarships. France, in December 1966, signed an agreement to assist in establishing an Electricians Training Center at Thon Buri.

HISTORICAL BACKGROUND

Before the establishment of a modern school system, formal education was provided chiefly by the Buddhist monks, for whom teaching was a regular and important part of their lives. They provided instruction for the many youths who, in accordance with Buddhist tradition, served for a short time in the temples, either as novices or as temple boys. Other children, with the exception of the sons of wealthy families, who were privately tutored, had little or no formal training.

The novices who were preparing for ordination as monks learned reading and writing in Thai and in Pali (the language of Theravada Buddhist writings), arithmetic and, above all, moral and religious precepts. The temple boys, who were essentially general servants to the monks enjoying far less prestige and gaining less merit than the novices, were permitted to join the classes. Students wrote out texts from the Buddhist scriptures which they memorized and chanted in unison.

Only if he remained in the *wat* (see Glossary) for a long period of time could a boy learn more than the rudiments of reading and writing. Those who did share the experience, however, were for the rest of their lives more respected members of the village community than those who did not, reflecting the widespread respect for knowledge and for the man of knowledge.

The existence of *wat* schools and of a group of monks accustomed to teaching greatly facilitated the modernization of the education system, a process which began in the latter half of the nineteenth century. The initiative in this development was provided by King Mongkut (1851–68) and his son, King Chulalongkorn (1868–1910), who, having come in contact with representatives of Western nations, were the first to recognize the need for changes in the educational system. Their chief concern was to increase the efficiency of the government and to develop a group of officials qualified by training to deal with the Western nations.

Under King Mongkut, who had spent more than 20 years in the Buddhist priesthood, and had also had many Christian missionaries as teachers and friends, Western advisers were engaged for the government and English tutors appointed for the royal children. In addition, government officials and royal princes were sent abroad to further their studies.

In 1871, King Chulalongkorn founded the first institution giving modern education—a school in the palace for children of the nobility. Here the future civil servants of the country received a basic education, which included courses in the English language for advanced students. Many of his sons and sons of noblemen went to Europe for further study. Facilities within the country were improved as the King encouraged the establishment of private schools by Thai and by foreign missionaries. Later in his reign King Chulalongkorn decreed that every *wat* should offer instruction to children of its locality, the first instance of the government showing concern for the education of the general population.

With the establishment of the Department of Education in 1887 (which became a Ministry in 1892), schooling came to be the responsibility of the central government. Under the leadership of Prince Damrong Rachanuphab, who had studied in England and who subsequently became Minister of the Interior, plans were made for a system of national primary education. For many years foreign advisers, usually English, were attached to the Ministry of Education, and the Thai program for national education was patterned largely on that of the English schools. A study was made also of the Japanese system, and features of it, particularly those concerning moral training (defined in terms of duties of citizens to their country and Buddhist ethics), were incorporated into Thai education.

During the early twentieth century the government took the initiative in building up a system of state schools and also assumed some control over existing *wat* schools. Although the development of state schools was hindered by lack of funds, by

1921, 4,000 such schools had been established. Government supervision of schools was gradually extended as education officers were assigned to the districts and then to the provinces. Facilities for higher education were expanded with the founding of Chulalongkorn University in Bangkok in 1917, combining the existing Civil Service College and the Medical School.

In 1921, by royal decree of King Vajiravudh (1910–25), primary education of children between the ages of 7 and 14 was made compulsory. Existing schools, however, could not accommodate all children, and those living too great a distance from a school were exempt. Serious attempts at systematic enforcement of the law throughout the country began only after 1935, when, in keeping with the democratic ideals of the new regime, greater emphasis was placed on widespread primary education. The Constitution of 1932 had provided for a fully elected parliament which would come into being as soon as half the population had completed 4 years of primary education or within 10 years, whichever was sooner. Therefore, the compulsory education law was enforced more consistently. Despite some progress, the feeling among national leaders at the close of the 10-year period was that the educational level of the population had not been raised sufficiently to permit the election of a national assembly by popular suffrage.

The 1932 Constitution, as amended in 1952, contained the provision that, after 5 years, the people of any province could elect all their representatives in the National Assembly when 50 percent of its population had completed a primary education. In March 1957 the government announced that in the total of 71 provinces, more than half the population in each of 14 provinces had completed primary education. Accordingly, in March of the following year, elections were held in five of these provinces for the representatives who were to replace the appointed members.

The procedure was discontinued after Prime Minister Sarit Thanarat took direct control of the country in October 1958 and placed it under martial law. Nevertheless, his administration gave new impetus to education by increasing budgetary appropriations for education and by establishing a committee at the national level to formulate plans for expanding facilities and improving the curriculum. Before 1958 the expenditure on education had averaged from 12 to 15 percent of the national budget; but under Prime Minister Sarit it was increased to 15 to 18 percent of the total. Most of this sum was spent for primary education.

THE EDUCATIONAL SYSTEM

The educational program is divided into four levels. The preprimary level varies from 1 to 3 years. The primary level includes grades 1 to 7 of which grades 1 to 4 represent a compulsory general course. The extension of compulsory attendance of the primary level up to and including grade 7 was under progress in 1967. The secondary level consists of two stages, a 3-year lower and a 2-year preuniversity course. In addition, there are several kinds of higher education and vocational education at three levels: elementary, intermediate and advanced.

A large majority of the schools are government controlled. In 1964, the country had a total of 27,319 preprimary, primary and secondary schools of which only 2,250 were private. There were, however, additional privately owned vocational institutes and teaching establishments offering specialized courses.

Each cycle of the primary and secondary programs ends in a competitive examination for admission to the next cycle—a procedure which tends to decrease enrollment at successive levels. The largest number of dropouts and repeaters are at the end of the fourth year of primary work, after the third year of secondary work and again at the end of the preuniversity course. The competitive examination procedure reflects an effort to maintain a uniform educational standard throughout the kingdom and at the same time to single out the students best qualified to continue to higher levels of education.

Administration and Finance

Centralized control has been characteristic of the state school system since its inception. Following the 1932 coup d'etat, the national government tried briefly to decentralize the school system and encouraged local authorities to take more initiative in providing education, but it was soon apparent that local funds were insufficient for the task. Since then the trend has been toward increasingly greater centralization of responsibility, with the line of authority descending from the Ministry of Education to the village school. Local schools maintained by communes (tambon) are under the jurisdiction of the administrative officers of the provinces or districts and those maintained by municipalities are supervised by local officials under the Ministry of the Interior.

The Ministry of Education has various means of control. Since the government budget is the source of nearly all funds spent on education, it exercises control through the allocation of these funds. In addition, the teaching and administrative staffs of all except private schools are employees of the Ministry.

The Ministry's regulations determine school hours, curricula, textbooks and examinations, and also contain rules concerning the dress of students and the style of new schools built in the villages.

Administrative control of the Ministry is exercised by the minister of education, a Cabinet member, who is assisted by a staff in which his immediate deputy is the under secretary, a civil servant. The minister supervises the work of the Under Secretary's Office, the Educational Planning Office, and of eight other departments: Physical Education, Teacher Training, Educational Techniques, Secondary Education, Elementary and Adult Education, Vocational Education, Religious Affairs and the Fine Arts Department. The National Education Council, under the Office of the Prime Minister, has important policymaking responsibilities in the drafting and implementation of long-term projects designed to improve various critical areas of the educational system.

The so-called local (communal) and municipal schools, in contrast to the national government schools, offer only primary level instruction. Although they are operated and partially financed by local authorities, the government pays the teachers' salaries, furnishes a minimum of equipment and provides a partial grant toward construction of new buildings. Since 1963, the national government has tended to assume a growing share of responsibility in the management and direction of local schools.

In the case of the national government schools the entire cost of construction and maintenance is borne by the central government. Originally established as models for the local municipal schools, they offer secondary and vocational training as well as primary level instruction.

The system of school supervision followed in the Central Region differs from that in effect elsewhere in the country. Schools of all types in that region are supervised by officials of the Ministry of Education in Bangkok, rather than by provincial or district education officers. Control is consequently somewhat closer than in outlying areas.

In the budget of fiscal year 1966–67, the Ministry of Education was allocated 2,427.8 million baht (see Glossary), or 16.81 percent of the total, surpassed only by economic services.

Of the 2,427.8 million baht allotted to the Ministry of Education for 1966, some 507.4 million represented an investment for the expansion of school facilities and services on the primary and secondary levels and for the extension of higher education to provincial areas. About 54.8 percent of the total appropriation was spent on elementary education, notably on projects to extend the compulsory education from 4 to 7 years. More than 14.5 percent was spent on higher education and 11.2 percent on technical education. The main effort in the latter field was to provide vocational education facilities for students who failed to qualify for institutions of higher learning. Some 8.5 percent was allotted to secondary education with a view to increasing the number of classrooms and teachers, and providing teaching aids.

Preprimary and Primary Education

Preprimary education, more commonly known as kindergarten, is mainly provided by private individuals and organizations rather than by the government. In 1964, there were 50,982 preprimary pupils of which only 7,388 attended public schools. The preprimary program varies in length from 1 to 3 years, depending on the school, and pupils are taught the rudiments of reading and writing. Such schools are important in the system, because a number of primary schools accept only those students who have acquired some reading and writing facility.

Primary schools which enrolled 4,768,000 pupils in grades 1 to 7 in 1966, have been in the focus of government attention in the field of education. As a result an impressive number of schools have been built, particularly in the hitherto neglected North and Northeastern regions. New schools were also opened in the southern half of the Peninsula but the pace of building them was slower than elsewhere.

Efforts of the Ministry of Education to enlarge the network of primary schools were complemented by the Border Patrol Police, which established some 200 schools during 1965–66 in the villages located in the North and Northeast. The schools offer instruction in primary grades 1 to 4. The same areas also benefited by schools started by the Mobile Development Units organized by the Army.

The prescribed curriculum for the lower primary grades (1 to 4) gives emphasis to arithmetic and to reading and writing the Thai language. From 1 to 3 hours each are devoted to geography, history, nature study, civics, morality, health education, singing and drawing, handicrafts and physical education. In the upper primary grades (5 to 7) a combination of academic subjects and basic vocational knowledge and skills are emphasized. Since 1963, curricula in the lower primary schools have been modified. Three hours a week are spent on basic sciences, mathematics, health education and art education. Thai social and language studies still receive the main emphasis, however, with 6 to 7 hours each week (out of a total of 25) devoted to them. In the upper primary grades the main emphasis is on practical arts and crafts to which 6 to 8 hours a week are allotted, and the study of English has been introduced. Government officials also reported in 1964 that social subjects in primary school curricula in the Northeastern Region were designed to stress qualities "which will help consolidate unity and maintain national culture and eliminate the possibility of becoming victim to political propaganda and subversion."

The large majority of children who should be in primary school were, in fact, enrolled in 1966 although the degree of compliance with the compulsory education law varied locally. Under the law children may be exempted from attendance by permission of the district education officer. Some handicapped children in the compulsory age bracket do not attend school because of the scarcity of special facilities. In 1964 there were five schools catering to the needs of these children. The government has also built three boarding schools in Kanchanaburi, Nonthaburi and Chiang Rai to accommodate children living in remote areas who are unable to commute to schools because of lack of transportation.

Among the children enrolled in school, haphazard attendance habits undoubtedly contribute to the high proportion of examination failures. Children are economically useful from an early age and parents prefer to have their help at home. Education officials reported in 1964 that between 20 and 25 percent of lower elementary grade students fail their examinations which terminates their studies in grade 4.

Despite efforts to build new school buildings, only some 42.7 percent of public primary schools were located in modern, well-equipped buildings in 1964. More than 46 percent of the schools were conducted within the local *wat* where, in many instances, several classes were held in the same room. Often there were no desks, for these had to be provided locally, and no equipment other than a blackboard. Students had to buy their own textbooks and as a result, in many schools only the teacher had copies. Under these circumstances the students wrote the teacher's words on their slates and memorized their lessons, just as they had in the traditional temple schools. Even when textbooks were available the traditional method of learning by memorization persisted.

In spite of progress in the field of primary education, the lack of teachers, especially of adequately trained teachers, slows the process of learning. Crowded classrooms are commonplace in many areas. The teacher shortage and poor quality of teaching appear to be most severe in the Northern and Northeastern regions. Because of better qualified teachers urban children are, as a rule, more successful than rural children in passing the primary school examinations. In Bangkok and the larger towns teachers are much better qualified, classes smaller, equipment better and more value is attached to education. In the villages, many students spend 2 or more years in each grade, and some reach the age of 15 before they finish primary school. Because many students must repeat one or more of the lower grades, the age variation in class is often considerable.

To extend the scope of primary schooling the government introduced school broadcasts in 1958. In 1964 approximately 2,000 schools had been equipped with receivers to tune in on these broadcasts.

The United States Operations Mission (USOM) has offered material and financial assistance in kind and money to help solve teaching supply shortages in rural schools of the remote areas. In 1965 USOM planned to supply 4,000 schools in the Northeast with a minimum of two readers and one arithmetic textbook per student and to furnish other supplementary teaching aids. USOM also planned to distribute some 1.4 million additional school texts by the beginning of the 1966 school year.

Secondary Education

Secondary school facilities are limited and competition for admission is intensifying as more children complete the primary course and wish to continue their education. The prerequisite for entrance into the civil service, formerly completion of the lower secondary stage, has been raised to completion of the upper secondary stage for most positions.

In response to the growing demand the government has been making a determined effort to extend secondary education facilities, its immediate goal being the provision of two secondary schools in each district. The government reported in 1964 that during the early 1960's the number of public secondary schools increased at the rate of some 20 a year and that the majority of the new schools were located in the various districts. In 1963, for example, 17 secondary schools were opened in the districts and two in the metropolitan area.

According to government figures, the total enrollment in public and private secondary schools was 311,664 in 1964. The number of students were about equally divided between public and private schools. Estimates on the number of secondary school students for 1966 varied between 376,000 and 743,000. In late 1966, the number of secondary schools totaled 1,470.

Financial considerations as well as the lack of facilities have prevented a great many students from pursuing secondary schooling. Although some government scholarships for needy students are available, students enrolled in public secondary schools must pay tuition and, even when no tuition is charged they must cover expenses for books, school supplies, and, in many cases, the cost of room and board away from home.

In 1961 the secondary school program was divided into a 3-year lower (lower *matayom*) and a 2-year higher (upper *matayom*) course. The students' ages ranged from 14 for the first year of the lower level to 18 in the last year of the upper level. Satisfactory completion of 7 years of primary school work is the prerequisite for entrance into the first grade of the secondary level.

The secondary education curriculum has two branches—the general academic branch and the vocational training branch. Both have a common core of liberal arts and basic science subjects but the academic branch stresses theoretical instruction and provides the foundation for further studies in higher educational institutions.

Vocational Education

One of the problems of education in the country has been its predominantly academic emphasis in areas where the majority of the children will later follow agricultural vocations. In the effort to cope with this problem, the Ministry of Education has given much attention to the development and improvement of education in the rural areas and has set out to provide instruction more appropriate in content. Special emphasis has been placed on assisting institutions which train teachers for vocational schools. The government offers approximately between 10,000 and 14,000 scholarships each year for students who wish to attend vocational training courses. Various ministries provide specialized training schools, including schools for telegraphy, railway engineering, nursing and aeronautical engineering.

According to official statistics, there was a total of 202 vocational and technical schools with 39,402 students enrolled in 1964. Other sources reported in 1966 that vocational training was provided in some 210 schools with an approximate total enrollment of 45,000. The training consisted of a number of courses, varying from 1 to 5 years, corresponding to the lower and upper secondary stages of academic work. Enrollment tended to be highest in the upper-level courses.

The oldest multivocational school in the country, the Technical Institute of Bangkok, was established in 1952 and is among the best such schools in Southeast Asia. The United States economic aid program assisted in establishing and equipping the Institute, and 30 Thai instructors in the school have received training in the United States. The Institute established regional branches at Songkhla on the Peninsula in 1955, at Nakhon

Ratchasima in the Northeast in 1956, and at Chiengmai in the North Region in 1957. In 1966 the United States awarded $1.1 million for the Institute's expansion and for the improvement of its facilities.

The Thewes Vocational School in Bangkok trains mostly instructors for boys' trade schools. It has building trade, machine, metal and carpentry shops as well as radio and electricity laboratories. The Thewes School has received about $120,000 worth of equipment for its library, shops and laboratories from the United States Operations Mission (USOM).

The Technical Institute in Thon Buri trains mainly engineers. A similar institution in Ubon Ratchathani in the Northeast, is the recipient of regular grants from the United Nations Special Fund. Another center for the training of engineers is the Southeast Asia Treaty Organization (SEATO) Graduate School of Engineering in Bangkok which offers courses in structural, highway and hydraulic engineering. SEATO has 20 other trade schools in the country. These have been equipped with USOM assistance, and annually graduate approximately 2,200 students trained to be technical supervisors, foremen, vocational teachers, and skilled laborers for the armed forces (see ch. 22, Labor).

The government also organizes short training courses in various vocations. One type of program is the experimental multivocational mobile units which tour the country, giving 4 to 6 months' courses in dressmaking, hairdressing, cooking and homemaking. There are also many agricultural extension schools which provide instruction in basic agriculture in self-help settlements. In addition, numerous private vocational schools offer short courses in typing, shorthand, hairdressing, mechanics and other subjects. In the program of vocational education, emphasis is being placed on the improvement of regional facilities.

Special programs for the improvement of rural education have been developed with assistance from the United Nations Educational, Scientific and Cultural Organization (UNESCO). One such project is the Regional Educational Development Project including Higher Education, under which teachers and trainees work together with students and villagers to improve living conditions in the rural areas.

Teacher Training

In 1967 the lack of trained teachers continued to be the greatest single obstacle to the improvement of Thai education. In 1964 the country had 158,920 teachers, but it was estimated that about 8,500 more would be needed annually to keep pace with the rapid expansion in education. In establishing hundreds of new schools each year, the government recruited teachers from all possible sources and in many instances Buddhist monks with academic qualifications were employed to serve as teachers in local and municipal schools. In addition, several members of the United States Peace Corps have served as teachers in the Thai schools since January 1962.

The officially prescribed training for primary school teachers consists of 7 years of primary and 3 years of lower secondary schooling to be followed by a 2-year course in a teacher training institution or completion of the 2-year upper secondary level. In addition, there is a higher certificate course of 2 years' duration, following the completion of the upper level of secondary school. Holders of the higher certificate teach grades 5 to 7 in the primary schools, but the majority is usually assigned to teach the lower secondary classes. To increase the supply of teachers, the government has had to employ a large number of uncertified teachers. In 1965, more than half of the teachers were without formal training for teaching and of those who have had formal training the majority had only 1 to 2 years of schooling in the upper secondary level.

Several problems face the government in trying to obtain a more adequate supply of teachers. Salaries have not kept pace with the cost of living and, in spite of several revisions of the pay scale, the teacher's real income is still below the prewar level. The salary varies with the qualifications of the teacher, so that most of them receive the minimum pay. In Bangkok the teacher's income places him in the middle class with the lower echelons of government employees. In the rural areas the teacher is considered to be slightly better off, for he can supplement his income by growing some of his food.

Another difficulty in providing rural teachers, however, is the preference of the better educated for urban life. The teacher-training schools are in Bangkok and the larger towns. Having gone to one of these to study, few qualified teachers wish to return to the village, and this perpetuates the differences in quality between education in rural and urban areas.

The government, recognizing the urgency of the country's need in this particular field, is now placing much greater emphasis on the training of teachers. As a result, enrollment in the country's 31 teacher-training schools in 1964 had risen to 18,727 as compared to 14,367 in 1961. The number of graduates from teacher-training schools in 1964 totaled 1,729 which represents a slight decrease compared to 1,763 graduates in 1961.

Training is provided free of charge, but students must pay for room and board and buy their own books. Approximately 4,000 scholarships annually are offered in this field, and teachers who undertake additional studies are entitled to receive their full salary while doing so.

The establishment and improvement of the College of Education in Bangkok, intended to be a model for other schools is a major effort toward improving the quality of teacher education. With financial and technical assistance from the United States, the course of instruction was extended to 4 years and a graduate school was established. In 1964 the enrollment of students in the college totaled approximately 1,600; the number of graduates was 684.

In every province, as well as in Bangkok, there is inservice training of teachers and refresher courses are offered in the summer. Several American educators worked with the College and with other teacher-training institutions, and several hundreds of Thai teachers and administrators had received their training abroad, principally in the United States. The United States has assisted the teacher-training program, not only by providing equipment and facilities, but also by advising education officials on the revision of the curriculum. The training centers, in which not only Thai students but also some from nearby Laos and Cambodia are enrolled, are in the Northeastern Region at Nakhon Ratchasima, Udon Thani and Ubon Ratchathani.

A general education development project has as its main objective increasing the number of teachers and improving their qualifications. Training centers have been established in various regions; short courses are being given there, introducing new teaching ideas and methods.

Membership in the Teacher's Institute, a government-sponsored organization established in 1944, is required of all teachers. The Institute's governing board, chosen every 4 years, is made up of six representatives of the Ministry of Education and nine teachers who have had at least 10 years' teaching experience and who are elected by the organization's membership. It was designed as a means of ensuring greater contact between teachers and the Ministry. Its function includes the handling of teachers' placements, promotions, transfers and resignations. It selects candidates for further studies, and it also publishes two teachers' journals.

Adult Education

Most of the facilities in adult education are on the primary level. Their main function is to provide literacy courses and basic vocational training. According to official statistics, 14,464 persons in 1964 were attending adult education courses; 5,875 were enrolled in primary level, 4,101 in secondary level and 4,488 in vocational courses. In addition to the adult education courses given by schools, the government has dispatched mobile education units to more than 2,000 remote localities.

In the North Region, a special school for adults, emphasizing the study of home economics and agriculture, operates in Chiengmai.

Private Schools

Private schools fill an important role, especially in preprimary and secondary education. Because they substantially assist the government in expanding educational services, some of them are subsidized by government funds. The subsidies usually take the form of supplements to teachers' salaries and funds for the maintenance and expansion of physical facilities.

In 1964 there were 2,924 private schools of which 2,250 represented preprimary (kindergarten), primary and secondary schools. The remainder were vocational institutes and special courses. Enrollment in all categories of private education totaled 838,142. The schools varied greatly in size and standards of excellence, ranging from some highly respected institutions in Bangkok run by various Christian mission groups and the Chinese community to small, country schools with low teaching standards.

The government has encouraged the maintenance of private schools, provided that their administrators conform to state regulations regarding the qualifications of teachers and the content of the curriculum. Schools which have attained excellent reputations may be allowed to deviate from the prescribed curriculum and to give their own examinations.

The early schools established by foreign missionaries provided the first Western education available in the country. Since then, Thai teachers and administrative personnel have largely supplanted foreign teachers and, in accordance with official regulations, they now give instruction almost exclusively in the Thai language.

Some missionary schools offering both primary and secondary education are among the best in the country, and often the children of the elite are educated here. Outstanding in this category are the Bangkok Christian College, the Master Dei College, the Assumption College and the Wattana Academy, all in Bangkok, and the Prince Royal College in Chiengmai.

The Chinese schools, which as a group were set up somewhat later than the mission schools, were usually established by one of the various Chinese regional associations, which were in turn based on a common dialect. They taught the children in the Chinese language and according to the pattern of education in China.

Chinese primary and secondary schools, first established in

1911 were of prime importance in fostering Chinese national feelings in their communities and in imparting Chinese cultural values. These educational activities were sharply curtailed in 1933 by the Thai government, which at that time embarked on a policy designed to assimilate the national ethnic minorities and to inculcate complete loyalty to the Thai government in the population. Teachers in all Chinese schools were required to be literate in Thai and, by regulation, Thai was established as the language of instruction. Only 10 hours per week could be devoted to a foreign language—a schedule which did not allow for teaching of the complex system of Chinese writing. The Chinese failed to comply fully with this ruling, however. As a result, during the late 1930's—a period of intense nationalism in Thai politics—the majority of Chinese schools were closed and hundreds of children were sent by their parents to study in China or Malaya.

Many Chinese schools reopened after World War II. As Communist strength on the Chinese mainland increased, the pressure for closer control of the Chinese schools intensified. Regulations were more rigorously enforced, and a decree was issued in 1947 forbidding the continued operation of Chinese secondary schools. In the succeeding period a number of teachers were dismissed, a ban was placed on the use of certain textbooks and many schools closed their doors. Regulations restricting Chinese education to the 4 years of primary school were continued by the new government following the coup d'etat of 1958, and other control measures remained in effect as well.

Regulations still in force in 1967 included the requirement that teachers in Chinese schools pass a test representing the equivalent of primary grade 4 of the Thai schools. The Ministry of Education kept a close scrutiny over curriculum and instruction. Textbooks featuring Chinese patriotic themes and songs could not be used, and only 10 hours of Chinese language instruction per week was allowed. As a result, the students gained only a minimal knowledge of Chinese history, geography and literature, and a limited reading ability in the Chinese language.

Chinese schools, despite these regulations, were not excluded from the program of financial subsidies which the government was extending to private schools. Government aid to Chinese schools was usually granted providing they conformed with official rules and were in good standing. The basic financing, however, continued to come from one of the numerous benevolent and fraternal associations of the Chinese community which have been established throughout the country. Such associations usually have special school committees which assign funds for school maintenance and for payment of teachers' salaries.

In 1966 there were 167 Chinese schools in the country with a total enrollment of about 40,000. Most of the schools were located in the Bangkok-Thon Buri area, in the nearby central lowlands and in the Peninsula.

Government regulations limit the operation of Chinese schools to instructions on the primary level but Chinese children may obtain their secondary and higher level education by attending night school or by home tutoring. The night schools are mainly language-teaching institutions. Many of them have expanded their curriculum and offer high-level instruction in academic and vocational subjects. The Chinese language night schools may operate only in the Bangkok area; in 1966, their enrollment totaled about 15,000.

Higher Education

The country's five principal universities, as well as most of its other institutions of higher learning are located in Bangkok. To answer the growing demand for university education throughout the country the government, since 1963, has begun the construction of three additional institutions of higher learning in Chiengmai (North Region), in Khon Kaen (Northeast) and in Pattani (Peninsula). In 1966, however, only Chiengmai University was completed.

In 1964 the total university enrollment was 45,980. Less than half of the students were women. During the same year, 4,835 persons graduated from universities as compared to 2,807 in 1961. The highest number of graduates in 1964 was in the fields of education, law, social sciences, commerce and accounting, and public health. All universities, as well as the Office of the Superintendent for Thai Students Abroad are administered by the Office of the Prime Minister.

Chulalongkorn University, founded in 1917, is the oldest university and has the highest academic standards. Four-year courses are offered in seven faculties: Arts, Education, Commerce and Accounting, Science, Engineering, Architecture and Political Science. Natural Science and engineering appear to be popular fields of studies. Graduate-level instruction is also provided in 18 fields, including history, education, psychology and nuclear physics. In 1964 the university enrollment totaled 6,473.

Thamassat University, also called the University of Moral and Political Sciences, was founded in 1934. It includes the Colleges of Law, Commerce and Accounting, Political Science, Economics, Social Administration, Public Administration and Liberal Arts; there is also a graduate division. In 1964 it had a student body of 28,408, representing the largest university enrollment in the country.

The Medical Sciences University in Bangkok which was separated from Chulalongkorn University in 1948, includes three Schools of Medicine—at Sirraj and Chulalongkorn hospitals in Bangkok and at Chiengmai Hospital in Chiengmai—as well as the Schools of Dentistry, Pharmacy, Public Health, Tropical Medicine, Medical Science, Medical Technology, and Nursing Midwifery and Health. The 1964 enrollment totaled 3,339 students.

Kasetsat University (or the University of Agriculture), organized in 1948, provides instruction in agriculture, economics, and cooperative science, veterinary science, forestry, fishery science and irrigation engineering. Enrollment in 1964 was 2,393.

Silpakorn University, also called the University of Fine Arts, is composed of four Colleges: Painting and Sculpture, Thai Architecture, Decorative Arts and Archeology. The number of students enrolled in 1964 was 471.

Chiengmai University opened in 1964 with an enrollment of 291. It offered instruction in agriculture, medicine, engineering, accounting, public administration and commerce.

Construction of Khon Kaen University in the Northeast was begun in 1963. The university will offer courses in agriculture, engineering and science.

Government officials reported in 1964 that Pattani University in the Peninsula will be ready to receive students in 1966. No data was available, however, on enrollment or courses offered at this institution.

In addition, there are two Buddhist ecclesiastical colleges in the capital under royal patronage. They offer programs of general and religious higher education for members of the Buddhist priesthood.

Since 1961 the government has worked actively to improve higher education. Plans have been made and partially initiated to increase the number of professors and to reduce the ratio of teacher and students to 1:12. Several fields of study have been added to the curricula, and standards of admission have been raised. The improvement of many graduate and research facilities was under progress in 1966.

In an attempt to encourage research in the fields of the natural and social sciences and its application to Thai society, the government has established the National Research Council and the International Institute for Child Study. The main emphasis of research at the Council has been in the field of health and medicine whereas at the Institute it has been psychology and child development.

Since higher education facilities are limited at home, and

great prestige is attached to foreign training, a growing number of students pursue or complete higher education in foreign countries. In 1966 there were approximately 4,000 Thai students abroad, about 1,700 of whom were in the United States. The majority of the rest studied in Canada, England, France, West Germany, Japan, Pakistan and the Philippines.

EDUCATION AND SOCIETY

Apart from the goal of mass literacy, the government's interest in educational content is primarily that it serve to develop loyalty to the government among all the people of the country and that it facilitate the assimilation of diverse groups in the society.

The government is making special efforts to promote national unity. The dialect of the Central Region is the medium of instruction throughout the country. Regional script has never been taught, and dialect speech in school has been discouraged. Group sports, Boy Scout training for boys and Junior Red Cross training for girls are included in the interests of physical health and the spirit of group cooperation. Basic principles of health and sanitation are taught.

The emphasis on patriotism is apparent in the curriculum itself and in other school activities. Certain courses lend themselves easily to a nationalistic treatment. Thus the classes in Thai history stress the roles of the heroes of Thai history and sometimes the roles of the present leaders of the government. In the civics course the pupils learn about the nature of the government, but the approach to the subject is defined in terms of duty—the student's duty to school, family, society, King and the government. In the course on morality the student is taught Buddhist ethics. Since 1958 increased emphasis has been placed on Thai culture, Buddhism and the royal family. Instruction throughout is strongly anti-Communist.

Other aspects of school life also encourage nationalism among the students. Each morning, in private as well as in public schools, there is a flag-raising ceremony at which the national anthem is sung. On national holidays the children are expected to participate in special formations as a group. For major holidays, such as Chulalongkorn Day, Bangkok students participate in elaborate commemorative ceremonies at the statues of King Chulalongkorn. In the provinces students from several villages commonly go to the office of the district administrator who conducts the proceedings. After the day's proclamation is read the students give three cheers. There may then be speeches, group singing and a service led by the monks. At these occasions the students must wear the prescribed school uniform—blue shorts and white shirts for the boys, blue skirts and white blouses for the girl—though at other times deviation from prescribed dress is overlooked. A short Buddhist ceremony is observed on the first and last days of the school year as well as on major holidays.

Respect for learning and knowledge among the Thai stems from the Buddhist tradition. The purpose of learning, according to Buddhist doctrine, is the acquisition of religious merit through knowledge of sacred things. It was believed that right understanding leads to right action and thus increases one's store of merit, and advances one on the path to *nirvana*. Literacy, accordingly, was respected as a means of participating more fully in the religious life. Great value was placed on the basic knowledge of reading, writing and of moral precepts disseminated by Buddhist monks among the many youth who served as temple boys in the *wat* before the introduction of the modern school system (see ch. 12, Religion).

The modern Thai tend to regard education primarily as a means for economic, professional and social advancement. The primary goal is the acquisition of a degree of higher learning, especially since government officials have repeatedly stressed the importance of such degrees to persons interested in advancement in the civil service.

Special prestige is attached to degrees acquired at institutions of higher learning abroad. The government has granted automatic salary raises to holders of degrees from foreign universities and has granted leave to many civil servants to study abroad. Key government posts are held by graduates of foreign schools. Nearly half of the Thai students abroad in 1965 were government officers or holders of government scholarships.

Learning by memorization and rote is still customary in most of the schools. Class discussions and teaching by question and answer are rarely practiced, and independent inquiry by students is not encouraged. Furthermore, the Thai have been accustomed by tradition to relate learning to abstract matters and are generally reluctant to apply knowledge to solve practical problems. These attitudes have hampered the government in implementing its educational reforms, especially those in the vocational field, and have generally delayed the training of manpower versed in technological and administrative skills (see ch. 22, Labor). Many wealthy parents send their children to study abroad because they feel that the most pragmatic teaching methods practiced in foreign schools provide a better preparation for professional advancement in the country's progressing economy and modernizing administration.

The Thai-Malays of the Peninsula, and the Chinese closely associate education with the inculcation and strengthening of cultural and moral values characteristic of their respective countries of origin. The enforcement in Chinese schools and in schools attended predominantly by the Thai-Malays of educational policies stressing Thai nationalism and assimilation, has created some resentment in both ethnic communities.

Among the hill peoples, the interest in education has been growing during the 1960's. The Miao, inhabiting the remote and mountainous sector of the northern border region have urged the government, through their village councils, to provide more schools for the area. Young and old Miao have come to value literacy in Thai because it enables them to trade more successfully. Group members with a rudimentary education in Thai find a wider choice of occupations and may seek and acquire jobs in the cities. It has been generally agreed among the Miao, however, that education should be limited to boys.

CHAPTER 11

ARTISTIC AND INTELLECTUAL EXPRESSION

The arts and sciences in Thailand have emerged from a synthesis of various culture patterns and civilizations. Foreign elements in literature and in the visual and performing arts have undergone an extensive process of creative transformation and have acquired a distinct character reflecting the interests and needs of Thai society.

The predominant cultural influences derive from India and China. Hinduism and Buddhism, the most important sources of Thai artistic and intellectual expression, originated in India and came to the Thai people through such other countries as Burma, Ceylon and Cambodia. Much was also drawn from the traditions of neighboring countries. The Thai system of writing was derived from the Khmer version of Sanskrit script. The exchange of artistic and literary styles, forms and methods was increased by local wars. Artists and writers were considered legitimate spoils of war and, after capture, were taken to the court of the conqueror.

The best examples of Thai architecture, sculpture and painting are those created between the fourteenth and eighteenth centuries, an era which is generally regarded as the golden age of Thai arts. A period of decline, which began in the middle of the eighteenth century, was characterized by excessive ornamentation and general stagnation in the visual arts. During the twentieth century the novelty of Western, machine-made products had a stultifying effect on the development of traditional crafts since the younger generation of artists tended to adopt Western art forms. Thai life and landscapes have remained the principal subjects of their paintings and sculptures, however.

Thai kings have been instrumental in the introduction of Western ideas and customs. Their example encouraged the adoption and assimilation of Western scientific and technological achievements as well as some theories of government and social development. By the late 1960's Western influence had emerged as a primary force in modifying Thai society and in influencing the visual and performing arts and political thought.

Thai culture, in turn, has influenced neighboring countries. The Thai features which are evident in some of the court music and dances of Burma date back to the Burmese conquest of Ayutthaya in 1763. Thai influence may also be detected in Laotian and Cambodian art and architecture. The dances of the Cambodian Royal Ballet have been adapted from the Thai version of the ancient Khmer ritual of Angkor Wat. Cambodian and Laotian scholars have extensively utilized Thai technical and scientific terms of Pali and Sanskrit origin. The country has traditionally served as a training ground for Laotian and Cambodian teachers who have adopted many of its educational practices and theories. The Dhammayuttika sect of Theravada Buddhism organized by King Mongkut (Rama IV, 1851–68) was adopted by Cambodia and became the religion of the Khmer court (see ch. 12. Religion).

Until the mid-1920's the royal court was the principal patron and arbiter of arts and scholarship. After the coup of 1932 these functions were largely taken over by the government, although the royal family remained a significant influence through its active support of official cultural programs and its traditional role in the formation of artistic and literary tastes, especially among the aristocracy. The government's main endeavor has been the revival of traditional drama, dance and literature and the rejuvenation of the ancient crafts of metalworking and silk weaving. The Fine Arts Department under the Ministry of Education is responsible for the implementation of official cultural policies and programs. Silpakorn University (the University of Fine Arts) under the Office of the Prime Minister is an important center for the study and research of the traditional arts and their adaptation for use in radio and television.

Largely as a result of the government's cultural policies, Thai art has gained much appreciation in the West during the 1960's. Thai temple dancers have performed with great success in Western countries, including the United States. Decorative articles have also received growing attention by Western students of Thai art and are in great demand by collectors. These include items carved of teakwood, bronzeware and silverware ornamented with rich designs featuring scenes from traditional literary works and the famous nielloware (metal objects decorated with inlaid designs).

THE VISUAL AND PERFORMING ARTS

Historically, Thai art may be divided into six schools or periods: Chiengsaen (or Chiengmai), 1050–1550; Sukhothai, 1250–1450; Uthong, 1250–1450; Ayutthaya, 1350–1767; Ratanakosin ("National" or Bangkok), 1782–1868; and Modern Revival, twentieth century.

The Chiengsaen period, recently termed "Chiengmai" as a result of archaeological discoveries, spans the migratory centuries of Thai history and extends into the era of the Kingdom of Chiengmai, thus becoming "northern" art (see ch. 3, Historical Setting). Within this period appear the first efforts toward a uniquely Thai mode of expression, utilizing certain features of surrounding cultures.

In the eleventh and twelfth centuries Chiengsaen pottery and metalwork were closely akin to the Chinese Nanchao art. By 1200, however, the Thai migrants had begun to accept some models and methods from the remains of the Dvaravati art of the Mon to the south (sixth to eleventh centuries) and from the Khmer art which was superimposed on the Dvaravati. Chinese influence predominated until 1250, but after the establishment of the Kingdom of Sukhothai new varieties in art rapidly appeared. Although Chiengsaen art continued to flourish for two more centuries, it lost its preeminent place to the Sukhothai school.

From 1250 to 1450 the artistic expression of the Thai peoples of the Chao Phraya basin was influenced by three major schools— Chiengsaen, Sukhothai and Uthong—which represented the three stages of Thai cultural development. Chiengsaen artists continued to produce objects which indicated some Chinese influence. Buddhist images were patterned, as elsewhere in the Buddhist world, on conventional Indian models, particularly of the Pala and Sena schools, but produced in Chiengsaen in the Chinese medium of bronze and with some Chinese interpretation. The art of casting bronze was learned from the Chinese in the Nanchao era and became a northern Thai specialty. Chiengsaen products were acclaimed throughout southern Asia as the acme of such work.

By the middle of the thirteenth century, Khmer control over the Chao Phraya basin was beginning to give way to the emerging power of the Thai Kingdom of Sukhothai. Direct contact with India, Ceylon and China brought waves of new styles and concepts. Bold and radical changes were made on foreign models until a unique Thai style was achieved, and experiments made then largely decided the later patterns of Thai artistic development.

The predominant influence on painting was Ceylonese; on architecture it was a combination of Chinese and Khmer. In sculpture a pure Thai style emerged out of Ceylonese and Chiengsaen influence. Buddha images became elongated, graceful and contemplative, with an oval face and aquiline features, in direct contrast to the squat, rounded and smiling Buddha of Khmer style. Similarly, the buildings of Sukhothai were contrasts of horizontal and vertical perspectives rather than the symmetrical stone masses of the Khmer.

The third school of the period, that of Uthong in the lower Chao Phraya valley, was almost completely under Khmer influence. Thai artisans accepted it with little adaptation; their product was essentially a Thai phase of Khmer art.

The period of synthesis in Thai culture extended from 1350 to 1767, the era during which Ayutthaya was established and became the paramount power in the Chao Phraya basin. The linear elegance of Thai sculpture, painting and architecture was at its height from about 1550 until 1650 and began a rapid decline after 1700. By 1750 sculptors and architects were producing monumental works characterized by excessive ornamentation.

The establishment of Bangkok in 1782 marked the beginning of the fifth school of traditional Thai art, the Ratanakosin. It was a period of little accomplishment, in which the decadence of the late Ayutthayan era continued. A few fine pieces of art and architecture were produced, largely as slightly modified copies of late Sukhothai types, but by 1868 traditional Thai sculpture, architecture, painting, music, ornamentation and handicrafts were stagnant.

Sculpture

Buddhism was the dominant influence in traditional sculpture. Most pieces which have been discovered are portrayals of the Buddha, usually in one of three poses: seated, with legs crossed or folded before him and in a mood of contemplation; reclining; or walking. Images of the seated Buddha range from the colossal bronzes of the late Ayutthayan era to minute necklace charms produced in all periods. Images of the reclining or walking Buddha are rare, though the walking Buddhas are considered some of the finest examples of art in the Buddhist world. Buddha has also been portrayed, probably by non-Thai artists, in the form of an Indian god, but this form is very rare.

The sculptures of Buddha served as vehicles and expressions of Buddhism and were to be "reminders of the doctrine," not portraits of an individual. Only certain poses were appropriate, and the physical appearance of the images of Buddha was governed by religious purposes and ideals. The artist was not portraying an ordinary human form, but the Enlightened One, the lord Buddha in his existence before entering *nirvana* (release from the endless and painful cycle of rebirth). Buddha was unique among men, and the sculptures depict his idealized form rather than his actual appearance. Because Thai sculptors believed that such physical elements as muscles, bones and veins would destroy the aura of contemplation achieved by the Enlightened One, they were not portrayed. The only realistic statues of Buddha are those which represent his search for enlightenment through asceticism and fasting. Such statues are uncommon and afford a striking contrast to the serenity of the other images of the Enlightened One.

Through the centuries Thai artists developed a unique style in Buddha images. Stone, which was popular in neighboring countries, was not commonly used. Bronze was the most acceptable material, and the more common images were of stucco.

By the fourteenth century a Thai style had developed which made extensive use of bronze as a medium. The bulk and heaviness of the Khmer image, so complementary to stone, was no longer imitated. Instead, the Thai bronze castings, which followed the Chinese method, had a smoothness and sheen ideally balanced by the elongated gracefulness admired in Sukhothai.

Buddha images of Sukhothai, which are considered the finest examples of pure Thai sculpture, represent an idealized conception of the Sakyamuni (one of Buddha's titles, meaning "teacher of the Sakya clan"). He is portrayed in stylized form, reflecting a deep spiritual quality and contemplative attitude. His face is long and oval shaped; his nose is chiseled and aquiline; and his mouth is small and delicate. The eyebrows, eyelids and chin are represented by sharp incised lines. The downcast eyes suggest spiritual contemplation and compassion. The hair consists of shell-shaped curls, and the flame-shaped crown extends upward. These characteristics distinguish the Thai representation of the Buddha from the more realistic and humanized Khmer versions.

Although much later than in their other art forms, the Thai love for adornment eventually destroyed the early elegance of their sculpture. In the late Ayutthaya period the Buddha began to be adorned with a crown, necklace, rings and an elaborate robe. Worshipers earned merit by plastering bits of gold leaf upon the stucco images. Thai sculpture came to be represented by the unrefined images completely encrusted with gems and colored glass. In the nineteenth century some fine images were produced, but as careful copies of Sukhothai and Ayutthaya types. By 1867 only Buddhist amulets were being made, many by Chinese artisans in Bangkok. Traditional Thai sculpture had almost disappeared.

Sculpture remained stagnant from the 1860's until 1947 when a Thai artist educated in France, Paitun Muangsomboon, became much acclaimed in Europe as well as in the elite circles of Bangkok. Using the forms, methods and media (marble and granite) of the West, Paitun made little attempt to portray Thai subjects. Sitthidet Sanghiran, Sawang Songmangree and Khien

Yimsiri are other notable sculptors using Western media. More important for the country are the attempts of two Thai artists to revive the casting of bronze. Piman Moolpramook and Vichitr Chaosanket have since 1946 experimented with Buddha images and religious subjects.

Thai sculptors are being trained and employed by Silpakorn University (University of Fine Arts) and the Fine Arts Department of the Ministry of Education. Thai artists are experimenting with both traditional concepts and modern techniques. Their work has been exhibited both at home and in foreign countries, and some examples have been used in official capacities. The trend seems to be toward a development of a new conceptual framework which would involve more originality and individuality.

Architecture

Thai architecture also gives evidence of native adaptation of Indian and Chinese influences. Except for the addition of the stupa (a commemorative or reliquiary structure), the basic forms, purposes and construction materials have remained virtually unchanged since the close of the thirteenth century. Thai buildings usually follow the pattern of the rural wooden thatch-roofed house, sometimes duplicating the concave slope of thatch after it becomes old and wet. Before 1900 wood was used almost exclusively as the construction material. The earlier Thai structures, which were rectangular in plan, had a rigid horizontal line, with walls low in relation to length. Superimposed upon the walls was a step-like progression of roofs, usually three, but the number depended upon the length of the building.

With the acceptance of Buddhism and contact with Khmer culture, the Thai in the Sukhothai period superimposed upon their architecture a new perspective, that of the vertical line. From the Khmer they adopted the *phra prang* (the Khmer version of the Indian stupa) and created from this square, massive stone tower a circular, graceful wooden structure. The Thai heightened the base of the stupa and, in place of the squat beehive chamber the Khmer erected on top of the base, created a graceful spire. Within this upper portion was the chamber within which religious or royal relics were housed.

In addition to the *phra prang,* the Thai adapted a type of stupa directly from Indian and Ceylonese models, which were received by the Thai in the early Sukhothai era. Called in Thailand the *phra chedi,* this rounded stupa is considered the most inspired Thai architectural achievement. The tapering base (drum) remained, but instead of the elongated chamber at the top a domed chamber was added, capped by a towering graceful spire (throne and umbrella). Four corner spires, each surmounting a Buddhist relic, accentuated the height of the central spire. In itself, the *phra chedi* achieves most perfectly the Thai architectural concept of contrast between horizontal and vertical line.

For the Thai, however, the ideal linear contrast was achieved not within one building but within a group, such as a *wat* (walled compound containing a Buddhist temple and associated buildings) or palace compound. The functions of the buildings governed their form, and the arrangement within the compound was as important as the form of the individual structure.

Other classic Thai structures were the *bot*, the *vihara*, the *mondop* and the *prasad*. The *bot*, a rectangular structure with superimposed roofs, contained the primary Buddha image in the typical *wat*. The *vihara*, built on the same plan as the *bot*, contained the lesser Buddhist relics in the *wat* and was also used for a preaching hall. The *mondop*, a cubical with a steeped-back pyramidal superstructure tapering to a spire, was frequently used as the *wat* library. Adapted from the stupa, the superstructure of a *mondop* resembled a much modified *phra chedi* and a *vihara*. The *prasad*, or palace throne hall, was traditionally a rectangular structure with superimposed roofs. A superstructure resembling the Thai crown indicates the royal purpose of the building. One of the finest examples of Thai architecture is the Chakkri (Grand Palace) in Bangkok, a group of buildings finished about 1840.

Architecture suffered the progressive accumulation of ornamentation that marked the decadence of Thai art. In the earlier periods a careful use of gilded ornament, such as the *cho fa* (a horn-like extension at the end of each ridgepole), and glazed tile accentuated the white-walled mass of the building. For contrast with the luxuriant vegetation of the forest, roofs were tiled, and *phra prang, phra chedi, mondop* and *prasad* structures were encrusted with colored glass mosaics. Initially, the ornamentation did not obscure the gracefulness of the building, but in the eighteenth century, all art forms were overwhelmed by excessive decoration. Though there was renovation of traditional architecture in the next century, it was smothered by the adoption of steel and concrete structures in the twentieth century.

Since 1932 there have been attempts to harmonize traditional Thai and modern Western architecture. The buildings of Thammasat University (the University of Moral and Political Sciences) and some of the recently built hotels and restaurants in the capital represent the new trend which combines modern architectural concepts and traditional decorative techniques. Conscious efforts are being made to achieve harmony and to avoid excessive detail and ornamentation. Thai furniture and art objects are increasingly being utilized. Traditional Thai art concepts are being experimented with to arrive at more diversified and practical application in modern use.

Painting

Classical Thai paintings reflect stylistic characteristics of the Sukhothai and Chiengsaen period. The two types of classical painting are the murals in the temples and manuscript illustrations. Murals usually portray celestial beings worshiping the Buddha, episodes from the different lives of the Buddha or scenes from the daily life of the people. Illuminated manuscripts deal exclusively with religious subjects.

Thai painting began as monochrome linear composition, relying upon the location and size of figures to give perspective. The only surviving examples of the Sukhothai period show influences of Indian and Ceylonese models; however, there seemed to be a considerable amount of Thai creative interpretation. This trend was also evident in several early Ayutthaya murals.

In the late Ayutthaya period a subtle polychromatic effect was achieved by the careful blending of earth colors and natural pigments, and gold leaf was discretely applied to provide vivid contrast. Chinese influence was reflected in the stylized treatment of water, trees and rocks. The Thai styles of Chiengsaen and Sukhothai periods gained increasing prominence and became the foundation of the classical style.

The classical period of Thai painting opened with the seventeenth century, and the conventions and formulas developed then continued to govern the style of Thai painting well into the middle of the nineteenth century. Certain gestures, similar to those used in the classical dance, were used to suggest particular emotions and moods. The portrayal of persons was governed by status distinctions. Royal and celestial beings were classically conventionalized in form and gesture, serenely expressionless, with great refinement of line and harmonious color. The established symbolism of dress and appurtenances was faithfully followed. There was some compromise between the classical and realistic styles in portraying nonroyal personages of the court, but the distinguishing marks of rank were always clear. The common people were portrayed realistically in dress, gesture and expression.

The classical style, which combined idealized and realistic portrayals, crystallized further in the early Bangkok period. Classical convention was adhered to until, toward the end of the period, it deteriorated into a rigid formula, copied over and over again by Bangkok artists.

By 1850 painting had reached a nadir similar to that of the other arts. It was virtually impossible to revive the traditional art because of the scarcity of historical examples. Murals of the Sukhothai period had disappeared because their earth colors had not withstood the heat and damp, and the destruction of Ayutthaya in 1767 had left few examples of earlier styles which might have provided guides for a revival of traditional art.

Since 1945 Thai painting has been the most prolific of the rejuvenated arts, though traditional Thai principles are largely obscured. Chitr Buabusaya, onetime director of the School of Arts and Crafts, encouraged a school of Western-oriented artists, including Amnat Puang Samniang, Samit Distaphundhu and Chalerm Makeerah; Chitr Buabusaya himself is perhaps the best known. Apai Saratani is the sole painter attempting to rediscover the Thai tradition of subdued colors and linear composition.

Since the late 1950's interest in traditional painting and drawing has been gradually increasing. Thai painting, interior decoration, sculpture and architecture are among subjects offered at Silpakorn University. A few collections of traditional drawing and painting have been published, showing the various styles and conventional forms. These books are designed mainly to encourage young artists to create works in the classical tradition. The books reflect the influence of Western styles and techniques, however, especially in color applications. The three-dimensional representation of figures, formerly absent in traditional works, has become characteristic in these new handbooks. Reproductions and imitations of traditional masterpieces have also become widely available, although most are designed for tourist and popular consumption and few are of notable quality.

Multicolored rubbings of the stone bas-reliefs of temple walls represent a relatively new form of representation which has become popular since the early 1960's. Mulberry paper and silk have been used as rubbing materials, and the finishing strips near the edge are made of brocade.

Drama and Dance

Khon and *lakhornram* (traditional Thai dance dramas) were played for royalty and the aristocracy only. The meticulously trained dancer-actors were permanently employed by the king and by the court nobility. The performances were held at the royal court and in the palaces of the aristocracy.

Kohn is dance drama based upon the *Ramakian,* the Thai version of the Indian *Ramayana* (Sanskrit epic poem of the adventures of Rama). It is the most formalized of all Thai drama: actor-dancers, who are trained for their roles from the age of 6, are masked, and onstage movements are highly stylized and conventionalized. The *khon* requires four categories of actors; human male, human female, demoniac and simian. Once trained for one category, an actor does not perform in another. Originally, all actors were males; it is believed that women first acted in *khon* plays in the early nineteenth century. The plot is narrated in verse in the form of a recitation alternated with choral singing. Music is provided by a *piphat* (a band which uses only wind and percussion instruments).

Khon productions were so lengthy—some lasted 20 hours—that they were staged on two successive days. The duration of the performance was governed by the length of the episode. Traditionally, it was impossible to conclude a performance with the death of the hero Rama or his brothers; the episode must continue until they had been reborn. King Rama II (1809–24) wrote a version of the *Ramakian* which allowed shorter stagings, and contemporary adapters have achieved 3-hour performances.

Lakhornram (sometimes shortened to *lakhorn*) is a less formal and more popular dance drama. Movements are more graceful and less formalized than those of the *khon*, and the actor-dancers are unmasked and allowed to speak their own lines. The narration is in verse form, sung by a chorus. In addition to incidents from the *Ramayana*, Jataka tales (legends of the previous incarnations of Buddha which teach a moral lesson) and folk stories are produced. Humor also appears in certain *lakhornram*, thereby increasing its popularity.

The third traditional drama form is the *nang* (shadow play). Cowhide figures are held against a screen, and shadows are cast by means of lanterns. Bearers of the figures dance their part, the movements being the same as those of *khon* and *lakhornram*. Narration is provided by a chorus and an orchestra. *Nang* staged in daylight uses cowhide figures painted for identification.

The *hun* (Thai marionette) performance utilizes elaborate models portraying characters from classical tradition. These figures are manipulated by strings from below. The narration takes the form of songs, accompanied by a small orchestra. This form of dramatic presentation has become almost extinct, however, and a popular version of the *hun*, called *hun krabok*, is taking its place. In this form smaller and less elaborate models are used; its lighter and more humorous stories appeal to a larger audience.

After the coup d'etat of 1932, dance drama declined since the king and members of the aristocracy could no longer afford to maintain an entourage of dancers and musicians. *Khon, lakhornram* and *nang* survive only by the efforts of interested students, the elite and the Fine Arts Department. The theater at the Silpakorn University produces traditional dance drama annually from October to May. Much-abbreviated productions of *lakhorn-ram* for television enjoy limited popularity, and brief excerpts from the classical dance are performed at most official functions.

The *liké* is the most popular form of dance drama. It is usually performed by itinerant troupes in provincial towns, in small *liké* theaters, or in the villages in the *wat* or on the main square. *Liké* performances are light and spontaneous, virtually unrelated to the formalism of court productions. During the 1960's these performances of *liké* plays appealed mostly to the older generation and to the lower classes, although adapted versions have been produced for modern television audiences.

The *liké* is believed to have developed in the nineteenth century from Malay origins, modified by influences of Thai classical dance drama. Music is provided by a *piphat* band, and the lines are sung or spoken by the actors themselves. The plot has been mainly historical; the dialogue is spontaneous, witty and risqué, with an emphasis on wordplay. Since 1955 the government has encouraged an anti-Communist theme in *liké* plots.

In the North and Northeast there are similar popular entertainments. The *molam* of the Northeast consists, as in Laos, of a declamation sung to the accompaniment of the Laotian *khene*, an oversized seven-tone panpipe. The declamations, improvised after the style of *liké* verse, are set to traditional melodies using simple Lao verse forms and may cover any subject, from the beauties of nature to topical local gossip or national events. The *molam* is also performed in rural Central Thailand, but there it is called *lam tat* and uses different musical accompaniment. In the North, where the analogous musical form is called *saw*, the flute is substituted for the Lao panpipe. In all of these forms the performers are professional entertainers, although more restrained amateur productions are sometimes produced in schools for special occasions.

Another popular entertainment in the Northeast is the *molammu*, which is dance drama similar to the *liké* except that Lao verse forms, language and instrumentation are used. The *molammu*, rather than the *liké*, will be found at rural temple fairs, commemorations of the dead and other social events. Although *liké* theaters are found in the provincial capitals, the *molammu* is more popular than the *liké* in the Northeast.

Under King Rama VI (1910–25) a more sophisticated type of drama was developed which appealed to the educated and official circles. The King, who was himself a distinguished dramatist and writer, was greatly interested in the theater. He established theaters within the palace grounds in Bangkok. In addition, he wrote, directed and supervised the production of many plays during his reign. His dramatic works include plays based on classical Sanskrit themes, translations from Shakespeare and light, humorous dramas depicting contemporary Thai scenes. This type of drama represents the first major attempt to use Western methods and techniques in dramatic presentation, but traditional themes and concepts were not totally overlooked.

Since 1932 Western ideas have influenced Thai dramatic works. In many instances historical and traditional themes are used, but with Western presentation techniques. Luang Vichitr Vadhakarn (1898–1962), a government official, wrote plays based on historical legends and enlivened by semipopular music with the main objective of arousing nationalistic sentiment among the people. With the introduction of motion pictures and television, Western influence on Thai drama has become more pronounced. Life in contemporary society is dealt with in Thai context, and some historical tales and legends are reinterpreted. Adaptations of traditional drama have a limited following, and *like'* and its regional variations still serve as the primary form of dramatic entertainment to the general public.

In addition to classical dances of the court, folk and regional dances are performed in various parts of the country. The *ram wong* (circle dance), a modified folk dance, is still popular in spite of the growing popularity of Western-style dances, and its influence seems to have spread to several other countries of southeast Asia. Accompanied by whatever local musical instrument is available, the *ram wong* is lively and gay. The women form a wide circle and face inward; the men stand behind also facing inward. The steps are simple and repetitious, and primary emphasis is placed on hand and arm movements. In the *ram wong* the dancers may utilize an array of dance motions in combinations according to their will.

The *fon lep* (temple dance of the North) retains its traditional popularity and is frequently performed, particularly in Chiengmai. At *wat* festivals and in Buddhist processions dancers move in stylized, serene and slow motions suggesting spiritual tranquillity and contemplation. The simplicity of the *fon lep* provides a direct contrast to the intricate character of the classical court dance of Bangkok, which is replete with Indian and Khmer influence. The *fon lep* was performed by hundreds of dancers in northern costume for the royal family during the royal visit to Chiengmai in 1961 and 1962.

In the Northeast the *ram kratopmai* (touching poles dance) is still performed. It involves dancing between moving bamboo poles, similar to the *tinikling* dance of the Philippines. The southern *manohra* reflects Malay and Indonesian influences.

In Bangkok and in the larger towns Western-style dancing has gained popularity, especially among the young generation. Latin American and discothèque-style dances have become popular during the 1960's.

Music

Thai music has a seven-note scale of the same octave spread as the Western scale, but the half-tone intervals are not used. Harmony is unknown; a certain variation is achieved by counterpoint. No compound meters exist; all music is in either 2/4 or 4/4 time.

Melodies traditionally were not written down but were passed from generation to generation by wandering minstrels. About 1,200 have been preserved over the past 500 years, all by anonymous composers. They are categorized into 36 groups, each of which serves a particular function or mood. For instance, one group of 13 melodies is for anger; one of 21, for sorrow; one of 7, specifically for the Buddhist ideal of contemplation; and 2 of 4 melodies each, for joy and excitement.

There are perhaps 50 kinds of musical instruments in Thailand, many of which are local types of flutes, stringed instruments, drums, percussion-melodic pieces and gongs. Modified copies of ancient Indian instruments are sometimes used. In 1934 the Fine Arts Department initiated a continuing project of collecting and recording all the different types and preserving the art of playing them. Many Thai can play at least one instrument, and local combinations of all sorts are played at festivals.

Formalized music to accompany *khon* and *nang* dance dramas was played by a type of band called the *piphat,* which uses only wind and percussion instruments. The one type of wind instrument used is a woodwind with reed, played in the manner of the clarinet. Percussion instruments are either melodic (capable of playing a scale) or rhythmic, without specific pitch. The melodic section comprises several kinds of instruments similar to the xylophone, and one type, consisting of small discs or chimes hung in a rattan frame, produces an effect like the glockenspiel or the celesta. The rhythm section has drums—some played with the bare hands and some with sticks—and gongs in different groupings. Bands may be made up of from 5 to 20 or more pieces.

Song festivals and local dancing are traditional in the provinces. At village festivals in the Central Plain the men often engage women in song contests. The soloists sing their verses accompanied by the rhythmic chanting of the others. The lines are risqué and humorous, using the play on words which is so popular with the Thai. Often the chorus sings a nonsensical background, the last syllable of which the soloist uses in his verse. It is a quick, spontaneous affair much enjoyed by the audience.

Itinerant minstrel troupes still thrive, visiting *wat,* village and family festivals to provide music and songs for the celebrations. In the remote villages, especially in the Northern and Northeastern Regions, flirtations are still frequently carried out in terms of songs and music.

Toward the close of the nineteenth century, when traditional drama was no longer performed, the training of musicians ceased. Prince Damrong Rachanuphab, former Minister of the Interior, attempted in 1930 to record as much of the traditional music as possible with the Western musical notation system. As a result of a few similar attempts to continue this effort, much of the traditional music was transcribed and some of it was published in 1951.

The Fine Arts Department has been instrumental in preserving and reviving traditional music. Serious efforts by the government began in 1946 when appropriations were made to increase the salaries of Thai musicians and dancers. Sangkhitsala, the open-air music hall, was established, and traditional music is performed there once a week for 5 months annually. Although public response has not been very warm, the musical programs continue. The Fine Arts Department also trains and supports a *piphat* orchestra to record and broadcast traditional music.

Western popular music (military marches, popular songs and jazz) has had a strong impact upon Thailand, resulting in blends of Thai and Western melodies and instrumentation and in the introduction of harmony. In the 1890's some traditional Thai melodies were transcribed for a royal marching band using Western instruments. After 1920 drama achieved popularity partially because of the melodic tunes used in the productions. Luang Wichit Watthakan capitalized upon the popular taste in music and drama by filling many of his plays with tunes which were sung and played all over the country. More recently, traditional Thai melodies have been transcribed for the Western scale. Western musical films have developed among the Thai a taste for Western popular tunes. A few Thai educated abroad are dedicated to American jazz. King Bhumibol Adulyadej is an accomplished amateur musician and composer.

Another influence of the West may be found in the development of Thai popular music. These are songs patterned after Western songs, using Western scales and techniques, though modified by

Thai themes and melodies. Another type of popular modern music consists of the adaption of Thai lyrics to purely Western popular melodies.

Crafts

The Thai are highly proficient in metalworking. Best known is their nielloware (*thom*) or silver holloware featuring etched patterns. A black metallic powder is packed into the etching, and heat is applied until the powder fuses and sets. Elaborately wrought ceremonial swords were formerly much in demand and are still popular with collectors. The craftsmen of Chiengmai are famous for their Buddha images, bells and dragons cast in brass.

The carving of teakwood bookcases decorated with lacquer work or gold and silver inlays is practiced on a small scale. Painted lacquer utensils are also popular.

Traditional methods of weaving and embroidery are still practiced in some aristocratic households. In the rural areas, especially in the Northern and Northeast Regions, many women still weave traditional garments, such as women's skirts (*phasin*) and men's lower garments (*phakhaoma*), either from homegrown and homespun cotton or silk yarns, or from purchased commercial yarns. Synthetic dyes are widely used in preference to earth and vegetable dyes of the past, both in the homespun products and in commercial products of the newly developing silk industry.

Silk weaving has been revived on a commercial scale since the 1950's, both in provincial centers and in Bangkok. Thai silk imprinted with traditional patterns is in great demand, notably by foreign consumers. Domestic demand has also increased since Queen Sirikit popularized the wearing of garments made of Thai silk.

LITERATURE

Thai literature derives in part from traditional tales depicting the life of the people and the historical experiences of the nation. These tales have been passed from generation to generation through oral communication with the result that differing versions of the same story are common. The oral literary tradition has served as an important source of inspiration for classical and popular literature. Its fundamental traits are an appreciation of wit and humor and the love of life and nature. Written literature did not develop until after the national Thai script was created by King Rama Khamhaeng in 1293.

With the influence of the existing Mon and Khmer cultures in the Chao Phraya basin and through direct contacts with India and Ceylon, the character of Thai literature was transformed. The introduction of Buddhism and Hinduism superimposed a new value system upon the society. Religious doctrine and the quality of virtue and justice became the main subjects, particularly in classical literature. Sacred Buddhist texts in Pali, the Jataka tales, the Hindu epic poem *Ramayana* and several secular Sanskrit writings provided the basis for early literature and their literary forms.

Classical (1293–1850)

Classical literature was fostered by royal patronage. It was written by members of the king's court, the aristocracy and by an organized group of writers, such as the Krom Alak (Royal Scribes) maintained by the king. Several Thai kings were notable poets themselves who worked in collaboration with their own Krom Alak.

Until 1800 all classical literature was in verse. Five main categories of poetic forms may be distinguished as well as many subcategories. The *chan* and *kan* forms were of Indian origin and were used mainly in works concerning religion or deeds of the king. The less elaborate poetic forms, which have become popular since the late Ayutthaya period, are the *khlong* and *klon,* which appear to be indigenous. *Rai* is free poetry, essentially rhymed prose. The poems are narratives or expressions of the poets' feelings on love, separation and similar subjects.

Acoustic effects, including assonance, alliteration, internal and external rhyme and tonal harmony, are most important in Thai poetry. Double entendre, allegory, metaphor and simile figure prominently among the favorite poetic techniques.

During the reign of King Narai (1657–88), the "golden age" of classical literature, a favorite court pastime was the composition of clever verse in addition to the more lengthy and serious literary works. King Narai and several members of his court were distinguished poets in their own right. According to tradition, the most brilliant young poet of his court was Siprat, the master of repartee and short verse, who is recognized for his wit, scintillating humor and penetrating satirical observations of society. His long poem *Kamsuan* (Lamentations) is considered a masterpiece.

Another brilliant period in classical literature was during the reign of King Rama II (1809–24) who was himself a noted poet. His court poet, Sunthorn Phu (1786–1855), popularized *klon* and helped to make literature known to the common people.

Most historical literature tends to glorify kings, princes and national leaders in their heroic deeds, such as the defense of the kingdom or their military conquests. King Rama II wrote the

194

epic poem *Yuan Phai* acclaiming the victory of King Trailok over the kingdom of Lannathai. The liberation of the Thai kingdom from Burmese rule in 1593 by Prince Naresuan is exalted in the epic poem *Taleng Phai* written by Prince Patriarch Poramanuchit (1790–1853).

Much of the original Thai literature which derives from local folklore and legends follows the theme of the nobility struggling to preserve honor and virtue and pursuing love with the aid of the supernatural. Generally there is a happy ending, and justice prevails. *Phra Law* is the most notable example of the early literature. It is a tale of romance and adventure involving a lifelong rivalry between two clans in the North which ended with the tragic death of the hero. Written in the style of mixed verse and poetic prose called *lilit*, the work has had considerable influence on Thai literature. *Phra Law* is traditionally ascribed to King Trailok (1448–88), but it has been so embellished through the centuries that it is not known which of its parts is the original.

The romance of *Phra Aphai Mani* written by Sunthorn Phu may also be included in the category of Thai literature derived from folklore and legend. *Khun Chang Khun Phaen,* by Sunthorn Phu, deals with a romantic triangle against the backdrop of middle-class society in the late Ayutthaya period.

Another type of purely Thai literature is the lyric travel poem called the *nirat*. It is generally an allegory of love and the pain of separation, exalting the beauty of nature and travel. One of the best examples is *Nirat Narin* (1809), composed by Narinthibet, a young poet during the reign of Rama II.

Buddhist literature, both canonical and noncanonical, has provided inspiration for many Thai classical masterpieces, such as the *Traiphum,* attributed to a fourteenth-century king of Sukhothai. This account of Buddhist cosmology vividly describes heaven, earth and hell with the purpose of illustrating the operation of *karma* (the law of cause and effect) which is the central Buddhist doctrine (see ch. 12, Religion).

Jataka tales furnish plots for many Thai works. The most widely known in the *Mahachat,* which is the story of the next-to-the-last reincarnation of the Buddha. For several centuries it has been rewritten in almost every generation, and since the monks have frequently drawn sermon texts from it, it is widely known by the peasantry. The *Samutthakhot,* considered the best of *chan* poetry, was begun during the reign of King Narai and was completed by Prince Patriarch Poramanuchit of Bangkok. It is a noncanonical Buddhist work which originally was in Sanskrit.

The most important Hindu influence on Thai classical literature is the epic poem *Ramayana,* called *Ramakian* in Thai. There are three extant versions, one written by King Rama II specifically for *khon* staging. Because the writers of the *Ramakian* frequently improvise by causing the characters to accomplish heroic deeds in Thai settings, these versions differ greatly from the original ones.

Secular Sanskrit writings also inspired several Thai master-pieces, one of which is *Anirut,* written by Siprat, the brilliant young poet believed to have lived during the reign of King Narai.

Another representative literary work of foreign origin is *Inao,* a tale from the cycle legend of Panji, the Javanese hero-king. Two versions of this story were written in the eighteenth century, and the version for the classical dance drama was written by King Rama II.

In addition to written works, the literary heritage includes legends, tales, anecdotes, adventure stories and proverbs. The world portrayed was one in which each individual must watch out first and foremost for himself and his own interests. There was little sympathy for the dupe. These tales and anecdotes were sung by minstrels and dramatized by wandering troupes.

In 1802 a new trend was begun in Thai literature. The Chinese classic *San Kuo Chih Yen I* (Romance of the Three Kingdoms) was rendered into Thai by Chao Phraya Phra Khlang and was entitled *Sam Kok.* This book was the first major Thai work in prose.

Modern (1900–   )

Since the early 1900's, Western literary forms and techniques exerted a prominent influence on Thai literature. The drama, the essay, the short story and the novel were introduced, and prose gained prominence as the main form of literary expression. King Rama VI (1910–25) himself was a prolific and important writer. He translated into Thai poetic forms such well known Shakespearean plays as *Romeo and Juliet, The Merchant of Venice* and *As You Like It.* The Hindu epic poem *Mahabharata* inspired several of the king's dramatic poems. He also wrote numerous essays on the subject of Thai national consciousness. His greatest works include dramatic poems such as *Phra Ruang, Matthanapatha* and *Huachai Nakrop.* A literary club, organized under royal patronage, included such leading modern literary figures as Prince Phitthayalongkorn, Prince Damrong Rachanuphab, Chao Phraya Thammasakmontri and Phraya Chaisurin. After the coup of 1932, however, royal patronage of literary endeavors came to a halt.

Contemporary writers and novelists capitalized on the Thai

readers' traditional love for romance and adventure. Many of the classical works were transcribed into simple prose. Novels and short stories became popular, and their readers increased with the rising literacy rate.

Among the better known works published since 1940 is *Yellow Race, White Race* by Prince Akat Damakoeng. The novel deals with problems faced by a European-educated Thai who returned to his country. Similar realistic themes were featured by a new group of authors, including Dokmai Sot, Kukrit Pramoj, Luang Vichitr Vadhakarn and Chot Phraphan. Most of the new authors come from the ranks of the aristocracy or the educated elite.

A number of scholars, including Prince Chula Chakrabongs, have written historical biographies and essays in social criticism and psychology. The readership of such works, however, tends to be limited.

Although prose has emerged as the favorite literary style of readers during the 1960's, some of the classical forms were being revived. Government-owned television channels have featured a number of *khlong* and *klon* type verse plays and poetry contests. Some of the Thai classics, including *Phra Law,* have been translated into English.

INTELLECTUAL TRENDS

In the field of intellectual expression, the Thai approach appears to have been mainly pragmatic and practical. The primary concern seemed to be daily life and how to achieve the most harmonious function and the fullest possible enjoyment and appreciation of it. Before the modern era Thai scholars produced chronicles of events, simple lists of plants, treatises on astrology for court ritual, compilations of medical practices (chiefly Indian) and compendia of military theory (see ch. 12, Religion). Laws were collected and codified according to royal intents and purposes (see ch. 3, Historical Setting).

Philosophical and metaphysical questions arising from Buddhist and Hindu doctrines and traditional animistic beliefs have been discussed in all periods. The system of merit and the doctrine of *karma* serve as basic guidelines for traditional behavior. Certain philosophical positions on ethical problems—such as justice, charity and good government—are woven into various legends and into stories by various authors. In recent years there have been formal debates on the proper interpretation of passages and concepts in the Tripitaka (Buddhist scripture). Various interpretations of *nirvana,* the soul (*winyan*), the nature of *karma* and other doctrines have been discussed both formally and informally (see ch. 12, Religion).

Personal and collective experiences were the basis of certain values and beliefs which have been preserved in a collection of proverbs, maxims and aphorisms. The earliest-known compendium of this type is the *Maxims of Phra Ruang,* attributed to the first king of Sukhothai. Commentaries on manners, behavior, family life, military conduct and national values have usually appeared in verse form; the most recent are the *Sawatdi Raksa* of Sunthorn Phu and the commentaries on court practices written by King Rama V. *Kritsana's Exhortations to Her Sisters* by Prince Patriarch Poramanuchit expounds the ideals of Thai womanhood.

In the nineteenth century Western ideas and concepts swept the country, and many of the traditional ideas and values were modified. Science and technology have emerged as new fields of inquiry. Education has become a major concern of the government. Students and officials have been sent abroad, particularly to European countries and to the United States. Fields of Western thought which have been explored include the physical and biological sciences, medicine, engineering, economics and administration. At the same time, a reexamination of Buddhist philosophy has been undertaken with a view to applying its main tenets to contemporary life.

CHAPTER 12

RELIGION

The established religion of Thailand is Theravada Buddhism. Theravada (the Doctrine of the Elders) is also known outside of the country as Hinayana (the Exclusive Way or Lesser Vehicle) Buddhism in contrast to Mahayana (the Expansive Way or the Greater Vehicle) Buddhism of China and Japan. Other religions that are represented include Brahmanism, Islam and Christianity as well as Confucian ethical teachings and the animism of the hill peoples. In the mid-1960's, however, their followers made up less than 7 percent of the population, and none of those beliefs was expanding rapidly.

Buddhism is a vital force permeating the daily lives of the people. The country is often referred to as land of the yellow robes, an allusion to the seeming omnipresence of Buddhist religious figures.

Theravada Buddhism is the official religion of the country, and under the constitution the king, although the protector of all religions, must be a Buddhist. Instruction in Buddhist morals must be given in all schools except those in Moslem areas where local officials may exercise an option to omit it. Buddhist observances usually accompany the celebration of national holidays and other official occasions.

Beside its formal division between laymen and religious officials, Buddhism in Thailand has an elaborate ecclesiastical structure. The structure comprises an hierarchical organization of the Sangha (the Buddhist order) and a large number of *wats* (a walled compound containing a Buddhist temple and associated buildings), some of which are subsidized or maintained by the state. The ordinary rural *wat* is both the religious and the social focus of the village. The urban *wat* occupies an important but less central position in the community.

Buddhism in Thailand has absorbed many beliefs and practices from other religious systems. Pre-Buddhist Hindu philosophies held that the universe was eternal, self-creating, cyclical and in a constant state of change. Life itself was seen as an expression of this transitory reality. The individual was born and reborn in a series of incarnations which were higher or lower depending upon the moral quality of his actions in his previous existences. Buddha neither denied nor affirmed these concepts, because his primary concern was winning freedom from frustration and pain rather than offering metaphysical explanations of the universe.

The concept of *karma* (the whole ethical consequence of one's acts) was apparently accepted with little question by Buddha's early disciples. Buddha himself spoke in terms of *karma*, but he evidently did so only to clarify his teaching in the intellectual idiom of the day. The concept of *karma*, however, became and remains a central doctrine of all schools of Buddhism.

Like other scriptural religions Buddhism's formal doctrine is intertwined with customs, attitudes, traditions and daily actions that are not sanctioned in writing. Some of these derive from the Indian milieu in which Buddhism developed; others were added after Buddhism reached the mainland of Southeast Asia. The result has been a complex of belief and practice which is in many ways uniquely Thai and which penetrates virtually every phase of the nation's life. Cosmological and astrological concepts influence not only religious ritual but many aspects of political and economic life. Beliefs about the supernatural continue to affect human relations, work, recreation and the arts.

The doctrine of *karma* is basic to an understanding of the hierarchical structure and the temporal social values of the traditional Thai society. The Buddhist code defines the ethical and moral system and provides the justification for the Sangha. Ideally every man aspires to enter the Sangha, at least temporarily, sometime during his life. Religious themes and moral prescriptions shaped an artistic tradition which is still vigorously alive. Popular religious beliefs and institutions are changing, but in a society which has taken so much of its character from them, they do so slowly.

HISTORICAL BACKGROUND

Only a small part of the Thai religion is recorded in scriptural writings. The Theravada scriptures, the Tripitaka (Three Baskets or Collections), are written in Pali, which is the canonical language of Theravada Buddhism, rather than in Sanskrit, which is the principal scriptural language of the Mahayana schools. The Tripitaka has also been written in Thai and the other Southeast Asian languages. It consists of the Vinaya, the rules of the monastic order, the Sutras, the texts giving the teachings of the Buddha, and the Abhidharma, the philosophical speculations. To these was added the Traiphum ("Three Places"—earth, heaven and hell) which was compiled in the fourteenth century and gave a vivid picture of the universe.

According to tradition Buddhism entered Southeast Asia in the third century B.C. The first Pali inscriptions found in the area, however, indicate only that it was well established sometime between the third and sixth centuries A.D.

While Buddhism was expanding into Southeast Asia it was experiencing a profound change in its Indian homeland. After the reign of Asoka, who was king of the Indian state of Magadha in the third century B.C., Mahayana Buddhism developed a different interpretation of the Buddha's teachings from Theravada Buddhism.

Mahayanism revised the basic teachings of the Buddha on two points. Instead of upholding individual salvation through individual effort, the new form declared that the moral ideal was the happiness of all living creatures and that living beings as a whole are aided in their struggle toward *nirvana* by the actions of the individuals who have achieved enlightenment but who defer entering into *nirvana* in order to help others achieve the same goal. Such a redeemer is called a *bodhisattva*.

To the followers of the Mahayana schools Gautama was one of many *buddhas* (persons who have reached "enlightenment") who had been and were to be incarnated. Moreover, *buddhas* and some of the *bodhisattvas* acquired the status of supernatural beings, who were conscious of human needs and responsive to prayers and offerings. Salvation was not restricted to the few who could maintain the strict "Eightfold Path" of the Theravada doctrine; it was available to many through devotion to a *buddha* or a *bodhisattva*. The human life of Gautama, although it was not denied, was regarded as a manifestation of the cosmic force which reveals itself in countless other *buddhas,* who are not merely his predecessors or destined successors but all the rulers of paradises in other worlds.

After the reign of Asoka Theravada and Mahayana Buddhism coexisted in India for several centuries. Mahayana gradually gained greater favor, but in time it was displaced by new forms of Hinduism. Both schools spread into central and eastern Asia, and Mahayanism became dominant.

Documentary evidence suggests that the Thai, who were living in the Yunnan area of China in the early Christian centuries, were at least superficially exposed to Theravada and Mahayana Buddhism. Buddhism, however, initially played a relatively minor role among those who subsequently moved into the area that is now the Northern Region. It did not become a sustained, permeating force in the society until the periods of strong Buddhist influence from Burma in the eleventh century and from Ceylon in the thirteenth century. The Ceylonese influence was the most important because it was associated with the Theravada teachings, which were the dominant forms of Buddhism in twentieth century Thailand.

The pattern of Thai religion has three main components, which are commonly distinguished by their origins. They are Theravada Buddhism, Brahmanism-Mahayanism and, as a term of convenience, animism. Although these three components have not always been in perfect harmony, they have normally reinforced one another in an integrated religious complex.

Formally Theravada Buddhism is concerned with the individual's release from suffering and his attainment of *nirvana* through discipline, virtuous conduct, meditative concentration, transcendent comprehension and devotional practice. Orthodox Theravada Buddhism, however, does not provide supernatural beings to intercede for men in their difficulties and crises. Early converts retained their old gods and demons but envisaged them as subject to the same law of *karma* as were all living beings. People could then continue to pray to the old gods, who were now transformed into Buddhist saints or angels, and to explain ill chance and sickness as the action of demons and malevolent spirits, who could be placated. Believers could also seek spiritual solace and otherworldly goals in the teachings of the Buddha. To the average villager the two realms of belief complement each other by one answering the problems which the other ignores or handles in an emotionally unsatisfactory way. Together they form the one system that is Thai Buddhism.

COSMOLOGY

Traditional Thai beliefs about the cosmos were derived from ancient Indian sources and were acquired primarily from the Khmer. Among them was the important belief that mankind was constantly influenced by forces which emanated from the directions of the compass and from the stars and planets, and which could produce either prosperity or havoc. It was necessary, therefore, that individuals, social groups and especially the state act in harmony with these astral forces. Individuals followed the signs offered by astrology, the lore of lucky and unlucky days, and many other rules. Harmony between the kingdom and the universe was achieved by organizing the state as a microimage of the universe. Brahman priests or astrologers were the intermediaries between the court and the forces of the cosmos. An essential component of traditional belief was this concept of the Kingdom as the Image of the Universe.

The Kingdom as the Image of the Universe

The royal palace formed the magical center of the traditional Thai kingdom. Around the palace lay the city which was known as the "Heavenly Royal City" or the "City of the Thewa" and which in its physical plan both copied and symbolized the universe. The royal palace was the residence of the sacrosanct Thai monarch, his queens and court officials, who bore titles that corresponded to those of their celestial counterparts. The king was regarded as an incarnation of one or sometimes two gods—usually Siva or Vishnu—who flew down from their heavens at the time of his coronation and entered his body. After the death of the king his corpse was covered by a cloth that symbolized Siva's death shroud.

The king's throne faced the east, and a division arose between right-hand and left-hand positions. Right-hand positions were associated with the south and the military; those on the left were associated with the north and civilian functions. There were also queens, great administrative divisions, departments and offices, and provinces of the right and left. During the Sukhothai and the early Ayutthaya periods the kingdom had five divisions: the capital city and four principalities of the north, south, east and west. When the kingdom expanded the system or organization became more complex, but the division of the country into right-hand (southern) and left-hand (northern) sections continued. During the reign of King Chulalongkorn the traditional Thai state was modernized and remodeled into a Western European pattern, but many ancient ceremonies and festivals were maintained for a number of years. Recently the government has revived a number of these festivals and rituals in a reaffirmation of the values and the continuity of Thai civilization.

Astrology

In modern Thai society the harmony desired between the individual and the cosmos is still sought through the use of astrology. The timing of many important occasions, such as housewarmings, marriages and cremations, is seldom set without consulting an astrologer or a monk who will make lunar calculations to ensure an auspicious date. Lucky and unlucky dates vary according to the year, month and birthday of each person. In November, March and July Tuesday is considered an unlucky day on which to start an important undertaking. Certain specific dates, such as the thirteenth, fourteenth and fifteenth of every lunar month, are lucky or auspicious. Most religious ceremonies are held on the eighth day of the waxing moon, the day of the full moon or the eighth and fifteenth days of the waning moon. Much of this old belief is declining, but elements of it, especially in the villages, still persist.

Supernatural Beings

Supernatural beings are also subject to the laws of *karma*. Their attributes and relative positions are determined by their merits or demerits in previous incarnations. They can be categorized as *thewada* (gods of various grades who inhabit the heavens), *chao* (guardian spirits) and *phi* (goblins and ghosts), which may be good or evil. Most of the deities of the Hindu pantheon have declined in importance among the whole population, although Indra (Phra In in Thai), "the protector of the earth" and everything on it, and a few others are sometimes invoked in fortunetelling and prayers.

The abode of the *thewada* is in the heavens above Phra Meru. They are beings who may at one time have been human and who have risen to their exalted state through accumulated merit. Each of the six heavens inhabited by ordinary *thewada* and the nine heavens inhabited by Brahmanic *thewada* are ruled by a king. The most important kings are versions of the Indian deities Siva, Brahma, Vishnu and particularly Indra. Other deities include "The Master of Heavenly Spirits" and "The Lord of Death" who, assisted by minor demons, presides over hell. Active belief in this pantheon appears to be dying out, and young people are increasingly vague in their knowledge of it.

The most important *chao* are those of the house compounds. Fixed on a post in the compound of most houses in the Central Region is a small spirit dwelling. Food offerings are made to the *phra phum* (the spirit of the place) on the anniversary of his installation in the house, the New Year and other special days. The spirit is told of the arrival of guests who are to stay any length of time, of projected journeys by members of the family and of births and deaths. Its help is also sought during illness and misfortune.

Other spirits protect gardens, the ricefields and the *wats*. The spirit of the ricefield is worshiped only once a year at the beginning of the rice planting; the Rice Goddess receives offerings when the seedbed is to be prepared and when the harvest is due. The Mother Earth Goddess often receives offerings at transplanting time (see ch. 20, Agriculture).

The Lao villagers of the Northeast and Northern Regions do not have *phra phum* shrines in their house compounds, but they may have a community spirit house where the spirits of the founders of the village are honored annually in the sixth lunar month. Each family in the village and the representatives of any offshoot hamlets take an offering, which is usually a parboiled chicken, to the village shrine in the sacred grove. There the ancestral spirits are informed of births, deaths, animals owned, trips planned and other matters, and the spirits' protection from illness, ghosts and evil spirits and their help in bringing on the rains is sought. The ancestral spirits are remembered only as a group, and it is not clear whether any other spirits beside the actual "founding fathers" are included. The spirit house, which is big enough to hold a seated man, is made in the form of a dwelling rather than in the form of a Buddhist temple like the *phra phum* shrines. Most of these spirit houses are quite old, and they will probably not be rebuilt. Many villages have already discontinued the custom and have cut down the sacred grove to make additional farmland.

One class of *phi*—mostly jungle dwellers—consists of such malevolent beings as vampires, weretigers and will-o'-the wisps and such benevolent beings as tree spirits. A very large tree is thought to harbor a powerful spirit, and passers-by will make token offerings. River and mountain spirits are important locally. The river spirits often receive elaborate offerings during Loi Kathong, the Festival of Floating Lights (see ch. 8, Family).

The ghosts of persons who died violently under mysterious circumstances or whose funeral rites were improperly performed are another class of *phi;* almost all of these spirits are malevolent. In contrast the ghosts of notable people, who reside in small shrines along the roads and who are referred to as "spirit lords," are often petitioned in prayers and can enter and possess the bodies of mediums to give oracles. Among the more important of the spirits and ghosts is the *phi bop* (ghoul spirit), which is a disembodied evil spirit that may enter human beings at the instigation of a witch and consume their internal organs. Although it is usually regarded as having a human collaborator, it may be found free-floating near slaughterhouses.

Although the government actively seeks to discredit belief in spirits and refuses to hear witchcraft cases in the law courts, most farmers apparently still partially believe in them. The spirits provide an explanation for illness, accidents and ill chance, and the rituals designed to placate them give the farmer the feeling that he is taking active steps against troubles with which he would not otherwise be able to cope.

KARMA, SOUL AND REINCARNATION

Central to the structure of Buddhist beliefs is the doctrine of *karma* which states that every act, word and thought has its consequences. These consequences are the result not of the intervention by any supernatural being but of the operation of cosmic principle. Evil acts have such evil consequences for the doer as suffering misfortune in this world, or being reincarnated in hell or as an animal in some future existence. Good acts yield such good consequences as prosperity in this world, birth in heaven or a high position in the world in some future state.

Each higher incarnation brings one closer to *nirvana,* but probably most persons aspire to a less elevated reward, such as rebirth in this world with happiness, wealth or honors, or rebirth in a lower heaven with the luxury of many wives and retainers.

A concomitant of the belief in *karma* is the view that all forms of existence are related because every form originates in a previous one. The entity which undergoes reincarnation is not, however, the soul in the sense of personality minus body but an envolving complex of attributes, merits and demerits. It is this complex which seeks and may achieve perfection as it passes from existence to existence.

The three components of a human being are *kai* (a material body), *khwan* (the body-spirit or life-soul) and *winyan* (an "ego" soul). The two souls are often not distinguished. The *khwan* can reside either inside or outside the body. When it is inside it acts as a life-soul bestowing life, health, success, wealth and prosperity. Usually, it resides in the head, but it may reside in other parts of the body. If it leaves the body, wanders away or becomes lost or injured the individual sickens or dies. A timid and easily frightened person is said to have "a tender and delicate *khwan.*" A present is "things for *khwan.*" When one has a great fright he says his *"khwan* is lost." When a baby cries out in sleep or fright the mother pats its breast gently saying, "Oh dear *Khwan,* please stay with the body." Sick children have their wrists tied with a piece of unspun thread to "bind in the *khwan.*"

The *winyan,* which is a more abstract concept, is the soul that endows an individual with thought, will, perception and consciousness. It represents the individual's share of the universal or cosmic intelligence.

The Thai theory of the soul plays an important part in the beliefs about disease and the afterlife. Disease is believed to be the loss of the *khwan,* the intrusion of a foreign spirit in the victim's body or an imbalance of the body's components. A foreign spirit can enter the body either by its own volition or by being projected into it by a witch; the common treatment in either case is exorcism. In the imbalance of the body's components the element that most commonly causes difficulty is "wind" (see ch. 9, Living Conditions).

THE PATH TO NIRVANA

Nirvana, which is the ultimate and complete state of content-
ment and fulfillment, can be achieved at the end of a final
incarnation by recognizing the Four Noble Truths and by following the Eightfold Path.

The Four Noble Truths are that all life is sorrow, sorrow is
the result of desire, cessation of desire ends sorrow and cessation
of desire is attained by following the Eightfold Path. The Eightfold Path, which is known as the Middle Way, includes right
understanding, right purpose, right speech, right action, right
livelihood, right effort, right attentiveness and right concentration.

Those seeking perfection must abstain from eight actions:
taking a life, taking what is not given, indulging in improper
sexual pleasure, speaking a falsehood, drinking intoxicants, eating after the hour of noon, attending entertainments and using
bodily adornments, and sleeping or lying on a comfortable cotton-
filled mattress. The first five are commonly accepted as the minimal requisites of social ethics and religious morality. People may
explicitly promise to keep all eight on Wan Phra, which is the
Buddhist "duty day" that occurs 48 times in the lunar year.
Monks observe all these precepts as part of the 227 rules of the
Patimokkha, which is translated as "that which should be made
binding." For the monks, however, the third rule requires
chastity and not merely the avoidance of improper pleasures.

THE SANGHA

Membership in the Sangha offers the best way for a devout
man to follow the Eightfold Path to *nirvana.* It does not guarantee his success, but it provides him the best environment in
which to seek his salvation. Women may not join the Sangha,
but a son who belongs may earn merit for them. Women may also
acquire merit by following the precepts, attending religious services and giving offerings and donations. The more devout may
become nuns in order to observe greater moral and spiritual
discipline than would be possible in a secular environment. Buddhist nuns numbering about 30,000, in early 1967, were found
largely in urban areas.

The organizational structure of the Sangha is important to
the strength of Buddhism. Its hierarchical system permits the
maintenance of close supervision and good discipline according
to the rules of the Vinaya Pitaka (Collection of Monastic Discipline and Morality), one of the books of the Buddhist scriptures.
It also facilitates the flow of information and instruction between
the levels of the hierarchy.

The head of the Sangha is the Supreme Patriarch, who is officially known as *sakala sanghaparinayaka somdech phra sangharaja* and who is appointed by the king in consultation with the leaders of the order of monks. Until the Sangha Act of 1962, which came into effect in January 1963, Sangha organization was a tripartite system composed of the executive council, legislature and the judiciary. Members of the executive council were appointed by the Supreme Patriarch and were subject to government approval. Members of the legislative branch, which had a maximum of 45 members, were appointed by the Supreme Patriarch on the basis of seniority and eligibility. This group was chiefly concerned with administrative regulations and monastic duties and discipline. Furthermore, it made recommendations to the Supreme Patriarch about appointments to the judiciary.

After the reorganization of the Sangha in January 1963 the tripartite system was replaced by a single administrative body, which was presided over by the Supreme Patriarch. This Sangha Supreme Council includes all dignitaries in the Sangha holding the rank of *somdech phra raja gana,* which is next in order to the Supreme Patriarch, and selected officials holding the next lower rank of *phra raja gama.* Those whom the Supreme Patriarch appoints have a 2-year term of office, but they may be reappointed. The Supreme Council has legislative and judicial powers and functions because it enacts laws governing the Sangha, it is empowered to reorganize the national administration of the Sangha and it is authorized to prescribe punishments and try infractions of ecclesiastical law.

Below the Supreme Council the organization of the Sangha corresponds to the major administrative units of the national government. In 1964 there were regional, provincial, district and precinct levels of ecclesiastical administration. The more than 20,000 monasteries are the basis for this hierarchical system.

Buddhism in Thailand has two sects. The older and larger sect is the Mahanikaya; the other is the Dhammayuttika sect, which was founded in 1933 by King Mongkut to enable monks to live a more scholarly and disciplined life. The ration of monks in the Mahanikaya sect to those in the Dhammayuttika sect is 35 to 1. The differences between the sects concern only minor points of discipline rather than interpretations of doctrine. The Dhammayuttika is more intellectual and conservative, but both sects are equally esteemed by the public.

Liaison between the Sangha and the government is maintained through the Department of Religious Affairs in the Ministry of Education. The Department keeps records of things like ecclesiastical property and membership. It also operates a large publishing office that prints textbooks, which are written by monks, and books about Buddhism for the general public. Through the Department the government supervises the 115 royal *wats,* which it has supported since the inauguration of the constitutional government in 1932. There are two ecclesiastical colleges, under royal patronage in Bangkok, which grant an equivalent of the bachelor of arts degree and which train monks in languages, comparative religions, philosophy, science and Buddhist studies. Graduates are expected to become teachers in the *wat* schools.

The government is the legal owner, in the name of the Sangha, of all *wat* lands. *Wat* grounds are considered sacred and cannot be used for secular purposes unless a ceremonial act of annulment is performed. The *wats* control nonsacred income-earning land, which is administered for the Sangha by a government agency. Public schools in which monks teach are operated within *wat* grounds. *Wat* aid to the indigent is an important contribution to public welfare.

In the mid-1960's there were 150,000 monks and 87,000 novices living in more than 23,000 *wats.* Less than half of these *wats* had *uposatha* (halls of ecclesiastical rites) in which ordination ceremonies could be held; in the remainder only ordinary religious services were conducted for the monks and the laity.

Many villages have no resident monks and depend upon the services of monks from *wats* in neighboring communities. Others have only one or two monks or novices in their *wat* compound. Such *wats* are supervised by the abbot of the nearest residential *wat* in the commune. When a full complement is required for certain ceremonies and religious functions, other monks come from a nearby *wat.*

Authority within the Sangha is relatively light, and within the limits of monastic discipline, monks and novices enjoy a freedom of choice in the exercise of their vocation. Some may specialize in certain non-Buddhist activities, such as spirit healing or fortunetelling; others may devote themselves to personal projects, such as raising money to build a road. If a monk wants to go to another *wat,* he tells his abbot and leaves. Villagers whose *wat* has no monk may invite a man of their choice without consulting his abbot.

CEREMONIES

State Ceremonies

Both before and after the establishment of constitutional rule some of the traditional state ceremonies, in which Theravada

Buddhism played a permanent part, fell into disuse. After World War II, however, official interest in the old observances has revived, and some new ones have been instituted. Among the most important celebrations are the memorial day of the Ghakri dynasty (April 6), Chatra Mongkhon, or Coronation Anniversary (May 5), Pued Mongkhon, or Plowing Day (May 11), the Queen's Birthday (August 12), Chulalongkorn Memorial Day (October 23), the King's Birthday and National Day (December 5) and Constitution Day (December 10).

In the past state ceremonial occasions were confined to Bangkok, but the government has now extended their observance to provincial capitals, district seats and village schools. Every program follows a common pattern. Schools within a short distance of the administrative centers must send their classes to the observances. A government officer reads the proclamation of the day, which is followed by speeches, a brief religious service and the singing of patriotic songs. Schools some distance from a town hold their own observances and report on them to the district office. On some holidays commune headmen (*kamnan*) and village headmen (*phy yai ban*) as well as schoolchildren are required to attend the ceremonies at the district headquarters. These official holidays, which are designed to increase national consciousness and patriotism, have only limited significance for most villagers.

Agricultural Ceremonies

The farmer traditionally marks the growth of the rice crop by ceremonies propitiating the spirits of the grain and the soil and any other supernatural beings that may be involved. Only remnants of these elaborate rites remain, but most peasants still make simple offerings to the spirits during seeding, transplanting and threshing. The government has revived some of the old Brahamanic ceremonies and sponsors a Buddhist ceremony of blessing seed rice.

An important rural celebration is the winter fair, which opens about December 5 and lasts for approximately a week. These fairs were originally local agricultural festivals held at the village *wat* after the harvest season. The authorities have adopted the idea and have inaugurated annual provincial fairs. Each district is invited to display its agricultural produce and handicrafts. Prizes are awarded for the best stalls and for the best displays of rice by individual farmers. Patriotism and national unity are stressed in the ceremonies.

Family-Centered Ceremonies

Buddha prescribed no ceremonies for birth, death and marriage, but the Hindu rites, which were retained and adopted by the people, involve the participation of Buddhist monks. The resulting ceremonies, which are held in the house rather than in the *wat*, have no scriptural sanction. The monks participate only to chant the appropriate Buddhist sutras (scriptural texts) or to provide holy water.

The propitiation of an individual's *khwan* is a basic feature of Thai family rites. Any ceremony for the welfare of a person, animal or plant is referred to as the "making of *khwan.*" On important occasions, such as birth, ordination into the priesthood, marriage, return from a long journey or the reception of an honored guest, a *khwan* ceremony is performed.

Of all the life-cycle and family-centered ceremonies funeral rites are the most elaborate. When a person is dying he is made to fix his mind upon the Buddhist scriptures or to repeat some of the names of Buddha. If the last thoughts of the dying person are directed toward Buddha and his precepts, the fruits of this meritorious act will be reaped by the deceased in the next incarnation. After death other meritorious acts are performed for his benefit, such as attendance at the wake and giving food to the officiating monks. Every effort is made to banish sorrow, loneliness and the fear of spirits by means of music and fellowship.

Confirmation is a modern ceremony first introduced by King Chulalongkorn, who feared that boys going to Europe for an education before they had entered the Sangha might be lost to Buddhism. The ceremony involves taking an oath of reverence to Buddhism, and it includes rites derived from those performed at the ordination of novices.

Wat-Centered Ceremonies

Ceremonies in the *wat* consist of those which benefit the entire community and those which primarily affect the Sangha. The first type includes the rites held on such occasions as Makha Buja (an important February holiday which marks the beginning of the season for making pilgrimages to Phra Buddha Baht, or Buddha's Footprint Shrine), Wisakha Bucha (a festival commemorating Buddha's birth, enlightenment and death), Khao Pansa (the holiday marking the beginning of a 3-month Buddhist lent) and Thot Kathin (a festival during which robes and other items are given to the monks by the laity). Ceremonies of the second type include ordination, confession, recitation of the 227 monastic rules and distribution of new robes after Thot Kathin.

Of all the ceremonies affecting the Sangha ordination is the one that most involves the laity, in both physical participation and spiritual benefit. Frequently, before a young man makes his initial entry into the Sangha a ceremony is held in the home of the aspirant (*naga*) which prepares him for the ordination. His *khwan* is invited to enter the Sangha with him; otherwise, evil and illness may befall him. He is informed of his parents' happiness with his decision, of the sacrifices they have made for him and of the life of austerity and discipline he is to begin. At this ceremony the *naga* is dressed in clothing that symbolizes the garments of Siddhartha Gautama Sakyamuni, who became the Buddha. After receiving a blessing he is led on horseback to the temple as a royal prince wearing a crown, shaded by an umbrella and escorted by flagbearers, musicians and others. The escort carries the gifts of flowers, cloth, candles, incense and food for the *naga* and for the monks who will ordain him. In the villages this phase of the ceremony, although still colorful, is abbreviated and simplified in comparison to its elaborate urban version.

At the *wat* the procession circles the hall of ecclesiastical rites, three times in clockwise direction, which symbolizes a joyous occasion. The aspirant is presented to the monks, exchanges his princely garments for simple white ones and takes his place before the *khana song*, which constitutes a validating quorum of monks for the ordination. The aspirant asks three times in Pali to take refuge in the Buddha, in his teachings (in the Dharma) and in the Sangha. After a brief sermon the officiating monk hands him the yellow robes. Having donned them the aspirant bows and presents gifts to two monks (*achan* or instructors); he then asks again for refuge and to be given the precepts. An instructor leads him in the proper Pali responses, which include recitation of the 10 precepts that govern novices. The ceremony ends at this point if the novice expects to remain only for a few days in the Sangha; if he wishes to become a regular novice he bows to the officiating monk and asks him to become his mentor. His acknowledgment of his acceptance ends the ceremony, unless he is ordained as a monk on the same day.

If a youth, after a period of service as a novice, wishes to become a monk his ordination will be marked only with simple festivities by friends and relatives of the family. Before the day of ordination villagers will assemble to prepare the personal items needed by a monk and the offerings of candles, flowers and money. Food is provided by the novice's family, and work is accompanied by conversation and pleasantries. On the day of ordination relatives and friends travel by foot or bus to the hall of ecclesiastical rites of the *wat* where the ceremony is held.

The ordination ceremony is a simple one. The novice is questioned about his eligibility by one of the monks, after which the novice asks to be admitted to the Sangha. His mentor then formally sponsors him and invites further interrogation of the novice, who is questioned twice more before the *khana song*. The *khana song* is asked three times to voice any objections it may have to admitting the novice into the Sangha or to show its consent by silence, and the ceremony is concluded.

THE WAT IN VILLAGE LIFE

In the country the social life of the community revolves around the *wat*, which is in contrast to the situation in urban areas where the *wat* is only one among many institutions. Besides its religious activities a village *wat* may function as a charitable agency, recreation center, dispensary, school, community center, place of safe deposit, community warehouse, home for the psychotic and the aged, employment agency, news agency, public guesthouse and information center.

The *wat* is a walled compound containing both small and large buildings. Its principal axis runs east to west, and the entrance is on the east. The number and arrangement of the buildings vary. A large *wat* may have a temple for lay worshipers (*vihara*); a temple for monks (*bot*); a dormitory for monks, novices and temple boys; a library, a number of public halls (*sala*); a stupa (*chedi*); and frequently, the public primary school. Separated from the rest of the village by tall coconut palms and fruit trees, the *wat* is surrounded by a cool grove and is shaded by coconut, betel palm and sacred bodhi trees. *Wats* are usually situated on the edge of the larger villages and towns, but in small villages the *wat* is adjacent to the physical center of the village.

Monks and novices play a major role in both the religious life and the secular affairs of the village. Their services are indispensable to the observation of marriage and funeral rites. In addition, they help to preserve the social stability of the community by their example of patience and serenity. They may give free medical diagnosis and treatment, act as arbiters in personal quarrels or serve as bankers in the safekeeping of a villager's savings. Many monks and novices participate actively in construction works around the village, such as helping to build a bridge or a primary school.

It is one of the duties of the monks to beg for their daily food. In central and southern Thailand individual families provide cooked rice, curry and other foods, but in the north some villages are divided into sections that provide food for the monks on a particular day. Giving food to the monks brings the donor merit because the monk is regarded not as a beggar but as one who grants the laity the privilege of gaining merit by feeding him.

He does not thank the donors for their gifts, which are usually offered with some respectful phrase, such as "Honor be to you."

The most meritorious act that a rural Thai male can perform is to join a *wat* as a novice or a monk for a period of time. The only requirements are that he be at least 20 years of age, healthy, free from debt, have the consent of his parents or wife, understand the rules and prescriptions of the order and show at least a token knowledge of Pali. Although most men can meet the requirements many never enter the Sangha because of economic and personal reasons.

The importance of the *wat* in the life of the people is suggested by the magnitude of their contributions which are made in cash, gifts and volunteer labor. The daily food offerings are only one of the farm household's contributions to the support of the *wat* and its residents. Religious expenditures consume from 5 to 10 percent of the annual cash income of the average farm family. Villages are called upon at irregular intervals to make sizable contributions of money or labor for repairs or for erecting new buildings. When the support needed is greater than the community's resources word is sent to neighboring villages, which usually send help. People do not feel imposed upon when asked to contribute to the building fund of a *wat* in another village because this gives them an opportunity to acquire merit and the assurance of reciprocated help in the future.

MODERN TRENDS IN BUDDHISM

Western philosophical and scientific thought, to which an educated urban minority has been exposed for a century, has both challenged dogmatic religious belief and stimulated new affirmations of Buddhist faith. In this small but influential group some individuals have developed a sceptical indifference to or a positive disbelief in the assertions of Buddhism. Others, however, have found in science a support for Buddhist teaching and an aid in removing the accretions of superstition, which have accumulated over the centuries. These modern Buddhists base their ideas on the teachings and principles revealed in the actions of Buddha himself, which they see as devoid of occultism and in correspondence with verifiable reality. Accordingly, such doctrines as the Law of Karma, the Four Noble Truths and the Eightfold Path are not matters for religious faith but demonstrable propositions for rational comprehension. Faith, a prop in the early stages of understanding, becomes increasingly unnecessary as the individual progresses along the path to enlightenment, which in shown by the Buddha.

The neo-Buddhists are generally more interested in Buddha's

moral example than in his metaphysics. They stress both his sympathetic, compassionate nature and his love and respect for people. For some Buddhists even desire is meritorious when it is directed toward such social goals as the elimination of poverty, ignorance and disease. Many persons believe that the reward for following the Eightfold Path is not postponed to future existences but that it comes in the present life in the form of spiritual and psychological well-being and serenity. Some neo-Buddhists not only reject the notion of heavens and hells but interpret *nirvana* as nothing more than the extinction of the individual.

Neo-Buddhist ideas seem to be spreading, but they do not represent an organized movement with a well-defined doctrinal position. They continue to be significant as an effort to reinterpret the traditional religion in the light of scientific knowledge and to adapt it to the needs of a society that is changing under the impact of the modern world.

RELIGIOUS MINORITIES

The religious affiliation of the large ethnic Chinese minority, which numbers 2.6 million, is difficult to identify. Some have adopted the Theravada beliefs of the Thai, and many participate in the activities of the local *wats*. Most Chinese, however, consciously retain the mixture of Confucian social ethics, formal veneration of ancestors, Mahayana Buddhist doctrines and Taoist supernaturalism that is characteristic of the popular religious tradition in China. To the Chinese community as a whole neither organized religion nor theological speculation has a strong appeal. Besides the monks, most large Chinese temples have lay associations attached to them.

Chinese monks are distinct in many respects from Thai Buddhist monks who dress in saffron-colored robes, beg for their food each morning, are free to leave the Buddhist order at any time they choose and participate fully in the lives of those around them. In contrast Chinese monks wear loose-fitting, long-sleeved jackets and trousers, receive their food from the temples to which they are attached and must upon entering the priesthood take a vow of celibacy and lifetime service. Chinese monks play a minor role in the lives of those who attend *wat* services and are usually consulted only at times of misfortune or death.

The influence of Islam is confined chiefly to the southernmost provinces where the vast majority of the country's Moslem believers are found. Numbering about 1 million persons they are predominantly ethnic Malay. The remainder are Pakistani im-

215

migrants in the urban centers and ethnic Thai in the rural areas of the Central Region.

Except in the small circle of theologically trained believers the Islamic faith in Thailand, like Buddhism, has become integrated with many elements of Brahman and animistic beliefs and practices. It would be impossible to draw a line between the shamanistic superstitions which are found in the Malay culture and those elements which are Islamic. Shamanistic exercises, which are intended to drive off evil spirits, exhibit many Islamic influences, while Islamic ceremonies invariably contain aspects of superstitious belief.

In the mid-1960's the country had over 1,350 mosques, and a national Islamic Center was being built. All but five of the mosques were associated with the Sunni branch of Islam; the remainder were of the Shia branch. These mosques were attended by 19,000 religious dignitaries. Each mosque had three formally appointed officials, the *imam* (priests), its chief figure, the *katib* (preacher) and the *muezzin* or *bial* (the Moslem crier).

One of the duties of the *imam* is to provide religious instruction to the Moslem children of the village. The instruction is available early in the morning before classes begin in the village school. Those who want to continue their religious education may attend a *pondok* (religious secondary school), of which there were 190 in 1964, with an enrollment of 10,800 students.

The Hindu population of the country in the mid-1960's was estimated at 7,000. There were three centers of worship, which were located in Bangkok and which had a combined attendance on religious holy days of about 200 persons. Hindus also maintained a public library, a cemetery of their own and a school for over 200 pupils.

The Christian population both Catholic and Protestant is less than 100,000. A high percentage is Chinese, although there are several Catholic Lao communities in Nong Khai Province in the Northeast Region and several Vietnamese Catholic communities in southeastern Thailand. The Christian missions have had only modest success in winning converts among the Thai, but they have played an important role as agents for the transmission of Western ideas to the Thai. They have opened hospitals, introduced Western medical knowledge and sponsored some excellent private elementary and secondary schools. Through their schools the missions have been able to reach many of the Thai urban elite who plan to have their children complete their studies abroad in English or American Universities.

CHAPTER 13

SOCIAL VALUES

Despite variations between the rural and urban populations, heightened by Western influence in urban centers, the ethnic Thai, who make up nearly 90 percent of the population, are a relatively homogenous people, unmistakably united by tradition, custom, social patterns, language and basic values.

A sizable Chinese minority, in 1967 numbering more than 2.6 million, in an estimated population of 34.2 million, stems from a culture distinctively different from that of the Thai, although many of its members are of mixed Thai-Chinese ancestry, and the group as a whole has made important adjustments to the Thai environment. The Malays of the Southern Region are ethnically distinct from the Thai but are closer to them in basic social values and orientation than are the Chinese. Other minorities are too small or too isolated to enter importantly into the dominant Thai pattern of life and outlook.

The basic values of Thai culture were developed in a predominantly rural society, but in their essentials they have been upheld by townsmen and villagers alike. Western influences and domestically generated social, economic and political change are inevitably altering the Thai inventories of good and evil, of virtue and vice. The traditional terms, however, still remain as basic reference points on the list, and there is no indication that they will soon be displaced. These key values may be considered as falling into three categories—spiritual development and the attainment of merit; individual responsibility; and status ranking and authority. From them may be derived the image of the ideal person as conceptualized by the Thai.

Most Thai feel that both men and women should be moderate in demeanor, respectful to elders and social superiors, self-reliant, generous, honest and self-disciplined. Traditionally, the ideal man was, and generally remains, the Buddhist monk—an individual devoting himself to the attainment of ultimate perfection by personal discipline, meditation and virtuous behavior. On a more practical level he is depicted as one who has served in the Buddhist temple for some months or years, has attained merit from this and other activities, is a good provider for his family and is an active leader in his community. The ideal woman is pictured as a good wife and mother, respectful, obedient and helpful to her husband, a wise manager of the family purse and a devout Buddhist.

A major goal of most Thai is the attainment and accumulation of merit, achieved by serving at least temporarily as a monk, by conforming to the Buddhist moral code and by performing meritorious acts. Among the rural male population service in the Sangha (Brotherhood of Monks) is the main path to social esteem and prestige. Theravada Buddhism provides a comprehensive system of moral values and ethical precepts, but within wide limits the individual is free to interpret its principles and rules for himself and to follow those which he finds most congenial, trusting that the merit accumulated thereby will counterbalance the demerits of his lapses (see ch. 12, Religion).

Of the values associated with merit-making, one of the most important is generosity. Any act of giving, regardless of whether the recipient is a temple, an individual monk, a relative or a friend, brings the donor some degree of merit and the expectation that he will be rewarded. Certain kinds of generosity are more virtuous than others. Contributing money for the construction of a temple, for example, is one of the most meritorious acts one can perform, second only to becoming a monk.

The Thai say that to gain merit by generosity a person must sincerely want to give and must not later mar the act with regrets. For example, when a number of Thai peasants were asked the question, "Who would receive more merit, a farmer who gave 30 baht (see Glossary) and had no regrets or a farmer who gave 50 baht but wished he had given only 25?" all but a few answered that the first farmer would. But practical accounting is also important. When asked, "Who would receive more merit, a farmer who gave 25 baht with no regrets or a farmer who gave 1,000 baht and wished he had given only 25?" more than half thought that more merit would result for the second farmer. Their explanation was that so much good would be realized from the 1,000 baht that the donor, even though he regretted all but 25, would eventually gain more merit.

One of the fundamental values of the Thai is individualism. It is expressed in the feeling that, within wide limits, each person is and should be responsible only to himself and that his actions are no one else's concern. Individual freedom of action is highly prized.

Living in a society in which few social relationships are institutionalized or even clearly defined, but are patterned after the basic patron and client model, the individual has great latitude for the expression of idiosyncrasies. Deviant behavior may not be condoned, but it is considered the concern of the individual, and he will not be interfered with except in extreme cases. There is also a strong disposition to avoid face-to-face conflict. If a villager gets too far out of line, negative sanctions of noncooperation and ultimately social ostracism may be imposed by his fellows. Expulsion from the village is the ultimate sanction, usually reserved for persons believed to be witches (possessed by a *phi bop*, a ghoul spirit) (see ch. 12, Religion). In the city there is more opportunity than in the villages to deviate from accepted standards of conduct and more likelihood of intervention by the agencies of the law. Everywhere, however, the range of permissive social behavior is relatively wide.

The individualistic nature of Thai culture, placing responsibility for self squarely on the individual, is reflected in the pattern of status ranking and authority. The concept of *karma,* by which persons attain particular positions in life according to their merit, militates against any concept of social equality between men. Thai society is an elaborate hierarchy of status in which each individual sees himself as above or below but seldom precisely equal to those around him. A feature of this pattern is a system of highly formalized respect usages which are expressed in language, gesture and posture. Perhaps the first social act a child learns is the gesture of respect (*wai*), which is made by pressing the palms together as in prayer. The gesture is used in a variety of ways, from simple salutations, particularly between persons of different status, to veneration of Buddha. Similarly, there are prescribed ways of sitting in the presence of superiors and of handing items to them or receiving items from them.

Instructions in morality given to Thai public school children stress the desirability of behaving properly toward superiors and subordinates. In a lesson summarizing desirable personal characteristics children are cautioned to show proper deference to their superiors, not to be concerned with their own comfort before the comfort of superiors and, if they become superiors, wherever they go, to look after the comfort of their inferiors.

The hierarchical system stratifies individuals rather than social groups, and although the authority of persons in high places is readily accepted, the individualistic values of the Thai work against the dictatorial exercise of authority by individuals. A superior must act with tact and some delicacy if he wishes to retain the acceptance of his position by subordinates. Only where compliance to the demands of authority can be compelled, as by the state through its legal machinery, is more direct application of authority feasible. Even here the government has found it better to persuade and lead the people than to command them. The Prime Minister has instructed district officers to respect the traditions of the society and administer their districts paternalistically rather than autocratically. In the village the headman leads by persuasion and by guiding villagers to a consensus in the village meetings rather than by decree.

The Thai expect leaders to exercise authority, however, and the concept of what constitutes the legitimate exercise of authority is broad. The Prime Minister, for example, at one time advised the people not to wear highly colored or bold-patterned clothing or to roll their sleeves, commenting that these things were in bad taste and were the mark of hooligans. There was no indication of any general feeling that the Prime Minister had invaded an area of personal liberty; it is also significant that his wishes were by no means universally followed. If authority is exercised discretely and in conformity with Buddhist concepts of virtue and righteousness, the Thai are willing to accept it over a broad range of activities and interests. Aside from recognition of the power of government to compel, authority is respected, but the Thai also insist that authority respect their integrity and independence of action.

The family is not the tightly organized group familiar in societies in which descent is reckoned only through the male or female line and in which the extended family group has a primary claim on its members throughout life. The basic loyalty of the individual is to the family group forming his household, but the strength of kinship bonds outside the household depends largely on the accidents of proximity and personal preference. Among the people generally, kinsmen may maintain warm personal relations with one another throughout their lives, but only the nearest relatives have binding claims, and the ties between friends and neighbors are often as close as those between all but immediate kinsmen.

Friendships play an important role in the life of the Thai peasant, particularly among the men. Friends are often described as "die friends" or "eating friends." The "die friendship" is an ideal not often realized, for it requires a willingness to sacrifice even life itself, if necessary, for the sake of the friend. In the past members of bandit gangs sometimes made such formal pacts with each other. Less binding but often close "eating friendships" are formed between men of about the same age. Formalized friendships between adolescent boys involving reciprocal duties and privileges on the pattern of "blood brotherhood" can be found in the Northern and Northeast Regions. Such friends are called *siu*.

A value resembling the Chinese concept of "saving face" is that of *kreng chai*. The term is usually used in reference to one's attitude toward superiors. *Kreng chai* involves the desire to be self-effacing, respectful, humble and extremely considerate, as well as the wish to avoid embarrassing other people or intruding or imposing upon them. Since the Thai abhor being thought weak, cowardly or afraid, the concept of *kreng chai* can be used to rationalize weaknesses where they exist. Thus, an employee can say to himself, "The thing which prevents me from criticizing my employer is not fear of him but rather thoughtfulness in not wanting to upset and disturb social relationships; I don't want to put my employer in an embarrassing situation."

Such attitudes help explain why the Thai like to use a middleman in negotiations or in other relationships where the principals might risk embarrassment if they dealt with each other directly. The middleman can cushion, absorb or cover up aggression, lack of generosity and fear.

Moderation and serenity are among the most important Thai social values. Moderation is thought of as a means to good health and the keynote of successful social relationships. One should be friendly, pleasant and polite to other people—not too involved, yet not too distant—and moderation should be maintained even in the closest relationships. Children are taught to show respect and deference to parents, but they are not expected to be compulsively dutiful or obedient. Serenity, mildness and nonaggression are perhaps most frequently named as the most important of all personal values. One may be educated, industrious and generous, but if he is not self-controlled he cannot be a really good man.

Most statements of praise or admiration will include references to a person's ability to refrain from showing his feelings. In the Thai view men who never show their feelings help everyone to live more happily together. They are thoughtful persons—serious persons, who do not want to cause trouble. Similarly, most statements of condemnation include comments on the offender's belligerence and aggression. Persons who lie, gossip, use rude or insulting language or who persistently irritate or threaten others are almost universally disliked.

People tend not only to avoid unhappy or emotionally charged situations but to take whatever pleasure they can in the passing moment. As a consequence most observers have characterized the Thai as fun-loving, carefree and endowed with a delightful sense of humor. Others, however, assert that all these manifestations of affability, politeness and apparent gaiety may not be expressions of carefree lightheartedness but techniques of implementing the main rule of social intercourse, which is, "avoid face-to-face conflict." Such traits permit the individual to keep the most persons at a distance by confining their social intercourse to the entertaining, jovial and inconsequential. The only way to establish greater intimacy is to establish oneself as a superior or an inferior in the basic patron-client relationship (see ch. 7, Social Structure).

Until the relative status of two persons is established, it is difficult to speak or act properly. Polite speech requires the use of personal pronouns and polite particles based on status differences, since there are no neutral terms, and it is the province of the superior, rather than the inferior, to initiate action. For this reason the polite course in dealing with strangers is to grant them nominally superior status by using the pronouns and particles one would use toward a superior until their status is known. On first encounters it is usual to ask a number of personal questions: the person's age, his plans and the cost of his clothes. This usage has, in fact, come to be regarded as an expression of polite interest.

The picture of the Thai as uncomplicated, amiable and carefree must be qualified in various ways. In some rural areas actual cases of theft are almost never encountered; nevertheless, frequent references to stealing are heard in conversations. In other regions thievery is fairly common, especially in bad crop years. Individuals who help themselves to other persons' property sometimes use force but more often use stealth. Fear of such thieves causes rural families seldom to leave their homes unattended.

The term *chai yen* (literally, "cool heart") is roughly the equivalent of composure and self-control. A person should have *chai yen* and not *chai ron* (literally, "hot heart"), that is, impulsiveness, impatience, quick temper and oversensitiveness. Hostility and aggressive feelings are often, however, expressed indirectly, as by insulting an animal or child in the hearing of the person at whom the feelings are directed, or vicariously, as by watching aggressive sports, such as boxing, soccer or cockfights. Gossip and backbiting, although disapproved of, provide indirect release of such feelings.

A person with *chai yen* is never caught unaware or uncomposed. He does not permit himself to be found in an embarrassing situation, but if found out despite himself, he maintains a calm and serene demeanor. Although *chai yen* is a generalized attitude, appropriate to all aspects of life—work, friendship and responsibility—it shows up most clearly in situations of stress. A person with *chai yen* ignores an insult; he seldom becomes angry but by his cool demeanor lets his antagonist appear foolish.

A related concept, expressed by the word, *choe,* indicates "indifference," "unconcern" or "disinterest." Whereas *chai yen* is complimentary, *choei* is often not. The person who is *choei* is simply indifferent to and uninterested in other persons as persons. Such a person can tell a lie successfully, duping others with a straight, or "poker," face. *Choei* carries no necessary connotations of mendacity and dishonesty and under some circumstances can be complimentary. A monk, for example, might be pleased to be thought *choei,* since it resembles the Buddhist virtue of *uppekha* (detachment from persons and things), implying not indifference, however, but objectivity and impartiality. For most laymen, on the other hand, *choei* implies a callous coldness and indifference that are not entirely admirable.

To feel that things are not intrinsically important, to be coolhearted and to be as uninvolved as possible, are—if not carried too far—general Thai values. Contrasting but not conflicting with the value of detachment are the three other chief virtues of Buddhism: compassion for others (*karuna*), loving kindness (*metta*) and emphatic joy (*mudita*), which find expression in hospitality, generosity, friendship and courteous consideration of others.

SECTION II. POLITICAL

CHAPTER 14

THE GOVERNMENTAL SYSTEM

The government in mid-1967 was based on the Interim Constitution of 1959 which provides for a political system of executive primacy. Official efforts to replace the interim version with a permanent constitution continued, but there was little indication of when the new constitution would be adopted and promulgated. A new draft constitution, however, was in the final stage of deliberation.

Thailand is a unitary state with a highly centralized government in which all important agencies of power and initiative are concentrated in Bangkok. The territorial administrative units in the provinces, districts, communes and villages exist to implement the decisions of the central authorities; there is little local initiative or flow of power from the provincial and local levels to the capital.

The King represents a strong and unifying national symbol. He exercises his limited powers through the executive, legislative and judicial branches into which the government is divided. The political role of the monarch is, however, largely confined to ceremonial functions.

The chief executive of Thailand in 1967 was Prime Minister Thanom Kittikachorn, who succeeded the late Prime Minister Sarit Thanarat in December 1963. Prime Minister Thanom was assisted by a small group of military and police officers and a body of professional, high-ranking civil servants. These officials rule the nation with a firm hand, and as the government was constituted in 1967, they were not answerable to any constitutional bodies in the conduct of state affairs.

The centuries-old autocratic tradition persisted in spite of recent but limited experience with a Western form of representative government. In the mid-1960's there was little significant indication of any popular pressure for a system of government with strong parliamentary control over the executive establishment.

THE TRADITIONAL PATTERN OF RULE

In ancient Siam the monarchical rule was paternalistic. The King was called *pho khun,* which means father-lord, or father-ruler. The introduction of Brahmanism in the fifteenth century brought with it the Khmer doctrine of the divinity or near-divinity of the king, and he was thenceforth regarded as *cakra-vartin* (universal sovereign) and *bodhisattva* (one destined to become a *buddha*). He personified all virtue as well as the symbol of authority, and his actions or commands were not questioned. He could be addressed only in a special language of deference, and all persons were required to prostrate themselves in his presence.

The King, who was both sacred and remote, stood alone above the law. He appointed all officials and held the power of life and death over all his subjects. In theory he owned all land and was the recipient of all state revenues; there was no distinction between his personal and public funds.

Certain theoretical limitations were inherent in the Brahmanic concept of the kingship. Under the ancient Hindu-Buddhist code of law called the Thammasat, the King was bound to uphold the four principles of justice: to assess the right and wrong of all services or disservice rendered to him; to uphold the righteous and the truthful; to acquire riches only through just means; and to maintain the prosperity of the state only through just means. In addition, the Thammasat required him to abide by the 10 "kingly" virtues (almsgiving, morality, liberality, straightfor-wardness, gentleness, self-restriction, nonanger, nonviolence, forbearance and rectitude) as well as the five moral precepts (not to kill; not to steal; not to commit adultery; not to tell an untruth; and not to take intoxicating drinks). If the King did not rule justly, tradition sanctioned his overthrow.

In the nineteenth century the old absolutist rule was altered in form by the impact of Western ideas, particularly after the reign of King Mongkut (1851–1868). Missionaries, traders, journalists and advisers to the government had gradually introduced new concepts of freedom and equality. Furthermore, young Thai had been sent abroad in increasing numbers to learn the ways of the West; they did not number more than 300 at any time, but their influence was significant. In Europe they absorbed the novel doctrine of parliamentary democracy. King Chulalongkorn (1868–1910) voluntarily modified a number of the more extreme features of monarchical rule. The old system itself, however, remained untouched, and there were few indications of popular dissatisfaction with it. It was not until the early 1930's that the small group of European-educated officials and intellectuals began to seriously question the absolute monarchical rule (see ch. 3, Historical Setting).

EVOLUTION OF CONSTITUTIONALISM

Since the coup of 1932, Thailand has had seven constitutions. The most recent is the Interim Constitution promulgated in 1959, which remained in effect in mid-1967. In order to replace this interim version with a permanent document the government in mid-1967 was giving final readings to a draft constitution for adoption and promulgation in the near future.

The first constitution promulgated in June 1932 was written by the civilian promoters of the 1932 coup. It ended the long era of absolutist monarchy and introduced a system of parliamentary government and limited kingship. Under the new system the king was stripped of all real powers except those of amnesty and the prerogative to propose amendments to acts passed by a unicameral legislature, which was not obligated to accept his proposals. Sovereign power was theoretically vested in the people and was to be exercised on their behalf by the king and by the legislative, executive and judicial branches of the government. In reality all power was retained and exercised by the small group of coup leaders.

The first constitution of June 1932 was succeeded within two decades by five other versions: December 1932, May 1946, November 1947, March 1949 and March 1952. Although there were variations in defining the structure of government and in prescribing the powers and the responsibilities of governmental agencies, certain themes remained unchanged. The king was placed "above politics" and was vested with only nominal powers. The principle of a separation of powers was upheld, but the government was dominated by an oligarchical, executive leadership. There was little communication between the government and the people.

The surface features of government looked like those in any number of other states, but these external features were the least significant. Imported ideas and institutions did not sweep away the habits and beliefs of centuries; rather, the new had to accommodate the old. Although the coup of 1932 introduced forms of constitutionalism, much of the spirit and many of the techniques of absolute rule continued to underlie subsequent governments.

The Interim Constitution of 1959

When Field Marshal Sarit took personal control of the government in 1958, the 1952 Constitution was abrogated, and on January 28, 1959, the Interim Constitution was promulgated. Despite official efforts to substitute a permanent version for the interim one, the 1959 Constitution remained the basic law of Thailand in mid-1967 (see fig. 11).

The Interim Constitution is a short document containing only 20 articles and is reportedly based on the 1953 constitution of Egypt. It specifies three separate branches of government: legislative, executive and judicial, which exercise their powers in the name of the King, who is the head of state.

Legislative power is vested in the Constituent Assembly, which is responsible for the drafting of a permanent constitution, in addition to its legislative functions. The Assembly consists of 240 members who, along with its president, are appointed by the King. Only one article of the Constitution deals with the judiciary, and it states that "Judges are independent in conducting trials and giving judgments in accordance with the law."

Although the Constitution states that "sovereign power emanates from the people," it is evident throughout the document that sovereign power is exercised by the executive branch, which is not subject to removal by either parliamentary action or periodic election. The Constitution contains no provision for the removal of the Prime Minister. All Cabinet members are accountable only to the Prime Minister.

The most striking feature of the Constitution is Article 17, which defines the constitutional emergency powers of the executive branch. It states:

> During the enforcement of the present constitution, wherever the Prime Minister deems appropriate for the purpose of repressing or suppressing action whether of internal or external origin which jeopardize the national security of the Throne or subvert or threaten law and order, the Prime Minister, by resolution of the Council of Ministers, is empowered to issue orders or take steps accordingly. Such orders or steps shall be considered legal.

The only limitation on this emergency power is that such orders or steps shall be "made known" to the Constituent Assembly. The Constitution contains no reference to the rights and duties of citizens.

The Draft Constitution

The Draft Constitution was written by the Constitution Drafting Committee of the Constituent Assembly established in 1959. When it is promulgated, it will represent the eighth basic law since 1932. In mid-1967 there was no definite indication of when it would be ready for promulgation, but government leaders continued to express the hope that it would be soon.

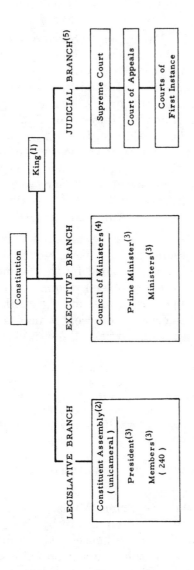

LEGISLATIVE BRANCH

Constituent Assembly[2]
(unicameral)

President[3]

Members[3]
(240)

Constitution

King[1]

EXECUTIVE BRANCH

Council of Ministers[4]

Prime Minister[3]

Ministers[3]

JUDICIAL BRANCH[5]

Supreme Court

Court of Appeals

Courts of
First Instance

(1) The King is nominal head of state. Legislative, executive and judicial powers are exercised in the name of the King.
(2) Duties include legislative functions and drafting of Constitution.
(3) Appointed by the King.
(4) The Council of Ministers is also the Cabinet, which is independent of the legislative branch and not subject to any
   periodic change through election. All laws, royal rescripts and royal commands must be countersigned by the
   Prime Minister or a minister.
(5) Judges chosen by Judicial Service Commission and appointed by the King.

Figure 11.—Constitutional Structure of Thailand in mid-1967.

In broad outlines the Draft Constitution describes Thailand as "a democratic state with the King as the Head of State." It declares that sovereign power is vested in the people and is exercised by the King through the legislative, executive and judicial branches of government. It further states that the King is also the Upholder of Religion and the Supreme Commander of the Armed Forces; functionally, his power is largely nominal and symbolic.

According to the draft the Parliament (National Assembly) consists of two chambers, the lower house which is composed of popularly elected representatives and the upper house which is appointed by the King. All bills are initiated by the lower house. Parliament may exercise broad but imprecisely defined, supervisory powers over the Council of Ministers or the Cabinet, which is collectively responsible to the legislature. In joint session it may open a general debate into the affairs of the executive establishment and pass a vote of no confidence in the Cabinet. The proposed governmental system has the appearance of parliamentary supremacy as does the system in Great Britain, but actually the proposed powers of Parliament are carefully circumscribed.

The draft is framed so that in times of national emergencies legislative powers may be preempted and exercised by the King through the executive establishment headed by the Prime Minister. For example, if certain fiscal problems require urgent and secret deliberation the King may issue, presumably on the advice of the Prime Minister, an "emergency decree," which is to have provisionally the force of an Act. Article 176 stipulates that:

> During a state of war or state of emergency . . . and when the normal exercise of the legislative power through Parliament may be inconvenient or unfit for the situation, Parliament may resolve to let the King exercise the legislative power through the Council of Ministers by means of issuing a Royal Decree which shall provisionally have the force of an Act.

Moreover, the initiation of money bills requires the prior consent of the Prime Minister.

The document provides that the Prime Minister be appointed by the King and be subject to countersignature by the President of Parliament (president of the upper house), who himself is a loyal appointee. The executive branch is given no express power to dissolve the lower house of Parliament, but because of the extraordinary discretionary powers that are conferred upon the King, it may counterbalance the legislature by exercising a broad range of emergency powers in the name of the King.

THE CENTRAL GOVERNMENT

The government is theoretically organized on the principle of separation of powers. There are separate and clearly distinct executive, legislative and judicial establishments which, in addition to a constitutional monarchy, compose the central government.

The Monarchy

The King is constitutionally the head of the state, and although all power is exercised in his name, he has very little real power. Since the coronation of King Bhumibol Adulyadej in 1950, the prestige of the throne has been greatly enhanced. The relationship between the King and the government has since been most cordial (see ch. 15, Political Dynamics). The influence of the monarchy upon national politics is slight, and its real significance lies in its symbolic representation of national unity.

The King is aided by three agencies: The Privy Council which advises the monarch and, under certain conditions, appoints a regency to exercise royal powers; the Office of the Royal Household which organizes ceremonial functions and administers the finances and housekeeping of the royal court; and the Office of His Majesty's Private Secretariat which performs clerical and secretarial tasks for the King.

The Executive Establishment

The executive branch dominates the other divisions of the government. It makes and implements policy, uses the legislature as an advisory body and supervises the operation of the judiciary. The executive branch is organized into 12 ministries, whose chiefs are all members of the Council of Ministers (the Cabinet) and whose work is supervised and coordinated by the Prime Minister (see fig. 12). In addition, there are a number of quasi-autonomous bodies that perform certain specialized functions under ministerial supervision.

The Council of Ministers frames and implements all important national policies and is the center around which the entire political system revolves. Besides the heads of the 12 ministries it contains their under secretaries, the Prime Minister and two deputy prime ministers. Ministers are chosen by the chairman of the Council of Ministers (the Prime Minister), who is selected by the Constituent Assembly and appointed by the King. The Cabinet meets frequently and formulates legislative proposals and executive policies.

The Office of the Prime Minister

The most important member in the Cabinet is the Prime Minister, who holds the ultimate powers of appointment, investi-

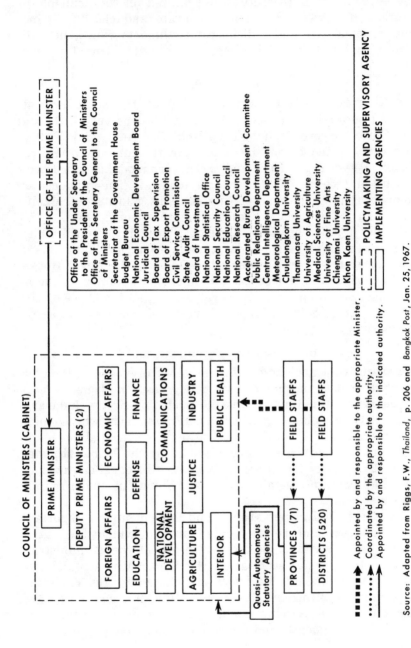

COUNCIL OF MINISTERS (CABINET)

OFFICE OF THE PRIME MINISTER

PRIME MINISTER

DEPUTY PRIME MINISTERS (2)

FOREIGN AFFAIRS
ECONOMIC AFFAIRS
EDUCATION
DEFENSE
FINANCE
NATIONAL DEVELOPMENT
COMMUNICATIONS
AGRICULTURE
JUSTICE
INDUSTRY
INTERIOR
PUBLIC HEALTH

Quasi-Autonomous Statutory Agencies

PROVINCES (71)
FIELD STAFFS
DISTRICTS (520)
FIELD STAFFS

Office of the Under Secretary to the President of the Council of Ministers
Office of the Secretary General to the Council of Ministers
Secretariat of the Government House
Budget Bureau
National Economic Development Board
Juridical Council
Board of Tax Supervision
Board of Export Promotion
Civil Service Commission
State Audit Council
Board of Investment
National Statistical Office
National Security Council
National Education Council
National Research Council
Accelerated Rural Development Committee
Public Relations Department
Central Intelligence Department
Meteorological Department
Chulalongkorn University
Thammasat University
University of Agriculture
Medical Sciences University
University of Fine Arts
Chiengmai University
Khon Kaen University

- - - POLICYMAKING AND SUPERVISORY AGENCY
IMPLEMENTING AGENCIES

■■■■ Appointed by and responsible to the appropriate Minister.
••••• Coordinated by the appropriate authority.
→ Appointed by and responsible to the indicated authority.

Source: Adapted from Riggs, F.W., *Thailand*, p. 206 and *Bangkok Post*, Jan. 25, 1967.

Figure 12.—The Executive Establishment of Thailand in 1967.

232

gation and review. He countersigns all royal decrees, appoints and dismisses other Ministers, presides over Cabinet meetings and controls their agenda. He also appoints and removes civil servants holding the ranks of Permanent Under Secretary and Head of Department. In the doctrine of emergency power, the Interim Constitution promulgated in 1959 authorizes the Prime Minister to take all steps necessary to maintain security and to aid economic progress in a national emergency. He must inform the legislature of such measures, but it has no power to veto them. The Prime Minister supervises the Office of the Royal Household and heads the National Economic Development Board, the National Security Council and the National Research Council. In 1967 Prime Minister Thanom was also the Supreme Commander of the Armed Forces.

The duties and functions of the Office of the Prime Minister are complex and extensive. Placed directly under the Prime Minister, it has the responsibilities of policy formulation, coordination and supervision. Its scope and powers have grown so large since October 1958 that the Office of the Prime Minister has become a government within the government.

Administrative Agencies

Administrative bodies fall into two categories; ministries and quasi-autonomous agencies that are created by statute. All ministries are organized within the same basic pattern (see fig. 13). In 1967 there were twelve ministries: Interior, Defense, Foreign Affairs, National Development, Finance, Industry, Economic Affairs, Communications, Public Health, Justice, Education and Agriculture. The political head of each ministry, who is responsible to the Prime Minister, is a Minister of State. The top civil service official in each ministry is the Permanent Under Secretary of State, who is responsible to the Political Minister. Aided by one or two deputy under secretaries and a small staff, he advises the minister, handles nonpolitical matters and represents the ministry on many boards and committees. Below the Permanent Under Secretary are the various departments, usually three or more in each ministry. Each department headed by a Director General is divided into three or more divisions. These divisions consist of several sections. In addition, many of the departments with countrywide responsibilities maintain provincial and district staffs.

Outside the ministries but subject to their direct control and supervision are a number of quasi-autonomous state enterprises, such as the Port of Bangkok Authority, the Railroad Organization, the Yanhee Electric Authority, the Metropolitan Electricity Authority, the Provincial Electricity Authority, the Thai Mari-

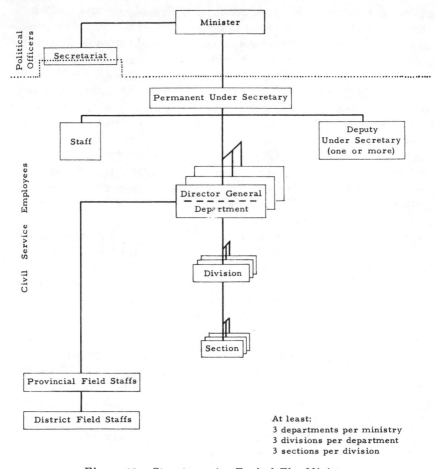

Figure 13.—Structure of a Typical Tha Ministry.

time Navigation Company Ltd., the Tourist Organization of Thailand, the Fuel Oil Organization and the Telephone Organization of Thailand (TOT).

The Legislative Establishment

The major characteristic of the Thai legislature, which was established in 1932 without any institutional basis in national tradition, has been its weakness vis-a-vis the executive establishment. This is the result of persistent misgivings among the ruling elite about the capacity of the electorate and its representatives to participate in the process of government without a lengthy period of tutorial control by the executive. This distrust has been reflected in most of the changes in the structure and the composition of the legislature, which have been instituted by successive governments since 1932. Except from 1946 to 1949, the executive branch has always had the power to appoint at least half the legislature or to appoint all the members of the upper house, during the years when it was a bicameral body. The executive branch, therefore, has usually been assured of a parliamentary majority; hence, the legislature has been largely an instrument of Cabinet rule and has had little influence in the political process.

Between 1934 and 1939 the National Assembly showed a considerable degree of independence. More than one Cabinet was dissolved by a vote of no confidence, and even during World War II the legislature occasionally refused to bow to the executive. After World War II the Assembly found it difficult to preserve the initiative it had developed before the war. The return to power of the military faction in the November 1947 coup further weakened the Assembly as an active force in the nation's politics and government, and it eventually resulted in the Assembly's secondary position to the executive branch (see ch. 15, Political Dynamics).

In October 1958, when Field Marshal Sarit assumed control of the government, he abolished the National Assembly and established a Constituent Assembly that, in addition to legislative functions, was vested with the task of drafting a new constitution. These two responsibilities of the Assembly are conducted separately. Its meetings are normally open to the public, unless closed sessions are requested by the Cabinet or a group fo assemblymen. Parliamentary organization and procedures follow the patterns of European legislative bodies. Most bills and all important bills are drafted in the ministries or the Office of the Prime Minister. After transmission to the Assembly, such bills are then either referred to committee for examination or are introduced directly on the floor, where they are brought to a vote after the third reading. One-third of the total membership constitutes a quorum of which a simple majority is required for the passage of most bills.

Prime Minister Sarit's view was that the Constituent Assembly should serve only as an "advisory body" and should not be given "the right to control the executive branch." In November 1960 the Assembly taking its cue from the Prime Minister voted that its members "had no right to submit questionnaires to Cabinet Ministers on matters within their fields of responsibility." The chief importance of the Assembly has been to legitimize the acts of the executive.

The Judicial System

The Law for the Organization of Courts of Justice, which was promulgated in 1934, continues in its amended form to provide for three levels of courts: the Courts of First Instance, the Court of Appeal and the Supreme Court. The independence of judges in conducting trials and giving judgment is protected by the amended Judicial Service Act of 1954.

The courts are supervised by two separate bodies, the Ministry of Justice and the Judicial Service Commission, which was established in 1954. The Ministry appoints and supervises the administrative personnel of the courts and is responsible for reform in judicial practice and procedures. The Commission is responsible for ensuring the independence of the court system. It appoints, removes and transfers judges on the recommendation of the Council of Ministers, usually on the recommendation of the Minister of Justice. Judges may be removed only on grounds of misconduct or incapacity determined by a board of discipline and the Judicial Service Commission. The compulsory retirement age is 60 and may be extended to 65.

The Judicial Service Commission is an independent statutory body and is composed of eleven members; three are ex officio, namely the President of the Supreme Court, who presides over its sessions, the Chief Judge of the Court of Appeal and the Under Secretary of State for Justice; four are elected from among the senior judges of the Supreme Court; the remaining four are selected from a list of retired judges.

In the mid-1960's there were 108 Courts of First Instance located in nine judicial regions. Eighty-three of these are provincial courts with unlimited jurisdiction in civil and criminal matters. Twenty are magistrate courts, which are situated at the district level in some of the larger provinces, and deal with petty civil and criminal offenses to relieve the burden on the provincial courts. Of the five remaining courts three are located in Bangkok: the Central Juvenile Court, the Civil Court and the Criminal Court. The last two have unlimited original jurisdiction in their respective spheres of competence for Bangkok and the provinces. Criminal offenses committed on the high seas and outside the country by Thai citizens are tried by the Criminal Court. There are two additional juvenile courts in Songkhla and Nakhon Ratchasima, respectively.

The Court of Appeal (Uthorn Court) which is composed of a chief judge and 51 other judges, sits in Bangkok and hears appeals from all the Courts of First Instance throughout the country. It is divided into 17 divisions dealing with civil, criminal and bankruptcy matters. At least two judges must sit at each hearing. Cases of exceptional importance must be heard by the plenary sessions of the court. This court considers appeals on questions of both law and fact, and it may reverse, revise or remand lower court decisions.

The Supreme Court (Dika Court), which is also located in Bangkok, is the highest court of appeal in all civil, criminal and bankruptcy cases. In addition, it has jurisdiction over election disputes. This court consists of the President and 21 judges, and the appeals are heard by 3 judges. Although decisions of the Court are final, the King may be petitioned for clemency in criminal cases.

Cases can be initiated either by the public prosecutors, who are officials of the Ministry of the Interior rather than of the Ministry of Justice, or by the injured person. There is no provision for trial by jury. The judiciary as a whole enjoys a reputation for honesty and competence.

LOCAL GOVERNMENT

The local government comprises administrative units at provincial, district, commune and village levels, as well as at the municipal level. Although self-governing powers are exercised through elective bodies by some of these units, they are quite nominal. The local government bodies constitute an integral part of the national administrative system as implements of policy and control for the central government. The government hierarchy, however, extends only to the district level, and the central government has no regular civil service officials working below that level. The Department of Local Administration in the Ministry of the Interior is responsible for the control and the supervision of all field administrative affairs.

In 1965 there were 71 provinces (*changwat*), 520 districts (*amphur*), 21 subdistricts (*king amphur*), 4,926 communes (*tambon*), 41,630 villages (*muban*) and 120 municipalities (*tesaban*). The division of the country into nine administrative regions (*phak*) was discontinued in 1956.

Province

Each province is headed by a governor (*phuwarachakan* or *kha luang*), who is appointed by and responsible to the Minister of the Interior, and consists of from six to eight districts. The Governor carries out the policies of the central government, supervises the overall administration of the province, coordinates the work of the various ministry representatives from Bangkok and maintains law and order within his jurisdiction. He reviews the reports of district officers and gives final approval to the election of commune headmen. The Municipal Act of 1953 also empowers him with a supervisory responsibility over municipal government. His staff consists of a deputy governor, an assistant governor, a public prosecutor, a chief of police and senior officers from the central ministries, such as Finance, Education, Agriculture and Public Health. The central government representatives are legally responsible to their respective ministries in Bangkok, but they are required to coordinate their activities with the provincial governor.

The Governor also presides over a provincial board composed of the senior civil servants under his administration. It has only advisory functions, and it serves as a channel for the transmission of policy directives from the central government to the district administrations and for coordinative purposes among the various ministry representatives. Formal meetings of the board are usually held once a month and are attended by the district officers.

In the provinces self-governing powers are vested in an elective council, which is composed of a minimum of 24 popularly chosen representatives. The council elects its president from among its members. It exercises only a limited power of check and balance in relation to the provincial executive authority. The budget and the police of the provinces are directly controlled by the Ministry of the Interior. Similarly, provincial councils may be dissolved by the Ministry.

District

The district is a subdivision of the province and has no corporate status. Consisting of 8 to 12 communes it is under the general charge of a district officer (*nai amphur*), who is appointed by the Minister of the Interior and who reports directly to the governor of the province. The district officer stands on the lowest level of central government authority; hence, he is the most important link between the government and the people. Larger districts may be divided into two or more subdistricts in which each is headed by an assistant district officer.

The duties of the district officer are varied and extensive. He is the chief executive and chief magistrate in his district and is responsible for ensuring the execution of laws and policies of the central government. Assisted by 3 to 10 officials he supervises the collection of taxes; issues certificates of birth, marriage, divorce and death; registers schoolchildren, aliens and buffaloes; arbitrates land disputes; and administers local elections.

The district officer also convenes monthly meetings of the headmen of the communes and villages to inform them of government policies and to instruct them in the implementation of these policies. At these meetings commune and village leaders may discuss their various problems and exchange views.

Because of the importance of these officials in effecting social changes at the village level the Ministry of the Interior has instituted a periodic training program in techniques of community development and human relations. In the early 1960's the central government attempted to bring the government to the people and to improve public attitudes toward local authorities by enrolling district officers and some provincial governors in a short-term training program dealing with government policy, human relations, national security, techniques of Communist insurgency, the organization of civil defense and the responsibilities of leadership.

Commune

Each commune is headed by a chief called the *kamnan,* who has a quasi-official status. He is chosen by the headmen of the villages that comprise the commune from among themselves and is confirmed in office by the provincial governor. The duties of the *kamnan* are few, but his prestige is considerable. He is in charge of recording vital statistics, assists the district officer in maintaining public peace and helps him collect taxes. He supervises and coordinates the activities of village headmen and convenes a monthly meeting of the headmen before his monthly meeting with the district officer; thus, the *kamnan* serves as an intermediary between the district officer and village chiefs.

The *kamnan* is not a civil service official, but he is entitled to wear an official uniform. He is paid a small monthly stipend by the central government. He has a small staff and is assisted by a commune executive committee, *(kana kamakarn tambon),* which is composed of the commune doctor, all the village headmen, the irrigation headman and one to five other locally influential persons appointed by the district officer. This committee is headed by the *kamnan.*

In addition, the *kamnan* is assisted by the commune council *(sapa tambon),* which consists of popularly elected members from each village, and the village headmen, who are members ex officio. The council is vested with very limited self-governing powers, but in the mid-1960's 59 commune councils were given official recognition as legitimate self-governing bodies.

Village

For administrative purposes the government defines a village as consisting of at least five households. Villages normally vary in size from 50 to 200 households. In 1965 there was a total of 41,630 villages; each was in the charge of a headman or *pu yai ban,* the "elder man of the village."

The *pu yai ban* is chosen, as he has been throughout most of

Thailand's history, by villagers. Every resident 21 years of age (18 if married) may vote. The term of office is formally fixed at 5 years, but the headman tends to remain in office until death or retirement. Although entitled to wear an official uniform, the village chief is not a regular government official. He receives a small stipend for services rendered, which are similar to those performed by the commune chief.

There are few formal prerequisites for the office. The government requires that candidates be 21 and able to read and write, but in practice the latter requirement often is not met. Village mores impose other requirements: the candidate should be married and at least of middle age; he should be of good moral character and not overly fond of gambling or addicted to narcotics; and he should have spent several months in a monastery as a novice or a monk and have been in frequent attendance at ceremonies in the local *wat*.

The office of headman is declining in importance. Frequently, a headman does not preside over a natural community but one that was created for administrative purposes through the consolidation of a number of adjacent settlements. Expansion of the power of the central government has made him little more than an appendage of the district officer.

Municipality

Before 1932 all towns and cities were governed by appointed officials. In 1933, however, a Municipality Act was passed that provided for self-government in urban areas. The act, which was amended in 1953, establishes three classes of municipalities: the commune (*tambon*), which consists of a group of contiguous villages; the town (*muang*), which includes the capitals of provincial governments and towns where the population exceeds 10,-000 with an average density of not less than 3,000 people per square kilometer; and the city (*nakhon*), which must have a population exceeding 50,000. There are 35 commune, 82 town and 3 city municipalities.

Theoretically, municipal governments possess legislative as well as executive functions, which are carried out through municipal councils (*sapa tesaban*) and municipal executive committees (*kana tesamonthri*). In practice, the executive organs have usually dominated the elective councils. Municipal council members are all popularly elected, and the councils range in size from 12 to 24 depending on the class of the municipality.

The municipal executive committee headed by the mayor consists of 2 to 4 members, who are appointed by the provincial governor and subject to approval by the elected council; thus, in theory, the committee is responsible to the municipal council.

The committee is required to resign collectively if the council rejects the annual budget proposal submitted by the mayor. The execution of this responsibility is often hampered by the intervention of the provincial and central authorities.

Local taxation does not produce sufficient revenue to meet the expenses of the municipalities, and all of them rely on the central government for budgetary support. Accordingly, the central government exercises considerable control over municipal finances and administration through the Department of Local Administration, the Ministry of the Interior and the various provincial administrations. The Ministry of the Interior reviews public works proposals, checks financial reports and conducts field inspections. The provincial governor has the authority to review municipal budgets, appoint and impeach municipal officials and under certain circumstances, to dissolve municipal councils and assemblies. Because the powers of the Ministry of the Interior have usually been exercised through the provincial authorities this dual jurisdiction over municipal affairs has occasionally produced administrative confusion and delay.

The government believes that the successful working of municipal government would provide a "short cut" to democracy. Two bodies have been created since 1958 to advance the achievement of this goal. The League of Municipalities of Thailand, which operates under a president and executive board elected by the mayors of the country, was formed in 1959 to promote lateral cooperation among municipalities and to maintain direct communication with cities abroad. In 1962 the Municipal Advisory Board, whose chairman is the Under Secretary of the Ministry of the Interior, was created to advise the Minister of the Interior in the general field of municipal activities.

CIVIL SERVICE

Employment in the civil service has always been a prestigious occupation in Thailand. Civil servants are accorded great deference, and the attainment of official position has been the principal means of achieving high social status. The majority of college students aspire to careers in the government service.

The theory and practice of civil service that is found in Western nations were first introduced under the Civil Service Act of 1928 and have since been continually modified and improved. The present civil service system is based on the Civil Service Act of 1954.

The civil service system covers the personnel of all ministries except the military personnel. It also applies to provincial and district government officials, schoolteachers and university professors, members of the police establishment and foreign service officials. Judges, public prosecutors, municipal employees, and officials of local administrative units in communes and villages are not included in the system. By 1965 there were at least 250,000 regular civil servants.

Regular civil servants are administered by the Civil Service Commission, which is a statutory body headed by the Prime Minister and placed directly under the Office of the Prime Minister. Schoolteachers and university professors are, however, administered separately by the National Education Council and by a University Personnel Commission (see ch. 10, Education).

Since its creation in 1929, the Civil Service Commission has worked to build a modern, standardized personnel system. Employment and promotion are based on public examination. Official codes of conduct have been promulgated. Salaries have been standardized for the various grades. Pension arrangements for most categories of the service have been adopted. Women are admitted to the service on an equal basis with men, but few have entered.

Officials are divided into five main grades: fourth grade, administrative-clerical; third grade, administrative including senior officers in districts or sections; second grade, executive including the most important district officers, governors of small provinces and division chiefs; first grade, executive including governors of larger provinces and officials who have held second-grade offices for at least 3 years; and special grade, only the very highest officials including directors general and under secretaries and their deputies.

Until 1941 the civil service showed steady improvement in efficiency and integrity. Wartime inflation, however, reduced the small, fixed incomes in the lower grades of the civil service to the point where they were roughly half that of the average unskilled laborer, and the continuing inadequacy of government pay after the war became a major source of dissatisfaction. In 1959 the Civil Service Act was amended to provide substantial salary increases for career and politically appointed officials, and legislation was enacted imposing heavy penalties on dishonest officials.

Because the civil service has traditionally been barred from participating in politics the bureaucracy, except for a handful of high-ranking officials, has been little affected by the internal shifts in power relations in Bangkok. Consequently, the career officials have been a source of administrative stability. Civil servants have been taxed, however, with a disposition toward bureaucratic delay and a reluctance to accept responsibility. The failure to delegate sufficient discretionary authority to the lower echelons and the practice of referring minor matters to the highest level for action have resulted in considerable congestion at the top of the decisionmaking structure.

ELECTIONS

The concept of election is rooted in the ancient practice of choosing village headmen who acted as the villagers' spokesmen. Between 1932 and 1957 there were seven general elections and numerous other elections for provincial and municipal assemblies, but only a small portion of the people have participated in elections of any kind above the village level. In the general elections of 1933, 10 percent of the electorate went to the polls; in 1937, slightly over 20 percent; in 1946, about 30 percent; in 1948, around 16 percent; in February 1957, about 37 percent; and in December 1957, 30 percent of the electorate voted in the general elections. Even in Bangkok only 35.8 percent of the electorate voted in the elections of December 1957.

Since 1957 no national elections have been held. The government in mid-1967 was considering the possibility of holding general elections within 6 months after promulgation of a new permanent constitution.

The Electoral Law of February 1956 was the most recent in a series of electoral reforms that sought to secure broader popular participation in the electoral process. Like the Political Parties Act of 1955 the Electoral Law of 1956 was a product of Phibun Songkhram's democratization reform program. It established legal safeguards to ensure accurate voter registration, secret balloting and fair campaigning; it broadened the electorate; and it liberalized qualifications for candidacy to the assembly. The Electoral Law of 1956 also sought to prevent dishonesty in elections by authorizing each party and candidate to name a poll watcher at each polling place, by establishing a system of district committees appointed by the district officers for the inspection of ballots and by fixing severe penalties for election irregularities.

In spite of these safeguards there were discrepancies between the law and its practice in national elections. National elections were characterized by irregular practices. Most voters seemed guided in their choice by personal and local concerns—a feeling of obligation to a candidate, requests from local leaders or the dictates of status or position.

The election of village headmen is a traditional institution that is more meaningful and important to the majority of the population than are the national elections. Political activity at the village level is entirely devoid of party identifications, and campaigns for the office of headman are conducted on an informal basis by the candidates among their fellow villagers. Candidates cultivate the favor of the priests of the local *wat* because although they do not vote, their opinions are solicited by the voters and carry great weight. The most effective guarantee of election is the endorsement of the incumbent headman. All adult male villagers participate in the election of the headman, and their choice must be approved by the district officer. Voting closely follows kinship and friendship lines. The candidate with many relatives and friends, therefore, stands the best chance of election.

CHAPTER 15

POLITICAL DYNAMICS

For centuries the government in Thailand was autocratic in form and authoritarian in spirit. Power was the privilege of a small elite (partly hereditary and partly appointive), who were not accountable to the people for their conduct and whose authority was enhanced by an aura of divinity attached to the highest levels of office. Even lower officials were regarded as a class above the ordinary people. Personalities rather than philosophies or institutions became a key factor in shaping the political destiny of the country. There were few moral issues to dispute because almost the entire community shared the doctrines of Buddhism.

The economic order was simple, stable and regarded by the people as reasonably just. Questions of foreign policy sometimes disturbed Thai political life, particularly during the seventeenth and twentieth centuries, but in recent Thai history political turmoil has usually resulted from factional struggles for power at the apex of the governing hierarchy.

There has never been any significant indication of popular resentment of or opposition to this autocratic tradition. Elite rule buttressed by Buddhist precepts and conventions was accepted as the natural order of society; it went unquestioned because those who ruled were believed to possess superior ability and moral excellence. The common man exhibited little interest in affairs beyond his own village, and high policy and national contests for power were subjects too remote for his comprehension.

The autocratic tradition and the decisiveness of personality have manifested themselves in certain characteristics of modern Thai politics: the use of the coup d'etat rather than the use of the electoral process as the major instrument of leadership change; the frequent modification and the occasional suspension of parliamentary and electoral processes; the widespread public indifference to politics; and the absence of any effective source of policy discussions and initiative besides the bureaucratic elite.

Politics, after the coup d'etat of 1932, was a series of competitive efforts between a limited number of civilian and military leaders that culminated in the emergence of the military as the dominant force after 1947 (see ch. 3, Historical Setting). These leaders experimented with several different constitutions designed to accommodate changing political situations. They tried a system of politics and government based on elected assemblies and political parties, which would allow broad popular participation in public affairs. In late 1958, however, Thai leaders decided that an extended period of political tutelage was needed for an orderly evaluation of the political system (see ch. 14, The Governmental System).

All organized political activities have been banned since October 1958, when Field Marshal Sarit Thanarat personally assumed control of the government and proclaimed martial law, which was still in force in mid-1967. Professional and other voluntary organizations are not numerous, and they exert very little political influence. The ban on partisan politics has left the country with almost no institutional channels for broad political participation.

In 1967 Prime Minister Thanom Kittikachorn's Cabinet, which has held office since the death of Field Marshal Sarit in December 1963, was seriously considering the revival of party politics and the reestablishment of national elections. There was, in mid-1967, no firm indication of when this plan would be implemented. It appeared that the government's readiness to permit the resumption of partisan politics depended in part on the outcome of counterinsurgency efforts in both Thailand and South Vietnam (see ch. 27, Public Order and Safety; ch. 28, The Armed Forces).

Since the mid-1960's the government has been progressively concerned about the growing Communist terrorist activities in the North and Northeast Regions and the Peninsula, or Southern Region. Thai leaders asserted that the subversive campaign was directly related to the intensified Communist insurgency in South Vietnam and that the Communist terrorists were aided, trained and controlled by Communist China and North Vietnam.

Political groups who possessed varying degrees of direct and indirect influence were the Chinese, Malay and Vietnamese minorities. The Chinese had to be considered because of their powerful economic position and their close ties with Thai political leaders; the Malays, because of their historic separatist sentiments and their antipathy toward the Buddhist rulers in Bangkok; and the Vietnamese, because of their potential as a fifth column in the event of a massive Communist insurgency.

POLITICAL BACKGROUND

The concept and practice of political competition through organized parties and electoral processes were first introduced to the country after the coup of 1932. The center of political power shifted from the royal family to the civilian and military leaders, most of whom came to positions of power and influence through coups and countercoups.

The coup of June 24, 1932, was executed by a group of about 50 civilian and military officials, who replaced the absolutist monarchy with a limited parliamentary form of government. Pridi Phanomyong, who was the civilian leader of the group, sought to establish a socialist economic order, but his opponents led by Phraya Manopakon branded the proposal as Communist, forced Pridi into exile and passed a sweeping anti-Communist law. In June 1933 the regime of Phraya Manopakon, which had been suspected of plotting to restore the absolutist monarchy, was ousted by the military leaders. The new regime under Phya Phahon recalled Pridi from France in September 1933, exonerated him of alleged Communist affiliation in early 1934 and later that year appointed him Minister of the Interior.

The Phya Phahon regime (June 1933 to December 1938) was divided into two major factions: the civilian group led by Pridi and the army group led by Field Marshal Phibun Songkhram. The army faction gradually increased its influence through a program stimulating militant Thai nationalism. In 1935 Phibun established an ultranationalist youth group (*yuwachon*), which resembled those groups in Germany and Italy at the time. In 1937 he announced that the interests of the nation would advance only as its military power grew and that Japan, Germany and Italy were the models Thailand should follow. In December 1938 he became prime minister and began to consolidate his power.

Phibun vigorously pursued a militantly nationalistic policy. He launched a so-called Pan-Thai Movement, which stressed the ethnic and historical connections between the Thai in Thailand and the Thai peoples in Laos, the Shan States in Burma and Yunnan in southwest China. Repressive measures were taken against the economically powerful Chinese minority. These efforts, however, had little impact on the society as a whole.

Toward the end of World War II Pridi's civilian group replaced Phibun's leadership through either Phibun's reluctant consent or a coup. Khuang Aphaiwong, one of the leaders of the anti-Japanese Free Thai Movement and an intimate associate of Pridi, became the new prime minister. In late 1945 the formation of political parties was permitted, and in the general elections of January 1946. Pridi's civilian faction swept the field. In a short time personal rivalry developed between Pridi and Khuang, who, despite Pridi's apparent objection, was confirmed as prime minister by the newly chosen parliament.

In spite of the split within the civilian faction, it appeared that Thailand would inaugurate a new era of democratic growth and liberalism in politics, but too many factors militated against such an outcome. Enthusiasm for democratic, partisan politics was felt only by a relatively small number of the educated urbanites; the rural population generally seemed uninterested in the shifting politics in Bangkok. The widespread dislocation of the society in the aftermath of war led to a weakening of civic attitudes and conduct among some of the leaders of the new regime and among the bureaucrats. In March 1946 Pridi succeeded in forcing the resignation of Prime Minister Khuang through a parliamentary maneuver, but he was unable to improve the situation. The Pridi regime encountered another difficulty because of widespread rumors about the mysterious circumstances surrounding the death in June 1946 of the popular young King Ananda Mahidon (Rama VIII). Because of the loss of public confidence in the government, Pridi resigned in August 1946. He was succeeded by one of his followers, Thamrong Nawasawat.

In November 1947 a group of army officers headed by Phibun Songkhram again seized control of the government and removed the civilian leaders; some were imprisoned and others, including Pridi, were forced to flee. The post of prime minister was offered to Pridi's rival, Khuang Aphaiwong, who was assured of noninterference by the military and who took office as a caretaker prime minister until the general elections of January 1948. The Khuang Cabinet was returned to office by the electorate, but 3 months later Phibun removed Khuang by a bloodless coup.

From 1948 to 1951, Prime Minister Phibun had to contend with the activities of the domestic opposition and with a continuation of wartime inflation. In October 1948 several high-ranking army officers were arrested for allegedly plotting against the regime. In February 1949 Pridi and his Free Thai followers supported by a small group of naval officers made an abortive attempt to overthrow the government. In June 1951 elements of the navy, who were apparently jealous of the army's long predominance in national politics and who were, thus, amenable to the influence of Pridi, again rebelled and succeeded in kidnaping Prime Minister Phibun while he was attending a public function. The army, air force and national police remained loyal to Phibun and suppressed the uprising, which was the most serious armed clash since 1932.

In November 1951 Phibun was ousted by elements of the military and police forces under General Sarit Thanarat and Police General Phao Siyanon, who charged the Phibun regime with failure to contain the internal Communist threat, to curb inflation and to eliminate corruption. The coup leaders set aside the 1949 Constitution that barred members of the armed forces from holding political office and engaging in political activity, and they restored the more authoritarian Constitution of 1932, which had provided for greater executive initiatives and powers.

Phibun was reinstated as prime minister 10 days after his removal apparently because of mutual jealousy and suspicion between Sarit Thanarat and Phao Siyanon. Phibun's previously unchallenged authority was reduced, and he came to hold the balance of power between the factions of Phao and Sarit. The new regime launched an intensified anti-Communist drive, which culminated in the passage of an Anti-Communist Activities Act in November 1952.

After Phibun's return from a visit to the United States and Great Britain in mid-1955, the government initiated a series of reform measures designed to broaden the area of public political participation and to secure greater popular support for official policies. The reform program, which was called *prachathipatai* (democratization), resulted in the enactment of laws providing for the formation of political parties, the liberalization of electoral laws to permit direct popular election, the decentralization of power and the institution of regular press conferences by the prime minister. The democratization program was apparently Phibun's effort to counter the increasing strength of the army and the police, and it was undertaken in anticipation of the approaching elections in February 1957.

This new policy inaugurated one of the more colorful and liberal years in Thai politics. The nation enjoyed a freer climate of public discussion, and a number of political parties competed vigorously against one another. Elections were held in February 1957, and the ruling party, Seri Manangkhasila, named after the villa where its founders met to debate political strategy, emerged victorious. The margin of victory, however, was small, and the party came under mounting criticism from opposition groups for alleged frauds in the election. Field Marshal Sarit, whose political differences with Phibun and Phao had become increasingly evident, dissociated himself from the ruling party and agreed with the opposition charges that the election had been "dirty from all sides." In September 1957 Sarit displaced Phibun and Phao in a bloodless coup d'etat.

New elections were held in December 1957 under an interim government headed by Pote Sarasin, who was then the Secretary

General of the Southeast Asia Treaty Organization (SEATO). The election gave no single political party a working parliamentary majority. Sarit organized a new ruling party, the National Socialist Party (Chat Sangkhom), that was a coalition of parties and individuals. The new government, which was formed under General Thanom Kittikachorn, Sarit's deputy, proved to be unstable because of intraparty wranglings over political and economic spoils. The inclusion of leftist politicians in the ruling party further complicated the situation because of their opposition to the government's pro-Western foreign policies (see ch. 16, Foreign Relations).

In October 1958 Field Marshal Sarit, who had remained in the background reportedly because of ill health, decided with the consent of General Thanom Kittikachorn to assume personal control of the government. Sarit proclaimed martial law, which was still in force in mid-1967, abrogated the Constitution, dissolved the National Assembly, banned political parties, closed a dozen or more newspapers suspected of leftist inclinations and arrested a number of persons suspected of leftist thought or activities. He reorganized the Office of the Prime Minister and brought nearly all policymaking and supervisory functions of the government under his direct control. In January 1959 an interim constitution legitimizing the new political order was promulgated (see ch. 14, The Governmental System).

Although Prime Minister Sarit ruled by decree and asserted that Thailand was not ready for a system of representative government based on popular mandate, he sought to curb the perennial accusations of misconduct among government officials, to strengthen internal and external security and to give the nation political stability and economic well-being.

After his death in December 1963 Sarit was succeeded by General Thanom Kittikachorn, who had been First Deputy Prime Minister and was widely respected for his integrity and dedication to duty. The new Prime Minister retained the previous Cabinet and vowed to continue the policies of the previous administration.

THE RULING ELITE

Political competition has been taking place mainly within the bureaucratic framework. Political power has been monopolized and exercised by a small number of ranking government officials; major political questions have usually been debated and resolved within this inner circle of ruling elite. Similarly, policies concerning the various aspects of nation-building and modernization have originated almost exclusively from this small group.

Political competition since 1932 has been largely a function of factional or clique rivalry among those in positions of power and influence. The basis of political power has been highly personalized and has been subject to informal political manipulations and shifting loyalties. The operation of the political system has, therefore, been generally determined by the attitudes, personalities and interaction of the small ruling group concentrated in Bangkok.

The members of this ruling circle are drawn primarily from the armed forces, the police and the executive branch of the government. At the apex of the ruling hierarchy is a group of about a dozen persons who are the ultimate holders and manipulators of power. These individuals occupy strategic positions in the Office of the Prime Minister and its subordinate bodies, the Ministries of Interior, Defense, National Development and Finance, and in other key agencies of the government. The principal means of rising to positions of political power and influence has been the demonstration of personal loyalty to a given leader.

Within the ruling group civilian elements have played a secondary role in the conduct of state affairs. Since 1958 shifts in control of the government from one faction to another have usually been achieved through coups supported by units of the armed forces, especially those of the First Army Area, which controls the capital city of Bangkok (see ch. 28, The Armed Forces).

When a particular regime has been replaced by a coup d'etat, only the members of the regime's dominant coterie in the central government or those directly responsible to it have been replaced. Minor members of the ruling group generally remained unaffected because their commitments and personal loyalties to the deposed regime or to its leader have been relatively weak or indirect. A new inner circle was then formed by the successful group, which often enlisted additional support from outlying or peripheral groups.

PARTY POLITICS

In mid-1967 there were no political parties; they had been banned since October 1958. The government, however, was considering the resumption af party politics after the promulgation of a new constitution. In March 1966 a new political parties act was drafted by the Ministry of the Interior to replace the Political Parties Act of 1955. The draft version stipulated: the formation of a party must be endorsed by at least 10 persons qualified to be elected to parliament; a party must have a minimum number of members, tentatively fixed at 500; a party must register with the authorities, and its leader and secretary general would be held responsible for conforming to the party's stated program and policy; and a party must be dissolved if it fails to obtain at least 10 percent of the total valid votes in a given election.

Before 1958 a typical party had only a rudimentary organization, was little concerned with issues and ideology and possessed little or no mass membership. It was more like a small social or political club that was held together by the prestige, power and skill of one or more prominent individuals. Party activities were limited in scope and were centered largely in Bangkok. Parties, as a whole, existed not so much to advance self-proclaimed political and social objectives as to promote the self-interest of the few in a given organization. Discipline was not strict; a man might be elected as a member of one party and vote with another one in the parliament.

The term "party" was first introduced to the country by the promoters of the coup d'etat of 1932. They formed a People's Party, but this organization was more an oligarchical governing body than a party as defined in conventional Western terminology. It was an exclusive political club and eventually faded from the scene.

Political parties in the modern sense first appeared late in 1945, while Pridi's civilian faction was in control of the government. The first was the Cooperation Party (Sahachip), which was formed by the Free Thai activists from the poverty-stricken Northeast Region. A large leftist coalition group called the Constitutional Front was formed under Pridi's direct leadership. Rival conservative and proroyalist elements rallied behind a Progressive Party. In early 1946 another conservative organization, the Democrat Party (Prachatipat), was established by Khuang Aphaiwong to counter Pridi's dominance in the government.

The Constitutional Front and the Cooperation Party were both forced out of power in the coup of November 1947, and after a brief interlude during which the goverment was controlled by Khuang's Democrat Party, the United Party (Sahaphak) under Phibun's leadership gained control in 1948. The United Party was renamed the Legislative Study Committee in 1951, and in 1955 it formed the nucleus of the Seri Manangkhasila Party. Although it was conservative and pro-Western, it was the only party with branch offices and at least a rudimentary organization in all 71 provinces. Its members held all of the appointed and more than half of the elected seats in the National Assembly. Its total disintegration, however, after the ouster of Phibun and Phao in September 1957 was a vivid illustration of the importance of personality in Thai politics.

After the elections of December 1957, Field Marshal Sarit formed a new ruling party, the National Socialist Party (Chat Sangkhom), into which anyone willing to support the new regime was invited. Sarit stated that its policy would be "50 percent nationalism and 50 percent socialism." The ambiguity of this policy and the heterogeneity of the views of the party members soon led to political confusion and contributed to Sarit's decision in October 1958 to ban party politics.

The leading opposition party from 1946 to 1958 was the Democrat Party, and it was the only party in continuous existence during that period. It drew its support from the civil service and the educated middle income group, particularly in the Bangkok-Thon Buri area, but was not favored at all by the military services. Although it consistently condemned the political views of the military, the Democrat Party tended to speak for royal interests and was criticized from the left as "royalist" and "feudalistic."

Another prominent opposition group was the Socialist Front, which was an electoral alliance of a number of leftist organizations formed shortly before the general elections of February 1957 to counter the conservative parties. The strength of the Socialist Front was drawn largely from the northeastern provinces. It advocated the eventual elimination of the monarchy, a socialist economy and a nonaligned foreign policy with a mildly anti-American but pro-Chinese Communist tendency. There was also a number of splinter parties whose influence on politics was minimal.

COMMUNIST MOVEMENT

Since its inception in the mid-1920's, the Communist movement in Thailand has failed to gain significant popular support. Its hard-core activists in 1967 were estimated to be between 1,000 to 2,000, in addition to 10,000 to 20,000 sympathizers. Support for the movement came chiefly from the Northeast Region and from the Peninsula in the south, but since the early 1960's the Communists have gained some followers in the Central Region, especially around Suphan Buri, northwest of Bangkok.

The Communists have made little progress, particularly among the indigenous Thai, partly because the country has never been under European colonial rule. This denied their organizers the issue of nationalism. Moreover, many Thai farmers own their land, and except in the backward northeastern provinces, they have been little affected by the extremes of poverty. A strong sense of national identity that is reinforced by a common language, customs and traditions and a strong attachment to the King and to the Buddhist faith have served as barriers to the acceptance of Communist dogma (see ch. 18, Political Values and Attitudes). Finally, the movement has been weak because of the general indifference of the people to all forms of organized political activity.

Background

From 1925 to late 1942 at least four separate Communist groups—Chinese, Thai, Vietnamese and Malay—operated clandestinely but exhibited little centralized coordination. Their respective leadership, organizations and strength remained obscure. Foreign Communist agents were periodically smuggled into the country to stimulate the movement, especially among the minority groups. One of the infiltrated agents was Nguyen Ai Quoc, who was later called Ho Chi Minh and who worked among the Vietnamese in 1928–29 in the guise of a Buddhist monk.

The Communist groups merged into a single organization called the Communist Party of Thailand (Pak Communist Thai) on December 1, 1942. This date has since been observed by the Party as the anniversary of its founding. The merger was possible because the presence of Japanese troops in Thailand, Vietnam, China and British Malaya served as the basis for an anti-Japanese united front among the four Communist groups. It remains unclear, however, whether the Party was allowed to participate in Pridi Phanomyong's wartime anti-Japanese Free Thai Movement, although a Soviet source claimed that the "working class" played an "active role" in this movement.

During the period of liberalization that followed World War II, the Communists emerged into the open; this action was aided by the repeal of the Anti-Communist Act of 1933, which was rescinded in October 1946 and which was to help ensure Soviet approval of Thailand's application for membership in the United Nations. Under the leadership of Secretary General Prasert Sapsunthon, who was an elected National Assemblyman from Surat Thani Province, the Party in December 1946 announced a moderate, although Communist, program, outlining political, social and economic objectives.

In 1948 the Party accused the United States of interfering in Thai internal affairs, but it was not until after October 1950 that the Communists began to attack the United States as the "main enemy of revolutionary struggle" in Thailand. The Party, which was then mostly under Chinese control, was outlawed in November 1952 by a new Anti-Communist Activities Act. This Act was still in force in mid-1967. The Central Labor Union, which was brought under Communist control by 1948, was also banned; the majority of its 50,000 members were Chinese (see ch. 22, Labor). Party activity, which was confined to clandestine circulation of propaganda leaflets, was further circumscribed after Field Marshal Sarit Thanarat assumed power in October 1958.

Internal Issues

After the Party was banned in 1952, the Communists exploited not only the traditional governmental neglect of the Northeast Region but also the poverty of the region and the strong separatist sentiments present in that area and in the Moslem-inhabited southern provinces of the Peninsula. The Northeast has long been a haven for disaffected political leaders, officials ousted from the capital and bandits. In the past, officials out of favor with top government leaders in the capital were often transferred to the Northeast Region. Many of these officials regarded themselves as "exiled"; hence, the morale of government administrators in that locality tended to be low. This area gradually became the center of leftist dissident movements.

The influential leftist Cooperation Party, formed in late 1945, drew its support from the Northeast Region and sought to obtain for it a larger share of political power and government resources. Most of the leftist politicians, who were suppressed by the successive army governments in the late 1940's and during the 1950's, came from this area. Many of them were participants in Pridi's wartime anti-Japanese Free Thai Movement and were removed from the Bangkok political scene after Pridi's fall from power in 1947 (see ch. 16, Foreign Relations).

Peoples of the Northeast Region have had strong separatist sentiments in the past, although these sentiments have diminished in recent years. Many share ethnic and linguistic affinity with the adjoining Laotians, and for generations many have had kinship ties with the Laotians across the Mekong (see ch. 5, Ethnic Groups; ch. 6, Language and Communication). They have traditionally regarded their rulers in Bangkok with reserve (see ch. 18, Political Values and Attitudes).

Before his death in 1952 Tiang Serikhan, a dynamic leftist, advocated independence for the Northeast Region and its own capital in Sakon Nakhon Province. Many of his followers later joined a secessionist group called the Solidarity Movement, which was led by pro-Communist Krong Chandawong. This group had several thousand followers, mostly in Sakon Nakhon. Many of them did not share Krong's Communist orientation and presumably left the organization once his views were exposed.

The hard-core pro-Communist remnants of the Solidarity Movement joined forces with the Communist Party of Thailand sometime before or shortly after Krong's arrest and execution in May 1961. At that time Thai authorities identified Krong as the ringleader of an alleged international Communist conspiracy to secede the 15 northeastern provinces with assistance from the Loatian Communists known as the Pathet Lao (see Glossary). Mass arrests followed, and by December 1961, 350 Communist suspects were taken into custody in Sakon Nakhon, Udon Thani and Nakhon Phanom.

Besides separatist sentiments, the Communists used Buddhist themes to gain local adherents. They established a clandestine front organization with a Buddhist facade called the Harmony-In-The-Doctrine Movement (Krabuankarn Smakhi Dharm).

In the Peninsula the Communists exploited the latent Moslem resentment against the Buddhist-oriented Thai authorities (see ch. 12, Religion). They also exploited the historic separatist sentiments current among the Moslem Malays, especially those in the provinces adjoining Malaysia (see ch. 18, Political Values and Attitudes). The Communists gained about 300 activists and a large number of sympathizers (possibly several thousand) among the more impoverished segments of the Chinese community. Moreover, they have collaborated with some 500 terrorists who are remnants of the Chinese Communist guerrilla fighters in Malays and who are allegedly receiving their orders from Peiping rather than from the Communist Party of Thailand (see ch. 27, Public Order and Safety).

POLITICAL GROUPING

Thailand's economic and professional organizations, except those within the Chinese community, are small and weak and have negligible political influence. Potential political groups, such as the urban workers, peasants, Buddhists, students, intellectuals and professionals, have not asserted themselves. Some of the large and cohesive ethnic minorities, however, are exceptions. The government has followed policies designed to heighten the difficulties of organizing these ethnic groups for political and social action. Nevertheless, because of their strategic position in the economy or a particular geographic location, these groups play either a direct or indirect political role of some importance. Outstanding among these groups are the Chinese, Malay and Vietnamese.

The Chinese

The Chinese minority has not taken a direct part in domestic politics. It has not organized its own parties nor has it supported its own candidates in national elections. For practical reasons most of the Chinese have avoided open identification with either the pro-Communist or pro-Nationalist Chinese regimes. Their primary concern has been successful trading, and their slight involvement in Thai politics has been influenced primarily by this consideration.

The Chinese, nevertheless, have been astute observers of Thai politics. In seeking protection for their powerful hold on the economy, they have cultivated personal relationships with leading Thai Cabinet ministers. They have also established business ties or partnership arrangements with Thai leaders, which have usually proved to be mutually beneficial. Politics and business have become so enmeshed that it is almost impossible to separate one from the other.

Because of nationalistic considerations Thai leaders have sought to curb, with only limited success, the increasing Chinese commercial influence in Thailand. Anti-Chinese nationalist sentiments have been encouraged periodically since the 1930's (see ch. 3, Historical Setting). Successive governments have attempted to institute measures against Chinese immigration, landownership and participation in certain trades and enterprises (see ch. 23, Domestic Trade). Many Chinese have been deported on charges of Communist affiliation or activity, and Chinese schools have been brought under strict government control (see ch. 10, Education).

By mid-1958 these discriminatory measures had apparently aroused strong Chinese resentment. A study conducted in September 1958 reported that a large proportion of the Chinese minority secretly favored the Chinese Communist regime over the Nationalist government in Taiwan. This apparent pro-Peiping sympathy was partly generated by the seemingly ineffective diplomatic representation of the Nationalist government in Bangkok. This trend was checked after the coup in October 1958 through more discriminate and intensified anti-Communist drives and through a more conciliatory approach toward the Chinese community.

In 1967, despite the reported pro-Peiping sentiments among the more impoverished segments of the community, the majority of the Chinese appeared less concerned with ideological questions than with the immediate issues of personal security and communal well-being. Should the Chinese choose to participate directly in politics, they could assert real power. This is possible partly because of their cohesive group structure and partly because of their numbers, which as a bloc of votes would be considerable, especially in the Bangkok-Thon Buri area.

The Malays

The 1 million Malays in Thailand are concentrated mainly in the southernmost provinces adjoining northern Malaysia. They are quite resistant to assimilation by the dominant Thai culture (see ch. 5, Ethnic Groups). A separatist movement has gained some adherents among the Malays, and it is seeking the integration of the four Thai provinces of Satun, Songkhla, Yala and Narathiwat with Malaysia. The separatists reportedly have been collaborating with the Communist terrorists in the region to their mutual advantage.

The Malay community became a political issue after World War II. The upheavals of the war, the economic distress of the postwar years and the growing nationalism among the Islamic peoples throughout Asia had a profound impact on the Malays in Thailand. The leaders of the community began to press for a special position for their people. Initially, the government refused to grant any concessions, and when the demands persisted the government attempted to suppress Malay leaders. Mounting communal friction and pressure eventually compelled the government to become more lenient, and in 1946 a commission was established to investigate Malay grievances. Beginning in 1948 some of the commission's recommendations were implemented.

Primary schools in the four southern provinces began to provide an hour of instruction daily in the Malay language and the Islamic religion. The government also allowed the Malays to submit marital and inheritance disputes involving Malays only to Malay officials for settlement under Islamic law.

Concessions were also made in the matter of political representation. Special committees, which are composed exclusively of Moslems, have been established in many of the southern provinces to advise Thai provincial administrators about local Moslem interests. The chairmen of these committees select one of their number as an adviser on Islamic affairs to the Minister of the Interior. The adviser then selects a number of prominent Moslems to act as a central advisory body on Islamic matters.

In 1967 Moslem leaders continued to reaffirm their allegiance to Thailand, but undercurrents of separatist sentiments, which were motivated by a historic opposition to the rule of the Buddhist-controlled central and local governments, still existed among much of the Moslem population.

The Vietnamese

In 1967 there were about 40,000 to 50,000 Vietnamese residents concentrated almost entirely in the northeastern border region, an area in which government security controls were notably weak. Many of them manifest their allegiance to Ho Chi Minh and to his Communist regime. They have persistently refused to be resettled in South Vietnam, where the Thai Government would like to send them. The South Vietnamese Government was reluctant to receive them because of their alleged pro-Communist orientation (see ch. 5, Ethnic Groups; ch. 16, Foreign Relations).

The Vietnamese lived in villages of their own, which were tightly controlled by their own clandestine organizations; took no part in local Thai politics; and outwardly refrained from actively identifying themselves with Thai Communist terrorists operating in the region. There were increasing indications, however, that this community was being infiltrated by Communist agents from Hanoi, and in 1967 it presented a major political and security problem (see ch. 27, Public Order and Safety). Early in 1967 Thai authorities detained 80 Vietnamese residents who were alleged Communist cadres.

CHAPTER 16

FOREIGN RELATIONS

In foreign relations Thailand was, in 1967, firmly anti-Communist. The emergence of China as a major Communist power in 1949 and the establishment of Communist North Vietnam in 1954 as an independent state with the implication of its influence spreading in Laos, Cambodia and South Vietnam, strengthened the Thais anti-Communist position. The country was a founding member of the Southeast Asia Treaty Organization (SEATO), established in September 1954 as a mutual defense alliance against any Communist aggression, direct or indirect, in the treaty area. In mid-1967 it remained a stanch supporter of SEATO (see ch. 28, The Armed Forces). Other conspicuous features of foreign relations have been the nation's persistent apprehension over the unstable political situation in neighboring Laos and its antagonism toward Cambodia, a legacy of the historic past and a derivation of mutual suspicion.

The country has been able to remain independent of foreign domination while its neighbors were subject to colonial rule by European powers. Independence has been maintained as a result of Thailand's realistic attitudes and practices in foreign relations and skillful diplomacy. Thailand has avoided quarrels with stronger states but has in the past warred against smaller neighbors to expand its power and enlarge its domains. It has made and broken alliances for strictly pragmatic purposes and has played off foreign powers against one another.

Lacking sufficient power confidently to challenge European nations, the Thai have obtained their objectives through persuasion and maneuvering. Westerners who have dealt with Thai diplomats have often remarked on their skill in careful, prolonged and complex negotiation. Thailand has also emphasized international law as the formal basis of relations among nations and has shown considerable respect for its norms. Similarly, a highly refined and elaborate system of protocol, rooted in age-old customs surrounding the king and his court, has been practiced. Although most of the ancient forms have been modified or discarded, Thai diplomacy is still notable for its delicate sense of propriety and style.

The anti-Communist orientation of the Bangkok government appeared likely to continue for at least so long as the militant and vocally aggressive anti-Thai attitude of Communist China persisted. Other contributing factors toward this orientation were the increasing signs of Communist terrorist activities within Thailand, the continuing Communist Pathet Lao activities in neighboring Laos and the stridently anti-Thai attitudes and policies of avowedly neutralist Cambodia. Thai leaders occasionally sounded a note of reservation that their commitment to the present policy might be subjected to "an agonizing reappraisal" if Western powers, implicitly the United States in particular, waver in their determination to defend Thailand against Communist threats. This was especially evident from 1960–62 when SEATO powers failed to act during the Laotian civil war and Thai leaders expressed apprehension that the United States favored the emergence of neutralist Laos and Cambodia.

HISTORICAL BACKGROUND

From the thirteenth to the early nineteenth century the Thai acknowledged Chinese superiority but paid tribute only irregularly. Historic Thai-Chinese relations were essentially commercial; even the tribute missions were made the occasion for profitable trade and barter. During these centuries the Chinese expressed little political interest in Thai affairs, and during the nineteenth century, when Western powers were concluding treaties and exchanging diplomatic missions with Thailand, the Chinese still considered it a tributary state and did not establish diplomatic relations as sovereign equals.

Beginning in the early seventeenth century, Thailand had to contend with the growing influence of foreign traders, mercenaries and missionaries. In the last quarter of the century attempts by France to bring the Thai court under its influence resulted in the wholesale ouster from the country of almost all Europeans for the next century and a half. As the British extended their influence over Malaya by the early nineteenth century, they clashed with the Thai who had claimed suzerainty over many of the small Malay principalities by right of conquest. By a succession of moves, beginning in the mid-nineteenth century and continuing until 1909, the British brought the entire Malay Peninsula under their protection and virtual rule (see ch. 3, Historical Setting).

Thailand was simultaneously meeting French expansion in the east. Its territorial losses to France between 1867 and 1907 were even larger than those to Great Britain. They were also more deeply felt since cultural affinity was stronger with the people of Laos and Cambodia, who were of Thai or Khmer extraction and who shared the Buddhist religion. Centuries of contact had also produced close economic and political ties among them. In fact, Thailand had, for centuries, exercised suzerainty over some of the areas ceded to France.

Thailand entered World War I on the side of the Allies in July 1917, mainly to obtain advantageous treaty concessions from European powers, France and Great Britain in particular, despite the pro-German views of a majority of the military establishment and the anti-French sentiments of the educated Thai. This act brought Thailand increasing respect and friendship from the major Western powers. After the war Thailand participated in the Paris Peace Conference and was the only Southeast Asian nation to become a charter member of the League of Nations.

World War I marked a turning point in Thai foreign relations, since it brought an end to European pressures and opened the way for eventual elimination of foreign treaty concessions. Foreigners obtained their special concessions through treaties, the first of which was made in 1664 between Siam and the Dutch East India Company. As expanded and elaborated in the 1855 treaty of friendship and commerce with Great Britain (commonly known as the Bowring Treaty), the treaty concessions gave foreigners immunity from the Siamese laws and courts (known as extraterritoriality) and gave them special privileges in matters of taxation and trade (see ch. 3, Historical Setting).

Pre-World War II Relations with the United States

Americans arrived relatively late in the country and had little influence over its affairs until 1920. The first, arriving early in the nineteenth century, were missionaries, and the missionary effort remained the dominant American concern throughout most of the century (see ch. 12, Religion). The United States had no territorial interest, and its commercial interest was small. Two diplomatic missions, those of Edmund Roberts and Joseph Ballistier, were sent to Thailand in the first half of the nineteenth century, but it was not until 1856 that the United States established permanent diplomatic relations. In that year Townsend Harris negotiated an agreement similar to the Bowring Treaty (see ch. 3, Historical Setting).

During the years when the country was under increasing pressure from France and England, it was finding the burden of extraterritoriality ever more onerous, but relations with the United States remained cordial. Although American citizens enjoyed extraterritorial privileges, there were few of them in the country, and they took only a minor part in Thailand's foreign commercial and other relations.

In 1920 a treaty with the United States ended extraterritoriality between the two countries and pointed the way to eventual abolition of the system of unequal treaty relations with European powers. In 1925 the American Francis B. Sayre, serving as foreign affairs adviser to the Siamese Government, began a series of negotiations with European countries to restore full fiscal and judicial autonomy to Thailand. In 1937 Foreign Minister Pridi Phanomyong negotiated with the United States a treaty which abolished the remaining tax and trade concessions enjoyed by Americans. Negotiations with other major powers soon followed; by the end of 1938 Thailand had recovered full fiscal and judicial independence and stood on a basis of sovereign equality with other nations. Through this long record of cordial relations, the United States had accumulated a fund of goodwill in Thailand.

Thai-Japanese Alliance: World War II

The startling victory of an Asian country over a major European power in the Russo-Japanese War of 1904–05 aroused admiration for Japan in Thailand and caused it to look toward Japan as a possible counterbalance to European power in the Far East. During the 1920's and 1930's, therefore, Thailand cultivated closer relations with the increasingly powerful island empire, although it did so rather cautiously for fear of antagonizing Great Britain. In 1933 Thailand was the only member of the League of Nations to vote against the censure of Japanese seizure of Manchuria, and it subsequently recognized the Japanese puppet state of Manchukuo. Japan was generous in its gratitude for this support, and thereafter the economic and cultural relations between the two countries became more intimate. Whatever ambivalence persisted in the orientation of Thailand's foreign policy during the rest of the 1930's was removed in 1939 when Philbun Songkhram assumed control of the government.

The new premier was convinced that war was imminent, that Japan and Germany would win it and that Japan was the proper model for Thailand to follow. Supported by a portion of the country's armed forces which shared the outlook of the Japanese militarists, Phibun launched a thoroughgoing policy of cultivating Japanese friendship and emulating Japanese methods.

Thailand entered World War II on the side of the Axis Powers in January 1942. Japanese troops landed on the southern coast of Thailand on December 8, 1941, and requested permission to move across Thailand to Burma. Thai leaders, faced with a virtual ultimatum, granted the request, apparently calculating that

Japan would sweep away American and European opposition and reign unquestioned in Asia and the Pacific. Later the same month Thailand and Japan concluded an offensive and defensive alliance containing secret clauses which pledged Japan's assistance to Thailand in recovering the territory it had lost in Malaya. Through the good offices of Japan the Vichy government of France had already returned, in May 1941, the territory which had been ceded to France in 1904 and 1907. In August 1943 Japan turned over to Thailand the four Malay states ceded to Great Britain in 1909 and the two Shan states of Kengtung and Mongpan in Burma.

Despite its alliance with Japan, Thailand was not recognized to be a hostile belligerent by the United States. Seni Pramoj, the Thai wartime ambassador to Washington, refused to officially convey his country's declaration of war to the United States Government. In 1945 the United States Secretary of State declared: "During the past four years we have regarded Thailand not as an enemy but as a country to be liberated from the enemy."

During the war the Thai people generally, some elements of the armed forces and many government officials proved by their actions that the presence of the Japanese was distasteful to them. Members of the Anti-Japanese Patriotic Thai, known as "Free Thai" agents, were trained in the United States and infiltrated Thailand. With the help of these agents and the Allies, the United States in particular, about 10,000 men were trained and equipped, and a guerrilla force of 50,000 more was raised clandestinely in the country. The underground was so extensive and had so effectively penetrated the government and the army that the United States received considerable wartime cooperation from Thai citizens and officials.

The Aftermath of War

When Japan was defeated in 1945, Thailand's overriding foreign policy objectives became the mitigation of the consequences of its wartime partnership with Tokyo and the restoration of amicable relations with the Allied Powers. This new policy orientation was discernible as early as July 1944 when, in the wake of Allied victories in the Pacific, the government of Phibun Songkhram was forced out of office on a vote of no confidence.

On August 16, 1945, 2 days after Japan's acceptance of Allied surrender terms, Thailand issued a "Peace Proclamation" which revoked its declarations of war against the United States and Great Britain. Seni Pramoj, a leading figure in the anti-Japanese Free Thai movement, became prime minister. These and subsequent efforts to regain the favor of the victors were aided by the fact that the United States, unlike Great Britain, France and China, was disposed to overlook Thailand's wartime alliance with Japan. Another favorable factor was the resistance to the Japanese, during the war, by the Free Thai underground, which had been supported by the United States.

Great Britain, at first inclined to deal severely with Thailand, presented to Bangkok a series of demands which were eventually mitigated through American intervention. In January 1946 Bangkok agreed to terms which included return of British territories acquired by Bangkok during the war, a free supply of 1.5 million tons of rice for delivery to places designated by the Allies, compensation for all damages to Allied property and payment for all costs involved in the maintenance of Allied troops in Thailand.

At first, Thailand refused to surrender to France the Cambodian provinces of Battambang and Siem Reap and the Laotian territory on the west bank of the Mekong, which it had lost in 1893 but repossessed in May 1941. This action was justified on the ground that Thailand had not declared war on France and that the treaty of cession with the Vichy government was still valid. A series of negotiations and border clashes between Thai and French forces proved indecisive. When it appeared, however, that Thailand's application for admission to the United Nations would be blocked by France, Thailand came to terms and agreed in November 1946 to retrocede the disputed areas.

Similarly, when confronted with the Soviet Union's opposition to seating Thailand in the United Nations, Bangkok conciliated Moscow by repealing the anti-Communist act of 1933. Thailand became a member of the world organization in December 1946.

DETERMINANTS OF POSTWAR FOREIGN RELATIONS

In modern times Thailand, alone among the nations of Southeast Asia, was able to retain its independence while others were falling under European colonial rule. This was achieved by balancing competing powers against one another and by remaining neutral regarding disputes affecting them in the region. From 1945 to 1949, for example, Thailand attempted to follow a middle path between the great power blocs. By the end of 1949, however, with the rise of Communist China, Thailand had become increasingly disturbed about the potential threat of the Communist regime whose nearest border is only 80 miles from Thailand's northernmost frontier.

With the Communist North Korean invasion in June 1950, the Chinese intervention late that year in Korea and the rapid expansion of Communist influence in Indochina, Thailand abandoned its traditional neutral policy and aligned itself firmly with the West, especially the United States. Thailand became the first Asian nation to send combat troops to Korea and extended diplomatic recognition to the anti-Communist state of Vietnam in Saigon, an action which promptly brought from Communist China the charge that Thailand was an "American stooge."

In September 1954 it joined SEATO in efforts to combat direct as well as indirect Communist aggression in the SEATO region. A temporary embargo was imposed on all trade with Communist China. Thailand opposed all diplomatic efforts to seat the Communist China regime in the United Nations. At the Bandung Conference of April 1955, and at many subsequent international conferences, Thailand took a vigorous anti-Communist stand. Despite its firm anti-Communist commitment, however, it apparently saw little or no direct threat from the distant Communist countries, such as the Soviet Union and Yugoslavia, with both of which Thailand maintained diplomatic ties.

With the exception of Cambodia, which Thailand tends to regard as being influenced by Communist China and by North Vietnam, Thailand's relations with all non-Communist Asian countries have been amicable. Thailand has consistently played an active peacemaking role in the region. The most notable achievement was its contribution toward the normalization in 1966 of diplomatic relations among three nations—Malaysia, Indonesia and the Philippines.

RELATIONS WITH NON-COMMUNIST ASIAN COUNTRIES

Cambodia

Thailand's relations with its neighbor Cambodia have been characterized by animosity and mistrust. The territories which were lost to France at the beginning of the century and which are now part of Cambodia have been the major source of friction, since Thailand has never accepted the loss as permanent. Although Thailand has suppressed its aspiration for regaining control of them by force and has adopted a more amicable policy, Cambodia appears to mistrust Thailand's motives and apparently believes it is only awaiting an opportune moment to begin an active campaign for the retrocession of the territories. Diplomatic relations, severed in 1961, have not been resumed, and evidence of Thai willingness to resume contact has not elicited a comparable response from Cambodia.

Border incidents arising from inadequately delineated frontiers have been one of the principal causes of strained relations. The most prominent instance was a dispute over the possession of an ancient Buddhist temple called Phra Viharn (Preah Vihear in Cambodian transliteration). The issue was whether the temple is situated in the Thai province of Sisaket or the Cambodian province of Kompong Thom. The Thai occupation of the temple by force in 1954 was followed by an exchange of accusations concerning border violations. When all bilateral efforts to settle the dispute through negotiations failed, diplomatic relations were suspended from November 1958 to February 1959. Relations were further worsened in October 1959 when Cambodia, over Thai protest, requested the International Court of Justice to assume jurisdiction of the dispute. The Court was petitioned to affirm Cambodian sovereignty over the location of the temple and to order the withdrawal of Thai armed forces from the territory.

When, in June 1962, the International Court decided in favor of Cambodia, Thailand's initial reaction was hostile. After observing that the president of the Court was a national of Communist Poland and that some of the judges were from countries which had been imperialist powers in Asia, Thailand termed the judgment "political" and temporarily withdrew its representatives from the SEATO Council and the Geneva Conference on Laos. A Cabinet minister vowed that Thailand would defend the temple "to the last drop . . . blood." The United States was also the object of protest for allowing Dean Acheson, then presidential adviser to the North Atlantic Treaty Organization (NATO) and former secretary of state, to represent Cambodia before the Court.

Nonetheless, Prime Minister Sarit announced that his government would abide, under protest, but the Court's decision so that the "good reputation" of Thailand would not be impaired and to prevent the dispute from working to the advantage of the Communists. Sarit, however, reserved the "inherent right" of Thailand to have recourse to any legal means to recover the temple "at an opportune moment." Thailand has since proposed a Thai-Cambodian condominium over the temple, but in the middle of 1967 Cambodia continued to retain possession of the temple.

Another source of conflict between the two nations has been the divergent international outlook of each country. Thailand has been irritated by what it felt to be the Cambodian policy of flirting with Communist China and North Vietnam. It has maintained that Cambodia, which had rejected SEATO, is not a genuine neutralist state and has deplored what it calls the practice of "playing up one side against another and taking benefits from all sides without morality or integrity." Diplomatic relations were broken off by Cambodia in October 1961 after Prime Minister Sarit had alleged that Cambodia had become a springboard of Chinese Communist aggression against Thailand and South Vietnam. This assertion was prompted in turn by an alleged statement by Prince Sihanouk, the Cambodian chief of state, that he would rather fight Thailand than Communists.

In early 1963 United Nations Secretary-General U Thant sought unsuccessfully to restore formal relations. With the intensification of the Vietnam conflict and increasing evidence of North Vietnamese participation in the Communist insurgency in South Vietnam, relations with Cambodia continued to deteriorate. In February 1966 Thailand charged Cambodia, before the United Nations, with permitting its territory to be used as sanctuary for the Vietnamese Communist insurgents and with allowing them to pass through its territory into Thailand. Cambodia rejected the allegation.

In June 1966 Thailand declared that its relations with Cambodia could be normalized should Cambodia be "freed from Communist influence and possesses full discretion and liberty to decide for itself." At the same time it appealed to the United Nations to help restore diplomatic ties. By November 1966, however, the United Nations efforts through Special Representative Herbert de Ribbing, who had visited both Bangkok and Phnom Penh, had proved fruitless. Through him, Cambodia was known to have demanded that Thailand formally consent to the Cambodian version of national boundaries and repudiate whatever its aspirations it might have with respect to the temple of Phra Viharn. Thailand was not prepared to accept these terms, but it counterproposed that official relations be first restored to provide a cordial atmosphere for border negotiations. Cambodia rejected the Thai proposal.

Laos

Relations with Laos have been generally cordial. In 1955, for example, a Thai spokesman proposed that Thailand and Laos, along with Cambodia, form a Buddhist anti-Communist bloc. He pointed out that the three countries are linked by religions, ethnic and cultural affinities and that closer relations would bring about mutual and economic advantages. While Cambodia remained cool to the idea, a leading Laotian newspaper urged in an editorial as late as March 1953 that Thailand and Laos should form a federation.

By the mid-1950's Bangkok had replaced Saigon as the landlocked Laos' principal outlet to the sea. Politically, however, Thailand was seriously concerned about the unstable internal conditions in Laos arising from the complex power struggle among pro-Western rightist, neutralist and Communist forces there. During the Laotian civil-war years in the early 1960's, it gave political and moral support to the pro-Western forces. When the war culminated in the formation in mid-1962 of a tripartite coalition regime including the Communists, Thailand remained skeptical of its durability and expressed concern that the coalition front might be dominated by the Communists. As a result, it exercised increased vigilance along its border with Laos to prevent Communist infiltration especially into its northeastern region.

In the mid-1960's the border vigilance was further stepped up in view of the Communist withdrawal from the coalition regime and overt initiation of antigovernmental activities in many parts of the country. Thai authorities frequently have stated that Communist agents from North Vietnam infiltrated into Thailand through Laos. Nevertheless, official relations between the two countries remained cordial in mid-1967 apparently because of the continued existence in Vientiane of a neutralist regime, whose downfall was a major political goal of the Hanoi-supported Communist Pathet Lao movement.

Burma

Relations with Burma, Thailand's historic enemy, have been friendly in recent years. The two countries cooperated actively in the suppression of occasional insurgent activities by the Burmese frontier peoples adjoining Thailand's northwestern border region. A treaty of friendship was agreed to in October 1957, and an agreement was reached in July 1960 facilitating movement between the two countries of those residing within 10 miles of the common frontier. In May 1963 they also signed a pact on border arrangements and cooperation which provided for the establishment of a ministerial-level committee. This committee is charged with the tasks of devising means of improving border security and of consulting on measures for economic and cultural cooperation between the two nations (see ch. 27, Public Order and Safety).

In November 1966 Prime Minister Thanom Kittikachorn paid a 3-day state visit to Rangoon at the invitation of the Burmese chief of state General Ne Win. Since the severance of diplomatic relations between Thailand and Cambodia in 1961, the Bangkok government has been represented by Burma in Phnom Penh.

Malaysia, the Philippines and Indonesia

Thailand has collaborated with the governments in Kuala Lumpur and Manila through a regional organization called Association of Southeast Asia (ASA). Established by Malaya (now Malaysia), the Philippines and Thailand in July 1961 as a nonpolitical body independent of any power bloc, the ASA sought to provide an effective forum for regional consultation, collaboration and mutual assistance in the economic, cultural, scientific and administrative fields. Its achievements have, however, remained largely on paper, especially since 1963, because of strained relations between Malaysia and the Philippines. In March 1966 its members met in Bangkok in an effort to revitalize the organization and to study ways and means of liberalizing trade among the member nations by lowering tariffs on goods traded among them (see ch. 24, Foreign Economic Relations).

Initially, the ASA hoped to include Burma, Cambodia, Ceylon and Indonesia, but these countries showed reluctance because two of its members, Thailand and the Philippines, were also members of SEATO. In June 1966, however, there was a preliminary hint that Indonesia, under new political leadership, was considering the possibility of joining in the ASA. It remained uncertain, however, whether the ASA would retain its name in such an eventuality.

Thai-Malaysian friendship has been especially evident in the two nations' combined efforts to suppress Communist rebels operating along their border regions. In March 1965 they signed a border agreement for further strengthening their collaborative counterinsurgency operations in the areas.

To help restore normal relations between Malaysia on the one hand and Indonesia and the Philippines on the other, Thailand has actively sought to mediate their differences. After Malaysia severed diplomatic relations with both Indonesia and the Philippines in September 1963, Thailand agreed to represent the Kuala Lumpur government in both Djakarta and Manila.

The Thai effort as peacemaker was rewarded in early 1966 when the Philippines and Malaysia reestablished formal relations, and again in June 1966 when Bangkok became host to a conference between Malaysia and Indonesia, as the result of which they agreed to cease their hostility against each other and normalize formal relations. It was after this conference that the Indonesia Foreign Minister Adam Malik confirmed a report that Thailand, Malaysia, Indonesia and the Philippines had agreed in principle to establish an organization for regional collaboration.

South Vietnam

Thailand has been especially concerned about the threat to its security posed by Communist insurgency in South Vietnam. Ambassadors were exchanged between the two countries soon after the Republic of Vietnam was proclaimed, and the need for solidarity to safeguard security was stressed during President Ngo Dinh Diem's visit to Thailand in 1957 and that of Thai Foriegn Minister Thanat Khoman to Saigon in 1959.

The relationship between Bangkok and Saigon has become

closer as a result of Cambodia's hostility toward them both while it maintained friendly ties with Communist China and North Vietnam. South Vietnam's Prime Minister Nguyen Cao Ky paid an official visit to Thailand in August 1965 reportedly to promote a new anti-Communist alliance based mainly on economic cooperation. After his visit Thailand agreed to train more South Vietnamese pilots and provide additional medical units to assist in South Vietnam's struggle against insurgency. In mid-1965 Thai aid to Saigon also included Thai aviation crews, cement and roofing materials. In October 1966, Thailand offered the equivalent of $20 million a year rice credit to South Vietnam. In January 1967 the Thai government also announced plans to dispatch a 1,000-man infantry battalion to South Vietnam (see ch. 24, Foreign Economic Relations; ch. 28, The Armed Forces).

Others

Diplomatic relations are maintained with all other Asian countries except the Communist states. Relations with Nationalist China, which decided in 1946 to exchange diplomatic envoys on an equal basis, the first time for these two countries, have been generally friendly. The countries, however, have been occasionally at odds over the issue of Chinese Nationalist irregular troops who continue to enter Thailand illegally from Burma across its northern frontier. Thailand has insisted that the Nationalist Chinese Government should receive these illegal entrants, but the latter has refused, alleging that it is troubled by increasing population and by the shortage of arable land.

With Japan there have been close cultural and economic relations since the early 1950's. Japan, long admired by Thailand for its economic, technological and cultural achievements, further gained the friendship of Thailand by agreeing in January 1962 to pay a longstanding World War II debt to the country (see ch. 24, Foreign Economic Relations).

The mutual anti-Communist cause has brought Thailand and South Korea closer since 1950. After the outbreak of hostilities in Korea, Thailand announced its support of United Nations intervention and sent to Korea about 2,000 troops, 2 corvettes, a transport ship, 2 airplanes and 40,000 tons of rice. Thai forces were withdrawn after the cessation of hostilities, but in June 1966, Thailand sent an infantry company to Korea to start a 1-year tour of duty as a contingent of the United Nations command there. Earlier, in February 1966, on the occasion of a state visit by South Korean President Park Chung Hee to Bangkok, the two nations had agreed to promote closer political, economic and cultural ties.

Relations with India are cordial. When India's Vice President,

Zakir Hussain, paid a visit to Bangkok in October 1966, Prime Minister Kittikachorn expressed the hope for improved relations in view of their traditional friendship and of their common dedication to the purposes and principles of the United Nations. Thailand, India and Pakistan were among the 23 nations which had sent delegates to the Asian Peoples Anti-Communist League (APACL) convention held in Seoul in November 1966.

Affiliated through SEATO, Thailand and Pakistan have maintained friendly relations. Since October 1965, when Pakistan broke off diplomatic relations with Malaysia, Thailand has represented Malaysian affairs in Pakistan.

RELATIONS WITH THE UNITED STATES

Thailand's traditionally cordial relations with the United States became progressively more cordial after the Communist takeover of mainland China in 1949. In April 1950, Thailand received its first direct aid from the United States, $10 million worth of arms and military equipment. Three months later, it signed an executive agreement providing for the exchange of students under the Fulbright Act. In September the two nations signed an Economic and Technical Cooperation Agreement, followed a month later by their first formal military aid pact.

Thailand joined SEATO in September 1954 and has generally regarded it as an effective and expedient military deterrent against Communist aggression. In March 1961, when the security of its own frontier was seriously threatened by the swelling tide of Communist Pathet Lao forces in Laos, Thailand requested SEATO to dispatch its troops to aid the anti-Communist Laotian forces. When the SEATO ministerial council refused to take such action and instead issued a vaguely worded warning to the Communists, Thailand demanded that SEATO be reorganized and that the rule requiring unanimity for action be revised (see ch. 28, The Armed Forces).

To allay Thailand's increasing apprehension, Secretary of State Dean Rusk issued in March 1962 a joint statement with Thai Foreign Minister Thanat Khoman in Washington, pledging United States determination to defend Thailand individually regardless of whatever action other members of SEATO might decide on. Secretary of State Rusk declared that this obligation of the United States does not depend upon the prior consent of all other SEATO members since this treaty obligation is individual as well as collective. Thailand was assured that American troops could be dispatched to the country within 24 hours to meet any crisis. Thus, when the strategic Laotian town of Nam Tha fell to the Pathet Lao forces in May 1962, the United States sent troops to Thailand at the request of the Thai government. Great Britain, Australia and New Zealand sent token forces.

This action did much to strengthen ties between Bangkok and Washington and to improve the Thai attitude toward SEATO. In 1964 the two nations began to undertake joint developmental efforts in the northeastern frontier region of Thailand to forestall Communist insurgency in the area. These efforts were further accelerated in 1965. With the intensification of Communist insurgency in South Vietnam, Thailand has actively supported United States counterinsurgency activities there. As a part of this effort and to improve Thailand's own defense capability against external Communist threat, the Bangkok government has allowed the United States to maintain troops, as well as to build and use military bases in the country for defensive measures (see ch. 28, The Armed Forces). The United States' presence in Thailand is based on the SEATO Treaty of September 1954, subsequently supplemented by the Rusk-Khoman joint statement of March 1962. The Thai Government has maintained that the United States bases are Thai bases, over which the Thai rather than the American flag flies.

In October 1966 Thailand, together with South Korea and the Philippines, cosponsored a conference which was held in Manila and was attended by the United States, Australia, New Zealand and South Vietnam. After the conference, which reaffirmed the participant nations' determination to support South Vietnam's anti-Communist cause, President Johnson visited Thailand and firmly assured the nation that it could "count on the United States to meet its obligations under the SEATO treaty."

In the same month Deputy Prime Minister and Minister of Interior Praphat Charusathien announced that Thailand and the United States agreed in principle that the United States military personnel violating Thai laws would be tried by a Thai court. He also stated that a status of forces agreement between the two nations embodying this principle was in the final stage of negotiation. In January 1967 a total of 35,300 members of the United States armed forces were in Thailand (see ch. 28, The Armed Forces). In March 1967 Thai and American officials in Bangkok jointly announced that "American planes are using Thai bases to bomb North Vietnam."

RELATIONS WITH GREAT BRITAIN AND FRANCE

Thai relations with Great Britian which, at the end of World War II, were initially strained because of Great Britain's severe war claims against Thailand, began to improve in 1950 as Thailand firmly aligned itself with the West in efforts to contain communism. London dropped its heavy damage claims and decided to accept very modest compensation. After becoming aligned with Great Britain through SEATO, Thailand expected it to take an active role in resisting Communist threats in Southeast Asia. The British Government, however, did not give direct aid until after the Laotian crisis of 1961. The situation between the two countries improved after mid-1962 when Great Britain sent a token force to Thailand in view of the rapidly deteriorating Laotian situation. In late 1963 Great Britain also offered to help Thailand in educational and economic matters. At about the same time London also announced a plan to construct an airfield in northeast Thailand under an agreement with the Bangkok government. By early 1965 the airfield was operating.

Relations with France have not always been cordial. During the Indochina War, Thailand did not oppose the Vietnamese independence movement against the French. Although allied through SEATO, Thailand, especially since 1962, has not been able to consider France as an active supporter. It has not accepted French President de Gaulle's proposal of August 1963 to neutralize and reunify the whole of Vietnam. Thailand has also deplored France's inactivity in SEATO and the French policy of seeming to favor Cambodia, to which Paris gave military aid.

RELATIONS WITH COMMUNIST CHINA

Policies pertaining to the Peiping regime are dictated in part by the geographical proximity of the two countries and in part by the anti-Chinese inclination—manifest since the late 1930's—of the Thai government which has varied in emphasis but not in direction. Thai authorities have generally admired the commercial acumen of the large Chinese minority, but have frequently questioned the political loyalty of this economically powerful group (see ch. 15, Political Dynamics).

Thailand has never recognized Communist China, which is regarded as the principal threat to its independence and territorial integrity. It condemned the Peiping regime as aggressor when the latter intervened in the Korean conflict. It has also imposed an embargo on the export of strategic materials to that country.

Thai apprehension regarding Communist China was heightened in January 1953 when the Peiping regime announced the establishment of an autonomous government for the Thai minority in Yunnan Province, less than 100 miles from northern Thailand. For centuries Thai peoples had been an important minority in this area. Since the announced objective of the autonomous government was to strengthen the defense of the Thai fatherland, Bangkok's leaders regarded it as a Chinese Communist-sponsored anti-Thai movement. In mid-1954 Pridi Phanomyong, an exiled former primer minister of Thailand then in Communist China, broadcast appeals to the Thai people to overthrow the pro-Western Bangkok government (see ch. 15, Political Dynamics).

Fear of spreading Chinese Communist influence has been further sustained by the intensified Communist insurgency in South Vietnam, which Thailand has blamed on both Peiping and Hanoi. Thailand has also expressed its uneasiness over the extension of Chinese Communist influence in Southeast Asia through the alleged Cambodian policy of accommodation to the Peiping regime. Thai hostility toward Peiping has been increased also by Chinese Communist open announcements in January 1965 of an avowedly anti-Thai and pro-Communist movement called the Thailand Patriotic Front (see ch. 15, Political Dynamics). The threatening attitude of Communist China toward Thailand was the subject of a communique issued by the SEATO Council of Ministers after meeting in London in May 1965. The communique noted a statement of Peiping's Foreign Minister Chen Yi to the effect that Thailand would be the next target of revolutionary warfare and that there would be a guerrilla war in Thailand by the end of 1965.

RELATIONS WITH NORTH VIETNAM

Relations with North Vietnam, which Thailand has not recognized, have been antagonistic because of the support given by the Hanoi government, along with Communist China, to the Communist elements in Thailand and to the Thai Patriotic Front (see ch. 15, Political Dynamics).

Thailand was ready to cooperate on the problem of repatriating some 80,000 Vietnamese nationals, most of whom had come to Thailand as refugees from the Indochina War and settled in the Thai northeastern provinces. The Thai government suspected many of them as pro-Viet Minh and hence a potential subversive threat (see ch. 5, Ethnic Groups). In August 1959 a 2-year repatriation agreement for those wishing to go to North Vietnam was negotiated, over South Vietnamese protest, between the Red Cross societies of the two countries, aided by the International Committee of the Red Cross. Under this agreement, which was renewed in December 1962, more than 40,000 persons had been sent to North Vietnam by July 1964.

Repatriation activities were suspended in August 1964 when Hanoi alleged that no more refugees could be accepted because of the United States' aerial attacks. The Red Cross societies of the two countries agreed to reconsider the matter when conditions permit. In mid-1967 more than 40,000 Vietnamese still remained in Thailand.

In mid-1967 Bangkok continued to ignore North Vietnamese charges that the Thai government permitted the United States to transform its country into a "new-style colony and military base in Southeast Asia." For its part, the Bangkok government continued to characterize the Hanoi regime as a tool of Communist China and also accused it of actively aiding and abetting Thai Communist rebels in and outside Thailand.

RELATIONS WITH INTERNATIONAL ORGANIZATIONS

Thailand was admitted to the United Nations in December 1946 and has since been a stanch supporter of its principles and activities, especially its peacekeeping missions through the world. Thailand was the first Asian nation to pledge support for the United Nations police action in Korea. In November 1956 it voted in favor of creating a United Nations Expeditionary Force to maintain peace in the Middle East. Similarly, it later supported the United Nations operations in the Congo.

Membership in the United Nations subsidiary organizations include: Food and Agriculture Organization (FAO), International Atomic Energy Agency (IAEA), International Bank for Reconstruction and Development (IBRD), International Civil Aviation Organization (ICAO), International Development Association (IDA), International Finance Corporation (IFC), International Labor Organization (ILO), International Monetary Fund (IMF), International Telecommunication Union (ITU), United Nations Educational, Scientific and Cultural Organization (UNESCO), Universal Postal Union (UPU), World Health Organization (WHO) and World Meteorological Organization (WMO).

Organizations maintaining regional representatives or missions in Bangkok in early June 1967 were: FAO, IBRD, ICAO, ILO, UNESCO and WHO. In addition, the Economic Commission for Asia and the Far East (ECAFE), a regional commission of the United Nations, has its secretariat in Bangkok. On a regional scale, Thailand is also associated with SEATO, ASA, the Committee for Coordination of Investigations of the Lower Mekong Basin, the Asian and Pacific Council (ASPAC) and the Colombo Plan (see ch. 24, Foreign Economic Relations; ch. 28, The Armed Forces).

MECHANICS OF FOREIGN RELATIONS

The making of foreign policies and conduct of external relations are the primary functions of the Ministry of Foreign Affairs, headed since 1959 by Thanat Khoman, who is generally regarded by his Asian as well as Western counterparts as an outstanding diplomat. Other influential Thai personalities in Bangkok's diplomacy include Prime Minister Thanom Kittikachorn; Deputy Prime Minister and Minister of Interior Prapart Charusathien; Deputy Prime Minister and former Minister of Foreign Affairs Prince Wan Waithayakorn; and Minister of National Development and former Secretary General of SEATO Pote Sarasin.

The conduct of foreign relations has been virtually an executive prerogative, subject to little or no scrutiny by other governmental authorities. In mid-1967 there was little evidence of any public criticism of foreign policies and relations.

The Ministry of Foreign Affairs is divided into six departments: Political, Protocol, Economic, Treaty and Legal, Information, and International Organization. The calibre of foreign service personnel is high and generally well trained. Thai regard a career in their foreign service as highly prestigious.

ATTITUDES TOWARD FOREIGN PEOPLES AND NATIONS

The vast majority of the people take little interest in foreign affairs and know little about its problems. Knowledge of foreign peoples and countries is very limited. Popular interest and understanding appears to be gradually increasing, however, as a result of expanding education and mass communications media, the growing numbers of tourists and the continued presence and activities of missions from international organizations.

Lacking the colonial history which has nourished intense fear and suspicion of the West among other Southeast Asian nations, Thailand does not recoil from close association with Western countries. It does not generally display the anti-Western nationalist sentiments of peoples long subject to foreign rule. These factors have helped create among the Thai peoples attitudes favorable to cooperation with nearly all countries for mutual benefits.

United States

The Thai people have had little or no cause to resent or suspect the avowed goodwill of American people and their government in relation to Thailand. Since the United States is generally regarded as not having had any territorial designs or other ulterior motives on the country, the people have held a friendly regard for it.

The people, urban dwellers in particular, appear to be favorably impressed with the technological achievements of the United

States. Among the more sophisticated Bangkok elite, America's interest in the welfare of the Thai people and its universal concern for national freedom are acknowledged. The traditionally favorable Thai attitude toward the United States was probably at a lowest point during the first half of 1962 when the Bangkok leaders resented what they termed the "American bias" in the Thai-Cambodian dispute over the temple of Phra Viharn; furthermore, SEATO's policy of moderation vis-a-vis the Laotian civil war then in progress was unfavorably viewed, especially among Thai official circles. The situation has appreciably improved since then because of the United States' demonstration of its firm intention to help defend the country against all external threats.

On official levels the Bangkok leaders are generally sensitive to any insinuations, Communist or otherwise, that Thailand is dependent on Washington and that it is something less than an equal partner in its relations with the United States. They continue to maintain the position that their security problem with the Communist terrorists is essentially an internal matter which should be met by their own resources. Foreign Minister Khoman declared in June 1966 that his country would ask for help from outside sources "only if the threat expands into an international problem and it is beyond our strength to deal effectively with it."

Asian Nations

Aside from a certain animosity toward Cambodia, the Thai attitude toward such non-Communist Asian nations as Japan, India, Indonesia, Malaysia, the Philippines, Burma and Laos has been generally friendly and cooperative. The Thai have always admired Japan as a model to be emulated. India is highly respected as the Buddhist holy land; the Thai are also favorably impressed with the neutralist orientation of India's foreign relations. The feeling of hostility with which the Thai have traditionally regarded Burma has gradually lessened in recent years through improved formal relations.

In contrast, the border tensions between Thailand and Cambodia have added popular resentment to Bangkok's growing suspicion of Cambodia as a pro-Chinese Communist state. The Thai, especially those in the Northeast, have tended to regard their Laotian neighbors as cultural cousins who speak the same language and share the same customs and faith. This attitude continued to be manifest in 1967, although internal tensions generated by the Communist Pathet Lao forces were viewed with increasing apprehension.

Communist Nations

Most Thai know very little about Communist nations and their ideologies. To them "communism" is simply a bad word heard constantly over the government radio, and they have some vague notion that it is associated with radical programs and China. In fact, the principal source of information in much of the country about communism is probably the government itself.

Communist China is viewed as the primary danger to Thailand by both the people and the ruling elite. When war broke out in Korea, the Thai government declared that it considered itself to be at war with communism—an indirect statement aimed at the Peiping regime. Internally, the government has intensified its antisubversive and anti-Chinese campaign, especially since the Peiping regime established the Thai autonomous regional government in Yunnan in 1953.

The Thai attitude toward North Vietnam is overtly hostile because of the latter's alleged involvement in the Communist terrorist activities in the Northeast. By contrast, Bangkok's attitude toward the Soviet Union and other East European Communist states appears to be less militant than it is in the case of the Peiping and Hanoi regimes. Although on several occasions Russian nationals have been expelled from Thailand on charges of subversive activities, it appears that Bangkok would be willing, under certain conditions, to establish closer relations with Moscow. Thailand's decision in September 1962 to formalize trade relations with the Soviet Union appeared to be a first step in this direction. This tendency may be attributed to the growing feeling among some educated Thai that the one-sided commitment of their country to the United States and other nations of the West may be politically inadvisable. Many of this group have asserted that Thai interests may be better served by joining the neutralist bloc or by adopting an independent Thai policy than by following the present unequivocally pro-Western course. The adoption of such a neutralist foreign policy would be entirely consistent with the jealously guarded tradition of national independence. With the increased signs of Communist threats from without, however, most educated Thai people are inclined to accept the pragmatic course of pro-Western commitment combined with the nationalist assertion of self-reliance.

CHAPTER 17

PUBLIC INFORMATION

In 1967 the principal channels of information for the people as a whole were radio, films and an informal network of word of mouth communication. Newspapers, books and magazines were read largely by members of the educated elite in the capital who, although relatively few in number, played a significant role in the formation of public opinion.

Radio broadcasting and television were virtually government monopolies. The most influential stations and channels were directed by the Public Relations Department of the Office of the Prime Minister, the Army, the National Police Department, the Ministry of Education and the Thai Television Company, Ltd., a partially state-controlled agency. Newpapers, publishing and motion picture companies were mainly private commercial undertakings. Privately owned information channels were subject to strict controls by the government and were at its disposal for use in building popular support for the government and its policies.

The exercise of censorship powers over privately owned news media has been adjudged necessary because of the threat of Communist subversion. Government regulations, therefore, forbid the publication of material which might endanger internal security or public morals or upset friendly relations with foreign governments.

The government regards radio as a "powerful instrument of information and enlightenment . . ." which, according to an official Thai publication, is "implicitly . . . subserving the policy of the government." In 1966 there were about 120 broadcasting stations in the country, and urban residents regarded radio to be the most reliable source of news. Special efforts have been made to reach larger segments of the rural population, notably those living in the less developed Northeast. Programs designed to solicit support for government policies and to warn against Communist subversion are combined with educational and cultural information, health advice and suggestions regarding community development. By 1967 broadcasts had become popular in the countryside, especially among the younger people. Most villagers, however, still depended on news gathered in the course of visits to friends, in the marketplace and from village monks.

In 1966 some 18 dailies were published in Bangkok and 1 was published in the provincial capital of Chiengmai. In addition, there were a number of weekly, semiweekly and other periodicals catering mainly to the interest of the urban population in sports, films and the lottery. In spite of close government control newspaper editors were free, within limits, to present to the public complete and unbiased coverage of news.

Television, already important in Bangkok and vicinity, was to be linked into a countrywide network. In 1966 plans were underway to survey suitable sites for establishing repeat stations which would be linked with the three regional stations, Khon Kaen (Northeast), Lampang (Northern) and Hat Yai (Southern).

In the course of official efforts to shape public opinion and to mobilize popular support, special attention has been given to the educated minority in Bangkok and in a few other urban centers. Since 1962, however, some information programs have been directed specifically to audiences in rural areas. In the provinces of the Northeast, where the people are vulnerable to Communist agitation stimulated from adjacent Laos, the government has expanded its efforts in the information field to win popular support.

Information programs addressed to domestic audiences concentrated on three related themes—prosperity and progress; internal order and stability; and the threat of Communist subversion. The government has emphasized that its primary concern was with economic and social development and has stressed the accomplishments brought about in these spheres. The need to strengthen national unity and to promote order and stability has also been accentuated. The third major theme, that of communism, has usually been treated as a threat to values and institutions to which the Thai are profoundly attached—independence, Buddhism and the throne (see ch. 13, Social Values; ch. 18, Political Values and Attitudes).

The main vehicles for information programs intended for audiences beyond the country's boundaries were the government-owned radio and reports of statements by Thai officials published in the press of friendly countries.

OFFICIAL CONTROLS

Regulation of the press in Thailand dates back to the reign of King Chulalongkorn (1868–1910), who initiated an informal type of censorship which he exercised according to his personal judgment. Since then the press has been subject to continuous government control, the severity of which varied considerably at different times.

In 1967 the legal provision for control was the Press Act of 1941 and Announcement No. 17 issued by the Revolutionary Party in October 1958. The Press Act contains some provisions to silence criticism of the government, but Announcement No. 17 is more specific and severe. It provides that all prospective newspaper publishers must apply for a license and that ". . . any newspaper publishing statements of a certain character shall be warned, impounded, and destroyed or undergo punishment in the form of withdrawal of the license of its publisher, printer or proprietor." Statements subject to punishment under the Announcement are those which "offend the King, . . . discredit the government, . . . contribute to the popularity or desirability of Communism . . . or constitute Communist subversive tactics; . . . those which are vulgar; . . . and likely to undermine the morals . . . of the nation; . . . those which divulge official secrets."

Although there is no prepublication censorship, the authorities carefully check the contents of newspapers to ensure that the provisions of the Press Act and Announcement No. 17 are not violated. The Anti-Communist Act of 1952 also is frequently invoked to censor material regarded as subversive by the authorities.

Article 33 of the Draft Constitution of 1966 provides that:

> A person enjoys full liberty of speech, writing, printing and publication. . . . Such liberty may be restricted only by the provisions of special law, enacted for the purpose of safeguarding the liberties of other persons, averting a state of emergency, maintaining public order or good morals or protecting youth against moral degeneration. . . . The closing down of a printing establishment or an order forbidding publishing work and (providing for) censorship of newspapers may not be effected except during a time of war, or state of war, or during the period when a state of emergency or martial law is declared . . . .

Martial law in the country has been in force since 1958.

In 1967 enforcement of the regulations was a responsibility of the Public Relations Department in the Office of the Prime Minister. The Department, headed in 1967 by Lieutenant General Kritcha Punnakanta, consisted of the Secretariat, News Division, Public Opinion Survey Division, Public Enlightenment Division, Radio Engineering and License Division, Foreign Affairs Division, and the Thai Information Services Division. Regional branches of the Department operated in Lampang, Khon Kaen, Surat Thani and Songkhla.

Broadcasting and television were supervised and coordinated by the Bureau of Radio and Television Services, a major agency under the Office of the Prime Minister. The Bureau included the Home Broadcasting Services and the Overseas Broadcasting Division. One of its principal functions was the enforcement of the Radio Communications Act. Although the latter contains no direct provision regarding the censorship of programs, the Bureau must ensure that "broadcasts are in good taste and do not threaten public order and security."

INFORMATION CHANNELS

Press

The earliest Thai newspapers were published under the auspices of foreign missionaries, the court and commercial companies. In 1844 a United States missionary, Dan Beach Bradley, published the first Thai-English semimonthly, *The Bangkok Recorder*. The newspaper carried political news, commercial announcements and reports from Europe and neighboring Asian countries. King Mongkut (1851–68) published the first *Royal Gazette* in 1866. The *Royal Gazette* lasted only a year, but King Chulalongkorn (1868–1910) in 1874 revived the publication and renamed it the *Government Gazette*. It has been published continuously, containing legal decrees, ministerial regulations and public announcements.

The first daily, the *Siam Daily Advertiser*, published in 1868, started as an English-language newspaper but soon carried parallel news columns in Thai and English.

During the early twentieth century newspaper publishing attracted the interest mainly of members of academic, religious and military establishments. Newspapers published under these auspices were mostly periodicals. After a temporary newsprint shortage during World War II many daily newspaper and periodicals were created during the 1950's.

Character and Scope

Thailand had 19 dailies in 1966; all except 1 were published in Bangkok. Thirteen were published in Thai, four in Chinese and two in English. Their estimated total circulation was over 500,000. Individual circulation figures, regarded as trade secrets, are difficult to ascertain. Press run figures, however, are available, and circulation estimates of daily newspapers, when given, are generally based on about two-thirds of the number actually printed.

In addition to the dailies, there are many weeklies, biweeklies and newspapers published 5 days a week. Their numbers in 1964 were estimated to vary between 37 and 51, with a total circulation of approximately 157,000. More than half of these newspapers, however, have press runs of less than 4,000, and only a few have individual circulations of more than 1,000 or 2,000.

Thai government press officials estimated in 1964 that an average of one newspaper copy was available to every 100 persons. A large majority of the newspaper readers reside in Bangkok, Thon Buri and in the provincial capitals. Most newspapers are bought daily from newsstands, and each copy is read by four to five persons.

Most of the newspapers are privately owned and published for profit. A few are backed by politicians supporting the government. Others are controlled by wealthy entrepreneurs. The Thai Commercial Company and the Dhana Karn Phim Company are among the major newspaper publishing enterprises in the Bangkok metropolitan area. Several of the nondaily newspapers and periodical magazines are published by some of the ministries, branches of the Army, members of the aristocracy, church dignitaries and intellectuals.

In the strenuous competition for readers the press tends to rely heavily on sensational news stories and human interest features. International news occupies usually no more than 1 page of an 8- to 12-page journal. Most newspapers have at least one editorial and an occasional political cartoon. Serialized fiction of love and violence, such as translated American Western stories, occupies a prominent place. Issues featuring a beauty contest story, the weekly lottery results or a boxing match, may double normal sales. Many readers, in fact, purchase newspapers mainly because of their interest in lottery results and sports news.

In provincial newspapers news items are largely reprints from the metropolitan press or are transcribed from Bangkok broadcasts. Since 1963, however, the provincial newspapers have placed increasing emphasis on local news and regional events. This policy change became necessary because of the growing competition provincial newspapers faced from Bangkok dailies which have become available in many provincial areas as a result of the improved transportation network.

Advertisements are vigorously solicited and occupy extensive space. Most dailies devote 30 percent of their space to advertisements, and some of them as much as 50 percent or more. The nondaily newspapers, because their financial situation is more precarious than that of the major dailies, assign from 50 to 70 percent of their space to advertisements.

Daily newspapers have an average of 10 eight-column pages, 21½ by 15½ inches in size. The format of nondaily newspapers is the same, but the number of pages varies between 4 and 35. Photographs, drawings, color and cartoons are used freely both in dailies and nondailies.

In the Bangkok metropolitan area the technical equipment of newspaper publishing enterprises has markedly improved as a result of the growing number of rotary presses imported from Japan since 1961. In the provinces, on the other hand, few newspaper publishers have their own printing and engraving facilities except those located in the provincial capitals of the Northern Region where, in 1963, all but three of the newspapers had their own printing plants.

Mechanical typesetters are rare since the complexity of the Thai alphabet makes the production and retail costs of such equipment prohibitive. Since only the largest newspaper and book publishers rely on mechanical methods, a large number of skilled typesetters are employed. For example, an eight-page daily in Bangkok with a press run of 20,000 employed a staff of about 400 setters.

Major Newspapers

There is no single outstanding Thai-language newspaper, but some have attained somewhat greater prominence than others either because of circulation or influence (see table 1). One of the most widely read newspaper is *Phim Thai* (Thai Press), a popular, morning newspaper specializing in sensationalism. Edited in 1967 by Chayong Chawalit, it devotes little attention to political developments, on which its position is neutral. Extensive space is given to scandal stories and crime reports. Owned by the Thai Commercial Company, *Phim Thai* moved to new quarters in 1963, equipped with modern rotary presses.

Siam Nikorn (Siamese People) also owned by the Thai Commercial Company, has an estimated circulation of 20,000. Formerly a leftist newspaper, it has adopted a more moderate position and in 1967 was one of the leading dailies, popular with the better educated. Its coverage of international affairs is praised as complete and constructive.

Another important daily is *Siam Rath* (Siam State); royalist in orientation, it has considerable influence and is noted for high journalistic standards. Founded in 1950, it claims a circulation of about 30,000. Government officials and educated persons generally predominate among *Siam Rath's* readers.

Sarn Seri (Free Press) is another quite widely read Thai-language daily owned by the Dhana Karn Phim Company which is also the owner of the much larger newspaper, *Thai Raiwan* (Thai Daily).

286

Table 1.—*Thailand Daily Newspapers, 1967*

Name of Newspaper	English Translation	Place of Publication	Estimated Circulation
Thai Language:			
Chao Thai	Thai People	Bangkok	9,600
Khao Panit	Trade News	_ _do_ _	8,000
Kiatisak	Fame	_ _do _ _	35,000
Kon Muang	People of the North	Chiengmai	5,000
Lak Muang	Pillar of the City	Bangkok	14,000
Phim Thai	Thai Press	_ _do_ _	65,000
Prachathipathai	Democracy	_ _do_ _	12,000
Sarn Seri	Free Press	_ _do_ _	35,000
Siam Nikorn	Siamese People	_ _do_ _	20,000
Siam Rath	Siam State	_ _do_ _	30,000
Siang Angtong	Voice of Angtong	_ _do_ _	20,000
Thai Raiwan	Thai Daily	_ _do _	100,000
Thai Rath	Thai State	_ _do_ _	120,000
Chinese Language*:			
Sakol	Universal Daily	_ _do_ _	5,000
(Shieh Chieh Pao)			
Sing Siang Yit Pao	Daily Siam Star	_ _do_ _	45,000
(Hsing Hsien Jih Pao)			
Siri Nakorn	Pride of the City	_ _do_ _	28,000
(Ching Hua Jih Pao)			
Thong Hua	China Daily	_ _do_ _	25,000
(Chung Hua Pao)			
English Language:			
The Bangkok Post		do_ _	13,000
The Bangkok World		do_ _	13,000

*The Thai title is listed first, followed by the Chinese title in parentheses.

Source: Adapted from the *Thailand Official Yearbook, 1964* p. 413; U.S., United States Information Agency, Research and Reference Service, *The Overseas Chinese in Thailand: A Communications Factbook, 1966*, pp. 17, 21; U.S., United States Information Service, *Thailand: County Data, 1966;* and *Editor and Publisher, International Year-book, 1967*, p. 528.

Kon Muang (People of the North), the only nonmetropolitan daily, is published in Chiengmai. Founded in 1961, it has modern printing facilities and has attracted many readers in the provinces of the Northern Region.

There are four Chinese-language dailies, all established after World War II and owned independently. They are usually pro-West in orientation and abstain from commenting on Thai political events. The standards of the two leading Chinese dailies, in respect to news coverage and presentation, are comparable to those of the better metropolitan dailies in the United States. They report extensively on international events and devote much space to commercial and financial information. Unlike their Thai counterparts, Chinese dailies publish both morning and evening editions and are distributed through circulation agents.

Sing Siang Yit Pao (Daily Siam Star) and *Siri Nakorn* (Pride of the City) are the most important among the Chinese dailies. With estimated circulations of about 45,000 and 28,000, respectively, they appeal mostly to educated readers. *Sakol* (Universal Daily) and *Thong Hua* (China Daily), with circulations of approximately 5,000 and 25,000, respectively, feature general news, interspersed with reports on crime and fiction items. They appeal mostly to readers in the middle and lower income groups.

The English-language daily, *The Bangkok Post,* reported a paid circulation of 13,000 in 1967. Started in 1946 as a commercial venture by a United States journalist, the controlling interest later was sold to Lord Thomson, a Canadian newspaper publisher who continued the editorial policy of its founder. *The Bangkok Post's* format is essentially that of a United States small-town newspaper, and it gives extensive coverage to international news. It achieved recognition as an established institution in the foreign community and among the Western-educated Thai.

The other equally prominent English-language daily, noted for the feature articles contained in its Sunday supplement, is the *Bangkok World* with approximately the same circulation as the *Post.* The *Bangkok World* in 1967 was purchased by Lord Thomson, who already owned *The Bangkok Post,* and by Cowles Communications, Incorporated, of New York.

Among the nondailies published in the Bangkok-Thon Buri area, *The Standard,* an English-language weekly, is edited by Princess Ngamchitr Prem. Intended for "officials, diplomats and socialites . . ." it features international news and publishes special articles on the cultures of countries represented by embassies in Bangkok. *Nakorn Thai* (Thai City) is a 5-day newspaper specializing in general news and lottery results. The *Weekly Bangkok Times,* with a press run of 20,000, is one of the most widely read nondaily newspapers in the metropolitan area. It concerns itself mainly with religious affairs and with Thai cultural and religious traditions. *Siang Chiengmai* (Voice of Chiengmai) and *Siang Rath* (Voice of the People)—the latter published in Nakhon Ratchasima—are the most popular nondaily newspapers in the Northern and Northeast regions, respectively. *Nakornsarn* (City Publication) serves the northeastern border province of Nakhon Phanom. *Thai Taksin* (Southern Illustrated Newspapers) is a popular newspaper serving the Southern Region.

Periodicals

A variety of magazines are financially unstable and have small circulation. Some of them are of general interest, but many of them are specially devoted to sports, motion picture stars, television, fashion or other popular subjects. Women's magazines, patterned after those in the United States, include *Satri Sarn* (Women's Magazine) and an English-language publication, *The Lady*. The latter is edited by Princess Ngamchitr, who also is editor of *The Standard*. Professional magazines are limited to a small group, including *Chang Ahkas* (The Air Engineer's Digest), published by the Thai Air Force Engineering Department, and *Vithya Sastr* (The Science Review), published by the Science Association of Thailand.

Nine Chinese periodicals were published in Bangkok in 1966. *Lien Yu* (Friend Magazine) with a circulation of 4,000 to 5,000 is among the most popular ones. It is published monthly and features general pictorial news. The rest of the Chinese periodicals—mostly weeklies—have estimated circulations of between 1,000 and 3,000; they feature motion picture news, serialized fiction and some current news items.

Books

Five commercial book publishers and the Fine Arts Department of the Ministry of Education published a total of 4,198 books in 1964. All five companies were in Bangkok, where most of their readers were found. Books of fiction were the most popular, followed by books dealing with social sciences, religion and history. In addition to the domestic output, bookstores carried sizable stocks of imported works, must of which were from the United States and Great Britain.

News Agencies

The country has no national news agency. Eighteen foreign press agencies and newspapers, with offices or part-time representatives in Bangkok, distribute and gather news. From the United States are the Associated Press, the Columbia Broadcasting Company, the New York Times, the United Press International, Newsweek and Time-Life; from Japan are the Kyodo News Service, the Jiji Press, and a newspaper, *Mainichi Shimbun;* and, from other parts of the world, Agence France-Presse. The West German Newspaper and Radio Service, the Overseas Chinese News Agency (Taiwan), the Pan Asia Newspaper Alliance, the Press Trust of India, Reuter-ComTel of Great Britain and the Soviet news agency, Tass.

Some of the Bangkok newspapers subscribe to the regular services of these agencies or monitor their dispatches which are broadcast to subscribes at dictation speed from Manila or Singapore. Others adapt news items from their competitors or rely on news releases by foreign embassies. Since coverage of foreign news in most of the Thai press is scanty, at best, newspapers are at little competitive disadvantage in printing foreign dispatches a few days late. The larger newspapers employ full-time reporters, assisted by a large number of part-time writers who gather local news.

Radio

Public radio broadcasting began in 1931. In 1966 the number of broadcasting stations was estimated at approximately 160. Since no license is required for the establishment of a broadcasting station, the consequent proliferation of stations has created problems in the allocation of wavelengths and in the government's efforts to control broadcasting. Most of the stations are owned by the government, directly or indirectly. Some are maintained by wealthy individuals. In 1966 the Thai Radio Control Commission recommended to the Cabinet that the number of stations be reduced to 35. According to recommendations, 25 of the remaining stations would be controlled by the Ministry of Defense, 1 by the National Police Department and 9 by the Public Relations Department.

The most powerful and influential facility is the National Broadcasting Station, commonly known as Radio Thailand (see table 2). It is controlled by the Public Relations Department in the Office of the Prime Minister and is financed by government subsidies. In 1963 Radio Thailand expanded its technical network by building several additional transmitters in the provinces, and its budget for that year exceeded 30 million baht (see Glossary). In 1966 Radio Thailand had a total of 14 mediumwave and shortwave transmitters.

Most of the radio stations are controlled by the Royal Thai Army, the Office of the Prime Minister and by various ministries. At least 11 of the stations belong to various branches of the Army. Others are operated by—the Ministry of Interior through its respective subdivisions, including the National Police Department and the Bureau of Provincial Administration; the Ministry of Education; the Ministry of Communication; the Royal Household; and by the Office of the Prime Minister, through the Public Relations Department. Still other stations are operated by Chulalongkorn and Kasetsat Universities, both of which are under the direct jurisdiction of the Office of the Prime Minister.

The Thai Television Company, organized in 1953, operates three radio stations in addition to the country's television network. The majority of its stock is owned by the Public Relations Department.

More than half of the country's radio stations are located in or near Bangkok. Most of the rest are in the Northeast and the

Table 2.—*National Broadcasting Stations in Thailand, 1966*
(Radio Thailand)

Location	Power (in kilowatts)	Wavelength (in meters)	Frequency (in kilocycles)
Bangkok	10	361.40	830
Do	10	323.60	927
Do	5	62.11	4,830
Do	1	49.20	6,070
Do	2.5	48.70	6,160
Do	1	47.02	6,380
Do	2.5	41.75	7,185
Do	2.5	41.07	7,305
Do	{ 2.5 / 50	31.07	9,655
Do	50	25.19	11,910
Do	50	25.12	11,945
Do	50	19.50	15,386
Khon Kaen	50	468.80	640
Nakhon Pathom	100	361.40	830

Source: Adapted from various government sources, 1966.

Northern Region. In 1966 the towns of Lop Buri (75 miles north of Bangkok) and Nakhon Ratchasima (175 miles northeast of Bangkok) had six broadcasting stations each, all of them affiliated with the military or the police forces. Chiengmai had six stations, three of which were under military control.

Transmitters are generally low-powered, ranging from 250 watts to 100 kilowatts. The Bangkok station of Radio Thailand, in 1966, broadcast from 12 transmitters—four were powered by 50 kilowatts and broadcast on shortwave; and two were powered at 10 kilowatts and broadcast on mediumwave. The remaining six broadcast on shortwave and their power ranged from 1 to 5 kilowatts. Plans were under way in 1966 to add two 100-kilowatt transmitters to Radio Thailand's Bangkok facilities. Radio Thailand, in 1966, had regional stations at Khon Kaen in the Northeast and at Nakhon Pathom, 30 miles west of Bangkok. Both broadcasted on mediumwave powered by 50 and 100 kilowatts, respectively.

In 1966 the Public Relations Department operated 10 regional stations, all broadcasting on mediumwave. The Northern Region had two stations, one at Chiengmai and the other at Lampang, powered at 500 watts and 10 kilowatts, respectively. An additional station, to be provided with a 100-kilowatt transmitter, is planned in Chiengmai for broadcasts to the hill peoples. The Northeast had one station, a 10-kilowatt installation, at Ubon Ratchathani. In the Central Region two stations, each powered at 1 kilowatt, were at Thon Buri, 30 miles west of Bangkok. The South had five stations, three at Surat Thani and one each at

291

Prachuap Khiri Khan and at Hat Yai; all except the 10-kilowatt transmitter at Surat Thani were powered at 1 kilowatt.

Because of topographic factors and the lack of relay facilities, all transmissions are given by radio signals. Many places in the mountains of the North and Northeast, however, have very poor reception. In the absence of network broadcasting each station originates its own programs or features the tape-recorded broadcasts of Radio Thailand's Bangkok's stations.

Radio Thailand broadcasts both to domestic and foreign audiences. The combined broadcasting output of its transmitters is 66 hours a day. Domestic broadcasts are on mediumwaves, in Thai, Chinese, Malay, Lao, Mon and English. Stations located in the Northern and Northeast regions also broadcast in languages spoken by the hill people.

Stations in Bangkok and vicinity and those in the Northern Region broadcast on an interrupted daily schedule, usually for several hours in the morning, midday and evening. The transmitters of the Army Signal Corps, Navy and Police radio stations broadcast between 10 and 24 hours a day. Special programs for rural areas are broadcast 4 hours every day from Bangkok from a station under the auspices of the Ministry of Agriculture and the Public Relations Department.

On the average, between 7 and 8 percent of broadcasting time is devoted to news. There is great variation, however, in the number of broadcasting hours devoted to news each week by individual stations. The radio station of the National Police Department (Siang Samyod) devotes 15 hours and 35 minutes a week to newscasts, but news in the program of the Thai Television Company's AM–FM (amplitude modulated-frequency modulated) station totals only 35 minutes for the same period of time.

Daytime serial dramas are popular and are regarded by many listeners as the highlight of daily programs. Stations owned by wealthy individuals devote most of their time to broadcasts of musical and literary programs.

Most stations, including those owned by the Army, rely heavily on commercials for revenue. Programs frequently consist mainly of jingles advertising soft drinks and similar products, interrupted by brief broadcasts of news and music.

Prime Minister Thanom Kittikachorn in 1966 considered the amount of radio advertising to be excessive and in September of that year issued an order banning commercial advertising on radio programs. All 81 stations controlled by the Army were affected by the order. The government's own radio stations, however, were allowed to continue to broadcast commercials. Although the ban on radio advertising deprived many stations of their principal source of revenue, only about 10 discontinued operations as a result of the order.

In 1966 the number of radio sets was estimated at 3.5 million or 1 for about every 8 persons. Most are owned by residents of Bangkok and its vicinity and by residents of large provincial towns. During the mid-1960's, however, few villages of any size were without at least one receiving set. In 1966 United States aid to Thailand included a $900,000 grant to increase the number of village radios.

Most radio receivers in the cities are imported from England, the Netherlands, West Germany and Japan. The battery-powered sets most often encountered in the villages generally are designed only for longwave or mediumwave reception. By mid-1967 transistor radios were being manufactured domestically and were very popular in cities as well as in the rural areas. The government has sought to develop community listening centers in the villages, but formal group-listening is not popular. It is customary, however, for small groups to gather in private homes or coffeeshops to hear radio programs.

There are no Chinese radio stations, but Chinese rebroadcasts may be heard in Bangkok and Chon Buri through the facilities of the Thai Rediffusion Company which is owned partly by the government and partly by a private Chinese concern. The Company operates two channels, one in Thai and one in Chinese. Receiving sets may be hired by subscribers for the equivalent of about 30 baht a month. Broadcasting hours on the Chinese channel are daily from 6 a.m. to 11 p.m. in Bangkok, and from 6 a.m. to 10:30 p.m. in Chon Buri. Only a few of the programs are commercially sponsored, and there is little advertising. The principal dialect used is Teochiu, followed by Cantonese, Hakka, Mandarin and Hainanese. It has been estimated that approximately 89 percent of the Chinese listen to broadcasts regularly. Musical shows, newscasts and dramas are the favorite programs.

Television

Television was initiated in 1955. In 1966 the country had five television stations, three of which (located in Lampang, Khon Kaen and Hat Yai) were operated by the Public Relations Department. The Department also controlled Television Channel 4 (HST–TV) in Bangkok through the Thai Television Company, in which it is a major shareholder. Television Channel 7 (HSA–TV), also located in Bangkok, is operated by the Army.

The most highly powered station is HST–TV which transmits on 10 kilowatts. The Khon Kaen station is powered by 6 kilowatts, the Army's by 6 to 8 and the Lampang by 2 kilowatts.

Hat Yai's low-powered television transmitter operates on a half kilowatt (500 watts).

Transmission of the Thai Television Company's HST–TV and the Army's HSA–TV in Bangkok may be received by at least 10 million people living mainly in the Central Region. The two stations telecast approximately 100 hours per week. The number of television receiving sets in 1966 totaled about 300,000.

About 60 percent of the television programs are live, the rest are transmitted from video tapes. The Thai Television Company's channel operates daily from approximately 5 p.m. to 11:30 p.m., featuring news, sports, religion, music and drama. At least two films and three live shows are transmitted every evening. In addition, there are special programs for women and children. Live transmission of boxing and soccer matches and of events featuring the Royal Family is especially popular. The Army's HSA–TV station transmits similar programs daily for approximately the same number of hours.

All television stations make extensive use of video taped programs from the United States showing Western stories and crime pictures. Plans were in progress in 1966 to improve and extend television facilities so that the respective stations may be linked into a countrywide network.

Films

Films, especially foreign films, are popular in the towns and are attracting growing rural audiences as new facilities become available. In 1966 about 70 percent of the people in Bangkok and over 50 percent of the provincial population attended film shows at least once a week. The influence of foreign films is evident in the modes of dress and behavior of the younger urban generation and in the wide interest in movie magazines and newspaper articles dealing with European and United States screen stars.

The country has three domestic film production companies, Aswin Studies, the Thai Film Company and the Far Eastern Film Company, all of which produce feature and documentary films. Most films, however, are imported. In 1964 imports totaled some 400 feature films, of which 202 were supplied by the United States. During the same year, feature films from the United States played in 28 theaters in Bangkok and in approximately 120 theaters in the provinces. Other foreign film sources included Hong Kong, the United Kingdom, Japan, and India.

Films were exhibited in various parts of the country in some 373 theaters with a combined seating capacity of 123,727. In Bangkok most motion pictures are shown in large, comfortable, air-conditioned theaters. In the provincial capitals the facilities are less sophisticated, although the motion picture theaters are usually among the most modern buildings in town.

In Bangkok crowds line up three or four times a day at film theaters, some of which show Hollywood productions almost simultaneously with their release in the United States. In the countryside peasants often walk for miles to sit under the open sky or in a building where a mobile projection unit sets up a screen. Tent theaters, sometimes showing old, silent serials dating back to the early days of motion pictures, have become a common attraction at rural fairs.

Slapstick and action pictures are most popular, partly because the handicap of a sound track in a foreign language is felt less when the plot is obvious and simple. Thai is seldom dubbed, and then mostly on newsreels and documentary films which are shown for informational and educational purposes. In the case of feature films a narrator is occasionally used, or a group of actors read the lines over a loudspeaker. Most commonly, subtitles are used; in Bangkok they are often in Thai at the bottom of the screen, and in Chinese on the side.

About six of the motion picture theaters in Bangkok show Chinese films regularly. They originate in Hong Kong and Singapore, and most of them are dubbed in Teochiu which is the dialect generally spoken by the Chinese residents of Bangkok; the rest are in Mandarin and Cantonese. The most popular style of action picture is the historical drama, and approximately 75 percent of the films shown deal with this subject matter.

Chinese films are also shown outside of Bangkok, particularly in the cities on the Peninsula, each of which shows an average of about one Chinese film a month, or one every 2 months.

All domestic and imported films are subject to close scrutiny by a board of censors represented by members of the National Police Department, the Ministry of Education and the Press Association of Thailand.

Informal Communication Channels

In traditional Thai society the gathering and exchanging of information took place mainly in the course of social contact. This tradition accounts for the continued reliance, especially in rural areas, on informal communication channels. Furthermore, the price of newspapers and radio sets and the essentially localized interest of the rural population tend to limit the use of these formal media. Interest in foreign movies is largely a matter of entertainment. The peasant is accustomed to being told what he must know about secular affairs by his village headman and the local teacher, and about spiritual matters by the monks of his village. He tends not to question matters which seem to him to be beyond his ability to influence or control.

Education and new economic and technical knowledge are, however, breaking down the barriers which isolate the village. The continuing expansion of government services in the fields of health and education, the proliferation of new ones, such as agricultural extension and cooperation, and the development of better roads—all increase contacts of the rural Thai with the outside world. Even without recourse to formal information media, the rural Thai are constantly and increasingly exposed to new knowledge and ideas. It is now a custom, partly as a matter of prestige, for the headman and the schoolteacher in a village to subscribe to a Bangkok newspaper.

Much of the outside influence still seeps in through personal contact and word of mouth. News is carried by the Chinese rice peddlers; it also travels along the rivers and canals on the long trains of barges which return empty from Bangkok after discharging their rice; and the occasional traveler or returning pilgrim or soldier brings back news and impressions of the world outside. There are indications that a growing interest in affairs outside the village is beginning to be reflected in the greater influence and importance of radio, film and press as sources of information throughout the rural area.

The most important informal communication channels among the Chinese are the trade guilds, benevolent and religious societies, dialect associations and social clubs. Although the main function of such organizations is to offer services and mutual aid, they exert considerable influence in guiding the opinions of and transmitting information to the Chinese community (see ch. 5, Ethnic Groups; ch. 9, Living Conditions).

GOVERNMENT INFORMATION ACTIVITIES

Domestic information activities are centered in the Public Relations Department. Its principal subdivisions implementing the information programs are the Thai Information Services Department, the Public Enlightenment Division and the News Division.

One of the main functions of the Public Relations Department is the production of a daily news bulletin in Thai and English for free distribution to the press. The Department also issues specific types of information to domestic audiences and distributes limited information abroad about Thailand. A news briefing for members of the press is given daily by the Department. The News Division is responsible for the preparation of a government news service file, which is made available to the local press at nominal cost.

Government publications include the Royal Thai *Government Gazette,* periodicals issued by the various ministries, posters and pamphlets on cultural or educational subjects, and textbooks published by the Ministry of Education. These publications, except the school texts, contain domestic and international news, policy statements by various government officials—all stressing themes regarding anticommunism, Thai national interest and current economic and social developments.

Since 1963 the government also has published a number of bilingual (Thai-English) books and pamphlets designed to give information to both domestic and foreign audiences on Thai history and culture and on the state of social, economic and technical progress in the country. The most comprehensive of these is the *Thailand Official Yearbook,* published in English by the Office of the Prime Minister. A publication of some 700 pages, it contains sections on Thai history, economics, communications, living conditions, education, religion, sports and tourism. The Ministry of the Interior has published a series of bilingual pamphlets dealing with problems and social economic conditions among the hill people. Government information also reaches the public by the broadcasting stations operated by the various ministries, the National Police Department and the Army.

In the fight against Communist subversion the government has utilized special units and agencies, operating mainly in the Northeast, to promote community development, health measures and new agricultural techniques. The Thai Army, for example, directs the Mobile Development Units which initiate roadbuilding and other crash programs designed to improve living conditions in the villages. Mobile Information Teams, aided by the United States Information Service, move from village to village showing documentary films on health and education interspersed with anti-Communist messages. The Accelerated Rural Development Program, initiated in 1962 to develop the Northern Region and the Northeast, offers courses to potential village leaders on the principles of self-government.

In 1965 exhibits shown at night fairs, some of them sponsored by the United States Information Agency, included explanations of improved animal and fish raising techniques along with films showing singers who interspersed popular tunes with health advice (see ch. 9, Living Conditions). The effectiveness of these programs in the areas which have been particularly susceptible to the Communist threat is unknown, but there has been much response to information on various aspects of community improvement, particularly when such information was linked with entertainment, such as film shows and traditional forms of singing.

Government information programs are supported by the Communications Media Branch of the United States Operations Mission (USOM). A Thai-American Audio Visual Service was established in 1956 to produce educational and information material. The Service has been equipped with printing presses, graphic materials and a movie production unit. It has prepared a number of documentary films, posters and pamphlets, mainly on health and agricultural improvement, and has conducted a survey on channels of communication in the villages.

Programs directed at foreign audiences in 1964 included broadcasts in English, French, Chinese, Malayan, Vietnamese and Cambodian by the Overseas Broadcasting Division of Radio Thailand. Overseas broadcasts were powered by a shortwave transmitter on 25.6 meters, or 11,715 megacycles utilizing an all-directional antenna. Two broadcasts were transmitted daily to the United States and Europe, respectively from 4:15 a.m. to 5:15 a.m. and from 10:25 a.m. to 11:55 a.m. Greenwich mean time.

FOREIGN GOVERNMENT INFORMATION ACTIVITIES

The most active information programs from abroad are conducted by the United States Information Service (USIS) and its radio branch, the Voice of America (VOA).

In 1966 the USIS headquarters was in Bangkok, and a branch office was in Chiengmai. Four small centers were also maintained in Nakhon Ratchasima, Songkhla, Udon Thani and Ubon Ratchathani. The information program included the operation of fixed and mobile lending libraries, distribution of news and feature material about the United States, showing of documentary films in urban areas, educational exchange activities and the radio broadcasts of VOA.

In 1966 VOA broadcasts were every half hour from 6 a.m. to 9:30 a.m. In the afternoons the broadcasts were continuous from 4 p.m. to 11:30 p.m. The featured programs included "Letters to the Editor and Viewpoints," "Issues in the News," "Short Stories" and "Forum Lecture." In addition, Radio Thailand features USIS broadcasts 31½ hours each week.

In addition to the radio programs, information about the United States may also be obtained from branch offices of the Asia Foundation, the Fulbright Foundation, the Institute of International Education and the Peace Corps, all located in Bangkok. The American University Alumni Association in Bangkok, formed by Thai graduates of institutions of higher learning in the United States, promotes educational and cultural exchanges between the two countries and engages in charitable activities.

The United Kingdom maintains Bangkok offices for the British Information Services and the British Council. The British Information Service distributes press releases and operates film libraries and a mobile film unit. The British Council obtains scholarships for qualified Thai youths for study in the United Kingdom, and helps the Ministry of Education in the recruitment of English teachers for Thai secondary schools and English lecturers for Thai universities. The Council also offers English-language instruction and operates a lending library.

In 1966 programs of the British Broadcasting Corporation from London and from relay stations in the Far East were heard in Thailand from 6 a.m. to 8:30 a.m. and from 4 p.m. to 11:50 p.m. The broadcasts featured news, commentary, music, sports and cultural programs.

The Alliance Francaise, sponsored by the French Government, has a 7,000-volume library in Bangkok and offers language classes, exhibits, plays and film shows. West Germany has an extensive information program through the German Institute in Bangkok and Chiengmai which, in addition to language instruction, offers programs featuring the culture and institutions of Germany. The Institute in Bangkok maintains a library, a musicroom and periodically holds exhibits and film shows. Japan, India and Nationalist China also maintain information offices in the capital.

Communist Countries

Communist propaganda reaches Thailand through the Voice of the People of Thailand, a clandestine radio station which first began to broadcast in 1962. By 1965 the station had changed its name to Voice of Free Thailand and broadcast six times a week for a total of 28 hours from studios located in Communist China. The station stressed the theme of a "national liberation war" against the United States. During the same year the station announced the formation of the Thailand Patriotic Front "a political organization willing to cooperate with all compatriots . . . who love peace and democracy" to oppose military, economic and technical agreements between Thailand and the United States (see ch. 15, Political Dynamics). In 1966 the broadcasts denounced the Thai Government for being guilty of war crimes in sending volunteers to South Vietnam, at the instigation of the United States.

Some propaganda dissemination is conducted by Communist agents and small bands of armed Communist guerrillas operating mainly in the Northeast and in the Northern Region. In the

Northeast such bands, after surrounding a village and summoning the people by beating the headman's drum, subject the listeners to an hour-long barrage of propaganda denouncing the government and accusing it of turning the country into a colony of the United States.

The usual "revolutionary appeals" against a "corrupt" government and "landlords" have generally failed with the Thai villagers who elect their own headmen and most of whom own their plots, however small. Moreover, the Royal Family enjoys universal popularity, and pictures of the King and Queen are generally found in most homes of the remotest villages.

The government has shown some concern about the possibility of Communist propaganda influencing the North Vietnamese refugees living in the Northeast along the Mekong River. Most of the refugees listen to Radio Hanoi which is clearly received in the area. In general, however, the North Vietnamese refugees have refrained from carrying out overt propaganda activities and have complied with Thai government regulations restricting their movements.

Much of the propaganda emanating from Communist China is directed at the Chinese community in Thailand. Chinese listeners can easily tune in on the frequent broadcasts of Radio Peking which are audible throughout Southeast Asia. The programs, transmitted on shortwave lengths, are in Chinese and in various Chinese dialects. They feature news, commentary and music. Many of the broadcasts, apparently appealing to the national feelings of the expatriates, stress the cultural and historical heritage of China. The programs are interspersed with reports on the economic and technical "achievements" of the country under Communist rule. Radio Peking also caters to Chinese listeners by offering language instruction in the Mandarin dialect, the mastery of which has always been considered a matter of prestige.

CHAPTER 18

POLITICAL VALUES AND ATTITUDES

Buddhist influences, omnipresent in the life of nearly every Thai, determine his sociopolitical beliefs and his attitudes toward government and national politics. The Buddhist concept of merit, for example, is largely responsible for the Thai deference to authority and status. The traditional pattern of respect is based on the Buddhist teaching that a person holding positions of power and influence has earned highly coveted merit in this or a previous existence; such a person is thought to be rewarded by supernatural sanction (see ch. 12, Religion; ch. 13, Social Values).

Although the coup of 1932 ended the long era of absolute monarchy, it brought about little radical change in the traditional patterns of popular respect for the monarch and for the government. The people, especially in the rural areas, continued to believe in the inviolability of authority, and, on the whole, they still remained convinced in 1967 that high officials in Bangkok and provincial governors were naturally superior and that they should be accorded unquestioning deference. By the 1960's expanded activities of all levels of government seemed to have considerably broadened the horizons of many villagers. They were responding, in increasing numbers, with varying degrees of enthusiasm, to the policies of the central government. In this process the government's developing capacity to communicate with the people and the rapidly expanding educational opportunities apparently have played a significant role (see ch. 10, Education; ch. 17, Public Information).

The members of the ruling hierarchy, however, have not found it necessary to justify their pattern of rule to the ruled because the authority and power do not derive from any popular mandate. Power and prestige are still buttressed by the Buddhist concept of merit and by the popular notion of cosmology. The ruling elite continues to regard its primary mission as a paternal one of leading the people, and political forms and methods used by the government seem to matter little to the people so long as the authorities are not oppressive.

Except among the disaffected segments of minority groups, popular loyalty to the King and the nation, in mid-1967, was not seriously questioned. The bulk of the people seemed content with the actions or policies of the central government and its local officials.

In addition, the concept of nation has become a powerful factor in shaping the attitudes of both the ruling elite and the politically awakening segments of the population, especially in the urban areas. Both are politically articulate and extremely conscious and proud of their nation's heritage of independence. They consider themselves intensely loyal to the nation, and, accordingly, any expedient to protect its integrity and freedom is regarded as legitimate.

DETERMINANTS OF VALUES AND ATTITUDES

Most Thai, both rural and urban, have a great emotional attachment to the doctrines and rites of Buddhism, which is constantly woven into their thoughts and actions. It influences their attitudes toward authority, their way of life and all fortune or misfortune which they encounter in their daily existence (see ch. 12, Religion; ch. 13, Social Values).

Religious devotion and the attainment of merit are the central values and themes in Thai culture. The individual's concept of religious merit is closely connected with his attitudes toward government and hierarchy. The people regard the entire universe as a hierarchy of living beings who are ranked within it according to the amount of merit they have acquired through the quality of their actions in this or in previous existences. They regard those holding positions of power and influence as deserving such positions because of their individual merit. Deference is accorded to anyone who holds an accepted position of authority, whether he is a village elder, a monk or a government official.

On the other hand, the Thai also believe that a person elevated in a social hierarchy should behave in a manner befitting his high position. He is expected to be more benevolent, more benign, more honest and more just than his subordinates if he wishes to maintain their acceptance of his superior status.

The Thai also realize, however, that through the workings of secular power a person may acquire a status or position which is greater than is justified by the amount of merit he has accumulated. This imperfection in the justice of the universe permits evasion of the demands of authority and, in extreme cases, even rebellion against it. If a person in a high position acts tyrannically or abusively, such action allows others to evade him or to transfer their allegiance to someone else whose conduct is more in line with Buddhist precepts.

Respect for authority and status is an important feature of Thai political values. Much of this respect has its roots in the Thai tradition of an absolute king. To their own early paternalistic concept of the king as a father-lord (*pho khun*), the Thai added the Khmer concept of divine king (*devaraja*), which supplied the rationale for the absolutist rule of the kings of Ayutthaya (see ch. 3, Historical Setting). The king stood at the apex of the human pyramid of merit and, thus, of status. This status provided him with supreme civil and military authority and invested him with an aura of the supernatural. He not only symbolized the order of society but also justified it (see ch. 7, Social Structure). This heritage accounts in large measure for the continued popularity of the king as the most enduring symbol of national unity.

ATTITUDES TOWARD THE GOVERNMENT

In the past, few questioned the authority or actions of government officials, the *kha rachakan* (lit., servants of the king). The popular notion of government did not extend beyond the district level, and many Thai had only a limited knowledge of events in Bangkok. The people did not feel that affairs of state were the concern of anyone other than public officials and unquestioningly accepted official decrees. They were indifferent to events which had no immediate bearing on their personal affairs. If any law or obligation was excessively abusive or demanding, it was simply ignored or evaded. Only in extreme cases have the people rebelled against the authorities.

Popular attitudes toward the government in mid-1967 remained substantially the same as in the past, except perhaps among some of the people in the Northeast Region and among the ethnic minorities (see ch. 5, Ethnic Groups; ch. 15, Political Dynamics). In 1932, when the absolute monarchy was overthrown by a group operating under democratic slogans, very few of the ancient practices and attitudes of authoritarian rule changed. The bulk of the people were unaffected and unconcerned by the formal shift of power. The government leaders also persisted in their traditional patterns of rule. All governments since 1932 have acted on the assumption that their mission was to lead and guide the people. Blessed by stable political and social order, the people had few reasons to alter radically their traditional pattern of obedience and, hence, continued to be passive and acquiescent.

ATTITUDES TOWARD POLITICS

Politics has been monopolized by a limited number of public officials and career politicians in Bangkok, just as the functions of government before 1932 were the exclusive domain of the king and court officials. Most of the people in mid-1967 continued to be indifferent to the manner in which major political decisions were made in the capital as well as to organized politics, or the lack of it, within the country (see ch. 15, Political Dynamics).

The Western concept of political representation or accountability is alien to the Thai culture. It was introduced by the coup group of 1932. As embodied in the first Thai constitution, the concept of representative democracy was a formal attempt to transfer power and prestige from the monarch to a broader segment of the population (see ch. 14, The Governmental System). Functionally, the idea of equality or popular sovereignty was little understood by the people, who continued to believe that a person's access to power was determined essentially by his moral or ethical excellence. Moreover, subject to the vagaries of politicians and aspirants to power, the new political concepts were not firmly institutionalized.

A village study conducted in 1957 showed, for example, that most voters went to the polls in national elections simply because they were told to do so by their headmen or local officials. The act of voting was regarded less as an exercise of civic right than as a fulfillment of social obligation to their local leaders or an attempt to comply with the expressed wishes of district officials.

In ordinary situations the Thai are inclined to act less as joiners than as independents. This predisposition is based on the Buddhist precept that an individual is answerable only to himself for his personal conduct. Many Thai are likely to seek the path to self-perfection in individual rather than group action. Because of this cultural orientation, organized political activities or official efforts to mobilize the people on the basis of abstract ideology, or issues far removed from any given locality, have failed to enlist much popular response. The government itself continued to maintain that the people themselves were not yet adequately prepared for participation in the Western form of democratic political processes.

ATTITUDES OF MINORITY GROUPS

The attitudes of the minority groups differ somewhat from those of the ethnic Thai. Until recently the Chinese were under the most pressure and had the most reason to feel that they were being discriminated against and that their problems were not receiving adequate attention. By and large, however, for a number of practical reasons, they have not expressed serious opposition to the government. First, the majority of ethnic Chinese are Thai nationals and thus are not directly affected by the government's anti-Chinese measures. Second, even those Chinese who are not Thai citizens have been able, for the most part, to evade Thai restrictive actions by one means or another. Third, increasing numbers of Thai-born Chinese are able to seek careers not only in business but also in government service.

Politically, the majority of the Chinese tend to stay unattached to any outside political groupings. They are primarily concerned with keeping their shops open, maintaining their trades, avoiding government officials and evading official decrees. Their allegiance to the king and to Thailand has never become a serious political issue, although many ethnic Thai appear to believe that psychologically the Chinese have a great emotional and romantic attachment to mainland China.

Malays in the Peninsula Region express less concern about discrimination by the government than about Bangkok's insufficient consideration for their religious, linguistic and other cultural characteristics. Since the war the Malays, through their religious leaders, have loudly voiced their complaints against the policies of the central government. Some concessions have been made to them, and their dissatisfaction appears to have lessened, at least temporarily. In mid-1967, however, there were continued indications that some Malays resented the staffing of government posts at the district level with predominantly Thai rather than Malay officials.

The political grievances of the Lao of the Northeast are primarily an outgrowth of the relatively depressed economic conditions of their area. In the past the government paid little attention to this region, and its inhabitants reacted by developing a strong minority consciousness—a feeling that they were being ignored because they were Lao and that the Thai, their cultural cousins who ruled in distant Bangkok, were biased against them (see ch. 5, Ethnic Groups). Their dissatisfaction found expression through certain leftist and pro-Communist politicians and more recently through Communist subversive activities in the region (see ch. 15, Political Dynamics). To placate the Lao, the successive governments of Prime Minister Sarit Thanarat (1959–63) and Prime Minister Thanom Kittikachorn have been carrying on an extensive program of public welfare and economic development.

The Vietnamese in the Northeast Region are strongly nationalistic and have shown little inclination to be assimilated into Thai society. They live in separate villages under the tight control of their own leaders. Many of them display pictures of Ho Chi Minh on the walls of their homes and are said to be pro-Communist. Although they have not openly shown opposition to the Thai authorities, they are reportedly under the strong influence of Communist North Vietnam.

NATIONAL SYMBOLS

The King

For centuries one of the important functions of the government was to conduct elaborate ceremonies, rituals and acts of religious merit that are regarded as efficacious in bringing to the people not only spiritual benefits but a host of material benefits. These ceremonies, as well as other displays of power and wealth by the state, made it possible for the people to see in their king the living symbol of the hierarchy of respect that was operative throughout Thai society. The court and the capital represented to the people the highest realization of their cultural values.

Before 1932 the monarch had held power and prestige by virtue of his representing both political powers and religious sanctions. The 1932 coup separated the power from the absolute monarch but failed to divert some of the traditional royal prestige to other symbols of government, such as the flag, the Constitution, the national anthem and the white elephant. Although the king was reduced to the position of being merely one of a number of national symbols, the people continued to respect their monarch much more than any other leader or emblem of the state.

Popular respect for the king is enhanced in part also through the playing of the royal anthem (Sanrasorn Phra Barami—literally, Anthem Eulogizing His Majesty) at all public functions attended by the king or the queen; it is also played at the end of public entertainments. Adopted in 1872, the royal anthem is translated into English roughly as follows:

We, Your Majesty's loyal subjects,
With deep, heart-felt reverence,
To the supreme Protector of the Land,
The Highest of the House of Chakri,
Under his benevolent rule, we his subjects,
Receive protection and happiness,
Prosperity and peace;
And we pray that whatsoever He may wish,
The same may be fulfilled;
Thus we offer him our *Cha Yo* [hurrah, cheer or victory].

Other Symbols

The official flag is a 3- by 5-foot rectangle. In the center is a dark-blue horizontal stripe which runs throughout its length and which is flanked on each side by white horizontal stripes, outside of which are red horizontal stripes. The flag is referred to as the "Trairange" (Tri-Color): the dark-blue signifying kingship; the white, religion and purity; and the red, the nation.

The state emblem is an immortal mythological bird with the features of a man. Known as the Garuda, this bird served as the mount of Phra Narai, who in reincarnation became Phra Ram, the heroic king and conqueror in the *Ramayana*, the famous Hindu religious epic.

The national anthem, adopted in 1934, is played on all ceremonial occasions of national importance and while the national flag is being raised or lowered. Its music was composed shortly after the 1932 coup; its words, as presently constituted, were written by Colonel Luang Saranuprabhandh (Nual Pacheenpyak) in 1939. The literally translated text of the anthem is roughly as follows:

> Thailand is the unity of Thai blood and body.
> The whole country belongs to the Thai people,
>   maintaining thus far for the Thai.
> All the Thai intend to unite together.
> The Thai love peacefulness, but will not fear to fight.
> They will never let anyone tyrannize their independence.
> They will sacrifice every drop of their blood to
>   contribute to the nation, will serve their country
> with pride and prestige—full of victory. *Cha Yo.*

Most national holidays and festivals are of a religious nature. They serve to evoke the sense of devotion to the king, Buddhism and the nation. Some are celebrated by the lunar calendar, and hence their dates vary from year to year. The following holidays are observed by the solar calendar: New Year's Day (January 1); Chakri Day (April 6), which commemorates the founding of the current Chakri dynasty; Songkran (April 13), marking the New Year's day based on the ancient Maha Sakaraj calendar, now practically out of use in Thailand; the Queen's Birthday (August 12); King Chulalongkorn Memorial Day (October 23); the King's Birthday and National Day (December 5), which is regarded as the most important national holiday; and Constitution Day (December 10), celebrating the promulgation of the first permanent Thai constitution on December 10, 1932.

Important holidays celebrated by the lunar calendar include Makha Buja (usually in February), the first day of the season for making pilgrimages to Phra Buddha Baht (Buddha's Footprint Shrine), Phra Chai (Buddha's Shadow on the Side of the Hill), Phra Taen Sila and Phra Taen Dong Rang; Chatra Mongkhon (Coronation Day—in May); Peja Mongkhon (Ploughing Festival—in May), signaling the start of the cultivation season; Visaka Buja (a 3-day festival usually in May), commemorating the triple episode of the birth, enlightenment and the passing into *nirvana* of the Lord Buddha; Asalaha Buja (in July), celebrating the delivery of the first sermon of the Lord Buddha; and Khao Pansa (in July), marking the beginning of a 3-month Buddhist period of fasting. During this period, which coincides with the rainy season, monks are not permitted to pass the night outside the *wat* (walled compound containing a Buddhist temple and associated buildings).

SECTION III. ECONOMIC

CHAPTER 19

CHARACTER AND STRUCTURE
OF THE ECONOMY

Thailand has a prosperous agrarian economy which grew between 1950 and 1960 at the rate of 5 percent a year, accelerating to 7 percent during 1960–65. The boom conditions characterizing the 1960's have buoyed the confidence of the business community. The accelerated business activity, the rapid expansion of the construction industry and a good year in agriculture are expected to show a rise of 10 percent in gross national income during 1966, considerably exceeding the annual goals of the country's new Five-Year Plan for National Economic and Social Development (1967–71).

Expansion has been shared by all sectors of the economy with the exception of forestry. Along with the gain in total output and an accompanying growth of exports, a significant diversification of economic activity has taken place. The principal exports are, as they have been throughout the modern period, rice, rubber, tin and teak. Rice continues to be the most important single product of the economy, but the largest recent increases in agricultural output have been in other crops, especially corn, tapioca, fibers and a variety of fruits, vegetables and livestock products. An industrial sector, though small, has expanded rapidly as a result of the establishment of enterprises producing light industrial goods, such as textiles, paper, cement, glass and sugar, and a few large-scale units for tin smelting and oil refining. Almost every year more manufactures are produced locally. Tin production has continued at peak levels, and power, communications, transportation and construction have greatly increased their contribution to the national income.

Foreign exchange reserves have been accumulating at a rapid rate, and the country's international credit rating is high. Since 1955 prices have been remarkably stable, and the baht (see Glossary), maintained at approximately 21 baht to the United States dollar, is considered one of the world's hard currencies.

The widening trade gap resulting from the fast growth of imports over exports continues to be more than closed by capital inflow and income from tourism and other services. Capital formation, which has increased continually in practically all sectors since 1952, and the remarkable rise in deposits in financial institutions also demonstrate the vigor of the Thai economy.

Although the signs of progress in modernization and diversification are indicative of a new trend, development has been handicapped by deficiencies in power, transportation and communications; scarcity of capital for development purposes; and shortages of technical and managerial skills in many fields. Loans from the International Bank for Reconstruction and Development (IBRD) have financed the development of hydroelectric power and the improvement of transportation and communications. The government is using its revenues and foreign loans from the United States and other countries to establish a number of enterprises. It is also offering inducements to foreign private capital to exploit mineral resources and establish industries.

Training programs have been undertaken at home, and with the assistance of the United States Agency for International Development (AID), the government is sending hundreds of its citizens to the United States to study in special fields. A number of fellowships for training in Thailand have also been provided by the United Nations and its specialized agencies.

Prospects for continued economic growth are favorable. Farmers have demonstrated their ability to adopt new crops for which there are domestic or foreign markets. Irrigation and flood control projects have added, within the past 10 years, a large acreage to land under cultivation, an important factor in the increase in agricultural output. Of the country's rich mineral resources only tin has been exploited to any degree, although government policy favors further development of minerals and metal production.

The goals of the Six-Year Economic Development Plan (1961–66), which is aimed generally at building up an infrastructure of communications, transportation and hydroelectric power, were more than met, and the new Five-Year Plan (1967–71) is well under way.

STRUCTURE OF THE ECONOMY

The structure of the economy has changed considerably in the course of development. The gross national product almost tripled between 1951 and 1965, from 28.2 billion baht to 80.2 billion baht. Agriculture, including livestock, forestry and fisheries, contributed the largest single share. The decrease, however, from almost 50 percent of the gross national product in 1951 to 32.8 percent in 1965, despite a 7 percent increase per year in agricultural output over that period, reflects the growing importance of other sectors of the economy. Within the agricultural sector crops and livestock made by far the largest contribution—86 percent in 1951, 88 percent in 1961 and 75 percent in 1965. The share contributed by fisheries rose from 4 percent in 1951 to 13 percent in 1965. Forestry's share, having fallen from 10 percent in 1951 to 6 percent in 1961, increased to 12 percent in 1965.

After agriculture, wholesale and retail trade is the most important sector of the economy. Its contribution to the gross national product has averaged 18 percent over the 15-year period with only minor fluctuations. It is followed by manufacturing, which has averaged 12 percent, and services, which has averaged 8 percent. Notable gains have been registered in construction, in communications and transportation and in electricity and water supply. From a negligible 1.6 percent in 1951, construction's contribution to the gross national product rose to 5 percent in 1965; communications and transportation, from 3 percent to 7 percent; and electricity and water supply, from 0.1 percent in 1951 to 0.7 percent in 1965. Mining and quarrying maintained an average contribution of 1.5 percent throughout the period, rising to 2 percent in 1965. Banking, insurance and real estate contributed 4 percent in 1951, 2 percent from 1957 through 1962 and 4 percent again in 1965.

Agriculture continues to be the main economic activity despite the growing importance of other sectors of the economy. It employs more than 12 million men and women, most of them raising irrigated rice on their own small farms clustered around scattered hamlets. Rubber production, begun before World War I, is still important for export, and new markets at home and abroad have resulted in increased output of other crops, such as sugarcane for the government's new refineries, fiber crops for the new gunny sack factories, corn for shipment to Japan and tapioca for export to Germany. As a result of the increasing prosperity domestic demand has grown for coconuts, fruits and vegetables. Where irrigation and flood control permit, these other crops are grown in addition to rice, a practice which is becoming more widespread as irrigation projects are completed.

Livestock, forestry and fishing, though overshadowed by crop production, occupy a significant place in the economy. The livestock population, even though decimated by disease during World War II, was largely reconstituted by 1955 as a result of a massive disease eradication program carried out by the government with the assistance of the United States. Since that year livestock has continued to increase, and it contributed almost 4.2 billion baht to agricultural income in 1965. The most important are buffaloes (essential to wet-rice cultivation), cattle, pigs and poultry. Almost all farmers own some livestock, but their numbers are highest in the forests and grasslands of the Northeast where buffaloes and cattle have long been raised for sale to rice farmers throughout the country.

The forests, which cover more than 50 percent of the country, have decreased in their importance as a source of income. Teak exports were especially important. Only half of the lands, however, are accessible, and these have been drastically overcut. To conserve the country's forest resources, the government instituted a rotation system of cutting, under which large areas were conserved for specified periods for reforestation. As a result, there has been a general decline in the cutting of teak as well as most other varieties of rare woods. Production of charcoal, firewood and other forest products, however, has more than doubled in the last 15 years. Forestry still contributes over 2 billion baht to the national income and in 1960 employed about 36,000 persons (see ch. 22, Labor).

In the agricultural sector, fishing ranks next to farming in importance. Fish, caught offshore and in rivers, ponds and canals, provide a major item of the national diet. Over 110,000 persons were employed full time as fishermen in 1960 and, in 1965, the commercial catch alone added over 2 billion baht to the national income. Fishing is, however, a part-time activity of some member of almost every family, and it is estimated that fishing's actual contribution to the national income is double the value of the commercial catch.

After agriculture the next largest segment of the population, about 770,000 in the 1960 census, is engaged in wholesale and retail trade, activities which contributed more than 14.9 billion baht to the national income in 1965. Most retail trade is in local produce and consumer goods sold either by vendors or in city and town markets; the bulk of wholesale trade is in imports and commodities for export. Commerce centers in Bangkok, a city of over 2 million people in 1967, the hub of the transportation system and the country's chief port. Through Bangkok, exports originating largely in the rural areas are shipped abroad, and from it most imports are distributed to the entire country. To a large extent, domestic retail and wholesale trade are dominated by the Chinese, who developed the distributive system over the last hundred years. Europeans and Americans play an important role in the import and export trade.

Trade is significantly influenced by the adequacy of transportation and communications facilities. Waterways are the oldest and most important means of inland transport, carrying more than three-fourths of the freight traffic. They are, however, confined to the Central Plain. Almost 2,300 miles of railroads radiating out from Bangkok to major centers within the country and to connecting links with rail lines in Cambodia and Malaysia are the only year-round means of interregional transportation. The highway system, almost 8,000 miles of roads, spans the length and width of the country, but numerous stretches of it are subject to flooding during the wet season. Many roads are used mainly as feeders for the long, heavy hauls which are made by railroad or by water.

The spectacular rise in contribution to the national income of transportation and communications from 883.4 million baht in 1951 to almost 6 billion baht in 1965 reflects the modernization and expansion of the transportation and communication networks which have taken place during the past 15 years. This includes not only the rehabilitation of the railroads and the replacement of obsolete rolling stock, the construction annually of 100 miles of all-weather highways and the motorization of most long-haul craft on the waterways, but also the expansion of air services and of the telegraph, radio and television networks. This sector of the economy, one of the fastest growing, employed over 165,000 persons in 1960 (see ch. 2, Physical Environment).

Service occupations—government, the professions, education and personal and domestic service—engaged approximately 800,-000 persons in 1965, and the contribution to the national income was valued at 6.9 billion baht. Governmental and educational services registered the largest share—52 percent of the total. The decline from 64 percent in 1961 reflected the increasing share attributable to hotels and restaurants, which more than doubled between 1957 and 1965. Over the same period the value of personal services, such as laundries, barbershops and beauty shops rose only 32 percent, and the share contributed by domestic servants and the professions showed an even greater lag, rising by only 26 percent. Recreational services, including theaters and motion picture houses, more than quadrupled their contribution over the same 8-year period, but the total share remained negligible.

Banking and finance, including banking institutions, insurance companies, moneychangers and pawnshops, employed almost 10,000 persons in 1960. Between 1951 and 1965 the contribution of banking and finance to national income almost tripled, rising from over 1.1 billion baht to over 2.9 billion baht, an indication that this sector of the economy was keeping pace with the general expansion.

Industry is on a small scale; emphasis is placed on the processing of agricultural commodities and the fabrication of a few consumer products and building materials. Its contribution to the national income tripled between 1951 and 1965, from over 3.2 billion baht to 9.7 billion baht. It employed almost 500,000 persons in 1960. Except in the production of cement and gunny sacks and in the processing of agricultural products, no branches of industry have achieved sufficient volume to satisfy the country's needs, and most manufactured goods continue to be imported. Many of the large industrial enterprises are entirely or partially owned by the government, and most of the smaller enterprises are owned and operated by private domestic capital, both Thai and resident Chinese. The government is seeking to promote industrial development by attracting both domestic and foreign capital in offering various guarantees and facilities for desired industries. Sizable investments in the Thai economy have been made by United States, British, Australian, Swiss, German and Japanese firms. An annual net capital inflow has characterized the 1960's.

The government actively participates in all economic activity in the country, except possibly some phases of agricultural production. It owns and exploits forests and mineral resources, processes agricultural products, manufactures numerous items, monopolizes transportation and communications, engages in both foreign and domestic trade and functions as banker for credit, savings and finance purposes. As the largest holder of fluid funds, the government must act as entrepreneur and take the initiative in economic development. The attitude of the government toward private enterprise is in general that of laissez-faire. While it does not interfere, it nevertheless competes at every level and in almost every field.

A conservative fiscal policy has given the country an excellent credit rating. The baht, backed by 100 percent reserves in foreign exchange and gold, is one of the most stable currencies in the world. Loans to Thailand by the IBRD and the United States Export-Import Bank are evidence of the government's financial soundness.

While conservative fiscally, the government has followed an aggressive policy in its economic development program. Postwar development efforts have concentrated on transportation, communications, power and irrigation; notable progress has been made in all these fields. The National Economic Development Board, created in 1959, drew up both the Six-Year Plan and the new

Five-Year Plan, through which investment in all branches of the economy is coordinated.

THE ECONOMIC DEVELOPMENT PLANS

In 1961 the Six-Year Economic Development Plan (1961–66), the first coordinated program for the economic development of the country, was formulated. Its principal objective was to raise the standard of living of the people by building a dynamic basis for continuous growth. Specific targets were set which included a 5 percent annual increase in gross national product and an estimated rate of capital information of not less than 15 percent.

During the first 3 years of the plan the increase in gross national product exceeded the target, with real growth averaging about 6 percent annually. By 1963 agricultural development, industry and mining had more than met their targets, and electric capacity had almost achieved the 1966 target. Expansion and improvement of health services were moving ahead of targets, and the education program had made progress. On the other hand, highway construction and communications programs had fallen behind schedule.

The plan was revised in 1965 by drawing up a less conservative Three-Year Economic Development Program (1964–66) which called for a public expenditure target of nearly 20 billion baht, an increase of almost 70 percent over the 11.8 billion baht spent in 1961–63 and also called for in the second 3-year period. The difference between the original and revised figures lay largely in the inclusion in the revised plan of development expenditures by state enterprises and local governments. Major emphasis was given to infrastructure projects (highways and communications network and power) and to education, health and social welfare. Domestic resources were to account for about 70 percent of the plan's financial requirements, and foreign loans and grants, for the remainder. Adherence to the projects was expected to assure a continued aggregate gross national product growth rate of approximately 6 percent and a per capita rate of approximately 3 percent.

By the end of the fifth year of the Six-Year Plan the growth of the economy had exceeded its set targets. The 80.2 billion baht value of the gross national product for 1965 surpassed the goal of 77 billion baht for the end of 1966. In 1965 the per capita income rose to 2,500 baht, whereas the target set for 1966 was only 2,400 baht. This per capita income was about 25 percent higher than the average income of 1958, although since that time the population had grown at the rate of 3.2 percent per year.

The new Five-Year Plan for National Economic and Social Development (1967–71) was promulgated October 1, 1966. The primary overall target is a 7 percent annual growth rate in gross national product. Development expenditure will amount to 52.7 billion baht compared to 33.6 billion baht in the previous 6-year period. Transportation and communications will continue to receive the greatest emphasis since the government feels that its previous expenditures in this sector have been justified by its success in stimulating private economic activity. Highway development in the largest component; projects include the construction of more than 2,000 miles of new highways and improvement of about 3,000 miles of existing highways. In irrigation the plan envisages the construction of 11 irrigation projects in the Northeast and 2 in the Southern Region. Expenditures on agriculture will rise sharply to 23 percent of the total, to enable the country to achieve greater productivity and accelerate overall rural development.

In addition to specific targets five policy objectives have been outlined. They are to alleviate the severe regional inequalities, to develop the potential of Thailand's human resources more fully, to make more effective use of the substantial investments in national infrastructure under the earlier plan, to strengthen the efficiency of private economic activity and to maintain a stable monetary environment in which economic growth results in real increases in the standard of living.

CHAPTER 20

AGRICULTURE

Agriculture, including animal husbandry, forestry and fishing, continued to provide employment in the mid-1960's for about 82 percent of the working population and contributed the largest single share—32.8 percent in 1965—to gross domestic product. Export of agricultural products, of which rice was still the most important, accounted for at least 50 percent of the country's foreign exchange earnings and for an appreciable part of government revenues. The economy, as for centuries, continued to be predominantly agricultural, based on rice—the staple food of the people.

Annual crop output has been adversely affected at times by weather conditions. Monsoon rains, if unusually heavy, cause extensive flood damage, and lack of large-scale water storage facilities, particularly in the northeastern part of the country, results in drought damage during a protracted dry season.

Agricultural production has increased fairly steadily since World War II. It is expected to continue to do so in the foreseeable future, and the government is directing its efforts toward that end. Although rice will continue to dominate the economy, the economic development program calls for increased diversification as well as expansion. Development plans cover a wide range of activities, including irrigation, rice seed breeding, the use of fertilizers, pest control, sericulture, planting of rubber, cotton and other upland crops, and the marketing of vegetables and fruits. A program for improving pasturage and for increasing livestock and meat production is also under way.

Thai farmers have demonstrated a remarkable adaptability to changing market conditions, and new agricultural products, such as tapioca, kenaf (a fiber crop used in making gunny sacks) and corn, have been capturing a growing share of exports. Thailand's farmers have a higher standard of living than those in most other Southeast Asian countries. Although their average income figured in money is low, few need to worry about food, shelter or clothing. Most rural communities are still largely self-sufficient, and the average farm family owns or rents the land it cultivates.

317

LAND UTILIZATION

Thailand is part of monsoon Asia, lying entirely within the tropics. Of the total land area of 126.9 million acres, more than 51 percent, or about 65 million acres, is forest or grazing land. Miscellaneous uncultivated land or unused land, including roads, rivers, canals, urban areas, railways and airports, is estimated at almost 25 percent, or over 31.5 million acres. Only 20.5 percent of the total land area, or approximately 26 million acres, is under cultivation, and about 62 percent of the cultivated area, or 16.1 million acres, is in rice paddies (see table 3). It is estimated that 19.8 million additional acres could be brought under cultivation.

Between 1960 and the end of 1964 total farmland was expanded by over 4 million acres, 94 percent of which was in the Central Region and the Peninsula, reflecting the success attending the government's programs for land reclamation and the extension of the irrigated area. About 1.4 million of the newly cultivated acres was in rice paddies, of which over 900,000 acres was in the Central Region, the remainder distributed in the other three regions. In the same period the area planted to rubber and coconut palms increased by a million acres, largely in the Peninsula, and the planting of upland crops had also expanded by over 1.5 million acres, almost 1.3 million acres in the Central Region.

The pattern of land utilization varies from one region to another. In the mountainous north the stands of teak and other valuable trees constitute the Northern Region's main contribution to the national economy. Only about 8 percent of the total land area is in farmholdings, but most of it is irrigated and can be cropped the year around. In the Northeastern Region about 19 percent of the land is cultivated, but soil, infertility and water scarcity severely limit farm production. The Central Region, with its rich alluvial soils, on the other hand, produces a large percentage of the country's rice crop. Over 26 percent of the region is under cultivation, most of it in rice paddies. In the Peninsula 27.3 percent of the land area is under cultivation, the greater portion of it planted to rubber, coconut and fruit trees, which are favored by the region's sandy soil and frequent rainfall.

IRRIGATION AND FLOOD CONTROL

Irrigation and flood control are vital necessities in Thai agriculture. Paddy rice, the main crop, needs about 70 inches of rain to grow and mature. Although Thailand, with the exception of

Table 3.—*Land Utilization in Thailand, by Geographical Regions, 1964*
(in thousands of acres)

	Northern	Northeastern	Central	Peninsula	Total	Percent
Farmland:						
Rice paddies	1,055	6,111	7,695	1,291	16,152	12.7
Rubber and coconut	28	139	277	2,035	2,479	1.9
Fruit trees	133	357	1,091	1,200	2,781	2.2
Upland crops [1]	376	1,297	2,773	216	4,662	3.7
Total cultivated area	1,592	7,904	11,836	4,742	26,074	20.5
Farm woodland	47	658	812	122	1,639	1.3
Miscellaneous farmland	100	332	1,010	301	1,743	1.4
Total farmland	1,739	8,894	13,658	5,165	29,456	23.2
Other Land Areas						
Forest and grazing	16,593	16,772	22,743	9,242	65,350	51.5
Swamps and lakes	8	156	101	247	512	0.4
Unclassified [2]	3,752	16,202	8,948	2,975	31,577	24.9
Total other land areas	20,353	33,130	31,792	12,464	97,739	76.8
GRAND TOTAL	22,092	42,024	45,450	17,629	127,195	100.0

[1] Includes corn, beans and sugarcane.

[2] Includes roads, rivers, canals, urban areas, railways, airports, as well as miscellaneous uncultivated and unused land.

Source: Adapted from Thailand, Ministry of Agriculture, Office of the Under Secretary of State, Division of Agricultural Economics, Agricultural Statistics Section, *Agricultural Statistics of Thailand, 1964*, pp. 176, 177.

the Peninsula where rains are heavy and occur the year around, has a rainy season beginning in May and ending in October, the rains are uncertain, and great fluctuations are common from year to year and from place to place. Most of the country, therefore, is dependent on the flooding of rivers for sufficient water to produce the rice harvest. River floods, however, often result in widespread damage to the paddy fields and the rice crop.

Of an estimated 10 million acres of irrigable land, about 5 million acres was under irrigation in 1964, an increase of 1.5 million acres since 1962. The most extensive single irrigated area lies in the Central Region, which is crisscrossed with canals, both ancient and modern. Many of the modern canal projects, follow the old canals dug by the Thai peasants. The first large-scale water control project, which involved the drainage of a vast swamp located between the lower reaches of the Nakhon Nayok and the Pa Sak to the northeast of Bangkok, was initiated in the late nineteenth century.

In 1889 digging was begun on the Khlong Rangsit which was designed to provide not only irrigation but transportation. Exits and entrances on the Chao Phraya and the Nakhon Nayok Rivers were provided with locks so that water in the canal might be held at higher levels for some time. As a result an additional 50,000 acres of land could be cultivated. Subsequently, similar canals were built in the southern part of the Central Region to the south of Bangkok.

The government's interest in the further development of water control was urgently revived by the low water levels of the years 1911, 1912 and 1913. In 1916 the government launched the South Pa Sak Canal Project (south of Sara Buri). Completed in 1922, it made about 269,000 acres irrigable. A few additional irrigation works were completed in the 1930's. After the suspension of activity during World War II, construction was resumed with new vigor. In 1952 the Great Chainat Project in the Central Region was begun by the government, assisted by an $18 million loan from the International Bank for Reconstruction and Development (IBRD), or World Bank, to cover the foreign exchange costs.

The Chainat Project consists of a large diversion dam on the Chao Phraya at Chainat (approximately 100 miles north of Bangkok) and an extensive system of lateral canals and drainage ditches on both banks of the river, extending throughout its lower reaches from Chainat to the Gulf of Siam. The dam was completed in 1956, the canal system in 1964. The Project provides improved water control on 1.4 million acres, supplemental water for about 860,000 acres and new irrigation for 80,000 acres. It is estimated that the Project has increased production of rice by 957,000 metric tons a year and permits a dry-season crop in the northern part of the Project, which yields 100,000 metric tons yearly of other crops.

An additional government undertaking is the Khuan Phumiphon (dam) in the Yanhee multipurpose project farther to the northwest on the Ping River. In addition to providing hydroelectric power and flood control, it makes double cropping possible on lands which have been producing only marginal crops. Its flood control aspects have also increased the effectiveness of the Chainat Project.

In the Northern Region 13 government projects completed by 1964 provided irrigation for about 400,000 acres. Others, either under construction or planned, are expected to further increase the irrigated area.

In the Northeast Region the total irrigated area remains small, although a pond irrigation program, referred to in the Far East as tank irrigation and started in 1951 with financial and technical assistance from the United States, is being developed. Runoff water during the rainy season is caught and held in large ponds for irrigation, watering livestock and household use.

By 1964, 108 such reservoirs had been constructed. Although many are used for domestic water supply only, it is estimated that they have a total storage capacity sufficient to furnish irrigation to supplement the rainfall on 129,000 acres.

In the Peninsula, with its heavy, year-round rainfall, there is less need for irrigation than in the rest of the country, but the problem of flood control and drainage is greater. By 1964, 10 projects affecting some 130,000 acres had been completed or were under construction.

LAND TENURE

Most agricultural land is owned and cultivated by peasant farmers operating on a small scale. Behind this circumstance lies a traditional system of land distribution which survived until the reign of King Chulalongkorn (Rama V, 1868–1910). Under this system the king, who in theory owned all land, dispensed holdings to officials, nobles and other free subjects. The grants, which were determined according to a system of ranks known as the *sakdi na* grades, ranged from 10 acres for commoners to 4,000 acres for officials of the highest grade. Although land thus allotted was subject to recall by the crown if it was left uncultivated for 3 years, the beneficiaries could transmit their holdings to their heirs or sell or mortgage them.

The operation of the *sakdi na* system and the plentifulness of land made it possible for the freeholding peasantry to survive and to increase its holdings alongside the huge estates which the notables were able to maintain through the use of slaves. Since the abolition of slavery and the abandonment of the system of *corvée* (unpaid labor due from a vassal to his lord), the number and size of the large estates have steadily declined. The system of inheritance has also militated against land accumulation. Children, both sons and daughters, inherit land equally through the father, the family head. The house and house compound, however, are usually inherited by the daughter, or son if there is no daughter, who remains with the parents. Some of the children, particularly daughters, are endowed with land at the time they establish separate households with their spouses (see ch. 8, Family). According to the 1963 Census of Agriculture, less than 6 percent of all farms were 24 acres or more. Most of the larger farms were in the Central Region around Bangkok, where there has been an increase in commercial vegetable gardening. In the country as a whole, farms averaged about 9 acres.

About 82 percent of the farmers own and operate their own farms. In the Northeast and the Peninsula, the proportions are 90 and 84 percent, respectively, and in the Central and Northern Regions, 75 and 74 percent, respectively. Renting land is more common in the fertile area of the Central Region, within easy access to a large city, where population pressure and land values are relatively high, and in the Northern Region, where the hilly character of the country limits the land area and irrigation increases land values by making double cropping possible. Even within these two regions the practice of renting land is limited.

The usual term of tenancy is the 1-year verbal contract (which may be renewed), with rent payable either in cash or in kind. Payment in kind amounts to about 50 percent of the crop, with the tenant furnishing work animals and implements. Payments in cash are highest in the North, where double cropping increases the productivity of farms.

PRODUCTIVE ACTIVITIES

Farming, animal husbandry and fishing are the major productive activities. Farming, in which rice cultivation predominates, is by far the most important. Over 55 percent of the cultivated area is planted in rice, almost 25 percent in upland crops and the remainder in rubber, field crops and tree crops, including coconuts. Pigs and poultry are numerous everywhere. Buffaloes and cattle are used as draft animals on the farms, elephants serve to haul logs in the forests, and horses and mules, are used as pack carriers in the mountains. Logging has long been well developed but has been hampered since World War II by past overcutting of valuable woods. Fishing, both marine and fresh water, ranks next to farming in its contribution to the economy as well as in its provision of an important part of the diet.

Farming

Rice

Both glutinous and nonglutinous rice in literally thousands of local varieties is grown in Thailand, glutinous mainly in the North and Northeast and nonglutinous chiefly in the Central Region and the Peninsula. Glutinous rice is preferred for home consumption in the North and Northeast and for candy and cakes in the rest of the country, whereas nonglutinous rice is produced largely for export. The maturation period of rice ranges, according to the variety, from 70 to 180 days. The selection of types grown depends on the amount and duration of the local water supply. In irrigated areas high fields, which receive less water, require use of the faster maturing varieties just as do "dry" ricefields, where rainfall is unreliable.

Annual production of milled rice from 1929–30 to 1947–48 fluctuated between 2.4 and 3.5 million metric tons. Beginning in 1949 production steadily increased, reaching a peak in 1957 of

Table 4.—*Output of Thailand's Major Crops, 1959–65*
(in thousands of metric tons)

Year	Rice	Rubber	Tobacco	Cotton	Sugarcane
1959	7,053	174.0	67.1	37.4	4,988
1960	6,770	170.8	74.1	45.5	5,382
1961	7,834	186.1	48.4	38.3	3,984
1962	8,177	195.4	47.9	41.3	3,154
1963	9,279	198.2	46.6	48.6	4,733
1964	10,168	210.5	62.8	49.1	5,074
1965	9,640	n.a.	n.a.	n.a.	n.a.

n.a.—not available.

Source: Adapted from Thailand, Ministry of Agriculture, Office of the Under Secretary of State, Division of Agricultural Economics, Agricultural Statistics Section, *Agricultural Statistics of Thailand, 1964*, pp. 46, 60, 76, 99–101.

about 8.3 million metric tons. In 1958 a serious drought caused production to drop to about 5.6 million metric tons. It recovered to 7.8 million metric tons in 1961 and continued to rise to 10.2 million metric tons in 1964 (see table 4). The area planted in rice has more than doubled since before World War II, increasing from about 7 million acres in 1939 to almost 16.2 million acres in 1964. Almost all of the new acreage was planted to wet rice.

Agricultural techniques have not changed greatly from those of 100 years ago. Methods of cultivation vary locally with climate, terrain and the nature of the soil and fall into two main categories: wet land and dry land cultivation. Wet land rice is cultivated either by transplanting or broadcast-planting; dry land rice is planted by dibbling, which involves using a pointed stick to make a hole in the ground into which a few seeds are dropped. The hole is then closed with the foot. All three techniques are traditional in Thailand and other parts of Asia.

Nearly 80 percent of the wet rice is produced by transplanting. The season begins in late April or May after the first rains have softened the ground for plowing. The seeds, which have been sprouted in a special frame, are planted in a nursery plot and allowed to grow while the fields are being plowed, harrowed and flooded by rains or by water admitted through the low dikes around each plot. In 4 to 6 weeks, when they are about 15 inches high, the densely growing plants are pulled up and transplanted to the fields, where they will mature. This task is carried out by both men and women, who work in rows, planting small clumps at intervals of about a foot.

In broadcast-planting the fields are prepared in the same way, but the grain is sown broadcast directly on the field. This method uses less labor but more seed, and the yield is about 50 percent smaller.

Floating rice, which is grown in the lower reaches of the Chao Phraya delta, is also broadcast and allowed to become established before the annual flood. While the floodwaters cover the field, the rice grows rapidly and, supported by the water, reaches a great length, its tip just above the waterline. The rice is harvested after the water has receded.

From planting to harvest, the rice crop requires little work. Reaping of the grain is done by hand with knives and sickles. The stalks are tied into sheaves and brought to the threshing floor, where they are beaten against a large bamboo basket or trampled by buffaloes or cattle.

Slash-and-burn shifting cultivation is practiced by most of the hill tribes. This method involves cutting down the trees and shrubs on the land to be cultivated, allowing them to dry and burning them just before the rainy season. In the cleared field a few seeds are dropped into holes made at intervals with a dibble stick. The seeds germinate with the first rain, and growth depends on rainfall and humidity. Rice and perhaps some vegetables are planted in these burned-over fields for 2 or 3 years, or until the soil loses its fertility and yields diminish, after which the cultivator shifts to a new piece of land. Many groups still plant the opium poppy despite the ban on this crop.

The average farmer owns or rents at least one water buffalo. Buffaloes are used for plowing, harrowing, threshing and sometimes for hauling, although bullocks are more frequently used for hauling. Buffaloes must be registered with the district officer and identified by some distinguishable feature. When a buffalo dies, the farmer, out of a sense of indebtedness to the animal for its services to him, in many cases does not eat the meat himself but gives it away. The bones are buried; the skin is used for making rope, although a part may be sold to a musician for a drumhead; and the horns are sold to a Chinese for making combs or used by the farmer as hooks for clothing or harness.

The tools used in rice cultivation are simple: a wooden plow with an iron share, a wooden harrow and a wooden-handled steel sickle. Except for the steel and iron parts, which are purchased in the market towns or from traveling vendors, most farm tools are made by the farmer himself or by the village carpenter.

The farm household of five or six persons (husband, wife, children and sometimes a grandparent or a son-in-law or daughter-in-law) can cultivate as much as 6 acres of paddy fields without hiring or borrowing additional labor except for transplanting and harvesting.

At about the age of 6, children are given such tasks as feeding chickens, caring for the animals and helping to grind rice. By the age of 15 they are doing full-time work along with the adults. Women take care of the house and the house-compound. They participate in planting the rice seedlings and do most of the transplanting. They also help with the threshing and grinding but usually do not plow or harrow.

Although the basic economic unit in the village is the household, certain forms of economic cooperation—nowadays less often than formerly—augment the household's labor resources for such heavy tasks as housebuilding and such urgent ones as transplanting and harvesting. Assistance may be reciprocal, as when a villager agrees to help in a neighbor's fields in return for an equal amount of work later in his own; or assistance may be given without expectation of direct and immediate return, as when people gather to do the heavy work on a neightbor's new house or when a tenant or debtor responds to a request for aid by his landlord or creditor. Increasingly, these traditional practices, particularly in regard to agricultural tasks, are being replaced by wage labor.

The production of commercial rubber, started in the southern peninsula in 1908, did not exceed 50,000 metric tons annually until the boom which followed World War II. Annual postwar production ranged from 98,000 metric tons in 1953 to 210,500 metric tons in 1964. Practically the entire output has always been exported. World War II gave impetus to the domestic manufacture of rubber products, but local manufactures still consume only an insignificant proportion of total production.

By 1964 the area planted to rubber, mainly in the Peninsula where climate, soil and rainfall are most favorable, totaled about 1.8 million acres, double the acreage planted in 1955. Government policy has been directed at encouraging the small Thai producer and restricting the growth of large plantations, traditionally owned by the Chinese. Accordingly, about 90 percent of the rubber acreage was in holdings of 20 acres or less. Only half a dozen estates were in the 1,000-acre range and only one was foreign owned. Of the larger holders the great majority are Thai-Chinese; of the 90,000 smallholders, most are Thai Moslems. The tappers are also mainly Thai Moslems—whether owner-tappers or share-tappers who tend the Thai-Chinese estates.

The estimated capital required to become a small rubber grower was about $100 in 1952 and not much more in 1964. This included a nominal fee to the government for unoccupied land (available to Thai nationals only), the outlay for seedlings from selected stock, supplied at nominal cost by the Department of Agriculture, and the cost of tools. The smaller grower may process the rubber into sheets or sell it in liquid form. Seedlings require about 6 years to become tappable, and during this time the new grower usually works as a tapper for one of the larger holders.

The rubber grower sells his product to a merchant, who is nearly always Chinese. The smaller growers sell raw sheets; the larger growers usually operate their own smokehouses and sell smoked sheets. The rubber merchant does the sorting, grading, packing and exporting.

Before World War II the government encouraged the production of rubber by exemption from taxes, licenses and export duties and by giving technical assistance to growers. Since World War II a small duty on rubber exports maintains a fund used to furnish growers with seedlings to replace old trees. Land is still available for rubber planting, so expansion of production can continue. The future of the rubber industry in Thailand, however, is uncertain. Such an industry, resulting from external demand and consequently depending primarily on export for its market, is at the mercy of world prices. The same high prices which encouraged rubber production also stimulated the development of synthetic rubber. It is not likely that Thai industrialization at its present rate of development will result in a substantial increase in domestic consumption in the immediate future, and the ability of Thai rubber to compete with synthetics in the world market is very uncertain.

Other Crops

Fruits are numerous in kinds and excellent in quality; included are: durians, mangosteens, mangoes, pineapples, oranges, pomegranates, jackfruit, tamarinds, guavas, a great variety of bananas and many others. They are grown supplementary to other crops in all parts of the country where climate permits. Orchards are well kept, and more care seems to be given to fruitgrowing than in many other tropical countries. Since the end of World War II, production has increased steadily, rising from 2 million metric tons valued at 1.8 million baht (see Glossary) in 1951 to 2.5 million metric tons valued at 2.8 million baht in 1960. Fruit surpassed rubber in 1952 in its contribution to the national income, becoming the second most important crop after rice. Most fruit is consumed locally, but expanding markets have developed in Singapore and Hong Kong.

Coconuts are the next most important crop after fruits, having contributed about half a billion baht annually to the national income since 1956. Mostly grown on plantations in the Peninsula, coconuts supply food, sugar and wine. The meat yields a fatty oil used for cooking, lighting and soapmaking, and the husk provides a fiber which can be made into mats and rope. Some copra is exported.

Vegetables, such as onions and various kinds of peas and beans, are sometimes grown as field crops but are more often raised in small garden patches. The betel vine, a climbing species of pepper, the leaf of which is chewed with the nut of the betel (*areca*) palm, is also grown in gardens. Consumption of this mild stimulant is declining. Cardamoms are grown and exported, and nutmegs are cultivated in the south. Yams, gourds of many kinds, chili peppers, eggplant and cassava (tapioca) are found in garden patches in most villages. In the southeast cassava in grown commercially to be processed into tapioca flour for export.

During the first half of the nineteenth century sugar was the principal export to Europe, but by 1899 export of cane sugar had ceased, and sugar factories, unable to compete with the foreign product, were deserted. Coconut and palm sugar continued to be made as before, and cane sugar was produced on a small scale for family use.

Sugarcane in the mid-1960's was grown commercially in some districts of the northern, northeastern and southeastern parts of the country but mainly in the Central Region. In 1965, because of depressed prices for sugar in the world markets, production was markedly reduced, and a large proportion of the crop was grown for home consumption, crudely refined or eaten raw.

Cultivated area, total output and average yield have risen steadily since World War II. Annual cane production increased from 839,000 metric tons in 1950 to over 5 million in 1964, and it is estimated that acreage planted to sugarcane more than quadrupled from 1947 to 1964. Since 1960, when refined sugar production of 100,000 metric tons exceeded domestic consumption requirements, the surplus has been exported. By 1965 domestic consumption had reached 130,000 tons; total production, however, had risen to 250,000 tons.

Tobacco has long been grown in various parts of the country, principally the North and the Northeast. In some localities it is cultivated as a second crop in the ricefields during the dry season. The best crops, however, are grown in the light, rich, alluvial soil on the banks and islands of the upper Chao Phraya River and its tributaries. In the North, tobacco is the principal agricultural product after rice.

The government in 1941 purchased the properties of the British-American Tobacco Company and now operates a monopoly, with exclusive rights to buy, sell at wholesale and manufacture all tobacco products. This is a very successful operation. Production of flue-cured, Virginia type tobacco averaged about 16,000 metric tons yearly from 1945 to 1949. This increased to 74,100 metric tons in 1961 but decreased to 62,800 metric tons in 1964. Acreage devoted to tobacco in 1964 was estimated to be nearly three times that of the immediate postwar period. Much of the crop is consumed locally in roll-your-own cigars and cigarettes and homemade chewing tobacco.

Cotton is the most important fiber produced. Output more than doubled to 49,100 metric tons between 1950 and 1964, but domestic production still supplies only a minor part of the cloth and other cotton needs of the country. The cotton grown is short staple, but efforts are being made to introduce some long staple varieties. In addition to cotton, jute and kenaf are the major domestically produced fiber crops. Because of the large domestic requirement for these fibers for bags, the goverment has adopted various measures to stimulate production. Seeds are supplied free of charge, capital is lent to the farmer without interest, and research stations have been established to assist in the education of planters. Output of jute increased from 1,300 metric tons in

1955 to 6,500 metric tons in 1964, and production of kenaf increased from 9,800 metric tons to 303,100 in the same period.

Until 1950 corn was not considered an important crop. Little was exported, and farmers did not often use it for animal feed because rice was cheaper and more plentiful. With increasing foreign demand, corn has become a leading export commodity. The area planted increased more than 10 times between 1951 and 1964, while during the same period production rose from 41,698 metric tons, valued at 35.8 million baht, to 935,000 metric tons, valued at more than 1 billion baht.

Output of oilseeds has increased substantially since 1950, and it is expected that the trend will be maintained. Oilseed crops, especially peanuts and soybeans, are prospering as a result of the new irrigation projects. In many places oilseeds are sown as a second crop after the rice harvest.

Sesame oil, extracted by means of rough wooden presses, is used for cooking, especially where coconut oil is not easily obtainable. Residue from the extraction is used for feeding cattle or as a fertilizer.

Except for corn, fruits, tapioca and kenaf, for which there is a growing export market, there is little trade in most of these crops except locally. Imports of processed fruits and most vegetables have been banned for several years to conserve foreign exchange.

Animal Husbandry

Almost every farmer raises some livestock. The most important are buffaloes, cattle, pigs and poultry. The forest and grasslands could support a great increase in the number, and expansion of livestock raising for export is an essential part of the plan to improve economic conditions in the Northeast. The problems of breeding, feeding, credit and transportation must, however, be overcome.

The main buffalo- and cattle-raising area is the Northeast. The animals are used for draft; buffaloes in the rice paddies and cattle on drier farms. Cattle are also raised for meat and provide about half of that consumed. In 1964 the Ministry of Agriculture estimated that there were almost 7 million buffaloes and over 5 million cattle in the country.

Pigs are raised everywhere, some for sale in Bangkok and other urban markets. Many farmers buy small pigs, fatten them and sell them to the Chinese in the markets. Since 1952 numbers have increased steadily to 4.3 million in 1964. Chickens, ducks, geese and other poultry are raised even more widely than pigs.

With the exception of some commercial duck farms on the out-skirts of Bangkok, most poultry is raised for family use.

Elephants play an important role in the logging industry and are found mostly in the Northern Region. Those in captivity have decreased from more than 13,000 in 1950 to about 11,000 in 1964. The horse—the small Yunnan pony—is used as a pack animal by the mountain peoples of the North. Their numbers have also declined from over 200,000 in 1950 to an estimated 179,000 in 1964.

Forestry

About 50 percent of the country is wooded, the tree cover varying from the dense growth of the Peninsula and the moun-tains of the North to the open forests of the Northeast. In central Thailand the forest area is small compared with open land; in the other three regions of the country the presence of man is marked by little more than patches and narrow belts of cleared land along banks of streams and other favorable spots. Except for minor private holdings the forest area is all public land.

Beginning in 1940 five major European companies obtained leases allowing them to work one-third of the concessions; a few domestic firms worked another third; and the remainder was reserved by the government. Leases were not renewed in 1955. The government decided to divide the industry between the government-owned Forest Industry Organization and a new com-pany, in which the government held 20 percent of the share capital and the five foreign companies held 80 percent.

Forest products are important in the economy, both for their utility locally and for the value of teak in foreign trade. Accord-ing to the 1960 census, over 36,000 people were employed in logging and allied occupations. The forests contain many woods other than teak which make good timber; among them are rose-wood, ebony, sapan and box. Other trees are valued for their oils, resins and gums.

The production of lac has long been important to the local economies of the North and Northeast in that it provided needed employment. Recently lac has reached significance as an export item as a result of the high postwar prices and recognition of the product's good quality. Seed lac and stick lac are shipped to the United States; shellac goes principally to the United Kingdom.

Other primary products important in domestic consumption include saw logs, pulpwood, charcoal and firewood. The cutting of rattan canes is a recognized business in some areas, and the demand for bamboos for temporary buildings, fishing poles, traps and numerous other domestic uses creates employment for a number of woodsmen.

The teak forests, now as in the past, are the most valuable and important government property in the country. The nation's teak is considered the finest timber in existence and the best in the world for shipbuilding. The teak zone extends over the whole northern portion of the country. Within it the teak tree grows only in certain localities where general conditions, especially the soil, are suitable. The whole area is traversed by a vast number of waterways, which provide the principal means to transport the teak to market.

Trees to be felled are selected and girdled by a forest officer. Girdling consists of cutting a ring around the trunk through to the heartwood in order to kill the tree and season the wood slowly. This must be done 2 years before the tree is felled in order that it will have dried enough to float. Felling operations take place during the rainy season. One or two elephants are harnessed to each log, which is then dragged to the nearest stream to be carried down by the flooding waters. The logs have to be floated singly until they pass the many rapids, below which there are rafting points.

Production has varied considerably since 1950. A major reason for yearly variations is the dependence on rainfall to raise the water level in the rivers high enough to float the logs. Demand and price also influence output, and their effect is complicated by the 3- to 4-year lag between the time of felling and the time the log reaches Bangkok. Estimates, however, indicate that teak production has decreased from a high of about 480,000 cubic yards in 1954 to a low of approximately 170,000 cubic yards in 1961. This was followed by a slight rise each subsequent year to 187,000 cubic yards in 1964.

The Forest Department was established in 1896, and a system of controls was inaugurated which kept the leasing of timberland in the hands of the government, set standards for felling and reserved certain areas for research or for exploitation by the Department. Leases were given for a period of 15 years, restrictions were changed from time to time and the number of concessionaires was steadily reduced.

Fishing

Fishing ranks next to agriculture in importance among the basic industries of the country. Fish is the principal source of protein in the general diet, and practically the entire mainland population devotes a part of its time to fishing for its own needs.

Every meal from infancy until old age consists principally of rice eaten with fish in some form—fresh, salted, dried or pickled. Thailand's rivers and canals, and even the marshes and rice-fields when flooded, abound with fresh-water fish of considerable variety. The sea waters along the 1,200 miles of coast also have sizable resources. Marine fishing grounds comprise about three-fourths of the shore waters of the Gulf of Siam and a long section of the eastern shore of the Indian Ocean between Burma and Malaya. The Gulf of Siam is rather shallow, and all parts are usable for fishing, but the area along the northern shore is exploited the most. A variety of nets, traps and other devices is used for both fresh-water and marine fishing.

Fishing activities have received added stimulus since 1951, when a program, aided by United States funds and technical advice, was started to explore and develop new fishing grounds in and around Thailand, to improve fishing methods, to promote new fishing industries and to expand marketing operations. This program has had significant success. Imported trap nets bring in a catch two to seven times greater than native traditional types. Culture of pondfish, including *talapia,* a South African importation, has made tremendous strides. A modern wholesale fish market, with freezer, cold storage plant and connecting technical laboratory, is in operation in Bangkok. A marine station has been established on the outer Gulf of Siam for experimental and exploratory fishing. A small-scale, village-level operation to produce fish meal and oil has been started and has developed into a new village industry to supply feed to farm animals.

In 1964 over 5,000 fishing boats were registered, almost double the number in 1950. All but a few hundred in 1964 were motorized, a reversal of the situation in 1950. The catch in 1964 totaled 577,000 metric tons, more than triple that of 1950. In the opinion of a United States fisheries expert, the country has only begun to produce what it can in fish and fish products.

Commercial fishing, both marine and fresh-water, centers around Bangkok and the fish markets there. It is estimated that the annual catch brought to the Bangkok market is between 40,000 and 50,000 metric tons, of which marine fisheries contribute more than 70 percent. Approximately 14 percent of the farm families derive income from fish, a part of which also goes to the Bangkok market. Most of the fish marketed in Bangkok is sold fresh to the consumer; the remainder is smoked, dried, pickled or made into sauce or paste. Two groups of selling agents —usually Chinese—handle these commodities in Bangkok; one group specializes in fresh fish, the other in cured or processed fish. Selling is only one of the activities of a selling agent. He also grants short-term loans or otherwise finances ventures of his clients, the fishermen; he retails all supplies the fishermen need.

Each consignment of fresh fish is sold at auction—singly for very large fish, but usually by the basket. Salted fish are sold by weight. Deductions are made for selling commission, watchman services and loading. Charges by the Chinese porters for unloading are determined by the location of the place at which the agents take delivery.

Prices fluctuate according to supply, and quick delivery by the fisherman is essential since he has a greater chance of securing a good price if his fish reach the market first. To the fisherman with small capital and only sailing boats, uncertain prices mean involuntary idleness, having to dump the catch into the sea, salt curing which ties up capital, or selling to salt curers at a lower price. The expansion of refrigeration and storage capacity, one of the projects advanced with United States financial and technical aid, has improved the situation. One day a surplus can be stored to meet shortages of other days, thus minimizing price fluctuations and saving the fishermen unnecessary risks. Refrigerated railway cars would make it possible to provide fresh fish to the northern and northeastern provinces and would thus improve the diet in those areas.

COOPERATIVES AND CREDIT

The cooperative movement began under government sponsorship in the 1920's. Progress was slow. In 1963, the latest year for which data is available, there were 9,876 credit cooperatives with 130,707 members; 410 land cooperatives with 19,278 members; and 271 cooperative credit federations, formerly called provincial cooperative banks, with 1,593 members. The Bank for Cooperatives, established by the government in 1947, began operations with a capital of 10 million baht. The Bank lends money to cooperative societies at 6 to 7 percent interest, and they in turn charge their members 8 to 10 percent.

Net profits of the credit cooperatives are disposed of as follows: 90 percent to the Reserve Fund, for future services to the societies themselves; 5 percent ot the Cooperative Public Welfare Fund, for promotion of public welfare in the community; and 5 percent to the Central Cooperative Fund Account of the Ministry of National Development, in case any society should be insolvent when liquidated. Taken as a whole, the cooperative credit societies are developing on a sound economic basis.

Until 1940 the development of cooperative societies was confined to agricultural credit societies. Since that time, other types have been organized, including those for land purchase, colonization, land improvement and producer marketing. The first cooperative stores were set up in 1938 in both rural and urban areas. A wholesale society in Chiengmai acts as a central purchasing agent for cooperative stores in that district.

It is estimated that only about 10 percent of agricultural credit is provided by cooperative credit societies, about 2 percent by commercial banks and the remainder by private lenders. Interest rates are high compared with Western standards; the system of repayment in kind makes it impossible to determine interest rates with any exactness. While the legal maximum interest rate is 15 percent, private loans carry much higher rates, and loans involving payment in kind are said to run as high as 60 to 120 percent. Many loans, however, are obtained interest-free from friends or relatives. The moneylenders may be either Thai or Chinese. Despite the popular belief that the Chinese hold most of the agricultural debt and charge high interest rates, several studies made during the past three decades showed that their rates, on the whole, were lower than those of the Thai moneylenders and that their holdings were less important. A survey made in 1952–53 indicated that less than one-third of the farmers queried had resorted to borrowing in the preceding 5 years. Of those who had, most reported borrowing from relatives. The highest rates of interest on loans were paid to landlords.

The problem of debt received considerable attention in the 1920's and 1930's. The severe crop failures between 1912 and 1920 and the depression of the 1930's not only increased the debts of the farmers but also made existing debts more onerous. The problem of agricultural debt became a political issue during the last years of the absolute monarchy and the first years of the constitutional regime. The price inflation during and after World War II greatly reduced the burden of earlier debts, and the high prices paid for rice enabled many farmers to settle their debts.

Commercial banks have not been prepared to make loans to farmers, and the government had not in the past made a serious effort to establish a farm bank system. Early in 1966, however, the government announced that a Bank for Agriculture and Agricultural Credit, incorporating the Bank of Cooperatives, would be set up. The new bank was to have seven branches: two in the North; two in the Northeast; two in the Central Region and one in the South. A 5-year agricultural credit program had been drawn up, and a sum of 400 million baht was to be lent the new bank by the World Bank, the Agency for International Development (AID) or the Asian Development Bank.

THE ROLE OF GOVERNMENT

Primary responsibility in the government for the promotion and improvement of agriculture, animal husbandry, forestry and fishing rests with the Ministry of Agriculture, which was established as an independent ministry in 1934. The duties of the Ministry include conserving and developing natural resources, regulating agricultural production, engaging in research and experimentation, giving demonstrations and providing advice and information on subjects within its purview, distributing improved seeds and combating agricultural diseases and pests.

Within the Ministry are the Departments of Agriculture, Rice, Fisheries, Livestock, and Forest. Under the Ministry's general supervision are the Ma Bon Rubber Estate Organization, the staff of which operates the government-owned rubber plantations, the office of the Rubber Replanting Aid Fund, the Fish Marketing Organization, the Cold Storage Organization, the Forest Industry Organization and the Thai Plywood Company.

Offices acting as field agents of the various departments within the Ministry are located in the provinces: rice offices in 63 provinces, agricultural offices in 69, veterinary offices in each of the 71, forest offices in 62 and fisheries offices in 24. These offices are part of the provincial administration and generally report to their respective departments in the Ministry of Agriculture through the governor of the provinces.

The rice offices are concerned solely with rice cultivation; otherwise their functions are similar to those of the agricultural offices. Both offices give advice and information to farmers, help distribute seeds and combat crop pests, and collect statistics on land under cultivation, on crop yields and on the economic status of farm families. The veterinary offices give technical advice on livestock breeding and care, help distribute forage and administer the giving of vaccine and serum to livestock, check livestock for disease and collect statistics on stock and on the economic status of stockbreeders. The forest offices give technical advice to those engaged in forest industries; assist in reforestation; license and inspect the operations of loggers, sawmill operators and charcoal burners; help collect fees and duties; and collect statistics on forest timber and on timber cut. The fisheries offices advise fish breeders and fishermen, issue licenses and collect taxes from fishermen, and collect statistics on the fish catch and on the economic status of fishermen.

Extensive research has been carried out since the 1930's by various institutions within the Ministry of Agriculture. The Research and Experiment Station Division of the Department of Agriculture operates 17 experimental stations located throughout the country. These stations undertake experimental research relating to upland field crops, fiber crops and fruits in order to develop improved seeds, to determine the proper growing and harvesting season and to learn the most efficient methods of planting, cultivating and harvesting these crops. Other divisions in the Department of Agriculture which engage in research are the Rubber Division, the Plant Industry Division (research on insect pests and plant diseases) and the Agricultural Chemistry Division (research on soil analysis and utilization of fertilizers).

The Rice Breeding Division of the Department of Rice conducts research in the development of better rice seeds and operates 16 experimental stations located throughout the country. Research into all other aspects of rice cultivation—soils, water, climate, fertilizers, mechanization and standardization—is under the jurisdiction of the Technical Division of the Department of Rice.

Three divisions of the Department of Livestock Development are engaged in research. The Animal Husbandry Division operates eight livestock stations to carry out improved breeding experiments, the Animal Nutrition and Forage Crops Division seeks to improve animal nutrition and forage crops and the Veterinary Research and Education Division undertakes to improve the quality and production of vaccine and serum used in the prevention and treatment of animal diseases.

The Division of Fisheries Investigation is the research division of the Department of Fisheries. It operates a technological laboratory and 14 experimental stations: 11 inland, 2 near brackish water and 1 on the seacoast. All stations are equipped with hatchery facilities and laboratory equipment for conducting research experiments. The Forest Department includes the Silviculture Division, which carries out research on the care and protection of forests, and the Forest Products Research Division, which is in charge of research and development in the utilization of timber and minor forest products.

The research divisions of the Ministry have received equipment and technical assistance from the United States Operations Mission (USOM), the Food and Agriculture Organization (FAO), of the United Nations and the Colombo Plan (see Glossary). Advisers from these organizations are training some technicians on the job, while others are receiving training abroad financed by these agencies.

The leading institution for agricultural education is Kasetsat University, located at Bang Khea, just northwest of Bangkok. It was founded in 1943, amalgamating previous schools of agriculture and forestry. Faculties include agriculture, animal husbandry, forestry, fisheries, a college of veterinary science and a school of irrigation engineering. The University is a government department under the Office of the Prime Minister and is entirely dependent on the government for budgetary support. It has received financial assistance, technical aid and scholarships for its graduates from FAO, USOM, the Rockefeller Foundation and various private firms. Most United States assistance has been given through contracts with Oregon State College and since July 1962 with the University of Hawaii. The contracts provided professors, established research and extension projects and assisted in the development of the curricula and the improvement of teaching methods. Under the project, large quantities of laboratory and plant equipment and teaching aids have been imported, and 14 buildings have been constructed. The United States has also assisted in the establishment of 16 vocational agriculture schools located throughout the country.

Agricultural Extension

In order to carry to the individual farmer the knowledge gained through research and experiment, eight regional agricultural centers have been established with United States assistance. Since the beginning of the program in 1951, approximately 1,200 Thais have received at least 6 months preservice training and been assigned to the field. Of these 187 have completed training abroad under the participant program. The broad objectives are: to increase farm production through extension methods which teach and encourage the adoption of improved cultural practices and to strengthen local self-help through the development of farm organizations.

Current plans call for training 100 new district (*amphur*) officers a year, thereby attaining a ratio of 1 agricultural officer for every 2,000 farm families in the Northeast by the end of 1967. A Northeast Regional Extension Headquarters has been established at Khon Kaen to coordinate area extension and research activities and serve as an extension training center. The center is equipped with facilities to accommodate classes of 100 and a production workshop for extension information activities.

Farmers' extension clubs have been organized by extension officers with United States assistance and serve as channels through which new agricultural practices are introduced to farmers. By 1965 there were 360 such clubs with 18,000 members.

Accelerated Rural Development

The Thai Government and the United States have launched the Accelerated Rural Development program in six of the northeastern provinces. It is designed to counter the threat of insurgency and to strengthen links between the central government and rural communities. Specific targets are to coordinate the planning and accelerate the rural development programs in the provinces of Ubon Ratchathani, Nakhon Phanom, Sakon Nakhon, Udon Thani, Loei and Nong Khai; to create, train and equip an organization in each of these provinces which will be able with local initiative to plan, design and construct rural roads, water facilities and other small-scale public works; to develop a Thai regional technical assistance center that can provide the necessary facilities, such as training and other specialized services for the six provinces. Projects are expected to reflect felt village needs and are planned to stimulate local participation in their implementation and maintenance. A sum of about 4 million baht has been allotted to the program, and a temporary office has been set up near Nakhon Ratchasima.

Agri Business

Agri Business is a program set up jointly by Thailand and the United States to arouse interest on the part of private investors in the agricultural and industrial development of the Northeast. The program calls for the expansion of agriculture and the establishment by the private sector on sound business principles of industries using agricultural products as raw materials.

With World Bank loans, United Nations technical assistance and the aid of Australia and other Southeast Asia Treaty Organization (SEATO) allies, the Thai Government has been building irrigation dams and roads and, in partnership with the United States, has been working on various development projects in the Northeast. To complete the economic structure, the resources of the private sector are being mobilized through the Agri Business program to utilize the fruits of these development programs. Industries envisaged include plants to process castor beans, cotton, jute, kenaf and other commodities whose output is being increased in the various projects. At the same time cultivation is to be encouraged of crops suitable for various parts of the Northeast which are not now planted but provide raw material for industries. The agricultural part of Agri Business calls for provision of fertilizer on credit to farmers to boost their output. Farm equipment and modern techniques are also to be made available for production of raw materials to supply the new industries.

CHAPTER 21

INDUSTRY

Industry is of minor but increasing importance in the country's economic life. Mining, which over a 10-year period averaged a contribution of 1.5 percent to gross domestic product, began improving in 1964, reaching 2.1 percent in 1965. The contribution of manufacturing rose from 11 percent in 1950 to 13.5 percent in 1965, most of the growth occurring after 1960. Between 1950 and 1960 the number of workers engaged in manufacturing more than doubled to over 400,000. With the exception of a few hundred plants built after 1950 most manufacturing is on a small scale. It is confined largely to processing agricultural commodities and fabricating a few consumer products and building materials. Except for a small steel mill, there is no heavy industry.

Available data on the principal industries show a generally rising trend in production (see table 5). Only the processing of agricultural products and the production of cement have, however, achieved sufficient volume to satisfy the country's needs. On the whole, Thailand must continue to depend on imports for its manufactured goods.

The government has increased its efforts to encourage the establishment of new industries and to modernize existing ones; there are signs of progress, but development is limited in scope. The rate of further industrial development will depend on ability to overcome deficiencies in transportation, power and communications; to increase the supply of domestic capital, which generally prefers short-term investment rather than long-term industrial ventures; and to train technicians and managerial personnel essential to profitable operation.

The government is aware of these problems and is taking steps to solve them. The Industrial Investment Promotion Act of 1954, followed by that of 1960, which was revised in 1962, and the Six-Year Economic Development Plan (1961–66) are evidence of Thailand's desire for industrialization and its recognition that such a program requires careful planning.

Some Thai think that improving agricultural methods and marketing rather than industrialization is a means of raising the standard of living. It is doubtful, however, that the average

Table 5.—Production in Major Industries in Thailand, 1956 and 1961–65

Item	Unit	1956	1961	1962	1963	1964	1965
Cement	Metric tons	397,608	800,284	967,475	997,231	1,059,136	1,247,998
Cotton textiles	Thousands of square yards	10,637	86,588	109,437	140,046	189,399	n.a.
Gunnysacks	Thousands	3,562	8,842	10,816	23,129	33,511	39,892
Sugar	Metric tons	42,332	120,000	151,344	125,031	167,973	319,976
Paper	do	2,732	3,627	5,768	7,890	13,577	13,330
Tobacco	do	8,461	9,739	9,739	10,148	10,409	10,057

n.a.—not available.
Source: Adapted from *Far Eastern Economic Review Yearbook 1967*, p. 369; and Thailand, *Bank of Thailand Monthly Report*, May 1962, p. 59.

farmer is concerned with such questions or is even aware of the program of diversification being planned. He knows the savings in time and labor of taking his paddy to the nearby rice mill instead of processing it for home consumption by the crude method he once used. In general, he prefers factory-made textiles to home-woven ones, although he complains that they are not sturdy enough for work clothes, which he may continue to weave at home. Beyond these few instances in which commercialization has directly impinged upon his individual experience, however, he remains indifferent to industrialization.

The government has quite another viewpoint. Primarily dependent on a few exports for most of its revenue, it is conscious of being at the mercy of fluctuating world prices. It feels that increased revenues and economic security can only be achieved by diversification and expansion of commerce and industry.

Although Thailand will not be transformed into an industrial nation in the foreseeable future—if ever—it has an excellent potential for diversification of its economy by further development of manufacturing.

NATURAL RESOURCES

Natural resources in the form of raw materials are adequate for the substantial development of industry, and the country's many rivers have a great hydroelectric power potential. Agricultural products for processing, canning and preserving are plentiful and varied. Mining has played a large part in the economy for many years, and discoveries of additional mineral deposits since World War II are increasing its importance. Substantial progress in industrialization, however, has been hampered by lack of available electric power.

The country's hydroelectric potential in the Mekong and other rivers is estimated to be 2.6 million kilowatts. By 1967 only small quantities of hydroelectric power were in use, generated by two installations completed in 1965 and 1966, respectively. Plans on the large-scale exploitation of hydroelectric energy, however, were well advanced, and work on a number of hydroelectric power projects was in progress (see fig. 14).

Little systematic investigation of mineral deposits was undertaken before World War II. After the war, however, the Department of Mines in the Ministry of Industry (which in 1964 became the Department of Mineral Resources of the newly organized Ministry of National Development), with the technical assistance of the United States Geological Survey, carried out reconnaissance to locate mineral deposits which were worth developing commercially. Further geological investigations have

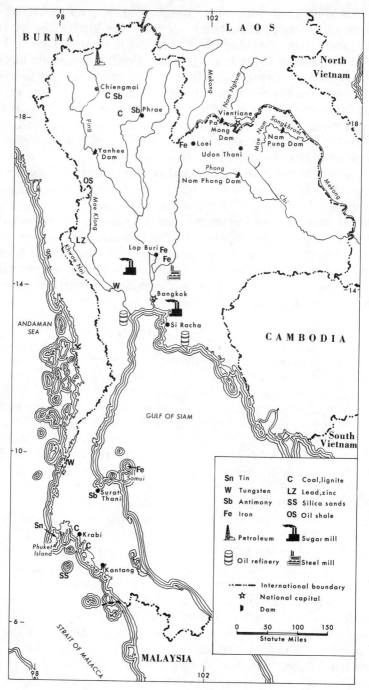

Figure 14.—Major Mining and Industrial Installations in Thailand.

been undertaken by the United States Agency for International Development (USAID). These surveys have served to train Thai geologist and engineers in specialized fields of geology. As part of the same United States technical aid program, Thai engineers trained in the United States have carried out experimental mining projects for practical instruction in modern methods of mechanized mining, at the same time training junior engineers, miners and machine operators.

The Mineral Experimental Center in Bangkok was opened in 1956. This is a modern laboratory for which the United States supplied all the equipment. Thai technicians trained in the United States direct operations of the Center.

In 1965 three mineral development projects were underway: the Copper Exploration Project to explore known copper deposits in various provinces; the Non-Metallic Minerals Exploration Project to determine commercially exploitable deposits of fluorite, lignite and phosphate; and the Mekong Basin Minerals Survey Project. The last, part of the Lower Mekong Development project, is for the purpose of estimating the amount of electric power required from the development of the Pa Mong Dam, on the Mekong, to supply the potential mineral industries in the area. The first two projects are financed by the government of Thailand and the third by the United Nations Special Fund.

Minerals

A wide variety of minerals including tin, tungsten, lead, zinc, antimony, iron, gold, precious and semiprecious stones, salt, lignite, oil shale, petroleum, asphaltic sand and glass sand occur in Thailand (see ch. 2, Physical Environment). Tin is by far the most important industrially. It is found mainly in the South (frequently called the Peninsula), where the mining areas extend from the southern tip of Burma to the Malaysian border. Tungsten deposits are mined extensively in many localities along the Burma border and in the mountainous areas in the central part of the Peninsula. Exploitation of the other minerals is on a smaller scale (see fig. 14).

Fuel and Power

Fuels are scarce and inadequate to meet the country's present power requirements. With the inauguration in 1961 of the first stage of the Khuan Phumiphon (dam) construction project (commonly known as the Yanhee Project), exploitation of hydroelectric power began. Sources of firewood, which supply much of the power and are used even by the railroads, are exhausted. Lignite deposits and petroleum reserves have been discovered and some are being exploited, but much of the power produced in the country is from imported crude oil that is processed domestically.

The most promising lignite deposits are those in the Northern Province around Mae Mo, southeast of Chiengmai, and in the Southern Province along the Strait of Malacca Coast, at Ban Pu Dam in Krabi Province and at Kantang in Trang Province. Only the Mae Mo and Ban Pu Dam Fields are being exploited.

A petroleum deposit estimated at 5 million barrels has been discovered adjoining the Burma border in Chiang Mai Province, and an experimental plant for refining the petroleum has been in operation since 1955. Exploitation of the oil shale reserve located at Mae Sot in Tak Province on the Burma border is hampered by difficulty of access through heavily forested rugged hills.

A complete oil refinery, including a catalytic cracking plant capable of producing a range of refined products totaling about 1.5 million tons, opened in late 1964 at Au Udom in Si Racha district, about 80 miles southeast of Bangkok on the Gulf of Siam. The refinery is capable of producing gasoline and aviation jet fuels, as well as fuel oil, kerosene and bitumen. It has a capacity of 36,000 barrels per day and is expected to supply most of the requirements for petroleum products for the next few years despite the expanding needs of industry, public utilities and private motor vehicle owners. It supplements the products of the other refineries, including the refinery at Ban Bang Chak about 60 miles southwest of Bangkok operated by the Ministry of Defense.

The Si Racha refinery is owned and operated by a Thai company, the Thai Oil Refinery Company (TORC), with financial and technical support from British, French, American and West German companies. It was incorporated in Thailand in 1964 and is subject to Thai laws. The Thai company will operate the refinery for 10 years, after which time it will be handed over to the Thai Government. In the intervening period 25 percent of the net profits are to be paid to the government.

A French consortium extended a 10-year credit covering the $28 million required for construction of the TORC refinery at an interest of 5.65 percent per year on deferred payment terms. Three Thai banks and one United States and one British bank in Thailand jointly financed the operating expenses of about 300 million baht (about $15 million). The Royal Dutch Shell group of companies acted as technical advisers and agreed to operate the plant; Thai specialists were sent to Great Britain, the Netherlands and India to be trained in oil refining techniques. Two United States companies, ESSO and CALTEX, jointly with

Dutch Shell assumed responsibility for the regular supply of crude oil, for the offtake of the refined products and their distribution throughout Thailand and for disposal of any surplus. They purchase the refined products at world market prices.

The refinery products are shipped from Si Racha to the marketing installations in Bangkok in four British-built 2,000-ton capacity coastal tankers owned by another company, Thai Petroleum Transports. Their Thai crews were trained by British and Dutch experts.

Electric power production increased gradually over the 10-year period between 1950 and 1960, mainly in and around Bangkok, where 85 percent of Thailand's total power is consumed. Beginning in 1961, as new installations came into operation, power generation registered great increases each year. In 1950 generating capacity was 32,334 kilowatts for the entire country. By 1964 it had increased more than 10 times to 376,508 kilowatts as a result of the completion of a new power station in Bangkok, three generating plants at the Khuan Pumiphon (dam) in the Yanhee Project on the Ping River in northwest Thailand and the Krabi plant in the South. Electricity generation rose from 68.5 million kilowatt hours in 1950 to 827.4 million in 1964. Nevertheless, most of the country outside of Bangkok continues to suffer from a power shortage.

The Yanhee is the major multipurpose development project which was underway in 1967. It is expected that eight generators to be installed at the Yankee Project Dam will eventually have a capacity of 560,000 kilowatts, which it is calculated will supply Bangkok and the Central Region with sufficient electricity to meet their needs until 1975 or 1980. The dam, three generators and transmission lines to Bangkok were completed by 1963. The cost of the Yanhee Project, estimated at $100 million, has been financed in part by a loan of $66 million from the International Bank for Reconstruction and Development (IBRD).

The Krabi Power Plant, with a capacity of 40,000 kilowatt hours, came into operation in 1963, and within 2 years demand had increased to such an extent that it was planned to double its capacity by 1968. The plant uses lignite from the Ban Pu Dam deposit. The Krabi Power Plant is a government undertaking financed in part with foreign funds; Austrian Government credits enabled two Austrian firms to provide not only technical personnel but also most of the electrical equipment.

Generating plants at dams on the Mae Nam Songkhram and Phong Rivers, the first installations in the Mekong Development Project, went into operation in 1965 and 1966, respectively. The Nam Pung Hydroelectric Plant on the Mae Nam Songkhram, northeast of Udon Thani, has a capacity of 6,300 kilowatts; the Nam Phong Hydroelectric Plant on the Phong River, southwest of Udon Thani, 25,000 kilowatts. They are expected to meet the requirements of the people in at least six provinces which previously had only 1,000 kilowatts of power capacity available (see ch. 2, Physical Environment).

Late in 1966 the Council of Ministers approved, in principle, an offer made by a United States company to build a pilot atomic powerplant with an estimated capacity of 12,500 kilowatts, the company to be granted a 15-year concession. The National Energy Authority has received a reactor from the United States, but in late 1967 it was being used solely for research purposes.

MINING

Mining of tin and other minerals is of great antiquity and continues to contribute important exports as well as raw materials required by the domestic economy (see table 6). Tin, tungsten, lead and antimony are mined almost entirely for export, and production is heavily dependent on world demand. Iron ore, lignite and cement are, in general, mined or quarried for domestic use, although Japan has been a heavy purchaser of iron ore in recent years. In 1960 almost 30,000 people (0.2 percent of the labor force) were employed in mining (see ch. 22, Labor).

Thailand is one of the world's major producers of tin. The richest sources, from which 80 percent of the country's annual production is derived, are located in the South. Most of the concessions are operated by British, Australians and Chinese. Mining methods vary from highly mechanized operations on a large scale to traditional practices utilizing the labor of thousands of Chinese coolies and Moslem Thai. Half of the tin produced is by dredging the sea bottom, and 40 percent is obtained by gravel pumps and hydraulic mines.

Table 6.—Ore Production in Thailand, 1958–64
(in metric tons)

Year	Tin*	Tungsten	Antimony	Iron	Lead
1958	10,892	605	n.a.	14,750	2,340
1959	13,433	463	19	6,074	3,300
1960	16,757	407	n.a.	11,475	4,600
1961	18,386	475	45	55,793	5,202
1962	20,323	394	33	45,308	5,550
1963	21,617	190	1,226	15,741	5,030
1964	21,635	397	2,819	190,955	8,125

n.a.—not available.
*Concentrates.

Source: Adapted from *Thailand: Statistical Yearbook, 1965*, p. 237.

Annual production, which fell off during and after World War II because of damaged equipment, regained its prewar production level by 1957. Until 1960, however, annual production was limited to 10,000 tons as a result of the quota imposed by the International Tin Council, of which Thailand is a member. This quota was raised in 1960 and 1961 and doubled to 20,000 tons in 1962. In the 1960's about 20 mines were in operation.

Thai tin used to be smelted in either Penang, Malaysia or Singapore, but Thailand has had its own smelter since August 1965, when the plant of the Thailand Smelting and Refining Company, Limited (Thaisarco) started to operate. Phuket Island, at the northern end of the Strait of Malacca, was chosen as the site because the major part of the tin ore produced is obtained from the seabed around it. The plant has an annual capacity of 20,000 tons of tin ingots and enjoys a statutory monopoly for smelting all tin concentrates in Thailand until 1970. Export of tin ore was prohibited by the government when the new smelter opened. Union Carbide Corporation of the United States owns 70 percent of the outstanding stock, and all the plant's output is sold to the United States.

Tungsten became increasingly important after World War II, as about 70 mines located in the northwestern and southern provinces came into operation. Demand, however, slumped in the late 1950's and production dropped from a high of 1,627 metric tons in 1952 to 190 metric tons in 1963.

Antimony is mined sporadically in the northern provinces of Lampang and Phrae and in the southern province of Surat Thani. Ore produced reached a high of 141 metric tons in 1954, fell to zero in 1958 and 1960 and rose to 2,819 metric tons in 1964.

Most of the lead produced is mined at Nong Phai, which is located on the divide between the Mae Klong and the Khwae Noi Rivers in Kanchanaburi Province, 125 miles northwest of Bangkok. Lead output rose to a high of over 12,500 metric tons in 1955 but steadily decreased each year to a low of 2,340 metric tons in 1958. Production rose in subsequent years to 8,125 metric tons in 1964.

Iron has been mined in many parts of the country for many centuries and smelted in simple charcoal furnaces to make the few implements needed by the farmers. From 1951 through 1960 annual production of iron ore fluctuated between 2,756 metric tons in 1954 to 14,750 tons in 1958. Most of the iron ore produced during this period was from a mine located near Lop Buri in central Thailand. Iron content of ore from this mine varies between 66.4 and 48.4 percent. It supplies a small charcoal blast furnace situated to the south of the mine, near Sara Buri.

In 1961 a new iron mine on Samui Island in the Gulf of Siam in the southern province of Surat Thani came into operation, boosting national production to 55,793 metric tons, of which about 40,000 metric tons came from Samui. Ore analyzes at 55 percent iron content or better. Most of it is shipped to Japan. This mine went out of operation in 1963 and national production sank to 15,741 metric tons. In 1964, however, as a result of the discovery of the new field of Loei in the Northeast and a Japanese purchase of 180,000 tons of ore, national production rose to over 190,000 tons.

Although there are a number of lignite deposits in the country, only those at Ban Pu Dam, which supply the Krabi Power Plant, and those at Mae Mo, in Lampang Province, are being mined. The Mae Mo mines were opened in 1955 by the government, with the assistance of the United States technical aid program. Production rose from 30,000 metric tons in 1955 to 137,075 in 1963, falling to 103,075 in 1964. Most of the output is used in the domestic thermal powerplants.

A survey of seven islands in the Bay of Krabi off the west coast has revealed the presence of some 15 million tons of high grade silica sands, averaging more than 95 percent silica content. The islands have been leased by the Thai Government to a Thai firm which is mining the sand and reexporting it to Japan for glassmaking.

MANUFACTURING

During the 1960's industrial growth continued at an increasing pace. An industrial census published at the end of October 1964 indicated that there were 29,242 factories distributed throughout the country, almost double the number in 1957. There were 9,395 factories in the Bangkok-Thon Buri metropolitan area; 6,434 in the Northeast; 5,158 in the North; 3,159 in the South; and 5,096 in the Central Region, excluding Bangkok and Thon Buri. Only 3 percent of these, employing about 150,000 persons, could be classified as large- or medium-scale industries; the rest are small-scale factories employing fewer than 50 persons and in most cases fewer than 20. The more typical producing unit is the small workshop employing only a few persons or using unpaid family labor. Most of the modern plants have been built since World War II and are owned and operated by the government.

With the exception of the small steel mill at Sara Buri, the Si Racha oil refinery and the tin smelter on Phuket Island, industry is chiefly confined to the processing of agricultural products and the manufacture of building materials and some consumer goods. As of 1960 manufacturing enterprises employed 471,027 persons, or 3.4 percent of the labor force (see ch. 22, Labor). Over 67 percent of the total was engaged in three industries: the largest group, 129,619, in the manufacture of textiles, knitwear and other wearing apparel; 99,913 in food processing, mainly in rice mills; and 89,768 in sawmilling and woodworking. Of the total engaged in manufacturing, 146,051 (31 percent) were self-employed and 79,446 were unpaid family workers. Only 11,-505 were employed by government factories.

Processing of Agricultural and Forestry Products

Rice milling with over 14,000 permanent and portable mills, is by far the most important industry in the country. About 140 permanent mills are located in Bangkok, the remainder in important centers upcountry. The portable mills move throughout the countryside with the seasonal cycle. The large Bangkok mills have an average capacity of 100 to 200 tons of rice daily; the upcountry mills, a daily capacity of 30 to 40 tons; and the portable mills, from 6 to 12 tons. Most rice, whether for domestic consumption or export, is processed in these mills.

Production of sugar is the next most important industry. Over 1,500 sugar mills are in operation, most of them small units. Of the 250 factory-plants, 12 are government owned. Two of them, built since World War II, are relatively large scale. One mill, opened in 1956 at Chon Buri, 45 miles southeast of Bangkok, has a cane-crushing capacity of 1,000 tons daily. A second, even larger plant with a daily cane-crushing capacity of 1,500 to 2,000 tons, located at Suphan Buri, 55 miles northwest of Bangkok, began operation in 1957. Before 1958 total annual production of all mills averaged between 40,000 and 45,000 tons, while consumption was estimated at 70,000 tons, the gap having to be met by imports. Since construction of the new mills, annual production has risen steadily. In 1959 it exceeded consumption requirements for the first time in Thai history. As production of refined sugar rose to 100,000 tons in 1960 and 120,000 in 1961, Thailand became a sugar exporter. By 1963 domestic consumption requirements were estimated at 121,000 tons, but production has continued to surpass that figure, increasing to 319,976 tons in 1965.

The spinning and weaving of natural fibers, including cotton, silk and jute, constitute one of Thailand's most important industries. In 1957 the cotton mills in the country had about 31,000 spindles; by 1963 the number had increased to 81,000. It is estimated, however, that at least 60 percent of the textiles used in the country have been woven on handlooms operated by farmers. By 1963 there were about 600 weaving mills in the country, many of them manufacturing Thai silk for the growing market at home and abroad. With increasing production as more plants come into existence, the pattern of this industry has become more diversified. Some of the establishments are modern factories, but most of them are mechanized or semimechanized, employing 20 to 30 persons. Official statistics of cotton textile production are based on returns from six factories and show that output increased from 10 million square yards in 1956 to over 189 million square yards in 1964.

Five gunnysack factories, using locally grown jute, are in operation; the newest ones started production in the 1960's. By 1965 output reached over 319 million sacks, more than 10 times the 1956 figure. Production, however, does not yet reach the level required for moving the rice harvest and for exporting the agricultural products.

The rubber industry has assumed increasing importance, and by the end of 1963 about 190 factories were using locally grown rubber to fabricate a number of rubber products. The largest was the Firestone Tire Plant, which had facilities to produce 270,000 tires per year.

Other manufacturing establishments which process agricultural products include cigarette and tobacco factories, flour mills, distilleries, canneries, dairies, tanneries and plants producing tea, vegetable oils, soap and carbonated beverages.

Forest products are an important source of income. Of these, teak and other rare woods rank first. In 1957, 1,736 sawmills were estimated to be in operation. Other than seven large mills located near Bangkok, most were portable and semiportable mills in use throughout the country. Five of the large Bangkok mills prepare lumber for export. The others supply the local market. The most important domestic use of lumber is in construction. Other woodworking industries include plywood, paper, matches and furniture.

Other Manufacturing

A plant for the manufacture of cement, built in 1913, was one of the first modern industrial establishments to be introduced. Before World War II production averaged 100,000 tons a year. After World War II capacity was rapidly expanded, and production more than tripled between 1956 and 1965, when it totaled over a million tons. Also owned by one of the cement companies is the small charcoal blast furnace located near Sara Buri. Associated with the furnace is a small iron and steel works with a daily capacity of 10 tons of steel. It produces steel bars, nails, bolts, screws and other finished products.

Many small units and medium-sized establishments for metal-working have been started since early in the 1960's. Additional plants assemble sewing machines, motorcycles, automobiles, trucks and tractors; others produce glass, pharmaceuticals, electric light bulbs, flashlight batteries and miscellaneous consumer goods.

In July 1966 the government approved the establishment of the first industrial estate on a 1,200-acre plot of land at Rangsit, about 25 miles north of Bangkok in Pathum Thani Province. The plan calls for the Ministry of Industry to divide the land into lots for lease, sale or rent to private companies. The Ministry will also provide power, water, roads and other essential facilities and services.

CONSTRUCTION

A vast upswing in construction has taken place since 1960—dams, factories, powerplants, highways and airfields. Most of these large projects have been carried out by foreign engineering firms using Thai labor. Simultaneously an indigenous building boom—new hotels, shops, business centers, apartments and both brick and wooden houses—has been underway in Bangkok and other urban areas. The number of persons employed in construction is unknown but must be appreciable.

As a result of the construction boom, the building materials industries have registered many new gains. There has been a rapid change to bricks and cement as construction materials for houses and buildings because of the timber shortage and the high cost of timber products. During the last few years local production of bricks, as well as cement, has increased greatly. Apart from ordinary bricks, decorative bricks, decorative concrete blocks and earthen and concrete tiles have been produced for some time. A recent addition in this group is lightweight hollow bricks, which permit economical multistory building projects. Precast concrete products, such as plain and steel-reinforced cement pipes, and prestressed concrete products, such as foundation piles, telegraph and electric poles, fenceposts, bridge girders and flat slabs, have been manufactured during the last few years. Plywood, veneer board, galvanized roofing sheets, teak parquet flooring, metal doors, and windows are also produced in the country.

Construction is regarded of such importance to rural development that the small construction projects are included in the programs of both Accelerated Rural Development and the Mobile Development Units operating in remote areas. The United States has contributed about $2 million worth of equipment and established a training program, jointly with the Ministry of Education, at the Khorat Technical Institute. The United States has also provided three Seabee Technical Assistance Teams, each team consisting of an officer, a medical corpsman and 12 noncommissioned officers, all specialists in one or more phases of construction. Although the teams have constructed roads and small dams, their main function is to train Thai construction chiefs, equipment operators and mechanics. By 1965 the teams had given on-the-job training to 66 Thai technicians, including 9 construction chiefs, 40 equipment operators, 11 mechanics and 6 builders.

HANDICRAFTS

Handicrafts are of great antiquity. Before the introduction of Western machine-made products in the last half of the nineteenth century, craftsmen provided most of the jewelry, textiles, furniture, pottery, metalware and other consumer goods used in the country. The impact of Western imports led to a decline in handicrafts, but many craftsmen are still to be found in every city and village. Their number and their total production remain far in excess of that of the factory industries. Furniture making, silk weaving and basketwork have been developed to a high degree of skill. Small-scale workshops also produce jewelry, including the famous Thai nielloware, toys and curios. Most luxury articles, such as silks, jewelry, ornamental metalware and carved rare woods, once designed for the nobility, are now produced for the tourist trade. In the villages cotton textiles, pottery and simple wooden tools made by craftsmen are still in demand, largely because they are inexpensive in comparison with imported machine-made products.

STRUCTURE AND OWNERSHIP OF INDUSTRY

Most of the older manufacturing industries such as rice milling and sawmilling, as well as small-scale workshops, are family owned and operated. The capital invested is domestic, either Thai or resident Chinese. Large-scale enterprises, on the other hand, are usually organized as limited companies. In many of these the government holds a majority of all of the shares; the remaining shares may be held by a company, a family, a partnership or by individuals. Other enterprises are operated directly by the government through the military authorities, the Ministry of Industry or another government agency. Between 1950 and 1960 capital from abroad that financed most of the country's industrial expansion was in the form of bank loans to government-sponsored enterprises. Since 1960 about one-third of registered capital in new industrial enterprises has been foreign private investment.

The chief foreign investors are Japanese, Nationalist Chinese, American, English, Malaysian and German. Of a total of 201 companies set up with foreign capital, 190 are joint ventures with Thai capital.

THE ROLE OF GOVERNMENT

Industry is dominated by the government. Government-operated factories produce cotton textiles, gunnysacks, paper and plywood, sugar, canned goods, ceramics, glassware, chemicals, pharmaceuticals, lacquerware, furniture, pins and paper clips. Other government-owned enterprises include cold storage plants and tanneries. The government has monopolies on the manufacturing of tobacco products, alcohol and playing cards and the processing of opium. It also operates all the public utilities. In 1958 the government stated its intention to dispose of its enterprises, with the exception of the public utilities, the manufacturing of cigarettes and the production of armaments, to private investors. By the end of 1966 no interested investors had been found.

A number of government-owned industries, as well as the utilities, are quasi-autonomous organizations which appear to come under the general supervision of the Government Enterprise Division in the Budget Bureau of the Office of the Prime Minister. The tobacco and opium monopolies are operated by the Ministry of Finance. Other government enterprises are under the jurisdiction of the Ministry of Defense, the Ministry of Agriculture and the Ministry of Industry. The Ministry of Industry includes a Department of Industrial Works, which manages several factories, and the Ministry of National Development has a Department of Mineral Resources, which is authorized to promote and control mining activities. Industrial development is the primary responsibility of the Industrial Investment Promotion Board, which reports directly to the Council of Ministers (see ch. 14, The Governmental System).

The government has adopted a policy of encouraging and promoting new industry. Preference is given to industries where domestic production is expected to conserve foreign exchange or provide substantial employment for Thai labor. There is little doubt that Thailand is anxious to encourage private investors to set up factories. As a measure to implement the government's policy, the National Assembly, on October 4, 1954, passed—and the King proclaimed—the Industrial Investment Promotion Act. This Act, liberalized by amendments in 1960 and 1961, was designed to attract domestic and foreign investment by offering various facilities and guarantees for the industries desired by

Thailand. Some 129 industries that could be promoted by the government were listed.

Under the Act the government guaranteed that it would not "initiate any industrial activity in competition with the industrial activity of the promoted person." Right to landownership and exemption from import duties on machinery brought in and from income tax on profits for the first 5 years of operation were granted. Capital and profits could be remitted abroad in foreign currency. Further privileges included exemption from or reduction of export duties for some years and protection of the product produced by control of imports of similar goods. The Industrial Investment Promotion Board was empowered to recommend a new enterprise for promotion and, upon approval of the Prime Minister, a ministerial regulation amending the list of promoted industries would be issued. The chairman of the Board was given the authority to issue promotional certificates to investors seeking to establish "promotable" industries. A new Industrial Promotion Act promulgated in 1962 offered all the rights and privileges given to investors under the former Industrial Investment Promotion Act. An added noteworthy feature of the new act was that it became possible to apply for promotional privileges even though a proposed enterprise was not listed among "promotable" industries.

Since the establishment of the Board of Investment in 1959, 540 applications for promotional privileges had been received by the end of 1963, and 217 promotional certificates had been issued, estimated to represent a capital investment of some 7 billion baht (over $330 million). During the same period 100 plants for which certificates had been granted had come into operation. Sources of investment were predominantly Thai and resident Chinese, but a fair amount of capital was foreign.

Another measure taken to encourage and expedite industrialization was the creation in 1959 of the Industrial Finance Corporation, which makes available medium- and long-term credit to industrial establishments. The Corporation is privately owned and controlled and will deal only with private industrial enterprises. An enterprise with government participation of over 15 percent of its registered capital is not eligible for assistance (see ch. 26, Banking and Currency).

Realizing the special problems faced by small-scale industries, in 1964 the Ministry of Industry set up a Loan Office to make short-term loans to such enterprises. Other measures included the establishment of a Small Industries Service Institute to render technical extension service to small private entrepreneur-industrialists. The Institute also served to train managers and skilled workers of small industries, develop prototypes of simple machinery and equipment and undertake techno-economic surveys of the provinces to determine what industries could be profitably set up and would be economically viable.

CHAPTER 22

LABOR

In 1966 the labor force was estimated to be 15 million persons aged 15 years and over, or about 45 percent of the population. Nearly half of the labor force was composed of women, who played a prominent role in the national economy.

Agriculture represented the largest sector; about 80 percent of the workers were engaged in farming, fishing, forestry and related occupations. About 7 percent were in commerce; 5.5 percent, in services; and 4.7 percent, in manufacturing. The proportion of wage and salary earners was relatively low because of many unpaid family workers, especially among farmers, craftsmen and those in commercial and service pursuits. The government was a major employer of wage- and salary-earning workers, many of them in the large, government-owned industrial enterprises or as clerical workers, teachers and professional employees in the civil service.

Unemployment rates in 1966 and 1967 were not significant, but underemployment existed because of the slower pace in agricultural work after planting and harvesting; because of low productivity, especially in the service and commercial sectors; and because of the limited scope of employment exchange services.

The labor force is expected to grow by more than 2 million persons between 1966 and 1971. Nearly half of these are expected to join the agrarian sector; most of the rest are likely to find work in commerce, manufacturing and the services.

There is a great shortage of labor possessing basic technical skills. There is an even greater need for intermediate-level administrative, business and technical expertise and for professional personnel in medicine, engineering and teaching. Several projects sponsored by the government and aiming at the expansion and improvement of vocational training were in progress during 1966. Many of these were aided by the United States and other free countries.

Labor unions and strikes have been outlawed since 1958. In spite of the ban on strikes a number of minor labor disputes and work stoppages occurred during the 1960's. Government officials, through the offices of the Department of Public Welfare, under the Ministry of the Interior, have played a prominent role in settling such incidents. The government's concern with labor was also reflected in the formulation of long-range manpower distribution and utilization policies incorporated in the new Five-Year Plan for National Economic and Social Development (1967–71) through the Manpower Planning Office of the Office of the Prime Minister (see ch. 19, Character and Structure of the Economy). The Department of Labor and the Department of Public Welfare, both under the Ministry of the Interior, are in charge of enforcing the legal provisions regarding workers' welfare, but in 1966 the scope of enforcement was limited to the Bangkok area.

THE LABOR FORCE

Composition

Rural Workers

The rural labor force, totaling between 11.6 and 13 million in 1966, was engaged mostly in agriculture, including forestry and fishing. A number of farmers, especially those from the Lao areas of the Northeast Region, supplemented their earnings by working for wages, mainly in the rice mills during the slack season between harvesting and planting. Handicrafts, pursued mostly with the help of wives, children and other family members, represented an important supplemental activity.

Nearly all the farmers of the Central Region and a high proportion of those in other parts of the country cultivate rice, the country's main export (see ch. 24, Foreign Economic Relations). Between 85 and 89 percent of the farmers own their land, generally about 10 acres, which they cultivate with the help of their families. Although the level of production in rural areas is not high in comparison to Western conditions, the favorable climate, rich soil and abundant natural resources guarantee a standard of living which most Thai find satisfactory. The relatively few tenant farmers pay rent in kind amounting usually from a half to a third of the harvest. Hired labor and tenant farming play a relatively small part, except in the lowlands along the Chao Phraya River (Central Plain) (see ch. 20, Agriculture).

In 1960 there were only about 319,000 wage laborers among the more than 11 million persons engaged in agriculture and livestock production. Data for more recent years are unavailable, but the proportion of wage earners in agriculture has probably remained low.

Hired labor is of slightly greater significance in the cultivation of rubber, the country's second most important export. In 1964 there were about 60,000 wageworkers on rubber farms.

The main source of income of the hill peoples of the Northern Region is the cultivation of the opium poppy. Some also engage in animal husbandry and raise small cash crops, such as rice, peppers and tea (see ch. 20, Agriculture; ch. 5, Ethnic Groups).

Animal husbandry, fishing and forestry are major economic activities of the rural labor force, but recent data regarding the number of persons in these occupations are not available. According to the census of 1960 fishing provided full-time employment for some 110,000 persons. Forestry and logging employed about 36,000 persons, most of whom were concentrated in the forests of the Northern Region, which produce teak, a major export. Over 10,000 women, principally unpaid family workers, were included in this group.

Urban Workers

About 1 million persons were engaged in commerce in 1966. A significant number of commercial jobs are held by women, who outnumbered their male counterparts in 1960. In 1963 nearly half of the workers in urban commercial enterprises were women. A large proportion of the urban workers are in retail trade, and most of the rest are in banking, insurance and real estate. Management and staff in commercial enterprises are predominantly Western, Chinese or Indian. In the 1960's, however, Western firms have tended to employ more Thai administrators and technical personnel than in the past.

The approximately 800,000 persons estimated to be in service occupations in 1966 ranged from physicians, lawyers and government officials to barbers, waiters and domestic servants. The government is the largest employer of professional and clerical workers. The vast majority of the better educated Thai are employed by the government to staff the ministries, the school system, the extensive administrative network and the judiciary. In 1964 the number of government employees totaled 253,765. The great majority (approximately 212,000) were employed by the Ministries of Education, the Interior and Public Health.

The services sector includes a large number of domestic servants, waiters and hotel employees, most of whom work long hours for below average wages. Since 1960 the demand for such workers, especially in the urban areas, has been steadily increasing.

About 690,000 persons were engaged in manufacturing in 1966 as compared to 471,000 in 1960. Most of them were independent artisans and craftsmen and members of their families who work with them. The majority of factories operate on a small scale.

Only 5 percent of the 30,672 manufacturing enterprises registered in 1966 employed more than 50 persons.

Among those employed in the manufacturing sector the largest number worked in rice and flour mills, sugar refineries, textile works, food-processing plants, sawmills and metal-working establishments. Women employed in manufacturing occupations worked mainly in food processing, spinning, weaving and finishing of cotton textiles, and the manufacturing of cord, rope and wearing apparel. Moreover, there were many self-employed women in the cottage industries, such as making of basketware and weaving silk and cotton.

Handicrafts have suffered from the competition of imported consumers goods, although since 1960 the government has promoted the revitalization and development of many traditional crafts. Private industry has also shown growing interest in promoting craft products. Weaving and basketry have remained important home industries. Silk weaving by hand looms is done on a relatively large scale, especially in the Northern and Northeast Regions.

Lacquer and nielloware (metal objects decorated with incised designs filled with black alloy) and bronzeware are made by individual artisans or by highly organized cottage industries in the Northern Region, mostly near the city of Chiengmai.

About 41,000 persons worked in mining, quarrying and related activities in 1966. One of the major extractive industries is the mining of tin in the Peninsula. The mining process itself requires little manpower, but a substantial number of persons are needed in auxiliary operations. There were about 110,000 construction workers in 1966, not including seasonal construction workers. The number of construction workers is expected to rise because of the expansion of the highway network and the building of airfields and military bases. The majority of workers in mining and construction are men, but many women perform heavy manual labor in road and building construction projects and in some aspects of mining operations.

Characteristics

Ethnic Factors

The Thai have traditionally preferred to work in agriculture. Before World War II nearly 80 percent of the nonagricultural labor force was Chinese. In 1957 official regulations were introduced forbidding the employment of aliens in rice cultivation; forestry; saltmaking; charcoal production and distribution; the processing of rice; the manufacture of soft drinks, lacquer and nielloware; taxi driving; and barbering. Partly because of the traditional occupational preferences of the Thai and the contributions of the Chinese labor force to the economy, the restrictions were not fully enforced. In 1963 Chinese constituted between 60 and 70 percent of the nonagricultural labor force and an even higher proportion of skilled laborers. Most Chinese worked in rice mills and sawmills, in various manufacturing enterprises, in tin mines and on rubber plantations. The proportion of Chinese is also high among construction workers, masons, carpenters, tailors, craftsmen, business entrepreneurs and petty vendors.

Most Malays in Thailand live on the Peninsula, where they are self-employed farmers, fishermen or craftsmen. Some also engage in small-scale rubber planting. On the shoreline many of them operate fishing sampans or serve as sailors in privately owned fishing fleets in the Pattani area.

The approximately 5,000 to 6,000 Indians residing mostly near Bangkok and other major urban centers are merchants specializing in the sale of jewelry, metalwork and textiles. Others are dairy operators or moneylenders, and some work as cabdrivers or night watchmen.

The 40,000 to 50,000 Vietnamese, mostly refugees from the Indochina War, live in the northeastern provinces. Most are retail business and service operators, dealers in local produce or small-scale farmers (see ch. 5, Ethnic Groups).

Skills and Training

In mid-1967 the supply of trained manpower continued to be inadequate to meet the current demand, an estimated 30,000 skilled workers annually. Only about 10 percent of the industrial labor force could be classified as skilled in 1966. There was a great need for metalworkers, mechanics, construction and transportation workers, craftsmen and production process workers. The shortage of middle-level manpower was critical, especially in community development, administration, trade and the services. In 1966 professional personnel constituted only a minute portion of the labor force—about 2 percent—although there was an urgent need for medical and paramedical workers, administrators, executives, engineers, agronomists, teachers and business specialists.

A gradual shift away from the traditional preference for agricultural employment was shown by the increasing number of young Thai enrolled in vocational training schools, especially in secondary-level courses. Much of the growing interest in acquiring industrial skills is attributable to the government's efforts to develop the industrial sector of the economy and to the expansion and improvement of vocational training facilities.

Such efforts are supported by the United States and by various international organizations. From the International Bank for Reconstruction and Development (IBRD) the Thai Government received a loan of $6 million in 1965 for the purpose of strengthening and enlarging 14 trade schools and 9 agricultural vocational schools. These schools plan to graduate about 2,100 skilled workers annually.

The Thailand Management and Productivity Center in Bangkok and the joint Thai-United States Accelerated Rural Development Program also are engaged in the training of skilled personnel. The Accelerated Rural Development Program emphasizes the training of heavy equipment operators, construction crews and mechanics. By 1966 the Thailand Management and Productivity Center had a total of 3,000 graduates. Between 1966 and 1971 it plans to graduate another 5,000 persons. The International Labor Organization (ILO) has offered its assistance in the establishment of the Bangkok Institute of Industrial Skill Promotion which is to be established during the same period (see ch. 10, Education).

UNEMPLOYMENT AND UNDEREMPLOYMENT

In 1960 only 0.5 percent of the economically active population was unemployed. In urban areas, however, the unemployment rate after 1960 was generally about 4 percent. Of a total of 1.3 million urban workers in 1963, 63,000, or 4.8 percent, were unemployed. In 1966 the combined rural-urban unemployment rate was between 1 and 2 percent. During that year between 4 and 5 percent of the urban workers were actively looking for work. Most of the unemployed in the urban and rural areas were between 15 and 24 years of age. They included a considerable number of students who had finished school and were looking for work.

Underemployment is extensive among both the rural and urban labor force. Between harvesting and planting their main crop, the farmers' work-pace slackens perceptibly, although they are busy repairing tools and buildings, caring for secondary crops and engaging in homecrafts. Rural underemployment has been somewhat reduced since 1963 because of the growing use of double-cropping made possible by irrigation. In the nonagricultural sector, notably in construction, many workers are active for limited periods of time only. Much underemployment is also the result of inefficient work practices. Such practices are especially widespread in the services, commercial occupations and transportation.

Much of the unemployment and underemployment, according to government officials, is present because of the lack of informa-

362

tion regarding employment opportunities. In 1966 the Department of Labor in the Ministry of the Interior operated employment exchange centers only in Bangkok and Nakhon Ratchasima. In the course of the Five-Year Plan for National Economic and Social Development (1967–71) additional ones will be opened in Songkhla, Chon Buri, Lampang and Khon Kaen. Officials plan to raise the number of employment exchange centers to a total of 15 by 1971.

WORKING CONDITIONS

The country's most extensive labor legislation, the Labor Code of 1956, became effective in January 1957. It limited the hours of work; regulated working conditions for women and children; provided for sick leave, workmen's compensation and severance pay; and established standards for industrial hygiene. The Code, however, was abrogated after the coup of Field Marshal Sarit Thanarat in October 1958. Since then Directive No. 19 of the Revolutionary Party, promulgated in October 1958, and other directives by the Ministry of the Interior have replaced or reinstated the provisions of the former Labor Code. In 1966 existing legal provisions were being revised and expanded in order to be incorporated into a new and more comprehensive labor act. The new act is designed to extend protection to agricultural and temporary workers who had been excluded from the provisions of earlier labor laws. The Industrial Factory Act was also under preparation in 1966; it will contain specific and detailed safety measures and will provide for a more adequate system of factory inspection.

In 1966 and 1967 the enforcement of existing labor laws was limited to the Bangkok-Thon Buri area. The government's provisions for labor inspection were not extensive enough to cover the many small enterprises and family craft shops located in the provinces. In addition to the shortage of labor inspectors, enforcement has been hampered also because many workers are uninformed regarding the contents and application of existing legal provisions. Foreign-owned firms are generally under fairly close scrutiny of labor inspectors, but almost all of these firms offer working conditions which well exceed the legal minima.

The responsibility for the administration of labor laws is vested in the Department of Labor and the Department of Public Welfare, both under the Ministry of the Interior. In 1967 the Department of Labor consisted of the Office of the Secretary, the Labor Research and Statistics Bureau, the Labor Administration Bureau and the Employment Services Bureau. One of the Department's important functions was to provide statistical and research data for government policies affecting the distribution of manpower and worker training. Manpower policies on a higher level are handled by the Manpower Planning Office in the Office of the Prime Minister. The Department of Public Welfare is responsible for the implementation of legal provisions pertaining to worker welfare and the settlement of problems arising from employer-employee relations, including disputes and work stoppages.

Hiring and Dismissal

Employers and jobseekers usually make their arrangements through personal contacts and individual intermediaries. Some groups, including the Chinese benevolent associations and the Organization for the Assistance of Ex-Servicemen, offer informal employment services.

Firms employing large numbers of unskilled workers, as in the case of many foreign enterprises, commonly rely on labor contractors. The contractor hires laborers for work in the mines, rice mills and sawmills; at the ports; and on construction jobs. He often acts as foreman and pays wages out of the money received by him under the contract—an agreement notorious for its abuse. Formerly, the contractor, particularly in mining areas, paid part of the wages either in food or in coupons for the purchase of commodities in a store run by him. Recently, however, the payment of wages in kind has been prohibited by law.

Legal provisions in force in 1966 provide that permanent workers and employees who have worked for more than 120 days must be given a reason for dismissal or may not be dismissed without cause and must be given at least 30 days of severance pay. Offenses justifying dismissal without compensation include willful acts of damage, negligence or violation of company regulations causing damage to the employer; unjustified absence for more than 7 days; dishonesty; and imprisonment because of criminal offenses.

Hours of Work and Wages

The maximum workweek, as established by law since the 1950's, is 48 hours. Persons in hazardous occupations have a 42-hour workweek. In some commercial establishments, on the other hand, employees work 64 hours a week. Western firms generally adhere to the 33-hour workweek of the Thai Government (6 hours of work per day, Monday through Friday, and 3 hours on Saturday). The workweek in modern Thai urban enterprises varies between 30 and 49 hours. Women and children are forbidden to do nightwork. Children under 12 may not work, and those between 12 and 16 years of age may work for only 36 hours a week. Regulations provide for a weekly day of rest and for daily rest periods. Employees and workers are entitled to at least 6 days of paid vacation, 13 days of paid public holidays and 30 days of sick leave each year.

Wages vary considerably according to geographical area. Women are generally paid less than men in comparable occupations. Foreign companies generally pay higher wages than Thai concerns, a circumstance which reflects both the special demands of the foreign concerns in respect to language abilities and other skills and the salary levels of their management staffs, many of whom are non-Thai. Chinese skilled laborers generally receive double the wages paid to Thai workers.

In mid-1965 unskilled workmen in Bangkok were paid approximately 21 baht (see Glossary) per day. Semiskilled factory workers received from 25.2 baht to 84 baht per day. The beginning salary of secretaries was about 525 baht per month. Those with multilingual and stenographic skills earned salaries as high as from 1,050 baht to 1,575 baht per month. Managerial workers generally were paid from 2,100 baht to 10,500 baht a month. The salaries of government workers ranged from 472.5 baht to 9,450 baht per month. Lower-level government salaries have generally been regarded as inadequate and were under review in 1966.

In large modern enterprises employees and workers receive low-cost housing and limited medical care. They also may buy food at cost in factory commissaries. Civil servants enjoy similar fringe benefits. Although wages in rural areas are lower than in the capital, the purchasing power of the baht is greater in the provinces. On rubber and fruit plantations in the Peninsula pay scales are similar to those of unskilled workers in the Bangkok-Thon Buri area. There is no minimum wage legislation. Employers, however, must pay the basic wage plus time-and-a-half for overtime work and double time for work on holidays.

Benefits

Regulations governing workmen's compensation and various welfare provisions for workers are contained in Special Announcement No. 2 of the Ministry of the Interior, issued in December 1958 and still in force in 1966. In accordance with the announcement, a monthly compensation at the rate of 50 percent of the salary or wage must be paid to workers who have contracted a work-connected disease, beginning with the eighth day of disability. For accidents resulting in permanent partial or full disability the same rate is payable for periods varying from 1 to 5 years. Death and survivorship benefits are covered by another announcement of the Ministry of the Interior, promulgated in October 1958.

Workers' health protection and industrial safety measures are also specified in the announcement. In accordance with these measures employers must provide safe drinking water, toilets and washing facilities. The services of a physician or nurse and first aid facilities must be available in commercial and industrial establishments employing 10 persons or more. Special provisions regulate health and safety rules for women and children.

Industrial safety standards are listed in the Factory Act of 1939. In accordance with its provisions dangerous machinery must be fenced in, and protective devices must be issued to persons working with explosives or chemically poisonous materials.

In the absence of comprehensive social security legislation private pension and life insurance plans are provided by some of the larger modern industrial and commercial firms. Government employees are eligible for a government-financed pension plan under the terms of which they are eligible at the age of 60 or, after 30 years of service, for retirement benefits proportionate to their salaries at the time of retirement.

THE LABOR MOVEMENT UNTIL 1958

A survey of the history of the labor movement before 1958 is useful for what it reveals about the character of trade unionism in Thailand, the direction taken by the labor movement and the attitudes toward labor affairs which probably continue to be held by business, government and the working force itself.

Labor Unions

The first workers' organizations were formed in the transport, shipping and rice milling industries. A benevolent association was organized among the Bangkok streetcar workers as early as 1897, but few other groups were formed until the 1920's.

In the absence of legislation recognizing or governing labor organization, unions were simply registered with the government as associations for the purpose of advancing the welfare of their members. There was no official recognition of collective bargaining, nor did it exist in practice. When a labor union or federation supported a worker's grievance, it was done on an informal and individual basis.

The membership and organization of most local unions were unstable. In a great many unions the workers carried on organized activity only when some crisis arose which demanded the more effective action which the group could provide, and the organization thus formed frequently dissolved once the dispute was settled. Some unions, however, did achieve a degree of permanence, especially in the transport and rice milling industries. Some of the strongest organizations were formed among self-employed persons rather than among wage earners. Of these the two most important groups were the motor-tricycle drivers and the peddlers. Unions were also established in the larger factories, both publicly and privately owned. Outside the Bangkok area unions tended to be organized by region rather than by industry and thus included in their membership persons in varied occupations. Although a few local labor unions developed gradually into organizations of some strength through the initiative of the workers themselves, national federations of local unions were usually the creations of interested political figures.

In 1929 the Communist-controlled General Labor Union and the Young Workers' General Labor Union were established. The rigorous enforcement of the Anti-Communist Act of 1933, however, effectively limited their activities and greatly reduced their membership.

Trade unions formed during World War II joined in establishing the Bangkok Federation of Trade Unions in 1944. In 1947 the Federation merged with the Central Labor Union, which was formed by wartime groups which had combined to resist the Japanese. By May 1947 the Central Labor Union was said to comprise 51 member unions; the strongest units were those organized among railroad and streetcar employees and busdrivers and among workers on the waterfront, in rice mills and in sawmills. Although the Union's membership was mainly Chinese, some Thai participation in each local union within the federation was required, and the leadership was predominantly Thai. The Central Labor Union, however, was known to be Communist dominated, and to counter its activities, various ministries of the government either sponsored or financed other labor-union organizations, such as the Thai National Trade Union Congress, the Free Workmen's Association of Thailand and the United Thai Federation of Labor.

The Thai National Trade Union Congress, under the name of the Thai Labor Union, was sponsored by Phibun Songkhram in 1948 as a counter to the Central Labor Union. The actual organizer of the Thai Labor Union in 1948 was Sang Pathanothai, a supporter of Phibun, who remained secretary general of the organization until 1953, when he resigned after a dispute with the Prime Minister. In December 1955 Prime Minister Phibun resigned from his position as "patron" of the Congress, and after the internal power struggle which followed, the Congress showed signs of Communist infiltration; members of the executive board attended May Day meetings in Peiping in 1957 and 1958. Declared ineligible by the government for recognition as a union and weakened by the coup d'etat of 1957, the Congress set up a sister organization, the Federation of Trade Unions of Thailand, in early 1958.

The constitution of the Thai National Trade Union Congress, adopted in 1951, stated its objectives as the promotion of labor welfare and cooperation between labor and capital. Membership was limited to persons of Thai citizenship who were approved by the general council.

The early government backing of the Congress enabled it to grow rapidly. Beginning among a group of harbor workers in 1948, it finally claimed a membership of 60 federations, unions and branches throughout Thailand which included 70,000 persons. Chinese workers were excluded from membership. The Congress was composed of occupational and regional unions (the strongest of which was the union of Motor Tricycle Drivers) and groups of small shopkeepers and peddlers. Employees in government-owned factories were also usually members of this federation. In the South, Congress membership extended to miners, rubber tappers and plantation workers and in the North, to tobacco and teak workers. Some farm and plantation laborers were also included.

The Free Workman's Association of Thailand, registered with the government in 1953, was formed with the motive of drawing Chinese workers away from the Communist-dominated Central Labor Union. The Association received considerable financial support from the Director General of the National Police Department, General Phao Siyanon, and, like the Congress, was linked to the political fortunes of Prime Minister Phibun Songkhram. Like the Congress also, it was weakened by Phibun's fall from power in 1957.

In contrast to the Congress, the Workmen's Association was not restricted in its membership to Thai nationals, and about 60 percent of its 14,000 members reportedly were Chinese. Its strongest components were dock and rice mill workers and the employees of privately owned factories. In the docks and rice mills it was thus competing directly with the Central Labor Union. Also, unlike the Congress, the membership was restricted to employed persons. The 45 chapters of the Association were nearly all in the Bangkok-Thon Buri area, and their affiliation with the Association was relatively loose.

The Overseas Chinese Labor Union of Thailand has been in existence since 1907 under various names; it became loosely affiliated with the Free Workmen's Association in the 1950's. It was mainly a benevolent association of Chinese workers loyal to the Taiwan regime. Although it reportedly had only 100 dues-paying members, the membership was thought to be larger.

The United Thai Federation of Labor was formed after the 1957 coup by Prayoon Chunswasdee, an editor who had left the Congress. Between September 1957 and October 1958 the Federation was active and enjoyed government backing.

Organized labor first gained recognition and legal protection by the Labor Act of 1956 which entered into force in February 1957. The Act gave workers the right to organize, strike and bargain collectively. It had been in force for only a brief period, however, when in October 1958 Field Marshal Sarit Thanarat placed the country under martial law. The Labor Act was rescinded, and all unions and union federations were abolished.

Strikes

Until the world depression and the overthrow of the absolute monarchy in the early 1930's there were few strikes in Thailand. Most of them were among the Chinese, and some were instigated by Chinese secret societies. Many strikes occurred, however, in the early years of the constitutional regime, and the government was drawn into mediating the grievances of striking Bangkok tramway workers. Chinese rickshaw pullers, rice mill workers and railway employees. Although the government did not hesitate to invoke police power against strikers, it also showed a new disposition to listen to workers' complaints. Before the war, however, the only action taken by the government to provide a permanent means of dealing with labor disputes was the appointment of a standing committee headed by the mayor of Bangkok. Although the committee seldom functioned and had no real power, it constituted a possible source of mediation.

Only among the Chinese did strikes have political overtones; however, they have been more closely connected to relations with China than with politics in Thailand. Early in World War II the Chinese dockworkers temporarily prevented the shipment of goods to Japan, and after the war they sought unsuccessfully to block the shipment of rice to the Chinese Nationalist armed forces.

In disputes between workers and employers between 1945 and 1958 labor organization became progressively more effective to the extent that there was increasing government intervention to prevent serious work stoppages. Strikes were frequent in 1946 and 1947, averaging about 40 a year, and they were motivated largely by the rapidly increasing cost of living.

Beginning with the premiership of Phibun Songkhram, the

government began to give special attention to the prevention of work stoppages, and after 1948 the number of strikes declined. Police intervention before the situation reached the stage of a strike was the usual pattern. If a labor dispute developed into a strike, the usual action taken by the strikers was, as in the past, to make a demonstration march to impress their demands on the government. In a number of cases Prime Minister Phibun himself acted as mediator. Work stoppages increased in the 1950's, however, and caused the government to launch a survey of labor conditions which culminated in the passage of the Labor Act of 1956, regulating trade unions and labor-management relations. After passage of the law strikes again increased but were brought to a halt by the imposition of martial law in 1958.

LABOR RELATIONS DURING THE 1960's

Although strikes were outlawed, a number of minor work stoppages occurred between 1964 and 1965, generally involving noncompliance on the part of management with provisions in current labor laws affecting workers' welfare. In August 1966, for example, workers employed on the construction of a United States military base in Nam Phong district in the Northeast went on a 40-hour strike because the employer stopped providing transportation to the worksite. Work was resumed after the transportation service was reinstated, and both skilled and unskilled workers were granted a wage raise and were promised medical and housing benefits.

Most work stoppages were resolved through conciliation and mediation services provided by the Department of Public Welfare, which usually ruled in favor of labor. Mediation by senior government officials of high prestige has also been an important means of settling disputes between workers and management.

The major event in labor relations during the 1960's was the passage of the Industrial Disputes Settlement Act of 1965, which became effective in April 1966. The Act legalized strikes, provided that they were preceded by attempts at settlement through arbitration or mediation and that a 30-day cooling off period had been observed. According to the Act, the right to strike does not apply to government employees; to railway, telecommunications and public utility workers; and to workers engaged in the production of fuel oil. By 1967 the new law had not been invoked frequently since many workers were uninformed of its provisions.

Serious tensions between workers and management are markedly absent. Benevolent employer paternalism, deeply rooted in Thai traditions, has been the chief characteristic of labor relations. The employer is considered responsible for his employees' welfare and is expected to treat his workers with courtesy and with respect for their human dignity. Subordination to the employer, on the other hand, is regarded as a natural relationship. Reprimands to the worker are issued in strict privacy to prevent loss of face in front of fellow employees. The latter represents a great personal calamity, although a reprimand given in private is accepted by the worker as a matter of course. In the small, family-run enterprises and craft shops employer paternalism manifests itself in courteous speech by the employer and by his avoidance of brusqueness and loud commands when dealing with workers. Many employers also grant token material favors on the occasion of family celebrations and religious holidays. Considerate treatment of the workers, however, is not incompatible with substandard working conditions and low wages. The majority of small enterprises, in fact, fail to comply with existing legal provisions regarding workers' welfare.

In modern enterprises, many of which are foreign owned, a personnel officer or industrial relations officer is sometimes appointed to handle employee relations. Some of these enterprises follow detailed procedures in settling grievances and other employee problems, but in many cases the management has adjusted its personnel policies to Thai traditions.

CHAPTER 23

DOMESTIC TRADE

Trade and public services—water and electricity supply, transportation and communications—had become by 1965 the most dynamic sectors of the Thai economy as a result of improvement in the communications network and increase in the power supply. Wholesale and retail trade alone contributed the second largest share after agriculture to gross domestic product. Volume of trade was expanding at a fast pace as newly constructed roads and railroads opened up previously inaccessible sections of the country and as the general prosperity sparked a rise in demand for all types of consumer goods. Train, bus, truck and air services had been speeded up and expanded; the number of passenger cars was increasing at the rate of five a day.

The 1960 census showed some 770,000 persons engaged in commerce, of whom about 42,000 were in wholesale and 728,000 in retail trade. Together they constituted about 5.6 percent of the economically active population. Men outnumbered women 4 to 1 in wholesale trade. In retail trade, however, 55 percent of the total were women, among whom many were unpaid family workers. As employers and individual independent traders, women held an appreciably less important place than men in both wholesale and retail trade, although about 800 of the 5,000-odd wholesale enterprises and about 163,000 of the 364,000 retail businesses were operated by women.

The generally small scale of trading operations, both wholesale and retail, and the large part played by unpaid family labor in retail are apparent. In wholesale trading there were about 1,300 employers, 34,900 employees, 3,700 persons operating independently and 2,100 unpaid family workers. In retail trading there were 7,000 employers, 52,000 employees, 357,000 working on their own account and 312 unpaid family workers. Over 70 percent of the wholesale businesses were operated by individual traders, sometimes assisted by unpaid family labor. The average number of employees in wholesale establishments having paid workers was 26, but if foreign firms were omitted it is probable that the average would be considerably lower. Only about 2 percent of retail businesses had paid employees, with an average of about 7 employees in each business. In the remaining 98 percent the proprietor worked alone or with the help of unpaid family labor.

The ratio of persons in wholesale to those in retail trade does not reflect the full extent of middleman operations in trading. It is probable that some of those classified as retailers also sell to other retailers. Furthermore, although private enterprise is clearly dominant in both wholesale and retail trade, the figures shown in the 1960 census—330 persons in wholesale trade and 280 persons in retail trade classified as government employees— do not indicate the full extent of government trading operations.

Transportation and communications provided employment for about 166,000 people, of whom about 23 percent were government employees. Even in transportation 96 percent of all enterprises were run by those working on their own account—in this case, usually without the aid of unpaid family labor, which accounted for less than 5 percent of all transportation workers as against over 40 percent in trade. The number of women workers in transportation was also small: 6 percent as against over 50 percent in retail trade.

DIRECTION AND COMPOSITION

Over four-fifths of the people derive a living directly from agriculture, forestry and fishing. The degree of self-sufficiency of rural communities almost everywhere is high. The production of agricultural surpluses—notably rice—for export, however, has increasingly monetized the economy, and although individual families produce for themselves a large part of the food they consume, most of them are dependent on cash income for the purchase of a number of articles of daily use and especially for a growing list of small luxuries. Many of these items are produced locally, but others, such as textiles, small pumping engines, transistor radios and even some foodstuffs, must be imported and the demand for them is increasing. The average income is not unduly low by Southeast Asian standards, and the standard of living has been slowly rising. Per capita cash income at the disposal of the rural people for purchase of goods from outside their communities remains small, but an appreciable part of it is available for buying items that are not strictly essential. The mode of life in rural areas is still very simple, but most rural families are able to afford some small amenities.

Bangkok-Thon Buri, where over half of Thailand's urban dwellers reside, provides the largest single market. Chiengmai, the only other urban enclave officially classified as a city, is the trading center of the North. About 120 towns and municipalities ranging in population from about 2,500 to 43,000 are variously seats of provincial administration, sites of local markets or of small-scale industry—particularly rice milling and sawmilling, and points of entry and exit for foreign commerce and tourist centers. Many of them derive much of their importance as staging and distribution points for goods moving to and from Bangkok.

Aside from the commerce between Bangkok and the provinces, there is little interregional trade. Rice, the basic item in the diet, is grown in every region and normally is available from local sources. The great majority of farmers produce the rice they consume. The other ingredients of the diet vary somewhat in different regions, but in the countryside, except for small amounts of imported items, most of them are produced by the consumers themselves or are obtained locally. The one important exception is salt. In a few instances it is obtained from local salt springs, but a major part of the salt consumed is derived from the salterns on the Gulf of Siam, southeast of Bangkok, whence it is distributed throughout the country.

Other essentials or rural life—wood, bamboo and other materials for houses, boats, plows and furniture, straw and reeds for baskets and hats, charcoal for fuel and in some areas even fibers for clothing—are obtained locally, rarely from other regions. There is, however, some movement of draft animals from parts of the country where conditions favor their breeding to areas where they cannot be raised as easily. The northern hill tribes number about 250,000 and engage in subsistence farming, gather forest products and raise livestock. They make exchanges with the lowland people for necessities they cannot produce themselves. Some groups at higher altitudes produce opium, and some of it apparently is traded clandestinely. Police frequently report the confiscation of consignments moving through illegal channels to Bangkok for shipment to foreign ports or for sale to local processors and retailers (see ch. 27, Public Order and Safety).

Throughout the rural areas the great bulk of the goods procured from outside the rural communities, whether essentials or minor luxuries, consists of semimanufactured goods produced in or imported through Bangkok. The dominant position of Bangkok can be seen by glancing at the transport network. All the major transport routes—highways, railroads, waterways and air routes—converge on Bangkok, and cross-country links are few.

Bangkok performs three major economic functions on behalf of the rural populace. It processes some of their products, such as rice and lumber, for export or for consumption in Bangkok. It manufactures various goods which are distributed in the provinces. It is an entrepôt from which the bulk of Thai exports, originating almost entirely in the rural areas, is shipped to world markets and through which passes the greater part of the country's imports.

An exception to this basic pattern is the distribution of tin and rubber produced in the Peninsula. Most of the rubber and almost all the tin are exported from small Peninsula ports. There has also been an increase in recent years of other exports from this region. The ships that carry these exports bring some return freight, which is distributed within the country from these Peninsular ports. Small quantities of goods also come overland from Laos, Cambodia and Burma, but these countries produce little that Thailand needs. The most important item is almost certainly smuggled opium originating in Laos, southern China and Burma, but the bulk of this probably goes to Bangkok for consumption or for clandestine export. Smuggled gems, mainly from Burma, also no doubt go largely to Bangkok (see ch. 27, Public Order and Safety).

The commodities moved from the provinces to Bangkok consist almost entirely of foodstuffs and raw materials. The major item, both in bulk and value, is rice. Meat, poultry, vegetables and fruit are also important. Production of corn (maize) is rising; some goes to Bangkok for domestic consumption, but it is increasingly being exported from Bangkok and from minor ports. Forest products make up much of the rest of the goods moving in trade. Of these, timber and charcoal constitute the bulk. Much timber, particularly teak, is floated down to Bangkok, where after milling it is either used locally or exported. Some rubber and a little tin go to Bangkok for domestic use and, in the case of rubber, for export. Small quantities of handicraft products also arrive from the provinces, but there has been a tendency for production of such items to shift to Bangkok workshops.

The countryside receives from the metropolis a variety of manufactures and semimanufactures. In bulk the biggest item is petroleum products—gasoline, diesel and fuel oil, kerosene and lubricants. Metals and metal products, cotton yarn and textiles, chemical fertilizers, paper products, books and periodicals, soap and cosmetics, beer and liquors, soft drinks, cigarettes, matches and canned and packaged foodstuffs make up most of the remainder.

STRUCTURE

Wholesale Trade

The distinction between wholesale and retail trade is less clear cut than in Western countries. Retailers usually maintain very small stocks, and consumers often buy in retail quantities directly from local wholesalers. Few wholesaler, however, have set up branch retail outlets of their own because it is difficult for large concerns to develop a sufficient turnover in a retail store to compete with the low overhead and flexibility in the operation of the small business run with family labor in a combined store and dwelling.

The few large merchant houses, whether of foreign or Thai ownership, are engaged largely, though by no means exclusively, in the distribution of imported products; most of them also do export business. They generally buy on their own account, but they sometimes also handle commission sales. They commonly have provincial depots, where they maintain stocks of goods for sale locally and assemble products of the countryside for dispatch to Bangkok. In general the large merchant houses are less specialized than merchandising establishments in the West.

There are many specialized importers operating on a small scale, but it is the large merchant houses that handle the greater part of imports. Wheat flour, some spices, hardware and motor vehicle spare parts are examples of goods handled mainly by small importers. Some of them are primarily retailers who import directly but also sell to other retailers. The small importers employ traveling salesmen who go out into the provinces and sell to upcountry stores.

There are a number of agents who collect orders for bulk commodities, such as grain, industrial chemicals and leaf tobacco in behalf of their principals overseas. They work only on commission and have no importing or distributing facilities of their own. A few commission agents specialize in obtaining bids from abroad for goods purchased by the government, but these agents have no monopoly on such business.

A number of European, Japanese and Hong Kong manufacturers have opened offices in Bangkok. Much of their business is with the government. In addition to their own products, they sometimes import noncompetitive products of other manufacturers. Some foreign film companies have distribution offices in Bangkok. An American chemical fertilizer firm recently began to organize a countrywide sales network.

The provincial wholesaler plays an important role as middleman between the ricegrowers and the millers. Some of the many small rice mills in the provinces buy rice directly from nearby growers and sell the milled grain directly to local retailers and consumers, but any of their milled rice that goes to Bangkok is handled by middlemen. The middleman in the rice business collects grain from the growers for dispatch to Bangkok or for processing in local mills, using small boats, trucks and carts. The collection points are commonly on waterways with warehouses and facilities for loading the boats, capable of carrying 20 to 30 tons, in which most of the rice is transported to the Bangkok mills on the Chao Phraya River and nearby waterways.

The middlemen's functions in the rice business are not limited to buying and selling rice. They advance money to ricegrowers and sell them goods from Bangkok for cash or on credit. They usually own warehouses and some transport equipment, though transport equipment often belongs to the operators themselves. The middlemen, who are almost all Chinese or of Chinese extraction, are criticized for taking too large a share of the profits of the rice trade, and attempts have been made by the government to break their hold on the business and limit their profits.

Government intervention in the rice export business in the period after World War II has weakened the position of the middlemen. The function they perform, however, involves sizable investment, assumption of considerable risk, intimate knowledge of markets and prices and hard work. It seems also that the middlemen compete vigorously among themselves. With the present structure of the Thai economy, it is questionable whether the middlemen receive unduly high rewards for their services.

Chinese middlemen also dominate the marketing of rubber. Acting either as agents for rubber merchants or buying on their own account, they buy rubber from the growers and smoke the sheets themselves for export. Sometimes these middlemen go to the growers; sometimes the growers bring rubber to them at a collection point near transport facilities.

Retail Trade

Except for the incursions into retail business by wholesalers and a few government cooperatives, retailing remains largely the province of small establishments run by shopkeepers, stallholders in permanent or temporary markets, vendors who ply their trade in boats on the waterways and itinerant peddlers. Department and self-service stores have made their appearance in Bangkok, and a number of cooperative retail stores have been established, mainly in the urban areas, but they do only a small part of the total retail business.

Production and retailing tend to be combined. The premises of many establishments serve as dwelling, workshop and wholesale and retail store. This is frequently the case in metalworking and in the manufacture of leather, wood, bamboo and rattan goods and is almost universal in tailoring and printing shops. Such businesses generally work to the customer's order.

The largest shopping district in Bangkok is Sampeng, with its Chinese atmosphere and concentration of stores and workshops of the same type in a particular section. Another important shopping area, which caters more to Westerners, is along New Road in the general vicinity of the main post office, the older Western-style hotels and most of the European and American banks and commercial houses. Near the Erawan Hotel a new and rapidly growing shopping area, which was built by the government in 1956, caters to the wealthier Thai, foreign residents and tourists. The city has several other shopping districts and a number of large markets dealing mainly in foodstuffs, some household supplies and cheap clothing. Retail stores, unhindered by zoning laws, tend to spring up in any place that offers a chance of business.

The colorful floating markets of Bangkok on the Chao Phraye River and adjoining waterways are a well-known tourist attraction. Customers arrive in small boats to buy fish and vegetables from boats or floating stalls tied up along the banks. Vendors of foodstuffs (cooked and uncooked) and other goods paddle from place to place selling to customers in other boats or on the banks. Stores along the banks selling textiles, household articles, cosmetics, toys or other items have landing stages for customers coming by boat.

In the provinces the principal retail trade channels are small stores, markets, vendors who come from Bangkok or other urban centers and local peddlers. The stores usually carry a wide assortment of goods, such as hardware, toilet articles, medicines, stationery and household articles. They are supplied in part by vendors from outside the area who are part retailers, part middlemen. The markets are stocked mainly with local produce, but they generally include some stalls—sometimes set up by itinerant vendors—displaying goods from outside. Street stalls for the sale of soft drinks, cooked foods and other things and the local peddlers supplement the retail facilities provided by stores and markets.

THE TRADING COMMUNITY

Thai

For a century or more trading has been carried on predominantly by aliens, most of them Chinese. Although the majority of the latter are Thai citizens by birth, as a group they remain culturally Chinese. The past neglect of commerce by the Thai reflects the orientation of the centuries-old agrarian society. Relatively favored by natural circumstances, the people have had little incentive to experiment with other than the traditional pursuits—government service, the professions, Buddhist religious vocations, landownership and farming. These, at different levels of social access, have offered most Thai a degree of economic security and occupational satisfactions with which commerce could not compete. There are indications that the popular attitude is changing with population growth and increasing urbanization. Public education and exposure to foreign influences are altering the outlook and arousing the ambitions of the younger generation. Encouraged by the government and finding opportunities in official measures designed to restrict the Chinese economic role, increasing numbers of Thai have been entering into commerce and industry, both at the higher and lower levels. The Thai have shown a particular interest in investing in hotels and massage parlors.

Chinese

Chinese traders have been entering Thailand for centuries, but the great flood of Chinese immigration occurred in the second half of the nineteenth century and the first quarter of the twentieth. These later immigrants were mainly impoverished farmers who provided a source of needed labor for the Thai. Starting mostly as unskilled workers, some of the immigrants never bettered themselves and either returned home with nothing to show for their venture abroad or lived out their days as common laborers in Thailand. Many, however, became skilled workers and artisans, and still more moved into trade, which at all levels they developed and dominated.

The occupational specialization of the Chinese resulted from various factors. It is doubtful that the Thai Government initially supposed that the immigrants would become permanent residents. It had what it apparently thought of as a temporary need for laborers, and it forbade the Chinese to own agricultural land and closed government positions to them. The Chinese immigrants themselves seem rarely to have regarded their stay in Thailand as permanent. Most had come looking for the livelihood the crowded farms of South China could no longer give them. Generally they sent an appreciable part of their earnings back to China to help maintain the families to which they hoped to return later. As the hope of better times in China faded and the immigrants, many of whom had married Thai women, became more securely established in the occupations open to them, the ambition to return to the homeland gradually disappeared. By that time the peasant origin of the majority of them had receded into the background, and commerce and manufacturing had become their traditional and preferred occupations.

While the Chinese collectively have a dominant position in commerce, Chinese trading enterprises on the average are small. Although a few Chinese traders in Thailand are quite wealthy, individual fortunes comparable to those of some Chinese commercial men in Singapore, Malaysia and Hong Kong are rare. Several business houses may be linked through the family ties of their proprietors, but in such cases there is no disposition to actually centralize management. Informal understandings about matters of common concern are no doubt reached by groups of Chinese businessmen, but there is no evidence of widespread monopolistic practices. In general Chinese traders compete vigorously, not only with non-Chinese, but also with one another.

Recent Chinese immigrants are the Haw, who are the shopkeepers, merchants and traders among the hill tribes. Controlling all financial activities in the hills by granting credit, they dictate prices and to a certain degree the commodities available for purchase by the tribesmen.

Other Traders

The Indians and Pakistani, a much smaller group than the Chinese, are also identified mainly with commerce. Some of them have Thai nationality, and most of them make Thailand their permanent home. A number retain close personal connections with their mother countries and even sometimes send their children there for education. Their principal line of business is textiles, but they are also to be found in jewelry and other trades, and some of them combine trading and moneylending. Indian textile merchants have established themselves not only in Bangkok, but also in provincial centers throughout the country. Within the last 10 years, the Vietnamese refugees also have entered urban businesses and trades as shopkeepers, mechanics, electricians, carpenters, barbers and the like. They exhibit the Chinese characteristics for enterprise and instinct for profit.

The rest of the trading community in Thailand is composed mainly of Europeans, Americans and Japanese, few of whom are permanent residents of Thailand. Their establishments are generally branches of concerns with head offices in foreign countries. The British are most numerous and do the largest volume of general trading, although their position in the community of Western traders is less prominent than it once was. If affiliated enterprises are considered as single businesses, there are about a dozen large, foreign merchant houses. The old, established British businesses are still the largest and most numerous, with Continental European, Japanese and American enterprises following in that order. Japanese trading concerns deal largely in Japanese goods in contrast to the Western firms, which do not confine themselves to merchandise made in their own countries. Western enterprises are not concentrated in one particular area as they are, for example, in Saigon, and the residences of foreign businessmen may be in one of several widely separated districts.

TRADE PRACTICES AND PROMOTION

Commercial Associations

Bangkok has seven chambers of commerce, all organized on a national basis—American, British, Chinese, Indian, Japanese, Dutch and Thai. All of them publish trade letters for their members, listing trade opportunities and giving general commercial news. The Chinese Chamber of Commerce publishes a *Trade Directory of Thailand* in Chinese, Thai and English. The Thai Chamber of Commerce puts out a directory of its own in Thai and English. All these directories are offered for sale. The Thai Chamber of Commerce also issues for general sale the monthly *Thai Chamber of Commerce Journal* in Thai and English, whereas the Indian Chamber of Commerce periodically issues pamphlets on trade relations between Thailand and various countries. The chambers of commerce, in addition to disseminating routine commercial information, seek to promote and defend the collective interests of their members.

There are several associations organized on a trade basis, such as the Rice Exporters Association. Like the chambers of commerce, they attempt to protect the general interests of their members, but their chief aim is to introduce and maintain various kinds of quality control. Neither the trade associations nor the chambers of commerce appear to have any political influence.

The directories published by the Chinese and Thai Chambers of Commerce are supplemented by two other trade directories published as commercial ventures. They are the *Siam Directory*, which now covers many aspects of Thailand other than trade, and the *Trade Guide for Thailand*. For credit and commercial rating information about particular concerns, the businessmen must look mainly to the banks since no organization in the country specializes in supplying such data.

Publicity and Market Information

Both the Thai and the Chinese welcome new types of goods, but once they have accepted a particular brand of any commodity they are not easily induced to try another even at a lower price. Once a brand has achieved a preferred position, the wise merchant will refrain as far as possible from making changes in its packaging and presentation since such changes are likely to arouse suspicion that the product also has changed.

The conservative attitude of the Thai in this respect makes them rather unreceptive to the kind of advertising of brand products common in the United States. Furthermore, the market is too small to justify mass advertising campaigns of such products, even though the press, radio and motion picture theater advertising rates are very low by American standards. The total newspaper circulation is still small and centered in Bangkok, and press advertising is directed mainly at the higher income groups. Radio and television advertising is growing in importance, but advertising in motion picture theaters is generally considered the most effective way to reach a mass audience. Advertising signboards are becoming more numerous and may be expected to continue to increase with the development of the highway network. Sound trucks are used mainly for advertising entertainments but are sometimes also used in the promotion of consumer goods. Exhibitions and fairs are being increasingly used as channels for trade promotion.

The existence of more than a dozen advertising agencies in Bangkok testifies to the growth of modern advertising methods in the country. However, personal calls, with demonstration of products and distribution of samples and publicity material, still remain the most effective way of selling many goods. Market research is in its infancy. There are two affiliated concerns, one Thai and one foreign, which do market studies.

Producers, on the whole, obtain data on prices from purchasing agents, who contact the individual on his own premises, with an offer to purchase his crop or product. Since the Thai radio does not carry information on market prices, merchants in provincial centers and market towns have price changes telegraphed to them from Bangkok. The Malays in the southern provinces listen to the Malaysian radio, which does carry such information, enabling merchants, fishermen and farmers to decide whether to market in Bangkok or in Malaysia.

THE GOVERNMENT'S ROLE IN TRADE

The government plays a part in domestic trade both through the operation of government enterprises and the regulation and promotion of private trade. The principal government departments concerned with trade are the Ministry of Economic Affairs, the Ministry of Agriculture and the Department of Credit and Marketing Cooperatives in the Ministry of National Development.

Four regional trade offices in the Ministry of Economic Affairs supervise and assist the 31 provincial trade offices. Among the responsibilities of the provincial offices are the registration and inspection of business firms, the inspection of weights and measures and the promotion of retail stores belonging the Thai nationals.

The Department of Internal Trade in the Ministry of Economic Affairs includes divisions engaged in rice control, trade control, promotion of Thai retail stores, purchase of goods for retail distribution and promotion of commercial enterprises in the provinces. The important Rice Control Division is responsible for procuring rice for export by the government, for registering rice traders and auditing their accounts and for controlling the quantity and quality of rice traded. The Trade Control Division is responsible for controlling commodities, other than rice, that are in short supply and for controlling the prices of certain exports. The Retail Shops Promotion Division has the task of helping retailers who are Thai citizens, mainly by registering them as being under official patronage, whereupon they become eligible to buy wholesale goods at reduced prices. Among the Division's other functions are the purchase and storage of goods, which are sold at favorable prices to retailers under official patronage, as well as to government stores. The Companies Promotion Division is charged with encouraging the organization and development of wholesale and retail enterprises by Thai citizens in the provinces. The Market Division is responsible for providing facilities for marketing farm products. Its activities include improving existing markets, promoting privately owned markets, operating markets itself and developing farm production and transport facilities. In Bangkok it operates the Central Vegetable and Fruit Market at Pak Klong Talat and the Central Market for Vegetable Producers on Maharaj Road.

The Department of Commercial Registration registers and inspects stores under the Business Registration Act; registers and checks the accounts of companies and partnerships under the civil and commercial codes; registers and audits the accounts of insurance companies and takes charge of the deposits they are required to make with the government. The department also registers trademarks under the Trade Marks Act and is responsible for the control of weights and measures.

The Department of Commercial Intelligence is concerned mainly with the collection and publication of statistics, but it also provides information on trade, organizes exhibits and runs a commercial training center.

The Minister of Economic Affairs has overall responsibility for the semiautonomous Public Warehouse Organization, which was established in 1955 as the successor to the Warehouse Division of the Internal Trade Department in the Ministry of Economic Affairs. The operational departments of the Public Warehouse Organization are the Rice Storage and Rice Mills Department and the General Warehouse Department. The former operates rice barns and mills, which through their purchases regulate prices in localities in which farmers are granted a minimum price for their rice, sells rice to wholesalers and consumers at moderate prices and endeavors to promote better production, storage, transport and selling methods. The General Warehouse Department does not operate any processing plants, but otherwise it performs for other farm products much the same functions as does the Rice Storage and Rice Mills Department for rice. Its capital is insignificant, as are its purchases and sales.

The Ministry of Agriculture has general responsibility for the Fish Marketing Organization, the Cold Storage Organization, the Forest Industry Organization, the Na Bon Rubber Estate Organizations and the Thai Plywood Company. The Fish Marketing Organization, established in 1953, buys directly from fishermen and sells in its own wholesale markets. It also assists in the establishment of cooperatives through which fishermen can sell their catch and buy equipment and supplies. The Cold Storage Organization, founded in 1958, operates cold storage facilities in which it stores seafood and other perishables which it buys and sells on its own account. It also provides cold storage facilities for the general public and manufacturers and distributes ice.

The Forest Industry Organization cuts timber, operates sawmills, sells lumber and manufactures and sells doors and windows. The Rafting Department of the Organization (150 miles north of Bangkok at Nakhon Sawan) floats teak logs to log depots and sawmills lower down the Chao Phraya. The Na Bon Estate Organization was created in 1959 to operate the government-owned Na Bon Rubber Estate established in 1941. The Organization seems to be concerned mainly with production and to have no sales or distribution functions. The same appears to be true of the Thai Plywood Company, which was founded in 1952.

In the Ministry of National Development is a Department of Credit and Marketing Cooperatives with divisions responsible for promoting the development of rice marketing cooperatives, marketing cooperatives for other agricultural products and consumers cooperatives. Cooperatives of these types are still few.

In general, government manufacturing enterprises sell to wholesalers and do no retailing. The Thai Sugar Industry Corporation, a government agency with a dozen sugar mills, not only wholesalers and retails its own product but acts as distributor for other producers. Since 1960 it has given cane growers and sugar producers a minimum price guarantee.

PUBLIC SERVICES

Between 1957 and 1965 electricity production grew at an average rate of 21.7 percent annually, with marked increases beginning in 1961 and 1962 mainly because of the establishment in 1960 of the Lignite Electricity Authority and the hydroelectric power station at Ban Khrua, north of Bangkok, followed by the Krabi Electricity Authority in the Peninsula and the hydroelectric power generated from the Khuan Phumiphon in the Yanhee multipurpose project. One of the important results of the expanded electricity supply was the reduction of rates in Bangkok and Thon Buri and in the surrounding provinces, the main beneficiaries being householders.

Between 1957 and 1965 water supply increased at an average rate of 13.1 percent annually. Between 1958 and 1959 the rate was 44.9 percent because many water supply authorities, both public and private, were opened in the provinces. During 1962 and 1963 the Bangkok and Thon Buri water supply authorities expanded their capacities and installed new pipelines.

While some progress has been made in improving telecommunications and mail services, they are still inadequate and constitute a serious handicap to business activity. Internal communications are by mail, telegraph, radiophone and teleprinter services (TELEX). Internationally, Thailand is serviced by surface and air mail, radio-telegraph, radio-telephone and the TELEX communication system. The TELEX system was introduced in 1963 and provides communication in printed form between subscribers in Bangkok and provincial towns and a large number of overseas subscribers.

All communications in Thailand are under the jurisdiction of the Telecommunications Project Administration Office (TPAO) which operates and regulates the network through the Telephone Organization of Thailand (TOT) and the Post and Telegraph Department.

In 1965 the first three zones of a five-zone microwave (radiolink) system for interregional communication was completed. This system, constructed at a cost of $25 million, provides direct microwave telephone links between 25 cities and towns in the Northeastern, Eastern and Central Regions of the country. Extension of the system to the other two zones is scheduled to be completed in 1967 and is being facilitated by a loan of $5.2 million from Western Germany, extended in September 1965. The project is expected ultimately to form part of a four-nation microwave network, with headquarters in Bangkok, connecting important towns in Thailand with those of Vietnam, Laos and Cambodia.

In mid-1966 there were 68 telephone exchanges in Thailand, 8 of which were in the Bangkok-Thon Buri metropolitan area. At the end of 1966 there were about 50,000 telephone lines in the capital serving about a half million households and businesses. Despite improvements, including the installation of a number of automatic telephone exchanges, there was a serious shortage, and phones were frequently out of order because of overloading. Bangkok has one of the lowest ratios of phones to population of any city in the world—1.7 phones per 100 persons in 1966. While the Telephone Organization has an expansion plan underway for the Bangkok area, larger than planned investments are needed to provide adequate service. Much of the value of the microwave system will not be realized until the bottleneck in Bangkok is overcome.

In 1964 there were 7,600 numbers on automatic exchanges in the provinces and 8,000 manual ones. The government is moving ahead with the hookup of telephone lines in major provinces with the national telecommunications system, although at a disappointingly slow rate of progress. Nationwide telephone service cannot be provided until the planned extension of the microwave system is complete.

Present telegraph service reaches only the principal commercial and railway centers. Radiotelegraphy is used largely for government messages across the country. Telegraphic services are to be improved in the late 1960's through replacement of old cables and through extension to areas not previously covered.

The postal service in the mid-1960's operated throughout the country from the General Post Office in Bangkok. There were 1,148 post offices of all classes, and mail was transported by surface and air by 400 contracted agents. Also, nearly 100 river craft served those living along the rivers and canals in the central provinces. There were, however, still many communities that did not have postal service. The government was trying to increase the efficiency of the postal system by increasing the number of post offices in the provinces and by gradually taking over those managed by district offices, railway postal agencies and private licensed postal offices.

In May 1966 Thailand became the forty-ninth member of INTELSAT, the international body that owns and operates the satellite communications system. It is making arrangements for the early installation of a temporary ground station that will permit limited satellite communications service beginning in early 1967 and a permanent ground station that will permit full-scale commercial service beginning in 1968. Benefits expected to emerge include continuous all-weather telephone, telegraph and radiophone contacts with the rest of the world; a reduction in the cost of the average phone call, cable, or radiophotograph and the emergence of Thailand as regional telecommunications hub, as its neighbors hook up to the system.

TRANSPORTATION

Responsibility for maintaining and developing transport and communications facilities rests with the Ministry of Communications. Within the Ministry are the Department of Land Transport, which licenses motor vehicles; the Department of Aviation, which controls air transport; the Harbor and Marine Transport Department, which registers marine craft and supervises habormasters and pilots; and the Post and Telegraph Department, which runs the country's mail and telegraph system. The Department of Highways in the Ministry of National Development is responsible for the planning and construction of the national roads.

Modern means of transport have been developed mainly by the government. The government owns the entire railway system, the only airline, the Bangkok local transport system and a coastal shipping line. Since World War II the government has received much assistance from the International Bank for Reconstruction and Development (IBRD or World Bank) and the United States in improving the railroads, harbor and airport facilities, and highways.

Waterways

Rivers and canals still carry a large part of the goods transported in Thailand despite the growing importance of railroads and highways. By far the most important river system is that of the Chao Phraya. Four rivers flowing southward from the mountainous country in the North—the Nan, the Yom and the Ping with its tributary, the Wang—unite near Nakhon Sawan to form the Chao Phraya. Farther south at Ayutthaya the Chao Phraya is joined by the fourth river, the Pa Sak. This great system of natural waterways is supplemented by canals in many places. In the southwestern part of the central lowlands, the Mae Klong River and its tributaries form a smaller but important system. The rivers draining the Khorat Plateau flow eastward to the Mekong, and their usefulness for transport is limited. The short rivers of the Peninsula are also of minor value as transportation arteries (see ch. 2, Physical Environment).

Waterways provide the principal means of transportation for about one-third of the freight carried within Thailand and for persons traveling in the country. Bulk cargo, such as petroleum, cement, construction materials, sand and gravel, moves largely by water. Up to 80 percent of rice transported in the Central Region is by water, first to the rice mills and then to Bangkok.

Craft used on the waterways range from sampans and rowboats to diesel and steam launches. In recent years the number of mechanically propelled craft has greatly increased. Capacity of watercraft is usually 10 to 30 tons and their draft up to 6 feet. Power craft consist mainly of diesel and steam launches, tugs, motorized barges and sampans. Diesel launches up to 75 feet in length are used for passenger service in the waterways in Bangkok and vicinity. Smaller launches are used for towing rice barges. In 1963 registered vessels and craft totaled 36,372 and had a gross tonnage of 317,679. Of these, 27 were steam launches, 23,061 motor launches and 13,284 barges.

Most of the larger boats carrying freight on the inland waterways are owned and operated by Chinese. Among the measures introduced in the 1930's to restrict Chinese economic activity in Thailand was a requirement that individual owners of registered boats and three-quarters of the crewmembers of boats owned by companies should be Thai nationals. Although it is unlikely that this regulation was strictly enforced, most of the boat operators in the 1960's are probably Thai nationals of Chinese origin.

All craft operating on the inland waterways and in Thai territorial waters, whether mechanically propelled or not, must register with the Ministry of Communications and pay the specified registration fees. Commercial transport of goods on inland waterways is in the hands of private operators, but various departments of government own boats for various purposes connected with their operations.

Coastal shipping, which consists primarily of transporting cargo between Bangkok and ports located along the east coast of the Gulf of Siam, accommodates the movement of some 75 percent of all goods in the Southern Region. Coastal vessels ply the southeast coast between Bangkok and Si Racha, Rayong, Chanthaburi and Trat, near the boundary with Cambodia, and the east coast of the Peninsula between Bangkok and Chumphon, Surat Thani, Nakhon Si Thammarat, Songkhla, Pattani and Narathiwat, just north of the border with Malaysia. On the west coast of the Peninsula others call at Phangnga, Takua Pa and at Ranong, east of the southern tip of Burma. Both Thai and foreign vessels, the latter mostly British ships coming from Penang and Singapore, are engaged in this trade. The government owns the most important Thai coastal shipping line, the Thai Maritime Navigation Company, Ltd., which was purchased from Danish interests.

Ocean shipping for Thailand is provided for by 28 international shipping lines serving Bangkok and operating on schedule. Three also load and discharge cargoes at Songkhla. All are foreign owned except the Thai Maritime Navigation Company, Ltd., which operates three 2,300-ton vessels between Bangkok, Malaysian ports and Singapore. Other than the scheduled lines, seven other lines operate on call or on a charter basis between Bangkok and foreign ports. In 1964 over 5,000 vessels carrying more than 5 million tons of cargo cleared Thai ports. The majority were of Panamanian, British, Norwegian and Japanese registry, in that order.

Ports and Harbors

Thailand has 1 principal and 19 minor ports. The principal port, Bangkok, which handles over 95 percent of the country's imports and nearly 75 percent of its exports, is a river port built between 1939 and 1954. It is located on the Chao Phraya River some 17 miles from its mouth on the Gulf of Siam. The harbor area extends about 3 miles above and 6 miles below the Royal Palace and is navigable for vessels up to 10,000 tons. Larger vessels tie up for lighterage at an open-sea roadstead in the Gulf, near the mouth of the river. The Port of Bangkok is well equipped with modern wharves with transit sheds and can berth 10 oceangoing vessels at any one time.

The port has, however, serious handicaps. The entrance channel has to be dredged at an annual cost of $2 million, a procedure which has not proved satisfactory. With the tonnage of incoming general cargo through the port increasing at a rate of 10 percent annually since 1957, congestion resulting from insufficient berths began to become a problem by 1962. Since 1964 proposals to relieve this congestion have included increasing wharf length and doubling midstream capacity. During 1966 the lack of facilities at the port was the subject of much discussion among shipping agents and businessmen generally, who complained that the congestion in the port was causing them much loss. The climax came with the announcement by some shipping conferences that they were making a surcharge for cargoes assigned to Bangkok. Thereupon, the government and port authorities instituted procedural changes that eased conditions in the port and announced a plan for extending the wharf area. The government is also considering the establishment of a seaport at or near Si Racha, on the Gulf of Siam, which could berth big ocean liners and cargo ships.

Songkhla, Phuket, Kantang and Pattani in the southern provinces handle most of the exports not shipped through Bangkok. These and other minor coastal ports have satisfactory harbors for coastal boats, but their entrances are restricted by sandbars. They have meager terminal facilities and limited capabilities for handling cargo. They are important, however, in coastal trade, serving as cargo transfer points for raw materials and forest products from the hinterland and for imports to the interior.

Most inland post facilities (landings or loading stations) for waterway transportation are limited in size and capacity and are maintained by carriers or municipal authorities. There are also a few privately owned landings. Storage facilities and cargo handling equipment are nonexistent, although loading stations may be permitted to store cargo in open-air lots for periods not exceeding 24 hours. Loading and unloading are performed by manual labor.

Railroads

Railways are the most important means of transport, carrying most of the domestic long-haul freight. The Thai railways (Royal State Railways) are government-owned and -operated. They have a network of approximately 2,275 miles of meter gauge, mainly single track. Lines radiate south, east and north from Bangkok, the hub of the system, providing connections with important administrative and commercial centers (see ch. 2, Physical Environment).

Railroads have played a vital part in stimulating the economic development of the country and breaking down the barriers of local particularism. Railway traffic has been increasing by about 4 percent annually, and the prospects are that it will continue to grow, highway construction notwithstanding. The chief item of rail freight into Bangkok is rice from the central valley, but hogs, cattle, hides and forest products are also important. Goods carried from Bangkok into the provinces include petroleum products, sugar, sea salt and a wide range of manufactured products.

Rolling stock at the end of 1964 consisted of 290 steam and 169 diesel locomotives, 774 passenger and passenger service cars; and 7,238 freight cars. As a result of general improvement of passenger services and increased speed of operations, the total number of passengers carried reached a record high of 46 million in 1966. Freight carried declined slightly in 1963 compared to 1962 because of strong competition from motor carriers and a shortage of freight cars but rose again to a high of 4.3 million tons in 1964. The average length of a freight haul in 1964 was 240 miles.

The four freight terminals located in the Bangkok area are equipped with minimal but adequate mechanical handling equipment (primarily forklift trucks). Terminal facilities elsewhere are quite limited. Most of the freight handling operations are performed at freight terminals in Bangkok and vicinity. The railway has six yards, with the main classification yard located at Bang Su, about 5 miles northeast of the main station at Bangkok. All major locomotive and rolling stock repair work is carried out at the Makkasan workshop in Bangkok. This workshop in 1964 produced 10 freight cars—the first made in Thailand—and put them immediately into service. A program for training workers and improving techniques had been initiated, and it was expected that by 1967 the shop would be able to produce all freight cars needed.

The first railroad in Thailand was opened in 1892 between Bangkok and Samut Prakan, at the mouth of the Chao Phraya. It carried mainly passengers and proved a financial success. The government eventually acquired it from its private founders.

In 1901 the government completed a line between Bangkok and Nakhon Ratchasima in the southeastern part of the Khorat Plateau, a distance of about 150 miles. The new link made an important contribution toward lessening the isolation of the Northeastern Region from the rest of the country. It was extended eastward to Ubon Ratchathani by 1926, and in 1941 a branch from Nakhon Ratchasima to Udon Thani in the north was put into operation. In 1955 the Udon Thani line was extended to Nong Khai on the Mekong, opposite Vientiane, the administrative capital of Laos, and new ferry facilities were built for the carriage of goods across the Mekong. The building of this extension, to which American aid funds made an important contribution, accelerated and cheapened the transport of goods to Vientiane from Bangkok, which is now the major port of entry for imports into Laos.

In 1901 the first short section of the 425-mile Bangkok-Chiengmai railroad line was opened. By 1909 this line had reached Den Chai 85 miles southeast of Chiengmai in the north. Because of the difficult terrain northwest of Den Chai and cessation of construction during World War I, the section to Chiengmai was not completed until 1921.

Construction of a railroad running southeast from Bangkok through Chachoengsao was started before World War I, and by 1926 it had reached the border and connected with the Cambodian line to Phnom Penh.

A line from Bangkok to Phet Buri, on the Peninsula, about 60 miles southwest of Bangkok, was completed in 1903. By 1922, under the direction of British engineers and with the aid of a loan of 4 million pounds raised Malaya, the line had been extended southward and linked with the Malayan system connecting Bangkok, Penang and Singapore by rail. Two short branches from Thung Song in the southern part of the Peninsula run northeastward to Nakhon Si Thammarat on the Gulf of Siam and southwestward to Kantang on the Strait of Malacca. The main line divides at Hat Yai near the Malaysian border, one section going southwest to Padang Besa, where it joins the Malaysian line to Penang, and the other continuing along the east coast of the Peninsula to Sungai Kolok. For strategic reasons the southern line, which altogether comprised about 850 miles of track, was built with the meter gauge of the railways of Malaya, Burma and Indochina. Other lines in Thailand at that time were standard gauge, however, so that rolling stock was not interchangeable. The economic advantage of a single gauge for the whole country eventually prevailed, and in the 1930's all lines were converted to meter gauge (see ch. 2, Physical Environment).

Since World War II a new Peninsular line has been constructed to serve the tin mining area of the west coast. It runs from a point north of Surat Thani on the main line southwest of Takua Pa on the coast and thence south to Phangnga. In 1961 a 45-mile stretch from Ban Pong northeast to Suphan Buri was completed, and a new line from Kaeng Khoi, 8 miles northeast of Sara Buri, to Bua Yai, 45 miles northeast of Nakhon Ratchasima, was under construction.

The more immediate concern of the State Railway, however, is not construction of new lines but improvement of existing facilities. With the assistance of World Bank loans amounting in all to $28 million, progress has been made in modernizing rolling stock and improving the tracks, but much work remains to be done. The railway development program under the original Six-Year Plan (1961–66) concentrated on increasing the carrying capacity and efficiency of the railway system. To improve the existing facilities the State Railway is shifting from steam to diesel; procuring new passenger and freight cars; replacing 50-pound rail with 70-pound rail, wooden sleepers with concrete sleepers and wooden bridges with steel or concrete bridges capable of carrying 15-ton axle loads; and improving station yards, railway junctions and signal systems. To facilitate the training of railway personnel, a training center was being constructed in 1966 near the Bang Su classification and freight yards, north of Bangkok.

In 1966 the State Railway announced plans for a new 5-year $100 million investment program, including purchase of diesel locomotives, diesel railcars and diesel switch engines. It is estimated by the State Railway that during the later 1960's passenger traffic will increase at a rate of 3 percent per year and freight traffic at a rate of 4 percent per year.

Highways

The economic expansion since 1950 has been accompanied by a tripling in road transport activity. Although both capital and maintenance outlays on roads have increased greatly, they have not been able to meet the needs created by this growth in traffic. As a result further major outlays are needed for the improvement of existing roads, as well as for new roads to open up the country.

The highway network in 1964 totaled 5,770 miles of trunk roads, of which 2,834 miles were paved with concrete or asphalt and 2,172 miles were gravel surfaced. The provincial highway system, mostly unpaved, totaled about 1,300 miles, and an additional 2,300 miles were officially reported to be under construction. A typical Thai road is 10 to 20 feet wide, with a loose laterite surface, unaligned and interspersed with poorly constructed wooden bridges. The surfacing, designed for wheel loads of 6,000 to 8,000 pounds, is inadequate for the heavy traffic that has developed. In addition many roads are usable only in the dry season. Consequently, many districts are cut off from communication with the rest of the country during the rainy season. With the exception of a few new roads, paved sections of the road network are in poor condition, and maintenance is minimal.

In 1964 there were 261,000 motor vehicles registered, of which 109,000 were in the Bangkok area. The total for the country included 69,300 passenger cars (including 12,500 taxis), 73,200 trucks, 11,300 buses, 87,400 motorcycles and 19,800 other vehicles.

Truck and passenger transport is carried out primarily by large privately owned companies or by small independent operators owning one or two vehicles. Intense competition for freight and passengers often drives down transport charges, resulting in lower standards of vehicle maintenance and quality of service. A government-owned enterprise, the Express Transport Organization, has a trucking monopoly in the area of railway stations in certain provinces and in the Khlong Toei port area of Bangkok. It has a concession to operate three bus routes and an inland waterway service in Bangkok and other monopoly privileges.

In 1966 the Express Transport Company, which had over 3,000 buses under its control, was planning to build a large terminal in Bangkok to accommodate the interprovincial buses coming into and going out of the city, thus centralizing control of its services. Also during the year 200 private bus companies engaged in interprovincial transport requested the government to set up a Transportation Bank for credit facilities to import vehicles and spare parts for their expanding fleet of buses.

Until World War II the government paid little attention to roadbuilding since it owned the railroad system and was reluctant to encourage road transport that might reduce railroad earnings. Roads were built only in parts of the country not served by railroads or as a means of access to the railroads. Bangkok could be reached only by water or rail, and to get to the airport at Don Muang it was necessary to take a train.

In sizable areas topography and weather no doubt slowed highway construction. On the Bangkok plain, roads can be built only by raising them above the level of the surrounding country. Even then they are liable to flooding during the rainy season. Rugged terrain in the north and west and in some parts of the Peninsula makes roadbuilding difficult and costly. Although the country as a whole is well supplied with roadbuilding materials, these often have to be transported long distances to the places where they are needed.

In 1950 the government, with a sharpened awareness of the economic, political and strategic necessity for an efficient national highway system, launched road improvement and new construction that would give the country a national system of 5,600 miles of all-weather highways. Priority was given to eight major highways: Bangkok to Chiang Saen on the border with Burma in the extreme north; Bangkok to Nong Phai on the Mekong, opposite the Laotian capital at Vientiane; Bangkok to the Malaysian border, along the east coast of the Peninsula; Chumphon, about midway down the Malaysian route to Phuket on the west coast of the Peninsula; Bangkok to Trat along the southeast coast; Bangkok to Aranyaprathet on the Cambodian border; Nakhon Ratchasima eastward to Ubon Ratchathani; and Tak, about midway along the Bangkok-Chiang Saen route, eastward to Nakhon Phanom on the Mekong, joining at Udon Thani with the Bangkok-Nong Khai route.

By 1967 substantial progress had been made toward completion of the program. The Three-Year Economic Development Program (1964–66)—the second half of the original Six-Year Plan —called for the expenditure of around $180 million on highways. Financing in the amount of about $70 million was arranged in the form of loans and grants from the International Bank for Reconstruction and Development (IBRD) and the United States, through the United States Export-Import Bank and the Agency for International Development (AID). An IBRD loan of $35 million (of which $10 million was later canceled at the government's request) was extended in 1963 to pay the foreign exchange cost of three sections of road in the North (Nakhon Sawan to Sara Buri, Loei to Khon Kaen and Udon Thani to Nakhon Phanom) and two sections in the South (Nakhon Si Thammarat southwest to Kantang, and Prachuap Khiri Khan southward to Chumphon). A $19 million Export-Import Bank loan was extended in 1963 to construct a section of the Bangkok-Trat Highway. A United States AID loan of $20.6 million was extended in May 1965 for a highway from Sara Buri north to Lom Sak, in the northern part of the Central Region, which would cut into a relatively isolated and underdeveloped area and link the United States-built Friendship Highway at Sara Buri with the East-West Highway at Lom Sak. The Nakhon Ratchasima-Nong Khai Highway, a 225-mile highway built with United States aid funds, was opened in January 1965, and in April 1966 a new section of highway was completed between Bangkok and Sara Buri, connecting Bangkok by all-weather roads with Nong Khai, on the Mekong River opposite Vientiane.

Highway construction and repair under the Three-Year Plan, however, did not proceed as fast as anticipated, and in September 1965 a 7-year (1965–71) highway development plan was announced. It involved 4,740 miles of asphalting and new road construction at a cost of $378 million, to be financed from budget allocations and foreign loans. In terms of road mileage and costs, greatest emphasis is placed on the Northeast and the South. While plans are fluid and continue to be linked to financing and technical capabilities, development of an efficient nationwide road network is the ultimate goal.

Air Transport

Thai Airways Company, Ltd. (TAC), the sole domestic airline, operates internally with a fleet of 11 aircraft and connects Bangkok with 21 provincial airports. In 1964 it flew 16.5 million passenger miles, 226,075 cargo-ton miles and 17,388 mail-ton miles. Additionally, Thai Airways International, Ltd., a joint venture with Scandinavian Airlines System (SAS), operates six chartered transports between Thailand and Hong Kong, Taipei, Osaka, Tokyo, Manila, Rangoon, Calcutta, Kuala Lumpur, Djarkarta and Saigon.

All civil air activity is under government auspices, and government-owned planes are utilized as commercial aircraft. Airline training is provided by the government and by a United States assisted civil aviation regional training center.

The first commercial airline to operate in Thailand was the Aerial Transport Company, organized in 1931 as a private concern under government control. In 1947 it was taken over by the newly formed government-owned Siamese Airways Company. Soon afterward the Thai Government entered into agreements with two American companies to run an international service from Thailand. In 1952 one of these companies merged with Siamese Airways to form the Thai Airways Company, and the other American concern withdrew. By 1962 the Thai Airways Company was entirely government owned. After a period of difficulty in the operation of its international service, Thai Airways entered into an agreement with the Scandinavian Airlines System for technical and financial assistance, reorganizing its overseas arm as Thai Airways International.

Don Muang, Bangkok's international airport, has excellent facilities and is a regular stop for about 20 international airlines. It also serves as a center for regional carriers because of its convenient interconnecting links with the major airlines and access to aircraft maintenance and repair facilities. The International Airport in 1964 accommodated 143,375 passengers, 918.9 tons of cargo and 374.6 tons of mail.

Other Means of Transport

Although mechanized transport is increasing fairly rapidly, on both land and water, men and animals still play a large role in the carriage of goods. Many boats are now motor driven, especially in the vicinity of Bangkok, but great numbers are still propelled by oars and paddles. On land carts drawn by water buffaloes and oxen and also by people are widely used to take produce to market and to shipping points on railroads, rivers and canals. Pack animals are also found in areas where roads are impassable for carts. The most common pack animals are oxen, but on the west coast of the Peninsula water buffaloes are often used. Elephants still haul logs in the northern forests and are sometimes found in mining districts. Among the northern hill tribes ponies and mules are the usual pack animals.

CHAPTER 24

FOREIGN ECONOMIC RELATIONS

Foreign trade reached a new high in 1966, and in the early months of 1967 no abatement of its upward trend was indicated. Increases were the result of larger shipments of the principal Thai exports and of accelerated domestic economic activity and rising incomes which stimulated a noteworthy expansion in the demand for imports. Thailand's economy, unlike that of many underdeveloped countries, no longer depended on the export of only one or two critical products. The former overwhelming dependence on rice was being reduced by significant increases in the export of several previously unimportant agricultural commodities. The trade deficit, although severe, was almost entirely offset by such invisible factors as tourism, insurance, spending by foreign military and diplomatic staffs and official transfer payments.

Foreign trade plays a dominant role in the Thai economy. The export of raw materials provides foreign exchange for the import of needed manufactured products, including the capital goods required for the expansion of industry, power, transport and communications. Direct levies on trade, particularly on exports, supply about half of the government's revenue, and earnings from foreign trade represent a substantial portion of the national income.

Exports and imports have steadily increased in both volume and value since 1950. From 1950 through 1960 four principal exports—rice, rubber, tin and teak—accounted for 89 percent of all export earnings. Beginning in 1961, however, the proportion of these four to total exports dropped to two-thirds, which reflected significant increases in exports of corn, jute and kenaf, tapioca and other agricultural products. Rice, while declining in relative importance, remains preeminent and in 1964 accounted for 36 percent of the value of all exports. Imports consist primarily of food, petroleum products, chemicals, motor vehicles, mining and industrial machinery, iron and steel, and cotton fabrics. Beginning in 1957 imports of producer goods as a proportion of total imports have increased significantly each year. With rate exceptions yearly value of imports exceeds that of exports, the deficit being met by grants, loans, debt settlement and tourist spending.

The government does not formally restrict the operations of private enterprises in trade, but it plays an active role in this sphere by engaging directly in export, import and distribution and thus competing with private business in all fields. It also maintains safeguards against foreign control of any segments of the economy, including foreign trade. After World War II various restrictions, including foreign exchange controls, were adopted to promote the recovery of the economy, which was suffering war-engendered ills. Most of these controls have been eased, and, in general, the government pursues a laissez-faire policy toward private enterprises. A complete ban, however, was placed on imports from Communist China in 1959.

HISTORICAL BACKGROUND

Until the fourteenth century, foreign trade was controlled closely by the king. Warhouses were maintained to store domestic taxes which were paid in the form of produce, such as rice, hides, tin, pepper, benzoin, beeswax, ebony, rosewood and many other items brought in from the provinces. The surplus beyond what was sold domestically was exported in the king's ships or, with royal approval, sold to foreign traders. Import trade was also controlled by the king. Foreign traders competed fiercely in the effort to ingratiate themselves with the king and his court.

Meanwhile, the country maintained a well-established commerce with countries contiguous to its frontiers and also with China and India. When Ayutthaya became the center of the kingdom in the fourteenth century, Indian merchants established an overland route to the capital from their previous west coast ports of call, and Chinese junks ascended the Chao Phraya River to transact business there.

When the Portuguese arrived in 1511 they found old communities of Indians and Chinese engaging in profitable trade in all the ports and at Ayutthaya. Ducth ships and merchants began to visit Siam in 1605, followed by the Japanese in 1606. The Japanese were interested in procuring firearms and ammunition, and in their opinion Siamese gunpowder was of "surprisingly good quality." The first British ships anchored in the harbor of Pattani—near the Malayan border— in 1612, and before the end of that year the British East India Company had opened two establishments, one at Pattani and one at Ayutthaya. The Dutch were so successful in competing for the King's favor that the trade with the Portuguese and English declined and, in the late seventeenth century, ceased altogether.

In 1685 Louis XIV of France sent to Siam a mission which negotiated a treaty reserving for the French 90 percent of the pepper produced in the country. French political maneuvering, however, which included an effort, aided by King Narai's first minister, Constantine Phaulkon, to bring a Catholic convert to the throne, provoked a rebellion at the Court which led to Phaulkon's execution. Thereafter, until the middle of the nineteenth century the kings of Siam discouraged commercial and diplomatic contacts with the West (see ch. 3, Historical Setting). After the Europeans had departed, late in the seventeenth century, trade increased with other countries of the Far East, and the Chinese resumed their preeminent position. By 1812 there was a large and flourishing trade carried by Chinese and Siamese junks, and scarcely a single European ship was involved.

In 1826 the British East India Company secured the right (by the Burney Treaty) for its ships to trade at Siamese ports. A similar treaty was negotiated by the United States in 1833. By 1840 one English business house had succeeded in establishing itself in the country; it imported cotton yarn and piece goods directly from Liverpool and exported limited amounts of tea, sugar, ivory, dyewoods, tin, lead and spices.

The number of Indian merchants in Bangkok increased. Vessels flying British and American flags appeared more frequently in the ports. The Chinese, however, retained their favored position. They were exempt from tonnage dues charged other foreign ships; they could also build ships, occupy houses and land, export rice and travel in the interior—activities forbidden to other foreigners.

King Mongkut (Rama IV) came to the throne in 1851 after having spent 27 years as a Buddhist monk. A scholar of ability, he had learned English in the course of his studies and was convinced that his country would benefit from cultural and commercial contact with the West. When Sir John Bowring went to Siam in 1855 to negotiate a new Anglo-Siamese treaty, his task was facilitated by the King's attitude.

The Bowring Treaty, which went into effect in April 1856, contained Siam's first grant of extraterritorial privileges in exempting British subjects in the country from the jurisdiction of the Siamese authorities. The treaty included the following important economic provisions:

> British subjects were given the right to trade freely in all seaports, to reside permanently in Bangkok, to buy and rent property in the environs of Bangkok and to travel freely in the interior.

Import and export duties were fixed:

(a) Import duty was fixed at 3 percent ad valorem for all articles, with two exceptions—opium was to be free of duty, but had to be sold to the opium concessionaire, and bullion was to be free of duty.

(b) Articles for export were to be taxed only once (whether inland, transit or export), and duties were specified on practically all major and minor products of the country.

British merchants could trade directly with individual Siamese.

The Siamese Government reserved the right to prohibit the export of salt, fish and rice, wherever these articles were deemed scarce.

By 1900 similar treaties had been concluded with the United States, Japan, Russia, France, Denmark, Portugal, the Netherlands, Germany, Sweden, Norway, Belgium, Italy, Austria-Hungary and Spain.

The expansion of the rice trade in the latter part of the nineteenth century brought the Germans to Siam and led to the establishment of some German-owned rice mills. By 1897 German vessels represented about 8 percent of steam tonnage. The North German Lloyd Company purchased the English shipping interests at a very high price in an effort to monopolize the entire trade, but it succeeded in securing no more than 50 percent of it.

The terms of the Bowring Treaty were substantially unchanged for 70 years. In 1926 complete control of customs duties was restored to the Siamese Government, but not until after the coup of 1932 and the establishment of constitutional government was a real effort made to break the virtual monopoly of trade held by foreigners, notably Chinese. In 1937 and 1938 the treaties with all the powers were revised on a basis of the principles of sovereign equality and full reciprocity. Since that time successive Thai governments have, with varying degrees of determination, sought to diminish the Chinese commercial role and expand that of the Thai. Semiofficial commercial undertakings were founded and financed with government funds. Certain functions were forbidden to the Chinese, and the government returned to more direct participation in trade.

Since World War II Thailand has renegotiated old trade agreements with the non-Communist countries of Europe and with the United States and Japan and made new trade agreements with Pakistan, Laos, South Korea, India, Ceylon, South Vietnam and Nationalist China. The Thai have sought by these measures to enlarge the markets for their planned expansion of exports and to improve their foreign economic relations. Economic cooperation between the United States and Thailand for the purpose of developing Thailand's economic resources and technical skills was instituted in 1950 and has had a marked effect on the growth of the economy. A proposal by Communist China to establish a number of light industries was declined, and trade negotiations opened by the Soviet Union in 1955 were not concluded until 1963.

BALANCE OF PAYMENTS

In the decade before 1961 Thailand's balance of payments registered surpluses in 1952, 1956, 1957 and 1961 and deficits in the other years. The favorable balance in 1952 resulted from the sharp increase in prices and in exports, created by the Korean war, of tin, rubber and some other commodities. The balance of payments position weakened in late 1952 as prices fell from their wartime peaks and government expenditures for imports mounted. The balance of payments was again unfavorable in 1953. The government reacted by reducing its expenditures and tightening import controls. It also acted to increase its revenues by raising tariffs and by improving efficiency of collection, particularly of foreign exchange, from rice exporters.

Deficits continued through 1954 and 1955 but ended in 1956 with rising prices and increased demand for rice and rubber. The balance remained favorable during 1957. Again in 1958 a fall in the world prices for rice and rubber combined with a high level of imports resulted in a deficit which continued through 1959 and 1960. A favorable balance developed in 1961, however, as a result of a sharp increase in exports in relation to imports and a large net inflow of foreign investment.

As a result of the fall in the value of exports in 1962 and 1963 while the value of imports continued to climb, the unfavorable trade gap again developed and widened. The balance of payments accounts beginning with 1963 are illustrative of the new trend (see table 7). The differential between exports and imports shows no sign of narrowing as both increase steadily in value. At the same time a sharp rise in invisibles, such as tourist spending and expenditures by international organizations and foreign firms for office space and services, more than offsets the outflow of funds for travel, investments and government investments abroad. The net gain in invisibles serves to reduce the unfavorable trade deficit.

Grants-in-aid have come largely from the United States and international organizations. That they were greatly diminished in 1961 reflected a shift in the foreign aid policy of the United States, the principal donor, which changed its form of assistance from grants to loans. As a result of the reversal of this policy in 1962, grants-in-aid reached new highs in 1963 and 1965.

The inflow of private capital continued to rise during the 1950's and 1960's, reaching a peak in 1963. At the same time the foreign liabilities of both government and commercial banks continued to show a great increase over assets as a result of repayments of foreign loans and the purchase of foreign securities.

Table 7.—Thailand's Balance of Payments, 1963–65
(in millions of baht*)

Account	1963	1964	1965
Current account			
Exports	9,577.7	12,165.0	12,663.5
Imports	−12,547.0	−14,015.0	−15,813.7
Invisibles	683.4	752.9	1,461.2
Total goods and services	−2,285.9	−1,097.1	−1,689.0
Grants-in-aid	944.8	601.3	1,323.1
Special yen account	58.2	58.2	58.2
Rice donated to UNICEF and other foreign countries	−2.6	−4.6	−2.4
Other	−7.1	−10.7	−6.0
Total	−1,292.6	−452.9	−316.1
Capital account			
Private capital	1,633.6	1,504.7	1,125.0
Official and bank capital	−937.3	−1,291.4	−1,434.8
Errors and omissions	596.3	239.6	625.9

*US$1 equals 21 baht.

Source: Adapted from *Bank of Thailand Monthly Report*, VI, December 1966, p. 51; and *Bank of Thailand Monthly Report*, V, December 1965, p. 51.

No information is available on remittances sent abroad by individuals and private firms. Some estimates of Chinese remittances are as high as $50 million per year, but authorities agree that they have substantially declined. Some writers content that the contribution of the Chinese to the economy of Thailand has always been greater than the monetary drain of their remittances. The large-scale trade in opium smuggled through the port of Bangkok in the early 1960's has been substantially reduced and the unreported influx of foreign exchange from this illicit export has materially diminished (see ch. 27, Public Order and Safety).

PATTERN OF FOREIGN TRADE

Before World War II foreign trade was carried on primarily with neighboring Asian countries, especially through the ports of Singapore and Hong Kong, and with the United Kingdom and Japan. Since 1950 the general trade pattern has been roughly the same, with the exception of the increased importance of the United States, which has become one of the foremost trading partners, following Japan and preceding the United Kingdom. Neighboring ports and countries in Southeast Asia, particularly Hong Kong, Malaysia, Singapore and Indonesia, have continued to be major sources of imports as well as important customers (see tables 8 and 9).

Table 8.—*Countries Supply Most Thai Imports, 1950–64*
(in millions of baht*)

Year	United States	Japan	United Kingdom	Germany	Total to all Countries
1950	385.6	529.4	255.2	32.7	2,576.2
1951	692.8	680.4	507.3	109.2	3,666.6
1952	1,995.5	1,024.8	888.0	236.9	5,456.9
1953	1,176.0	1,090.4	989.7	373.6	6,393.6
1954	1,331.4	1,521.8	933.7	506.0	6,950.4
1955	1,445.8	1,378.5	830.9	438.4	7,391.9
1956	1,175.3	1,256.7	876.7	462.1	7,448.4
1957	1,399.1	1,746.3	958.1	605.0	8,289.2
1958	1,418.4	1,890.1	870.3	539.9	7,983.0
1959	1,485.0	2,255.0	941.0	613.0	8,988.0
1960	1,605.0	2,463.0	976.0	811.0	9,622.0
1961	1,487.0	2,933.0	952.0	731.0	10,236.0
1962	1,950.8	3,357.4	1,024.0	827.8	11,503.7
1963	2,184.4	4,073.5	1,138.6	888.2	12,802.8
1964	2,300.0	4,704.3	1,326.3	1,093.0	14,253.5

*US$1 equals 21 baht.
Source: Adapted from *Thailand Statistical Yearbook, 1965*, p. 299.

Table 9.—*Countries Receiving Most Thai Exports, 1950–64*
(in millions of baht*)

Year	United States	Japan	United Kingdom	Germany	Total to all Countries
1950	862.3	397.3	94.2	8.7	3,423.8
1951	1,604.4	513.4	71.0	10.4	4,374.6
1952	1,300.7	716.5	17.4	8.3	4,551.2
1953	1,048.6	1,596.5	39.1	15.7	5,693.9
1954	1,351.0	1,322.0	126.1	49.5	6,105.9
1955	2,094.9	1,254.7	168.6	68.3	7,009.8
1956	1,719.2	589.1	214.2	90.7	6,716.5
1957	1,493.3	590.4	228.7	107.8	7,291.8
1958	1,158.7	484.5	335.7	111.4	6,192.6
1959	1,867.0	888.0	225.0	182.0	7,560.0
1960	1,204.0	1,530.0	377.0	431.0	8,614.0
1961	858.0	1,409.0	852.0	515.0	10,011.0
1962	824.6	1,353.0	470.3	522.0	9,529.2
1963	709.2	1,826.4	369.3	460.8	9,676.3
1964	546.8	2,672.9	576.7	571.0	12,339.2

*US$1 equals 21 baht.
Source: Adapted from *Thailand: Statistical Yearbook, 1965*, p. 299.

Exports to the United States rose from 862.3 million baht (see Glossary) in 1950 to a peak of over 2 billion baht in 1955. In that year the United States was the largest single customer, purchasing almost 30 percent of all exports. Thereafter, United States purchases gradually declined, reaching a low of 546.8 million baht in 1964. Over the same period imports from the United States increased from 385.6 million baht in 1950 to over a billion baht in 1952, a level which was maintained each year through 1961. In 1962, as a result of an increase in aid shipments, the value of imports from the United States began registering a sharp rise and reached over 2 billion baht in 1963 and 1964.

As a supplier of imports the United States is surpassed only by Japan, which has won a steadily increasing share of the Thai market. In 1964 imports from Japan, valued at over 4 billion baht, were double the value of imports from the United States. Exports to Japan, however, have shown wide fluctuations. Only in 1953 did they exceed imports from Japan, and at times they have been 3 to 1 in Japan's favor.

Trade with both the United Kingdom and West Germany has expanded since 1950. Imports from the United Kingdom rose from 255.2 million baht in 1950 to 888 million baht in 1952 and from 1953 to 1961 averaged over 900 million baht annually, rising to over a billion baht in 1962, 1963 and 1964. Thai exports to the United Kingdom sank to a low of 17.4 million baht in 1952 but, with the exception of 1959 when there was a small downswing, rose steadily each year to a peak of 852 million baht in 1961, but decreased in subsequent years. Trade with West Germany, which was relatively insignificant in the early 1950's, showed a spectacular rise by 1964, when Thai exports to Germany reached 571 million baht and imports from Germany over a billion baht.

After Japan, Thailand's principal trading partners in the Far East are Malaysia, Singapore, Hong Kong and Indonesia. Since 1950 this trade has shown almost continual expansion. They have, however, been more important as customers than suppliers, buying 30 percent or more of Thai exports annually.

Exports

The outstanding economic change since the Bowring Treaty of 1855 has been the marked growth of the volume and value of exports. The total value of exports increased almost tenfold between 1850 and 1900. From then until World War II it showed an almost unbroken upward trend. During the war, when the country was within the Japanese sphere, exports fell to 40 percent of their prewar value. Postwar recovery was rapid, climbing to over 12 billion baht in 1964 (see table 10).

Table 10.—*Value of Thai Exports, 1950–64*
(in millions of baht*)

Year	Rice	Rubber	Tin	Teak	Other	Total
1950	1,672.3	726.4	257.3	142.6	625.2	3,423.8
1951	1,823.1	1,469.1	187.2	158.1	737.1	4,374.6
1952	2,629.4	1,008.9	223.8	96.7	592.4	4,551.2
1953	3,746.8	751.5	299.9	133.3	762.4	5,693.9
1954	3,072.7	1,108.7	373.5	194.3	1,356.7	6,105.9
1955	3,094.2	1,801.9	440.5	264.3	1,408.9	7,009.8
1956	2,796.1	1,526.4	507.4	305.6	1,581.0	6,716.5
1957	3,309.2	1,410.0	531.2	261.7	1,779.7	7,291.8
1958	2,601.9	1,326.6	255.0	238.8	1,770.3	6,192.6
1959	2,576.0	2,336.0	434.0	244.0	1,970.0	7,560.0
1960	2,570.0	2,579.0	527.0	366.0	2,572.0	8,614.0
1961	3,612.0	2,130.0	615.0	253.0	3,401.0	10,011.0
1962	3,239.0	2,110.6	685.1	170.1	3,323.5	9,528.2
1963	3,423.9	1,903.2	740.9	136.7	3,471.6	9,676.3
1964	4,388.0	2,059.9	961.5	178.8	4,750.4	12,338.6

*U.S.$1 equals 21 baht.

Source: Adapted from *Thailand: Statistical Yearbook, 1965*, pp. 295, 336, 337, 340–345.

The principal export items since the middle of the nineteenth century have been rice, tin, teak and rubber. Rubber surpassed teak and tin in importance after World War II. Since 1955 corn, jute, kenaf and tapioca have become additional major export commodities.

For more than three-quarters of a century, until after World War II, rice consistently represented 60 to 70 percent of total exports. A sharp decline during World War II brought shipments to a low of less than 500,000 metric tons in 1947. Rice exports rose thereafter, and between 1951 and 1964 shipments fluctuated between slightly over a million to over a million and a half metric tons. Rising prices after World War II increased the value of rice exports to 3.7 billion baht in 1953. Because of a decline in world prices, this amount was not again attained in the 1950's. It was, however, almost equaled in 1961, when rice was in demand in almost every Asian country, and Thailand exported almost 1.6 million metric tons, a record amount, valued at 3.6 billion baht. As a result of the rise in the world rice price, earnings in 1962 and 1963 remained well above the 3 billion baht level and rose to a new record high of over 4 billion baht in 1964 (see table 11).

Major customers for rice are Malaysia, Indonesia, Singapore, Ceylon and Hong Kong. Intensive efforts to find new customers and to increase shipments to old customers are continuing.

Table 11.—Volume of Major Thai Exports, 1950-64
(in thousands of metric tons)

Year	Rice	Rubber	Tin
1950	824.5	109.1	10.7
1951	1,472.6	111.5	8.9
1952	1,560.9	99.8	10.5
1953	1,370.0	103.2	10.7
1954	1,005.0	136.3	10.0
1955	1,236.5	132.6	15.6
1956	1,265.0	136.2	17.6
1957	1,570.2	135.5	18.4
1958	1,132.9	135.5	9.1
1959	1,091.7	174.4	13.7
1960	1,202.8	169.7	17.1
1961	1,582.4	184.6	18.1
1962	1,271.0	194.2	19.8
1963	1,417.7	186.0	22.0
1964	1,896.3	217.0	22.3

Source: Adapted from *Thailand: Statistical Yearbook, 1965*, pp. 336, 340, 342; *Thailand: Statistical Yearbook, 1956-1958*, pp. 148-151; and *Bank of Thailand Monthly Report*, July 1962, p. 41.

Rubber is a relatively recent export, production beginning during World War I. It moved ahead of tin and teak in importance during World War II and has continued to rank second to rice as an export item since then, except in 1960, when it surpassed rice. In 1964 rubber exports reached a peak in quantity of 217,000 metric tons. As a result of the fall in the world price of rubber, valuation at over 2 billion baht, however, was less than in 1962, when a lesser tonnage was shipped. Japan, the United States, the United Kingdom and West Germany have been the leading buyers of Thai rubber.

Tin exports have also increased, although not as steadily as rubber. Thus, exports, which fell from 10,700 metric tons in 1950 to 8,900 metric tons in 1951, rose to 18,400 metric tons, valued at 531.2 million baht in 1957; dropped again the next year to 9,100 metric tons; and climbed to 22,300 metric tons, valued at almost 962 million baht in 1964. Until August 1965, when ore shipments were banned, most tin was shipped to Singapore and Malaysia for processing and reexport. Since that date all ore has been smelted at the Phuket plant of the Thailand Smelting and Refining Company (see ch. 21, Industry).

The government's policy of encouraging the growth of agricultural products other than rice, in order to diversify and improve the country's export potentialities, is reflected in the rapidly increasing importance of corn and kenaf as income-producing crops. Expanding foreign markets and relatively small domestic demands for these items give them added significance as export commodities. This is indicated by the rise in corn exports from approximately 40,000 tons in 1954 to more than 800,000 tons in 1965, while kenaf exports, during the same period, rose from zero to more than 320,000 tons. Other agricultural exports which are growing in importance include oilseeds, tapioca products and livestock.

Teak exports reached their maximum in both volume and value in the early part of the twentieth century, when they represented 11 percent of total exports, ranking second to rice. From 1950 to 1965 shipments fluctuated widely, and production decreased. Overcutting occurred in areas readily accessible to the road network, and as a result of the government's conservation policy, which was stepped up beginning in 1958, there has been a drastic decline in total production. About 50 percent of the total is exported, and the amount sold abroad is determined by the government. The principal markets have been the Far East and Thailand's neighboring countries; Europe and the United States have taken only a small part.

Imports

Between 1950 and 1964 imports increased more than fivefold, rising in value from approximately 2.6 billion baht in 1950 to more than 14.2 billion baht in 1964 (see table 12). Principal imports are manufactured goods, machinery and transport equipment, chemicals and pharmaceuticals, petroleum products, food and beverages. Although manufactured consumer goods remain a foremost category of imports, they were surpassed in 1964 by machinery and transport equipment.

The large increases which have been registered in consumer goods, in petroleum products and in chemicals reflect the expansion of the country's transportation system and the quickening tempo of its industrial development. Whereas in 1950 over 57 percent of imports were manufactured consumer goods, in 1964 they made up only 33 percent of the total. In the same period imports of machinery and transport equipment rose from 14 percent of total imports to 32 percent; imports of petroleum products, from 7 percent to over 10 percent; and imports of chemicals, from 6 percent to 10 percent.

Major suppliers are Japan, the United States, the United Kingdom, West Germany, Indonesia, Hong Kong and Singapore. Japan is the leading source of textiles and other light manufactures (included under manufactured goods in Thai statistics of imports) as well as iron and steel, chemicals, and machinery and transport equipment. The United States contributes machinery,

Table 12—Value of Major Thai Imports, 1950–64
(in millions of baht*)

Year	Food	Beverages and Tobacco	Mineral Fuels and Lubricants	Chemicals	Manufactured Goods	Machinery and Transport Equipment	Other Commodities	Total
1950	291.3	55.5	194.2	179.1	1,456.7	379.4	20.0	2,576.2
1951	497.5	96.4	266.7	227.9	1,934.6	577.2	66.3	3,666.6
1952	710.4	118.5	419.8	295.5	2,689.8	1,111.4	111.5	5,456.9
1953	630.3	136.8	471.8	337.8	2,933.4	1,366.0	517.5	6,393.6
1954	639.9	121.9	569.9	526.5	3,284.1	1,388.4	419.7	6,950.4
1955	661.8	158.5	691.8	580.7	3,677.5	1,383.1	238.5	7,391.9
1956	611.8	170.3	775.2	654.1	3,560.0	1,522.9	184.1	7,478.4
1957	693.7	203.4	928.1	753.9	3,640.1	1,907.3	162.7	8,289.2
1958	781.1	197.2	901.1	757.0	3,433.8	1,860.8	52.0	7,983.0
1959	813.0	171.0	945.0	922.0	3,603.0	2,200.0	334.0	8,988.0
1960	784.0	108.0	1,025.0	974.0	3,811.0	2,390.0	520.0	9,612.0
1961	754.0	198.0	1,010.0	1,030.0	4,220.0	2,461.0	555.0	10,236.0
1962	754.9	146.7	1,223.5	1,190.3	3,872.4	3,155.9	1,159.3	11,503.0
1963	811.7	144.5	1,221.0	1,242.5	4,187.6	3,903.0	1,292.5	12,802.8
1964	876.0	183.2	1,458.4	1,485.6	4,342.8	4,520.2	1,387.3	14,253.5

*U.S.$1 equals 21 baht.

Source: Adapted from *Thailand: Statistical Yearbook, 1965*, pp. 319–324; *Thailand: Statistical Yearbook, 1956–1958*; pp. 136, 138, 139; and *Bank of Thailand Monthly Report*, July 1962, p. 30.

motor vehicles and transport equipment, tobacco, chemicals and related products; the United Kingdom and West Germany, steel manufactures and chemical products. Indonesia is the primary source for petroleum products. Hong Kong and Singapore are also important sources of light manufactures and of certain food specialties which the Chinese community formerly imported from Communist China.

FOREIGN AID AND LOANS

The United States has been the largest single donor of aid and loans granted for the purpose of promoting Thailand's economic growth and strengthening its internal security. Expenditures for economic aid to Thailand from 1950 through June 30, 1965, including Food for Peace and Export-Import Bank loans, were reported by the United States Agency for International Development (AID) to total $431.7 million. This sum consisted of $296.3 million in grants and $135.4 million in loans. Military assistance grants from 1950 through June 30, 1964, totaled $531.1 million.

Loans from United States agencies were for the construction of powerplants, transmission lines, a regional telecommunications system, highways, irrigation projects, a dredge for the removal of sediment from Bangkok harbor and a modern abattoir near Bangkok.

Expenditures other than loans provide project assistance in the form of goods and services rendered directly to government agencies or autonomous enterprises, such as Thai Airways Company, Ltd. Projects have included power development, irrigation, installation of navigation communications and other equipment at airports, exploration for ground water, highway construction and establishment of agricultural extension centers. The United States has assisted government agencies, educational institutions and other public institutions in numerous training and demonstration activities, such as crop diversification and livestock improvement, teacher training, malaria eradication and medical education. It has also financed the services of United States government advisers and contractors training Thai technicians in the United States and other countries and supplies and equipment for training and demonstration purposes.

Military aid to Thailand includes delivery of tanks, planes, transport aircraft, troop landing ships, minesweepers, helicopters and guided missiles for use with aircraft. Major projects are the construction of highways, landing strips and aviation fuel storage depots; improvements to the naval base at Sattahip; and purchases of uniforms and field equipment. In 1967 military aid was also being given in support of the Thai Government's program for accelerating the economic and social development of the North and Northeast (see ch. 28, The Armed Forces).

West Germany in 1962 agreed to supply technical aid amounting to DM45 million (for value of the deutsche mark, see Glossary). Most of this was to be spent on a mining survey for iron and coal in northwestern Thailand, a rural development project at Sara Buri, a dairy project at Chiengmai and expansion of the Technical Institute of Bangkok. West Germany also lent Thailand DM156 million, DM109 million to be used in the Northeast for railway extension and for construction of a dam on the Nam Phong River, DM11 million to increase the capital of the Industrial Finance Corporation of Thailand, DM23 million for microwave equipment and engineering services to be used in the development of north-south telecommunications. Apart from government-level loans the West German Government has also made loans to private firms under Thai Government guarantees totaling 400 million baht. Private organizations in West Germany have also given technical assistance to Thai agencies and firms. An aid agreement with Denmark provided for technical assistance in setting up a dairy farm and a teak improvement center.

A further source of funds and technical assistance was created by the special yen agreement signed with Japan in January 1962. Japan agreed to repay the remainder of a special wartime loan amounting to 570 million baht in installments over 8 years, from 1962 to 1969 inclusive. The agreements also provided that the payments were to be used for procurement in Japan of capital goods, equipment and the services of technicians. In October 1966 Japan extended a credit loan to Thailand equivalent to $60 million for construction of a new bridge across the Chao Phrayo.

Various international organizations have also given financial and technical assistance to Thailand. Between 1950 and the end of 1966 the International Bank for Reconstruction and Development (IBRD) lent Thailand $137.8 million for railroad improvement, irrigation works, port development, construction of the Yanhee multipurpose project and the expansion of vocational education for agricultural industry. Over the same period, technical assistance amounting to $8.9 million was provided by the United Nations, and $7.4 million, by the United Nations Special Fund. Since 1947 the United Nations Children's Fund (UNICEF) has provided equipment and drugs for disease control, health services and improved nutrition. The World Health Organization (WHO) has been helping Thai medical authorities fight malaria, tuberculosis, leprosy and yaws and train nurses and public health technicians. The Food and Agriculture Organization (FAO) has given assistance in the development of agriculture, fisheries, forestry and cattle breeding. The International Civil Aviation Organization (ICAO), with the help of the United Nations Special Fund, has established a Civil Aviation Training Center in Bangkok. The United National Educational, Scientific and Cultural Organization (UNESCO) has given important help in the development of rural education and teacher training. The International Labor Organization (ILO) has been giving aid in industrial training and productivity; and the International Atomic Energy Agency (IAEA) has helped train Thai scientists in the use of radioisotopes in agriculture at Kasetsat University (University of Agriculture) and in medicine at Sirraj and Chulalongkorn Hospitals.

The Economic Commission for Asia and the Far East (ECAFE), one of the four regional commissions established by the United Nations in 1947, is located in Bangkok. It holds international meetings throughout the year on such topics as the development of industry and natural resources, trade promotion, economic research and planning, inland transport, flood control and agricultural progress. It has rendered the government of Thailand advisory services on such questions as railways, bridges, inland waterways, irrigation projects and population statistics. ECAFE has located its Asian Institute of Economic Planning in Bangkok, and Thailand stands to benefit from two of ECAFE's main regional projects, the Asian Highway, which runs through Thailand, and the Mekong Development Projects, which are designed to exploit the potentials of the great river and some of its tributaries in the fields of irrigation, navigation, flood control and hydropower.

Aid has also come from the Southeast Asia Treaty Organization (SEATO), which has established a graduate engineering school in Bangkok, sent Thai postgraduates abroad for advanced study and brought specialists to Thailand to teach and conduct research in geology, economics and veterinary medicine. SEATO operates two skilled labor projects in Thailand, one for training civilians, the other for military personnel. For civilians Thailand, the United Kingdom and the United States have cooperated in setting up 18 vocational schools in provincial towns and a Teacher Development Center in Bangkok, for industrial teacher training. For military personnel Thailand and Australia have jointly sponsored the establishment in Bangkok of a military technical training school which provides skilled workmen or instructors for the armed forces' workshops or schools. In 1962 a Thai-SEATO Community Development Technical Assistance Center was established at Ubon Ratchathani, a project designed to decentralize community development by having a regional center engage in analyzing the actual conditions and training experts to meet specific needs of the people in the area. The SEATO Cholera Research Project, founded in 1959, later converted into the SEATO Medical Research Laboratory, has proved useful to Thai doctors and students of medical sciences. Thailand also benefits from the SEATO meteorological telecommunications project linking Bangkok with Manila and from SEATO's scholarship and fellowship programs for study abroad.

Thailand has also received aid under the Colombo Plan (see Glossary). It has profited from the Colombo Plan scholarship program and from economic development projects, such as the feeder roads being built in the Northeast by Australia, which has also provided equipment for the telecommunications link between Thailand and Malaysia. In addition, Japan assisted Thailand in setting up the Virus Research Center and the Telecommunications Research Center as well as sending a group of roadbuilding specialists with appropriate equipment into the Southern Region to construct road outlets from villages to markets. The United Kingdom, under the Colombo Plan, established a cotton-ginning factory and has assisted in the expansion of the Faculty of Engineering at Chulalongkorn University.

THE ROLE OF GOVERNMENT

The government projects only a minimal role for itself in foreign trade. Exchange controls are based on the Exchange Control Act of 1942, which provides for a system of import licenses and export certifications, for control over funds available for imports as well as over the proceeds from exports and for regulation of all financial transactions involving foreign exchange. Controls are administered by the Exchange Control Officer of the Bank of Thailand. This system has been initiated to prevent the flight of capital and to reestablish a favorable balance of payments. As a result of success in maintaining a stable currency, universally accepted as freely exchangeable at a single uniform rate, the authorities gradually relaxed exchange controls. By the early 1960's these involved little more than the requirements that all foreign exchange transactions take place through the Bank of Thailand or its authorized agents, such as banks and companies operating under the Bank's supervision. Practically all issuances of exchange permits and foreign exchange transactions are handled by agents of the Bank, and only rarely does the Bank deal in foreign exchange or are applications for permits referred to the Exchange Control Officer.

414

Imports are comparatively free from restrictions, although 49 categories of goods require licenses and the import of a few items is banned to protect local industry. Controls are also exercised to exclude imports from Communist China. Whereas most types of goods can be exported freely, licenses are required for the export of rice, rubber, minerals and livestock. This measure is not designed to restrict exports, however, but is designed to establish a means of control.

Customs duties are primarily for revenue, even though increasing use is being made of the tariff to protect local industry. Import duty rates, while having undergone increases on most items beginning in 1955, are still moderate. Shipments abroad of rice, rubber and teak are subject to export duties, and a rice "export premium" is assessed on the individual trader's sales. Regulations regarding rice exports and sales are the responsibility of the Department of Foreign Trade of the Ministry of Economic Affairs. The establishment of other export and import duties is the function of the Customs Department of the Ministry of Finance.

After World War II the government declared a monopoly on the rice trade and engaged in government-to-government contracts to assure export of surpluses. Although the trade was profitable, the government abandoned the monopoly in 1955, and rice has since been exported by private traders. The latter are still predominantly Chinese, but increasing numbers of Thai, with special encouragement from the government, have been entering this field.

From time to time the authorities have imposed controls in order to increase the importation of essential commodities or to conserve foreign exchange. The most rigid import controls were exercised immediately after World War II, when there was an urgent need to improve Thailand's foreign trade position. By September 1955 import restrictions had been eliminated on all major items; those which remained applied only to a small portion of total imports.

INTERNATIONAL ORGANIZATIONS

Ten agencies of the United Nations have offices in Thailand; of these, six—ECAFE, the Technical Assistance Board (TAB), FAO, ICAO, UNICEF and UNESCO—maintain regional headquarters in Bangkok. There are also representatives of WHO, ILO, IAEA and IBRD.

The headquarters of SEATO and the Executive Agent of the Committee for Coordination of Investigations of the Lower Mekong Basin are also situated in Bangkok. Thailand is one of the four states represented on this Committee; the other three are Laos, Cambodia and South Vietnam.

Thailand in July 1961 joined with the Federation of Malaya and the Republic of the Philippines in forming the Association of Southeast Asia (ASA) for purposes of economic and cultural cooperation. The Joint Committee of Economic Experts has been established to consider common economic problems, and the Standing Committee on Trade Promotion is responsible for cooperation in the field of customs administration and joint participation in trade fairs held outside the area. In July 1962 the ASA states abolished visa requirements for officials, and the waiver of visa fees for nationals of ASA countries was agreed upon by all parties. A railway service has been inaugurated between Kuala Lumpur (in Malaysia) and Bangkok, and telecommunications have been set up between Malaysia and Thailand. ASA also proposes to set up a joint airline and to establish a joint shipping line. The participating countries expect to conclude a multilateral agreement on trade and navigation, granting each other most-favored-nation treatment on customs, tariff, foreign exchange and shipping.

CHAPTER 25

PUBLIC FINANCE

In August 1966 the Constituent Assembly approved a record budget for fiscal 1967. The Deputy Prime Minister, who was acting for the Prime Minister, explained to the Assembly that this Second Five-Year Plan would begin in 1967 and that the government would be compelled to incur the highest expenses of any previous period. He stressed the administration's determination to expedite national economic growth and to improve and strengthen the country's military and police capabilities in countering Communist subversive activities.

Since 1962 budgets have been characterized by a rapid increase in government expenditure. The main emphasis has been on national economic development, but special emphasis is also placed on public utilities, transportation and power. Although revenues have increased, larger budgeted deficits have been financed by borrowing. In general, however, actual expenditures have been less than budgeted figures; revenues have been larger than estimated; and deficits have been smaller than anticipated.

The government has rarely suffered from serious budgetary difficulties during the 75 years in which an official record of state finances has been kept. Until the 1960's there was a surplus of revenue over expenditure in the national account, which reflected both an economic growth that seldom encountered severe setbacks and an unhurried approach to projects for social and economic development. Beginning in 1961 the Six-Year Economic Development Plan, which required large-scale state borrowing, came into operation. A relatively large increase in the national debt took place, therefore, in the following few years; further increases were expected to finance the Second Five-Year Plan.

Since World War II Thailand has received large external loans from the International Bank for Reconstruction and Development (IBRD) and the United States, but there are no indications that it will have any difficulty in providing enough foreign exchange to meet its foreign loan obligations.

The central government collects and disburses almost all public funds. The revenue that local governments are permitted to collect directly is only a fraction of the revenue received by the central government.

Budgets, however, give only a partial picture of the government's fiscal activities. Itemized in the postaudited budget are tax revenues that have been collected and expenditures that were made by government departments. The government, however, owns and operates businesses and semiautonomous organizations whose earnings and expenditures are not included in the government budget. Additional difficulties in assessing actual government expenditures arise from the elimination of budgeted items or the introduction of government activities that are not budgeted.

EVOLUTION OF THE STATE FINANCIAL SYSTEM

Until 1892 state finances included only those of the Royal Household and the provincial administrations, which had a large measure of financial autonomy. The financial records that were kept were not made public. The keeping of complete records, which would permit comparisons to be made from year to year, would have been complicated because the change from the traditional practice of contributions to the state in the form of personal service and produce was a gradual process that was still continuing in the late nineteenth century. Labor service obligations were not completely abolished until 1899.

Before the administrative reforms that were introduced by King Chulalongkorn at the end of the nineteenth century, most of the revenue was spent on the maintenance of the court, the staging of elaborate ceremonies, the construction and upkeep of temples, and the military. The government did, however, promote some public works. In the mid-1800's it initiated and financially supported the construction of some canals for transport and irrigation, and in the last few years of the nineteenth century it began some railroad construction.

When the Bowring Treaty with Great Britain came into effect in 1856, official revenues included taxes on land, gardens and orchards, a capitation tax, customs duties, inland transit duties and income from certain monopolies (see ch. 16, Foreign Relations). Collection of taxes and monopoly revenue was given to Chinese agents; this system readily lent itself to abuse. The Bowring Treaty, which was followed by similar accords with 14 other countries between 1856 and 1900, imposed limitations on the rates at which certain taxes could be levied and on the government's monopoly powers.

Tax rates on the land held by nationals of the treaty countries could not be raised, and because the government could hardly discriminate against its own nationals a general freeze on land tax rates was imposed. Great Britain eventually accepted a change in this provision in order to permit land held by British subjects to be taxed at rates no higher than those on similar land in lower Burma. In 1906 the Thai Government carried out a thorough revision of the land tax.

More important than the treaty limitation on the land tax were the restrictions on customs and internal transit duties. Import duties could not exceed 3 percent ad valorem. Export duties, up to a specified rate, could be levied on 64 items of which 51 were exempt from internal taxes. Other items were exempt from export duty, but inland transit duties, up to specified maxima, could be charged. The treaty also provided that there should be no state trading or trading monopolies, although the government was allowed to continue to monopolize the sale of opium and the operation of gambling establishments.

The effects of this fiscal tutelage on Thailand's development are difficult to gauge. Without these limitations on its capacity to raise revenue the government might have played a more active role in social and economic development during the early part of the twentieth century. On the other hand the treaty restrictions, which were combined with the powerful influence of the British financial advisers employed by the Thai Government, may well have prevented some waste of national resources at a time when the government was taking its first steps toward modern administration. Moreover, the fiscal system resulting from the treaty provisions tended to encourage foreign trade and the production of commodities for which Thailand had natural advantages.

The treaty restrictions did not prevent the government from obtaining enough revenue during the time in which they were enforced. Following the reform of the public finance system introduced in 1892, there was a large increase in revenue, although no new taxes were imposed and some old taxes were rescinded. The increase was the result of direct tax collection by the government, the subsequent improvement in tax administration and the steady growth of the economy.

As the modernization in the administrative, social and economic spheres proceeded, the limitations on the country's fiscal autonomy became an anomaly. The government wished to be free not only to raise more revenue but to change the revenue structure. The major revenue sources were the gambling establishments and the opium monopoly, which together accounted for over two-fifths of the total revenue. Customs, and excise and inland transit duties accounted for about one-third, and direct taxes, which consisted of land and capitation taxes, comprised one-tenth of the total revenue. The heavy dependence on revenue from gambling and opium sales was considered damaging to Thailand's international prestige. Changing economic conditions also necessitated the revision of customs, excise and inland transit duties.

The government, therefore, steadily pressed through diplomatic channels for treaty revision; success came in 1926 with the restoration of fiscal autonomy. The government had abandoned its gambling monopoly in 1918 in order to strengthen its case for treaty revision. After obtaining fiscal independence in 1926 it raised the general level of import duties and abolished inland transit duties. Except during the Japanese occupation in World War II, therefore, import duties constituted the principal revenue source. The general rate of import duty was raised in 1926 from 3 to 5 percent ad valorem, but higher rates were imposed on some items, such as 10 percent on automobiles, 12 percent on alcoholic drinks and 25 percent on manufactured tobacco; specific rates were also set for sugar, matches, kerosene and benzine. Ten years later the import tariff was extensively revised and ad valorem duties were largely replaced by specific duties.

Before 1905 the land tax was comparatively low, and in some areas it was not collected at all. After the Bowring Treaty came into operation in 1856 until the end of the nineteenth century, remissions of the land tax were made on land newly taken into cultivation. The revision rates introduced in 1905 were graduated according to land fertility. In 1938 the land tax was again revised and was renamed the local development contribution.

The capitation tax developed from the ancient obligation to perform personal service. Throughout the nineteenth century acceptance of money payments in lieu of labor service became increasingly common. When labor service obligations were abolished in 1899 a revised capitation tax was introduced; its rates varied with the degree of prosperity of different areas. The capitation tax was abolished completely in 1938.

Revision of the land tax and abolition of the capitation tax were both part of a general reform of the system of direct taxation. It was designed to lighten the farmers' tax burden and to increase the contributions of the urban businessmen and the wealthier sections of the community. A beginning was made in 1932 with the establishment of an income tax, which was revised in the comprehensive Revenue Code of 1938. Since the enactment of the Code no fundamental changes have been made in the system of state finance.

THE NATIONAL BUDGET

The government is required by the Interim Constitution promulgated in 1959 to present parliament with a Budget Appropriation Estimates Bill 2 months before the beginning of each fiscal year. The draft Constitution of February 1966, which is being considered by the Constituent Assembly in 1967, merely states that "The annual budget of the State shall be promulgated in the form of an Act," and "If the Act is not passed in time for the near year, the Budget Act of the preceding year shall remain in force for the time being."

Preparation of the budget was transferred in 1959 from the Ministry of Finance to the Budget Bureau, which is a separate office directly responsible to the Prime Minister. Until 1961 the fiscal year in Thailand coincided with the calendar year. Since 1961, however, the fiscal year has extended from October 1 to September 30.

The annual budget for the next fiscal year is prepared by the Budget Bureau early in the current fiscal year. The Bureau notifies all government agencies and state enterprises to submit the plans and projects that they intend to implement in the next fiscal year and their estimated expenditures. During February the Bureau develops budget ceilings for the agencies, which are based on the data received from the agencies and which are submitted to the Cabinet. The Cabinet generally gives its approval near the end of February. From February through May the Bureau in cooperation with the agencies concerned reviews the estimated expenditures, which are submitted by the agencies.

During the same period the Budget Bureau studies in detail the likely receipts of the government. Subsequently, it prepares the budget documents consisting of a statement on fiscal and financial status and policy, information relating to receipts and expenditures and the annual appropriations bill. In the Thai budgetary process government expenditures must be legislated each year. Revenue collection does not require annual legislations because it is authorized by specific laws, such as the Revenue Code and customs duties ordinances.

When the budget documents are completed, the Budget Bureau submits the appropriation bill to the Cabinet for approval, which is normally rendered in mid-July. At the same time the Bureau is authorized by the Cabinet to submit the appropriation bill to the Legislative Assembly—since 1959 the Constituent Assembly has acted as the legislative body.

Three phases, which take 2 months, mark the consideration of the annual appropriation bill by the Assembly. In the first reading the bill is discussed and accepted in terms of the principles embodied in the bill; in the second reading the details of the bill are reviewed by the Budget Review Commission; and in the third reading the bill is accepted and authorized to become the annual appropriation act. In considering the bill the Assembly may reduce amounts, items or expenditures proposed by the government, but it may not increase the total proposed budget. The Assembly generally authorizes the bill in mid-September.

After the annual appropriation act is promulgated government agencies and state enterprises are required to secure an allotment authorization from the Budget Bureau before they can withdraw funds from the Bank of Thailand. To secure money for disbursement government agencies and state enterprises must submit payment petitions to the Comptroller General's Department in the Ministry of Finance, which checks whether the petitions are in accordance with authorized allotments. If they are correct disbursement by the Bank of Thailand is permitted.

Vouchers and other authenticated documents for budgeted expenditures by government agencies and state enterprises must be submitted to the National Audit Council secretariat. The Council, upon completion of its audit of the vouchers and other documents, prepares and submits an annual report to the Cabinet and the Constituent Assembly at the end of the fiscal year.

Besides the annual appropriation the government may submit a supplementary appropriation to the Assembly whenever the government finds it necessary to spend in excess of the amount authorized in the annual appropriation bill. The preparation of the supplement is not governed by the same procedure as the annual appropriation; the Director of the Budget Bureau is authorized to set the terms and the procedure. The disbursement of funds and the audit of payments made under the supplementary appropriation are governed, however, by the same rules and regulations as those applied to the annual appropriation.

The manner of compiling the budget estimates and the actual implementation of the budget have been strongly criticized. In 1959 the International Bank for Reconstruction and Development (World Bank) reported that the examination of requests for funds by the various government departments was cursory and that cuts were made arbitrarily. Other criticisms stated that appropriations were not strictly adhered to and that funds were often shifted from one category of expenditure to another. Certain revenues including the bulk of the revenue from the State Lottery Organization and the income derived by some departments from special funds were collected and disbursed outside the budget framework.

It was also stated that the audit system was generally inadequate and, in particular, that there was no proper scrutiny of the accounts of the semiautonomous government agencies, such as the Thailand Tobacco Monopoly, the Royal State Railway of Thailand, the Port Authority of Thailand, the Express Transportation Organization, the Fuel Oil Organization and the Government Savings Bank. Finally, in the absence of a proper cash budget it was impossible to obtain a precise idea of the state finances. There have been signs of improvement since the mission reported, but questionable or defective budgetary procedures remain.

Several reclassifications of the published budget figures in the 1950's and 1960's now make it possible to get a more accurate idea of the direction of state expenditure. Because of the frequent changes in the presentation of the accounts, however, accurate comparisons of budget figures cannot readily be made over any long period of time. Figures published by government bureaus since 1959 are advantageous in showing total revenue and expenditures, which are subdivided into expenditures by major functions and revenue by sources (see tables 13 and 14).

In 1958 and 1959 there were relatively large budget deficits of 312 million baht (see Glossary) and 406 million baht, respectively; in 1960 there was a small surplus of 74 million baht. In 1961, when the budget period was only 9 months, (a result of the shift in the fiscal year) the estimated revenue was 5.5 billion baht, and the expenditure was 6.1 billion baht with a deficit of 581 million baht. Actual revenue, however, was 163 million baht higher than the estimates, and expenditure was 446 million baht lower than the estimates; consequently, there was a surplus of 28 million baht. Beginning with the 1962 budget each budget has shown a deficit, and each succeeding deficit has been larger than that of the preceding fiscal year. Revenue collection has so improved that actual revenues greatly exceed estimates and actual deficits are quite small.

For both fiscal 1966 and 1967 deficits of 4,600 million baht were budgeted, and the Prime Minister promised that the government would increase public revenue by instituting additional efficiency improvements in the collection systems. Bond sales would also be instituted. Revenue collections throughout 1966 indicated that revenue would greatly exceed expectations.

PUBLIC EXPENDITURE

Current Expenditures

Social services, which include education, health and public welfare services, constitute the largest major category of expenditure. In 1959 this category accounted for 27.2 percent of the

Table 13.—Expenditures of the Thailand Government, by Major Functions, 1962–66
(in millions of baht[1])

Function	1962	1963	1964	1965[2]	1966[2]
Economic services	1,819.9	2,553.9	2,605.0	3,487.7	3,487.7
Education	1,520.9	1,743.6	1,922.1	2,150.9	2,425.6
Defense	1,534.8	1,635.6	1,754.6	1,962.8	2,163.8
Health and public welfare services	932.1	1,283.2	1,630.2	1,892.6	2,127.8
General administration	808.7	809.7	897.4	962.9	1,425.6
Internal peace maintenance	785.5	782.8	822.1	964.2	1,008.0
Debt repayment	1,091.9	1,213.5	994.4	687.8	779.0
Other	148.0	480.2	404.5	759.7	281.9
TOTAL	8,641.8	10,502.5	11,030.3	12,868.6	13,699.4

[1] US$1 equals 21 baht.
[2] Budgetary appropriations.

Source: Adapted from Thailand, Office of the Prime Minister, Bureau of the Budget, Financial and Legislative Division, *Budget in Brief—Fiscal Year 1966.*

Table 14.—Revenues of the Thailand Government, by Sources, 1962–66
(in millions of baht [1])

Sources	1962	1963	1964	1965 [2]	1966 [2]
Taxes and duties	7,371.0	7,934.8	8,856.2	9,235.4	10,377.6
Sales of goods and services	227.5	245.6	277.0	280.9	308.3
Profits from nonmonopolistic state enterprises	206.9	226.2	206.4	370.4	335.0
Other revenues	180.7	225.6	315.9	683.3	1,219.1
Total of receipts	7,986.1	8,632.2	9,655.5	10,570.0	12,240.0
Loans	1,394.1	1,691.2	1,001.8	1,850.0	2,200.0
TOTAL	9,380.2	10,323.4	10,657.3	12,420.0	14,440.0

[1] US$1 equals 21 baht.
[2] Estimates.

Source: Adapted from Thailand, Office of the Prime Minister, Bureau of the Budget, Financial and Legislative Division, *Budget in Brief—Fiscal Year 1966*, p. 23.

budget. This percentage has steadily risen, and in the 1965 and 1966 budgets it stood at 31 percent.

The second largest major category of expenditure is for economic services, which include transportation, electric power supply, telecommunications, agricultural and forestry services, irrigation, industry and mining. The share of this category in total expenditure is also increasing. Accounting for 22.7 percent in 1959 it rose to 29.6 percent in the 1966 budget.

Defense accounted for 22.4 percent of the total actual expenditure in 1959. It declined to 18 percent in 1962 and to 16 percent in the 1966 budget. If the new category of "internal peace maintenance" is added to the defense budget a defense expenditure of 27 percent in 1962 and 23 percent in 1966 results. The declining trend in the outlay for defense reflects a sharp increase in nonmilitary expenditure and a relative stability in the amount of military expenditure. This latter circumstance is partially due to the receipt of military aid and equipment from the United States (see ch. 28, The Armed Forces).

The remainder of the expenditure goes to the general administration, the servicing of the national debt, the Royal Household expenses and the items that cannot be allocated to any of the major categories.

Capital Expenditure

The proportion of total government expenditure devoted to capital expenditure on railroads and highways, irrigation and water supply, the postal and telegraph system, and agricultural and industrial development, which from the beginning of the century to World War II averaged about 10 percent, has increased markedly in the postwar period. From 1950 to 1960 it averaged 20 percent annually, and it rose from 22 percent in 1962 to 32 percent in 1965.

Before World War II capital expenditure was concentrated on railroad development and irrigation works; some funds were devoted to electric power and urban water supply. Although expenditure on railroads and irrigation has continued to be substantial, the heaviest outlays after the war have been for highways and other transport facilities, which include airfields and port improvements.

The government has made some investments in industrial enterprises in an effort to promote industrial development and not because of any ideological preference for public over private ownership. The question of public ownership of economic facilities has never been a serious political issue in Thailand because the economic outlook has been essentially pragmatic. The National Economic Development Board for the last 5 years has been offering to sell to private interests a number of government-owned factories (see ch. 21, Industry).

Government capital expenditure in the past was financed from current revenue rather than from borrowed funds, and it was not always budgeted. In 1953, however, the government obtained authority to borrow 4 billion baht over a 3-year period to meet current and expected deficits; the source of the funds was not specified. This has become the accepted pattern. The internal debt has risen considerably since the end of World War II, when it was very small in terms of the present value of the baht.

Some capital expenditure has been financed by foreign loans. In the first decade of this century loans were obtained from the United Kingdom for railroad construction, and an additional sterling loan, which was obtained after World War I, was used partially for railroad construction and irrigation works. By the end of World War II the outstanding balance on these loans was comparatively small. Since World War II external loans have been obtained from the World Bank, the United States Export-Import Bank and the United States Agency for International Development (USAID), West Germany and Austria for use in railroad, highway, hydroelectric power, irrigation, industrial and port development. All are longterm loans that were borrowed to finance projects requiring foreign currency. In August 1966 World Bank loans totaled $209.9 million; United States Export-Import Bank loans equaled $34.4 million; USAID loans totaled $74.2 million, West Germany lent 45 million DM ($11.25 million); and Austria lent $3.4 million. In addition, by August 1966 aid grants had been received from the United States ($337 million), the United Nations and its specialized agencies ($21.8 million), the Colombo Plan ($8.6 million), and from 12 other nations (9 European, the United Arab Republic, Israel and Nationalist China) a total $43 million was received.

SOURCES OF REVENUE

About nine-tenths of the total revenue receipts is derived from taxes, and the largest part of the tax revenue comes from indirect taxes. Nearly half of the tax revenue is derived from customs duties on imports and certain exports. In recent years there has been no decline in the importance of customs duties as a source of revenue, although internal taxes have begun to show improvement.

Import duties have until recently been used almost entirely to obtain revenue, but now they are being modified to protect and promote local production. The revised customs tariff that came into force in March 1960 exempted from import duties agricultural implements, electrical and water supply equipment, which is used by local authorities, and maps and students' writing materials. Duties on some basic chemicals, which are used in making pharmaceuticals, were raised to an extent that threatened to make some domestically manufactured drugs more heavily taxed than the imported products. In December 1960 duties were reduced on certain imported raw materials and components used by local industries. These included asbestos, iodine, ampoules and the glass tubes for their manufacture, raw silk, iron and steel sheets and egg-cleaning machines. The Industrial Investment Promotion Act exempted from import duty materials and equipment for factory construction. In August 1962 import duty increases were made to protect local industry. Duties on some pharmaceuticals were raised from 11 percent to between 30 and 80 percent ad valorem; on baskets and sieves duty was raised from 15 to 30 percent to 60 percent; on some textiles it increased from 22 to 35 percent; and on some processed milk the duty rose from 10 to 20 percent. At the same time the importation of gunny bags was prohibited. The increased duty on pharmaceuticals led to a rise in the price of existing stocks. This caused the government, which was already concerned about recent price increases, to threaten sellers with price control.

Thailand is reaching the stage where the advantages and disadvantages of protective customs need to be carefully weighed. The benefits of encouraging local production must be balanced against both the loss of customs revenue that cannot be easily regained by an increase in other taxes and the disadvantages of price increases that are caused by the higher cost of domestic products.

A duty on rubber exports was introduced in October 1960; these proceeds are used to help growers change to higher-yielding trees. The duty is imposed on a sliding scale varying with the price of rubber. Export duties are also imposed on rice and tin. As a source of revenue they have become much less important than they formerly were.

The principal direct tax, which is on income, provides only one-tenth of the total tax revenue. It is levied on individuals at progressive rates ranging from 10 percent on taxable income up to 10,000 baht a year to 50 percent on amounts above 400,000 baht per year. For companies and partnerships rates are progressive from 15 percent on amounts above 1 million baht. Provision is made for deduction—at the source—of income tax payments on employee salaries and on interest and dividends. If the payer is a government organization payments are made to suppliers, contractors and professional men. Before 1962 taxable income consisted of revenue from all sources less a general deduction of 20 percent of gross income up to a maximum deduction of 20,000 baht. In January 1962 additional allowances of 4,000 baht for the taxpayer, 2,000 baht for wife or husband and 1,000 baht for each child were introduced. Exemption from income tax was granted on the income of farmers for the sale of rice grown by them or their families and on the interest on government bonds, government provident funds and commercial bank deposits.

Besides the income tax on net profits, a business tax that is payable on gross revenue is levied against importers, exporters, producers, providers of various services, bankers, brokers, agents, insurers, and sellers of precious metals and immovable property. The tax rate varies from 1.5 to 25 percent and for most businesses does not exceed 5 percent. Hotel operators are required to pay 7.5 percent; night club and cabaret operators pay 10 percent; importers of a wide range of manufactured goods of a luxury or semiluxury type pay 12 percent; importers of passenger automobiles pay 20 percent; and importers of wines and liquors pay 25 percent.

The Industrial Investment Promotion Act exempted approved, new industrial projects from the business tax on imported machinery and accessories, and it granted total or partial exemption on raw materials for 5 years. Exemption from the business tax on exports may be granted at the discretion of the Board of Investment (formerly the Industrial Investment Promotion Board).

Other taxes covered by the Revenue Code are the signboard tax, stamp duties on documents, entertainment duties and the local development contribution. The rates of taxation on signboards depend upon whether the signboards have only Thai writing on them, Thai and foreign writing with the former covering an area not less than the latter, or the whole or larger part in foreign writing. The last type is subject to a tax 10 times larger than the first. Entertainment duties vary from 10 percent of the admission charge for sports gatherings approved by the minister of education to 50 percent for motion picture showings.

The local development contribution is a tax on land values, whose yield is intended for improvement in local facilities, such as roads, water supplies, schools and clinics. The tax collected in a province is allocated for use in that province. Landowners are exempt from the tax on a holding of 2 acres if the land is outside or in specified parts of a municipal area. Besides these exemptions, land is taxed on a sliding scale according to its assessed value. Cultivated farmland is taxed at half the ordinary rate, but unused land is taxed at twice the ordinary rate. Characteristics of land to which the ordinary rate applies are not detailed. The revenue yield from the local development contribution is small.

Like other countries where the great majority of the population is engaged in agriculture and where enterprises of all kinds are mainly small-scale family undertakings, collection of direct taxes is difficult. Strict enforcement of the income tax would necessitate a much larger corps of trained tax inspectors and severer penalties for evasion, and the increase in collection costs might well be disproportionate to the increase in revenue. Income tax collection has been improving, but the present heavy dependence on indirect taxation is likely to continue for a long time.

The general argument for direct rather than indirect taxes is that the latter tend to be regressive and to weigh more heavily on the lower income groups. In Thailand, however, the tax structure and the mode of living of the majority of the people do not impose a particularly large burden on the low income groups. The farming population is largely self-sufficient in acquiring its food and the materials needed for house construction; it is even able to supply a significant part of its own clothing needs. Luxury items are taxed heavily, but except for transistor radios, those items do not seem to have significantly entered into the simple life of the villager. Since World War II the government has, through state trading in rice and other means, kept down the price received by the farmers for their rice and diverted into the treasury part of the profits they might have received from a free market. The system has, until 1966, prevented excessive price fluctuations that might have upset the rural economy, and it has probably reduced the gains of the middlemen more than those of the farmers.

Revenue from monopolies and government enterprises is a fairly important budget item. The Tobacco Monopoly was established in 1941, when the government bought the properties of the British-American Tobacco Company in Thailand. Although the Monopoly was given the exclusive right to manufacture and sell all tobacco products, production and sale by private individuals of purely local products are still permitted.

The Monopoly is very profitable, and although a large part of its earnings is reinvested, it makes a sizable contribution to the general revenue; it is entered in the budget under taxes and duties. Other contributors are the railroads, the postal, telephone and telegraph systems, electric power enterprises, the Bank of Thailand and the State Lottery Organization. Among nonmonopolistic state enterprises government-owned industrial enterprises have not been profitable, and little revenue is derived from this source. In 1960 a proposal was made to transfer to general revenue a smaller part of the earnings of government commercial services and to leave a greater proportion within the services for development purposes.

THE NATIONAL DEBT

During the past 10 years Thailand's national debt, which includes short-term internal borrowing, has more than doubled. The per capita debt, however, is still low. The total debt at the end of May 1965 was 14.8 billion baht, of which 9.1 billion was internal and the remainder external. It amounted to one-fifth of the gross national product and was considerably less than 2 years' state revenue. The cost of servicing the debt has declined from 12 percent of annual government expenditure in 1962 to a little over 5 percent in 1965. About 70 percent of the internal debt is held by the Bank of Thailand in the form of government bonds and treasury bills; another 10 percent is held by the Government Savings Bank; the remainder is held by commercial banks and members of the public who purchased government bonds.

About two-fifths of the national debt consists of external borrowing and foreign currency obligations. Foreign borrowing was first used for railroad construction and irrigation works. Loans for railroads were obtained in 1905, 1907 and 1909. Two loans, which were obtained in 1922 and 1924, were used partly for railroad construction and irrigation works and partly to stabilize government finances. In 1945 repayments had reduced the amount outstanding on these early loans, which were in sterling, to the equivalent of approximately $9 million. Besides a credit granted by the United States in 1946, which had been repaid by 1954, no new foreign debts were incurred until 1950.

The World Bank made three loans totaling $25.4 million in 1950 for railroad improvement, irrigation and port development. Additional loans for railroad and port development, which amounted to $15.4 million, were granted in 1955 and 1956. In 1957 the Bank made a loan of $66 million for the Yanhee multipurpose project. It made a third loan in 1961 of $22 million for railroad development. In 1962 two loans were signed; one was $3.4 million for the development of irrigation at Phet Buri; the other was a Chao Phraya Project loan for the construction of dikes and ditches. In 1963 a second Yanhee project loan of $6.6 million was made for the development of power, and a loan of $35 million was granted for the construction of highways. In 1964 $2.5 million was lent to the Industrial Finance Corporation of Thailand to buy imported equipment, materials and services for industry, and a loan of $22 million was made for the development of an irrigation system along the Mae Klong River. In 1965 a third Yanhee project loan for $6 million was expected to cover foreign exchange costs of constructing an irrigation distribution system.

Between 1953 and 1957 the United States Agency for International Development (USAID) granted development loans totaling $20 million for the construction of powerplants, transmissoin lines and a regional telecommunications system. In 1958 a loan of $1.75 million was made for the purchase of dredging facilities, and in 1959 two loans, one for $20 million for electric power expansion and one for $750,000 for the purchase of a meat processing plant, were made. In 1962 the United States lent $11.1 million for an irrigation project in the Northeast Region and one in the Northern Region. In 1965 the United States made a loan of $20.6 million to build a 175 mile two-lane hardsurfaced highway.

Between 1952 and 1964 the United States Export-Import Bank granted numerous loans to Thailand. In 1952 a loan of $1.3 million was made to the Thai Maritime Navigation Company, Ltd. to purchase cargo vessels; in 1955 $1.3 million was lent to the Siam Cement Company to build a new cement plant. In 1959 $14 million was lent to the Yanhee Electricity Authority to build a powerplant, and a $100,000 loan was made to the North Star Company for water treatment and bottling equipment. In 1960 a loan of $200,000 was granted to the Yong Kee Liab Heng Company to purchase equipment for the production of oxygen and acetylene; a loan of $300,000 was given to the Department of Public Welfare in the Ministry of the Interior to purchase tractors. In 1961 small loans totaling $100,000 were made to the Thai Lignite Authority for the purchase of shovel loaders, to the International Engineering Company for the purchase of an excavator and to the Min Sen Machinery Company for the purchase of pumps. In 1962 a $10 million loan was granted the Yanhee Electricity Authority to build a powerplant; in 1963, $5 million was lent to the Firestone Corporation to build a tire factory; and in 1964, $2.1 million was granted to Pan American Airways for construction of a hotel.

In 1962 West Germany agreed to grant a loan of 100 million DM ($25 million) for construction of a railroad line from Kaeng Khoi to Bua Yai in the northeast and for construction of two small hydroelectric projects in the northeast at Nam Phong and Nam Pung. In 1963, 11 million DM ($2.75 million) was lent the Industrial Finance Corporation of Thailand (IFCT) for loans to medium-sized industries. In 1964 a loan of 13 million DM ($3.25 million) was granted for Yanhee power distribution, and in 1965, 23 million DM ($5.75 million) was lent to construct a telecommunications system between north and south. In 1965 an 11 million DM ($2.75 million) loan was made for the distribution of power from Man Phong, and in 1966 an additional 9 million DM ($2.25 million) was added to the Nam Phong loan to extend the irrigation works in the project.

In 1966 Austria granted a loan of $3.4 million to add a third steam generating plant to the Krabi Power Plant (see ch. 21, Industry).

The internal debt, which excludes short-term borrowing, increased after World War II from about 110 million baht to about 9.1 billion baht in May 1965. Government bonds, whose current issues pay an 8 percent tax-free interest, are held mainly by government financial institutions, although the proportion owned by the public shows some tendency to increase. About 5 percent of the total amount of internal loans is registered in foreign currency. These foreign currency loans were issued between 1949 and 1957 at moderate rates of interest and once constituted a high proportion of the long-term internal debt.

The ratio of external obligations in the total public debt is relatively high, although the debt is small in relation to the country's economic potential. It would not be difficult to increase internal borrowing substantially if suitable inducements were offered and greater efforts were made to interest the public in buying government bonds. Furthermore, Thailand does not suffer from any serious shortage of foreign exchange, which would necessitate recourse to external rather than internal borrowing. Its foreign creditors regard their loans as sound investments, and the payment of interest and the repayments of principal are made in foreign currency. The country's recourse to external borrowing in these circumstances suggests that motives other than financial need are present—among them the value placed by the government on the technical assistance and the administrative guidance accompanying foreign loans for specific projects. The Thai Government may also value the prestige derived from the ability to obtain and service loans from the World Bank.

Under the Six-Year Economic Development Plan, which was started in 1961, allocations to the Economic Development Fund were scheduled to total 21.3 billion baht for the period of the plan. According to tentative estimates 31 percent of the required funds would be supplied by budget revenue, and 2.2 percent of the funds would be profits from government enterprises; thus, the total would be 33.2 percent from current receipts. It was expected that 34.4 percent would come from internal borrowing and that 32.4 percent would come from external sources; 18.2 percent of the latter is to be derived from foreign loans and 14.2 percent from foreign grants. Execution of the plan has necessitated a large increase in the internal debt, and if serious inflation is to be avoided a much larger sale of government bonds to the public is needed. Since 1960 bond sales to the public have increased, but they are still below the level desired. Public investment in government bonds has been made more attractive by making them reimbursable on a 15 days' notice.

LOCAL GOVERNMENT FINANCE

The general trend of administrative reform during the past century has been toward the centralization of power. In public finance this has led to the collection of almost all the public revenue by the central government. Available information indicates that the total revenue collected by all local authorities is only about 2 percent of that collected by the central government. Local government revenues are supplemented by grants from the central government that are approximately equal to the revenue collected locally; thus, local government disbursements are about 4 percent of those made by the central government.

The World Bank mission in Thailand from 1957 to 1958 recommended that efforts be made to improve the efficiency of local administrations in order to give them enlarged responsibilities. It suggested they be given a new independent source of income in the form of local property tax. Municipal governments are empowered to impose a house tax, but the return is small. There was a possibility this source of local income might be improved when the Ministry of Education suggested in September 1962 that municipalities should increase the house tax to meet the cost of operating about 300 publicly supported schools, which the government proposed to give to them.

CHAPTER 26

BANKING AND CURRENCY

By 1965 banking had become Thailand's most lucrative business. The country's flourishing foreign trade and the increasing activity in other sectors of the economy had afforded the banks plenty of scope to expand their operations. Both deposits and loans had more than doubled since 1960, averaging an increase of 17.8 percent and 16.2 percent, respectively, per year, indicating a wider acceptance of commercial banking by the general public.

About one-third of all banking units, holding 75 percent of all deposits, was located in the Bangkok-Thon Buri metropolitan area, leaving much to be done by way of attracting funds, especially in the provinces, which were still outside the banking system. Despite the expansion in banking operations, capital and credit were still in short supply. Until the 1960's the government was almost the sole initiator of large-scale enterprise, more from lack of private venture capital than from any commitment in principle to public enterprise.

Thai currency is solidly backed by gold, foreign exchange and securities and has been remarkably stable, except during and immediately after World War II when the country suffered from inflation. The country's past financial record and its present strong international position encourage the belief that inflationary forces will be kept under control.

Modern banking in Thailand dates from over 60 years ago when foreign banks began to open branches in Bangkok. The first Thai bank was started in 1904, and foreign banks continued to dominate banking until World War II. Since then many new Thai banks and a few branches of foreign banks have been opened.

The government exercised no control over banking until 1928, when the Ministry of Finance issued a set of banking regulations. This was followed in 1937 by a Commercial Bank Act, which was revised in 1945 and 1962. The latest revision imposes much more stringent regulations on banks than existed before and strengthens the powers of the central bank over the commercial banks. The Commercial Bank Act of 1962, designed to increase confidence in banks, thereby encouraging the growth of banking habits among the people and the eventual lowering of interest rates, has been notably successful.

Central banking started in 1942, when the Bank of Thailand was established as the bank of issue, the chief custodian of government funds, a repository for the reserves of commercial banks and a rediscounter of their bills. Its effectiveness as an instrument of credit control has so far been limited.

THE CENTRAL BANK

In 1939 the government created the National Banking Bureau, which was designed to pave the way for setting up a central bank. The Bureau acted as a banker for the government and the commercial banks, but note issue remained in the Treasury Department of the Ministry of Finance.

The central bank—the Bank of Thailand—was founded in December 1942. It is an autonomous public institution but subject to the general supervisory authority of the Ministry of Finance. Its governor and deputy governor are appointed by the king; the nine other members of its Board of Directors are appointed by the Council of Ministers acting on the advice of the Ministry of Finance. Its capital of 20 million baht (see Glossary) was provided entirely by the government, and the net assets of the National Banking Bureau, amounting to 13.5 million baht, were transferred to it as a reserve fund. It took over from the Treasury Department the currency reserve and the sole right of note issue. The bank's net profits, after provision for reserves, are transferred to the general state revenue.

The bank has two main divisions: the Issue Department and the Banking Department. The former issues the currency and manages the currency reserve. This reserve may consist of: gold, United States dollars, sterling or other foreign currency as authorized by ministerial regulations, in the form of bank deposits abroad; foreign securities with interest and principal payable to the prescribed currencies; Thai government securities payable in the prescribed currencies or in baht; treasury bills bought or rediscounted by the bank (not exceeding 10 percent of the total note issue); and gold or United States dollars contributed to the International Monetary Fund (IMF). Formerly, the note issue had to be fully covered by gold, foreign exchange and foreign currency securities. This regulation, which proved unduly restrictive, was modified by the Currency Act of 1958, and it was provided that the amount in gold, foreign currency and foreign securities redeemable within 1 year from the date of purchase or deposit must not be less than 60 percent of the note issue.

The Bank of Thailand is strictly a central bank, and its Banking Department does not compete with the commercial banks, for which it functions as a bank of reserve. The Commercial Bank Act of 1945 empowered it to fix the minimum cash reserves of the commercial banks at a rate from 9 to 20 percent of their total deposits. At least half of these reserves had to be deposited with the bank. This provision, designed to give it a measure of control over the volume of commercial bank credit was little used. Until the revised Commercial Bank Act of April 1962 came into force, the bank kept the reserve requirement unchanged at 10 percent —a requirement which, because of administrative difficulties, it did not strictly enforce. In general, commercial banks have kept reserves that have varied greatly but usually have been well above the legal minimum.

The revised Commercial Bank Act of 1962 changed the reserve requirements and introduced new provisions regarding capital funds. These funds must not be less than a prescribed percentage of total assets, excluding cash, Thai government and other specified securities, and deposits with the Bank of Thailand and other banks. The bank is empowered to fix the percentage at not less than 5 and not more than 15 percent. The prescribed ratio in 1965 was 6 percent. Until June 1, 1965, up to a quarter of the reserve could be in the form of Thai government securities; after that date the bank raised the ratio to one-half. The cash reserves kept by banks in their own custody are no longer subject to any control.

A special proviso applies to branches of foreign banks, which are subject not only to the general regulation regarding capital funds but are also required to maintain capital assets of not less than 5 million baht. Of these assets, 2 million baht may be in the form of immovable property, and the remainder must be in the form of deposits in the Bank of Thailand over and above the normal cash reserve.

The foreign banks concerned have criticized the new capital requirements as an uneconomical use of resources and inappropriate to the situation of international banks. Although the requirements appear to strengthen the competitive position of Thai banks over foreign banks, some criticism has also come from Thai bankers. They point out the difficulty of increasing capital at short notice and argue that it is good banking practice to link the volume of lending not to capital funds but to deposits.

The revised Act provides for the fixing of maximum interest rates for both deposits and loans. Beginning on April 5, 1966, the maximum rate of interest payable by commercial banks on deposits other than interbank deposits may not exceed 0.01 percent per year for demand deposits and for time deposits of less than 3 months. Previously, the interest rate on such deposits was 0.5 percent per year. The interest rate on saving deposits with commercial banks for which passbooks are used in making deposits and withdrawals and for which the initial deposit was not less than 100 baht was lowered from 4½ percent to 3½ percent. The interest rate on special deposits (that is, against which a limited number of checks might be drawn each month) remained unchanged at 3 percent per year until July 1, 1966, when all such amounts were to be liquidated. Interest rates on time deposits of 3 to 12 months remained at 5 to 6 percent, and those of 12 months and over, at 7 percent per year.

The Bank of Thailand announced that, beginning on April 5, 1966, there would be a reduction from 10 to 13 percent to 9 to 14 percent per year in the range of interest rates charged by commercial banks on advances to exporters and manufacturers. The old rates will, however, remain in force until the expiration of existing contracts between commercial banks and borrowers, but not later than April 5, 1967. The interest rates of Thai banks have been higher than those of foreign banks, and the effect of the new regulations is to reduce the gap between the two.

The revised Commercial Bank Act, by strengthening the commercial banking system, has encouraged larger deposits, and this, as the authorities hoped, resulted in lower interest rates. Savings in Thailand are still kept largely in the form of currency and precious metals, and loans are made outside the banking system at rates of interest which may be as high as 1.5 to 2 percent a month, even on good security. It was estimated in 1961 that the weighted average of interest rates in the unorganized money market was approximately 21 percent per year. This situation, which is basically the result of the scarcity of capital, is aggravated by mistrust and ignorance of banks and—especially in the provinces—by lack of banking facilities, although many provincial branch banks have been opened in recent years.

The Bank of Thailand has always had authority to inspect the operations of commercial banks, but lack of staff has prevented it from doing so effectively. The revised Commercial Bank Act strengthens the Bank's inspection powers and imposes stricter reporting requirements on the commercial banks.

The bank manages the public debt and is the government's agent for exchange control. It effectively managed the multiple exchange rate system that was in operation during the first decade after World War II. Up to the end of 1960 foreign exchange derived from exports and other foreign transactions had to be sold to the bank, and foreign exchange required for imports and other foreign payments had to be procured through it. Since that time commercial banks and authorized exchange dealers have been permitted to deal in foreign exchange without prior bank approval. Some restrictions are designed to prevent loss of capital abroad. The bank operates an exchange equalization fund and buys and sells foreign exchange so as to prevent undue fluctuation in exchange rates. It also operates a clearinghouse.

OTHER GOVERNMENT BANKS

In addition to the Bank of Thailand, there are other government banks: the Government Savings Bank, the Bank for Agriculture and Cooperatives which incorporated the former Bank for Cooperatives, the Welfare Housing Bank and the privately owned but government-supported Industrial Finance Corporation. The government also has shareholdings in commercial banks.

The Government Savings Bank had its origin in the Treasury Savings Bank, which was created in 1913 under the Treasury Ministry (now Ministry of Finance). In 1929 the Savings Bank was transferred to the Post and Telegraph Department, and in 1946 it became a separate institution under its present name. It accepts savings deposits, issues savings banks and small denomination lottery bonds, makes money transfers and deals in government bonds. It transacts life, disability and endowment insurance business on a small scale, and it also carries on commercial banking operations, including the granting of loans.

Payment of all liabilities of the Savings Bank is guaranteed by the government, and the investment of its funds (mainly in government securities) is subject to regulation by the Ministry of Finance. It is the only bank operating under the Savings Account Law, and although other banks pay interest on current account deposits, they may not call them savings accounts.

As a savings institution, the bank has some defects. Although it uses post offices as agencies in many areas, branch facilities are inadequate in the provinces. All loans must be authorized by the main office in Bangkok, and the branches merely collect savings and do little to promote the bank's operations. In 1967 interest rates on deposits were modest, being 2 percent on deposits repayable on call and 5 percent on deposits repayable on 6 months' notice (raised from 3 percent as of April 1, 1965). The bank has, nevertheless, been reasonably successful. It his 850 depositors with deposits of only 135,234 baht at the end of its first year of operation. In 1963 the amount of deposits had risen to 1,723 million baht, and deposits continue to increase.

The Bank for Agriculture and Cooperatives was formally opened on November 1, 1966, for the express purpose of extending credit to farmers. All shares are held by the Ministry of Finance. The bank had an initial capital of 20 million baht, which it was expected would be built up to a billion baht in 10 years' time. The bank was authorized to extend credit to agricultural cooperatives and to groups of farmers not officially classed as cooperatives as long as the groups of farmers were supported by the Ministry of the Interior or the Ministry of Agriculture.

The new bank incorporated the former Bank for Cooperatives which was founded in 1947 to finance cooperative credit societies, of which there were 9,876 in 1963. It operated under the general supervision of the Ministry of National Development and the Ministry of Finance. Its initial capital was provided by the government, which also gave it loans and issued special cooperative bonds to help finance it. At the end of 1963 the loans advanced by the bank to all credit societies throughout the country stood at over 300 million baht.

The Welfare Housing Bank was established by the government in 1953. Little information is available about the bank, but the institution does not appear to have been very active.

The Industrial Finance Corporation of Thailand developed from the Industrial Bank, which was founded in 1953, to provide medium- and long-term financing for small industrial enterprises. The Industrial Bank's capital was fixed at 500 million baht payable in installments at the discretion of the government. Only a small part of this was actually paid in, so that by 1958 the bank was in serious difficulties and had virtually ceased operations. In 1959 it was replaced by the Industrial Finance Corporation, which is privately owned although backed by the government.

Under the provisions of the Industrial Finance Corporation of Thailand Act of 1959, the objectives of the corporation are to assit in the establishment, expansion or modernization of private industrial enterprises; and to encourage the participation of private capital, both internal and external, in such enterprises.

When the Industrial Finance Corporation of Thailand first came into existence, the Thai Government financed it with an interest-free loan of about 13 million baht from the proceeds of the liquidation of the government-owned Industrial Bank. In October 1962 a sum of 20 million baht from the 1962–63 budget appropriation was added to its resources as a long-term loan from the government, and in September 1965 the government made another loan of 30 million baht. The Corporation has also received a 20-year interest-free loan of 15 million baht from funds provided under the United States aid program. By the end of 1965 the Corporation's total resources were about 214 million baht, including a loan of 50 million baht from the International Bank for Reconstruction and Development (IBRD—World Bank) and another of 55 million baht from the Kreditanstalt für Wiederaufbau (Credit Institute for Reconstruction) of Germany, all in foreign currencies. In October 1966 the Chairman of the Board of the Industrial Finance Corporation of Thailand announced that the corporation was planning to issue loan shares of 30 million baht for public subscription. From its inception on October 6, 1959, to September 30, 1966, the corporation made 75 loans totaling 183 million baht to 65 companies.

In order to make low-interest credit facilities available to small industries, a government loan of 10 million baht a year for 3 years starting in 1963 was made to two local commercial banks, the Agricultural Bank and the Provincial Bank, at a 3 percent interest rate. Having contributed 10 million baht of their own funds, the banks had a total of 20 million baht to lend out each year to small-scale industrialists at an interest rate of 9 percent.

For the purpose of screening applications to the banks, a small Industry Loan Office has been established in the Department of Industrial Promotion (in the Ministry of Industry). After the office makes a technical assessment of each application, its recommendations concerning the application are submitted to a Loan Board for its final decision. The Loan Board is composed of officials of the Department of Industrial Promotion, representatives of the Ministry of Finance, the National Economic Development Board (in the Office of the Prime Minister), the Budget Bureau (also in the Office of the Prime Minister) and the managers of the two banks. If a loan is to be granted, the Loan Board prescribes repayment terms and interest rate to be charged by the banks.

In January 1966 the Agricultural Bank and the Provincial Bank informed all their correspondents of their decision to merge and continue their banking business as one institution to be named Krung Thai Bank. The new bank was to have a capital of 105 million baht, and the government was to own 80 percent of the shares.

COMMERCIAL BANKS

In 1967 there were 29 privately owned commercial banks in Thailand, of which 13 were branches of foreign banks. Just before World War II there were only 9 commercial banks, of which 6 were branches of foreign banks and 1 was locally registered but Chinese owned. Thus, not only has the number of banks tripled during the last 25 years, but the number of Thai-owned banks has significantly increased.

The first commercial bank in Thailand, a branch of the Hong Kong and Shanghai Banking Corporation, opened in 1888. The Chartered Bank of India, Australia and China established a Bangkok branch in 1893, and the French Bank of Indochina (Banque de l'Indochine) followed the lead of the two British banks in 1897. The business of these banks was primarily the financing of foreign trade, particularly with Europe.

The first locally organized bank was the Siam Commercial Bank, which was founded in 1906. Although a private institution, it received support from the government, which wished to end the foreign monopoly of banking in the country. The Siam Commercial Bank, like the foreign banks, engaged mainly in foreign trade financing, but it also did some mortgage business. No new locally organized banks appeared until 1934, when the Chinese-owned Tan Peng Choon Bank was established. This bank's principal business was financing trade with other Southeast Asian countries and China and remitting money to China on behalf of local Chinese residents.

In August 1960 it was reorganized under the name of the Thai Development Bank. The only other locally organized bank to open before World War II was the Bank of Asia for Industry and Commerce, which was started in 1939. Meanwhile, three more foreign branch banks, two Chinese and one British, had been established. These were the Sze Hai Tong Bank of Singapore (1909), the Bank of Canton (1919) and the British-owned Mercantile Bank (1933).

During and after World War II banking prospered. Regulations were lax, and minimum capital requirements were low. Between 1940 and 1958, 12 new local banks were established. They were the Siam City Bank (1941), the Provincial Bank (1942), the Bangkok Bank and the Bangkok Bank of Commerce (1944), the Bank of Ayutthaya and the Thai Famers Bank (1945), the Laem Thong Bank (1948), the Thai Danu Bank and the Union Bank of Bangkok (1949), the Bangkok Metropolitan Bank and the Agricultural Bank (1950) and the Thai Military Bank (1957). No new commercial bank was added to the list until 1965 when the Asia Trust Bank, a successor of Asia Trust, which had been a well-known financial institution since 1942, was opened. The total amount invested by the government in commercial banks is not known.

Eight new foreign banks have also opened since World War II. They are the Indian Overseas Bank and the Bank of China (1947), the Nationale Handelsbank (Dutch National Bank for

Commerce) and the Bank of America (1949), the Mitsui Bank (1952), the Bank of Tokyo (1962), the United Malayan Banking Corporation and the Chase Manhattan Bank (1964) which took over the operations of the Nationale Handelsbank.

Along with the establishment of new banks, there has been a spread of branch banking to different districts in the Bangkok Thon Buri metropolitan area, to the provinces and overseas. By the end of 1965 there were 484 commercial banking offices, more than double the number existing at the end of 1963. Of this total, 160 were in Bangkok and Thon Buri, the rest scattered in important commercial centers throughout the country. Ten branches of a Thai bank were located in 7 foreign countries. Local banks were opening branches as fast as permission was granted by the Bank of Thailand. The establishment of provincial branches has had the effect of attracting some formerly idle funds to Bangkok, where they can be put to work.

The commercial banks finance enterprises mainly by short-term loans, advances and overdrafts and by discounting trade bills. In 1967 the legal maximum rate of interest was 14 percent, reduced from 15 percent in 1966.

Deposits in commercial banks increased nearly tenfold and loans and advances about sixfold between 1952 and 1964, a most notable upsurge beginning in 1963. The cash reserve ratio in 1967, although still maintained at a fairly high level because more deposits were sight deposits, had sharply declined. The proportion of time deposits had, however, grown substantially. The bulk of advances by the commercial banks continued to be for the financing of foreign trade. Holdings of government securities, which yielded a poor return compared with that obtainable from commercial loans, were relatively small but had risen considerably since 1962.

The revised Commercial Bank Act of April 1962 tightened banking regulations by forbidding banks to make loans to their directors, to the spouses of directors or to partnerships in which directors or their spouses had unlimited liability; by limiting bank holding of immovable property; by forbidding the purchase or holding of stocks or debentures in a limited company in an amount exceeding 20 percent of the company's capital; by prohibiting the addition of charges for loans and supplementary payments on deposits designed to circumvent the maximum interest rate provisions; by requiring observance of minimum deposits requirements for letters of credit and security requirements for loans and of maximum charges for services as prescribed by the Bank of Thailand; by requiring reports and balance sheets in a prescribed form and independent auditing of accounts; by forbidding a director or officer of one bank to serve as a director or officer of another; and by empowering the minister of finance to take over control if a bank should suspend payments. The new rules indicate the nature of some of the defects in commercial banking in Thailand in the past, and their application should help to remove some of the present mistrust of banks.

At least some of the commercial banks, particularly foreign ones, continue to employ *compradors,* often Chinese or of Chinese origin, who function as intermediaries between the banks and borrowers and to some extent act as guarantors of loans. Men of good financial standing are valued by the banks for their personal knowledge of loan applicants. The *comprador* system has been criticized as increasing the cost of providing loan facilities. Because of the small scale of most business in Thailand, the small number of corporate enterprises, the defective accounting practices and the dearth of experienced banking officials, however, it seems likely that the *comprador* system will persist for some time.

OTHER SOURCES OF CREDIT

In addition to the ordinary commercial banks, a number of small Chinese private banks continue to exist. Established mainly in connection with the once-flourishing business of remitting funds to China, they are now less numerous because of the decline of that activity. They also accept deposits and extend credit at high interest rates to Chinese businesses. Gold dealers are another group which plays a role in business financing. Moneylenders continue to supply a large part of the small loans, particularly in the rural areas.

Credit is often extended by wholesalers to retail customers. Goods with a slow rate of turnover may be placed on consignment with a retailer, who may return them to the wholesaler if they prove to be unsalable. In the case of faster moving merchandise, the retailer may be given credit which is automatically renewed up to a maximum amount with every payment he makes, or goods may be delivered to him on condition that he pay the wholesaler as he sells them. Retailers often extend credit to their customers, although installment buying as practiced in Western countries is almost unknown.

In rural areas during the months before harvesttime when cash is short, storekeepers often allow farmers to postpone payment for purchases until they have received the proceeds from the sale of their new crops. Storekeepers sometimes combine moneylending with trade, especially in the countryside, and in both rural and urban areas many persons make a living from granting small loans at interest.

These various small-scale credit arrangements depend on the existence of personal relations between lender and borrower. It appears that the rate of default on loans is not great and that the high interest rates charged reflect capital shortage rather than the risk involved.

FINANCING OF INVESTMENT

Public Sector

Although the government, beginning in 1959, has introduced measures to encourage private foreign investment in new industrial ventures, it traditionally has been wary of large-scale private foreign investment. Old concessions granted for operating streetcars and electric-power plants and for exploiting teak forests were not renewed. The properties of the big foreign tobacco company were bought by the government, which until the opening of the Thai Oil Refinery in 1964, competed with the large foreign oil companies in the distribution of oil products.

This attitude toward large-scale private foreign ventures evidently reflected a sensitivity to the political dangers, real or imaginary, of foreign economic dominance, a desire to give as much economic opportunity as possible to the Thai and, perhaps, to obtain control of valuable sources of state revenue. A result has been that for several decades the government was almost the sole instrument for providing the capital needed for modern large-scale undertakings and almost the only large-scale entrepreneur. In the development of transport, public utilities and large-scale industry, indigenous private enterprise has played an inconspicuous role. The range of public enterprises is wide. It includes the railroads, the telegraph and telephone systems, a savings bank and other specialized banks, the Thailand Tobacco Monopoly and a number of manufacturing enterprises (see ch. 21, Industry).

Government enterprises and other government capital expenditure have been financed from ordinary revenue and from internal and external loans. The proportion of capital expenditure made from current government revenue has been high, and until recently, revenues from government enterprises easily sufficed to meet the cost of servicing the public debt. With the recent expansion of development expenditures and increased borrowing, this is, however, no longer true.

Private Sector

The commercial banks have provided little in the way of long-term investment capital either for industry or agriculture. They do some mortgage lending, but the bulk of their business is the provision of short-term financing, particularly for foreign trade. This short-term financing, of course, contributes indirectly to capital growth by making it possible for businessmen to allocate a large part of their own funds to long-term investment. The special banks established by the government to provide medium- and long-term loans to industry and agriculture have as yet made only a minor contribution.

In 1962 a group composed partly of Thai nationals and partly of foreigners started a stock exchange in Bangkok, and the shares of 11 companies were listed. In 1964 after 2 years of operation, it had made some progress but was still only moderately active. There were 19 companies listed, the market value of whose shares totaled about $53 million (1 billion baht). The annual trading volume was, however, only $3 million (60 million baht), not quite 6 percent of the total value of listed shares which compares unfavorably with the norm of about 10 percent in other major exchanges in the world. According to a member, the securities-holding Thai public like to hold onto its shares, and 80 percent of the listed shares were retained by their owners on virtually a permanent basis.

Meanwhile, the main source of new private capital funds continues to be private savings and the profits of existing businesses that are used for extension and diversification. Great numbers of the small- and medium-sized business enterprises in Thailand are partnerships—often confined to family members—in which the entire capital is provided by the partners.

In spite of government attempts to meet the need for long-term agricultural credit at moderate interest rates through the promotion of cooperative credit societies, many farmers who cannot finance improvements and extensions out of current income have recourse to moneylenders. The latter lend nominally on short terms but in practice often renew loans for extended periods as long as the high interest rate is paid. The problem of rural indebtedness is less acute in Thailand than in some countries but is by no means negligible.

CURRENCY

The unit of currency in Thailand is the baht, which foreigners —perhaps less commonly than formerly—often call the tical, a word of Malay origin. The baht is divided into 100 satang. Thailand has been a member of the International Monetary Fund since 1949, but did not at that time fix an initial par value for the baht because the monetary condition had not yet returned to normal after World War II. In recent years the domestic monetary situation has satisfactorily improved. The exchange rate has stabilized, the good reputation of the baht deriving in part from the very strong reserve position. Gold and foreign exchange had long exceeded the value of baht notes in circulation. On October 20, 1963, a royal decree was promulgated establishing the par value of the baht, fixing it at 0.0427245 grams of fine gold and giving it an exchange rate of 20.80 baht to 1 United States dollar. In August 1966 the baht was revalued upward to 20.75 to the United States dollar.

Originally, the baht was a piece of silver shaped like a bullet and of a fixed weight. The word in fact meant a weight of 15 grams (approximately a half ounce avoirdupois) and, as applied to the currency, was an abbreviation of "baht of silver." For small transactions cowrie shells were used. Facilities for coinage in Thailand in the nineteenth century were insufficient, and, in 1857, it was decreed that foreign coins should be legal tender. Most commonly used were Mexican dollars, then widely found in the Far East; Straits dollars in the south and rupees in the north were also used. With the opening of a new mint and the issuing of new flat coins, the old coins were gradually withdrawn. When foreign banks were established toward the end of the nineteenth century, they issued notes which had some degree of use as currency in Bangkok but were not legal tender. In 1902 when the Treasury Department began to issue notes, the foreign banks lost the right to note issue.

The currency consists of notes issued by the Bank of Thailand and subsidiary coins struck by the Royal Mint and issued by the Treasury Department in the Ministry of Finance. The notes are printed in England, and serial numbers are added in Thailand. Notes are issued in denominations of 100, 20, 10, 5 and 1 baht and 50 satang. Notes of 1 baht and higher are legal tender up to any amount. Since even sizable payments are often made in currency rather than by check, the fact that the highest denomination note is equivalent to less than US $5 is an inconvenience. During World War II the government issued 1,000 baht notes, but these were withdrawn after the war; the government is said to be reluctant to issue high denomination notes lest it create the impression that there is inflation and thereby cause loss of confidence in the currency.

Coins are issued in denominations of 1 baht and 50, 25, 20, 10, 5 and 1 satang. Special 20-baht silver coins and 1-baht nickel coins were issued in December 1963 to commemorate the 36th birthday of His Majesty the King. The older silver coins of 50, 25, 10 and 5 satang, nickel coins of 10 and 5 satang and bronze coins of 1 satang and ½ satang have almost all been withdrawn. They have been replaced by tin and new bronze coins of the same denominations, except the ½ satang coin, which is no longer issued.

Confidence in the paper currency is high within the country, as it has been during the 65 years that it has been issued, except during World War II and the period of postwar adjustment. In normal times the note issue has been strongly backed by gold and foreign exchange, and changes in the exchange value of the baht, other than ordinary market fluctuations, have had external rather than internal causes. While the tendency to hoard rather than invest persists, the fact that the bulk of hoarded savings is in the form of notes indicates that this does not arise from mistrust of the currency.

VOLUME OF MONEY AND PRICE LEVEL

Until 1902 Thailand was on a silver standard. Apart from the cowrie shells used for small payments and, from 1898 onward, the notes and current deposits of the foreign banks—which together constituted only a small part of the total—the money supply consisted of silver currency. Since Thailand mined no silver, the amount of silver currency in circulation varied with the balance of payments. A deficit decreased the amount in circulation and tended to depress prices; a surplus had the opposite effect, and over a period of time external payments and receipts were balanced automatically. The exchange rate was determined by the relative intrinsic values of different currencies.

Until about 1870 the price of silver in terms of gold did not vary much, and many countries were than on a silver standard. After that time the price of silver fell drastically, causing widespread abandonment of the silver standard. In relation to the gold standard pound sterling the baht fell from 8 to the pound in 1850 to 21 in 1902. The decline had disturbing effects on foreign trade, and, in 1902, Thailand stopped minting silver currency and unofficially moved off the silver standard onto a gold exchange standard at 20 baht to the pound sterling, a change which was made official with the passage of the Gold Standard Act in 1908.

Troubles with silver were not over, however. The currency in circulation was still silver coins, and, after 1902, the price of silver started to rise so that the intrinsic value of the baht had exceeded its face value. To prevent export of the currency it was necessary to change the rate of exchange, and, at the end of 1907, it was fixed at 13 to the pound. A short-lived rise in the price of silver after World War I necessitated an appreciation of the baht to 9.54 to the pound. In 1923 the rate was fixed at 11 to the pound. Gradually replaced by notes, silver coinage was reduced to a subsidiary fiduciary currency which by the 1960's had almost completely disappeared.

During World War II vast quantities of paper money were issued to meet the expenditures of the Japanese forces in the country, and with the increase in the volume of money in circulation came a rise in prices. After the war stringent foreign exchange controls and measures to reduce the volume of money in circulation restored financial stability. In terms of the pound sterling the baht in 1962 stood at 58, compared with 8 in the middle of the nineteenth century. Forces outside the control of the government—the fall in the value of silver and the effects of World War II—and not financial mismanagement have been responsible for this decline, and Thailand's one major inflation was mild compared with the war-engendered inflations in some other countries.

Government borrowing from the Bank of Thailand since 1952 has caused an almost continuous increase in the money supply from 5,074.7 million baht to 12,923. 7 million baht in 1964. This expansion has not been matched by increased production, and prices have again been rising. In October 1966 the government announced that a joint study of inflationary pressures would be made by the Budget Bureau, the Bank of Thailand and the National Economic Development Board. In early 1967, although the situation did not appear to be dangerous, the government's economic development plans could be seriously hampered if the inflationary trend continued. In spite of the tendency toward inflation, the exchange value of the baht has remained stable.

SECTION IV. NATIONAL SECURITY

CHAPTER 27

PUBLIC ORDER AND SAFETY

The government's overall commitment to the containment of communism in Southeast Asia and the increased scope of externally directed Communist subversion in the country's border areas produced pressures which, by mid-1967, had seriously affected conditions of public order and internal security. With extensive foreign assistance, principally from the United States, the government had undertaken expanded counterinsurgency programs to improve the economic, social and security conditions in troubled areas of the Northeast, the North and the southern portion of the Peninsula. These developments increased the burden on the Royal Thai National Police, commonly called the National Police Department, which in addition to maintaining law and order, was charged with active participation in the suppression of subversive elements and providing protection to the country and its people.

General conditions of public order and safety are normally good. Habits of obedience and respect for authority have been inculcated in the people by centuries of rule by absolute monarchs whose authority was both secular and religious. The moral sanctions of Buddhism and the pressures for conformity in the village communities where most of the people still live continue to reinforce the traditional value placed on personal restraint and public harmony. A potential source of friction exists in the ethnic minorities, but the vast majority of the population is united by its common heritage of Thai history, language and tradition.

Political coups have been frequent, especially since the end of the absolute monarchy in 1932, but even these have involved relatively little bloodshed. Riots and public disturbances requiring large-scale police action have been rare occurrences (see ch. 3, Historical Setting; ch. 15, Political Dynamics).

The maintenance of public order and the enforcement of laws are primarily the responsibilities of the National Police Department. Although a subdivision of the Ministry of the Interior, the Department itself is one of the strongest agencies of the central government. It controls all police activity and exercises strong influence in prosecutions in the courts and, therefore, on the application of the law. This highly centralized police organization is being assisted extensively in its modernization and training programs by the United States Operations Mission (USOM), Public Safety Division, and is rapidly improving in its overall effectiveness. Most of the force is concentrated in the densely populated Bangkok area and in the sensitive Northeast Region.

The Criminal and Civil Procedures Code enforced by the Department represents an amalgamation of Thai and Western concepts of justice. The influence of Thai tradition is notably apparent in the character of the moral propositions and the general definition of public order set forth in the Code. The establishment of a constitutional monarchy following the coup of 1932 brought about fairly extensive law reforms which were promulgated when the Code was revised in 1935.

INSURGENCY

The Communist subversive campaign in Thailand is a long-standing one which became increasingly serious in the early and mid-1960's. Three major areas, all along or near the borders, are involved: the Northeast Region, embracing the more remote districts of the provinces of Udon Thani, Ubon Ratchathani, Nakhon Panom, Kalasin, Sakon Nakhon and Nong Khai; the Southern Region, including parts of the provinces of Songkhla, Surat Thani, Trang, Phatthalung and Nakhon Si Thammarat; and the northern tier of provinces, including Mae Hong Song, Chiang Mai, Chiang Rai, Nan and Uttaradit. The Communist problem is not generally considered an indigenous one, but rather an externally directed effort and part of the general Communist aggression in Southeast Asia. The movement is predominantly controlled by Communist China, extensively assisted by North Vietnam and the Pathet Lao in Laos.

The problem of insurgency is more extensive in the Northeast than in the other two areas. It is the poorest part of the country and contains almost one-third of the population. Cut off from Bangkok by rough terrain and poor communications, the impoverished hinterland has long evidenced discontent and dissatisfaction with the lack of interest in the area shown by earlier Thai governments. Also, the people in the area have a strong ethnic link with the neighboring Laotians across the Mekong River and have developed a fairly extensive and homogenous river culture with them. Furthermore, about 40,000 refugees who

452

fled from Vietnam during the Indochina War (1946–54) are located in the region and have remained unassimilated.

The Communists have attempted to exploit the dissatisfaction in the Northeast by all means possible. Propaganda broadcasts have been intensified, agents have been infiltrated from Laos, Thai natives have been sent to Hanoi and Peiping for guerrilla training, revolutionary movements have been fostered and small bands of armed dissidents have been organized in scattered jungle areas. These armed bands have gradually increased their activities, and many incidents of terrorism, assassinations and armed clashes with Thai security forces had taken place. Estimates of the number of armed insurgents operating in the area vary greatly, but there are probably only 1,500 or slightly more. They exert some influence, however, and United States officials in Bangkok indicate that they may have several times as many followers and sympathizers. In a regional population of some 10 million, however, they remain a very small minority. The North Vietnamese have thoroughly infiltrated the Vietnamese refugees and exert a dominant influence over the community.

In the South the problem of active subversion is smaller, but of nearly equal intensity. The mountainous terrain and distance also isolate the region and the people from the capital. Most of the 2 million inhabitants are Malay Moslems who feel a closer affinity with the similar population of northern Malaysia than with the Thai Buddhists. A sizable minority of ethnic Chinese also live in the lower provinces and are a special target for exploitation.

The armed southern insurgents number 600 to 800 and are in part ethnic Chinese survivors of the 1948–60 guerrilla war in Malaysia who sought sanctuary on the Thai side of the border. For the most part, the subversive effort is fostered and controlled by the rather small Communist Party of Malaysia which is linked with the Communist activity in the Northeast. The actual number of sympathizers and supporters of the active insurgents and terrorists is unknown, but is has been estimated to be as high as 25,000. The Malaysian Government is cooperating with the Thai in launching joint counterinsurgency operations and improving the security of the area.

Communist agitation, recruiting and organization in northern Thailand was being stepped up in the mid-1960's, but most of the government's public order and security problems in the area were still associated with the 250,000 rather primitive, stanchly independent hill peoples who have little loyalty to, or contact with, the central government. Most of these peoples ar involved in the illegal growing and marketing of opium and in the illicit cutting to teak, which is the area's chief export. Shan and Karen tribesmen, in rebellion against the Burmese Government, move back and forth across the border; some have settled in Thailand and have added to the minority problem.

There are also over 3,000 organized Chinese Nationalist exile troops which operate rather freely in the area. Pushed out of Yunnan in 1949 by the Chinese Communists and forced out of Burma in 1960–62 by the neutralist government, they have refused repatriation to Taiwan and have established themselves in Thailand. Their principal income allegedly comes from serving as armed escort units for the opium caravans moving southward.

THE POLICE SYSTEM

The police system, organized into the National Police Department, is composed of the National Police Department Headquarters and four bureaus: the Provincial Police, including the Border Patrol Police; the Metropolitan Police; the Criminal Investigation Bureau; and the Education Bureau. The police organization, totaling over 60,000 personnel, is quasi-military in character, and all ranks, except the lowest (constable), correspond to military ranks. The annual police budget has been increasing steadily, and for fiscal year 1967 it will approximate the equivalent of $45 million.

The major operational units of the police system are the Provincial Police, the Border Patrol Police and the Metropolitan Police. Smaller units are supervised by the Criminal Investigation Bureau and include the Special Branch Police, Railway Police, Highway Police, Marine Police and Forestry Police. Together, these specialized units employ less than 4,000 men. The most important unit is probably the 1,500-man Special Branch Police which has the responsibility for detecting, investigating and apprehending subversive elements throughout the kingdom.

Within the Ministry of the Interior, but outside the Police Department, there is a Volunteer Defense Corps under the supervision of the Department of Local Administration. This completely volunteer organization is a part-time militia which functions as an auxiliary police force to supplement security measures at the village level. In time of full emergency, this force of more than 20,000 would be expanded and mobilized as a reserve force to serve under the Ministry of Defense (see ch. 28, The Armed Forces).

The formal functions of the National Police Department include more than the enforcement of laws and the apprehension and investigation of offenders. The Department also bears full responsibility for the internal security of the country under conditions of less than full insurgency. In case of invasion all components of the police system, except the Metropolitan Police, are expected to mobilize and bear the brunt of fighting until the Army can deploy its forces to the field. In case of war the mobilized police units would be placed under the Ministry of Defense and would serve with, but would not be incorporated into, military formations.

By mid-1967 the counterinsurgency role of the police had been modified to include cooperation with representatives of other government agencies. Realizing that the betterment of local conditions reduced dissatisfaction and the subversive potential in depressed areas, Bangkok authorities augmented the security efforts of the police by assigning teams of economic and sociological specialists to operate and improve living standards in rural areas.

National Police Department Headquarters

The National Police Department Headquarters administers all components of the police system. It is headed by a director general who is normally aided by two deputies and one assistant director general. The comprehensive scope of the functions preformed by the Headquarters is indicated by its numerous divisions, bureaus and offices. In addition to the usual headquarters administrative sections, it includes divisions dealing with legal affairs, prosecution, finance, supplies, research and planning, immigration, alien registration, tax controls, communications, technical services, medical service, welfare, crime detection and matters affecting foreign nationals. It also has an inspector general's office which is directly responsible to the director general. An air support division for the National Police Department was approved in 1966 and in early 1967 was undergoing planning and organization prior to activation.

Provincial Police

The Provincial Police, which includes the Border Patrol Police, comprises the largest component of the National Police Department, in terms of both manpower and geographic responsibility. They are charged with providing police services and protection to every city and town in Thailand, except the metropolitan Bangkok-Thon Buri area, and to all rural areas, except those contiguous to the land borders patrolled by the Border Patrol Police. With a strength of over 30,000, the Provincial Police bear the brunt of law enforcement activities and in many areas are the principal representatives of the central government's authority.

The Provincial Police are headed by a commissioner, who reports directly to the director general of the National Police Department. He is assisted by two deputy commissioners (one of whom is in charge of the Border Patrol Police) and four assistant commissioners. The country is divided administratively into nine police regions, headed by commanders who are responsible for police functions in the 71 provinces which include over 5,000 district and subdistrict police stations. Each region has a police headquarters which is responsible for the administration, operation and training of all police forces in that region. Each regional commander is in charge of the superintendents of the Provincial Police in the provinces (from 6 to 11) of his area. Each provincial superintendent of police, in turn, supervises the operation of the district (*amphur*) police stations and substations within his province.

In 1966 the Provincial Police, with the assistance of personnel operating under the Public Safety Division of the United States Agency for International Development as part of the USOM, extended their forces to township (*tambon*) and village level as an expanded counterinsurgency measure. In that year the first 50 township police stations were constructed in the Northeast, and sites for another 200 were selected and planned for activation by mid-1967.

Pilot models of improved village security organizations were also developed and established with USOM assistance. One plan envisaged a unit of 12 to 15 men selected from the village to augment police security operations. These units function under operational control of the Provincial Police and receive their training and equipment from them. A second plan attempts to accomplish these security objectives in the same manner, but the units are staffed by members of the Volunteer Defense Corps.

A further development in the Provincial Police action to suppress mounting insurgency was the activation and training of nine special action force groups by the fall of 1966. These groups, consisting of about 50 men each, received specialized counterinsurgency training and were assigned to regional police headquarters as quick-reaction, backup forces capable of reinforcing police units in trouble areas. Twenty-nine additional groups of this type are planned for activation with assistance and support from the United States.

Border Patrol Police

Although technically under the control of the commissioner of the Provincial Police, the Border Patrol Police operate with a great deal of autonomy. They are responsible for the maintenance of law and order within the country's border areas, and the protection of the borders against smuggling, illegal entry, infiltration of subversive elements and banditry. They are also charged with the support of civic action projects and counter-insurgency programs. With a strength of about 6,800 men, they operate closely with the Provincial Police with whom they are linked administratively.

Within each Provincial Police region, as appropriate, the regional commander is assisted by a deputy for Border Patrol Police affairs, who also acts as the commander of Border Patrol Police forces in the area. The Border Patrol Police usually maintain a separate area headquarters in the region from which all operations are coordinated and conducted. The basic operating unit is the line platoon which in 1966 was reduced in strength from almost 50 to 30 men. The personnel thus saved were organized into 10 heavy weapons platoons, one of each being assigned to area headquarters as a mobile reserve strike force. In mid-1967 additional mobile reserve platoons were being planned under joint Thai-United States projects in order that increased firepower and destructive force could be applied at opportune points in counterinsurgency operations.

In addition to the mobile reserve platoons operating within each police area, the Border Patrol Police operates a special Police Aerial Reinforcement Unit. This organization, centrally located with respect to the northern and northeastern border areas, is also capable of acting as a mobile strike force in support of police operations. In wartime it would act as an airborne guerrilla force, employing special forces methods and techniques.

In support of civic action programs conducted to counter subversion, the Border Patrol Police have become the continuing government presence in many of the border areas. As of mid-1967 they operated over 150 schools in remote areas in addition to constructing many others which were turned over to other agencies. They have built small airstrips for communications and the movement of supplies, established medical aid stations and dispensed limited assistance in agricultural projects. Working among some of the ethnic minorities, they have created development centers, complete with dispensaries, trading facilities and schools.

Metropolitan Police

The Metropolitan Police are assigned the responsibility of providing all police services for the capital city of Bangkok and the contiguous area of Thon Buri. They have a strength of about 6,000 and are commanded by a commissioner with the rank of police lieutenant general. He is assisted by a deputy commissioner and three assistant commissioners, all in the grade of police major general. Organizationally, the force is divided into three areas, each of which is under a Metropolitan Police division headed by a police major general who is assisted by three police colonels as deputy commanders. These divisions are the Northern Bangkok, the Southern Bangkok and Thon Buri. Together, these divisions encompass about 40 precincts which are patrolled on a 24-hour basis.

Other elements of the Metropolitan Police are in the Traffic Police Division, the Police Fire Brigade and four subdivisions: Mobile Patrol, Police Dog, Juvenile Aid and Building Safeguard. The Traffic Police Division has the additional functions: it provides mounted escorts to protect and act as guards of honor to the King; and it serves as a riot-control force to prevent unlawful demonstrations and disperse unruly crowds.

Rank Structure

Police ranks and grades (above the grade of constable which is equivalent to patrolman) parallel those of the military. Commissioned officer ranks include police general, police lieutenant general, police major general, police brigadier general, police colonel, police lieutenant colonel, police major, police captain, police lieutenant and police sublieutenant. Noncommissioned officer grades include police sergeant major (or ensign), police sergeant, police corporal, police lance corporal and constable.

Position assignments are generally commensurate with those held by officers of comparable rank in the Army. The various divisions in the Police Department Headquarters are headed by officials varying in rank from police lieutenant general to police lieutenant colonel. The major police forces are headed by commissioners with the rank of lieutenant general. The officers in charge of police regions and of the Border Patrol Police have the title of commander. Their ranks vary from police major general to police colonel. Each province has a superintendent of police who is usually a police colonel; the district station chief is generally a police captain, and substation chiefs are lieutenants or sublieutenants.

Training and Equipment

All police training is supervised by the Education Bureau of the Thai National Police Department. The training program is comprehensive, and the impact of United States advice and assistance has been great in expanding and improving facilities, methods and techniques. The installations involved in the training program include: the National Police Academy at Sam Phran, some 15 miles west of Bangkok; the Detective Training School in Bangkok; the Metropolitan Police Training School at Bang Khen, about 10 miles north of Bangkok; and the Noncommissioned Officer Training School also at Bang Khen. There are also four Provincial Police Training Schools, one each at Nakhon Pathom (about 30 miles northwest of Bangkok), Lampang (in the North), Nakhon Ratchasima (in the Northeast) and Yala (in the southern part of the Peninsula).

The growth of insurgency spurred the adoption of intensive counterinsurgency training to augment the conventional police training carried on at established institutions. In early 1965 the Border Patrol Police established a new training center at Phitsanulok, about 200 miles north of Bangkok, principally to retrain their line platoons in modern countersubversive techniques and in the conduct of counterinsurgency operations in jungle areas. The recently organized mobile reserve platoons also received training in newly acquired United States armament, including crew-served weapons. Similarly, the Provincial Police opened "Chaiya" (Victory) centers in well-dispersed areas—at Chiengmai, Udon, Nakhon Ratchasima and Pattani—to familiarize and train their personnel in modern counterguerrilla concepts. In mid-1967 all Provincial Police recruits were sent to the training center either at Udon or Chiengmai and required to complete successfully the counterinsurgency course before their permanent assignment to a police unit.

The Metropolitan Police have also improved and modernized their training in recent years. Their technical police work has improved and they have received additional modern equipment and assistance. In particular, their crowd-control effectiveness has markedly improved as have their communications control and overall mobility.

Equipment supplied by the United States has enabled the National Police Department to improve its capabilities in all phases of law enforcement and internal security. This equipment has included quantities of light infantry weapons, small arms, ammunition, technical devices, radios, vehicles and helicopters. Also considerable quantities of civic action commodities have been furnished, such as drugs, livestock, agricultural tools and school materials.

The National Police Department is affiliated with several international organizations and sends representatives to their periodic meetings. The Department is an active participant in the International Criminal Police Organization (Interpol) and exchanges information on the movement of criminals and contraband in international channels. The commissioner of the Metropolitan Police usually represents the Department at conferences of the International Association of Police Chiefs.

CRIMINAL LAW AND PROCEDURES

Legal Development

Ancient Siamese law was based on the Hindu Code of Manu, introduced in the Ayutthaya period (1350–1767). Over the centuries this code was augmented by numerous and sometimes conflicting royal laws and decrees. Moreover, different judges often interpreted and applied the same law differently. This resulting tangle of legal concept and arbitrary judicial decision came under strong criticism by the Western powers, whose nationals were settling in the country during the nineteeth century. Objecting to the complexities, cruel punishment, delays and injustices of the legal system, each Western state insisted that its nationals and others under its protection in Siam be subject only to the jurisdiction of its own extraterritorial courts. By the middle of the nineteenth century the system of extraterritoriality was firmly established and had further complicated the already confused legal structure.

Concerned by the limitations of the country's sovereignty and encouraged by treaty promises that extraterritoriality would be ended when the laws and judiciary were modernized, Siam's rulers set about making legal reforms. While earlier kings had attempted to codify existing law and to eliminate many of the most cruel punishments, King Mongkut (1851–68) upon his accession went further. He proclaimed the equality of all before the law, tried to improve standards of judicial honesty and competence and attempted to abolish the delays and conflicting rules which had become so much a part of the judicial administration (see ch. 3, Historical Setting).

In the reign of King Chulalongkorn (1868–1910) legal reform took a new direction. Previously the kings had tried to revise and adapt ancient Siamese law to meet modern needs. King Chulalongkorn believed that the problem would be solved not by revising the old system but by replacing it. His first important step was the creation of a Ministry of Justice in 1892, with powers extending to all the courts in the land. The Ministry, under Prince Rabi of Rat Buri, began reforming the system.

The first task was to create a modern, uniform system of courts. Up to that time, the head of each department of government had under his authority a court or courts to adjudicate the disputes of persons under his jurisdiction. Outside the capital, governors of circles (administrative regions composed of a number of provinces) and provinces had their own courts. In addition, the Court of Brahmins in Bangkok had jurisdiction over certain civil and criminal violations. Finally, there were the extraterritorial courts created by treaty to deal with cases involving foreign nationals or persons under foreign protection.

The process of dismantling this disorderly system and replacing it with a unified hierarchy of Siamese courts took place over the decade and a half ending in 1920. Most of the foreign courts operating under extraterritoriality treaties had been withdrawn by 1909, but an international court with European jurists sat in Bangkok until 1937.

During this period major innovations were made in the law. Under Prince Rabi's direction the existing statutory and customary laws were collected and codified, and by 1910 an enormous volume of new legislation had been enacted. In 1897 a commission, composed almost entirely of French and Belgian lawyers, was appointed to draw up a penal code. The commission, which worked continuously until 1924, completed the penal code and went on to draft a civil code, a commercial code, codes of civil and criminal procedure and a law of judicial organization. Together they constitute the substance of modern Thai law. They are predominantly Western in character with a remnant of indigenous Thai concept.

The establishment of a constitutional monarchy following the coup of 1932 brought about fairly extensive law reforms which were promulgated in a revised Criminal and Civil Procedures Code in 1935. These Codes were based fundamentally upon past experiences and Western practices which provide substantial safeguards in the administration of justice. Upon completion of these reforms in accordance with concepts of Western jurisprudence, the system of extraterritoriality was completely eliminated by 1938.

Penal Code

The first comprehensive penal code, promulgated in 1908 and amended four times, was superseded by the Criminal Code of 1956, which, however, preserves the main features of the earlier one. Like its predecessor, the new code incorporates features taken from French, Italian, Japanese, English and Indian sources but retains a trace of traditional Thai elements.

The explicitness and detail of its provisions suggest that its drafters were conscious of composing for judges, many of whom would have only a superficial acquaintance with the Western legal concepts which predominate in the document. For example, the Code begins by defining numerous terms, such as "fraudulent," "assault" and "official document." Instructions follow for the application of criminal law, and included are explanations regarding penalties, criminal liability, principals and accessories and judgments. The Code also specifies the actions to be taken in the case of repeated offenses and of offenses involving violations of several provisions of the law.

Twelve types of felonies are listed. Crimes against the security of the Kingdom include offenses against the King, the Queen, the Heir to the Throne and the Regent, as well as offenses against the internal and external security of the state and offenses damaging to friendly relations with foreign states. Crimes relating to public administration include offenses against officials and malfeasance in office. Crimes relating to justice, such as perjury and offenses against the police and members of the judiciary, constitute another category.

Other felonies include: crimes against religion; crimes against public peace and security; crimes relating to false money and the counterfeiting of seals, stamps and documents; crimes against trade, including the use of false weights and measures and the misrepresentation of goods; sexual offenses; crimes against the person; crimes against liberty and reputation, such as false imprisonment, kidnaping and libel; crimes against property; and such offenses as misappropriation and the receipt of stolen property. Misdemeanors include an assortment of petty offenses which are subject to occasional redefinition by the authorities. Misdemeanors are officially defined as offenses punishable by imprisonment for not more than 1 month or a fine not exceeding the equivalent of $50 or both.

Five penalties are recognized by the code: death, imprisonment, detention (restricted residence), fines and forfeiture of property to the state. Execution is by firing squad. The death sentence is mandatory for: murder or attempted murder of the King, the Queen, the Heir to the Throne or the Regent; offenses likely to endanger the life of the King; murder of a public official or of anyone assisting a public official while in the performance of his duty; murder of parents or grandparents; murder committed in perpetrating another offense; murder committed to escape punishment; premeditated murder; and murder accompanied by torture. Other murders are also punishable by death or by imprisonment. A sentence to life imprisonment normally expires in 20 years, which is the maximum prison term.

The Code provides that children under 8 years of age are not subject to criminal penalties; juvenile offenders between the ages of 7 and 15 are not subject to fine or imprisonment but may be restricted to their homes, placed on probation or sent to a vocational training school. The court may admonish the delinquent and release him, or the parents may be called before the court and given a warning. Parents may also be required to show that they have taken measures to ensure against the commission of another offense by the child for a period of as much as 3 years and to pay a sum not exceeding the equivalent of $50 in compensation for damages caused by the child within this period. If the offender has no parents or guardian, the court may appoint a guardian or place the child in an institution.

For offenses committed by minors over 14 but not over 17 years of age, the court may impose penalties in the form of fines or confinement which are half of those prescribed for adults committing the same crimes. If the court decided that punishment is unnecessary, it may proceed as it would for children between 7 and 15 years of age.

Criminal Courts

Criminal cases or points of criminal law come before three types of courts: the various courts of the first instance in the provinces; the Court of Appeals (Uthorn Court), in Bangkok; and the Supreme Court (Dika Court), also in Bangkok. Locally, district administrative officers are authorized to impose fines on petty offenders. The country is divided into nine judicial regions, each under the control of a chief justice of the region who has both judicial and administrative functions. He may sit as a judge in any of his regional courts, and in emergencies he may temporarily transfer a judge from one court to another in his region. The courts of first instance include the district and provincial courts, the Bangkok Criminal Court and the juvenile courts (see ch. 14, The Governmental System).

District or magistrates courts, with jurisdiction comparable to that of justice of the peace courts in the United States, have been established in the larger provinces to relieve the provincial courts of the burden of judging minor criminal cases. Three of these courts have also been created in Bangkok, one in the northern part of the city, one in the south and one in Thon Buri. The decisions of the district courts, of which there are 20 in the whole country, may be appealed to the Court of Appeals.

The 83 provincial courts exercise unlimited criminal jurisdiction within their respective provinces. In general they are comparable to the United States superior courts. Their decisions may be appealed to the Court of Appeals.

The Bangkok Criminal Court has unlimited jurisdiction over all major offenses committed in the Bangkok-Thon Buri metropolitan area. At the request of the minister of justice, the president of the Supreme Court may direct that any case of grave national importance be referred to the Bangkok Criminal Court for trial.

The Central Juvenile Court in Bangkok has jurisdiction over all offenses committed in Bangkok and Thon Buri by persons under 18 years of age. In 1962 an additional juvenile court was established at Songkhla in the South, and in 1964 a third started functioning at Nakhon Ratchasima in the Northeast. Both the Court of Appeal and the Supreme Court have sections dealing exclusively with juvenile cases referred to them.

The independence of the judiciary is prescribed by the Interim Constitution of 1959, but there are many inhibiting factors. Actually, the executive branch may establish or abolish courts on the recommendation of the Minister of Justice. Moreover, the Judicial Service Commission, appointed by the King upon recommendations of the Minister of Justice, is charged with recruiting appointing, transferring or removing judges. Also, judges' salaries are included in the budget of the Minister of Justice which is voted annually by the National Assembly (see ch. 14, The Governmental System).

Judges are recruited through competitive examinations held annually. Successful candidates are placed on a probationary status and receive judicial training for 1 year, after which they are eligible for appointment to full judgeships. There is a progressive system of promotion until retirement at age 60. Judges' salaries compare favorably with those of civil servants charged with comparable responsibilities. They are not regarded as civil servants, however, and are not subject to civil service controls.

Thailand does not employ the jury system. Court trials are heard by one or more judges, the number depending on the gravity of the charge. Subject to juridical regulations, which are established by the Supreme Court, trial procedure is left to the discretion of the presiding judges.

Procedures

Responsibility for the administration of criminal law is divided between the Ministry of Justice and the Ministry of the Interior. The National Police Department in the Ministry of the Interior is charged with the detection and investigation of crimes, with the collection of evidence and with bringing the accused before the court. The Public Prosecution Department, representing the state in criminal proceedings, is responsible for conducting prosecutions. The Ministry of Justice supervises the operation of the courts.

The Public Prosecution Department, directly under the Ministry of the Interior, works closely with the National Police Department. Since the Prosecution Department has no investigative staff of its own, it must rely on the police to document cases, which makes it dependent on the Police Department in its work.

The first step in a criminal case is the investigation, which is carried out by a police officer. Searches of the houses or persons of the suspect and others thought to be implicated with him may be made. Warrants for search or arrest can be issued by a court, by certain officials of the Ministry of the Interior, or by a senior police officer. The law specifies that search warrants must state the reason for the search, the identity of the place or person to be searched, the name and official position of the officer making the search and the nature of the offense charged.

Similar procedures generally apply for arrest warrants, but a senior police official may make an arrest without a warrant when a criminal offense of a serious nature has been committed, when the person arrested is taken in the act of committing a crime or attempting to do so or when a person is found in possession of a weapon or instrument commonly used for criminal purposes. Private citizens may arrest, without a warrant, anyone caught in the act of committing a serious crime.

An arrested person must be taken promptly to a police station, where the arrest warrant is read and explained to him. He may then be held or released on bail. The provisions for bail and security are defined by law.

Investigation following arrest may not begin until the complainant—either the authorities or a private complainant—has submitted and signed a full bill of particulars. At the beginning of the investigation, the accused must be warned that any statement he makes may be used against him in court. Threats, promises or coercion may not be used by the investigator to induce the accused to make self-incriminating statements.

When the investigation is completed, it is given to the public prosecutor who prepares an indictment which is given to the accused or his counsel. The accused is then brought into court and asked how he pleads. The decision as to acceptance of the case for trial lies with the judge.

Trials are normally held in open court, and the accused is presumed to be innocent until proved guilty. At the beginning of proceedings the accused is asked if he has counsel; if he wishes counsel, the court will appoint a defense attorney. During the trial the accused or his counsel may cross-examine prosecution witnesses and reexamine his defense witnesses. He also may refuse to answer questions or to give evidence that may incriminate himself. Judgment must be read to the accused in open court within 3 days after the end of argument. The presiding judge, after announcing the sentence, frequently cancels half of it if the accused has confessed to his crimes. If the convicted person wishes to appeal, he must do so within 15 days of the original decision, the appeal being made by petition. If the appeal is made against sentence, the Court of Appeals may reverse or reduce but cannot increase the sentence of the trial courts. Judgments must be carried out immediately.

Thai attitudes toward the criminal code and its applications by the courts are not clear. The vast majority of the people know little about the legal code or court procedures. For most of them, constitutional rights remain shadowy abstractions insofar as they are conscious of them at all, and questions of constitutional rights have concerned no more than an educated minority (see ch. 14, The Governmental System).

CRIME RATES

Published crime statistics are virtually nonexistent because the National Police Department, which is responsible for computing annual crime rates and indexes in each province, does not release its findings. The Ministry of Justice, however, has published some statistics indicating the increase of convictions in the courts of first instance and the nature of the crimes committed.

The major classes of offenses are: offenses against public administration; offenses against public justice (obstructing police, etc.); riot (general violence); offenses against morality; libel and slander; murder and assault; theft and armed robbery; petty crimes; and contraventions and violations (gambling, narcotics, tax evasion, etc.). In 1958 a total of 109,941 persons were convicted of these offenses, and some 22,000 were committed to prison. In 1963 convictions had risen to 185,316, and sentences of imprisonment to over 36,000. In May 1964 the latest published figures available relating to prison population showed that the total of imprisonments had reached almost 33,000 during the first 5 months of the year.

Regarded as the most serious crimes are offenses against the royal family or against the state (particularly those directly affecting national security), assassination of a public official or any murder involving cruelty or torture. The most common offenses, after violations of the antigambling laws, are theft and contraventions of the narcotics and excise laws. In general, organized crime is relatively rare, except for the illicit trade in opium which persists in spite of the progress of police reforms. In Bangkok and some of the larger towns the activity of gangs, mostly of youths, seems to be giving the authorities increasing concern. Increased insurgency has also given rise to offenses against the state and those involving general violence.

The highest incidence of crime appears to be in the group under 25 years of age. Of the total number of persons committed to prison in 1958, about 42 percent were under 25, and 11 percent were under 20. The lower incidence of crime in the latter group may be attributed in part to the fact that it includes youths of 18 to 20, many of whom are called to military service. Comparable percentages for 1964 were very similar, 32 and 12 percent, respectively. Most of these young offenders were said to be from the tenement districts of Bangkok and included a high proportion classed as hooligans.

THE PENAL SYSTEM

The penal system is administered by the Department of Corrections within the Ministry of the Interior. The government's announced policy in operating the system is to use prisons as a means of reducing crime by correcting the criminal's behavior and rehabilitating him as a useful member of society.

There are a total of 46 special institutions devoted exclusively to the confinement of prisoners: 7 central and 5 regional prisons; 23 prison camps; 7 correctional institutions; 1 detention home; and 3 reformatories. In addition, 84 provincial and district police stations are used as prisons for short-term offenders (up to 1 year), as well as temporary places of confinement; 71 are used additionally as temporary reformatories. The 45 Metropolitan Police stations in Bangkok and Thon Buri are also considered part of the penal system and are utilized as places of temporary confinement. The law provides that first offenders be segregated from habitual ones, and that prisoners also be confined, to the extent practicable, in separate groups according to the types of offense committed.

The seven central and five regional prisons house the bulk of prisoners with relatively long-term sentences, and plans are underway to improve their facilities and expand the capacities of five of them. Klong Pream, one of the oldest and largest, is scheduled to be rebuilt in the northern outskirts of the city of Bangkok and is designed, when completed in 1968, to have a capacity of over 6,000 inmates. One of the 23 prison camps not yet fully completed is at Pulao Terutao, the site of a former maximum security prison on an island in the Strait of Malacca near the Malaysian border.

All other prison camps are integral parts of the main prisons with which they are collocated. The size of the prison camps vary, as do the number of inmates which can be accommodated. The average inmate population of a camp is about 50 selected good conduct prisoners who engage principally in agricultural pursuits to prepare them for productive lives after release.

Among the seven correctional institutions, one at Ayutthaya

and one in Bangkok deal primarily with youthful offenders of 18 to 25 years of age with terms of 1 to 5 years. The Women's Correctional Institution is also located in Bangkok. The Medical Correctional Institution for drug addicts and other prisoners requiring medical supervision is located in Pathum Thani Province, to the northwest of Bangkok. Two minimum security institutions for short-term good conduct prisoners are maintained in the provinces of Rayong (75 miles southeast of Bangkok) and Phitsanulok (about 200 miles north of the capital). The maximum security institution for habitual criminals is operated in Nakhon Pathom, about 40 miles west of the capital.

Aside from the metropolitan, provincial and district police stations, there is only one principal detention home situated in Pathum Thani Province. Its inmates consist of persons with confinement terms of less than 3 months and those confined in lieu of payment of fines.

Of the three reformatories, the Ban Lat Yao (sometimes called Lardyao) facility, about 15 miles north of Bangkok, apparently receives the bulk of the more recalcitrant juvenile delinquents. Its capacity is about 2,000, and extensive programs are undertaken to rehabilitate offenders sent there. Those not rehabilitated are usually sent to the reformatory in Rayong Province which is operated on the prison farm principle. A third reformatory exists in Prachuap Khiri Khan Province, about 125 miles southwest of Bangkok, but it is used only to accommodate the overflow from the other two institutions.

Special facilities for juvenile offenders, called observation and protection centers and administered by the Central Juvenile Court and the Central Observation and Protection Center, under the Ministry of Justice, were instituted when juvenile courts were authorized in 1952 (see ch. 9, Living Conditions). Three of these centers now operate in Bangkok, Songkhla in the South and at Nakhon Ratchasima in the Northeast.

A center is attached to each juvenile court and assists it in caring for and supervising delinquent children charged with criminal offenses, both before and after trial. Probation officers, social workers, physicians, psychiatrists and teachers are assigned to the center. They help the court by collecting information on the background and home environment of youthful offenders, arranging for their release from police stations and taking them into custody until their cases are heard in court. They also accompany the children into court, supervise those placed on probation, arrange for their medical examinations and report to the court on their mental and physical conditions.

Health conditions in the prisons have gradually improved, but more hospital facilities are needed. In mid-1967 only three prison hospitals of 120-bed capacity each were operating, two in the Bangkok area, and one at Pathum Thani, some 25 miles to the north.

Since most of the prisoners are relatively uneducated, extensive special instruction classes are operated within prisons. On the average, over 20,000 illiterate prisoners are enrolled per year. Of this number, about half become reasonably literate. Prisoners are graded or classified as to conduct into six classes: excellent, very good, good, fair, bad and very bad. Those in the first three categories are considered "parole eligible" and are released on parole when they have completed two-thirds, three-fourths and four-fifths, respectively, of their terms.

Vocational training and workshops have been established in most of the prisons. Products from prison labor are sold, and 35 percent of the net profit is returned to the prisoners. A small portion, credited outright to the individual prisoner, may be spent during his time of imprisonment. A larger part is set aside so as to constitute a savings fund which is given to the prisoner upon his release.

SMUGGLING AND BLACK-MARKETING

Smuggling and black-marketing deprive the government of needed revenue, and the cost of controlling these activities is a considerable loss to the national economy. The principal clandestine trade is in opium, heroin and other narcotics. Thailand itself is a source of some opium, but much larger quantities are produced in nearby Yunnan Province of South China and in the hills and mountains of Burma and Laos across the Thai frontier.

Thai authorities are greatly concerned about the sale and use of narcotics (especially opium and heroin) in the country. Periodic drives against the traffic are undertaken, and the press has frequently reported the arrest of opium dealers and the seizure of their supplies. Most of the opium is seized in transit from northern Thailand whence it is carried by foot, motor vehicle, railway or airplane to Bangkok. At Bangkok some of the drug is sold to local dealers, but most of it is shipped to foreign ports, mainly to Hong Kong and Singapore. The trade is carried on by both small- and large-scale operators.

With the rise in insurgency, the smuggling of guns has increased sharply, and a sizable amount of "opium-for-guns" trade has been reported by the press.

The smuggling of other items is generally limited to small-scale operations by persons seeking quick profits in spite of the risk of fines and confiscation. The trade, some of which is into and some out of the country, involves a few food products and various items of consumer goods. Rice reportedly is smuggled out through Chiang Rai Province into Laos and Burma and into Yunnan Province in South China. Gem stones, mainly from Burma, are traded clandestinely in Bangkok. Thai customs officials occasionally arrest agents attempting to smuggle in wrist watches and platinum jewelry from Hong Kong. Some illicit gold traffic is carried on between Thailand and Laos. Other items of interest to smugglers include transistor radios; alcoholic beverages, particularly whiskey; and miscellaneous drugs, such as antibiotics.

CHAPTER 28

THE ARMED FORCES

The country's military establishment consists of the Royal Thai Army, the Royal Thai Air Force and the Royal Thai Navy, of which the Royal Thai Marine Corps is a component. By mid-1967 the estimated strength for all the armed forces approximated 130,000, about 0.38 percent of the total population. The Army numbered about 88,000 men, and the remainder was about equally divided between the Air Force and the Navy. All components had been provided with equipment supplied by the United States and were trained in accordance with American military concepts.

In addition to the regular military establishment, the Royal Thai National Police, also provided with United States technical assistance and equipment, served under the Ministry of the Interior and was charged with supporting the armed forces in any national emergency.

BACKGROUND

For a people regarded by themselves and others as generally peaceable, the Thai have had much experience in warfare. From early times, with few exceptions, the country's kings were military leaders, and the history of their reigns is replete with accounts of armed conflict. The Thai people, in contrast to their kings and nobles, had no initiative in the choice between peace and war, and there is no reason to believe that many of them were interested in taking up arms except to safeguard personal or community property or to ward off the threat of enslavement by an invading force.

In spite of their long history of warfare, no military cult or warrior class developed. Between wars the peasants went back to the land, and the few retainers and mercenaries who made up the permanent military establishment enjoyed no special privileges or prestige and exercised no particular influence in national life. The few military leaders with recognizable ability were usually members of the royal family or favorites with an aptitude for military organization and command. Their authority and tenure, however, were subject to the king's pleasure.

During the fifteenth and sixteenth centuries the Thai learned much from their campaigns against the Khmers (Cambodians) and the Burmese. The 17-year old King Trailok, who had ascended the throne in 1448, was greatly influenced by the captured Khmer leaders who had been brought back to Thailand. Following the Khmer example, he established civil and administrative areas in his kingdom and increased the proficiency of his army. His successor, King Rama Thibodi II (1491–1529), further developed the Thai military capability by devising a treatise on military warfare and by reorganizing the whole military system on the basis of compulsory service.

The Portuguese introduced firearms into Thailand in the early part of the fifteenth century and taught the Thai the arts of guncasting and fortifications. Portuguese were also employed by the king as bodyguards and served as instructors in musketry.

The Thai-Burmese struggle continued into the seventeenth century, and King Naresuan (1590–1605) contributed greatly to the emerging Thai military traditions. In 1593 he killed a Burmese crown prince in a mounted elephant duel and later died valiantly in battle against Burmese forces. His exploits are recounted in school texts as part of the nation's heritage of courage and valor. The Burmese were finally driven from Thai territory in 1769 by Taksin, a strong national leader who reunited the country, established the capital at Bangkok and set the stage for the development of the present Chakri dynasty of kings.

Thailand's history has been an almost constant struggle to maintain freedom and national identity, and emphasis has been placed on teaching it as a basis for developing patriotism and a strong national spirit. This historical emphasis, coupled with the time-honored value of respect for authority, taught from early childhool, inculcates in Thai youths those basic social attitudes which enable them to accept military life and become well-disciplined members of the armed forces. In addition, their high regard for the king is a binding force which tends to increase their loyalty to the nation, despite their slight concern for political affairs (see ch. 7, Social Structure; ch. 8, Family).

DEVELOPMENT OF MODERN FORCES

Although Thailand's relations with the Western world began in the fifteenth century, the first steps toward the development of modern fighting forces did not take place until the mid-nineteenth century under King Mongkut (Rama IV, 1851–68). Under his rule, and that of his son, King Chulalongkorn (Rama V, 1868–1910), the Thai were particularly receptive to Western ideas and methods. Military and naval cadet schools were established; foreign advisers in limited numbers were imported; and the reorganization of the Army along European lines was begun. In 1894 the Ministry of Defense was formed, and this gave the military, for the first time, a recognized position in the governmental hierarchy.

These developments laid the groundwork for the creation of a professional military officer class and for the establishment of a permanent and relatively modern military organization. The king maintained complete control, and the princes and other high-ranking members of the royal family continued to hold key positions. The crown prince in 1905 was by law commander in chief of the Army. In 1912 King Vajiravudh (Rama VI, 1910–25) headed the National Defense Council, composed of military and civilian officials. At this same time antimonarchical sentiment found its first clandestine expression in a small group of Army and Navy officers who resented Vajiravudh's policy of favoring palace guard-type units. Powerful princes of the time also indicated their displeasure at the King's practice of appointing commoners to high government posts, including military (see ch. 15, Political Dynamics).

In succeeding years the throne gave increasing attention to building a modern military force and soon began to use it to further the country's international interests. In World War I Thailand joined the Allied Powers and sent a small contingent of soldiers to France. The nation's demonstrated ability to develop its military arm by its own initiative and leadership, with its own resources and with limited foreign assistance, was effectively employed in the early 1920's as an argument in obtaining favorable revision of certain treaties (see ch. 3, Historical Setting).

In World War II, when invaded by the Japanese in December 1941, Thailand's policy of favoring the Axis Powers led first to a cease-fire after a short military engagement and then to an alliance with the Japanese. Very shortly thereafter, however, an extensive anti-Japanese underground was established which served the Allies' cause throughout the war. This action was an effective and important element in the emergence of postwar Thailand as a "liberated" rather than as a "defeated" country (see ch. 16, Foreign Relations).

Immediately after the war the military establishment was involved in periods of political instability, and little was done to improve its professional quality. In 1950 the Thai entered into various assistance agreements with the United States, including a Military Assistance Program (MAP). Under this arrangement a comprehensive postwar modernization program was initiated based on United States advice, materiel assistance and training. By mid-1967 the measures taken under MAP had transformed the Thai military into a force with greatly improved capabilities for national defense and internal security.

COUNTERINSURGENCY

The Thai Government's overall commitment to the containment of communism in Southeast Asia and the increased scope of externally directed Communist subversion in its border areas during the mid-1960's led the armed forces to stress the improvement of the country's counterinsurgency capabilities. The Army became increasingly more involved in supporting the counter-subversion efforts of the police and in furnishing military personnel for civic action work. Special United States support, particularly helicopters and communications equipment, was made available to increase the effectiveness of combined civil-military-police units operating to neutralize dissident elements in isolated frontier areas. The Army also participated in the development and employment of Mobile Development Units and in the carrying out of the Accelerated Rural Development Program.

Both the Mobile Development Units and the units of the Accelerated Rural Development Program were conceived as part of the national socioeconomic program to eliminate popular discontent and potential subversion by the improvement of conditions at the village level in the less developed provinces. The Mobile Development Units, as organized in mid-1967, were generally under military leadership and were composed of doctors, engineers, agronomists, social workers and minor officials who spent approximately 6 months in vulnerable areas working with villagers, identifying their needs and giving them the guidance, assistance and tools necessary to accomplish needed projects.

The units of the Accelerated Rural Development Program followed up on the work of the Mobile Development Units and laid the groundwork for longer term projects, such as the building of roads and the opening of markets for local products. A secondary objective of the Accelerated Rural Development Program was to decentralize governmental authority into the hands of local administrators and to preserve and expand community improvements. In late 1965 the government established in Bangkok the Counter Subversion Operations Command to coordinate the efforts of all national agencies engaged in counterinsurgency operations, particularly in the Northeast. In mid-1967 the military operations against guerrilla bands and terrorists had begun to show progress in improving the security and stability of threatened areas, and the civil aid programs were judged to be effective in reducing voluntary support for the active insurgent elements.

POSITION OF THE MILITARY IN GOVERNMENT

The acceptance of, and adaptation to, Western influences by the rulers of Thailand at the outset of the twentieth century affected the role of the military. By the 1930's many officers had attended European military schools where they learned not only new military techniques but also new social and political patterns and concepts. Similarly, considerable numbers of civilians had studied abroad during the same period and were concerning themselves with the problem of liberalizing the governmental system. They found the support they needed among some of the military leaders and, through the coup d'etat of June 1932, brought about the transformation of the absolute monarchy into a constitutional institution. The military leaders, who had played a secondary but essential role in the coup, were soon at odds with the new Prime Minister, Phraya Manopakon. Many feared that his ultraconservative policies would lead to reestablishment of the absolute monarchy. In June 1933 a group of Army officers, supported by a few civilian officials, seized power in a second coup (see ch. 3, Historical Setting; ch. 15, Political Dynamics).

Within a year the country had experienced two coups, one made possible by support of the armed forces, the other led by military officers. The pattern established by these events persisted, with coups taking place in November 1947, November 1951, September 1957 and the latest one in October 1958. All were carried out by military leaders assisted by the armed forces. Except for a brief period near the end of World War II and shortly thereafter, the military, particularly the Army, has exercised a dominant influence on the nation's political and economic affairs.

The decision of the Thai Government, under Field Marshal Phibun Songkhram, to ally itself with Japan in World War II foreshadowed a decline in the influence of the military, which began when Phibun, unacceptable to the Allies and mistrusted by the Japanese, was voted out of office by the Assembly in 1944. In 1945, with the fall of Japan, military influence was further diminished, and this trend continued through 1946 under Prime Minister Pridi Phanomyong, who had been a prominent liberal leader in the coup of 1932. In 1947, however, military leaders again seized power and have since retained it.

Shifts of power since 1947 have been caused by rivalry between military leaders. A feature of this contest has been that the achievement of high political office by an officer tended to weaken his personal connections and his influence within the military establishment. Phibun, who held office as prime minister from April 1948 to September 1957, was overthrown by a military group headed by Field Marshal Sarit Thanarat, who since 1944 had commanded Army troops in Bangkok where he was in an excellent position to control political activities among the military. After his death in December 1963, Sarit was succeeded by his deputy, Field Marshal Thanom Kittikachorn, who has continued the military regime.

Military leaders, when in power, have exercised their authority in the name of the king, and while some of them have suspended, modified or redrafted the Constitution, they have not formally challenged the constitutional principle. They have shown little disposition to alter drastically the basic political and economic order and, with modifications, they have tended to work through existing governmental institutions. Civilian career officials appear to have accepted without resentment the dominance of military men in the major executive positions of control.

In 1967 the two most powerful men in the Thai Government were Field Marshal Thanom Kittikachorn and General Praphat Charusathien. In addition to occupying the principal political post of prime minister, Marshal Thanom also held the position of supreme commander of the armed forces and minister of defense. General Praphat, while serving as deputy prime minister, concurrently held the positions of deputy supreme commander of the armed forces, commander in chief of the Royal Thai Army and minister of the interior. The Ministry of the Interior exercised the extremely important police functions and appointed and supervised local government officials.

MISSION

The armed forces, together with the National Police Department, have the threefold mission of maintaining internal security, guarding the life and property of the citizens and defending the country against external aggression. The most urgent of these missions has become the defense of the country against Communist-led insurgency, an incipient condition which has gradually intensified since the early 1960's. Thailand has also assumed limited military obligations as a result of membership in the Southeast Asia Treaty Organization (SEATO) and the United Nations.

The Army, oldest and largest component of the armed forces, is responsible primarily for planning and directing military operations to oppose any threat to the national security. It is also charged with training and equipping the ground forces in accordance with these plans. The Navy's mission of protecting the seaward approaches to the country would be carried out in cooperation with SEATO forces. An additional naval function is to assist in the suppression of subversive activity in the maintenance of internal security. The Air Force, newest of the three services, is charged primarily with giving maximum tactical air support to the ground and naval forces and to counterinsurgency units, including movement of personnel and equipment. Secondary missions include the coordination of civil and military aviation activities and the establishment of technical training courses for civil aviation specialists.

In peacetime all components of the National Police Department —except the Metropolitan Police, whose jurisdiction does not extend outside of the Bangkok-Thon Buri area—are responsible for maintaining the internal security of the country and for protecting its borders. The rise of Communist-sponsored subversion in border areas has resulted, since late 1965, in the involvement of armed forces and other agencies' resources in support of police efforts (see ch. 27, Public Order and Safety).

ORGANIZATION

High Command

Although the king is constitutionally the commander in chief of the armed forces, he actually has little direct military authority. Functional control of the armed forces until 1957 was exercised by the prime minister through the minister of defense. When Field Marshal Sarit came to power, he assumed direct control of the military establishment, and his authority was formalized in April 1960 by a royal decree designating him as supreme commander of the armed forces.

After Marshal Sarit's death in December 1963 his deputy, Field Marshal Thanom Kittikachorn, assumed this title and in mid-1967 exercised full authority of the office. Marshal Thanom is advised by the Council of Ministers (Cabinet) and the National Security Council (see fig. 15). He is assisted by a deputy supreme commander and an assistant supreme commander. Under the provisions of a draft of a new constitution which in 1967, was being considered for early approval and adoption, the king is reaffirmed as "head of the Thai Armed Forces," but other provisions in this document appear, in effect, to place actual control in the hands of the prime minister.

The National Security Council advises the prime minister on subjects that pertain to national security and that require Cabinet approval or action. The Council consists of the prime min-

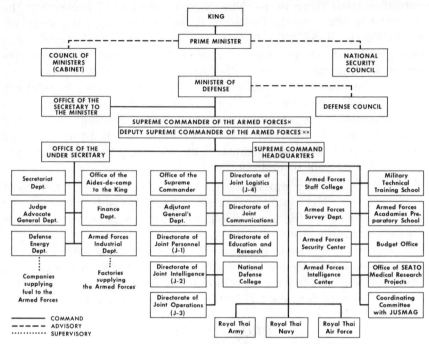

Figure 15.—High Command of the Royal Thai Armed Forces, 1967.

ister as chairman, the deputy prime minister as deputy chairman, the secretary general of the National Security Council, the ministers of defense, foreign affairs, the interior, communications and finance, and the supreme commander of the armed forces. In mid-1967 the prime minister (concurrently minister of defense and supreme commander of the armed forces) and the deputy prime minister (concurrently minister of the interior) dominated the Council.

The Ministry of Defense is charged with supervising the operation and administration of the Army, Navy and Air Force. It also coordinates policies and procedures for the armed forces and other governmental agencies concerned with the nation's security.

The Defense Council within the Ministry advises the minister of defense on military matters, particularly those pertaining to draft laws, budget allocations and the mobilization, training and deployment of the armed forces. The Council is composed of the minister of defense as chairman, the undersecretary and the deputy undersecretary of defense, the supreme commander of the armed forces and his deputy and assistant, the chief of staff of the Supreme Command, the commanders in chief and the deputy commanders in chief of the three military services, the chiefs of staff of the three military services, and not more than three additional general officers selected by the minister of defense for their outstanding ability.

The Ministry of Defense is organized into an Office of the Secretary to the Minister, the Office of the Undersecretary and the Supreme Command Headquarters. The Office of the Secretary to the Minister is concerned primarily with political affairs and with the preparation of matters to be considered by the Council of Ministers. The Office of the Undersecretary is responsible for functions not allocated to other offices in the Ministry.

The Supreme Command Headquarters, the most important in the military command structure, is responsible for maintaining the armed forces in a state of combat readiness. The Headquarters—under the supreme commander of the armed forces, assisted by the deputy and the assistant supreme commanders and by the chief of staff of the supreme command—is provided with administrative and general staff sections for exercising command over the three military services. The Headquarters also supervises the operation of certain special activities, projects and schools.

Each of the three armed services is headed by a commander in cheif who is responsible directly to the supreme commander of the armed forces. The functions of the commanders in chief are similar to those of their counterparts in the United States armed forces: army chief of staff, chief of naval operations and air force chief of staff. While the three military services are equal under existing laws, the Army, in fact, is the dominant component, and key positions both in the armed forces structure and other parts of the government are held by senior Army officers.

Field Command

The Royal Thai Army

The commander in chief of the Army is charged with carrying out the directives and missions issued to him by the minister of defense. He is assisted by a deputy commander in chief, two assistant commanders in chief, a chief of staff and a deputy chief of staff. The Army Headquarters is formed into five general sections: General Staff, Special Staff, Technical Staff, Training Staff and Area Commands and Combat Forces (see fig. 16). The functions and procedures of the General, Special and Technical Staffs are, in general, similar to those employed by the United States Army.

The Training Staff is concerned with the overall educational and training activities of the Army and the Army reserve personnel. It is composed of four groups: the Army Field Forces, comparable to the United States Army's Continental Army Command; the Army War College; the Command and General Staff College; and the Chulachomklao Royal Military Academy.

In addition to these groups, there is the Territorial Defense Department of the Ministry of Defense which plans and supervises the training of reserve personnel. Since organized reserve units are lacking, this Department is concerned chiefly with organizing and supervising the military training courses in schools and universities.

The Army is organized into regional Army area commands for tactical and administrative purposes. Each Army area is divided into military circles which are subdivided into military districts and provinces in which the tactical and service units of the combat forces are stationed. The chain of command proceeds from basic unit upward through military district and military circle headquarters to the Army area command headquarters to the commander in chief of the Army.

The Royal Thai Navy

The commander in chief of the Royal Thai Navy is assisted by the deputy commander in chief and the chief of the naval general staff. The highly centralized Naval Headquarters is divided into five groups: General Staff, Special Staff Logistics Service, Education and Naval Operations (see fig. 16). The functions of the first four of these groups are roughly similar to those of corresponding groups in the army command structure.

The Naval Operations Group includes the Royal Fleet, the Royal Marines and the Naval District. The commander in chief of the Royal Fleet is responsible for the training, employment and administration of the naval operating forces and for maintaining them in a state of combat readiness. The commander of the Royal Marines is responsible for training and equipping the naval landing forces. The commander of the Naval District is responsible for administration and discipline at both the naval base of Bangkok and the one at Sattahip, about 75 miles southeast of the capital.

The Royal Thai Air Force

The commander in chief of the Royal Thai Air Force is responsible for organizing, training and equipping the Air Force and coordinating its operations with those of other military forces to attain a unified defense of the kingdom. He is assisted by a vice commander in chief and a deputy commander in chief. The command structure consists of five groups: Air Force Head-

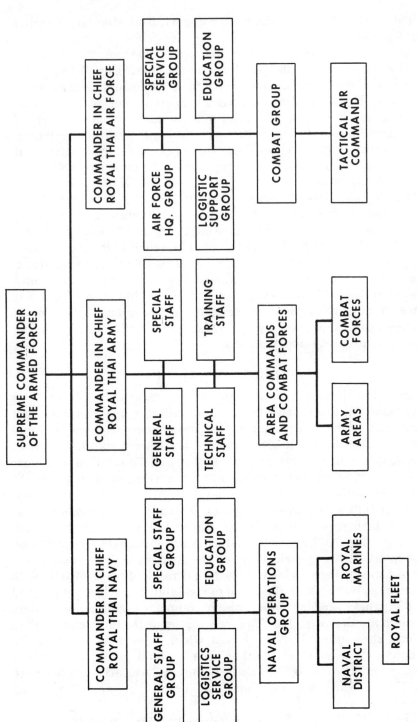

Figure 16.—Field Command of the Royal Thai Armed Forces, 1967.

481

quarters, Special Service, Logistic Support, Education and Combat (see fig. 16).

The Air Force Headquarters Group consists of the Office of the Secretary, the Office of the Commander, Don Muang Air Base and seven directorates to perform the usual general staff functions. The Special Service Group is composed of two directorates, Welfare and Civil Aviation, the latter being concerned with coordinating the activities of civil and military aviation. The Logistic Support Group and the Education Group carry out the normal supply and training staff missions common to a service headquarters.

The Combat Group's major element is the Tactical Air Command. The commander of the Tactical Air Command is responsible for all tactical air operations and exercises operational control over all tactical air wings. He also administers, organizes, equips and trains the tactical air squadrons and maintains them in a state of readiness for employment in support of naval and ground forces and counterinsurgency units. The Royal Thai Air Force Regiment, a smaller element of the Combat Group, is charged with safeguarding airfields and installations, including buildings, property and personnel.

FOREIGN INFLUENCE

From the time of their migration from South China, the Thai have adopted, from friends and foes alike, many concepts and ideas that have strongly influenced most aspects of the national life. Early contacts with the armies of the Khmer and the Burmese provided lessons in strategy and tactics, and Thai military leaders have learned from their defeats as well as from their victories.

The adaptability of the Thai and their willingness to accept Western influence and methods set the stage for the modernization of their armed forces during the early years of the twentieth century. Many officers attended European military schools, and first-hand battle experience was obtained by a 1,200-man Thai expeditionary force which served in France during World War I. During World War II the Thai established a well-organized anti-Japanese underground which supported the Allies' cause throughout the war. The Thai were among the first contingents to join the United Nations forces which undertook to repel the Communist invasion of South Korea in 1950. As of mid-1967 a small ground force (one infantry company) was still serving with the United Nations Command in the area on an annual rotating basis.

Since 1950 United States influence has been predominant. In that year the Thai recognized that a comprehensive modernization program would be necessary to revitalize its postwar forces and entered into an agreement with the United States to undertake such a program. Accordingly, since that time most of the equipment for all components of the armed forces has been received from the United States as has the instruction for its operation, maintenance and tactical employment. A sizable number of officers from all services attended military training courses in the United States, some as early as 1946. The impact of this long-term association with the United States instructors, and the accompanying familiarization with United States planning and training methods, has influenced the form and orientation of the entire military establishment.

The defense preparedness effort of Thailand has been enhanced as a result of the steady increase of North Vietnam's aggression against South Vietnam. In keeping with a 1962 pledge to defend Thailand against Communist aggression under SEATO, the United States has extensively improved many of the nation's military bases, airfields and naval facilities. In addition, the forward positioning in Thailand of military supplies that would be needed by Thai and allied troops to defend the country against outside attack has taken place.

Foreign influence, to a lesser degree, is received through Thailand's membership in SEATO whose permanent headquarters are in Bangkok. The tactical and strategic concepts of Thai commanders have inevitably been conditioned by cooperation with the armed forces of the other SEATO countries, including participation with them in joint field exercises. In addition to the United States, three other SEATO members—Great Britain, Australia and New Zealand have small military contingents in Thailand engaged in engineering and in air-support activities.

While Thailand has been a heavy recipient of military aid under SEATO arrangements, it has taken steps to recognize its responsibilities under the Treaty. Before the end of 1966 the Thai dispatched small air and naval detachments to assist South Vietnam in its war against North Vietnam. On January 23, 1967, Prime Minister Thanom Kittikachorn announced that a ground expeditionary force of about 2,400 men would be raised and sent to aid the South Vietnamese later of the same year.

ECONOMIC IMPACT

Manpower

Source and Quality

The main source of personnel for the armed forces is the Thai conscription system which, over the years, has produced reliable and hardy individuals, physically fit, adaptable and capable of performing military duties in a creditable manner. The manpower potential for the armed forces is basically the ethnic Thai who comprise close to 90 percent of the total population.

Most of the Thai soldiers come from families of farmers or fishermen. With this rural background, they are accustomed to working out of doors in tropical heat, humid climate and monsoonal rains. They are predominantly Buddhist, are well adjusted and possess a keen interest in learning and developing new skills. The average conscript accepts his military obligation as a patriotic duty.

Noncommissioned officers are, in most cases, former conscripts who have made military service a career. They are products of a selective system and are usually graduates of a noncommissioned officers candidate school. A limited number also are graduates of the reserve training programs conducted by the Territorial Defense Department of the Ministry of Defense.

The officer corps of the armed forces is generally composed of graduates of the service academies and officer candidate schools. It also includes a small number of reserve officers who have completed courses similar to those given to Reserve Officer Training Corps students in the colleges and universities of the United States. A few officers with special qualifications have been commissioned directly from civilian life.

Procurement

Conscription is authorized by the Military Service Act of 1954, which is a modernized version of a similar law passed in 1905. The service period in peacetime is 2 years, to be performed sometime between the ages of 21 and 30; in wartime it may be extended for the duration of the emergency. The tour of duty of conscripted soldiers was often shortened in all services to 18 months because of budgetary limitations, but in May 1966 the full 2-year term was reinstituted by Ministry of Defense order in view of the increasing Communist threat in border areas. The draft is conducted by the Army for all three services.

Under the Act each male adult of Thai nationality must register at the age of 18; at age 21 he is liable for compulsory service in the Army, Navy or Air Force. Upon notification of selection, he receives a medical examination to determine his fitness for military duty. On the basis of this examination, youths are divided into four categories: first, those who are fully qualified and thus eligible to serve in combat units; second, those with partial defects, held available for duty in service units; third, those with minor correctible defects or illnesses, held deferred until the next callup; and fourth, those who are physically disqualified and are therefore permanently exempted and released from all military obligation.

In addition to medical exemptions, release from military service is granted to persons in various occupations or professions. Amendments to the Act which became effective in 1964 granted exemptions to priests and monks, career teachers, cadets attending the military academies, persons undergoing military training, students in certain technical courses and persons convicted of a crime with a penalty of 10 years imprisonment or more. Waivers are usually granted to personal hardship cases. These include sole support of parents and support of minor children and students in the later stages of their education.

Conscripts, upon release from active military service, go into unassigned reserve status for a period of 23 years: 7 years in Class I (stand-by reserve); 10 years in Class II; and 6 years in Class III. Registered personnel who do not enter the service until age 30 are placed in Class II and, after the age of 40, pass to Class III. The class designation indicates the priority in which reservists would be called to active duty in case of mobilization.

Individuals of induction age are permitted to volunteer for service before being drafted. They must serve 2 years, but are usually given their choice of branch of service. Privates in the reserves may enlist for an unspecified term of service and receive a slightly higher rate of pay than conscripts. They are also eligible for promotion to noncommissioned officer grades if they are qualified and vacancies exist. Civilians with special qualifications may enlist in the armed forces to serve in specific assignments for a minimum period of 2 years.

The total induction each year averages about 30,000 men, far less than the total available. Accordingly, exemptions and waivers are granted liberally and only men in the best physical condition are selected for service. Inductees are customarily sent to the nearest Army, Navy or Air Force installation, where they are given uniforms and assigned to units for training.

Military Budget

Steps taken by the government to strengthen the Thai military posture are reflected in the steady rise of the military budget. Between 1962 and 1965 the military budget rose an average of slightly more than 8 percent per year to the equivalent of about $92.5 million. In 1966 the rise was more than 12 percent to $104.4 million. From 1960 to 1966 the military budget has rather consistently amounted to about 15 percent of the total national budget. The Thai fiscal year covers the period October

1 to September 30, having been changed from a calendar year basis in 1961.

The Army's allocated share of the budget has generally exceeded that of the Navy and Air Force combined. In fiscal year 1966 the Army received about $49.8 million; the Navy $18.1 million; and the Air Force, about $18.5 million. On the basis of the expected increasing percentage rise in military spending in fiscal year 1967 to an estimated $120 million, it is likely that the Army would receive about $60 million and the Navy and Air Force about $20 million each.

TRAINING

General

Training has increased in scope and intensity since the implementation of the United States Military Assistance Program (MAP) in 1950. With MAP support, and with the guidance of the Joint United States Military Advisory Group (JUSMAG)/ United States Military Assistance Command, Thailand (USMACTHAI), weapons were replaced by modern armament, and increased fund outlays were made for training purposes. Training facilities were expanded; military instruction courses in the United States were made available to Thai officers; and, in the mid-1960's, conventional training was augmented by the introduction of intensified programs dealing with counterinsurgency. By mid-1967 United States military advisers had increased in number, and a 350-man United States Special Forces Unit had been made available to assist in placing further emphasis on all aspects of counterinsurgency training.

School programs, special courses and training methods in the Royal Thai Army are patterned mainly on those of the United States. Conscripts are customarily assigned directly to a battalion or comparable unit stationed in the Army area in which they are inducted and undergo a 16-week recruitment training program. The first 8 weeks are devoted to basic training and the second 8 weeks to more advanced branch and specialist training.

The unit training cycle begins in June and generally extends through the following March. About 2 months are allocated for training and testing in squad, section and platoon tactics. The next phases of company- and battalion-level exercises follow progressively, and the cycle usually ends with some form of a regimental or combined maneuver.

Naval training is the overall responsibility of the Navy Education Group, and it too has greatly improved in quality and broadened in scope since 1950. Reorganization of the Navy took place in 1958 and, with the help of American advisers and the acquisition of materiel under the Military Assistance Program, a highly centralized training system was established. Almost all training agencies (including the Recruit Training Center at Klet Kaeo, just northeast of the Sattahip naval base about 75 miles southeast of Bangkok) are linked in a fairly well coordinated service-wide training program.

The course of instruction for basic naval training lasts 8 weeks for the regular recruits and 11 weeks for Naval Training School candidates. This course is devoted to the elementary aspects of seamanship, navigation, ordnance and gunnery, and damage control. Marine Corps recruits also attend the normal naval basic training course, but those selected for advanced training receive an additional 8 weeks of recruit training as well as training in special amphibious warfare along counterinsurgency lines.

Unit training is generally conducted at naval squadron level with assistance from the Fleet Training Command. Shipboard drills, including team gunnery and other underway training, take place throughout the annual training cycle. Underway training for fleet units is also part of the mission of the Fleet Training Command, and regular schedules are maintained throughout the training year. Unit and advanced training in the Marine Corps encompasses a 36-week cycle and is considered to be excellent, particularly with respect to special operations and counterinsurgency techniques.

Since 1950 Air Force training, with modifications for Thai conditions, has been basically the same as that of the United States Air Force. During World War II the Thai Air Force was an embryonic, developing organization which had extremely limited opportunities for training or for combat. After the war Thailand began to rebuild its air arm with the guidance, assistance and support of the United States.

Under the Education Group, the Directorate of Education and Training supervises all training activities. After assignment to the Air Force and completion of their basic training, recruits are selected for more advanced programs. Flight training (primary and advanced) is conducted at the Nakhon Ratchasima airbase in the Northeast, but it is planned to move this activity to a new facility in Nakhon Pathom Province by 1970. The predominant portion of the air technical training takes place at the school complex situated at Don Muang, some 15 miles north of Bangkok.

Schools

No single command or staff agency exercises general supervision over all the various military schools. Supervisory responsibilities are decentralized to the respective commanders in chief for the schools in their services. Matters affecting the whole system of military education or problems of coordination between schools are usually resolved within the Directorate of Education and Research, with advice from the general staff sections of the Supreme Command Headquarters. The Directorate also supervises the operation of the combined and special service schools, such as the National Defense College, the Armed Forces Staff College, the SEATO-sponsored Military Technical Training School and the Armed Forces Academies Preparatory School.

The National Defense College at Bangkok, organized in 1955, on the model of the United States National War College, is the highest level military school in the country. The 10-month course, conducted for about 40 high-ranking civilian officials and senior military and police officers each year, covers military, political and economic subjects. Its principal objective is to encourage understanding between military and civilian officials in those matters which are essential in the forming of policy, in planning and in directing national security interests.

The Armed Forces Staff College, also at Bangkok, was established in 1956 by the Ministry of Defense as the second highest military school. It is comparable to the United States Armed Forces Staff College at Norfolk, Virginia, and has an annual enrollment of about 35 senior officers selected from the three armed forces. The school's aim is to produce senior general staff officers qualified to serve on joint or combined staffs. Special emphasis is given to staff planning procedures and to the logistical and tactical responsibilities of commanders in joint and combined operations.

The SEATO-sponsored Military Technical Training School was opened in 1960 with the technical cooperation of the Australian Government. Its course of instruction covers 3 years and is designed to provide noncommissioned officers with specialty training in technical fields, including automobile mechanics, engineering and construction, radio and telecommunications maintenance and electronics.

The Armed Forces Academies Preparatory School in Bangkok provides 2 years of premilitary instruction to selected youths expecting to enter the service academies and the National Police Academy. Candidates for admission to the school must be between the ages of 15 and 19, and they must possess a secondary school education or its equivalent. They are chosen in a competitive examination, and usually there are more than 15 applicants for each of the almost 250 vacancies which are available each year.

Each of the three armed forces operates its own service academy of which the Army's Chulachomklao Royal Military Academy is the oldest, having been founded in 1887. These service academies are patterned after their counterparts in the United States and serve as the principal source of junior officers for their respective branches. The course of instruction in each is 5 years, and graduating classes are fairly uniform, approximating 175 in number.

The Army, Navy and Air Force maintain separate Command and General Staff Colleges for the training of selected officers in the rank of major or its equivalent in advanced military tactics and general staff techniques. For certain officers of the Army and Navy, generally in the grade of colonel and captain, respectively, provision is made for advanced study and preparation for higher command at their separately maintained War Colleges. Noncommissioned officer schools exist throughout the armed forces to provide the technical specialists as required. These schools are oriented primarily toward career enlisted men and offer courses of varying length in vocational specialities. In all three services some academic instruction along technical lines is made available to junior officers prior to certain assignments.

A sizable number of selected officers from the armed forces are sent abroad each year, most of them to the United States, to attend special courses and to receive advanced technical training. Others are assigned to United States units operating in the Pacific area for observer training under operational conditions. Australia, New Zealand and Great Britain have also participated in similar Thai training projects.

LOGISTICS

Transport, terrain, weather and limited industrial facilities create special difficulties with respect to procurement, supply, distribution, troop movement and evacuation. Logistical problems are paramount in all military operations, both conventional and counterinsurgency. The focal point in all armed forces logistic matters is the Directorate of Joint Logistics (J–4) within the Supreme Command Headquarters. This office acts as a planning and coordinating staff for the three military services and as the principal liaison channel for all contacts with foreign aid missions. Actual procurement and allocation of arms, equipment and supplies, however, rest with the individual service commanders who also control the facilities and support units within their respective forces.

A very heavy percentage of the armed forces materiel requirements must be acquired from outside sources. The bulk of these supplies are furnished by the United States and flow through MAP channels. In each military service a senior staff element has overall responsibility for logistical matters, but most of the actual supply functions are carried out by the technical services (quartermaster, ordnance, communications, transportation, etc.) or their equivalents. Most of the depots and support facilities are concentrated in the Bangkok area, including Don Muang airfield and the Sattahip naval base.

ARMS AND EQUIPMENT

Because of its agrarian economy and limited industrial facilities, Thailand has virtually no domestic military production serving the needs of its armed forces, particularly armament. Until the inception of the Military Assistance Program in 1950, armament of the armed forces consisted mostly of heterogeneous European and Japanese items. Since 1950 most of the obsolete materiel has been discarded and replaced by United States equipment, mainly of World War II vintage supplemented by increasing numbers of more modern types.

The Army's heavy weapons included: mortars, artillery, rockets, antiaircraft artillery, light tanks and armored personnel carriers. In view of the increasing insurgency along that Thai borders, the United States agreed in late 1966 to increase its military aid, principally in more advanced types of small arms, communications equipment, cross-country vehicles and helicopters.

Before World War II the Navy was equipped mainly with vessels from British, Italian and Japanese shipyards. In the postwar years these craft have been gradually replaced with United States and British World War II coast defense-type vessels. These include one destroyer escort, various types of escort ships, patrol boats, minesweepers, minelayers and antisubmarine craft.

In the Air Force all major items of equipment are of United States origin. Aircraft acquired since 1962 included some jet fighter planes, trainers and liaison planes and helicopters. In 1967 it was expected that increased United States aid would include more modern jet fighters and trainers, as well as additional light aircraft, transports and helicopters.

RANKS AND INSIGNIA

The rank structures of the three armed forces are similar to those of the comparable components of the United States Forces.

The king, as head of state, grants all commissions. Appointments to noncommissioned grades are authorized by the minister of defense. In theory, the authority and responsibilities of officers of various ranks correspond to those of their counterparts in the United States Forces. Since there seems to be a surplus of senior officers, staff and administrative positions in many instances are held by officers of higher rank than their assignments would warrant in the United States Forces. Commanders of tactical units, however, generally have ranks similar to corresponding United States unit commanders.

AWARDS AND DECORATIONS

Formal honors and symbols of merit occupy an important place in the Thai tradition, and officers and enlisted men receive and wear awards and decorations with great pride. The Thai Government grants numerous awards, and outstanding acts of heroism and courage receive quick recognition by superiors. There are no awards or decorations for Thai military personnel which are peculiar to any of the three services. All recognition for outstanding achievement is normally made in the name of the Royal Thai Government. Military personnel, however, are also eligible for foreign medals and decorations in addition to the many distinctive Thai awards (see table 15).

MILITARY JUSTICE

The military justice system of the Thai armed forces is administered by the minister of defense through his Judge Advocate General Department which supervises the various military courts appointed by the commanders in chief of the Army, Navy and Air Force. In structure and procedures the system is similar to that of the United States. Points of similarity include its uniformity of application in the three services, its decentralization of authority to subordinate commanders, its investigative and court-martial procedures and its close relation to the civil justice system. Wide variations, however, exist in both systems.

All serious cases are tried by appropriate courts. The military court system is administered by the minister of defense and is divided into three categories: the courts of first instance, which include those operated by military units as well as the formal courts within the various regions, provinces and at Bangkok; the Military Appeal Court; and the Military Supreme Court. The last two courts are located in the capital, and their judges are appointed by royal decree. The authority to appoint judges of the various military courts, however, has been delegated to

Table 15.—*Thai Military Awards and Decorations*
(In accepted order of precedence)

Title	Date Established	Remarks
Most Illustrious Order of the Royal House of Chakri.	1882	Awarded for meritorious service to members of the royal family and heads of state.
Ancient and Auspicious Order of the Nine Gems.	1869	Awarded to high government officials of the Buddhist religion.
Most Illustrious Order of Chula Chom Klao.	1873	Awarded for meritorious service to the sovereign; given in three classes.
Ratana Varabhorn	1911	An order of merit.
Honorable Order of Rama	1918	Awarded for military and naval service to the state; given in four classes.
Most Exalted Order of the White Elephant.	1861	Awarded for meritorious service to the state; given in eight classes.
Most Noble Order of the Crown of Thailand.	1869	Do.
Vallabhabhorn Order	1919	Awarded for personal service to the king.
Vajira Mala Order	1911	Do.
Rama Medal	1918	Awarded for gallantry in action.
Dushdi Mala Medal	1882	Awarded as token of royal appreciation.
Chakra Mala Medal	1873	Awarded to military personnel for 15 years' honorable service.
Chakrabarti Mala Medal	1873	Awarded to military personnel for 25 years' honorable service.
Rajaruchi Medal	1897	Awarded to officers and warrant officers of His Majesty Guard Regiment.
Rajaniyom Medal	1912	Awarded for lifesaving.
Chai Smorabhum Medal	1941	Awarded for service in the Indochina War.
Medal for Bravery	1941	Awarded to members of the defense and police forces for courageous actions during the Indochina War.
Border Service Medal	1941	Awarded for courageous and honorable service in a frontier area.
Home Front Service Medal	1941	Awarded to those who performed auxiliary war duties in support of the fighting forces during the Indochina War.

the minister of defense and the appropriate military commanders. In time of war a military court may be established when necessary by the highest ranking commanding officer present, who has under his command not less than one Army battalion or equivalent naval or air force element.

The types of penalties meted out to convicted officers and enlisted men are similar to those imposed by the military courts of the United States Forces. They may range from reprimand to death. In time of war, desertion, surrender to the enemy, treason and murder usually carry the death penalty. All sentences, however, are subject to possible reduction by the reviewing authority, and death sentences are automatically postponed for 60 days to permit petitioning of clemency from the king who is empowered to pardon any convicted person.

Thailand is a signer of the 1949 Geneva Convention dealing with prisoners of war. In keeping with this obligation, the government enacted a law in 1955 providing in effect that all rules and regulations of the convention would take precedence over any conflicting Thai laws concerning prisoners of war that were binding on either military or civilian courts.

BIBLIOGRAPHIES

Section I. Social

RECOMMENDED FURTHER READING

Among the sources consulted in the preparation of this section, the following are recommended as additional reading on the basis of quality and general availability.

Cady, John F. *Thailand, Burma, Laos, and Cambodia.* Englewood Cliffs: Prentice-Hall, 1966.

Evers, Hans-Deiter. "The Formation of Social Class Structure: Urbanization, Bureaucratization and Social Mobility in Thailand," *American Sociological Review*, XXXI, No. 4, August 1966, 480–488.

Fraser, Thomas M., Jr. *Fishermen of South Thailand.* New York: Holt, Rinehart and Winston, 1966.

Fulham, Parke. "Elites or Elections?" *Far Eastern Economic Review*, LI, No. 7, February 17, 1966, 273–275.

Geddes, W. R. "The Hill Tribes of Thailand." Pages 107–114 in Southeast Asia Treaty Organization, *Seminar on Community Development Proceedings, July 19–23, 1965.* Bangkok: SEATO, 1966.

Hall, D. G. E. *A History of Southeast Asia.* (2d ed.) New York: St. Martin's Press, 1964.

Hanks, Lucien M., and Hanks, Jane R. "Thailand: Equality Between the Sexes." Pages 424–451 in Barbara E. Ward (ed.), *Women in the New Asia.* Paris: United Nations Educational, Scientific and Cultural Organization, 1963.

Hanks, Lucien M.; Hanks, Jane R.; Sharp, Lauriston; and Sharp, Ruth B. *A Report on Tribal Peoples in Chiengrai Province North of the Mae Kok River.* (Comparative Studies of Cultural Change, Department of Anthropology, Cornell University.) Ithaca: Cornell University Press, 1964.

Hanks, Lucien M.; Hanks, Jane R.; and Sharp, Lauriston. *Ethnographic Notes on Northern Thailand.* (Data Paper No. 58, Southeast Asia Program, Department of Asian Studies, Cornell University.) Ithaca: Cornell University Press, 1965.

Hanna, Willard A. *Change in Chiengmai, VI: Visits to Three Wats.* (American Universities Field Staff Reports, Southeast Asia Series, XIII, No. 9.) New York: AUFS, 1965.

————. *Peninsular Thailand, I: The Dim Past.* (American Universities Field Staff Reports, Southeast Asia Series, XIII, No. 22.) New York: AUFS, 1965.

————. *Peninsular Thailand, II: The Border Provinces.* (American Universities Field Staff Reports, Southeast Asia Series, XIII, No. 23.) New York: AUFS, 1965.

Hanna, Willard A. *Peninsular Thailand, III. The Shores of Songkhla.* (American Universities Field Staff Reports, Southeast Asia Series, XIII, No. 24.) New York: AUFS, 1965.

_____. *Peninsular Thailand, IV: The Rubber of Haadyai and the Tin of Phuket.* (American Universities Field Staff Reports, Southeast Asia Series, XIII, No. 25.) New York: AUFS, 1965.

_____. *Peninsular Thailand, V: The Thai Muslim Centers of Pattani and Yala.* (American Universities Field Staff Reports, Southeast Asia Series, XIII, No. 26.) New York: AUFS, 1965.

_____. *Thailand's Strategic Northeast.* (American Universities Field Staff Reports, Southeast Asia Series, XIV, No. 1.) New York: AUFS, 1966.

Kaufman, Howard Keva. *Bangkhuad: A Community Study in Thailand.* New York: Augustin, 1960.

Kingshill, Konrad. *Ku Daeng, the Red Tomb: A Village Study in Northern Thailand.* Bangkok: Prince Royal's College (Distributed by Siam Society), 1960.

Kirsch, A. Thomas. "Development and Mobility Among the Phu Thai of Northeast Thailand," *Asian Survey*, VI, No. 7, July 1966, 370–379.

Klausner, William J. "Popular Buddhism in Northeast Thailand." Pages 71–92 in F.S.C. Northrop and Helen H. Livingston (eds.), *Cultural Understanding: Epistemology in Anthropology.* New York: Harper and Row, 1964.

Kunstadter, Peter. *The Lua' (Lawa) of Northern Thailand: Aspects of Social Structure, Agriculture and Religion.* Princeton: Princeton University, Center of International Studies, November 30, 1965.

Kusalasaya, Karuna. "Buddhism: Its Past and Present in Thailand," *Indo-Asian Culture*, XII, October 1963, 90–113.

Landon, Kenneth Perry. *Siam in Transition.* Chicago: University of Chicago Press, 1939.

LeBar, Frank M.; Hickey, Gerald C.; and Musgrave, John K. *Ethnic Groups of Mainland Southeast Asia.* New Haven: Human Relations Area Files Press, 1964.

Mills, Richard C. *Narrow is the Road: A Study of Social Forces and Drives Evident in Asian Young People.* Los Angeles: Claremore Fund, 1963.

Pendleton, Robert Larimore. *Thailand: Aspects of Landscape and Life.* New York: Duell, Sloan and Pearce, 1963.

Phillips, Herbert P. *Thai Peasant Personality: The Patterning of Interpersonal Behavior in the Village of Bang Chan.* Berkeley: University of California Press, 1966.

Shaplen, Robert. "Letter from Bangkok," *New Yorker*, XLIII, No. 4, March 18, 1967, 135–172.

Siffin, William J. *The Thai Bureaucracy: Institutional Change and Development.* Honolulu: East-West Center Press, 1966.

Skinner, George William. "The Thailand Chinese: Assimilation in a Changing Society," *Asia*, II, Autumn 1964, 80–92.

Southeast Asia Treaty Organization. *Seminar on Community Development Proceedings, July 19–23, 1965.* Bangkok: SEATO, 1966.

Thailand. Ministry of the Interior. Department of Public Welfare. "Report on Socio-Economic Survey of the Hill Tribes of Northern Thailand." Bangkok: September 1962 (mimeo.).

Thailand. Office of the Prime Minister. Editorial Board. *Official Yearbook, 1964.* Bangkok: Government House Printing Office, 1965.

Thailand. Office of the Prime Minister. National Economic Development Board. *National Income of Thailand, 1965.* Bangkok: 1965.

Thailand. Office of the Prime Minister. National Statistical Office. "Preliminary Socio-Economic Survey of the Hill Tribes in Thailand, 1955–66." Bangkok: n.d. (Unpublished manuscript not available for public distribution.)

U.S. Department of Defense. Military Assistance Institute. *Thailand: Country Study*, by Walter Frank Choinski. Washington: American Institute for Research, 1963.

Wilson, David A. *Politics in Thailand*. Ithaca: Cornell University Press, 1962.

―――. "Thailand." Pages 3–72 in George McTurnan Kahin (ed.), *Government and Politics of Southeast Asia*. (2d ed.) Ithaca: Cornell University Press, 1964.

Wood, William Alfred Rae. *A History of Siam, From the Earliest Times to the Year A. D. 1781, With a Supplement Dealing With More Recent Events*. (Rev. ed.) Bangkok: Siam Barnakich Press, 1933.

OTHER SOURCES USED

Alabaster, Henry. *The Modern Buddhist*. London: Trubner, 1870.

―――. *The Wheel of Law*. London: Trubner, 1871.

Anderson, J. P. "The Karens in Siam." (Translated from "Karererne i Siam," *Geografisk Tidsskrift*, XXXI, 1928, 233–242.)

―――. Some Notes About the Karens in Siam," *Journal of the Siam Society* (Bangkok), XVII, Pt. 2, October 1923, 51–58.

Andrews, James M., IV. "Evolutionary Trends in Body Build; Data from Thailand (Siam)," *Papers of the Peabody Museum of American Archaeology and Ethnology, Harvard University*, XX, 1943, 102–121.

Andric, John. "The Changing Face of Thailand," *Eastern World*, XVIII, No. 5, May 1964, 14, 15.

Anudhuvadi, Phya. *Buddhism in Simple Words*. Bangkok: Daily Mail Press, 1930.

Anuman-Rajadnon, Phya. *A Brief Survey of Cultural Thailand*. ("Thailand Culture Series," No. 2.) Bangkok: National Culture Institute, 1953.

―――. *Chao Thai and Some Tradition of Thai*. ("Thailand Culture Series," No. 6.) Bangkok: National Culture Institute, 1953.

―――. *The Cultures of Thailand*. ("Thailand Culture Series," No. 1.) Bangkok: National Culture Institute, 1953.

―――. *Loy Krathong and Songkram Festival*. ("Thailand Culture Series," No. 5.) Bangkok: National Culture Institute, 1953.

―――. *Phra Cedi* (The Stupa). ("Thailand Culture Series," No. 7.) Bangkok: National Culture Institute, 1953.

―――. *Thai Language*. ("Thailand Culture Series," No. 17.) Bangkok: National Culture Institute, 1954.

―――. *Thai Literature and Swasdi Raksa*. ("Thailand Culture Series," No. 3.) Bangkok: National Culture Institute, 1953.

Bacon, George Blagden. *Siam: The Land of the White Elephant, As It Was and Is*. New York: Scribner, Armstrong, 1873.

Bahm, A.J. *Philosophy of the Buddha*. New York: Collier Books, 1962.

Bank of Thailand. "Cost of Living Indices," *Bank of Thailand Monthly Report*, II, August 1962, 63.

Barnett, David. *The Mask of Siam*. London: R. Hale, 1959.

Bartlett, Norman. *Land of the Lotus Eaters*. New York: Roy Publishers, 1959.

Basham, A. L. "Jainism and Buddhism." In William Theodore de Bary (ed.), *Sources of Indian Tradition*. New York: Columbia University Press, 1958.

Benedict, Paul K. "Studies in Thai Kinship Terminology," *Journal of the American Oriental Society*, LXIII, 1943, 168–175.

———. "Thai, Kadai and Indonesian," *American Anthropologist*, XLIV, October-December 1942, 576–601.

———. "Tonal Systems in Southeast Asia," Journal of the American Oriental Society, LXVIII, October-December 1948, 184–191.

Benedict, Ruth. *Thai Culture and Behavior.* (Cornell University Southeast Asia Program, Data Paper No. 4.) Ithaca: Cornell University Press, 1952.

Bernatzik, Hugo Adolf. *Akha und Meau: Probleme der Angewandten Volkerkunde in Hinterindien.* 2 vols. Innsbruck: Kommissionverlag, Wagner'sche Univ-Buchdrukeri, 1947.

Bernatzik, Hugo Adolph, and Bernatzik, Emmy. *Die Geister der Gelben Blatter: Forschungsreisen in Hinterindien* (Spirits of the Yellow Leaf: Explorations in Further India). Munich: F. Bruckmann, 1938.

Binson, Boonrod. "The Mekong and Thailand's Power Programme," *Far Eastern Economic Review*, XXX, November 1960, 244, 245, 248–250.

Birasri, Silpa. *Thai Architecture and Painting.* ("Thailand Culture Series," No. 4.) Bangkok, National Culture Institute, 1953.

Blake, Wilfrid Theodore. *Thailand Journey.* London: Alvin Redman, 1955.

Blofeld, John E. *People of the Sun: Encounters in Siam.* London: Hutchinson, 1960.

Bohannan, Paul. "An Alternate Residence Classification," *American Anthropologist*, LIX, February 1957, 126–131.

Boribal Buribhand, Luang. *Thai Images of the Buddha.* ("Thailand Culture Series," No. 9.) Bangkok: National Culture Institute, 1953.

Bose, Phanindra Nath. *The Indian Colony of Siam.* Lahore: Punjab Sanskrit Book Depot, 1927.

Bowers, Faubion. *Theater in the East: A Survey of Asian Dance and Drama.* New York: Thomas Nelson, 1956.

Bowring, Sir John. *The Kingdom and the People of Siam*, I. London, John W. Parker, 1857.

Briggs, Lawrence P. "The Appearance and Historical Usage of the Terms Tai, Thai, Siamese, and Lao," *Journal of the American Oriental Society*, LXIX, April-June 1949, 60–73.

Brimmell, J.H. *Communism in Southeast Asia.* New York: Oxford University Press, 1959.

Busch, Noel Fairchild. *Thailand: An Introduction to Modern Siam.* Princeton: Van Nostrand, 1959.

Campbell, John G.D. *Siam in the Twentieth Century.* London: Edward Arnold, 1902.

Carter, A. Cecil. *The Kingdom of Siam.* New York: Putnam, 1904.

Chandavimol, Abhai. "Thailand: Educational Developments in 1960–61." Pages 374–377 in United Nations Educational, Scientific and Cultural Organization, *International Yearbook of Education 1961*, XXIII, Geneva: International Bureau of Education, 1962.

Chandruang, Kumut. *My Boyhood in Siam.* New York: John Day, 1938.

Charusathira, Prapas, General. "Thailand's Hill Tribes." Washington: Royal Thai Embassy, Office of the Public Relations Attache, n.d. (mimeo.).

Chemical Bank New York Trust Company. *Thailand.* (International Economic Survey, No. 130, May 1960.) New York: 1960.

Chen-Durizanga, Phra. *Thai Music.* ("Thailand Culture Series," No. 8.) Bangkok: National Culture Institute, 1953.

"Chinese in Siam," *Economist* (London), CCIII, June 30, 1962, 1321, 1322.

Choon, Silasuvan. "The Thai Political Traditions Which Influence the International Relations of Thailand," University of Michigan, 1939 (manuscript).

Chula Chakrabongse, His Royal Highness Prince. *Lords of Life*. London: Alvin Redman, 1960.

Close, Alexandra. "Thailand's Border Alarms," *Far Eastern Economic Review*, XLVIII, No. 9, May 27, 1965, 395–398.

Coast, John. *Some Aspects of Siamese Politics*. New York: International Secretariat, Institute of Pacific Relations, 1953.

Coedes, G. *Les Etats Hindouisés d'Indochine et d'Indonésie*. Paris: Boccard, 1948.

Cole, Fay-Cooper. *The Peoples of Malaysia*. New York: Van Nostrand, 1945.

Consultative Committee on Economic Development in South and South-East Asia, *The Colombo Plan*. (Tenth Annual Report, Kuala Lumpur, October-November 1961.) London: HMSO, 1962.

Conze, Edward. *Buddhism: Its Essence and Development*. Oxford: Cassirer, 1960.

Cornell University. *Area Handbook on Thailand*. (HRAF Subcontractor's Monograph.) Ithaca: 1956.

Coughlin, Richard J. "The Chinese in Bangkok," *American Sociological Review*, XX, June 1955, 311–316.

_____. *Double Identity: The Chinese in Modern Thailand*. Hong Kong: Hong Kong University Press, 1960.

_____. "The Pattern of the Chinese in Thailand," *Journal of the South Seas Society*, VIII, 1952, 1–3.

_____. "Some Social Features of Siamese Buddhism," *Asia: Asian Quarterly of Culture and Synthesis* (Saigon), II, December 1952, 403–408.

_____. "The Status of the Chinese Minority in Thailand," *Pacific Affairs*, XXV, December 1952, 378–389.

Credner, Wilhelm. *Siam das Land der Tai*. Stuttgart: J. Engelhorns Nachf., 1935.

Crosby, Sir Josiah. *Siam: The Crossroads*. London: Hollis and Carter, 1945.

_____. *Siam Past and Future*. London: Oxford University Press, 1945.

Curtis, Lillian Johnson. *The Laos of North Siam*. Philadelphia: Westminster Press, 1903.

Damrong Rajanubhab, His Royal Highness Prince. *A History of Buddhist Monuments in Siam*. (Trans., S. Sivaraksa.) Bangkok: Siva Phorn, 1962.

_____. "The Introduction of Western Culture in Siam," *Siam Society*, VII, 1959, 1–12.

Darling, Frank C. "Marshal Sarit and Absolutist Rule in Thailand," *Pacific Affairs*, XXXIII, December 1960, 347–360.

_____. "Modern Politics in Thailand," *Review of Politics*, XXIV, April 1962, 163–182.

De Berval, Rene. "Presence du Royaume Lao: Pays du Million d'Eléphants et du Parasol Blanc," *France-Asie* (Saigon), XII, March-April 1956.

De Young, John E. *Village Life in Modern Thailand*. Berkeley: University of California Press, 1955.

Dhani Nivat Kromamun Bidhyalabh, His Royal Highness Prince. *The Nang* (Shadow Play). ("Thailand Culture Series," No. 12.) Bangkok: National Culture Institute, 1954.

_____. "The Old Siamese Conception of the Monarchy." Pages 160–175 in *Siam Society—Fiftieth Anniversary: Commemorative Publication* (Selected Articles from *Siam Society Journal*), II. Bangkok: 1954.

Dhani Nivat Kromamun Bidhyalabh, His Royal Highness Prince, and Danit-Yupho. *The Khon.* ("Thailand Culture Series," No. 11.) Bangkok: National Culture Institute, 1953.

Dhuraratsadorn, Luang Boriphandh. "The White Meo." (Trans., E. Seidenfaden), *Journal of the Siam Society* (Bangkok), XVII, Pt. 3, 1923, 153–189.

The Directory for Bangkok and Siam—1932. Bangkok: Bangkok Times Press, n.d.

The Directory for Bangkok and Siam—1933. Bangkok: Bangkok Times Press, n.d.

Dobby, E.H.G. *Southeast Asia.* (6th ed.) London: University of London Press, 1958.

Du Bois, Cora. *Social Forces in Southeast Asia.* Minneapolis: University of Minnesota Press, 1949.

Dulyachindi, Medhi. "The Development of Labour Legislation in Thailand," *International Labour Review*, LX, 1949, 467–486.

Eberhard, Wolfram. "Kultur und Siedlung der Randvölker Chinas" (Culture and Settlements of the Border Peoples of China). *T'oung Pao* (Leiden), Supplement to XXXVI, 1942.

"Economic Development and Full Employment Programs in Thailand," *Industry and Labour*, XIII, April 1, 1955, 306, 307.

Eliot, Charles Norton Edgecumbe. *Hinduism and Buddhism: An Historical Sketch.* 3 vols. New York: Barnes and Noble, 1954.

Elwin, Verrier. "Chiengmai, Land of Smiles," *Geographical Magazine*, XXV, November 1952, 359–361.

Embree, John F. "Thailand: A Loosely Structured Social System," *American Anthropologist*, LII, April-June 1950, 181, 193.

Embree, John F., and Thomas, William L. *Ethnic Groups of Northern Southeast Asia.* (Yale University Graduate School, Southeast Asia Studies.) New Haven: Yale University Press, 1950.

Fairbank, John K., and Reischauer, Edwin O. *East Asia: The Great Tradition.* Boston: Houghton Mifflin, 1960.

Fall, Bernard B. "Informal Communications in Southeast Asia." Washington: June 1960. (Unpublished manuscript not available for distribution.)

Fifield, Russell H. *The Diplomacy of Southeast Asia: 1945–1958.* New York: Harper, 1958.

Finot, Louis. "Outline of the History of Buddhism in Indo-China," *Indian Historical Quarterly* (Calcutta), II, December 1926, 637–689.

Fogg, E.L. "Labour Organization in Thailand," *Industrial and Labour Relations Review*, VI, April 1953, 368–377.

Franke, O. *Geschichte des Chinesischen Reichs: Eine Darstellung Seiner Entstehung, Seines Wesens und Seiner Entwicklung bis zur Neuesten Seit,* II and III. Berlin: Walter de Gruyter, 1936 and 1937.

Franklin, Mary Anne. "English Is Rare For Me," *National Education Association Journal*, XLIX, May 1960, 37, 38.

Franzen, Carl G. F. "An Educational Frontier in Thailand," *School and Society*, LXXXIV, October 27, 1956.

Fraser, Thomas M., Jr. *Rusembilan: A Malay Fishing Village in Southern Thailand.* Ithaca: Cornell University Press, 1960.

Freyn, Hubert. "The Backward Village," *Far Eastern Economic Review*, XLVIII, No. 12, June 17, 1965, 580, 581.

———. "The Chinese in Thailand," *Far Eastern Economic Review*, XXX, December 29, 1960, 657–660.

Furnivall, John S. *Educational Progress in Southeast Asia.* New York: Institute of Pacific Relations, 1943.

Gandasena, Nai Chandr. "The Red Karen." (Trans., E. J. Walton), *Journal of the Siam Society* (Bangkok), XVII, Pt. 2, October 1923, 74–79.

Gard, Richard A. *Buddhism.* New York: Washington Square Press, 1963.

Gedney, William J. "Indic Loanwords in Spoken Thai." (Unpublished Doctoral dissertation) New Haven: Yale University, 1947.

"Geopolitics of Thailand," *World Affairs Interpreter*, XXIV, 1953, 273–283.

Gerini, Gerolamo Emilio. "On Siamese Proverbs and Idiomatic Expressions, *Journal of the Siam Society* (Bangkok), I, 1904, 11–168.

Gille, Halver, and Chalothorn, Thip. "The Demographic Outlook of Thailand and Some Implications." Pages 113–139 in "Seminar on Population in Thailand, 1963." Bangkok: n.d. (Unpublished manuscript.)

Graham, David Crockett. "The Customs of the Ch'uan Miao," *Journal of the West China Border Research Society* (Shanghai), IX, 1937, 13–70.

Graham, Henry M. "Some Changes in Thai Family Life: A Preliminary Study." Bangkok: Institute of Public Administration, Thammasat University, 1961 (mimeo.).

Graham, Walter A. *Siam: A Handbook of Practical, Commercial, and Political Information.* 2 vols. London: Alexander Moring, 1924.

Griswald, A. B. "Art from Siam," *Artibus Asiae*, XXIII, No. 2, 1960, 129–131.

———. "King Mongkut in Perspective," *Journal of the Siam Society*, XLV, Pt. 1, April 1957, 1–41.

Grousset, Rene. *The Civilization of the East: India.* New York: Knopf, 1931.

Haas, Mary Rosamund. "The Declining Descent Rule for Rank in Thailand." *American Anthropologist*, LIII, 1951, 585–587.

———. "Interlingual Word Taboos," *American Anthropologist*, LIII, No. 3, 1951, 338.

———. *Special Dictionary of the Thai Language*, Pt. II: English-Thai. Berkeley: Army Specialized Training Program, University of California, 1945.

———. *The Thai System of Writing.* 2 vols. Washington: American Council of Learned Societies, 1956.

———. *Thai Vocabulary.* (Program in Oriental Languages, Publications Series A [Texts], No. 2.) Washington: American Council of Learned Societies, 1955.

Hall, D. G. E. *A History of Southeast Asia.* New York: St. Martin's Press, 1955.

Hamilton, James W. "Effects of the Thai Market on Karen Life." (Paper Given at the 1961 annual meeting of the American Anthropological Association in Chicago, 1962.)

Hanks, Lucien M., Jr. "An Alternative to Innovation Through Expressed Wants." (Unpublished paper given at the annual meeting of the American Anthropological Association in Boston, 1955.)

———. "Changes in Family Life." (Unpublished manuscript dated June 1959.)

———. "Indifference to Modern Education in a Thai Farming Community," *Human Organization*, XVII, Summer 1958, 9–14.

———. "Merit and Power in the Thai Social Order," *American Anthropologist*, LXIV, No. 6, 1962, 1247–1261.

Harrison, Brian. *Southeast Asia: A Short History.* London: Macmillan, 1954.

Hoontrakul Lukhit. *The Historical Records of the Siamese Chinese Relations*. Bangkok: Thai Bithaya Press, 1951.

Humphreys, Travers Christmas. *Buddhism*. Middlesex: Penguin Books, 1951.

————. *Karma and Rebirth*. London: J. Murray, 1943.

Iijima, Shigeru. "Cultural Change Among the Hill Karens in Northern Thailand," Asian Survey, V, August 1965, 417–423.

Ingram, James C. *Economic Change in Thailand Since 1850*. Stanford: Stanford University Press, 1955.

International Bank for Reconstruction and Development. *A Public Development Program for Thailand*. Baltimore: Johns Hopkins Press, 1959.

International Labour Organisation. International Labour Office. *Report of the Ad Hoc Committee on Forced Labor*. (E/2431.) Geneva: ILO, 1953.

————. *Yearbook of Labour Statistics 1959*. Geneva: ILO, 1959.

Irwin, A. J. "Some Siamese Ghost-Lore and Demonology," *Journal of the Siam Society* (Bangkok), IV, Pt. 2, 1907, 19–33.

Jaiyanama, Nai Direck. *Lectures on Thailand*. Tokyo: Ko–A Nippon Sha, 1943.

Janlekha, Kamol Odd. "A Study of the Economy of a Rice Growing Village in Central Thailand." Unpublished Doctoral dissertation, Ithaca: Cornell University, 1955. (Library of Congress microfilm, No. 15,491-thesis.)

Jiang, J. P. L. "Chinese in Thailand: Past and Present," *Journal of Southeast Asian History*, VII, March 1966, 39–65.

Judd, Laurence Cecil. "A Study of the Central Organization of Tong Taa Village in Thailand." Unpublished Master's thesis. Ithaca: Cornell University, 1954.

Jumsai, Mon Luang Manich. *Compulsory Education in Thailand*. (United Nations Educational, Scientific and Cultural Organization Studies on Compulsory Education, VIII.) Paris: UNESCO, 1951.

Kahin, George McTurnan (ed.). *Government and Politics of Southeast Asia*. Ithaca: Cornell University Press, 1959.

Kassebaum, John C. *Thailand Economic Farm Survey*. Bangkok: Ministry of Agriculture, 1953.

Kerr, A., and Seidenfaden, E. "Ethnology." In Vol. I. of *Thailand: Nature and Industry* (2d ed.). Bangkok: Department of Commercial Intelligence, Ministry of Commerce, 1950.

"Ku De Ta to Gunjin to Seigi" (Coup d'etat and the Military and Politics), *Ekonomist* (Tokyo), XL, June 5, 1962, 6–17.

"Labor in Thailand," *United Asia: International Magazine of Afro-Asian Affairs* (Bombay), XII, No. 1, 1960, 244–251.

Lakshmipathy, V. "Labour Conditions in Siam," *Asian Labour* (New Delhi), I, October 1948, 142–159.

Landon, Kenneth Perry. *The Chinese in Thailand*. New York: Oxford University Press, 1941.

————. "The Monks of New Thailand," *Asia* (Concord), VL, 1940, 129–132.

————. *Southeast Asia: Crossroads of Religion*. Chicago: University of Chicago Press, 1937.

Lasker, Bruno. *Human Bondage in Southeast Asia*. Chapel Hill: University of North Carolina Press, 1950.

————. *Standards and Planes of Living in Southeast and Eastern Asia*. New York: Institute of Pacific Relations, 1954.

Leach, Edmund. "The Frontiers of 'Burma'," *Comparative Studies in Society and History* (The Hague), III, No. 1, 1960, 49–68.

Lee, S. Y. "Double Identity: The Thai Chinese," *Far Eastern Economic Review*, XXXII, June 1, 1961, 399–413.

Le May, Reginald Stuart. *An Asian Arcady: The Land and Peoples of Northern Siam.* Cambridge: Heffer, 1926.

———. *The Culture of Southeast Asia: The Heritage of India.* London: Allan Publications, 1954.

Li, Fang-Kuei. "A Tentative Classification of Thai Dialects." Pages 951–959 in Stanley Diamond (ed.), *Culture in History: Essays in Honor of Paul Radin.* New York: Columbia University Press, 1961.

Lithfield, Whiting, Bowne, *et al. Historical Growth.* (Bangkok-Thonburi City Planning Project, Technical Monograph, I.) Bangkok: Bangkok-Thonburi City Planning Project, 1959.

———. *Population.* (Bangkok-Thonburi City Planning Project, Technical Monograph, III.) Bangkok: Bangkok-Thonburi City Planning Project, 1959.

MacDonald, Alexander. *Bangkok Editor.* New York: Macmillan, 1949.

Malai, Huvanandana. "The Status of the Thai King." Ann Arbor: University of Michigan, 1939. (Manuscript).

Malakul, Mom Luang Pin. "Education in Thailand Today," *Bangkok Post* (Special Supplement), December 4, 1962, 21, 99.

———. Proposed Projects for the Development of Education in Thailand. Bangkok: Ministry of Education (1962?).

Manunet Banhan, Phya. *Siamese Tales, Old and New: The Four Riddles and Other Stories.* (Trans., Reginald Le May.) London: Noel Douglas, 1930.

Marshall, Harry Ignatius. "The Karen Peoples of Burma: A Study in Anthropology and Ethnology," *Ohio State University Bulletin* (Columbus), XXVI, April 29, 1922.

Matthew, Eunice S. "Cultural Values and Learning in Thailand," *Educational Leadership*, XVI, April 1959, 419–424.

May, Jacques Meyer. *Thailand.* Garden City: Doubleday, 1957.

Mayer, Paul A. *Thailand. A Market for U.S. Products.* (U.S. Department of Commerce. Bureau of International Programs. Supplement No. 3 to Part I, World Trade Information Service.) Washington: GPO, April 1962.

McFarland, George Bradley (ed.). *Historical Sketch of Protestant Missions in Siam, 1828–1928.* Bangkok: Bangkok Times Press, 1928.

McLeish, Alexander. *Today in Thailand.* London: World Dominion Press, 1942.

Methi, D. C. "Thailand's 1962 Budget," *Eastern World*, XVI, February 1962, 24–26.

Moerman, Michael. "Class and Culture in North Thailand." (Paper given at the 1961 annual meeting of the American Anthropological Association, Chicago 1962.)

Moffat, Abbot Low. *Mongkut: The King of Siam.* Ithaca: Cornell University Press, 1961.

Mookherji, Sudhansu Bima. "The Indian Minority in Southeast Asia," *Eastern World*, XIX, No. 819, August-September 1965, 14, 15.

Moore, Frank J. "Social Science Newsletter from Bangkok," (Correspondence of King Mongkut, Rama IV), November 1, 1951.

Moore, W. Robert. "Thailand Bolsters its Freedom," *National Geographic*, CXIX, June 1961, 810–849.

Mosel, James N. "Communications Patterns and Political Socialization in Transitional Thailand." Pages 184–228 in Lucian W. Pye (ed.), *Communitions and Political Development.* Princeton: Princeton University Press, 1963.

Mosel, James N. *A Survey of Classical Thai Poetry: Commentary and Thai Text to Accompany a Tape Recording of Thai Poetry.* Bangkok: Bangkok World Limited Partnership, 1959.

―――. "Thai Administrative Behavior." Pages 278–324 in William J. Siffin (ed.), *Toward a Comparative Study of Public Administration.* Bloomington: University of Indiana Press, 1959.

―――. *Trends and Structure in Contemporary Thai Poetry.* (Southeast Asia Program, Data Paper No. 43.) Ithaca: Cornell University, Department of Far Eastern Studies, August 1961.

"The Mrabri: Studies in the Field," *Journal of the Siam Society,* LI, Pt. 2, October 1963, 133–199.

Murray, Douglas P. "Chinese Education in South East Asia," *China Quarterly,* No. 20, October-December 1964, 67–96.

Muscat, Robert J. *Development Strategy in Thailand: A Study of Economic Growth.* London: Praeger, 1966.

"National Seminar on Population Problems of Thailand: Conclusions of the Seminar," *Studies in Family Planning,* No. 4 August 1964, 1–4.

Nghiep-Lenh-Thiev. "The Role of Traditional Medicine in the Vietnamese Society." N.pl.: n.d. (Unpublished manuscript not available for public distribution.)

Nuechterlein, Donald E. "Thailand: Year of Danger and of Hope," *Asian Survey,* VI, No. 2, February 1966, 119–124.

―――. "Thailand After Sarit," *Asian Survey,* IV, No. 5, May 1964, 842–850.

Obeyesekere, Gananath. "The Great Tradition and the Little in the Perspective of Sinhalese Buddhism," *Journal of Asian Studies,* XXII, February 1963, 139–153.

Ohya Anuman Rajadhon. *Introducing Cultural Thailand in Outline.* Bangkok: Fine Arts Department, 1963.

Ortiz, Elizabeth. "The Mekong Project of Vietnam," *Far Eastern Economic Review,* XXV, November 6, 1958, 596, 597.

"The Overseas Chinese," *Military Review,* XLV, No. 8, August 1965, 31–35.

Pacific Science Congress, Ninth. Publicity Committee. *Thailand, Past and Present.* Bangkok: 1957.

Pendleton, Robert Larimore, and Montrakun, Sarot. *The Soils of Thailand.* (Reprinted from the Proceedings of the Ninth Pacific Science Congress; XVIII—Soil and Land Classification.) Bangkok: Department of Rice, Ministry of Agriculture, 1960.

Perera, Walter (ed.). *Thailand Yearbook, 1964–1965.* Bangkok: Temple Publicity Service, 1965.

Pickerell, Albert G. "The Press of Thailand: Conditions and Trends," *Journalism Quarterly,* Winter 1960, 83–96.

Pramuanvitya, Udom. *Prime Minister Field Marshal Sarisdi Dhanarajata.* Bangkok: Kasemsomphon, 1962.

Pratt, James B. *The Pilgrimage of Buddhism.* New York: Macmillan, 1928.

Pringle, Richard. Bhindhuvatana, Songsang; and Kwasardr, Wang Chai. *Report on Land Development in Thailand.* Bangkok: U.S. Special Technical and Economic Mission to Thailand, 1952.

Prinyayogavipulya, Luang. *Concise Principles of Buddhism.* Bangkok: Sammajivasilpa (Foundation for Education in the Art of Right Living), Mulnidhi, 1957.

Punyasingh, Temsiri, and McGlasson, Maurice A. *A Changing Secondary Education in Thai Culture.* Bangkok: Chulalongkorn University, 1958.

Purcell, Victor. *The Chinese in Southeast Asia.* London: Oxford University Press, 1951.

Reeve, W. D. *Public Administration in Siam.* London: Royal Institute of International Affairs, 1951.

Sarasas, Phra. *My Country Thailand: Its History, Geography and Civilization.* Tokyo: Maruzen, 1942.

Sargent, Sir John, and Orata, Pedro T. *Report of the Mission to Thailand.* Bangkok: United Nations Educational, Scientific and Cultural Organization, 1950.

Sastrabuddhi, S. "Thailand: Educational Development in 1959–60." Pages 391–393 in United Nations, *International Yearbook of Education,* XXII. New York: 1960.

Satawethin, Chuea. *Wannakhadi Lae Prawatwannakhadi Thai* (Thai Literature and Its History). Thonburi: Thonburi Publishing, 1959.

Schweiguth, P. *Etude sur la Littérature Siamoise.* Paris: Imprimérie Nationale, 1951.

Seidenfaden, Erik. *The Thai Peoples,* I. Bangkok: Siam Society, 1958.

"Seven Bridges to Goodwill," *Army Digest,* XXI, No. 7, July 1966, 36–39.

Sharp, Lauriston. "Cultural Continuities and Discontinuities in Southeast Asia," *Journal of Asian Studies,* XXII, November 1962, 3–11.

————. "Peasants and Politics in Thailand," *Far Eastern Survey,* XIX, No. 19, September 13, 1950, 157–161.

Sharp, Lauriston, *et al. Siamese Rice Village: A Preliminary Study of Bang Chan, 1948–1949.* Bangkok: Cornell Research Center, 1953.

Shen James C. H. (ed). *China Yearbook 1961–62.* Taipei: China Publishing, 1962.

Shor, Edgar L. "The Thai Bureaucracy," *Administrative Science Quarterly,* V, June 1960, 66–68.

The Siam Directory—1960. (Compiled by Chamni Phimphisan and Associates.) Bangkok: n. pub., n.d.

The Siam Directory, 1962. (Compiled by Chamni Phimphisan and Associates.) Bangkok: Thai Inc., 1962.

The Siam Directory, 1963–1964. (Compiled by Chamni Phimphisan and Associates.) Bangkok: Thai Inc., 1964.

"Siam Heads Off Communism," *Economist,* CLXXIV, February 1955, 635, 636.

Sibunruang, J. Kasem. "Littérature Siamoise." Pages 1362–1383 in R. Queneau (ed.), Histoire de Littératures, I. Paris: Encyclopédie de la Pleiade, 1955.

Sien-chong, Niu. "The Overseas Chinese and Southeast Asia." *Military Review,* XLV, No. 8, August 1965, 29–31.

Silpha-Bhirasri. *Appreciation of Our Murals.* Bangkok: Fine Arts Department, 1959.

————. *A Bare Outline of History and Styles of Art.* Bangkok: Fine Arts Department, 1959.

————. *Modern Art in Thailand.* ("Thailand Culture Series," No. 14.) Bangkok: National Culture Institute, 1954.

————. *Thai Architecture and Painting.* ("Thailand Culture Series," No. 4.) Bangkok: National Culture Institute, 1953.

————. *Thai Buddhist Sculpture.* ("Thailand Culture Series," No. 10.) Bangkok: National Culture Institute, 1953.

Silpakorn Gallery. *The Origin and Evolution of Thai Murals.* (Published for the exhibition of photographs of Mural Paintings at the Silpakorn Gallery.) Bangkok: 1959.

Simoniya, N.A. *Overseas Chinese in Southeast Asia—A Russian Study* (translated by U.S. Joint Publications Research Service). (Southeast Asia Program, Department of Far Eastern Studies, Data Paper No. 45.) Ithaca: Cornell University Press, December 1961.

Sithi-Amnuai, Paul. "The Economy of Southern Thailand," *Far Eastern Economic Review*, XXXVIII, October 25, 1962, 237–243.

――――. "Thai Power Industry," *Far Eastern Economic Review*, XXXVI, May 10, 1962, 279, 282–287.

Sivaram, M. *Mekong Clash and Far East Crisis*. Bangkok: Thai Commercial Press, 1951.

――――. *The New Siam in the Making: A Survey of the Political Transition in Siam, 1932–1936*. Bangkok: Stationers Printing Press, 1936.

Siwasariyanon, Witt. "Thai Literature," Orient Review and Literary Digest, XI, August 1956, 4–10.

Siwasariyanon, Witt (ed.) *Aspects and Facets of Thailand*. Bangkok: Public Relations Department, 1958.

――――. *Vistas of Thailand*. Bangkok: Dhana Publishing Company, 1963.

Skinner, George William. "Chinese Assimilation and Thai Politics," *Journal of Asian Studies*, XVI, February 1957, 237–250.

――――. *Chinese Society in Thailand*. Ithaca: Cornell University Press, 1957.

――――. *Leadership and Power in the Chinese Community of Thailand*. Ithaca: Cornell University Press, 1958.

――――. *Report on the Chinese in Southeast Asia*. Ithaca: Cornell University Southeast Asia Program, 1950.

――――. "A Study of Chinese Community Leadership in Bangkok, Together with a Historical Survey of Chinese Society in Thailand." Unpublished Doctoral dissertation. Ithaca: Cornell University, 1954.

Smyth, H. Warren. *Five Years in Siam*. London John Murray, 1898.

Sonakul, Ayumongol. "Constantine Phaulkon of Siam," *Bangkok Post*, August 14, 1966, 18, 19.

Sparrow, Gerald. *Land of the Moon Flower*. London: Elek Books, 1955.

Spencer, J.E. *Asia, East by South*. New York: Wiley, 1954.

Srisavasdi, Boon Chuey. *The Hill Tribes of Siam*. Bangkok: Khun Aroon, 1963.

Stamp, Dudley L. *Asia: A Regional and Economic Geography*. (9th ed.) London: Methuen, 1957.

Stanton, Edwin F. "Communist Pressures in Thailand," *Current History*, XXXVIII, February 1960, 102–109.

Sullivan, Michael. "Archeology in Thailand Today," *Archeology*, X, March 1957, 11–17.

Sumitra, Sanon. "Thailand: Educational Progress in 1956–7." Pages 375–378 in United Nations, *International Yearbook of Education*, XIX. New York: 1957.

Suriyabongs, Luang. *The Buddhas' Doctrine of Truth (Dhamma) and Buddhist Religion as Practiced by the Holy Brotherhood in Siam*. (Trans., Krachang Bunnag.) Bangkok: Krungdebarnagar Press, 1936.

――――. *Buddhism: An Introduction*. Colombo: Lanka Bauddha Mandalaya, Ministry of Local Government and Cultural Affairs, 1957.

――――. *Buddhism and the Thai People*. Bangkok: Government Tourist Bureau, n.d.

Svasti Panish, Kaw. "Thailand: Educational Progress in 1958–9." Pages 409–411 in United Nations, *International Yearbook of Education*, XXI, New York: 1959.

506

"Symposium on Northeast Thailand," *Asian Survey*, VI, No. 7, July 1966, 349–380.

Textor, Robert B. "The Northeastern Samlor Driver in Bangkok." Pages 7–47 in United Nations Educational, Scientific and Cultural Organization, *The Social Implications of Industrialization and Urbanization*. Calcutta: 1956.

Textor, Robert B.; McCullough, James C.; Kanitayon, Kitima; and Wasi, Suchart. *Manual for Rural Community Health Workers in Thailand*. Bangkok: USOM and Royal Department of Health, 1958.

Thailand. Laws, Statutes, etc.
Labour Act, B.E. 2499. (Trans., U.S. Department of Labor.) Bangkok: 1957 (mimeo.)

Royal Thai Government Gazette (Trans., International Translations, Bangkok), II, No. 267, January 21, 1962; No. 272, February 28, 1962; No. 273, March 7, 1962; No. 279, April 21, 1962; No. 291, July 21, 1962; No. 292, July 28, 1962; No. 293, August 7, 1962; No. 297, September 7, 1962.

Thailand. Ministry of Education. External Relations Division. *Education in Thailand*. Bangkok: Religious Affairs Department Publishing, 1960.

Thailand. Ministry of Education. Fine Arts Department. *Ngansankheetsin khong Kromsilpakorn 2492–2494* (Work of the Fine Arts Department in Music and Drama 1949–1951). Bangkok: Thaphrachan Publishing, 1951.

Thailand. Ministry of Foreign Affairs. *Facts About the Relations Between Thailand and Cambodia*. Bangkok: 1961.

―――. Department of Information. Foreign Affairs Bulletin, I, December 1961-January 1962; February-March 1962.

Thailand. Ministry of the Interior. Department of Public Welfare. *Social Welfare in Thailand*. (DSS 2/59.) Bangkok: 1959.

Thailand. National Museum. *Album of Art Exhibits*, I. Bangkok: National Museum, 1955.

Thailand. Office of the Prime Minister. *Raingan khwankaona nai raya 3 pi haeng kanpatiwat: 20 Tulakhom 2504* (Report of the Progress Made During the Three Years of the Revolution, 20 October 1961). Bangkok: Samnak Tamniab Nayok Ratthamontri Publishing, 1961.

―――. Budget Office. *Budget in Brief: Fiscal Year 2505*. Bangkok: Government House Printing Office, 1961.

Thailand. Office of the Prime Minister. Bureau of the Budget. *Budget in Brief: Fiscal Year 1966*. Bangkok: Local Affairs Press, 1966.

Thailand. Office of the Prime Minister. National Economic Development Board. Central Statistical Office. *Bulletin of Statistics, July-September 1961*, X, No. 3, 1961.

―――. *Statistical Yearbook of Thailand 1956–1958*. (No. 23.) Bangkok: 1961.

―――. *Thailand Population Census, 1960 (Changwad Series: Whole Kindgom)*. Bangkok: Government House Printing Office, 1962.

Thailand. Office of the Prime Minister. National Statistical Office. *Bulletin of Statistics Quarterly*, XIV, No. 4, 1966.

―――. *Statistical Yearbook of Thailand, 1965*. Bangkok: 1966.

Thailand. Thailand Information Service. *Thai Information Service Bulletin*, No. 28, July 23, 1951: No. 41, September 6, 1951.

Thailand Directory—1961. (Compiled by Sanan Phiewnaun.) Bangkok: Mongkolkarnpim, 1961.

Thailand Directory—1962. (Compiled by Sanan Phiewnaun.) Bangkok: Hongkhon Publishing, 1962.

"Thailand." In *Far Eastern Economic Review Yearbook, 1965.* Hong Kong: Far Eastern Economic Review, 1964.

"Thailand." In *Far Eastern Economic Review Yearbook 1966.* Hong Kong: Far Eastern Economic Review, 1965.

"Thailand." In *Far Eastern Economic Review Yearbook, 1967.* Hong Kong: Far Eastern Economic Review, 1966.

"Thailand," *World Health,* XIV, January-February 1961, 28, 29.

"Thailand Today: A Special Survey of the Thai Economy," *Far Eastern Economic Review,* XXXII, June 22, 1961, 551–610.

Thibert, Marguerite. "Training Problems in the Far East," *International Labour Organisation Studies and Reports.* (New Series, No. 11.) Geneva: 1948.

Thompson, Peter A. *Lotus Land.* London: T. Werner Lourie, 1906.

Thompson, Virginia. *Labor Problems in Southeast Asia.* New Haven: Yale University Press, 1947.

————. *Minority Problems in Southeast Asia.* Stanford: Stanford University Press, 1955.

————. *Thailand: The New Siam.* New York: Macmillan, 1941.

Thompson, Virginia, and Adloff, Richard. *Cultural Institutions and Educational Policy in Southeast Asia.* New York: Institute of Pacific Relations, 1948.

Trager, Frank N. *Marxism in Southeast Asia.* Stanford: Stanford University Press, 1959.

Transportation Consultants, Inc. *Survey of Southern Ports in Thailand.* Washington: 1963.

Turpin, M. (comp.). *History of the Kingdom of Siam and of the Revolutions That Have Caused the Overthrow of the Empire, Up to A.D. 1770.* (Translated from French by B. O. Cartwright.) Bangkok: American Presbyterian Mission Press, 1908.

"Two Six Year Plans Unveiled," *Bangkok Post,* October 11, 1960, 1, 14.

United Nations. Department of Economic and Social Affairs. Statistical Office. *Population and Vital Statistics Report.* (Statistical Papers, Series A, Vol. XIV, No. 2.) New York: United Nations, April 1, 1962.

————. *Population and Vital Statistics Report.* (Statistical Papers, Series A, XVIII, No. 4.) New York: October 1, 1966.

United Nations. Technical Assistance Program. *Village Communities in N.E. Thailand.* (Survey of Thailand—UNESCO Fundamental Educational Center [TUFEC], Report No. TAA/THA/i.) New York: 1958.

United Nations Educational, Scientific and Cultural Organization. *Basic Facts and Figures: International Statistics Relating to Education, Culture and Mass Communication, 1960.* Paris: UNESCO, 1961.

————. International Documents Service. *World Survey of Education II: Primary Education.* Paris: 1958.

————. *World Survey of Education III: Secondary Education.* New York: 1961.

United Nations Educational, Scientific and Cultural Organization. Statistical Reports and Studies. *Statistics of Newspapers and Other Periodicals.* Paris: 1959.

United Nations Statistical Yearbook 1961. New York: United Nations, 1961.

U.S. Agency for International Development. Cambodia. "Lower Mekong Basin Development With Special Reference to Cambodia." Phnom Penh: AID, March 1962.

U.S. Army. Quartermaster Research and Engineering Center. Earth Sciences Division. *Special Report, S–1. Notes on Some Environmental Conditions Affecting Military Logistics in Thailand.* Natick: Quartermaster Research and Engineering Command Headquarters, 1962.

U.S. Department of Commerce. Bureau of International Commerce. *Overseas Business Report.* (OBR–66–60.) Washington: September 1966.

U.S. Department of Labor. Bureau of Labor Statistics. "Foreign Labor Information: Labor in Thailand." Washington: June 1959 (mimeo.).

––––––. *Labor Law and Practice: Thailand.* (BLS Report No. 267.) Washington, 1964.

U.S. United States Information Agency. *Country Data: Thailand.* Washington: 1966.

––––––. Broadcasting Service. *Voice of America Program Schedule: Far East.* Washington: n.d.

U.S. United States Information Agency. Research and Reference Service. "The Overseas Chinese in Thailand: A Communications Factbook." (R–19–66.) Washington: January 1966 (mimeo.)

U.S. United States Operations Mission to Thailand. *Assignment Thailand.* Bangkok: USOM, 1958.

––––––. *Private Enterprise Investment Opportunities in Thailand.* (2d ed.). Washington: USOM, 1966.

––––––. *Thai-American Economic and Technical Cooperation.* Bangkok: USOM, 1961.

––––––. *Thai-American Economic and Technical Cooperation.* Bangkok: USOM, 1962.

––––––. *Thai-American Economic and Technical Cooperation.* Bangkok: USOM, 1965.

––––––. Program Office. *Summary of U.S. Economic Aid to Thailand and Selected Statistical Data.* Washington: USOM, 1966.

U.S. United States Operations Mission to Thailand. Public Administration Division. *Organizational Directory of the Government of Thailand.* Bangkok: USOM: 1955.

––––––. *Organizational Directory of the Government of Thailand.* Bangkok: USOM, 1966.

University of Chicago. *Area Handbook on Malaya.* (HRAF Subcontractor's Monograph.) Chicago: 1955.

Vacha, Phya Srivisarn. "Kingship in Siam." Pages 237–246 in *Selected Articles from the Siam Society Journal,* III. Bangkok: 1959.

Varavetyaphisit, Phra. *Vannakhadi Thai.* Bangkok: Chulalongkorn University, 1959.

Vella, Walter F. *The Impact of the West on Government in Thailand.* (University of California Publications in Political Science, IV, No. 3.) Berkeley: University of California Press, 1955.

Videt-Yontrakich, Luang. *Certain Facts About Thailand.* Washington: n.pub., October 1965.

––––––. "Notes on Certain Facts about Thailand." Washington: Royal Thai Embassy, November 24, 1961 (mimeo.).

Vongsayanha, C. "Thailand: Educational Progress in 1957–8." Pages 110–112 in United Nations, *International Yearbook of Education,* XX. New York: 1958.

Wales, Horace Geoffrey Quaritch. *The Making of Greater India: A Study in South-East Asian Culture Change.* London: Bernard Quaritch, 1951.

––––––. *Prehistory and Religion in South-East Asia.* London: Bernard Quaritch, 1957.

Wales, Horace Geoffrey Quaritch. *Siamese State Ceremonies*. London: Bernard Quaritch, 1931.

Walter Reed Army Medical Center. Institute of Research. *Thailand*. (Health Data Publications, No. 6.) Washington: December 1966.

Wan Waithayakon, His Royal Highness Prince. "Thai Culture," *Journal of the Thailand Research Society*, XXXV, Pt. 2, September 1944, 135–145.

Warner, Denis. "Aggression by Seepage in Northeast Thailand," *Reporter*, XXVII, October 25, 1962, 33–37.

———. *Reporting Southeast Asia*. London: Angus and Robertson, 1966.

Watcharaphon, Prakat. *Ngan lae Chiwit khong Nakpraphan 40 Nampakka* (Work and Life of 40 Writers). Bangkok: Rungruangrat Publishing Co., 1962.

Wells, Kenneth Elmer. "Buddhism is Thailand: Its Sources of Strength," *International Review of Missions* (Edinburgh), XXIII, 1942, 199–204.

———. *Thai Buddhism: Its Rits and Activities*. Bangkok: Bangkok Times Press, 1939.

Wells, Margaret B. *Guide to Bangkok*. Bangkok; Christian Bookstore, 1959.

Wiens, Herold J. *China's March Toward the Tropics*. Camden: Shoestring Press, 1954.

Williams, Lea E. *The Future of the Overseas Chinese in Southeast Asia*. New York: McGraw-Hill, 1966.

Wilson, David A. "Thailand: Scandal and Progress," *Asian Survey*, V, No. 2, February 1965, 108–112.

Wolfstone, Daniel. "The Measure of the Mekong," *Far Eastern Economic Review*, XXXII, April 20, 1961, 125, 128–31.

Wood, William Alfred Rae. *Land of Smiles*. Bangkok: Krungdebarnagar Press, 1935.

Worawetyaphisit, Phra. *Wannakhadi Thai* (Thai Literature). Bangkok: Chulalongkorn University, 1959.

World Confederation of Organizations of the Teaching Profession. *Survey of the Status of the Teaching Profession in Asia*. (Prepared by E. W. Franklin.) Washington: 1963.

World Health Organization. *Health in South East Asia*. New Delhi: Statesman Press, n.d.

———. Regional Office for South East Asia. *Thirteenth Annual Report of the Regional Director to the Regional Committee for South East Asia*. N.pl.: July 1, 1960 to August 1, 1961.

Wright, Phillip. "Thailand's Chinese Question," *Reporter*, XXVI, April 26, 1962, 24–26.

Young, Ernest. *Kingdom of the Yellow Robe*. Westminster: Archibald Constable, 1898.

Young, Gordon. *The Hill Tribes of Northern Thailand*. Bangkok: Siam Society, 1962.

(Also consulted in the preparation of this section were:
Bangkok Post, from January 1, 1959, to December 31, 1962, and *Siam Rath*, from October 15, 1962, to January 15, 1963.)

Section II. Political

RECOMMENDED FURTHER READING

Among the sources consulted in the preparation of this section, the following are recommended as additional reading on the basis of quality and general availability.

Brimmell, J. H. *Communism in Southeast Asia.* New York: Oxford University Press, 1959.

Coughlin, Richard J. *Double Identity: The Chinese in Modern Thailand.* Hong Kong: Hong Kong University Press, 1960.

Darling, Frank C. "America and Thailand," *Asian Survey*, VII, No. 4, April 1967, 213–225.

————. "Marshal Sarit and Absolutist Rule in Thailand," *Pacific Affairs*, XXXIII, December 1960, 347–360.

————. "Modern Politics in Thailand," *Review of Politics*, XXIV, April 1962, 163–182.

————. *Thailand and the United States.* Washington: Public Affairs Press, 1965.

Fifield, Russell H. *The Diplomacy of Southeast Asia: 1945–1958.* New York: Harper, 1958.

————. *Southeast Asia in United States Policy.* New York: Praeger, 1963.

Hanks, Lucien M. "Merit and Power in the Thai Social Order," *American Anthropologist*, LXIV, No. 6, 1962, 1247–1261.

Hanna, Willard A. *Thailand's Strategic Northeast.* (American Universities Field Staff Reports, Southeast Asia Series, XIV, No. 1.) New York: AUFS, 1966.

Hollinger, Carol. *Mai pen rai (Means Never Mind).* Boston: Hougton Mifflin, 1965.

Mitchell, John D. "Thailand's Unexamined Media: Nondaily Newspapers and Radio-TV," *Journalism Quarterly*, XXXXII, Winter 1965, 87–97.

Nuechterlein, Donald E. "Thailand: Another Vietnam?" *Asian Survey*, VII, No. 2, February 1967, 126–130.

————. "Thailand: Year of Danger and of Hope," *Asian Survey*, VI, No. 2, February 1966, 119–124.

————. "Thailand After Sarit," *Asian Survey*, IV, No. 5, May 1964, 842–850.

————. "Thailand and SEATO: A Ten-Year Appraisal," *Asian Survey*, IV, No. 12, December 1964, 1174–1181.

————. *Thailand and the Struggle for Southeast Asia.* Ithaca: Cornell University Press, 1966.

Phillips, Herbert P. *Thai Peasant Personality: The Patterning of Interpersonal Behavior in the Village of Bang Chan.* Berkeley: University of California Press, 1966.

Riggs, Fred W. *Thailand: The Modernization of a Bureaucractic Policy.* Honolulu: East-West Center Press, 1966.

Shaplen, Robert. "Letter from Bangkok," *New Yorker*, XLIII, No. 4, March 18, 1967, 135–172.

Siffin, William J. *The Thai Bureaucracy: Institutional Change and Development*. Honolulu: East-West Center Press, 1966.

Skinner, George William. *Chinese Society in Thailand*. Ithaca: Cornell University Press, 1957.

_____. *Leadership and Power in the Chinese Community of Thailand*. Ithaca: Cornell University Press, 1958.

"Symposium on Northeast Thailand," *Asian Survey*, VI, No. 7, July 1966, 349–380.

Thailand. Office of the Prime Minister. Editorial Board. *Official Yearbook, 1964*. Bangkok: Government House Printing Office, 1965.

Theh Chongkhadikij. "Foreign Minister Thanat—An Evaluation," *Bangkok Post*, July 10, 1966, 15.

Thompson, Virginia, and Adloff, Richard. *The Left Wing in Southeast Asia*. New York: William Sloane Associates, 1950.

Williams, Lea E. *The Future of the Overseas Chinese in Southeast Asia*. New York: McGraw-Hill, 1966.

Wilson, David A. "Elections and Parties in Thailand," *Far Eastern Survey*, XXVII, August 1958, 113–119.

_____. "The Military in Thai Politics." Pages 253–276 in John J. Johnson (ed.), *The Role of the Military in Underdeveloped Countries*. Princeton: Princeton University Press, 1962.

_____. *Politics in Thailand*. Ithaca: Cornell University Press, 1962.

_____. "Thailand: Scandal and Progress," *Asian Survey*, V, No. 2, February 1965, 108–112.

_____. "Thailand and Marxism." Pages 58–101 in Frank N. Trager (ed.), *Marxism in Southeast Asia: A Study of Four Countries*. Stanford: Stanford University Press, 1959.

OTHER SOURCES USED

Atthakor, Bunchana. "Conditions in the Thai Northeast," *Far Eastern Economic Review*, XXXV, March 16, 1962, 597–599.

Ball, W. MacMahon. *Nationalism and Communism in East Asia*. (2d ed.) Carlton: Melbourne University Press, 1956.

Benedict, Ruth. *Thai Culture and Behavior*. (Cornell University, Southeast Asia Program, Data Paper No. 4.) Ithaca: Cornell University Press, 1952.

Berrigan, D. "Thailand Is on the Spot," *Reporter*, XXIV, January 19, 1961, 29–31.

_____. "Tidying Up in Thailand," *Reporter*, XIV, November 27, 1958, 27–29.

Blanchard, Wendell, *et al*. *Thailand*. New Haven: Human Relations Area Files Press, 1957.

Chatham House Study Group. *Collective Defense in South East Asia: The Manila Treaty and Its Implications*. London: Oxford University Press, 1956.

"Chinese in Siam," *Economist*, CCIII, June 30, 1962, 1321, 1322.

Coast, John. *Some Aspects of Siamese Politics*. New York: International Secretarist, Institute of Pacific Relations, 1953.

Cornell University. *Area Handbook on Thailand*. (HRAF Subcontractor's Monograph.) Ithaca: 1956.

Coughlin, Richard J. "Some Social Features of Siamese Buddhism," *Asia: Asian Quarterly of Culture and Synthesis* (Saigon), II, December 1952, 403–408.

Crosby, Sir Josiah. *Siam: The Crossroads*. London: Hollis and Carter, 1945.

———. "Siamese Imperialism and the Pan-Thai Movement," *Fortnightly*, CLXI (New Series, CLIII), May 1943, 300–307.

de Lapomarede, Baron. "The Settling of the Siamese Revolution," *Pacific Affairs*, VII, September 1934, 251–259.

De Young, John E. *Village Life in Modern Thailand*. Berkeley: University of California Press, 1955.

Dwivedi, O. P. "Bureaucratic Corruption in Developing Countries," *Asian Survey*, VII, No. 4, April 1967, 245–253.

Fall, Bernard B. "Red China's Aims in South Asia," *Current History*, XLIII, September 1962, 136–144, 181.

Fraser, Thomas M., Jr. *Rusembilan: A Malay Fishing Village in Southern Thailand*. Ithaca: Cornell University Press, 1960.

Freyn, Hubert. "Thailand's Political Parties," *Far Eastern Economic Review*, XXI, December 20, 1956, 799–801.

Fulham, Parke. "Elites or Elections?" *Far Eastern Economic Review*, LI, No. 7, February 17, 1966, 273–275.

Gordon, Bernard K. *The Dimensions of Conflict in Southeast Asia*. Englewood Cliffs: Prentice-Hall, 1966.

Hanrahan, Gene Z. *The Communist Struggle in Malaya*. New York: International Secretarist, Institute of Pacific Relations, 1954.

Heine-Geldern, Robert. *Conceptions of State and Kingship in Southeast Asia*. (Data Paper No. 18, Southeast Asia Program, Department of Asian Studies, Cornell University.) Ithaca: Cornell University Press, 1956.

Horrigan, F. J. "Provincial Government and Administration." Pages 41–72 in Joseph L. Sutton (ed.), *Problems of Politics and Administration in Thailand*. Indiana: Indiana University Press, 1962.

Institut Vostokovedeniia, Akademia Nauk, SSSR (Institute of Oriental Studies, Academy of Sciences, USSR). *Sovermennyi Thailand* (Modern Thailand). Moscow: Izdatelstvo Vostochnoi Literaturyi, 1958.

Jacobs, Milton. *A Study of Communications in Thailand with Emphasis on Word of Mouth Communication*. Washington: Special Operations Research Office, The American University, 1964.

Johnstone, William C. "The Appeals of Communism in Asia," *Annals of the American Academy of Political and Social Science*, CCXLII, July 1962, 105–110.

Kaufman, Howard Keva. *Bangkhuad: A Community Study in Thailand*. New York: Augustin, 1960.

King, John Kerry. "Thailand's Bureaucracy and the Threat of Communist Subversion," *Far Eastern Survey*, XXIII, November 1954, 169–173.

Kingshill, Konrad. *Ku Daeng, the Red Tomb: A Village Study in Northern Thailand*. Bangkok: Prince Royal's College (Distributed by Siam Society), 1960.

Koe, John. "What Chances for Democracy in Thailand," *Eastern World*, XVI, May 1962, 11, 12.

"Military In, Politicians Out," *U.S. News and World Report*, XLVI, June 1, 1959, 97, 98.

Mosel, James N. "Communications Patterns and Political Socialization in Transitional Thailand." Pages 184–228 in Lucian W. Pye (ed.), *Communications and Political Development*. Princeton: Princeton University Press, 1963.

Nairn, Ronald C. *International Aid to Thailand: The New Colonialism*. New Haven: Yale University Press, 1966.

Nippon ECAFE Kyokai (Japan ECAFE Association). *Tai no shakai kozo* (Social Structure in Thailand). Tokyo: Nippon ECAFE Kyokai, 1966.

"Peking and Thai Communists," *Far Eastern Economic Review*, XVII, October 14, 1954, 485, 486.

"Political Change in Thailand," *External Affairs*, II, March 1959, 53–56.

Rebrikova, Nina V. *Tailand.* Moscow: Gousudarstvennoye Izdatelstvo Vostochnni Literaturyi, 1960.

Reeve, W. D. *Public Administration in Siam.* London: Royal Institute of International Affairs, 1951.

Rose, Saul. *Socialism in Southern Asia.* New York: Oxford University Press, 1959.

Sander, S. W. "Report from Thailand: Communists Heating Up a Second Front in Asia," *U.S. News and World Report*, LXI, July 18, 1966, 42–44.

Sharp, Lauriston. "Peasants and Politics in Thailand," *Far Eastern Survey*, XIX, No. 19, September 13, 1950, 157–161.

Shor, Edgar L. "The Thai Bureaucracy," *Administrative Science Quarterly*, V, June 1960, 66–68.

The Siam Directory, 1963–1964. (Compiled by Chamni Phimphisan and Associates.) Bangkok: Thai Inc., 1964.

Simoniya, N. A. *Overseas Chinese in Southeast Asia—A Russian Study* (translated by U.S. Joint Publications Research Service). (Southeast Asia Program, Department of Far Eastern Studies, Data Paper No. 45.) Ithaca: Cornell University Press, December 1961.

Sithi-Amnuai, Paul. "Towards Stability," *Far Eastern Economic Review*, XXXVII, September 6, 1961, 423, 424.

Siwasariyanon, Witt (ed.). *Vistas of Thailand.* Bangkok: Dhana Publishing Company, 1963.

Skinner, George William. "Chinese Assimilation and Thai Politics," *Journal of Asian Studies*, XVI, February 1957, 237–250.

South Manchurian Railway Co. *Taikoku in Okeru Kakyo* (Overseas Chinese in Thailand). Tokyo: Mantetsu Toa Keizai Chosakyoku, 1939.

St. Clair, McKelway. "Siam Tries a People's Party," *Asia*, XXXII, November 1932, 555–561.

Stanton, Edwin F. "Communist Pressures in Thailand," *Current History*, XXXVIII, February 1960, 102–109.

―――. "Spotlight on Thailand," *Foreign Affairs*, XXXIII, October 1954, 72–85.

Sucharitkul, Sompong. "The Rule of Law in Thailand," *Journal of International Commission of Jurists*, I, August 1957, 23–42.

Sutton, Joseph L. (ed.). *Problems of Politics and Administration in Thailand.* Indiana: Indiana University Press, 1962.

Swygard, Kline R. "The Impact of Western Political Institutions in Thailand," *Western Political Quarterly* (Supplement), XIII, September 1960, 21–33.

Thailand. Laws, Statutes, etc.

Act Organizing the Office of the President of the Council of Ministers, *Royal Thai Government Gazette* (trans., International Translations, Bangkok), LXXXIII, No. 4, January 25-February 25, 1966.

Constituent Assembly. Constitution Drafting Committee. The Constitution of Thailand (Draft.) Bangkok: n.d. (mimeo.). (Unpublished manuscript not available for public distribution.)

"Expenditure Budget Act for the Fiscal Year B.E. 2510, "*Royal Thai Government Gazette* (trans., International Translations, Bangkok), LXXXIII, September 30, 1966.

Thailand. Office of the Prime Minister. National Statistical Office. *Statistical Yearbook of Thailand, 1965.* Bangkok: 1966.

"Thailand's Alien Fee Encourages Communism," *Far East Digest,* No. 66, October 1952, 48.

"Thailand's Secret of Tranquility," *Far Eastern Economic Review,* XXXIII, July 6, 1961, 13–15.

Thanat Khoman. "Some Facts and Considerations About our Foreign Policy." Pages 39–42 in Witt Siwasariyanon (ed.), *Vistas of Thailand.* Bangkok: Dhana Publishing Company, 1963.

Thompson, Virginia. *Minority Problems in Southeast Asia.* Stanford: Stanford University Press, 1955.

Uchida, Naosaku. *The Overseas Chinese: A Bibliographical Essay Based on the Resources of the Hoover Institution.* Stanford: Stanford University Press, 1959.

Udayanin, Kasem, and Smith, Rufus D. *The Public Service in Thailand: Organization, Recruitment and Training.* Brussels: International Institute of Administrative Sciences, 1954.

U.S. Congress. 89th, 2d Session. Senate. Committee on Foreign Relations. *U.S. Policy With Respect to Mainland China.* Washington: GPO, 1966.

U.S. Department of Commerce. Bureau of International Commerce. *Overseas Business Report.* (OBR–66–60.) Washington: September 1966.

U.S. United States Information Agency. *Country Data: Thailand.* Washington: 1966.

———. Research and Reference Service. "The Overseas Chinese in Thailand: A Communications Fact Book." (R–19–66.) Washington: January 1966 (mimeo.).

U.S. United States Information Service. *USIS Objectives.* Washington: 1966.

U.S. United States Operations Mission to Thailand. *Summary of U.S. Economic Aid to Thailand and Selected Statistical Data.* Washington: USOM, 1966.

———. *Thai-American Economic and Technical Cooperation.* Bangkok: USOM, 1965.

———. Public Administration Division. *Organizational Directory of the Government of Thailand.* Bangkok: USOM, 1966.

Vandenbosch, Amry. "Chinese Thrust in Southeast Asia," *Current History,* XXXVIII, December 1959, 333–338.

Waithayakon, Wan. "Communist Danger to Asia," *U.S. News and World Report,* XLV, October 31, 1958, 33.

Wales, Horace Geoffrey Quaritch. *Ancient Siamese Government and Administration.* London: Bernard Quaritch, 1934.

Warner, Denis. *Reporting Southeast Asia.* London: Angus and Robertson, 1966.

Wells, Kenneth Elmer. "Buddhism in Thailand: Its Sources of Strength," *International Review of Missions* (Edinburgh), XXIII, 1942, 199–204.

Wilson, David A. "Thailand." Pages 3–72 in George McTurnan Kahin (ed.), *Governments and Politics of Southeast Asia.* (2d ed.) Ithaca: Cornell University Press, 1964.

Woodman, Dorothy. "Corruption or Communism?—Dilemma in Siam," *Far East Digest,* Nos. 91 and 92, December 1954, 32, 33.

———. "Soldier and Statesman: Pibul and Pridi," *Asian Horizon,* I, Summer 1948, 9–21.

Wright, Phillip. "Thailand's Chinese Question," *Reporter,* XXVI, April 26, 1962, 24–26.

(The following periodicals were used in the preparation of this chapter: *Asian Recorder,* from January 1955 to January 1967; *Azia no Doko* (Asian Trends) [Tokyo] from January-August 1966; *Bangkok Post,* from January 1, 1957, to March 15, 1967; *Christian Science Monitor,* from January 1961 to May 1967; *Keesing's Contemporary Archives,* from January 1955 through May 1967; *New York Times,* for 1932, 1933 and 1939 and from 1941 through May 1967; and *Tonan Azia Yoran* (Southeast and South Asia Factbook), 1959-1966.)

Section III. Economic

RECOMMENDED FURTHER READING

Among the sources consulted in the preparation of this section, the following are recommended as additional reading on the basis of quality and general availability.

Ayal, Eliezer B., "Private Enterprise and Economic Progress in Thailand," *Journal of Asian Studies*, XXVI, No. 1, November 1966, 5–14.

_____. "Thailand's Six Year National Economic Development Plan," *Asian Survey*, I, No. 11, January 1962, 33–43.

Charoenchai, Bun. "Progress and Problems of Industrialization in Thailand," *Foreign Affairs Bulletin*, III, No. 5, April-May 1964, 469–490.

Darling, Frank C. "American and Thailand," *Asian Survey*, VII, No. 4, April 1967, 213–225.

Fraser, Thomas M., Jr. *Fishermen of South Thailand*. New York: Holt, Rinehart and Winston, 1966.

Fulham, Parke. "Elites or Elections?" *Far Eastern Economic Review*, LI, No. 7, February 17, 1966, 273–275.

Hanna, Willard A. *Peninsular Thailand, I: The Dim Past*. (American Universities Field Staff Reports, Southeast Asia Series, XIII, No. 22.) New York: AUFS, 1965.

_____. *Peninsular Thailand, II: The Border Provinces*. (American Universities Field Staff Reports, Southeast Asia Series, XIII, No. 23.) New York: 1965.

_____. *Peninsular Thailand, III: The Shores of Songkhla*. (American Universities Field Staff Reports, Southeast Asia Series, XIII, No. 24.) New York: AUFS, 1965.

_____. *Peninsular Thailand, IV: The Rubber of Haadyai and the Tin of Phuket*. (American Universities Field Staff Reports, Southeast Asian Series, XIII, No. 25.) New York: AUFS, 1965.

Hanna, Willard A. *Peninsular Thailand, V: The Thai Muslim Centers of Pattani and Yala*. (American Universities Field Staff Reports, Southeast Asia Series, XIII, No. 26.) New York: AUFS, 1965.

_____. *Thailand's Strategic Northeast*. (American Universities Field Staff Reports, Southeast Asia Series, XIV, No. 1.) New York: AUFS, 1966.

Nuttonson, M. Y. *The Physical Environment and Agriculture of Thailand*. Washington: American Institute of Crop Ecology, 1963.

Pendleton, Robert Larimore. *Thailand: Aspects of Landscape and Life*. New York: Duell, Sloan and Pearce, 1963.

Pombhejara, Vichitvong N. "The Second Phase of Thailand's Six-Year Economic Development Plan, 1964–1966," *Asian Survey*, V, No. 3, March 1965, 161–168.

Rice, Richard P. "Thailand," *International Commerce*, LXXIII, No. 2, January 9, 1967, 43.

Scholla, Paul F., and Associates. *Mining Resources and Mining Investment Potential in Thailand.* Bangkok: United States Operations Mission to Thailand, May 1965.

Simonet, Pierre A. "Harmonious Development in Thailand," Finance and Development, III, No. 3, September 1966, 194–201.

Thailand. Ministry of the Interior. Department of Public Welfare. "Report on the Socio-Economic Survey of the Hill Tribes in Northern Thailand." Bangkok: September 1962 (mimeo.).

————. Ministry of National Development. Department of Technical and Economic Cooperation. *Thailand: Facts and Figures, 1965.* Bangkok: 1965.

"Thailand." *In Far Eastern Economic Review Yearbook, 1967.* Hong Kong: Far Eastern Economic Review, 1966.

United Nations. Economic and Social Council. *An Evaluation of the Impact of the Technical Cooperation Programme of the United Nations Family of Organizations in Thailand.* New York: 1966.

U.S. Department of Commerce. Bureau of International Commerce. *Basic Date on the Economy of Thailand.* (World Trade Information Service "Economic Reports.") Washington: GPO, 1966.

U.S. Operations Mission to Thailand. *Thai-American Economic and Technical Cooperation.* Bangkok: USOM, 1962.

————. *Thai-American Economic and Technical Cooperation.* Bangkok: USOM, 1965.

OTHER SOURCES USED

"Aid and Finance." *In Far Eastern Economic Review Yearbook, 1966.* Hong Kong: Far Eastern Economic Review, 1965.

"Aid to Farmers in Thailand," *International Financial News Survey,* XVIII, No. 9, March 4, 1966, 74.

Andrews, James Madison. *Siam: Second Rural Economic Survey, 1934–1935.* Bangkok: Bangkok Times Press, 1935.

Andrews, Laurence E., Jr. *Status of the Minerals Industry in Thailand.* Bangkok: U.S. Geological Survey, 1965.

"ASA and ASPAC." *In Far Eastern Economic Review Yearbook, 1967,* Hong Kong: Far Eastern Economic Review, 1966.

"ASA and Maphilindo." *In Far Eastern Economic Review Yearbook, 1964.* Hong Kong: Far Eastern Economic Review, 1963.

Asian Annual, "Eastern World" Handbook, 1956. London: Eastern World, 1956.

"Bank Merger in Thailand," *International Financial News Survey,* XVIII, No. 15, April 15, 1966, 123.

Bank of Thailand. "Cost of Living Indices," *Bank of Thailand Monthly Report,* II, July 1962.

————. *Ten Years of the Bank's Operation, 1942–52.* Bangkok: n.d.

Bank of Thailand Monthly Report, V, December 1965; VI, December 1966.

Bever, Margaret. "Thailand to Increase Rice Output with Irrigation," *Foreign Agriculture,* XX, May 1956, 14, 15.

"Big New Mills." *In Far Eastern Economic Review Yearbook, 1961.* Hong Kong: Far Eastern Economic Review, 1960.

Binson, Boonrod. "The Mekong and Thailand's Power Programme," *Far Eastern Economic Review,* XXX, November 1960, 244, 245, 248–250.

Bowring, Sir John. *The Kingdom and the People of Siam.* 2 Vols. London: John W. Parker, 1857.

518

Brown, Glenn C. "Agricultural Financing in Thailand." Washington: May 4, 1966. (Unpublished manuscript not available for public distribution.)

Chang, C. M. "Birth Blues," *Far Eastern Economic Review*, XLVI, No. 13, December 24, 1964, 603.

Chinalai, Charoen. "Deficit Trading," *Far Eastern Economic Review*, LI, No. 8, February 24, 1966, 351.

————. "Nowhere but Up," *Far Eastern Economic Review*, L, No. 9, December 2, 1965, 427.

————. "Planning Ahead," *Far Eastern Economic Review*, LI, No. 11, March 18, 1966, 500.

————. "Thailand: Mopping Up," *Far Eastern Economic Review*, LII, No. 2, April 14, 1966, 77–81.

Close, Alexander. "Behind Bangkok's Boom," *Far Eastern Economic Review*, XLVIII, No. 8, May 20, 1965, 355–358.

"The Colombo Plan." In *Far Eastern Economic Review Yearbook*, 1966. Hong Kong: Far Eastern Economic Review, 1965.

"The Colombo Plan." In *Far Eastern Economic Review Yearbook, 1967.* Hong Kong: Far Eastern Economic Review, 1966.

"Colombo Plan: Hard Work Inside." In *Far Eastern Economic Review Yearbook, 1965.* Hong Kong: Far Eastern Economic Review, 1964.

Consultative Committee on Economic Development in South and South-East Asia. *The Colombo Plan.* (Tenth Annual Report, Kuala Lumpur, October-November 1961.) London: HMSO, 1962.

Cornell University. *Area Handbook on Thailand.* (HRAF Subcontractor's Monograph.) Ithaca: 1956.

Crane, David. "Grains of Sand," *Far Eastern Economic Review*, L, No. 12, December 23, 1965, 569.

————. "Moving Up," *Far Eastern Economic Review*, L, No. 1, October 7, 1965, 33.

————. "Thai Hopes," *Far Eastern Economic Review*, LII, No. 12, June 23, 1966, 610.

Crosby, Sir Josiah. *Siam: The Crossroads.* London: Hollis and Carter, 1945.

Daniel, K. "Bonn and Bongkok," *Far Eastern Economic Review*, XXXIII, September 21, 1961, 602.

Davies, Derek. "Refining with Thais," *Far Eastern Economic Review*, XLVII, No. 1, January 7, 1965, 21–23.

De Young, John E. *Village Life in Modern Thailand.* Berkeley: University of California Press, 1955.

Dhanit, Chalerm. "Five-Year Monopoly," *Far Eastern Economic Review*, XLIX, No. 9, August 26, 1965, 395.

————. "1966 Budget," *Far Eastern Economic Review*, L, No. 7, November 19, 1965, 325.

"ECAFE." In *Far Eastern Economic Review Yearbook*, 1967. Hong Kong: Far Eastern Economic Review, 1966.

"ECAFE: Collaboration Amid Conflict." In *Far Eastern Economic Review Yearbook, 1966.* Hong Kong: Far Eastern Economic Review, 1965.

The Economist Intelligence Unit, Ltd. *Quarterly Economic Review: Continental Southeast Asia*, No. 4, December 1966.

————. *Quarterly Economic Review: Continental Southeast Asia*, No. 47, September 1964.

"Finance for Industry in Thailand," *International Financial News Survey*, XVI, No. 11, March 20, 1964, 90.

Freyn, Hubert. "Lignite Power," *Far Eastern Economic Review*, XLVIII, No. 13, June 24, 1965, 609.

Freyn, Hubert. "Phuket—Boom Island," *Far Eastern Economic Review*, LII, No. 1, April 7, 1966, 30, 31.

———. "Planned Security," *Far Eastern Economic Review*, LI, No. 6, February 10, 1966, 232, 233.

———. "Rebels Undeterred," *Far Eastern Economic Review*, LII, No. 3, April 21, 1966. 147, 148.

———. "Rubber Growing in Thailand," *Far Eastern Economic Review*, XXXII, April 6, 1961, 11, 12.

George, Ted. "Thailand Creeps Up," *Far Eastern Economic Review*, LII, No. 9, June 2, 1966, 452, 453.

Gopalan, M. P. "The Launching of ASA," *Far Eastern Economic Review*, XXXIII, September 21, 1961, 548–552.

Graham, Walter A. *Siam: A Handbook of Practical, Commercial, and Political Information*. 2 vols. London: Alexander Moring, 1924.

Hornaday, Mary. "UN Tames Mekong River—Vast Impact," *Christian Science Monitor*, October 18, 1962, 3.

"IBRD Loan to Thailand," *International Financial News Survey*, XVIII, No. 43, October 28, 1966, 359.

"Import Controls in Thailand," *International Financial News Survey*, XVIII, No. 13, April 1, 1966, 106.

Ingram, James C. *Economic Change in Thailand Since 1850*. Stanford: Stanford University Press, 1955.

International Bank for Reconstruction and Development. *A Public Development Program for Thailand*. Baltimore: John Hopkins Press, 1959.

International Monetary Fund. *International Financial News Survey*. September 16 and 30, October 28, November 4 and 11, 1955; February 10, March 9 and 16, April 13, May 4, 1956.

Jones, Emily and Alan. "Taming the Mekong," *Far Eastern Economic Review*, XLIX, No. 10, September 2, 1965, 418–420.

Kantabutra, Bundhit. *The Economy and National Income of Thailand*. Bangkok: National Economic Development Board, September 1959.

Kaufman, Howard Keva. *Banghuad: A Community Study in Thailand*. New York: Augustin, 1960.

King, John Kerry. *Southeast Asia in Perspective*. New York: Macmillan, 1956.

Ladjinsky, W. I. "Thailand's Agricultural Economy," *Foreign Agriculture*, VI, 1942, 165–184.

Landon, Kenneth Perry. *The Chinese in Thailand*. New York: Oxford University Press, 1941.

———. *Siam in Transition*. Chicago: University of Chicago Press, 1939.

Langbell, Kenneth S. "Remember Sarit," *Far Eastern Economic Review*, LI, No. 1, January 6, 1966, 10, 11.

Lee, S. Y. "Currency Banking and Foreign Exchange of Thailand," *Far Eastern Economic Review*, XXX, November 24, 1960, 360–378.

———. "Thailand's New Bank Act," *Far Eastern Economic Review*, XXXVII, August 9, 1962, 261–265.

Matlock, Clifford C. "Self-Determined," *Far Eastern Economic Review*, LIV, No. 3, October 20, 1966, 141–145.

Mayer, Paul A. *Thailand. A Market for U.S. Products*. (U.S. Department of Commerce. Bureau of International Programs. Supplement No. 3 to Part I, World Trade Information Service.) Washington: GPO, April 1962.

McGillivray, Donald; Kuhl, Leonard, *et al.* "Corn in Thailand." (A report on the corn situation in Thailand, containing the findings of representatives of the U.S. Feed Grains Council and the Foreign Agricultural Service, United States Department of Agriculture.) N.pl.: September 29, 1962.

Muscat, Robert J. *Development Strategy in Thailand: A Study of Economic Growth.* London: Praeger, 1966.

"The 1963 Industrial Census of Thailand," *Foreign Affairs Bulletin,* IV, No. 6, June-July 1965, 1184–1188.

"Par Value of Thai Baht," *International Financial News Survey,* XV, No. 42, October 25, 1963, 374.

Pillai, Gopinath. "Border Worries," *Far Eastern Economic Review,* XLVII, No. 10, March 12, 1965, 429.

―――. "On the Upswing," *Far Eastern Economic Review,* XLVIII, No. 1, April 1, 1965, 7–9.

―――. "Smelter's Ban," *Far Eastern Economic Review,* XLVIII, No. 3, April 15, 1965, 135.

―――. "Thai Crisis," *Far Eastern Economic Review,* XLVIII, No. 11, June 10, 1965, 521.

―――. "Thailand's Flourishing Business," *Far Eastern Economic Review,* XLVIII, No. 4, April 22, 1965, 197.

―――. "The Widening Gap," *Far Eastern Economic Review,* XLVII, No. 4, January 28, 1965, 172, 173.

"Pulp on the River Kwai," *Far Eastern Economic Review,* XXXII, April 13, 1961, 119.

Reangsuwan, Chaveng, and Thomas, M. Ladd (eds.). *Ministry of Agriculture.* (Thailand Government Organization Manual Series, Pt. II.) Bangkok: Thammasat University, Institute of Public Administration, 1960.

―――. *Ministry of Communications.* (Thailand Government Organization Manual Series, Pt. VII.) Bangkok: Thammasat University, Institute of Public Administration, 1960.

―――. *Ministry of Cooperatives.* (Thailand Government Organization Manual Series, Pt. III.) Bangkok: Thammasat University, Institute of Public Administration, 1960.

―――. *Ministry of Economic Affairs.* (Thailand Government Organization Manual Series, Pt. VI.) Bangkok: Thammasat University, Institute of Public Administration, 1960.

"Regional Work By ECAFE." *In Far Eastern Economic Review Yearbook,* 1963. Hong Kong: Far Eastern Economic Review, 1962.

"Siam and Its Chinese Community," *Economist,* CLXXVIII, February 4, 1956, 373.

The Siam Directory—1962. (Compiled by Chamni Phimphisan and Associates.) Bangkok: Thai Inc., 1962.

The Siam Directory, 1963–1964. (Compiled by Chamni Phimphisan and Associates.) Bangkok: Thai Inc., 1964.

Sithi-Amnuai, Paul, "An Infant Industry," *Far Eastern Economic Review,* XXXV, March 1, 1962, 497,498.

―――. "Investment Law Simplified," *Far Eastern Economic Review,* XXXVI, April 5, 1962, 13–16.

―――. "A Plan for Thailand," *Far Eastern Economic Review,* L, No. 3, October 21, 1965, 129–132.

―――. "The Thai Cotton Industry," *Far Eastern Economic Review,* XXXIII, August 3, 1961, 233–237.

Sithi-Amnuai, Paul, "Thai Power Industry," *Far Eastern Economic Review*, XXXVI, May 10, 1962, 279, 282–287.

———. "The Thai Sugar Industry," *Far Eastern Economic Review*, XXXII, May 18, 1961, 310–312.

Siwasariyanon, Witt. *Life in Bangkok*. ("Thailand Culture Series," No. 16.) Bangkok: National Culture Institute, 1954.

Sung, Kayser. "Thailand's Drive for Industrialization," *Far Eastern Economic Review*, XXIX, July 28, 1960, 158–163, 193.

"Survey for Iron and Steel Industry in Thailand," *International Financial News Survey*, XVII, No. 49, December 10, 1965, 449.

"Thai Government Loan for Industrial Finance," *International Financial News Survey*, XVII, No. 47, November 26, 1965, 434.

Thailand. Report of the Financial Advisors Covering the Years B. E. 2484 (1941) to B. E. 2493 (1950). Bangkok: n.d.

Thailand. Laws, Statues, etc.

"Commercial Banking Act, B.E. 2505," *Royal Thai Government Gazette* (trans., International Translations, Bangkok), LXXXIX, Pt. 40, May 1, 1962; III, July 23, 1962.

———. Ministry of Agriculture. *Agriculture in Thailand*. Bangkok: 1961.

———. *Land Utilization of Thailand, 1959*. Bangkok: 1960.

———. *Thailand and Her Agricultural Problems*. (Rev. ed.) Bangkok: 1950.

———. *Thailand Economic Fary Survey, 1953*. Bangkok: 1953.

———. Office of the Under Secretary of State. Division of Agricultural Economics. *Agricultural Statistics of Thailand, 1957*. Bangkok: 1958.

———. *Agricultural Statistics of Thailand, 1964*. Bangkok: 1966.

Thailand. Ministry of Commerce. Department of Commercial Intelligence. "Fish Market of Bangkok." In *Commercial Directory of Thailand, 1949–50*. Bangkok: 1951.

———. "The Teak Industy," In *Commercial Directory of Thailand, 1949–50*. Bangkok: 1951.

Thailand. Ministry of Foreign Affairs. Department of Information. *Foreign Affairs Bulletin*. I, December 1961-January 1962.

Thailand. Office of the Prime Minister. *Raingan khwankaoma nai raya 3 pi haeng kanpatiwat: 20 Talakhom 2504* (Report of the Progress Made During the Three Years of the Revolution, 20 October 1961). Bangkok: Samnak Tamniab Nayok Ratthamontri Publishing, 1961.

———. Bureau of the Budget. *Budget in Brief: Fiscal Year 1966*. Bangkok: Local Affairs Press, 1966.

Thailand. Office of the Prime Minister. Editorial Board. *Official Yearbook, 1964*. Bangkok: Government House Printing Office, 1965.

Thailand. Office of the Prime Minister. National Economic Council. Central Statistical Office. *Statistical Yearbook, 1952*. Bangkok: 1954.

Thailand. Office of the Prime Minister. National Economic Development Board. *The National Economic Development Plan, 1961–1966;* Second Phase: 1964–1966. Bangkok: January 1964.

———. *National Income of Thailand, 1960*. Bangkok: 1961.

———. *National Income of Thailand, 1965*. Bangkok: June 1966.

———. Central Statistical Office, *Bulletin of Statistics, January-March 1962*, XI, No. 1, 1962.

———. *Statistical Yearbook of Thailand, 1956–1958*. (No. 23.) Bangkok: 1961.

———. *Thailand Population Census, 1960 (Changwad Series: Whole Kingdom)*. Bangkok: 1962.

Thailand. Office of the Prime Minister. National Statistical Office. *Statistical Yearbook of Thailand, 1965.* Bangkok: 1966.

"Thailand." *In Far Eastern Economic Review Yearbook, 1962.* Hong Kong: Far Eastern Economic Review, 1961.

"Thailand." *In Far Eastern Economic Review Yearbook, 1963.* Hong Kong: Far Eastern Economic Review, 1962.

"Thailand." *In Far Eastern Economic Review Yearbook, 1964.* Hong Kong: Far Eastern Economic Review, 1963.

"Thailand." *In Far Eastern Economic Review Yearbook, 1965.* Hong Kong: Far Eastern Economic Review, 1964.

"Thailand." *In Far Eastern Economic Review Yearbook, 1966.* Hong Kong: Far Eastern Economic Review, 1965.

"Thailand," *International Financial Statistics,* XX, No. 2, February 1967, 278–281.

"Thailand Raises Foreign Loan Ceilings," *International Financial News Survey,* IV, No. 15, April 19, 1963, 141.

"Thailand's Interest Rate Policy," *International Financial News Survey,* XVIII, No. 21, May 27, 1966, 177.

Thompson, Virgina. *Thailand: The New Siam.* New York: Macmillan, 1941.

Tonan Azia Chosakai (South and Southeast Asia Research Institute). *Tonan Azia Yoran, 1966* (South and Southeast Asia Fact Book, 1966. Tokyo: Tonan Azia Chosakai, 1966.

"Trade and Aid." *In Far Eastern Economic Review Yearbook, 1967.* Hong Kong: Far Eastern Economic Review, 1966.

Tulyayon, Niwat. "Thailand's Jute Industry," *Far Eastern Economic Review,* XXV, January 4, 1962, 19–22.

United Nations. Economic Commission for Asia and the Far East. *Agricultural Development of Thailand.* Bangkok: 1955.

––––––. *Economic Survey of Asia and the Far East (1954–56).* Bangkok: 1954–56.

––––––. *Financial Institutions and the Mobilization of Domestic Capital in Thailand.* Bangkok: 1950.

United Nations Statistical Yearbook—1961. New York: United Nations, 1962.

U.S. Agency for International Development. Bureau for the Far East. *United States Aid to Thailand: Background Paper.* Washington: 1966.

U.S. Agency for International Development. Statistics and Reports Division. *U.S. Foreign Assistance and Assistance from International Organizations. (July 1, 1945—June 30, 1962).* Washington: AID, October 5, 1962.

U.S. The Comptroller General. Report to the Congress of the United States— Examination of Economic and Technical Assistance Program for Thailand —International Cooperation Administration, Department of State—Fiscal Years 1955–1960. Washington: August 1961.

U.S. Department of Agriculture. *Foreign Commerce Weekly,* LVII, January 21 and 28, 1957.

––––––. Foreign Agricultural Service. *The Agriculture Situation in Thailand* (FTAP 42–56). Washington: 1955 and 1956.

––––––. "Thailand's People Introduced to Recombined Milk," *Foreign Agriculture,* XXI, March 1957, 16.

––––––. "Thailand's Tobacco Production," *Foreign Crops and Markets,* LXXIII, December 17, 1956, 7.

U.S. Department of Commerce. Bureau of Foreign Commerce. *Basic Data on the Economy of Thailand.* (World Trade Information Service, "Economic Reports," Pt. 1, No. 60–45.) Washington: 1960.

523

U.S. Department of Commerce. Bureau of Foreign Commerce. *Economic Developments in the Far East and Oceania—1959*. (World Trade Information Service "Economic Reports," Pt. 1, No. 60–7.) Washington: GPO, 1960.

———. *Import Tariff System of Thailand*. (World Trade Information Service "Operations Reports," Pt. 2, No. 61–1.) Washington: GPO, 1961.

———. *Licensing and Exchange Controls—Thailand*. (World Trade Information Service "Operations Reports," Pt. 2, No. 60–10.) Washington: GPO, April 1960.

U.S. Department of Commerce. Bureau of International Commerce. *Overseas Business Report*. (OBR–66–60.) Washington: September 1966.

U.S. Department of Commerce. Bureau of International Programs. *Economic Developments in Thailand—1961*. (World Trade Information Service "Economic Reports," Pt. 1, No. 62–43.) Washington: GPO, May 1962.

U.S. Department of Labor. Bureau of Labor Statistics. *Labor Law and Practice: Thailand*. (BLS Report No. 267.) Washington: 1964.

U.S. Department of State. Bureau of Public Affairs. Office of Media Services. *Thailand: Background Notes*. Washington: 1966.

U.S. International Cooperation Administration. *Thailand: United States Economic Cooperation, 1951–1956*. Washington: GPO, 1957.

U.S. Operations Mission to Thailand. *Private Enterprise Investment Opportunities in Thailand*. (2d ed.) Washington: USOM, 1966.

———. *Summary of U.S. Economic Aid to Thailand and Selected Statistical Data*. Washington: USOM, 1966.

———. *Thai-American Economic and Techanical Cooperation*. Bangkok: USOM, 1961.

———. *Thai-American Economic Cooperation 1951–56*. Bangkok: USOM, 1957.

———. *United States Economic and Technical Assistance to Thailand—1950 to Date*. Bangkok: USOM, 1959.

———. Development Assistance Committee. Coordination Group in Thailand. *Fourth Annual Compendium of Technical Assistance to Thailand, 1966*. Bangkok: 1966.

U.S. Operations Mission to Thailand. Public Administration Division. *Organizational Directory of the Government of Thailand*. Bangkok: USOM, 1962.

———. *Organizational Directory of the Government of Thailand*. Bangkok: USOM, 1966.

van Rijnberk, W. L. *Industrial Development Policy and Planning in Thailand*. (United Nations Programme of Technical Assistance, Report No. TAO/THA/14.) New York: United Nations, Department of Economic and Social Affairs, 1961.

Voorhees, Harold C. "Thailand Tempo Still Rising," *International Commerce*, LXXIII, No. 14, April 3, 1967, 32, 33.

Williams, Lea E. *The Future of the Overseas Chinese in Southeast Asia*. New York: McGraw-Hill, 1966.

Wolfstone, Daniel. "The Siamese Situation," *Far Eastern Economic Review*, XXXIX, January 31, 1963, 204–210.

———. "The Six-Year Plan in Outline," *Far Eastern Economic Review*, XXXII, June 22, 1961, 565–567.

Wood, William Alfred Rae. *A History of Siam, from the Earliest Times to the Year A.D. 1781, with a Supplement Dealing with More Recent Events*. (Rev. ed.) Bangkok: Siam Barnakich Press, 1933.

Wu, Michael. "Bangkok Ingenuity," *Far Eastern Economic Review*, XLV, No. 8, August 20, 1964, 349.

Zimmerman, Carl C. *Siam, Rural Economic Survey, 1930–31*. Bangkok: Bangkok Times Press, 1931.

(The following periodicals were also used in the preparation of this section: *Bangkok Post*, from January 1, 1957 through March 15, 1967; *Bank of Thailand Monthly Report*, from January 1962 through December 1966; *Far Eastern Economic Review* [Hong Kong], from January 4, 1962, through December 30, 1966; and *Three-Monthly Economic Review: Continental Southeast Asia* and annual supplements [London], from March 1957 through December 1966.)

Section IV. National Security

RECOMMENDED FURTHER READING

Among the sources consulted in the preparation of this section, the following are recommended as additional reading on the basis of quality and general availability.

Busch, Noel Fairchild. *Thailand: An Introduction to Modern Siam.* (2d ed.) Princeton: Van Nostrand, 1964.

Darling, Frank C. *Thailand and the United States.* Washington: Public Affairs Press, 1965.

Hall, D. G. E. *A History of Southeast Asia.* (2d ed.) New York: St. Martin's Press, 1964.

Insor, D. *Thailand: A Political, Social and Economic Analysis.* New York: Praeger, 1963.

Kaufman, Howard Keva. *Bangkhuad: A Community Study in Thailand.* New York: Augustin, 1960.

Kuebler, Jeanne. "Thailand: New Red Target," *Editorial Research Reports,* XI, No. 10, September 15, 1965, 665–682.

Moffat, Abbot Low. Mongkut: *The King of Siam.* Ithaca: Cornell University Press, 1961.

Nuechterlein, Donald E. "Thailand: Another Vietnam?" *Asian Survey,* VII, No. 2, February 1967, 126–130.

————. *Thailand and the Struggle for Southeast Asia.* Ithaca: Cornell University Press, 1966.

Pendleton, Robert Larimore. *Thailand: Aspects of Landscape and Life.* New York: Duell, Sloan and Pearce, 1963.

Reangsuwan, Chaveng, and Thomas, M. Ladd (eds.). *Ministry of Justice.* (Thailand Government Organization Manual Series, Pt. IV.) Bangkok: Thammasat University, Institute of Public Administration, 1960.

Riggs, Fred W. *Thailand: The Modernization of a Bureaucratic Polity.* Honolulu: East-West Center Press, 1966.

The Siam Directory, 1963–1964. (Compiled by Chamni Phimphisan and Associates) Bangkok: Thai Inc., 1964.

Siffin, William J. *The Thai Bureaucracy: Institutional Change and Development.* Honolulu: East-West Center Press, 1966.

Sucharitkul, Sompong. "The Rule of Law in Thailand," *Journal of International Commission of Jurists,* I, August 1957, 23–42.

Tarling, Nicholas. *A Concise History of Southeast Asia.* New York: Praeger, 1966.

Thailand. Laws, Statutes, etc.
The Criminal Code, B.E. 2499. Bangkok: International Translations, 1956.

Thailand. Office of the Prime Minister. Editorial Board. *Official Yearbook, 1964.* Bangkok: Government House Printing Office, 1965.

Thailand. Office of the Prime Minister. National Economic Development Board. Central Statistical Office. *Statistical Yearbook of Thailand, 1956–1958,* (No. 23.) Bangkok: 1961.

Warner, Denis. *Reporting Southeast Asia.* London: Angus and Robertson, 1966.

Wilson, David A. *Politics in Thailand.* Ithaca: Cornell University Press, 1962.

———. "Thailand: A New Leader," *Asian Survey,* IV, No. 2, February, 1964, 711–715.

———. "Thailand: Old Leaders and New Directions," *Asian Survey,* III, February 1963, 83–88.

Wood, William Alfred Rae. *A History of Siam, from the Earliest Times to the Year A.D. 1781, with a Supplement Dealing with More Recent Events.* (Rev. ed.) Bangkok: Siam Barnakich Press, 1933.

OTHER SOURCES USED

Bowring, Sir John. *The Kingdom and the People of Siam.* 2 vols. London: John W. Parker, 1857.

Busch, Noel Fairchild. *Thailand: An Introduction to Modern Siam.* Princeton: Van Nostrand, 1959.

"City With the Smile," *Eastern World,* XX, Nos. 7–8, July-August 1966, 23, 24.

Clubb, Oliver E., Jr. *The United States and the Sino-Soviet Bloc in Southeast Asia.* Washington: Brookings Institution 1962.

Darling, Frank C. "American Policy in Thailand," *Western Political Quarterly,* XV, March 1962, 93–110.

———. "Marshal Sarit and Absolutist Rule in Thailand," *Pacific Affairs,* XXXIII, December 1960, 347–360.

———. "Modern Politics in Thailand," *Review of Politics,* XXIV, April 1962, 163–182.

Dhiradhamrong, Abhiehart. "Defense Economy in Thailand," *Thai Journal of Public Administration* (Special Issue), III, July 1962, 187–190.

Freyn, Hubert. "Planned Security," *Far Eastern Economic Review,* LI, No. 6, February 10, 1966, 232, 233.

Fulham, Parke. "A Land at Peace?" *Far Eastern Economic Review,* LI, No. 6, February 10, 1966, 235–239.

Huff, Lee W. "Village Reactions to Local Threats: A Study in Northeast Thailand." (Unpublished paper given at the annual meeting of the American Political Science Association in New York, 1966.)

"Is This Where We Came In?" *Economist,* CCXX, No. 6419, September 1966, 894.

Kingshill, Konrad. *Ku Daeng, the Red Tomb: A Village Study in Northern Thailand.* Bangkok: Prince Royal's College (Distributed by Siam Society), 1960.

Murphy, Charles J. V. "Thailand's Fight to the Finish," *Fortune,* LXXII, No. 4, October 1965, 122–127.

Nuechterlein, Donald E. "Thailand: Year of Danger and of Hope," *Asian Survey,* VI, No. 2, February 1966, 119–124.

———. "Thailand and After Sarit," *Asian Survey,* IV, No. 5, May 1964, 842–850.

———. "Thailand and SEATO: A Ten Year Appraisal," *Asian Survey,* IV, No. 12, December 1964, 1174–1181.

Pacific Science Congress, Ninth. Publicity Committee. *Thailand, Past and Present.* Bangkok: 1957.

Shaplen, Robert. "Letter From Bangkok," *New Yorker,* XLIII, No. 4, March 18, 1967, 135–172.

Southeast Asia Factbook Thailand (Thai Kingdom). Tokyo: 1966.

Suporn Kanchanokamole. "Thai Decorations," *Bangkok World Magazine*, October 1966.

Thailand. Laws, Statutes, etc.
"Royal Decree on Organization and Duties of Services of the Army, Supreme Armed Forces Command, Ministry of Defense, B.E. 2508," *Royal Thai Government Gazette* (trans., International Translations, Bangkok), July 1965.

Royal Thai Government Gazette (trans., International Translations, Bangkok), II, No. 293, August 7, 1962; No. 300, September 28, 1962.

Thailand. Ministry of Foreign Affairs. Department of Information. *Foreign Affairs Bulletin*. IV, No. 6, 1965.

Thailand. Office of the Prime Minister. *Raingan khwankaona nai raya 3 pi haeng kanpatiwat: 20 Tulakhom 2504* (Report of the Progress Made During the Three Years of the Revolution, 20 October 1961). Bangkok: Samnak Tamniab Nayok Ratthamontri Publishing, 1961.

————. Budget Office. *Budget in Brief: Fiscal Year 2505*. Bangkok: Government House Printing Office, 1961.

————. Office of the Prime Minister. Bureau of the Budget. *Budget in Brief: Fiscal Year 1966*. Bangkok: Local Affairs Press, 1966.

Thailand. Office of the Prime Minister. National Statistical Office. *Statistical Yearbook of Thailand, 1965*. Bangkok: 1966.

"Thailand: China Shows Her Hand," *Asian Analyst*, September 1966, 18–21.

Trager, Frank N. *Marxism in Southeast Asia*. Stanford: Stanford University Press, 1959.

U.S. Agency for International Development. Public Safety Division. *Briefing Material*. Washington: 1967.

U.S. United States Operations Mission to Thailand. Public Administration Division. *Organizational Directory of the Government of Thailand*. Bangkok: USOM, 1962.

————. *Organizational Directory of the Government of Thailand*. Bangkok: USOM, 1966.

Wilson, David A. "The Military in Thai Politics." Pages 253–276 in John J. Johnson (ed.), *The Role of the Military in Underdeveloped Countries*. Princeton: Princeton University Press, 1962.

(The following periodicals were used in the preparation of this section: *Bangkok Post,* all from February 1966 through April 1967, *Christian Science Monitor, Economist, Evening Star, New York Times, U.S. News and World Report* and *Washington Post.*)

GLOSSARY

AID—See USAID.

amphur—District; an administrative subdivision of a *changwat* (province).

Angkor Wat—Ruins of an ancient Khmer Buddhist temple in northwestern Cambodia.

ASA—Association of Southeast Asia. Formed in July 1961 by Thailand, Malaya and the Philippines to foster mutual cooperation in economic, cultural and other fields.

Asian Highway—An ECAFE-sponsored project, designed to span Asia by two major routes: (1) from Iran to Indonesia; and (2) from Turkey to South Vietnam, a section of which is to pass through Thailand.

ASPAC—Asian and Pacific Council. Formed in June 1966 by nine non-Communist nations in the Asian and Pacific area to promote cooperation and solidarity among them. The participants are Australia, Japan, Malaysia, the Republic of China, New Zealand, the Philippines, South Korea, South Vietnam and Thailand.

baht—Thai monetary unit. The par value established on October 20, 1963, was fixed at 0.0427245 grams of fine gold, or an exchange rate of 20.80 baht to 1 United States dollar. In August 1966 the baht was revalued upward to 20.75 to the United States dollar; or 1 baht equals $0.0482.

Bhumibol Adulyadej, His Majesty King—King of Thailand (Rama IX) since June 1946. His name (pronounced Poo-mee-phon Ah-doon-yah-deht) often appears as Phumiphol or Phumiphon, Adulyadet, Adutdet or Adundet.

Buddha—Title meaning "The Enlightened One," which is given to Gautama Siddhartha (C. 563–483 B.C.), the founder of Buddhism (see ch. 11, Religion).

changwat (or *changwad*)—Province.

chao—Guardian spirits, usually associated with particular places.

chao phraya—Highest title formerly given to appointed officials outside the royal family.

Chao Phraya—The principal river in Thailand.

CIO—Congress of Industrial Organizations.

Code of Manu—Hindu law code on which ancient Siamese law was based; introduced from Burma during the Ayutthaya period (1350–1767).

Colombo Plan—The Colombo Plan for Cooperative Economic Development in South and Southeast Asia was published by the Commonwealth Consultative Committee on South and Southeast Asia on November 29, 1950, and was to be effective from July 1, 1951, to June 30, 1957. The terminal date was extended to 1961 and later to 1966. The Plan is an international cooperative effort to assist countries of the area to raise their living standards. Member nations in 1966 were Afghanistan, Australia, Bhutan, Burma, Cambodia, Canada, Ceylon, India, Indonesia, Japan, Korea, Laos, Malaysia, the Maldive Islands, Nepal, New Zealand, Pakistan, the Philippines, Thailand, the United Kingdom, the United States and South Vietnam. By mid-1966 no action regarding membership had been announced by the newly formed Republic of Singapore.

deutsche mark (*DM*)—The monetary unit of the Federal Republic of Germany (West Germany); par value is 4 to the United States dollar, or 1 deutsche mark equals 25 cents. Spot rate is 3.975 to the United States dollar; or 1 deutsche mark equals $0.2515.

Dika Court—Supreme Court.

DM—*See* deutsche mark.

ECAFE—Economic Commission for Asia and the Far East, a regional body of the United Nations.

ECOSOC—Economic and Social Council of the United Nations.

Export-Import Bank—An independent agency of the United States Government.

FAO—Food and Agriculture Organization, a specialized agency of the United Nations.

farang—Foreigner.

Hinayana—*See* Theravada.

IAEA—International Atomic Energy Agency, a specialized agency of the United Nations.

IBRD—International Bank for Reconstruction and Development, commonly known as the World Bank, a specialized agency of the United Nations.

ICAO—International Civil Aviation Organization, a specialized agency of the United Nations.

ICFTU—International Confederation of Free Trade Unions.

ILO—International Labor Organization, a specialized agency of the United Nations.

IMF—International Monetary Fund, a specialized agency of the United Nations.

Interpol—International Criminal Police Organization, a quasi-intergovernmental organization which aims to promote and facilitate cooperation among member nations on common criminal police problems.

JUSMAG—Joint United States Military Advisory Group.

kamnan—The headman, or chief official, of a commune.

kenaf—A valuable fiber plant grown in the East Indies but widespread in cultivation. The term also applies to its fiber which is used in ropemaking and canvas manufacture.

karma—A Hindu and Buddhist doctrine which teaches that the ethical consequences of one's acts determine one's lot in future incarnations or rebirths.

kha luang—Provincial governor.

khwan—The body-spirit or life-soul, generally thought to reside in the head, which activates the body and maintains its life. Illness and eventual death follow loss of the *khwan*.

klong—Canal.

ko—Island.

kwaeng court—District court.

like—The Thai popular drama.

Loi Krathong—The Festival of Floating Lights, celebrated, especially in the North, during the night of the first full moon in November.

MAAG—Military Assistance Advisory Group (United States).

Mahayana—A branch of Buddhism which is followed by a small minority of persons in Thailand and is also found in other countries of Southeast Asia and the Far East.

MAP—Military Assistance Program (United States).

Mekong Committee—Sponsored by ECAFE to develop water resources of the Lower Mekong Basin with a view to encouraging industrialization in the area. Its mission is to coordinate the planning and development of the various Mekong projects. Project activities are implemented through the cooperative efforts and financing of the four riparian countries (Thailand, Laos, Cambodia and South Vietnam), several United Nations agencies, and 11 donor nations: Australia, Canada, France, India, Iran, Israel, Japan, New Zealand, Taiwan, Great Britain and the United States.

Mekong River Development Plan—Designation of the consolidated plans developed by the Mekong Committee, *q.v.*

muang—A provincial capital or a town which has more than 10,000 and less than 50,000 inhabitants; also, a watercourse.

muban—Village.

nai amphur—Chief of district administration.

nakhon—A city of more than 50,000 inhabitants.

nam—Stream; also, a general term for water.

nirvana (Pali: *nibbana*)—Reunion with the ultimate cosmic reality which comes with enlightenment and release from all desire and from the cycle of reincarnation.

Pali—Scriptural language of Theravada Buddhism, derived from ancient India.

Pathet Lao—Literally, "Lao State." Refers to the dissident, Communist movement in Laos supported by North Vietnam.

phi—The spirits of natural objects, such as trees, rivers, etc., the personifications of some diseases and the disembodied souls of the dead, especially those who have died in childbirth, in infancy or by violence; also, older sibling.

phu yai ban—Village headman.

Phumiphol Adulyadet, His Majesty King—*See* Bhumibol Adulyadej, His Majesty King.

rai—Unit of area: 0.395 acre.

sala—An open-sided building commonly used as a meeting hall and lodging place for travelers.

samlor—A three-wheeled passenger vehicle propelled by an operator using a bicycle-type drive.

Sangha—Buddhist religious community or monastic order.

sapha changwat—Provincial assembly.

SEATO—Southeast Asia Treaty Organization. Formed by the United States, Great Britain, France, Australia, New Zealand, Pakistan, Thailand and the Philippines by the Manila Pact of September 8, 1954.

Six-Year Economic Development Plan—Thailand's economic development plan for 1961–66.

Songkran—A festival held in mid-April, at about the time of the onset of the monsoon rains, in celebration of the lunar New Year, which actually begins several months earlier.

TAB—Technical Assistance Board of the United Nations.

tambon—A commune or administrative unit comprising a group of villages.

Theravada—(Literally, Way of the Elders)—A branch of Buddhism, also known as Hinayana, which is found in Thailand and other countries of Southeast Asia.

thewada—Gods of various grades who inhabit the heavens of the Brahmanic cosmology which has become part of Thai Buddhist belief.

UNESCO—United Nations Educational, Scientific and Cultural Organization, a specialized agency of the United Nations.

532

UNICEF—United Nations Children's Fund, a specialized agency of the United Nations.

USAID—United States Agency for International Development.

USIS—United States Information Service.

USOM—United States Operations Mission.

Uthorn Court—Court of Appeals.

Viet Cong—Condensed from the term Viet Nam Cong San, meaning Vietnamese Communists (sometimes translated as Vietnamese communism). The term is generally applied to the supporters and participants in the Communist-controlled subversive insurgency in South Vietnam. Communists, including the insurgents themselves, avoid use of the term, preferring to operate under the guise of Nationalists.

Viet Minh—Contraction of Viet Nam Doc Lap Dong Minh (Vietnam Independence League), established in 1941 as a coalition of Vietnamese Communist-Nationalist groups which actively opposed the French and Japanese during World War II and spearheaded Vietnamese resistance to French rule in the early years of the Indochina War (1946–1954), by which time the Viet Minh came to be dominated by the Communists.

VOA—Voice of America.

wai—Gesture of respect made by pressing the palms of the hands together, as in prayer. Used for salutations, both in greeting and farewell.

wat—Walled compound containing a Buddhist temple and associated buildings.

WFTU—World Federation of Trade Unions, the Communist-dominated labor union federation.

WHO—World Health Organization, a specialized agency of the United Nations.

INDEX

Army Quartermaster Subsistence Division: 147
Army War College: 480
arts: background, 179–180; predominant influences, 179; visual and performing, 180–182
asbestos: 29
Asia and Pacific Area Council (ASPAC): 11
Asia Foundation: 298
Asia Trust Bank: 442
Asian countries: attitude toward, 279, 280; non-Communist, relations with, 267–273
Asian Development Bank: 334
Asian Highway: 11, 413
Asian Institute of Economic Planning (Bangkok): 413
Asian Peoples Anti-Communist League (APACL): 273
asphaltic sand: 29
Associated Press: 289
Association of Southeast Asia (ASA): 11; Joint Committee of Economic Experts, 416; projects, 416; Standing Committee on Trade Promotion, 416
Association of Southeast Asian Institutions of Higher Learning (ASAIHL): 159
Assumption College (Bangkok): 171
astrology: 203–204
Aswin Studios (films): 294
atomic powerplant: 346
attitude toward animism and witchcraft, 205
Australia: aid, 11, 338, 413, 414, 483, 488, 489; investment, private, 314; relations with, 274
Austria: 345, 427, 433
authority: use of and attitude toward, 220, 301, 302, 303
Ayutthaya (kingdom): history, 41, 42, 51, 52–53

baht (monetary unit): history, 447; value, 309, 314, 446, 447, 449
balance of payments: 403–404 (table 7), 414
Ballistier, Joseph (U.S. envoy): 263
Ban Pu Dam: 344, 345
Bandung Conference: 267
Bang Pakong River: 22
Bangkok (capital city): 15, 107; description, 32–33, 135; eating hab-

its, 138; as economic hub, 375; education and training, 144, 166–174 *passim;* employment exchange center, 363; employment of villagers, 121; family patterns, 122; films, 294, 295; health services and facilities, 134, 147–153 *passim;* housing, 139, 142; international organizations, offices, 415; language, 90; as nation's capital, 2; naval base, 480; newspapers, 282, 284, 285; population, 111–114, 148; port and port facilities, 15, 39, 312, 390; shopping area, 379; television, 293; water supply, 148
Bangkok Bank: 442
Bangkok Bank of Commerce: 442
Bangkok Christian College: 171
Bangkok Criminal Court: 463
Bangkok Federation of Trade Unions: 367
Bangkok Institute of Industrial Skill Promotion: 362
Bangkok Metropolitan Bank: 442
Bangkok Post (English-language newspaper): 288
Bangkok World (newspaper): 288
Bangkok-Thon Buri area: banks and banking, 435, 443; Chinese schools, 173; disease, 148; factories, 348; labor law enforcement, 363; newspapers, 288; police, 457–458; politics, 253, 257; population, 74, 257; public services, 386–397 *passim;* trade market, 374
Bank for Agriculture and Agricultural Credit: 334
Bank for Agriculture and Cooperatives: 439, 440
Bank of America: 443
Bank of Asia for Industry and Commerce: 442
Bank of Ayutthaya: 442
Bank of Canton: 442
Bank of China: 442
Bank for Cooperatives: 333
Bank of Thailand (central bank): 422, 430, 431, 449; description and functions of, 436–439, 443, 447; Exchange Control Officer, 414
banks and banking: background, 435–437; central (*see also* Bank of Thailand), 436–439; commercial, 438, 441–444, 445–446; *comprador*

system, 444; deposits, commercial banks, 443; farm bank system, 334; foreign, 437, 441, 442, 443; government, 439–441; interest rates, 437–438; number of, 441–442; place in economy, 313–314; savings, 438, 439,448

barite; 29

barter: 137, 138

beliefs and practices, popular: 153–155

beriberi: 186

betel nut: 135

Bhumibol Adulyadej (King): 231

bibliographies: economy, 517–525; national security, 526–528; politics, 511–516; social structure, 495–510

Bilauktaung Range: 13, 14, 27

birth control: 145

birth rate: 63

black-marketing: 469–470

Board of Investment: 354, 429

boats: required registration, 389

bonds, government: 433, 434

books: 289

Border Patrol Police, 14, 88, 454–459 *passim;* schools staffed by, 104

borders: Burmese insurgent activities, 270; communist infiltration, 67, 270; communist subversion and terrorism, 10, 81, 474, 477; disputes, 13, 267–268; Nationalist Chinese army irregulars, 272; Pathet Lao threat, 273

boundaries: changes, 42; natural inland, 13; outer, 13; provinces, 14

Bowring, Sir John: 401

Bowring Treaty: 263, 401–402, 418

Boy Scouts: 113, 175

Bradley, Dan Beach (publisher): 284

British (people): in trade, 381

British-American Tobacco Company of Thailand: 328, 430

British Broadcasting Corporation: 299

British Council: 299

British East India Company, 54, 55, 400, 401

British Information Service: 102, 299

Buddhism: arts and intellectual expression, influence on, 179–198 *passim;* attitude toward education, 176; background, 200–202; central doctrine of (*karma*), 197, 200–206

passim, 214, 219; and health, 151, 153, 154, 155; influence of other systems, 199–200, 202; modern trends, 214–215; *nirvana*, 207, 215; popular beliefs and practices, 153–154; and public order, 451; reincarnation, 205–206; Buddhism: two sects, 208; values and attitudes, influence on, 217–223 *passim;* 301, 302

Buddhists (*see also* monks, wats): ecclesiastical colleges, 174; merit-earning, 137, 154, 176, 207–214 *passim*, 218, 301–303 *passim;* schools (*see under* wats); as soldiers, 484; Thai, family system, 119–128

budget: constitutional provision on form of, 421; criticism, 422–423; military, 485–486; police, 454; state, 417, 421–423

Budget Bureau: 421, 422, 441

Budget Review Commission: 422

buffalo: 84, 312, 322, 325, 329, 397

Bureau of Radio and Television Services: 284

Burma: attitude toward, 279; cultural borrowing from, 8; relations with, 41, 42, 52, 53, 54, 270

Burney Treaty: 401

Cabinet. *See* Council of Ministers

caloric intake: 415

CALTEX (oil company): 344

Cambodia: attitude toward, 10, 279; boundary dispute, 13, 267–268; cultural influence, 8, 46, 48; relations with, 10, 261, 262, 263, 267–269; in Thai history, 42–55 *passim*

Cambodian Royal Ballet: 180

canals: 320, 388

capital, foreign: 310, 314, 315, 352, 353, 354, 404

Catholic Association of Thailand: 141

Catholic Family Movement: 141

cattle: 329

cement: 350, 351

censorship: 281, 282, 283, 295

central bank. *See* Bank of Thailand

Central Hospital of Bangkok: 152

Central Juvenile Court: 142, 143, 236, 464, 468

Central Labor Union: 254, 367, 368

Central Observation and Protection

Chinese Chamber of Commerce: 75, 113, 382
Chitr Buabusaya (artist): 187
cholera: 134, 149
Chot Phraphan (writer): 197
Christianity: 84, 85, 216
Chula Chakrabongs, Prince (writer): 197
Chulachomklao Royal Military Academy: 480, 489
Chulalongkorn Medical School and Hospital: 153, 413
Chulalongkorn University: 161, 173, 414
cities. See Bangkok, Bangkok-Thon Buri area, Chiengmai, Nahkon Ratchasima, urban areas
Civil Aviation Training Center (Bangkok): 413
Civil Court, 236
civil service: 112, 166, 241–243
Civil Service Commission: 242
climate: viii, 14–15, 23–26
coal: 27
Cold Storage Organization: 335, 385
College of Education (Bangkok): 170
Colombo Plan: x, 159, 336; aid grant total, 427; types of aid, 414
Columbia Broadcasting Company: 289
Command and General Staff College (Army): 480
commerce: employment in, 359
commercial associations, 382
Committee for Coordination of Investigations of Lower Mekong Basin: 22, 415
communes: government, 238
communication (see also information, public; newspapers, radio, television): development, 316; employment, 374; informal channels, 295–296; place in the economy, 311, 313; services, 386–387; Thailand-Malaysia, 416; summary, ix
communism (see also communists, counterinsurgency): background of and support for, 253–256; counteractivity, 158, 172–173, 249, 254, 257, 297, 367, 451, 474–475, 476; government policy toward, 58–59, 249, 254, 261, 266, 267, 280
Communist China: activity in Southeast Asia, government concern, 275–276; attitude toward, 280; citizens in Thailand, 74; ethnic kin of hill people in, 84; refugees from, 66; relations with, 275–276; subversion campaign and terrorist activities, 246, 299–300, 452; trade restriction, 400, 415
communist countries: attitude toward, 280; relations with, 10
Communist Party of Malaysia: 453
Communist Party of Thailand (Pak Communist Thai): 254, 255
Communist Pathet Lao: 256, 262, 273, 279, 452
communists: activity, and Thai foreign policy, 10–11; infiltration, 67, 259, 270; and labor unions, 367, 368; terrorism and subversion, 3, 66, 67, 81, 246, 259, 262, 299, 451, 452–454, 474, 476, 477
Community Development Technical Assistance Center, Thai-SEATO (Ubon Ratchathani): 413
Companies Promotion Division (internal trade): 384
comprador system: 444
concubinage: 125
conscription system (military): 483, 484–485
Constituent Assembly: 228, 417, 421, 422; responsibilities, 235
constitution: changes, 4 5: draft (1966), 228, 230, 283, 421, 477; first (1932), 57, 227; interim (1959), 227–228, 421, 464; military attitude toward, 476
Constitutional Front (political party), 252
constitutionalism: evolution of 227–230
construction: 351–352
consumer goods: 139
consumption levels: 140
conventions and customs: 98, 117
cooperation: tradition of, 108
Cooperation Party (political party): 252, 255
cooperatives: 333–334, 378, 385
copper: 27, 343
Copper Exploration Project: 343
corn: 329, 399, 408, 409
cosmology: 202–205
Cosmopolitan Club: 114

539

cost-of-living index: 140
cottage industries: 360
cotton: 328, 349, 399
Council of Ministers (Cabinet): 236, 346, 353, 421, 436, 477, 479; functions, 231
Council of Social Welfare of Thailand: 141
Counter Subversion Operations Command: 474
counterinsurgency: 451, 474–475, 476; training, 459, 486, 487
Court of Appeals (Uthorn Court): 236, 463, 464
courts: viii, 235–237; civil, 236; criminal, 236, 463–464; of First Instance, 236; juvenile, 142, 143, 236, 464, 468; Supreme Court, 237, 463, 464
courtship: 120, 124, 127–128
Cowles Communications, Inc. (publishing): 288
Crawfurd, Dr. John (of British East India Company): 54
credit (see also banks and banking, interest, loans): agriculture, 333–334, 440, 444; industry, 344, 345, 441; international rating, 309; sources, 444–445
crime rates: 466–467
Criminal Court: 236
Criminal Investigation Bureau: 454
criminal law: development, 460–471; felonies, types of, 462; penal code, 461; penalties, 462; procedures, 464–466
Crippled Children's Welfare Center: 141
crops (see also opium and specific crop): 82–86 passim, 317, 326–329, 349, 408, 409; production, 323 (table 4)
cultural influences: 4, 7–8, 42–48 passim, 109; predominant, 179
currency (see also baht): 446–449; stability, 309, 314, 435; volume and price level, 448–449
customs duties: 415

dams: 23, 230, 321, 343, 345, 348
dance drama: 187–191
death: chief causes, 149; rate, 63, 64, 134, 150
debt, public: external, 431–433; internal, 433–434; total, ratio of external obligation, 433
Defense Council: 478–479
de Gaulle, Charles: 275
Democrat Party (Prachatipat): 252, 253
Denmark: x, 412
Department of: Agriculture, 326, 335, 336; Aviation, 388; Commercial Intelligence, 384; Commercial Registration, 384; Corrections, 143; Credit and Marketing Cooperatives, 383, 385; Customs, 415; Fine Arts: 180, 184, 191, 192; Fisheries, 335; Foreign Trade, 415; Forests, 335; General Warehouse, 385; Harbor and Marine Transport, 388; Highways, 388; Industrial Promotion, 441; Industrial Works, 353; Internal Trade, 384, 385; Irrigation, 142; Labor, 358, 363; Land Transport, 388; Livestock Development, 335; Local Administration, 237, 241; Medical Sciences, 152; Mineral Resources, 341, 353; National Police, x, 142, 281, 290, 291, 292, 295, 297, 368, 451, 454, 455, 458, 459, 464, 466; Post and Telegraph, 386, 388, 439; Public Prosecution, 464; Public Relations, 281, 283, 290–293 passim, 296; Public Welfare, 88, 141, 142, 358, 363, 370, 432; Rafting, 385; Rice, 335; Rice Storage and Rice Mills, 385; Thai Information Services, 296; Territorial Defense, 480, 484; Treasury, 447
Detective Training School (Bangkok): 458
development and improvement (economic and social): government plans, 3, 9–10, 134, 142, 157, 158, 309, 310, 314, 315–316, 339, 358, 363, 395, 396, 417, 433
Dhana Karn Phim Company (publishing): 285, 286
dialect associations: 113
diet: 135, 145–147, 333
disease: 133, 143–151 passim; leading causes, 134; religious beliefs, 206
districts: government, 238
divorce: 124
Doi Intharnon (mountain): 18
Dokmai Sot (writer): 197

family: 119–131, 325; adolescence and adulthood, 127–128; assistance, 143; basic concept of the system, 123; Chinese, 129–130; ethnic minorities, 128–131; extended, 120, 131; fragmentation or dissolution, 121; hill people, 84, 85, 129, 130–131; Malay, 130; names, 121; nuclear, 119, 120, 122, 130; obligations, 123; rural, 115, 120–121, 130–131; strength of relationship, 220; Thai Buddhist; 119–128; urban, 121–122, 129

family planning service: 145

Far Eastern Film Company: 294

farmers (see also land: holdings; land: tenure): 108, 116, 317; agriculture extension clubs, 337; attitude toward industrialization, 341; cash income, 144; and communism, 253; credit, 333–334, 440, 444; government assistance to fiber crop producers, 328; in labor force, 358; living standard, 135; religious expenditures, 214

farming: 323–325

Federation of Trade Unions of Thailand: 368

Fernandez, Duarte (envoy of Portuguese India): 51

fibers: 328; processing, 349

films: 294–295, 377

finance, public (see also budget; debt, public; expenditures, public; revenue): 417–434; local, 434; state, 418–420; summary, ix

Firestone Corporation: 350, 432

fiscal year (Thai): 485

fish industry: 31, 312, 331–333

Fish Marketing Organization: 335, 385

fish meal and oil: 332

Five-Year Plan for National Economic and Social Development (1967–71): 3, 9–10, 158, 309, 310, 316, 358, 363, 417

flag: 306–308

floating markets: 36, 379

flood control. See irrigation and flood control

food (see also diet): 138, 146; begging by monks, 213–214; imports, 399, 410 (table 12); religious offerings, 204, 212; sanitation, 147; supply, 135

Food and Agriculture Organization (FAO): 146, 277, 336, 337, 415; types of aid, 413

foreign aid (see also loans: foreign; military: aid): 411–418; agriculture, 321, 333, 334, 336–338; education, 159, 168, 170; health and welfare, 134, 142–153 passim; industry, 343, 344–345, 346, 351; irrigation and water control, 22–23, 310, 320, 321; security, 451, 452, 456; training, 310, 361, 362, 393; transportation and communications, 310, 387, 388, 393–397 passim; sources, types, projects, amounts, 9, 411–414; summary, x

foreign exchange; 353, 417, 433, 438–439; controls, 400, 414; earnings, 317; rate, 447; reserves, 309

foreign policy: 10; and communism, 58

foreign relations (see also organizations, international and specific countries and organizations): 10, 261–280; attitudes toward foreign peoples and nations, 278–280; background, 42, 51–52, 262–266; diplomatic skill, 261; influential personalities, 278; non-Communist Asian countries, 267–273; peacemaker role, 267, 271; policy-making and conduct, 277; recent, determinants of, 266–267; in World War II, 264–266

Forest Industry Organization: 330, 335, 385

forestry: 330–331; place in the economy, 312; products, 330, 350

forests: 29

France: aid, 344; background of relations, 51, 55, 56–57; recent relations, 262–267 passim, 275

Free Thai Movement (anti-Japanese): 247, 252, 254, 255

Free Workmen's Association of Thailand: 367

French Bank of Indochina (Banque de l' Indochine): 442

Friendship Highway: 396

friendships: 220–221

fruit: 327

fuel: 343–345

Fuel Oil Organization: 423
Fulbright Foundation: 298
funerals: 211

gem stones: 27
General Labor Union: 367
General Post Office: 387
Geneva Conference on Laos: 268
Geneva Convention: 493
geographic regions: 2–3, 18, 19 (fig. 3), 20, 21
German Institute (information program): 299
Germany, Federal Republic of: aid, x, 159, 344, 412; imports from, 293; information program, 299; loans, projects, and amounts, 387, 427, 432–433; trade, 293, 406, 409, 411; trade agreements 11
glossary: 529–533
gold: 27
government (*see also* Department; government policy; Ministries): administrative bodies, 233–234; administrative divisions, viii, 14; attitude of people toward, 4, 301, 303–304; autocratic tradition, 245; background, 3–5; central, 231–237; communism in Southeast Asia, attitude toward, 451; constitutional structure (mid-1967), 229 (fig. 11); constitutionalism, 227–230; communes, 238; coup of 1932, 4, 57–58, 247; coup of 1958, 5; democratic processes, 4, 249; district, 238–239; education, attitude toward, 157, 158, 175; ethnic minorities, attitude toward, 70; executive branch, 231, 232 (fig. 12), 233–234; legislative branch, 234–237; local, 237–241; judicial system, 235–237; under martial law, 283; modernization, 3, 56; monopolies, 353; municipal, 240–241; opium trade, attitude toward, 82–83; participation in economic activity, 314; position of the military in, 475–476; private enterprise, attitude toward, 314; private foreign investment, attitude toward, 445; provincial, 237–238; public ownership of economic facilities, attitude toward, 426; publications, 297; role in agriculture, 335–338; role in industry, 353–355; role in trade, 383–386,

414–415; summary, vii; system of, 225–244; traditional pattern, 226–227; use of authority and reactions to, 220; village, 239–240
government policy: agriculture, 408; arts, 180; assimilation, 103–104; toward the Chinese, 70, 76–77, 78; on communism, 58–59, 249, 254, 261, 266, 267, 280 ethnic minorities, 70–81 *passim*, 87, 256; forestry, 330, 331; industry, 339, 340, 353; labor unions and strikes, 357; language, 89, 90, 103–105; mineral resources, 310; Moslems, 81; political parties, 246, 247, 249–255 *passim;* polygamy, 125; prisons, 467; private enterprise, 400; private schools, 171, 177; public information media, 281, 284–285; rubber production, 326; trade, 400
Government Savings Bank: 423, 431, 439
Great Britain: aid, 344, 414; background of relations with, 51–57 *passim;* financial effects of Bowring Treaty, 418–419; as export market, 330; imports from, 294; information activities, 299; investment, private, 314; military aid, 11, 483, 489; trade, 404, 405, 406, 409, 411; relations with, 262–266 *passim*, 274–275
Great Chainat Project (water control): 320–321
gross national product (GNP): contribution of economic segments, 310–311; growth, 310; per capita, 133; targets, 315, 316
gypsum, 29

handicrafts: 85, 193, 352, 360, 376
Harmony-in-the Doctrine Movement (Krabuankarn Smakhi Dharm. Communist front organization): 256
Harris, Townsend (U.S. diplomatic envoy): 263
headman, village: 84, 85, 86, 116, 126, 148, 210, 239; election, 243
health (*see also* diet, disease, hospitals, sanitation): films, mobile information teams, 297; government expenditures, 134, 424 (table 13); immunizations, 134 mobile units, 133; popular beliefs and practices,

153–155; in prisons, 468–469; public, 145–155; services and facilities, 134, 151–153; summary, viii
Health Training Demonstration Center (Thon Buri): 153
helminthiasis (parasitic worm infestation): 150
highways. See roads and highways
hill peoples: 2, 7, 61; assimilation, 83; basis of economy, 82; cash income source, 359; education, 158, 177; as ethnic groups, 70, 82–86; government policy toward, 87–88; language, 89, 103; living conditions: 138; major tribes, 70; number of, 63, 69; public order and security problems, 453; radio broadcasts to, 291, 292
Hindus and Hinduism: 179, 194, 196 216
history (see also kings): 1, 41–59 Ayutthaya era (1350–1767), 47–53; Bangkok era (1767–1932), 53–57; Chakkri dynasty, 54–55; constitutional era (1932–   ), 57–59; kingdoms, 43, 44 (fig. 9), 45–57; Nanchao era (c. A.D. 650–1253), 43–45; origins of Thai people, 71
Ho Chi Minh (President, North Vietnam): 254, 258, 306
holidays and festivals: 129, 175–176, 199, 210, 211, 307–308
Hong Kong: opium, 469; trade, 327, 404–411 passim, 469
Hong Kong and Shanghai Banking Corporation: 442
hospitals: 134, 144, 145, 149, 151–152; prison, 469
houseboats: 139
household: 120, 121, 128, 130; expenditures, 140; rural, 115, 325; unit, 84, 85
housing: conditions and programs, 142; public, 139, 142; standards, 139; supply, 136, 138–139
Housing Bank: 142
humor: 98
Hunter, John (English resident merchant), 54
Hussain, Zakir (Indian Vice President): 273
hydroelectric power: 22, 23, 343, 345–346; potential, 341;

illegitimacy: 124

illiteracy: 157; prisoners, 469
immigration: 65–67; illegal, 77; quotas, 66, 76, 77; repatriation of refugees from communist countries, 66
immunizations, 134
imports: controls, 414, 415; duties, 427–438; major sources, 405 (table 8), 409; principal, 399, 409; summary, ix; volume and value, 399–400, 409, 410 (table 12), 411
income: national, 309, 312–314; personal, 133, 315, 374
India: attitude toward, 279; cultural influence, 8, 46, 48, 179, 181, 183, 184; films from, 294; relations with, 272–273
Indian Chamber of Commerce: 382
Indian Overseas Bank: 442
Indians: attitude toward, 79; economic activity, 78–79, 361, 381; as ethnic group, 78–79; population, 63
Indonesia: attitude toward, 279; relations with, 270–271; trade, 405, 407, 409, 411
Industrial Finance Corporation of Thailand: 412, 431, 432, 439, 440–441
Industrial Investment Promotion Board: 353, 354
industrialization: 135, 352–354
industry (see also specific industry): 339–355; attitude toward development, 339–340; government monopolies, 353; modernization and development, 338–346 passim, 351–355 passim; new projects tax exemption, 429; place in the economy, 314; production, 340 (table 5); small, credit to, 441; status of, 309; structure and ownership, 314, 352–353; summary, viii; technical extension service, 354–355
Industry Loan Office, 441
infant mortality rate: 63, 134
inflation: 434, 449
information, public: 281–300; channels, 281, 284–296; foreign government activities, 298–300; government activities, 296–298; Mobile Information Teams, 297; official controls, 282–284; program themes, 282

inheritance system: 120, 123, 124, 126, 129, 130, 322
insurgency: 452–454
Institute of International Education, 298
intellectual trends: 197–198
interest rate: 437–438, 445; maximum legal, 334
International Association of Police Chiefs: 459
International Atomic Energy Agency (IAEA): 277, 413, 415
International Bank for Reconstruction and Development (IBRD): 36, 277, 310–441 passim; criticism of budget, 422; loan total, 422; types and amounts of loans, 412
International Civil Aviation Organization (ICAO): 277, 413, 415
International Committee of the Red Cross: 66, 276
International Conference of Social Workers: 142
International Court of Justice: 268
International Criminal Police Organization (Interpol): 459
International Development Association (IDA): 277
International Engineering Company: 432
International Finance Corporation (IFC): 11, 277
International Institute for Child Study: 174
International Labor Organization (ILO): 277, 362, 413, 415
International Monetary Fund (IMF): 11, 277, 436, 446
international organizations (see also specific organization): discussion, 11; loan totals, 427; membership, x, 10, 266, 347, 387, 459; offices in Thailand, 415; types, projects, and amounts of aid, 412–414
International Telecommunication Union (ITU): 277
International Television Satellite (INTELSAT): 387
International Tin Council: 347
International Union of Child Welfare: 142
investment: 354; foreign, 314, 352, 353, 445; industrial enterprises,

426; private, 314, 352, 445; public, financing of, 445–446
iron: 347–348, 399, 408
irredentist movements: 91
irrigation and flood control: 22, 23, 133, 318–319; development plans, 316, 320, 321
Israel: aid, 427

Japan: aid, x, 159, 412, 414; attitude toward, 279; as export market, 348; imports from, 293, 294; private investment, 314; relations with, 264–266, 272, 473, 475; trade, 293, 294, 348, 404, 406, 409; trade agreements, 11
Japanese (people): in trade, 381
Jiji Press (news agency): 289
Johnson, Lyndon B. (U.S. President): 274
Joint United States Military Advisory Group (JUSMAG): 486
judges: 464
Judicial Service Commission: 236, 464
judicial system (see also courts): 5, 235–237; military, 491, 493; summary, viii
Junior Chamber of Commerce: 114, 175
jute: 328, 349, 350, 399

kamnan (commune chief): 239
Kantang (port): 391
Karachi Plan: 158
Karen (people): 83–84; language, 103, number of, 83
karma (central doctrine of Buddhism): 197, 200–206 passim, 214, 219
Kasetsat University (University of Agriculture): 147, 174, 336, 413
kenaf (fiber crop): 317, 328, 329; export, 399, 408, 409
Khien Yimsiri (sculptor): 183
Khmer (people): 46, 61, 80
Khon Kaen (town): agriculture extension center, 337; education, 173; health, 149; television, 293
Khon Kaen University: 174
Khorat Plateau: 14; Lao (people), 72; principal town, 2; roads, 38; salt springs, 29; soil, 26; water transport, 37
Khorat Thai (people): 72

Lao, 99; Malay, 81, 89, 101, 104, 258; Mon-Khmer group 80, 81; and national unity, 3, 7; official national, 72, 89, 90; Pali and Sanskrit, 102; of the press, 284, 287, 288; of radio broadcasts, 292, 293, 298; "royal", 92; summary, vii-viii; of trade publications, 382; used by Vietnamese, 80, 90

Lao (people): 72; language, 90, 99; political attitudes, 305; religion, 204–205

Laos: attitude toward, 279; communist infiltration from and subversion, 67, 452; relations with, 261, 262, 263–269–270

law (see also courts, criminal law); history, 49–50

Lawa (people): 80, 86, 103

lead: 27, 347

League of Municipalities of Thailand: 241

League of Nations: 263, 264

leprosy: 134, 143, 148, 151

lignite: 344, 348

Lignite Electricity Authority: 386

Lisu (people): 86, 103, 131

literacy rate: 157, 158

literature: 193–197

livestock: 83, 84, 85, 136, 144, 146, 329–330; place in the economy, 311

living conditions: 133–155

living standard: 9, 135–140, 315, 317, 339, 358, 455

Loan Board: 441

loans: farm bank system, 334; foreign 310, 314, 320, 334, 345, 362, 386, 411, 412, 417, 427, 431–433; personal, rural areas, 44; small industry, 354

(Lu (people): 74

Luang Phra Bang Mountains: 18

Luang Saranuprabhandh (Nual Pacheenpyak), Col. (lyricist): 307

Luang Vichitr Vadhakarn (writer): 190, 197

Luang Wichit Watthakan (playwright): 192

machinery: import, 399, 409; tax exemption, 429

Mae Klong River: 22, 388, 432

Mae Nam Songkhram River: 345

Mahayana Buddhism: 201

Mainichi Shimburn (news agency): 289

malaria: 134, 135, 143, 149, 150

Malaria Eradication Project, 150

Malay (people): 3, 7; attitude toward government, education, 81, 177; communist activity among, 256; cooperation in counterinsurgency operations and security, 453; economic activity, 81, 82, 361; as ethnic group, 70, 81–82; family, 130; language, 81, 89, 101, 104, 258; living conditions, 137; marriage, 123; number of, 70; and politics, 81, 246, 255–258 passim, 305; religion, 215; social values, 217

Malaysia: attitude toward, 279; relations with, 270–271, 416; trade, 405, 406, 407

Malik, Adam (Indonesian Foreign Minister): 271

malnutrition: 133, 145

manganese: 27

manufacturers: offices in Bangkok, 377

manufactures: trade, 376

manufacturing: 339, 348–351; employment, 359–360

Marines, Royal Thai: 480, 487

market information: 383

marriage: 123–125, 128, 129; ceremony, 137; Chinese, 129; remarriage, 124

Master Dei College (Bangkok): 171

Medical Correctional Institution (Pathum Thani Province): 468

Medical Sciences University (Bangkok): 174

medicine: Chinese oriental, 155; traditional, 154

Mekong Basin Minerals Survey Project: 343

Mekong River: 13, 19, 266, 300, 396, 452; and communist infiltration, 67; development plan and projects, 11, 22–23, 345, 413; population crossing, 72; water transport, 37

Mao (people): 130–131

Mercantile Bank: 442

Metropolitan Police: 454, 457–458, 459

Metropolitan Police Training School (at Bang Khen): 458

Miao (people): 82, 84–85, 177

Miao–Yao(people): 103

midwives and centers: 152, 155

migration: internal, 65

military, the: (*see also* Air Force, Army, Marines, Navy): 471–473; agreements, x; aid, x, 10–11, 411, 413; arms and equipment, 490; awards and decorations, 491, 492 (table 15); background, 471–472; budget, x, 485–486; conscription, x, 483, 484–485; counterinsurgency training, 486; coups, 247, 475; defense expenditures, 424 (table 13), 426; economic impact, 483–487; field command, 479–480, 481 (fig. 16), 482; foreign influence, 482–483; high command, 477, 478 (fig. 15), 479; justice system, 491, 493; logistics, 489–490; mission, 476–477; modernization, 472–474; organization, 477–482; position in government, 475–476; rank and insignia, 490–491; schools, 487–489, 480; service, 127; soldiers, fishermen and farmers as, 484; summary, x; training, 480, 482, 483, 486–489

military Technical Training School (SEATO-sponsored): 488

milk and dairy products: 146

min Sen Machinery Company: 432

Mineral Experimental Center (Bangkok): 343

minerals: 26–27, 28 (fig. 6), 29, 341; development projects, 343; production, 346 (table 6)

mining: 339, 346–348; employment, 360; ore production, 346 (table 6)

Ministries: Agriculture, 292, 329, 335, 353, 383, 385, 440; Communications, 388, 389; Defense, 290, 344, 353, 454, 473–484 *passim;* Economic Affairs, 383, 384, 385, 415; Education, 102, 143, 144, 158–172 *passim,* 180, 184, 281, 295, 299, 359, 434; Finance, 353, 415, 421, 422, 435, 436, 439, 440, 441, 447; Industry, 147, 351, 352, 353, 354, 441; Interior 141, 142, 237, 241, 251, 297, 358, 359, 363, 432, 440, 452, 454, 464, 476; Justice, 142, 143, 236, 464, 466, 468; National Development, 142, 333, 341, 353, 385, 388, 440; Public Health, 144–153 *passim,*

359; structure of a typical ministry, 234 (fig. 13)

minority groups (*see also* Chinese, hill peoples, Indians, Malays, Moslems, Vietnamese): 6–7; Americans, 63; assimilation, 177; attitudes, 304–306; Burmese Shan and Karen tribesmen, 454; communist movement among, 254; Europeans, 63; Khmer, 46, 61, 80; Kui, 61, 80; political influence, 256–259; Westerners, 63, 86–87

missionaries: 51, 84, 95, 160, 263, 284; influence, 216

Mitsui Bank: 443

Mobile Development Units: 297, 351, 474

molybdenum: 27

Mon (people): 63, 80

monarchy: background, 109; hierarchical tradition in social order, 7

monks: 109, 199, 200; ceremonies, 211–213; Chinese, 215; contribution to village life, 213; description, 207–209; as ideal man, 217; liaison with government, 208–209; as medical practitioners, 152, 155; ordination, 211–213; number in *wats,* 209; status, 8, 115–116, 127, 218; teaching, 159; vocabulary of address, 92

monogamy: 120

moral values: 218

Moslems: 215–216; advisory committees to provincial administrators, 258; communist activity among, 256; economic activity, 326, 346; separatist sentiments, 255, 256, 258

mosques: 216

motor vehicles: number registered, 394

Mun River: 20, 22

Municipal Advisory Board: 241

music: 191–193

Na Bon Rubber Estate Organization, 335, 385

Nakhon Chai Si River, 22

Nakhon Nayok River: 320

Nakhon Ratchasima (or Khorat, town): 15; air base, 487; description, 33; employment exchange center, 363; highway, 395, 396; radio, 291; railroad, 392; rural development office, 338

549

143; politics, and political attitudes, 252, 255, 305; population density, 62; radio, 281, 291; railroads, 412; refugees, 66, 79; religion, 204; roads, 133, 414; schools, 133; vegetation, 29

Northern Region: animals, 30; communist activities, 246, 299, 453; crops, 328; description, 2, 18; development work with hill people, 88; education, 158, 164, 165, 171; factories, 348; family systems, 120, 130–131; farm credit, 334; handicrafts, 193, 360; irrigation and water control, 321, 432; land tenure, 322; land use, 318; language, 90; living conditions, 139; minerals, 26, 27, 29; population density, 62; radio, 291, 292; religion, 204; roads, 37–38, 396; soil, 26; vegetation, 29; villages, 31; vocational training, 144 Yuan (people), 69, 73

nutrition: 145–147

obeisance: basic gesture, 126
oil. *See* petroleum
oil refinery: 344
oil shale, 27
oil seeds: 329
opium: 63, 82–88 *passim*, 138, 144, 325, 353, 359, 376, 404, 418, 420, 453, 454, 466, 469
Oregon State College: 337
Organization for the Assistance of Ex-Servicemen: 364
organizations: (*see also* international organizations, labor unions, monks, political parties): Chinese benevolent associations, 141; Chinese regional, 171; commercial, 382; dialect, 113, 129, 130; economic and professional, 256; farmers' extension clubs, 337; health and welfare, 134, 141; literary, 194, 196; political, 247–256 *passim*, 276; private social and voluntary, 108, 113, 114, 175; secret societies, 75, 113; surname group, 130
Overseas Chinese Labor Union of Thailand: 368
Overseas Chinese News Agency (Taiwan): 289
oxen: 322, 397

Pa Mong Dam: 23, 343

Pa Sak Canal Project: 320
Pa Sak River: 388
painting, 181, 186–187
Paitun Muangsomboon (sculptor): 183
Pak Thai (people): 73
Pakistan: 273
Pakistani (people): 78, 215, 381
Pan American Airways, 432
Pan Asia Newspaper Alliance (news agency): 289
Park Chung Hee (South Korean President): 272
Pasteur Institute (Bangkok): 151, 152
Patriarch Poramanuchit, Prince: 195
Pattani (port): 39, 391
Pattani University: 174
penal system: 467–469
Peninsula Region: boundaries, 13; buffaloes, 397; coastal shipping, 389; coconuts, 327; communist activities, 246, 253, 255, 256, 452, 453; description, 3, 14, 20–21, disease, 149, 150, 151; education, 164, 167; ethnic groups, 63, 69, 73, 74, 81, 123; factories, 348; family organization, 119, 130; flood control and drainage, 321; health, 150; irrigation, 316; land tenure, 322; land use, 318; language, 90, 101; living conditions, 137, 139, 143; minerals, 26, 29; political attitudes, 305; ports, 39–40, 389, 391; power, 386; radio, 291; railroads, 34, 35, 393; rivers, 389; roads, 38–39, 414; rubber, 326; rural development, 144; social values, 217; soils, 26; temperature, 26; tin, 26, 346; trade, 376; vegetation, 30; vocational training, 144; wages, 365; wild animals, 31
periodicals: 288–289
petroleum: 27, 29, 344; products, 399, 409
Phanom Dongrak Range: 3, 13, 19, 27
Phao Siyanon (Police General): 249, 252, 368
pharmaceuticals and biologicals: 152
Phaulkon, Constantine (Greek adventurer): 52
Phetchabun Mountains: 3, 19
Phibun Songkhram (Field Marshal

and Prime Minister): 77, 91, 93, 243, 247, 264, 367, 475, 476
Philippines: 270, 274, 279, 416
Phim Thai (Thai Press): 286
Phitthayalongkorn, Prince (writer): 196
Phong River: 23, 345, 346
Phra Bamras Naradura (Minister of Public Health): 151
Phra Ram (Phra Narai, heroic king): 307
Phra Viharn (temple): border dispute over, 267–268
Phraya Chaisurin (writer): 196
Phraya Manopakon (Prime Minister): 247, 475
Phuket Island: 13, 14, 347, 348; port, 40, 391; roads, 38; tin, 13, 26
Phuthai (people): 73
Phya Phahon (political leader): 247
Piman Moolpramook (sculptor): 184
Ping River: 22, 321, 345, 388
police: (*see also* Departments of: National Police: border patrol, 454, 456–457; metropolitan, 454, 457–458; mobile reserve platoons, 457, 459; operational units, 454, 455–457; counterinsurgency role, 455; provincial, 454, 455–456; ranks and grades, 458; training and equipment, 458–459 Police Aerial Reinforcement Unit: 457
political parties: government policy, 5, 113, 246, 249, 250, 253, 255; from 1945, 252–253
politics (*see also* elite: ruling; political parties): 245–259; attitude toward, 5, 114; background, 4–5, 247–250; bibliography, 511–516; influence of economic and professional organizations, 256; importance of the Chinese, 70; importance of hill peoples, 70; locus of power, 4, 5–6; power mobility, 251; separatist sentiments and movement, 255, 256, 258; values and attitudes, 301–308
polygamy: 120, 124–125, 129, 131
population: 43, 61–67; density, 62–63, 64 (fig. 10); structure, 61–63; summary, vii
Port Authority of Thailand: 423
ports and port facilities: 15, 35 (fig. 8), 39–40; coastal, 389–391; inland, 391; summary, ix

Portuguese (people): 472
Pote Sarasin (Prime Minister): 249
power (*see also* electric power, hydroelectric power): 345–346;
Pra Pradang Home: 145
Praphat Charusathien, General (Deputy Prime Minister and Minister of Interior, mid–1967): 274, 476
Prasert Sapsunthon (political party leader): 254
Prayoon Chunswasdee (editor, labor organizer): 369
press: character and scope, 284–286; regulation, 282–284
Press Association of Thailand: 295
Press Trust of India (news agency): 289
Pridi Phanomyong (Prime Minister): 58, 247, 248, 252, 254, 255, 264, 276, 475
Prime Minister, Office of: 152, 163, 180, 242, 250, 251, 281–284 *passim*, 337, 353, 354, 358, 441; duties and functions, 231, 233, 235; emergency power of, 228
Prince Royal College (Chiengmai): 171
prisons. *See* penal system
private enterprise: government policy toward, 400
Privy Council: 231
Progressive Party: 252
property: inheritance, 120, 123, 124, 126, 129, 130, 322
prostitution: 144
protein: intake, 145; source, 146
proverbs: 98
provinces: 14, 16 (fig. 2), 17; government, 237–238; police, 454, 455–456, 458, 459
Provincial Bank: 441, 442
Provincial Highway Development Program (1964–70): 37
Provincial Police: 454, 455–456, 458, 459
Provincial Police Training Schools, 459
pu yai ban. See headman
public order and safety (*see also* criminal law, military, penal system, police): 451–470 public services: 353, 386–388; improvement and expansion, 387–388, 390, 393–394, 395–396

551

359; living standards, 135–138; mobile development units, 144; radio, 281–282; schools, 104; settlement: 31–32; social relationships, 116; social structure, 114–117; teachers, 169; trade, 375; underemployment, 362; weaving, 193

Rusk, Dean (U.S. Secretary of State): 10, 273

salt: 29

Salween River: 13

Samui Island: 27, 348

Sangha (Buddhist Brotherhood of Monks). *See* monks

sanitation: 134, 139, 147–148

Sarit Thanarat, Marshall (Prime Minister, 1957–63): 5, 161, 225, 227, 235, 246, 268, 305, 363, 369, 476, 477

Sarn Seri (Free Press): 286

satellite communication service: 387–388

Sattahip (port): development, 15; facilities and repair shop, 39; naval base, 411, 480, 487

savings: 438, 439, 448

Sawang Songmangree (sculptor): 183

Sayre, Francis B. (U.S. foreign affairs adviser): 264

Scandinavian Airlines System (SAS): x, 396, 397

scholarships and fellowships: 159, 166, 167, 299, 414

School of Arts and Crafts: 187

sakdi na system (social and functional ranking): 110, 321–322

schools (*see also* military: schools; teachers; wats: schools): age of entry, 126; boarding, 165; built and/or operated by border police, 457; Chinese, 6, 75, 100, 104, 171–173; enrollment, 166, 167; facilities, 163–164; local (communal) and municipal, 162, 163; private, 160, 166, 171–173; rural, 104; tax support, 434; vocational and technical, 167–168

Science Association of Thailand, 289

sculpture: 181, 182–184

security, national (*see also* Army, Marines, Navy, police, public order and safety): 451–493; bibliography, 526–528

self-government: training, 144

Seni Pramoj Prime Minister: 265

Seri Manangkhasila (political party): 249, 252

services: employment, 359, 360; place in the economy, 313

Seven-year highway development plan (1965–71): 396

sewage disposal: 134, 139, 147, 148

Shan (people): 73–74

shipping: coastal, 389; line, ASA proposed, 416

Shongkhla (port): facilities, 15

Si Chang Island: large vessel berth, 39

Si Racha (town): proposed seaport at or near, 390

Siam Cement Company: 432

Siam City Bank: 442

Siam Commercial Bank: 442

Siam Directory: 382

Siam Kikorn (Siamese People, newspaper): 286

Siam Rath (Siam State, newspaper): 286

Siddhartha Gautama Sakyamuni (Buddha): 212

Sihanouk, Prince (Cambodian chief of state): 269

silk: 193, 349, 352

Silom Club: 114

Silpakorn University (University of Fine Arts): 174, 180, 184, 187

Silvera, Carlos Manual (Portuguese envoy), 54

Sing Siang Yit Pao (Daily Siam Star, Chinese newspaper): 288

Singapore: 404–411 *passim;* trade, 327; opium, 469

Siprat (poet): 194, 196

Sirraj Medical School and Hospital (Thon Buri): 152, 153, 413

Sitthidet Sanghiran (sculptor): 183

Six-Year Economic Development Plan (1961–66), 9, 134, 142, 157, 310, 314, 315, 339, 417, 433

slavery: 3, 45, 48, 50, 56, 109

Small Industries Service Institute: 354

smuggling: 469–470

social problems: control, 144–145

social security: proposed, 143

social services: expenditures, 423

social structure (*see also* elite, the; status): 107–117; attitudes and

position, 374–376; early, 51–55 *passim;* ethnic groups engaged in, 378, 379–382; floating markets, 36; and foreign relations, 11; government role, 383–386; market information, 383; publicity, 382–383 traders, 378, 379–382; trading centers, 375; wholesale and retail, 11, 378–379

trade, foreign: 399–411, 414–415; back ground, 400–403; controls, 414–415; pattern, 404–411; present status, 399–400

Trade Control Division: 384

Trade Directory of Thailand: 382

Trade Guide for Thailand: 382

trade publications: 382

trade unions. *See* labor unions

trademarks: registry, 384

training: airline, 397; counterinsurgency, 459; foreign aid for, 310; medical, 135; military, 480, 482, 483, 486–489; police, 458–459; self-government a n d administration, 144; teachers, 168–170; technical, 393; vocational, 144, 145, 159, 164, 167–168, 357, 361–362, 469

transportation: 34, 35 (fig. 8), 36–40, 388–397; air, 396–397; development, 316; employment, 374; equipment, 409; government owned, 388; men and animals as transport means, 397 place in the economy, 311, 313; private expenditures, 140; truck and passenger, 394

Transportation Bank: 395

treaties and agreements: ASA trade and navigation, 416; early, 51–57 *passim,* 263–274 *passim,* 401–402; financial effects of restrictions, 418–420; military, x, 11, 473; summary, x

Tripitaka (Buddhist scripture): 197, 200

tuberculosis: 134, 148, 149

tungsten: 27, 347

typhoons: 26

U Thant (UN Secretary-General): 269

unemployment and underemployment: 357, 362–363;

Union Bank of Bangkok: 442

Union Carbide Corporation; 347

unions. *See* labor unions

United Arab Republic: 427

United Malayan Banking Corporation: 443

United Nations: 10, 11, 134, 158, 168, 261–279 *passim,* 310, 336, 338, 415; aid, types and amount, 412; aid total, 427; forces, participation in, 482; membership, x, 266, 277

United Nations Children's Fund (UNICEF): 142, 143, 149–153 *passim,* 412, 415

United Nations Educational, Scientific and C u l t u r a l Organization (UNESCO): 142, 277, 415; types of aid, 413

United Nations Expeditionary Force: 277

United Nations Special Fund: 343: aid, type and amount, 412

United Party (Sahaphak): 252

United Press International: 289

United States (*see also* United States aid): attitude toward, 87, 278–279; communist propaganda against, 299, 300; economic cooperation, 402–403 as export market, 330, 347; films, 294; influence on military, 482–483, 486–493 *passim;* information services, 298–299; investment, private, 314; military advisers, 486, 487; news agencies, 289; personnel, effects of presence, 135, 139; relations with, 262–268 *passim,* 273–274; student exchange, 273; Thai students in, 175; trade, 404–409 *passim*

United States aid: agriculture, 312, 321, 334–338 *passim;* change of policy (1962), 403; education, 159, 166–170 *passim;* equipment and training, 310, 474, 483, 486, 490; expenditures (1950–65), 411; farm credit, 334; grant total, 427; health and welfare, 134, 142–147 *passim,* 150, 152, 153; fishing, 332, 333; industry, 343, 344, 346, 351, 361; irrigation 321; Mekong Basin project, 23; military, 10, 11, 273, 426, 473, 474, 483, 486, 490; natural resources, 341, 343, 344; projects and loan amounts, 432; security, 451, 452, 456, 459; transportation, 388, 392, 396, 397; types, projects, 411–432; for village radios, 293

United States Agency for International Development (AID) (*see also* U.S. Operations M i s s i o n, U.S. (AID Public Safety Division): x, 134, 310, 334, 343, 396, 411, 432; loan totals, 427, 432

United States (AID) Public Safety Division: 456

United States Export-Import Bank: 314, 396, 411; loan total, 427; projects and loan amounts, 432

United States Food for Peace: 411

United States Geological Survey: 341

United States Information Agency (USIA): anti-communist and community improvement efforts, 297

United States Information Service (USIS): 298; health and education films, 297

United States Military Assistance Command, T h a i l a ñ d USMAC-THAI): 486

United States Military Assistance Program (MAP): 473, 486, 487, 490

United States Operations. Mission (USOM): 134, 142–147 *passim*, 150, 152, 153, 159, 166, 168, 298, 336, 337; Public Safety Division, 452

United States Peace Corp: 144, 169, 298

United States Special Forces Unit: 486

United Thai Federation of Labor: 367, 369

Universal Postal Union (UPU): 277

University of Hawaii: 337

University of Medical Sciences (Bangkok): 152, 153; Faculty of Public Health, 147

University Personnel Commission: 242

urban areas: 15; family, 121–122, 129; government, 240–241; health, 147, 148, 149, 152, 153; living conditions, 138; population, 62; sanitation, 147; settlements, 32–34; structure of the society, 111–117

urbanization, 140

Vajira Hospital (Bangkok): 152

vegetation: 29, 30 (fig. 7)

venereal diseases: 149

Vichitr Chaosanket (sculptor): 184

Vietnamese (people): 7, 63; economic activity, 79, 361, 381; as ethnic group, 79–80; language, 90; and

politics, 246, 258–259, 305; refugees, 79, 300, 452–453; repatriation of nationals, 276

villages: 15; antimalaria measures, 150; characteristics of villagers, 116; elections, 243; government, 239–240; hill people, 82–87 *passim*; importance of *wats*, 199, 213–214; political activity, 243; social institutions, 115; tradition of cooperation, 108; types, 31–32

Virus Research Center: 414

vocational training. *See under* training

Voice of America (VOA): 298

Voice of Free Thailand (broadcast from Communist China): 299

Volunteer Defense Corps: 454, 456

voting: 4, 244, 304

wages: 365

Wang River: 22

water (*see also* irrigation and flood control): 139; improvement projects, 135; pollution, 147; potable, 143, 144, 147; supply, 134, 143, 147, 386

watercraft: 389

waterways: 15, 36–37, 313, 388–390, 391

wats (Buddhist temple compounds): 99, 115–116, 137, 139, 141, 154; architecture, 185; ceremonies, 211; description, 213; education, 176; festival dance, 190; importance in village life, 199, 213–214; land ownership, 209; music, 192; number of monks in, 209; schools, 110, 159, 160, 165, 176

Wattana Academy (Bangkok): 171

wealth: attitude toward, 133; and house and furnishings, 136; and influence, 116–117; and polygamy, 125; and surname group leadership, 130; and women in family, 121

welfare: 140–145; child, 142–143; government expenditures, 134; and health expenditures 424 (table 13)

Welfare Housing Bank: 439, 440

West, the: attitude toward, 4; early contacts, 51–52; and foreign policy, 10; influence of, 3, 4, 110, 122, 135, 136, 138, 139, 146, 179, 187–198 *passim*, 216, 217, 226, 241, 452, 461, 472, 475, 482

West German Newspaper and Radio Service: 289

Westerners: 86–87

women: Chinese, 75, 76; employed, 359, 360; farm work, 325; higher education, 173; ideal, 218; legal status in concubinage, 125; magazines, 289; married, status of, 128; merit-earning, 207; in the population, 62; position in family, 121–122; in trade, 373; wages, 365; work hours, 364

Women's Correctional Institution (Bangkok): 468

workmen's compensation: 365

workweek: 364

World Health Organization (WHO): 142, 143, 147–153 *passim*, 277, 412, 415

World Meteorological Organization (WMO): 277

World War I: government position and military contribution, 473

World War II: anti-Japanese underground, 482; government position and after effects, 264–266, 473

writing: basis of, 46–47; Chinese, 99, 172; derivation, 179; Lao, 99; systems, 94–95

Yanhee project (multipurpose water project): 23, 321, 343, 345, 386, 431, 432

Yao (people): 85

Yom River: 22, 388

Yong Kee Liab Heng Company (oxygen and acetylene): 432

Young Men's Christian Association (YMCA): 141

Young Women's Christian Association (YWCA): 141

Young Workers' General Labor Union: 367

Yuan (people): 73

Yugoslavia: 10, 267

☆ U.S. GOVERNMENT PRINTING OFFICE: 1968—O 307–333